T0211892

Lecture Notes in Computer Science 12934

More information about this subseries at http://www.springer.com/series/7409

Carmelo Ardito · Rosa Lanzilotti ·
Alessio Malizia · Helen Petrie ·
Antonio Piccinno · Giuseppe Desolda ·
Kori Inkpen (Eds.)

Human-Computer Interaction – INTERACT 2021

18th IFIP TC 13 International Conference
Bari, Italy, August 30 – September 3, 2021
Proceedings, Part III

 Springer

Editors
Carmelo Ardito (iD)
Department of Electrical and Information
Engineering
Polytechnic University of Bari
Bari, Italy

Alessio Malizia (iD)
Computer Science Department
University of Pisa
Pisa, Italy

University of Hertfordshire
Hatfield, United Kingdom

Antonio Piccinno (iD)
Computer Science Department
University of Bari Aldo Moro
Bari, Italy

Kori Inkpen (iD)
Microsoft Research
Redmond, WA, USA

Rosa Lanzilotti (iD)
Computer Science Department
University of Bari Aldo Moro
Bari, Italy

Helen Petrie (iD)
Department of Computer Science
University of York
York, UK

Giuseppe Desolda (iD)
Computer Science Department
University of Bari Aldo Moro
Bari, Italy

ISSN 0302-9743 ISSN 1611-3349 (electronic)
Lecture Notes in Computer Science
ISBN 978-3-030-85612-0 ISBN 978-3-030-85613-7 (eBook)
https://doi.org/10.1007/978-3-030-85613-7

LNCS Sublibrary: SL3 – Information Systems and Applications, incl. Internet/Web, and HCI

This Springer imprint is published by the registered company Springer Nature Switzerland AG
The registered company address is: Gewerbestrasse 11, 6330 Cham, Switzerland

Welcome

It is our great pleasure to welcome you to the 18th IFIP TC13 International Conference on Human-Computer Interaction, INTERACT 2021, one of the most important conferences in the area of Human-Computer Interaction at a world-wide level. INTERACT 2021 was held in Bari (Italy) from August 30 – September 3, 2021, in cooperation with ACM and under the patronage of the University of Bari Aldo Moro. This is the second time that INTERACT was held in Italy, after the edition in Rome in September 2005. The Villa Romanazzi Carducci Hotel, which hosted INTERACT 2021, provided the right context for welcoming the participants, thanks to its liberty-period villa immersed in a beautiful park. Due to the COVID-19 pandemic, INTERACT 2021 was held in hybrid mode to allow attendees who could not travel to participate in the conference.

INTERACT is held every two years and is well appreciated by the international community, attracting experts with a broad range of backgrounds, coming from all over the world and sharing a common interest in HCI, to make technology effective and useful for all people in their daily life. The theme of INTERACT 2021, "Sense, Feel, Design," highlighted the new interaction design challenges. Technology is today more and more widespread, pervasive and blended in the world we live in. On one side, devices that sense humans' activities have the potential to provide an enriched interaction. On the other side, the user experience can be further enhanced by exploiting multisensorial technologies. The traditional human senses of vision and hearing and senses of touch, smell, taste, and emotions can be taken into account when designing for future interactions. The hot topic of this edition was Human-Centered Artificial Intelligence, which implies considering who AI systems are built for and evaluating how well these systems support people's goals and activities. There was also considerable attention paid to the usable security theme. Not surprisingly, the COVID-19 pandemic and social distancing have also turned the attention of HCI researchers towards the difficulties in performing user-centered design activities and the modified social aspects of interaction.

With this, we welcome you all to INTERACT 2021. Several people worked hard to make this conference as pleasurable as possible, and we hope you will truly enjoy it.

Paolo Buono
Catherine Plaisant

Preface

The 18th IFIP TC13 International Conference on Human-Computer Interaction, INTERACT 2021 (Bari, August 30 – September 3, 2021) attracted a relevant collection of submissions on different topics.

Excellent research is the heart of a good conference. Like its predecessors, INTERACT 2021 aimed to foster high-quality research. As a multidisciplinary field, HCI requires interaction and discussion among diverse people with different interests and backgrounds. The beginners and the experienced theoreticians and practitioners, and people from various disciplines and different countries gathered, both in-person and virtually, to learn from each other and contribute to each other's growth.

We were especially honoured to welcome our invited speakers: Marianna Obrist (University College London), Ben Shneiderman (University of Maryland), Luca Viganò (King's College London), Geraldine Fitzpatrick (TU Wien) and Philippe Palanque (University Toulouse 3 "Paul Sabatier").

Marianna Obrist's talk focused on the multisensory world people live in and discussed the role touch, taste and smell can play in the future of computing. Ben Shneiderman envisioned a new synthesis of emerging disciplines in which AI-based intelligent algorithms are combined with human-centered design thinking. Luca Viganò used a cybersecurity show and tell approach to illustrate how to use films and other artworks to explain cybersecurity notions. Geraldine Fitzpatrick focused on skills required to use technologies as enablers for good technical design work. Philippe Palanque discussed the cases of system faults due to human errors and presented multiple examples of faults affecting socio-technical systems.

A total of 680 submissions, distributed in 2 peer-reviewed tracks, 4 curated tracks, and 3 juried tracks, were received. Of these, the following contributions were accepted:

- 105 Full Papers (peer-reviewed)
- 72 Short Papers (peer-reviewed)
- 36 Posters (juried)
- 5 Interactive Demos (curated)
- 9 Industrial Experiences (curated)
- 3 Panels (curated)
- 1 Course (curated)
- 11 Workshops (juried)
- 13 Doctoral Consortium (juried)

The acceptance rate for contributions received in the peer-reviewed tracks was 29% for full papers and 30% for short papers. In the spirit of inclusiveness of INTERACT, and IFIP in general, a substantial number of promising but borderline full papers, which had not received a direct acceptance decision, were screened for shepherding.

Interestingly, many of these papers eventually turned out to be excellent quality papers and were included in the final set of full papers. In addition to full papers and short papers, the present proceedings feature's contributions accepted in the shape of posters, interactive demonstrations, industrial experiences, panels, courses, and descriptions of accepted workshops.

Subcommittees managed the reviewing process of the full papers. Each subcommittee had a chair and a set of associated chairs who were in charge of coordinating the reviewing process with the help of expert reviewers. Two new sub-committees were introduced in this edition: "Human-AI Interaction" and "HCI in the Pandemic". Hereafter we list the sub-committees of INTERACT 2021:

- Accessibility and assistive technologies
- Design for business and safety-critical interactive systems
- Design of interactive entertainment systems
- HCI education and curriculum
- HCI in the pandemic
- Human-AI interaction
- Information visualization
- Interactive systems technologies and engineering
- Methodologies for HCI
- Social and ubiquitous interaction
- Understanding users and human behaviour

The final decision on acceptance or rejection of full papers was taken in a Programme Committee meeting held virtually, due to the COVID-19 pandemic, in March 2021. The technical program chairs, the full papers chairs, the subcommittee chairs, and the associate chairs participated in this meeting. The meeting discussed a consistent set of criteria to deal with inevitable differences among many reviewers. The corresponding track chairs and reviewers made the final decisions on other tracks, often after electronic meetings and discussions.

We would like to express our strong gratitude to all the people whose passionate and strenuous work ensured the quality of the INTERACT 2021 program: the 12 sub-committees chairs, 88 associated chairs, 34 track chairs, and 543 reviewers; the Keynote & Invited Talks Chair Maria Francesca Costabile; the Posters Chairs Maristella Matera, Kent Norman, Anna Spagnolli; the Interactive Demos Chairs Barbara Rita Barricelli and Nuno Jardim Nunes; the Workshops Chairs Marta Kristín Larusdottir and Davide Spano; the Courses Chairs Nikolaos Avouris and Carmen Santoro; the Panels Chairs Effie Lai-Chong Law and Massimo Zancanaro; the Doctoral Consortium Chairs Daniela Fogli, David Lamas and John Stasko; the Industrial Experiences Chair Danilo Caivano; the Online Experience Chairs Fabrizio Balducci and Miguel Ceriani; the Advisors Fernando Loizides and Marco Winckler; the Student Volunteers Chairs Vita Santa Barletta and Grazia Ragone; the Publicity Chairs Ganesh D. Bhutkar and Veronica Rossano; the Local Organisation Chair Simona Sarti.

We would like to thank all the authors, who chose INTERACT 2021 as the venue to publish their research and enthusiastically shared their results with the INTERACT community. Last, but not least, we are also grateful to the sponsors for their financial support.

Carmelo Ardito
Rosa Lanzilotti
Alessio Malizia
Helen Petrie
Antonio Piccinno
Giuseppe Desolda
Kori Inkpen

IFIP TC13 – http://ifip-tc13.org/

Established in 1989, the Technical Committee on Human–Computer Interaction (IFIP TC 13) of the International Federation for Information Processing (IFIP) is an international committee of 34 member national societies and 10 Working Groups, representing specialists of the various disciplines contributing to the field of human–computer interaction. This includes (among others) human factors, ergonomics, cognitive science, and multiple areas of computer science and design.

IFIP TC 13 aims to develop the science, technology and societal aspects of human–computer interaction (HCI) by

- encouraging empirical, applied and theoretical research
- promoting the use of knowledge and methods from both human sciences and computer sciences in design, development, evaluation and exploitation of computing systems
- promoting the production of new knowledge in the area of interactive computing systems engineering
- promoting better understanding of the relation between formal design methods and system usability, user experience, accessibility and acceptability
- developing guidelines, models and methods by which designers may provide better human-oriented computing systems
- and, cooperating with other groups, inside and outside IFIP, to promote user-orientation and humanization in system design.

Thus, TC 13 seeks to improve interactions between people and computing systems, to encourage the growth of HCI research and its practice in industry and to disseminate these benefits worldwide.

The main orientation is to place the users at the center of the development process. Areas of study include:

- the problems people face when interacting with computing devices;
- the impact of technology deployment on people in individual and organizational contexts;
- the determinants of utility, usability, acceptability, accessibility, privacy, and user experience ...;
- the appropriate allocation of tasks between computing systems and users especially in the case of automation;
- engineering user interfaces, interactions and interactive computing systems;
- modelling the user, their tasks and the interactive system to aid better system design; and harmonizing the computing system to user characteristics and needs.

While the scope is thus set wide, with a tendency toward general principles rather than particular systems, it is recognized that progress will only be achieved through both general studies to advance theoretical understandings and specific studies on practical issues (e.g., interface design standards, software system resilience, documentation, training material, appropriateness of alternative interaction technologies, guidelines, integrating computing systems to match user needs and organizational practices, etc.).

In 2015, TC13 approved the creation of a Steering Committee (SC) for the INTERACT conference series. The SC is now in place, chaired by Anirudha Joshi and is responsible for:

- promoting and maintaining the INTERACT conference as the premiere venue for researchers and practitioners interested in the topics of the conference (this requires a refinement of the topics above);
- ensuring the highest quality for the contents of the event;
- setting up the bidding process to handle the future INTERACT conferences (decision is made at TC 13 level);
- providing advice to the current and future chairs and organizers of the INTERACT conference;
- providing data, tools, and documents about previous conferences to the future conference organizers;
- selecting the reviewing system to be used throughout the conference (as this affects the entire set of reviewers, authors and committee members);
- resolving general issues involved with the INTERACT conference;
- capitalizing on history (good and bad practices).

In 1999, TC 13 initiated a special IFIP Award, the Brian Shackel Award, for the most outstanding contribution in the form of a refereed paper submitted to and delivered at each INTERACT. The award draws attention to the need for a comprehensive human-centered approach in the design and use of information technology in which the human and social implications have been taken into account. In 2007, IFIP TC 13 launched an Accessibility Award to recognize an outstanding contribution in HCI with international impact dedicated to the field of accessibility for disabled users. In 2013, IFIP TC 13 launched the Interaction Design for International Development (IDID) Award that recognizes the most outstanding contribution to the application of interactive systems for social and economic development of people in developing countries. Since the process to decide the award takes place after papers are sent to the publisher for publication, the awards are not identified in the proceedings. Since 2019 a special agreement has been made with the *International Journal of Behaviour & Information Technology* (published by Taylor & Francis) with Panos Markopoulos as editor in chief. In this agreement, authors of BIT whose papers are within the field of HCI are offered the opportunity to present their work at the INTERACT conference. Reciprocally, a selection of papers submitted and accepted for presentation at INTERACT are offered the opportunity to extend their contribution to be published in BIT.

IFIP TC 13 also recognizes pioneers in the area of HCI. An IFIP TC 13 pioneer is one who, through active participation in IFIP Technical Committees or related IFIP groups, has made outstanding contributions to the educational, theoretical, technical, commercial, or professional aspects of analysis, design, construction, evaluation, and use of interactive systems. IFIP TC 13 pioneers are appointed annually and awards are handed over at the INTERACT conference.

IFIP TC 13 stimulates working events and activities through its Working Groups (WGs). Working Groups consist of HCI experts from multiple countries, who seek to expand knowledge and find solutions to HCI issues and concerns within a specific domain. The list of Working Groups and their domains is given below.

WG13.1 (Education in HCI and HCI Curricula) aims to improve HCI education at all levels of higher education, coordinate and unite efforts to develop HCI curricula and promote HCI teaching.

WG13.2 (Methodology for User-Centred System Design) aims to foster research, dissemination of information and good practice in the methodical application of HCI to software engineering.

WG13.3 (HCI, Disability and Aging) aims to make HCI designers aware of the needs of people with disabilities and encourage development of information systems and tools permitting adaptation of interfaces to specific users.

WG13.4 (also WG2.7) (User Interface Engineering) investigates the nature, concepts and construction of user interfaces for software systems, using a framework for reasoning about interactive systems and an engineering model for developing UIs.

WG 13.5 (Resilience, Reliability, Safety and Human Error in System Development) seeks a framework for studying human factors relating to systems failure, develops leading edge techniques in hazard analysis and safety engineering of computer-based systems, and guides international accreditation activities for safety-critical systems.

WG13.6 (Human-Work Interaction Design) aims at establishing relationships between extensive empirical work-domain studies and HCI design. It will promote the use of knowledge, concepts, methods and techniques that enable user studies to procure a better apprehension of the complex interplay between individual, social and organizational contexts and thereby a better understanding of how and why people work in the ways that they do.

WG13.7 (Human–Computer Interaction and Visualization) aims to establish a study and research program that will combine both scientific work and practical applications in the fields of human–computer interaction and visualization. It will integrate several additional aspects of further research areas, such as scientific visualization, data mining, information design, computer graphics, cognition sciences, perception theory, or psychology, into this approach.

WG13.8 (Interaction Design and International Development) is currently working to reformulate their aims and scope.

WG13.9 (Interaction Design and Children) aims to support practitioners, regulators and researchers to develop the study of interaction design and children across international contexts.

WG13.10 (Human-Centred Technology for Sustainability) aims to promote research, design, development, evaluation, and deployment of human-centered technology to encourage sustainable use of resources in various domains.

New Working Groups are formed as areas of significance in HCI arise. Further information is available at the IFIP TC13 website: http://ifip-tc13.org/.

IFIP TC13 Members

Officers

Chairperson

Philippe Palanque, France

Vice-chair for Awards

Paula Kotze, South Africa

Vice-chair for Communications

Helen Petrie, UK

Vice-chair for Growth and Reach out INTERACT Steering Committee Chair

Jan Gulliksen, Sweden

Vice-chair for Working Groups

Simone D. J. Barbosa, Brazil

Vice-chair for Development and Equity

Julio Abascal, Spain

Treasurer

Virpi Roto, Finland

Secretary

Marco Winckler, France

INTERACT Steering Committee Chair

Anirudha Joshi, India

Country Representatives

Australia
Henry B. L. Duh
Australian Computer Society

Austria
Geraldine Fitzpatrick
Austrian Computer Society

Belgium
Bruno Dumas
IMEC – Interuniversity
Micro-Electronics Center

Brazil
Lara S. G. Piccolo
Brazilian Computer Society (SBC)

Bulgaria
Stoyan Georgiev Dentchev
Bulgarian Academy of Sciences

Croatia
Andrina Granic
Croatian Information Technology
Association (CITA)

Cyprus
Panayiotis Zaphiris
Cyprus Computer Society

Czech Republic
Zdeněk Míkovec
Czech Society for Cybernetics
and Informatics

Finland
Virpi Roto
Finnish Information Processing
Association

France
Philippe Palanque and Marco Winckler
Société informatique de France (SIF)

Germany
Tom Gross
Gesellschaft fur Informatik e.V.

Ireland
Liam J. Bannon
Irish Computer Society

Italy
Fabio Paternò
Italian Computer Society

Japan
Yoshifumi Kitamura
Information Processing Society of Japan

Netherlands
Regina Bernhaupt
Nederlands Genootschap
voor Informatica

New Zealand
Mark Apperley
New Zealand Computer Society

Norway
Frode Eika Sandnes
Norwegian Computer Society

Poland
Marcin Sikorski
Poland Academy of Sciences

Portugal
Pedro Campos
Associacão Portuguesa para o
Desenvolvimento da Sociedade da
Informação (APDSI)

Serbia
Aleksandar Jevremovic
Informatics Association of Serbia

Singapore
Shengdong Zhao
Singapore Computer Society

Slovakia
Wanda Benešová
The Slovak Society for Computer
Science

Slovenia
Matjaž Debevc
The Slovenian Computer Society
INFORMATIKA

Sri Lanka
Thilina Halloluwa
The Computer Society of Sri Lanka

South Africa
Janet L. Wesson & Paula Kotze
The Computer Society of South Africa

Sweden
Jan Gulliksen
Swedish Interdisciplinary Society for
Human-Computer Interaction
Swedish Computer Society

Switzerland
Denis Lalanne
Swiss Federation for Information
Processing

Tunisia
Mona Laroussi
Ecole Supérieure des Communications de
Tunis (SUP'COM)

United Kingdom
José Abdelnour Nocera
British Computer Society (BCS)

United Arab Emirates
Ahmed Seffah
UAE Computer Society

ACM

Gerrit van der Veer
Association for Computing
Machinery

CLEI

Jaime Sánchez
Centro Latinoamericano de Estudios en
Informatica

Expert Members

Julio Abascal, Spain
Carmelo Ardito, Italy
Nikolaos Avouris, Greece
Kaveh Bazargan, Iran
Ivan Burmistrov, Russia
Torkil Torkil Clemmensen, Denmark
Peter Forbrig, Germany
Dorian Gorgan, Romania

Anirudha Joshi, India
David Lamas, Estonia
Marta Kristin Larusdottir, Iceland
Zhengjie Liu, China
Fernando Loizides, UK/Cyprus
Ochieng Daniel "Dan" Orwa, Kenya
Eunice Sari, Australia/Indonesia

Working Group Chairpersons

**WG 13.1 (Education in HCI
and HCI Curricula)**

Konrad Baumann, Austria

**WG 13.2 (Methodologies
for User-Centered System Design)**

Regina Bernhaupt, Netherlands

WG 13.3 (HCI, Disability and Aging)

Helen Petrie, UK

**WG 13.4/2.7 (User Interface
Engineering)**

José Creissac Campos, Portugal

**WG 13.5 (Human Error, Resilience,
Reliability, Safety and System
Development)**

Chris Johnson, UK

**WG13.6 (Human-Work
Interaction Design)**

Barbara Rita Barricelli, Italy

WG13.7 (HCI and Visualization)

Peter Dannenmann, Germany

**WG 13.8 (Interaction Design
and International Development)**

José Adbelnour Nocera, UK

**WG 13.9 (Interaction Design
and Children)**

Janet Read, UK

**WG 13.10 (Human-Centred
Technology for Sustainability)**

Masood Masoodian, Finland

Conference Organizing Committee

General Conference Co-chairs

Paolo Buono, Italy
Catherine Plaisant, USA and France

Advisors

Fernando Loizides, UK
Marco Winckler, France

Technical Program Co-chairs

Carmelo Ardito, Italy
Rosa Lanzilotti, Italy
Alessio Malizia, UK and Italy

Keynote and Invited Talks Chair

Maria Francesca Costabile, Italy

Full Papers Co-chairs

Helen Petrie, UK
Antonio Piccinno, Italy

Short Papers Co-chairs

Giuseppe Desolda, Italy
Kori Inkpen, USA

Posters Co-chairs

Maristella Matera, Italy
Kent Norman, USA
Anna Spagnolli, Italy

Interactive Demos Co-chairs

Barbara Rita Barricelli, Italy
Nuno Jardim Nunes, Portugal

Panels Co-chairs

Effie Lai-Chong Law, UK
Massimo Zancanaro, Italy

Courses Co-chairs

Carmen Santoro, Italy
Nikolaos Avouris, Greece

Industrial Experiences Chair

Danilo Caivano, Italy

Workshops Co-chairs

Marta Kristín Larusdottir, Iceland
Davide Spano, Italy

Doctoral Consortium Co-chairs

Daniela Fogli, Italy
David Lamas, Estonia
John Stasko, USA

Online Experience Co-chairs

Fabrizio Balducci, Italy
Miguel Ceriani, Italy

Student Volunteers Co-chairs

Vita Santa Barletta, Italy
Grazia Ragone, UK

Publicity Co-chairs

Ganesh D. Bhutkar, India
Veronica Rossano, Italy

Local Organisation Chair

Simona Sarti, Consulta Umbria, Italy

Programme Committee

Sub-committee Chairs

Nikolaos Avouris, Greece
Regina Bernhaupt, Netherlands
Carla Dal Sasso Freitas, Brazil
Jan Gulliksen, Sweden
Paula Kotzé, South Africa
Effie Lai-Chong Law, UK

Philippe Palanque, France
Fabio Paternò, Italy
Thomas Pederson, Sweden
Albrecht Schmidt, Germany
Frank Steinicke, Germany
Gerhard Weber, Germany

Associated Chairs

José Abdelnour Nocera, UK
Raian Ali, Qatar
Florian Alt, Germany
Katrina Attwood, UK
Simone Barbosa, Brazil
Cristian Bogdan, Sweden
Paolo Bottoni, Italy
Judy Bowen, New Zealand
Daniel Buschek, Germany
Pedro Campos, Portugal
José Creissac Campos, Portugal
Luca Chittaro, Italy
Sandy Claes, Belgium
Christopher Clarke, UK
Torkil Clemmensen, Denmark
Vanessa Cobus, Germany
Ashley Colley, Finland
Aurora Constantin, UK
Lynne Coventry, UK
Yngve Dahl, Norway
Maria De Marsico, Italy
Luigi De Russis, Italy
Paloma Diaz, Spain
Monica Divitini, Norway
Mateusz Dolata, Switzerland
Bruno Dumas, Belgium
Sophie Dupuy-Chessa, France
Dan Fitton, UK
Peter Forbrig, Germany
Sandnes Frode Eika, Norway
Vivian Genaro Motti, USA
Rosella Gennari, Italy

Jens Gerken, Germany
Mareike Glöss, Sweden
Dorian Gorgan, Romania
Tom Gross, Germany
Uwe Gruenefeld, Germany
Julie Haney, USA
Ebba Þóra Hvannberg, Iceland
Netta Iivari, Finland
Nanna Inie, Denmark
Anna Sigríður Islind, Iceland
Anirudha Joshi, India
Bridget Kane, Sweden
Anne Marie Kanstrup, Denmark
Mohamed Khamis, UK
Kibum Kim, Korea
Marion Koelle, Germany
Kati Kuusinen, Denmark
Matthias Laschke, Germany
Fernando Loizides, UK
Andrés Lucero, Finland
Jo Lumsden, UK
Charlotte Magnusson, Sweden
Andrea Marrella, Italy
Célia Martinie, France
Timothy Merritt, Denmark
Zdeněk Míkovec, Czech Republic
Luciana Nedel, Brazil
Laurence Nigay, France
Valentina Nisi, Portugal
Raquel O. Prates, Brazil
Rakesh Patibanda, Australia
Simon Perrault, Singapore

Lara Piccolo, UK
Aparecido Fabiano Pinatti de Carvalho, Germany
Janet Read, UK
Karen Renaud, UK
Antonio Rizzo, Italy
Sayan Sarcar, Japan
Valentin Schwind, Germany
Gavin Sim, UK
Fotios Spyridonis, UK
Jan Stage, Denmark
Simone Stumpf, UK
Luis Teixeira, Portugal

Jakob Tholander, Sweden
Daniela Trevisan, Brazil
Stefano Valtolina, Italy
Jan Van den Bergh, Belgium
Nervo Verdezoto, UK
Chi Vi, UK
Giuliana Vitiello, Italy
Sarah Völkel, Germany
Marco Winckler, France
Dhaval Vyas, Australia
Janet Wesson, South Africa
Paweł W. Woźniak, Netherlands

Reviewers

Bruno A. Chagas, Brazil
Yasmeen Abdrabou, Germany
Maher Abujelala, USA
Jiban Adhikary, USA
Kashif Ahmad, Qatar
Muneeb Ahmad, UK
Naveed Ahmed, United Arab Emirates
Aino Ahtinen, Finland
Wolfgang Aigner, Austria
Deepak Akkil, Finland
Aftab Alam, Republic of Korea
Soraia Meneses Alarcão, Portugal
Pedro Albuquerque Santos, Portugal
Günter Alce, Sweden
Iñigo Aldalur, Spain
Alaa Alkhafaji, Iraq
Aishat Aloba, USA
Yosuef Alotaibi, UK
Taghreed Alshehri, UK
Ragaad Al-Tarawneh, USA
Alejandro Alvarez-Marin, Chile
Lucas Anastasiou, UK
Ulf Andersson, Sweden
Joseph Aneke, Italy
Mark Apperley, New Zealand
Renan Aranha, Brazil
Pierre-Emmanuel Arduin, France
Stephanie Arevalo Arboleda, Germany
Jan Argasiński, Poland

Patricia Arias-Cabarcos, Germany
Alexander Arntz, Germany
Jonas Auda, Germany
Andreas Auinger, Austria
Iuliia Avgustis, Finland
Cédric Bach, France
Miroslav Bachinski, Germany
Victor Bacu, Romania
Jan Balata, Czech Republic
Teresa Baldassarre, Italy
Fabrizio Balducci, Italy
Vijayanand Banahatti, India
Karolina Baras, Portugal
Simone Barbosa, Brazil
Vita Santa Barletta, Italy
Silvio Barra, Italy
Barbara Rita Barricelli, Italy
Ralph Barthel, UK
Thomas Baudel, France
Christine Bauer, Netherlands
Fatma Ben Mesmia, Canada
Marit Bentvelzen, Netherlands
François Bérard, France
Melanie Berger, Netherlands
Gerd Berget, Norway
Sergi Bermúdez i Badia, Portugal
Dario Bertero, UK
Guilherme Bertolaccini, Brazil
Lonni Besançon, Australia

Laura-Bianca Bilius, Romania
Kerstin Blumenstein, Austria
Andreas Bollin, Austria
Judith Borghouts, UK
Nis Bornoe, Denmark
Gabriela Bosetti, UK
Hollie Bostock, Portugal
Paolo Bottoni, Italy
Magdalena Boucher, Austria
Amina Bouraoui, Tunisia
Elodie Bouzekri, France
Judy Bowen, New Zealand
Efe Bozkir, Germany
Danielle Bragg, USA
Diogo Branco, Portugal
Dawn Branley-Bell, UK
Stephen Brewster, UK
Giada Brianza, UK
Barry Brown, Sweden
Nick Bryan-Kinns, UK
Andreas Bucher, Switzerland
Elizabeth Buie, UK
Alexandru Bundea, Germany
Paolo Buono, Italy
Michael Burch, Switzerland
Matthew Butler, Australia
Fabio Buttussi, Italy
Andreas Butz, Germany
Maria Claudia Buzzi, Italy
Marina Buzzi, Italy
Zoya Bylinskii, USA
Diogo Cabral, Portugal
Åsa Cajander, Sweden
Francisco Maria Calisto, Portugal
Hector Caltenco, Sweden
José Creissac Campos, Portugal
Heloisa Candello, Brazil
Alberto Cannavò, Italy
Bruno Cardoso, Belgium
Jorge Cardoso, Portugal
Géry Casiez, France
Fabio Cassano, Italy
Brendan Cassidy, UK
Alejandro Catala, Spain

Miguel Ceriani, UK
Daniel Cermak-Sassenrath, Denmark
Vanessa Cesário, Portugal
Fred Charles, UK
Debaleena Chattopadhyay, USA
Alex Chen, Singapore
Thomas Chen, USA
Yuan Chen, Canada
Chola Chhetri, USA
Katherine Chiluiza, Ecuador
Nick Chozos, UK
Michael Chromik, Germany
Christopher Clarke, UK
Bárbara Cleto, Portugal
Antonio Coelho, Portugal
Ashley Colley, Finland
Nelly Condori-Fernandez, Spain
Marios Constantinides, UK
Cléber Corrêa, Brazil
Vinicius Costa de Souza, Brazil
Joëlle Coutaz, France
Céline Coutrix, France
Chris Creed, UK
Carlos Cunha, Portugal
Kamila Rios da Hora Rodrigues, Brazil
Damon Daylamani-Zad, UK
Sergio de Cesare, UK
Marco de Gemmis, Italy
Teis De Greve, Belgium
Victor Adriel de Jesus Oliveira, Austria
Helmut Degen, USA
Donald Degraen, Germany
William Delamare, France
Giuseppe Desolda, Italy
Henrik Detjen, Germany
Marianna Di Gregorio, Italy
Ines Di Loreto, France
Daniel Diethei, Germany
Tilman Dingler, Australia
Anke Dittmar, Germany
Monica Divitini, Norway
Janki Dodiya, Germany
Julia Dominiak, Poland
Ralf Dörner, Germany

Julie Doyle, Ireland
Philip Doyle, Ireland
Fiona Draxler, Germany
Emanuel Felipe Duarte, Brazil
Rui Duarte, Portugal
Bruno Dumas, Belgium
Mark Dunlop, UK
Sophie Dupuy-Chessa, France
Jason Dykes, UK
Chloe Eghtebas, Germany
Kevin El Haddad, Belgium
Don Samitha Elvitigala, New Zealand
Augusto Esteves, Portugal
Siri Fagernes, Norway
Katherine Fennedy, Singapore
Marta Ferreira, Portugal
Francesco Ferrise, Italy
Lauren Stacey Ferro, Italy
Christos Fidas, Greece
Daniel Finnegan, UK
Daniela Fogli, Italy
Manuel J. Fonseca, Portugal
Peter Forbrig, Germany
Rita Francese, Italy
André Freire, Brazil
Karin Fröhlich, Finland
Susanne Furman, USA
Henrique Galvan Debarba, Denmark
Sandra Gama, Portugal
Dilrukshi Gamage, Japan
Jérémie Garcia, France
Jose Garcia Estrada, Norway
David Geerts, Belgium
Denise Y. Geiskkovitch, Canada
Stefan Geisler, Germany
Mirko Gelsomini, Italy
Çağlar Genç, Finland
Rosella Gennari, Italy
Nina Gerber, Germany
Moojan Ghafurian, Canada
Maliheh Ghajargar, Sweden
Sabiha Ghellal, Germany
Debjyoti Ghosh, Germany
Michail Giannakos, Norway

Terje Gjøsæter, Norway
Marc Gonzalez Capdevila, Brazil
Julien Gori, Finland
Laurent Grisoni, France
Tor-Morten Gronli, Norway
Sebastian Günther, Germany
Li Guo, UK
Srishti Gupta, USA
Francisco Gutiérrez, Belgium
José Eder Guzman Mendoza, Mexico
Jonna Häkkilä, Finland
Lilit Hakobyan, UK
Thilina Halloluwa, Sri Lanka
Perttu Hämäläinen, Finland
Lane Harrison, USA
Michael Harrison, UK
Hanna Hasselqvist, Sweden
Tomi Heimonen, USA
Florian Heinrich, Germany
Florian Heller, Belgium
Karey Helms, Sweden
Nathalie Henry Riche, USA
Diana Hernandez-Bocanegra, Germany
Danula Hettiachchi, Australia
Wilko Heuten, Germany
Annika Hinze, New Zealand
Linda Hirsch, Germany
Sarah Hodge, UK
Sven Hoffmann, Germany
Catherine Holloway, UK
Leona Holloway, Australia
Lars Erik Holmquist, UK
Anca-Simona Horvath, Denmark
Simo Hosio, Finland
Sebastian Hubenschmid, Germany
Helena Vallo Hult, Sweden
Shah Rukh Humayoun, USA
Ebba Þóra Hvannberg, Iceland
Alon Ilsar, Australia
Md Athar Imtiaz, New Zealand
Oana Inel, Netherlands
Francisco Iniesto, UK
Andri Ioannou, Cyprus
Chyng-Yang Jang, USA

Florian Mathis, UK
Andrii Matviienko, Germany
Peter Mayer, Germany
Sven Mayer, Germany
Mark McGill, UK
Donald McMillan, Sweden
Lukas Mecke, Germany
Elisa Mekler, Finland
Alessandra Melonio, Italy
Eleonora Mencarini, Italy
Maria Menendez Blanco, Italy
Aline Menin, France
Arjun Menon, Sweden
Nazmus Sakib Miazi, USA
Zdeněk Míkovec, Czech Republic
Tim Mittermeier, Germany
Emmanuel Mkpojiogu, Nigeria
Jonas Moll, Sweden
Alberto Monge Roffarello, Italy
Troels Mønsted, Denmark
Diego Morra, Italy
Jaime Munoz Arteaga, Mexico
Sachith Muthukumarana, New Zealand
Vasiliki Mylonopoulou, Sweden
Frank Nack, Netherlands
Mohammad Naiseh, UK
Vania Neris, Brazil
Robin Neuhaus, Germany
Thao Ngo, Germany
Binh Vinh Duc Nguyen, Belgium
Vickie Nguyen, USA
James Nicholson, UK
Peter Axel Nielsen, Denmark
Jasmin Niess, Germany
Evangelos Niforatos, Netherlands
Kent Norman, USA
Fatima Nunes, Brazil
Carli Ochs, Switzerland
Joseph O'Hagan, UK
Takashi Ohta, Japan
Jonas Oppenlaender, Finland
Michael Ortega, France
Changkun Ou, Germany
Yun Suen Pai, New Zealand

Dominika Palivcová, Czech Republic
Viktoria Pammer-Schindler, Austria
Eleftherios Papachristos, Denmark
Sofia Papavlasopoulou, Norway
Leonado Parra, Colombia
Max Pascher, Germany
Ankit Patel, Portugal
Fabio Paternò, Italy
Maria Angela Pellegrino, Italy
Anthony Perritano, USA
Johanna Persson, Sweden
Ken Pfeuffer, Germany
Bastian Pfleging, Netherlands
Vung Pham, USA
Jayesh Pillai, India
Catherine Plaisant, USA
Henning Pohl, Denmark
Margit Pohl, Austria
Alessandro Pollini, Italy
Dorin-Mircea Popovici, Romania
Thiago Porcino, Brazil
Dominic Potts, UK
Sarah Prange, Germany
Marco Procaccini, Italy
Arnaud Prouzeau, France
Parinya Punpongsanon, Japan
Sónia Rafael, Portugal
Jessica Rahman, Australia
Mikko Rajanen, Finland
Nimmi Rangaswamy, India
Alberto Raposo, Brazil
George Raptis, Greece
Hanae Rateau, Canada
Sebastian Rauh, Germany
Hirak Ray, USA
Traian Rebedea, Romania
Yosra Rekik, France
Elizabeth Rendon-Velez, Colombia
Malte Ressin, UK
Tera Reynolds, USA
Miguel Ribeiro, Portugal
Maria Rigou, Greece
Sirpa Riihiaho, Finland
Michele Risi, Italy

Paul van Schauk, UK
Koen van Turnhout, Netherlands
Jean Vanderdonckt, Belgium
Eduardo Veas, Austria
Katia Vega, USA
Kellie Vella, Australia
Leena Ventä-Olkkonen, Finland
Nadine Vigouroux, France
Gabriela Villalobos-Zúñiga, Switzerland
Aku Visuri, Finland
Giuliana Vitiello, Italy
Pierpaolo Vittorini, Italy
Julius von Willich, Germany
Steven Vos, Netherlands
Nadine Wagener, Germany
Lun Wang, Italy
Ruijie Wang, Italy
Gerhard Weber, Germany
Thomas Weber, Germany
Rina Wehbe, Canada
Florian Weidner, Germany
Alexandra Weilenmann, Sweden
Sebastian Weiß, Germany

Yannick Weiss, Germany
Robin Welsch, Germany
Janet Wesson, South Africa
Benjamin Weyers, Germany
Stephanie Wilson, UK
Marco Winckler, France
Philipp Wintersberger, Austria
Katrin Wolf, Germany
Kim Wölfel, Germany
Julia Woodward, USA
Matthias Wunsch, Austria
Haijun Xia, USA
Asim Evren Yantac, Turkey
Enes Yigitbas, Germany
Yongjae Yoo, Canada
Johannes Zagermann, Germany
Massimo Zancanaro, Italy
André Zenner, Germany
Jingjie Zheng, Canada
Suwen Zhu, USA
Ying Zhu, USA
Jürgen Ziegler, Germany

Partners and Sponsors

Partners

International Federation for Information Processing

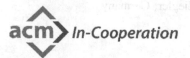

In-cooperation with ACM   In-cooperation with SIGCHI

Sponsors

EULOGIC

eusoft
more than a lims

Experis™
ManpowerGroup

exprivia

openwork
Just solutions

ORA ZERO
GROUP

sincon
ICT SOLUTIONS

Contents – Part III

Human-Centered AI

Human-Centred Development of Sustainable Technology

Human-Robot Interaction

Information Visualization

Interaction Design and Cultural Development

Games and Gamification

Diegetic and Non-diegetic Health Interfaces in VR Shooter Games

Kay Köhle[1], Matthias Hoppe[1], Albrecht Schmidt[1], and Ville Mäkelä[1,2,3(✉)]

[1] LMU Munich, Munich, Germany
[2] Bundeswehr University Munich, Munich, Germany
kay.koehle@campus.lmu.de,
{matthias.hoppe,albrecht.schmidt,ville.maekelae}@ifi.lmu.de
[3] University of Waterloo, Waterloo, Canada

Abstract. The player's *health* is one of the most pervasive components in computer games. However, in virtual reality games, it is unclear how different representations of player health function compared to traditional flat-screen games. Because the viewpoint changes based on the player's head movement, non-diegetic UI elements may not be ideal. Also, the sense of embodiment in VR provides opportunities to experiment with diegetic ways of communicating the player's health. To investigate different implementations of player health in VR games, we developed three health interfaces and evaluated them in a shooter game. The health interfaces included: **1)** A non-diegetic health bar, visible on the screen at all times, **2)** A diegetic health value on a virtual wristwatch, and **3)** A diegetic physical interface, where lost health results in trembling and slower movement. 37 participants played the game using all three health interfaces and provided feedback. We found that all three interfaces had their own strengths. The non-diegetic health bar was seen as suitable for multi-player games, while the wristwatch was seen as suitable for single-player, story-driven games. The physical interface was liked for its impact on gameplay, and was also seen as suitable for story-driven games.

Keywords: Virtual reality · Games · Diegetic interfaces · First-person shooters · Game design

1 Introduction

In many computer games, players face a variety of challenges like hordes of enemies that attempt to harm the player. The player's *health* is at the center of this type of gameplay. Health is reduced, for example, when enemies hit the player, or if the player stumbles into a trap. When health is reduced to zero, the game typically ends, or other repercussions are faced.

Electronic supplementary material The online version of this chapter (https://doi.org/10.1007/978-3-030-85613-7_1) contains supplementary material, which is available to authorized users.

Traditionally, player health is represented on the screen as a *non-diegetic* user interface element, like a progress bar or a numerical value. Non-diegetic elements exist outside of the story and space of the game [1,2]. In contrast, *diegetic* elements exist in the game world (e.g., they might also be perceived by other characters). Diegetic representations of player health also exist; for example, the player character may start limping when they are close to death, or they may have visible wounds. Audio cues, like shortness of breath and an elevated heartbeat, are common additional diegetic representations.

In virtual reality (VR) games, however, it is unclear how different health interfaces function. In particular, due to the sense of embodiment in VR, we can experiment with novel diegetic health interfaces that directly affect the player. To investigate different ways of communicating the player's health in VR games, we developed three health interfaces and evaluated them in a shooter game. 37 participants played the game using all three health interfaces and provided feedback. The health interfaces included: **Overlay:** A non-diegetic health bar, visible on the screen at all times, **Wristwatch:** A diegetic health value on a virtual watch, attached to the user's wrist, and **Physical:** A diegetic, movement-based health interface, where low health causes trembling and slower movement.

We found that all three interfaces have their unique strengths. Participants appreciated that the **overlay** was quickly available, stating that it is suitable for multi-player games. The **wristwatch** was appreciated for its balance of unobtrusiveness, immersion, and accuracy, and it was seen as suitable for single-player and story-driven games. The **physical** interface was appreciated for its direct impact on gameplay, and it was seen as suitable for story-driven games. The interfaces were rated equally for presence. Our work is useful for designing interfaces in VR, and for directing future work in physical interfaces in VR.

2   Background

Diegetic and non-diegetic interfaces have been studied in games and beyond, and both in traditional computer games as well as in VR games. Iacovides et al. [3] found that a diegetic interface was more immersive than a non-diegetic interface in a 2D first-person shooter. Raffaele et al. [6] found that players consistently rated diegetic UIs more immersive in VR games. Similar results were obtained by Salomoni et al. [9]. Diegetic cues have also been studied in other areas of VR, like guidance [8] and cultural heritage [1].

We are not aware of existing research that investigates diegetic cues in VR beyond their effect on immersion. Also, despite some research on health interfaces in flat-screen computer games [5], we are not aware of prior work that investigates health interfaces in VR. Especially, in VR we can use not only "traditional" diegetic UIs (e.g., health displayed on a virtual screen), but we can also make players *experience* the diegetic UI, as we can manipulate the way players move and interact in VR. We hypothesize that this could add to the player experience, creating, e.g., a stronger sense of danger, but also feelings of victory and triumph. With this work, we aim to close these gaps.

3 Study

We conducted a study where participants played a VR shooter game with three different health interfaces (Fig. 1).

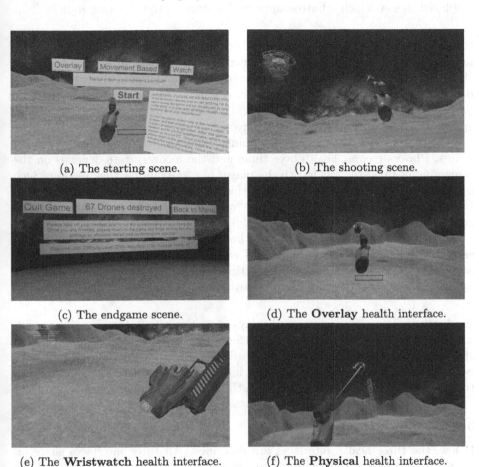

(a) The starting scene.

(b) The shooting scene.

(c) The endgame scene.

(d) The **Overlay** health interface.

(e) The **Wristwatch** health interface.

(f) The **Physical** health interface.

Fig. 1. The VR shooter game and the tested health interfaces.

3.1 VR Shooter Game

We implemented a VR shooter game using Unity and the SteamVR, containing the typical gameplay elements for shooters. The game is divided into three scenes.

Start. In the start scene, a menu and instructions for the game and the study are displayed (Fig. 1a). Two guns are hovering in front of the user, roughly at eye height, which the player can grab by touching them with their virtual hands and pressing the trigger buttons on the controllers.

The guns can then be used to shoot at one of the three buttons (by pointing and pressing the trigger) to activate one of the health interfaces. The order of the health interface buttons is randomized, but the player can choose any one of them. Upon selection, a brief explanation of the selected health interface is displayed, below which a button appears for starting the shooting round.

Shooting Round. The shooting round contains the main gameplay. The round lasts for four minutes, during which drones appear around the scene. The drones shoot at the player, whose task is to avoid getting hit and destroy as many drones as they can by shooting at them. All shots leave a red trail so that the player can follow where they are going. The drones die in one hit. The drones spawn in a half-circle in front of the player.

The player starts with 100 health points. Each hit damages the player by 10 points. Players recover health over time, and the recovery rate depends on the remaining health—the less health the player has, the quicker they recover. Such mechanisms are common in games, so that players can experience the thrill of barely surviving. Moreover, we did not want players to die too early, so they could properly experience each health interface.

After the four minutes are up, or the player's health has been reduced to zero, the round ends. Interactions and events in the round are supported by audio cues. This includes the round starting, the round ending, shooting, drones appearing, drones getting hit and destroyed, and the player getting hit.

Endgame. The endgame scene displays statistics about the shooting round, and instructions for the next steps in the study (Fig. 1c). At this point in the study, the user is asked to take off the headset and fill in forms on their computer before returning to the game. The user has options to quit the game, or return to the main menu to select another health interface and play another round.

3.2   Health Interfaces

Below, the three health interfaces are described. All three interfaces share an identical visual and auditory cue. The edges of the screen turn red as the player gets hurt, and the strength of the effect was determined by how much health was left (seen in Figs. 1d and 1f). Similarly, a heartbeat audio cue is played when the player gets hurt, which gets more intense as health decreases.

These two shared effects were added because they are commonly used in games as additional cues. Moreover, while our investigation was not focused on auditory cues, it did not make sense to leave out auditory cues entirely, as they are part of a complete gaming experience.

Overlay. The Overlay condition displays a traditional, two-dimensional health bar (Fig. 1d). It stays visible on the screen, following the player's head movements. This health interface was included because it is a typical non-diegetic representation of player health, used in games for several decades.

Wristwatch. The Wristwatch condition displays health as a numerical value on the player's wrist (Fig. 1e). This health interface was included because it has been used in VR shooting games (e.g., Half-Life: Alyx [11]). This health interface is diegetic, i.e., it exists in the game world, and players need to lift their arm and turn the watch towards them to see it.

Physical. The Physical condition is an experimental health interface where, when player's lose health, their movements become slower and twitchy, to represent the "reality" of being hurt. The player's real pointing location is displayed as a transparent gun (Fig. 1f), as opposed to the current pointing as a result of slower movement. This interface was included because we wanted to experiment not only with typical diegetic and non-diegetic interfaces, but also physical interfaces that VR makes possible.

3.3 Study Design

The study was of within-subjects design, where participants played three rounds of the shooter game, once with each health interface. Between the rounds, participants filled in a questionnaire that enquired about their experience with each interface. The study was designed as a remote study, so that people could participate from their own homes using their own VR equipment. In addition, we set up a physical testing space, where participants could attend the study with no human contact. The study procedure was exactly the same regardless of how participants attended the study. For an in-depth description of our remote study design and procedure and a discussion on lessons learned, see Rivu et al. [7].

3.4 Recruitment and Participants

We advertised the study through social media and targeted forums like VR-related subreddits in Reddit, where we expected to get in contact with people who own a head-mounted display. In our advertisement mail, we provided a registration link. Registered participants then received instructions by email and a link to download the VR shooter game. In addition, we recruited local participants via university mailing lists.

A total of 37 participants completed the study (24 male, 11 female, 2 undisclosed). Their average age was 23 (SD = 6.6). Several additional participants attended but did not fully complete the study, and so their data was excluded from the analysis. 13 participants attended the local study and used the HTC Vive Pro. 24 participants attended remotely using different HMDs, the most popular being the HTC Vive Pro and the Valve Index (7 participants each), and the HTC Vive (6 participants). Most participants (27) reported playing 0–5 h of VR games weekly; the remaining ten participants played more. Participants played other digital games more actively: 0–5 h per week (10 participants), 5–10 h (14), 10–15 h (4), 15–20 h (2), and 20+ h (7).

3.5   Procedure

The VR game placed participants immediately in the Start scene, where they could review the instructions to the game and the study, and play the first round with one of the health interfaces. Once the round was over, the endgame scene was displayed, and a feedback questionnaire was automatically opened on the default browser of their computer. At this point, the game asked participants to take off their HMD, fill in the questionnaire, and then return to the game. Participants repeated this procedure three times, which took around 40 min.

We chose to have participants fill in the questionnaire outside of VR because the questionnaire was long and we included open-ended questions that could not be reasonably answered in VR. The questionnaire contained the Slater-Usoh-Steed presence questionnaire [10], the Game Experience Questionnaire (GEQ) [4], and custom statements and open-ended questions. Four custom statements asked about the interface's suitability for different kinds of games (Fig. 2). One additional statement asked for an **overall rating** for the interface on a 10-point scale (1 - "very bad", 10 - "very good"). The open-ended questions asked what the participant liked and disliked about the interface.

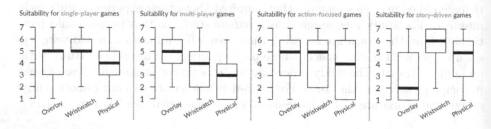

Fig. 2. Participants rated the suitability of the three health interfaces on four dimensions: single-player, multi-player, action-focused, and story-driven games. The ratings were on a 7-point scale (1 = not suitable at all, 7 = very suitable).

4   Results and Discussion

In this section, we present the results and discuss implications for design for each health interface. We conducted thematic analysis on the participants qualitative feedback, and statistical analyses on the participants' subjective ratings using Friedman's test and the Wilcoxon signed-rank test. The preferences are shown in Fig. 2.

There were no significant differences between the interfaces' **overall scores** ($X^2{}_F(2) = 2.17$, p = .339). The Overlay and Wristwatch received a median rating of 7/10, and the Physical received a median rating of 6/10.

With the GEQ, we tested against the seven experience components [4] separately. Only one of them, *Sensory and Imaginative Immersion*, had significant differences between the interfaces ($X^2{}_F(2) = 13.52$, p = .001): the Wristwatch was rated significantly higher than the Overlay (T $= 192.50$, z $= -3.31$, p $=$ .001). Hence, overall the differences between the GEQ scores were minimal.

There were no significant differences between the health interfaces' *presence* scores in any of the six tested dimensions [10]. This is an interesting finding. Previous research suggests that diegetic interfaces result in a higher sense of presence [3,6,9], but this was not the case in our study.

4.1 Overlay

The most common positive traits for the non-diegetic Overlay interface were that it offers a clear way to judge the player's health status (12 participants), that it is always visible and accessible anytime (11), and that it is immediately understandable and familiar (5). At the same time, it was commonly perceived to be intrusive, i.e., in the way of the player's view (14). Moreover, participants criticized that it was not always clear when health changed as their was no clear association with gameplay (5), and that it hurt the game's immersion (5).

The Overlay was seen as significantly more suitable for *multi-player* games (MD $= 5$, Friedman: $X^2{}_F(2) = 13.61$, p $= .001$) than the Wristwatch (MD $= 4$, Wilcoxon: T $= 324.50$, z $= -2.79$, p $= .005$) and Physical interfaces (MD $= 3$, Wilcoxon: T $= 430.50$, z $= -4.09$, p $= .000$). This is likely due to the competitive nature of multi-player games, where accuracy and efficiency (i.e., that health information is available with a glance) may be favored over immersive, less efficient interfaces.

While the individual positive and negative traits of the overlay are not surprising, it is somewhat surprising that overlay-like UI elements still seem to have a useful function in VR games, as they do bring the benefits of clarity, efficiency, and familiarity. Some of the negative traits of overlays could be alleviated with further design choices. In some games, the health bar could be part of a diegetic interface, like an augmented helmet that the player's avatar is wearing. At the same time, the health bar could be made transparent, becoming opaque only when health actually changes – this would make it less intrusive and also better highlight the exact moments when the player is hit.

4.2 Wristwatch

The most common positive traits for the Wristwatch interface were that it offers a clear and accurate way to assess health status (10 participants), it is immersive (9), unobtrusive (8), and that it blends well into the VR action (7). For negative traits, participants commonly stated that checking health was impractical during intense action (8), and that participants had to actively choose to check their health status in order to remain aware of it (8).

The Wristwatch was seen as significantly more suitable for *single-player* games (MD $= 5$, Friedman: $X^2{}_F(2) = 6.54$, p $= .038$) than the Physical interface (MD $= 5$, Wilcoxon: T $= 333.00$, z $= -2.55$, p $= .011$) and the Overlay (MD $= 4$, Wilcoxon: T $= 328.50$, z $= -1.99$, p $= .047$). Similarly, the Wristwatch was seen as significantly more suitable for *story-driven* games (MD $= 6$, Friedman:

$X^2 \ _F(2) = 33.18$, p = .000) than the Physical interface (MD = 5, Wilcoxon: T = 375.00, z = −3.44, p = .001) and the Overlay (MD = 2, Wilcoxon: T = 502.50, z = −4.48, p = .000).

This above preferences seem logical considering the identified positive and negative traits; diegetic interfaces are perceived as more immersive [6,9], which is likely rated as a more important trait in story-driven games than, e.g., competitive multi-player games.

Based on the participants' comments and rating, the wristwatch seemed to be the most well-rounded and the most liked health interface in our study. In the future, haptic cues could be added to the controllers whenever the player gets hurt, to make those exact moments more clear. Clearer audio cues about getting hit could also be used.

4.3   Physical

The most common positive traits for the Physical interface were that it impacts gameplay, i.e., there are consequences for getting hurt (7), and that it is unobtrusive (5), and immersive (4). However, most players complained that it was hard to tell how much health they actually had (23). Moreover, some participants stated that the slow movement was frustrating (4), and that it was annoying that the game got harder when they were already hurt (3).

The Physical interface was seen as significantly more suitable for story-driven games (MD = 5) than the Overlay (T = 364.00, z = −2.72, p = .006), but the Wristwatch was the most preferred. The Physical was not seen as suitable for multi-player games (MD = 3). This seems logical, as the intensity of the interface might enhance a story-driven game's story and setting, but might be not work in a competitive environment.

The clearest downside of this interface was that it does not communicate the exact health status. To overcome this, the Physical interface could be easily combined with another health interface, like the Wristwatch.

Despite the criticism towards the Physical interface, we believe we have only begun to uncover the potential of physical interfaces in VR. We already observed positive effects, e.g., its direct impact on gameplay. Investigating physical interfaces further, not only for player health but for other gameplay functions, like altered states (e.g., boosts and debuffs), is a clear direction for future work.

5   Conclusion and Future Work

Our work suggests that both diegetic and non-diegetic interfaces might have their place in VR games. Our three tested health interfaces were equal in terms of presence and received comparable overall and game experience ratings. Still, we uncovered unique positive and negative traits, and we also found clear differences in terms of what types of games each health interface might fit in. Non-diegetic interfaces might be useful in competitive multi-player games, where clarity and quick access to information are important factors. In turn, diegetic interfaces might fit better in single-player and story-driven games, where immersive experiences and consistency may be highly valued factors. Our work here provided initial insight into the design of health interfaces for VR; future studies should investigate diegetic and non-diegetic health interfaces more systematically. We also believe that future VR research should dive deeper into physical interfaces. Their direct and observable impact on gameplay and interaction can be utilized for many novel possibilities in VR games and beyond.

References

1. Caggianese, G., Gallo, L., Neroni, P.: Exploring the feasibility of diegetic user interfaces in immersive virtual exhibitions within the cultural heritage. In: 2018 14th International Conference on Signal-Image Technology Internet-Based Systems (SITIS), pp. 625–631 (2018). https://doi.org/10.1109/SITIS.2018.00101
2. Cecchi, A.: Diegetic versus nondiegetic: a reconsideration of the conceptual opposition as a contribution to the theory of audiovision. In: Worlds of Audiovision, pp. 1–10 (2010)
3. Iacovides, I., Cox, A., Kennedy, R., Cairns, P., Jennett, C.: Removing the HUD: the impact of non-diegetic game elements and expertise on player involvement. In: Proceedings of the 2015 Annual Symposium on Computer-Human Interaction in Play, CHI PLAY 2015, New York, NY, USA, pp. 13–22. Association for Computing Machinery (2015). https://doi.org/10.1145/2793107.2793120
4. IJsselsteijn, W.A., de Kort, Y.A., Poels, K.: The game experience questionnaire, pp. 3–9. Technische Universiteit Eindhoven, Eindhoven (2013)
5. Peacocke, M., Teather, R.J., Carette, J., MacKenzie, I.S., McArthur, V.: An empirical comparison of first-person shooter information displays: HUDs, diegetic displays, and spatial representations. Entertain. Comput. **26**, 41–58 (2018). https://doi.org/10.1016/j.entcom.2018.01.003. https://www.sciencedirect.com/science/article/pii/S1875952117300435
6. Raffaele, R., Carvalho, B., Silva, F.: Evaluation of immersive user interfaces in virtual reality first person games. In: 24° Encontro Português de Computação Gráfica e Interação, pp. 123–126 (2017)
7. Rivu, R., et al.: Remote VR studies - a framework for running virtual reality studies remotely via participant-owned HMDs. CoRR **abs/2102.11207** (2021). https://arxiv.org/abs/2102.11207
8. Rothe, S., Hußmann, H., Allary, M.: Diegetic cues for guiding the viewer in cinematic virtual reality. Association for Computing Machinery, New York (2017). https://doi.org/10.1145/3139131.3143421
9. Salomoni, P., Prandi, C., Roccetti, M., Casanova, L., Marchetti, L., Marfia, G.: Diegetic user interfaces for virtual environments with HMDs: a user experience study with oculus rift. J. Multimodal User Interfaces **11**(2), 173–184 (2017)
10. Slater, M., McCarthy, J., Maringelli, F.: The influence of body movement on subjective presence in virtual environments. Hum. Factors **40**(3), 469–477 (1998). https://doi.org/10.1518/001872098779591368
11. Valve: Half-life: Alyx. Game [Windows] (2020)

Encouraging Chemistry Learning Through an Augmented Reality Magic Game

Ana Margarida Sousa(✉) and Teresa Romão

NOVA LINCS - FCT, Universidade Nova de Lisboa, Campus da Caparica,
2829-516 Caparica, Portugal
amdd.sousa@campus.fct.unl.pt, tir@fct.unl.pt

Abstract. Chemistry is often labelled as a difficult subject, which challenges come mostly from topics that require abstract thinking, leading to a negative attitude by the learners. Studies show that augmented reality (AR) is potentially useful for education purposes, particularly in the representation of abstract concepts by depicting them through virtual objects. This paper presents an AR educational mobile game, named "Magic Elements", targeting children from 9 to 12 years old. The game was designed to promote a positive attitude towards chemistry, teaching children basic concepts while creating climate change awareness. As climate change is having a profound impact on Earth and urgent actions need to be taken, the game also addresses this topic relating chemistry with the real world and promoting sustainable habits among children from an early age. Tangibles and storytelling are explored to engage and sensitize children. Our findings show a positive outcome, as well as a considerable increase in the acquired chemistry knowledge and awareness towards climate change.

Keywords: Mobile game · Chemistry education · Climate change · Learning · Augmented reality · Tangible interfaces · Storytelling

1 Introduction

Chemistry topics such as atoms, molecules, and the periodic table itself are the fundamental base for understanding more advanced concepts [19], but students often struggle to comprehend it as it requires abstract thinking [12]. Thus, chemistry is often regarded as a difficult topic, which can demotivate children even before they tackle the subject in school [17].

As climate change is having a profound impact on Earth and urgent actions need to be taken, we decided to address this topic relating chemistry with the real world and contributing to promote sustainable habits among children from an early age.

Nowadays, children have a strong relationship with technology, particularly with mobile devices and digital games, which can be used for entertainment and learning. Augmented reality technology has shown great potential for educational purposes [23], specifically chemistry, since it allows the representation of 3D models, helping to understand abstract concepts, like atoms and molecules, while also building motivation [3, 4,

C. Ardito et al. (Eds.): INTERACT 2021, LNCS 12934, pp. 12–21, 2021.
https://doi.org/10.1007/978-3-030-85613-7_2

8, 15, 21]. AR technologies can be combined with physical objects, allowing users to interact with the augmented world, and helping them to visualize and control 3D models in an easier way, improving their visual and spatial skills [9, 10, 13, 15, 19]. Several studies also show that storytelling can be an advantageous tool as it helps to explain complex matters, connect different concepts [5], facilitate engagement and maintain motivation [18, 22].

Therefore, we designed and implemented a mobile serious game targeting children (9 to 12 years old) that combines AR, tangibles and storytelling, aiming to achieve three main goals: (1) foster an attitude change regarding chemistry by generating motivation and demystifying the idea that chemistry is a hard subject (2) promote the retention of some knowledge regarding the topics (chemistry concepts and climate change) addressed in our game (3) sensitize children for climate change and create a desire to implement small environmentally friendly practices in their daily routines.

2 Related Work

AR is defined by Azuma [1] as any system that has the following three characteristics: (1) combines real and virtual (2) is interactive in real time (3) is registered in three dimensions. Recent years have seen significant advances in AR technologies, leading to the proliferation of several studies which have demonstrated great potential of this technology in the education field. In a recent study [8], results suggested that the field with most potential to use AR technology is science education where, specifically in chemistry, 3D demonstrations of chemical bonds and molecules can be developed to envision micro models. Since AR works like a bridge between the real and virtual world [1, 14], this allows its combination with physical objects, improving user's visual and spatial skills [15] and making the control of virtual objects more manageable [10]. Studies also indicate that AR can be used in education to draw users' attention, increasing motivation and academic achievements, allowing students to interact with the learning subjects, unlike traditional approaches that put the learner as a passive element during the learning process [8, 15].

Multiple chemistry games and applications using augmented reality were already created, such as Núñez et al. AR system for teaching Inorganic Chemistry [15] and Chen application to learn amino acids [3], as well as other chemistry applications focused on the topics of atoms and molecules, such as Augmented Chemistry [19], Taçgin et al. application [21], The Table mystery [2] and Periodic Fable [16]. Interestingly, all these applications also incorporate tangible objects, usually used to control the movement of 3D virtual objects that represent chemistry abstract concepts, such as molecules. Most of these applications do not involve a playful component, and do not provide specific goals to the users, allowing them to freely explore the world of atoms and molecules. The Table mystery, although providing specific goals and challenges, requires a lengthy system set-up. Moreover, these applications do not explore the integration of chemistry with climate change.

3 Magic Elements

We created a mobile game to be played by 9 to 12 years old children that seeks to motivate them to learn chemistry and promote their awareness towards climate change. It combines AR techniques, tangible objects and storytelling. The use of the mobile phone as the AR display can be advantageous due to its portability, affordability and simplicity [7]. Touchscreens are also the preferred device of our target group, who can handle them easily [11]. We also explored cards as physical objects, in terms of promoting 3D spatial perception abilities since this can be an advantageous object to be used, given its portability. Besides conveying chemistry concepts, the story behind the game raises users' awareness towards climate change.

The development of the game described in this paper followed a user-centered design methodology, involving an iterative design process with several design, implementation and evaluation cycles that help to improve the system's quality, functionality and interface.

To ensure that the concepts covered in the game were suitable for our target group and well presented, we had the collaboration of a chemistry teacher that analysed our approach and game concept during the preliminary design, which at the time allowed us to identify some concepts that were too advanced and to correct some details that could lead to confusion in understanding the concepts. Also, she validated the final version of the game and, in this later stage, she claimed that the addressed concepts were appropriate for our target group, pointing that the way they were approached in the game allows children to understand them rather than memorize them, while transmitting the message that chemistry can be fun. As a teacher, she stated that she would advise younger students to install the game since she thinks it will encourage them a lot to learn about the subject.

3.1 Game Description

The fictitious premise of Magic Elements happens in Lemuria, a virtual magic world that is suffering with climate change. To fight it, the player as to perform some tasks during a game level and find an exit (that leads to the next game level), leaving the current place in a limited amount of time. To better explain the dynamics of the game, we next describe the main actions that take place during the first game level, showing the corresponding game screens in Fig. 1.

The first three magic objects that the player needs to collect in the first game level are the glasses (allowing the player to see abstract models such as atoms, molecules and macromolecules), a magic wand (to manipulate and interact with abstract models) and a multiplier (to multiply a molecule forming a resource, e.g. reproduce a water molecule to create a considerable amount of water). The hypothetical use of magic by the player during the game gives him more freedom to manipulate and interact with abstract models, like atoms and molecules, while it clarifies the idea that that interaction and manipulation is not possible in the real world.

Unlike the glasses and the wand, which are visibly available to be collected by the player, the multiplier can only be collected after the player opens the chest (Fig. 1.a) which in turn can only be opened with a key. To earn the key, the player needs to perform an activity by entering a portal that firstly leads to an AR closet, where the player chooses their magic accessories needed to perform the following activity. After choosing the magic accessories, the player performs an AR activity to "build" an atom of a certain element using paper cards. The card allows the player to visualize an animation of the atom electronic cloud. He then needs to stop the electrons of the electronic cloud model (Fig. 1.b), which will show the Bohr model visualization. The element card follows an atomic notation, showing the atomic symbol, the mass number and the atomic number of the element, indicating the number of subatomic particles of that element (Fig. 1.c). The player can add the subatomic particles (electrons, protons and neutrons) to the Bohr model of the chemical element's atom by scanning its corresponding card and consequently clicking a button labelled "Add (name of the subatomic particle)" until it reaches the number of each particle depicted in the card (Fig. 1.d). When the atom is fully built, the player can visualize it in 3D by moving the card around (Fig. 1.e).

Afterwards, he returns to Lemuria main environment and, with the key he won by performing the AR activity, he can now open the chest and collect the multiplier. After collecting all the items pictured in the door (glasses, wand, multiplier) (Fig. 1.a - center), the door opens, placing the player closer to the exit. At the other side of the door the player can talk with Carol that assigns him the mission of filling the lake with water. In order to create water, the player needs to collect the water spell, which is visibly available to be collected by the player (only at the other side of the door). The spell shows the atoms needed to compose the water molecule. The atoms can be gathered by splitting greenhouse gases (GHGs) molecules (which are abundant in Lemuria) using the magic wand and consequently collecting the atoms that made up the split molecule (Fig. 1.f). To create the water resource, the player goes to the laboratory, uses the water spell and chooses the required atoms in the periodic table shelf (Fig. 1.g). Before using the multiplier to reproduce the water molecule and produce a considerable quantity of water, the water molecule can be visualized using AR during its creation process in the lab (Fig. 1.h). Finally, after creating water, the player can use the boat to leave the current place and go to the next game level.

The remaining game levels are identical to the first one in terms of actions, however they take place in different Lemuria environments, that must be explored by the player, and comprise different challenges in terms of assigned missions and resources that need to be created. For example, in the second game level the player needs to create dioxygen to open a cave entry.

At the end of each game level, a score for that game level is calculated. Besides the score, a game level is marked with one (low score), two (medium score), or three (high score) stars. This technique has as main purpose to encourage the user to repeat the game levels, reviewing some concepts addressed in that game level, and increasing his score.

Since all game levels have a limited time to be completed, it may happen that the player can't win a game level at the first try. Therefore, the game level has several checkpoints that save the actions of the player, so he doesn't lose all of his progress if he wants to retry the game level. However, this will affect his final score in the level.

There are some data (such as game items and missions) that needs to be stored and accessible for the player at any time in the Lemuria place. Figure 2 illustrates the interface elements of our game, showing the main controls, game level information, and

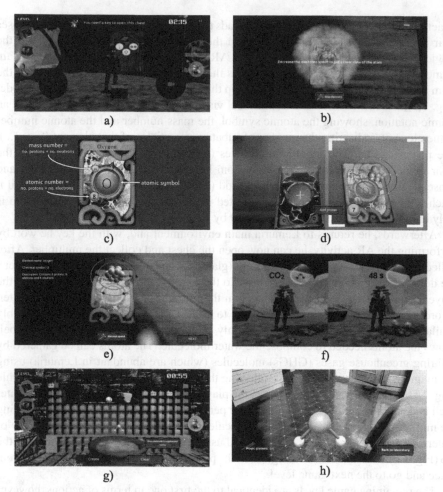

Fig. 1. Magic elements' first level game flow. a) The player needs to open the chest to access and collect the multiplier. b) Oxygen atom electronic cloud. c) Oxygen paper card. d) Subatomic particle (proton) card (left) and Oxygen card (right). e) 3D model of the atom. f) Splitting a CO_2 molecule to further collect its atoms (on the floor). g) Laboratory with periodic table shelf. h) Molecules AR 3D visualization and manipulation.

data access buttons corresponding to the spells book, the inventory (where the magic objects, atoms, and resources are stored), and the missions list. During the first game level we developed an interactive tutorial which provides the player, at some moments of the game, with guidance text (in the top center of the screen) accompanied by an animation that specifies which control the player should use.

The character depicted in the information panel (Fig. 2 – top center) is Auberon, who guides the player throughout the game, giving him clues and tips. In each game level, the player can talk to two other characters: Carol and Vinicius. Besides attributing missions to the player, Carol also shares her personal stories that aim to sensitize children

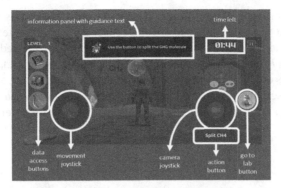

Fig. 2. Scheme of the Lemuria place interface

to climate change using evidences (e.g. climate change impacts with animals and plants, climatic phenomena). Vinicius, a Lemuria activist, shares some tips and small individual practices to soften climate change, to be implemented on Earth, where there is no magic and which can be adopted by children.

The current version of the game contains two fully developed game levels. New content (e.g. more GHG molecules, chemical elements, missions and stories) can be easily added to new game levels.

4 Evaluation

This section describes the last user tests performed on the current game version. Previous informal tests were conducted within each iterative design cycle to inform the design.

In this user studies, we mainly intended to evaluate whether (1) the game motivated the participants, promoting a positive attitude regarding chemistry; (2) the children retained some knowledge regarding chemistry; (3) the game sensitized children for climate change. Before the actual testing phase, the children's guardians were informed about the purpose of the study, data recording procedures and confidentiality and they signed a consent document to allow their children to participate in the study. To compare the results before and after the participants play the game, they had to answer a pre-test and a post-test questionnaire using Google Forms. Both questionnaires included the same questions regarding chemistry and climate change. The pre-test questionnaire also included an initial part focused on the participants' demographic data and the post-test questionnaire a final part concerning the participants' game experience. The questionnaires were carefully created to be suitable for our target group, containing a non-complex language and some instruments from the Fun Toolkit [20], such as the smileyometer, as well as the 5 Degrees of Happiness [6] (using pictorial representation).

4.1 Participants

Despite our initial idea being to perform tests on a larger scale, given the current pandemic situation, instead of performing the user tests at schools, we had to find individual users that fit our target group, having different profiles (so that the results were as rich as possible), and who were available and willing to test the game. We tested a total of 8 children (5 boys and 3 girls). Four of them were 10 years old (5th grade), two of them were 12 years old (7th grade), one of them was 11 years old (6th grade), and, lastly, one of them was 9 years old (3rd grade). All of them were new to chemistry, as at school none of them had the discipline yet. According to the results, most of the participants (seven - 87.5%) have their own smartphone, which operating system is often (five - 62.5%) Android.

4.2 Results

The game promoted a positive attitude regarding the chemistry topic. We asked the participants whether they considered chemistry a hard topic, using a smileyometer scale where 1 means "Very difficult" and 5 means "Very easy". In the pre-test we obtained a mean score of 3.12 (SD ± 0.99) that increased to a mean score of 4.50 (SD ± 0.76) in the post-test.

In order to evaluate the educational effectiveness of the game, the pre-test and post-test questionnaires contained the same questions (14 multiple-choice questions in total) focused on chemistry. To quantify the results, a percentage score was attributed to both tests, according to the number of correct answers.

The results, summarized in Table 1, were very positive and showed a substantial improvement between the pre-test and the post-test. The mean score increased from 10.7% (SD ± 6.8%) to 59.2% (SD ± 20.9%). Although the pre-test results were more consistent as none of the children had studied the topics at school, all the participants obtained higher grades in the post-test than in the pre-test questionnaire.

To evaluate whether the game promoted climate change awareness, the pre- and post-test questionnaires also included some questions regarding this topic. According to the pre-test answers, only five (62.5%) of the participants could already point out some daily individual practices to soften climate change. However, in the post-test questionnaire, all participants knew what the practices were, reported in Vinicius's stories, giving 100% of correct answers. Four (50%) of the participants remembered some climate change consequences reported in Carol's stories.

Table 1. Summary of acquired knowledge (knowledge test scores)

	Mean	SD	Lowest	Highest
Pre-test	10.7%	6.8%	2.4%	24.4%
Post-test	59.2%	20.9%	26.7%	86.7%

Concerning the game experience, participants considered the game fun. When asked how fun was the game, using the 5 Degrees of Happiness scale (where 5 is the most positive answer), a mean of 4.38 (SD ± 0.74) was obtained. All participants deemed the game useful and important. When asked why, they stated the game helps them to learn new things, with 50% specifying that it teaches important subjects, such as chemistry and how to fight the climate change. To conclude the questionnaire, we asked the participants if they wanted to play the game again, using the 5 Degrees of Happiness scale (where 1 means "Yes, a little bit" and 5 means "Yes, a lot!"), obtaining a mean of 4.75 (SD $\pm$ 0.71).

During the tests we could notice that the participants were enjoying the game, understanding the concepts, and we could hear some comments such as "Oh, so this is what (some concept) means!", showing satisfaction for being able to understand it.

All participants stated that they want to install the game, not only for the enjoyable experience, but also because it made them feel like they were learning important concepts in a "non-boring" way. They also stated that, now that they played the game, they think it will be easier for them to understand the concepts when they learn it at school. Finally, we could also notice some interest from the children's parents, who thought the game was a great initiative mainly because they noticed a positive reaction by their children at the end of the session.

Although some aspects of the game needed to be improved, such as the player movement controls, in general the evaluation results were very positive. Both the questionnaire and the participants' own reactions and comments show that they enjoyed the game, not only because it made them feel competent for learning new important concepts in such a short time, but also for the fun of the game itself.

5 Conclusions

Even before children approach chemistry as a school subject, the idea that many of them have is that chemistry is a difficult topic. To change their attitude towards chemistry, looking at it as a more pleasant topic and motivating them to learn chemistry, we created "Magic Elements", an educational mobile game aimed at children from 9 to 12 years old based on AR and tangible objects, containing a unique storyline. We also explored its use to raise awareness towards climate change. Our results reinforce the positive effects of using narrated games, as well as AR technologies and tangible interfaces in promoting children's motivation, constructing knowledge and developing awareness. According to the results of the user evaluation, the game also promoted a more positive attitude towards chemistry and sensitization regarding climate change. Further testing sessions, as well as a longitudinal study, are needed to better understand its potential, as well as to help to eliminate further design issues.

Acknowledgments. This work is funded by FCT/MCTES NOVA LINCS PEst UID/CEC/04516/2019.

References

1. Azuma, R.T.: A survey of augmented reality. Presence **6**(4), 355–385 (1997)

2. Boletsis, C., McCallum, S.: The table mystery: an augmented reality collaborative game for chemistry education. In: Ma, M., Oliveira, M.F., Petersen, S., Hauge, J.B. (eds.) Serious Games Development and Applications. SGDA 2013. Lecture Notes in Computer Science, vol. 8101, pp. 86–95. Springer, Berlin, Heidelberg (2013). https://doi.org/10.1007/978-3-642-407 90-1_9

3. Chen, Y.C.: A study of comparing the use of augmented reality and physical models in chemistry education. VRCIA 2006. In: Proceedings of the 2006 ACM international conference on Virtual reality continuum and its applications, pp. 369–372 (6 2006). https://doi.org/10. 1145/1128923.1128990

4. Fjeld, M., Voegtli, B.M.: Augmented chemistry: an interactive educational workbench. In: Proceedings of the International Symposium on Mixed and Augmented Reality (2002)

5. Gils, van F.: Potential applications of digital storytelling in education. In: 3rd Twente Student Conference on IT (2005)

6. Hall, L., Hume, C., Tazzyman, S.: Five degrees of happiness: effective smiley face likert scales for evaluating with children. In: IDC 2016, pp. 311–321 (2016). https://doi.org/10.1145/293 0674.2930719

7. Jeong, E.J., Kim, D.J.: Definitions, key characteristics, and generations of mobile games. Hershey: Idea Group (2009)

8. Koçak, Ö, Yılmaz, R.M., Küçük, S., Göktaş, Y.: The educational potential of augmented reality technology: experiences of instructional designers and practitioners. J. Educ. Future 15, 17–36 (2019)

9. Kubicki, S., Wolff, M., Lepreux, S., Kolski, C.: RFID interactive tabletop application with tangible objects: exploratory study to observe young children' behaviors. Pers. Ubiquitous Comput. 19(8), 1259–1274 (2015). https://doi.org/10.1007/s00779-015-0891-7

10. Lin, J.W., Cheng, P.W., hung Lin, C., Lin, I.C.: Intuitive 3d flight gaming with tangible objects. In: SIGGRAPH 2016, July 2016. https://doi.org/10.1145/2945078.2945156

11. Liu, F.: Design for kids based on their stage of physical development (July 2018). https:// www.nngroup.com/articles/children-ux-physical-development/. Accessed 06 Feb 2020

12. Mahdi, J.G.: Student attitudes towards chemistry: an examination of choices and preferences. Am. J. Educ. Res. 2(6), 351–356 (2014)

13. Maier, P., Klinker, G., Tönnis, M.: Augmented reality for teaching spatial relations. Conf. Int. J. Arts Sci. 369–372 (2009). ISSN: 1943-6114

14. Milgram, P., Kishino, F.: A taxonomy of mixed reality visual displays. IEICE Trans. Inf. Syst. 77(12), 1321–1329 (1994)

15. Núñez, M., Quirós, R., Núñez, I., Carda, J.B., Camahort, E.: Collaborative augmented reality for inorganic chemistry education. In: IASME International Conference on Engineering Education, pp. 271–277 (2008)

16. Olim, S.C., Nisi, V.: Augmented reality towards facilitating abstract concepts learning. In: Nunes, N.J., Ma, L., Wang, M., Correia, N., Pan, Z. (eds.) ICEC 2020. LNCS, vol. 12523, pp. 188–204. Springer, Cham (2020). https://doi.org/10.1007/978-3-030-65736-9_17

17. Osborne, J., Simon, S., Collins, S.: Attitudes towards science: a review of the literature and its implications. Int. J. Sci. Educ. 25(9), 1049–1079 (2003)

18. Padilla-Zea, N., Gutiérrez, F.L., López-Arcos, J.R., Abad-Arranz, A., Paderewski, P.: Modeling storytelling to be used in educational video games. Comput. Hum. Behav. 31, 461–474 (2013)

19. Piyawattanaviroj, P., Maleesut, T., Yasri, P.: An educational card game for enhancing students' learning of the periodic table. In: ICEMT 2019: Proceedings of the 2019 3rd International Conference on Education and Multimedia Technology, pp. 380–383, July 2019. https://doi. org/10.1145/3345120.3345165

20. Read, J.C.: Validating the fun toolkit: an instrument for measuring children's opinions of technology. Cogn. Technol. Work **10**,119–128 (2008). https://doi.org/10.1007/s10111-007-0069-9

21. Taçgin, Z., Uluçay, N., Özüağ, E.: Designing and developing an augmented reality application: a sample of chemistry education. J. Turkish Chem. Soc. Sect. C Chem. Educ. **1**, 147–164 (2016)

22. Waraich, A.: Using narrative as a motivating device to teach binary arithmetic and logic gates. ACM SIGCSE Bull. **36**, 97–101 (2004). https://doi.org/10.1145/1026487.1008024

23. Wu, H.K., Lee, S.W.Y., Chang, H.Y., Liang, J.C.: Current status, opportunities and challenges of augmented reality in education. Comput. Educ. **25**, 41–49 (2013). https://doi.org/10.1016/j.compedu.2012.10.024

Engagement and Discrete Emotions in Game Scenario: Is There a Relation Among Them?

Renan Vinicius Aranha[1,2]([envelope]), Leonardo Nogueira Cordeiro[2],
Lucas Mendes Sales[2], and Fátima L. S. Nunes[1,2]

[1] Interactive Technologies Laboratory, Escola Politécnica - Universidade de São Paulo - USP, São Paulo, Brazil
[2] Laboratory of Computer Applications for Health Care, School of Arts Sciences and Humanities - Universidade de São Paulo - USP, São Paulo, Brazil
{renanvinicius,leonogueirac,lucasm1sales,fatima.nunes}@usp.br
http://www.poli.usp.br
http://lapis.each.usp.br

Abstract. Analysis of user engagement is a factor of great importance for different computational applications, especially games. The knowledge of this information allows evaluating the software and making possible enhancing the software. However, analyzing user engagement is still a challenge. The most common approach in the literature has been the application of questionnaires at the end of the interaction process. Although some studies investigate the use of emotions to measure user involvement, the analysis of facial expressions has been little explored in this context. This technique has the main advantage of using a camera, dispensing other invasive sensors. This paper presents an investigation to evaluate whether discrete emotions can be related to engagement in game scenarios. Two studies were conducted with 48 volunteers playing games to discover if there is relation between emotions recognized by facial expressions and engagement measured in two different ways (by software and by user's self-assessment). Our analysis comprises about 38 h of games and more than one million records of emotional states. The results indicate that there is no universal relation between discrete emotions and engagement, suggesting that the game context can influence users' engagement.

Keywords: Games · Engagement · Discrete emotions

1 Introduction

The term "engagement" is widely used in the context of games to define an ideal state, in which the player is experiencing positive involvement with the game [30]. In a more practical sense, an engaged player is not bored when using the game and is willing to continue exploring the game and its challenges. Although the

© IFIP International Federation for Information Processing 2021
Published by Springer Nature Switzerland AG 2021
C. Ardito et al. (Eds.): INTERACT 2021, LNCS 12934, pp. 22–42, 2021.
https://doi.org/10.1007/978-3-030-85613-7_3

term engagement has been widely used, identifying if a person is engaged or not can be a complex task.

Firstly, there is no universal understanding from theorists about what this term represents [11,12,19]. Possibly, as a consequence, there are different approaches and methods to measure engagement, which can provide different results. Nowadays, a state-of-the-art approach to measure the user's engagement consists in applying questionnaires [6,19,30]. Some questionnaires are well-known and validated by other studies, as the User Engagement Scale (UES) [29] or the Game Engagement Questionnaire (GEQ) [8]. Despite its several benefits, the application of questionnaires can imply some disadvantages, since it usually interrupts the interaction process, breaking the focused engagement [31]. To avoid the interruption of the experience, this approach is more recommended to be used at the end of the interaction.

A promising approach consists in analyzing the user's physiological responses, such as heart rate, in addition to the aforementioned techniques. This approach, sometimes providing data in real time, has been explored both in research and in the gaming industry [30]. An interesting point of this approach is the possibility to collect data without interrupting the interaction process, besides improving the analysis with a kind of information that probably not even the user is aware of.

However, most of the initiatives are based on sensors coupled to the user body [30], and some of them can cause discomfort to the user – a scenario that has changed in the last few years with the development of wearable sensors. Additionally, this kind of measure is usually adopted in laboratory-based studies, since some sensors are not common and may require training in handling and use.

Conversely, facial expression recognition (FER) can infer the users' emotions in real time without involving the use of specific sensors [3]. FER can use popular devices, such as webcam or a smartphone camera to acquire images, and be used to analyze the player's emotions even remotely. Despite these advantages, the relation of the data provided by this technique with engagement have been little explored when compared to the traditional physiological measures.

In this challenging scenario, a few companies and researchers have been investigating the automatic measurement of users' engagement by analyzing facial expressions. At least two commercial software, named Affdex SDK [1] and FaceReader [27], provide indicators of engagement in their interfaces. In both cases, the engagement is computed considering the user's facial expressions. However, the weight of each facial expression, emotion, or action unit (AU) [15] in the engagement measurement is not explained in detail in either case [1]. Additionally, both software imply paid licenses, which can reduce or make the adoption of this technique impracticable in many contexts.

In the academic scope, some studies explore machine learning techniques to predict user engagement from facial expressions. In general, these studies involve a step of manual classification of facial images, which are used to train Artificial Intelligence algorithms [9,23]. However, finding a relation between the discrete emotions and engagement remains a challenge, since there is no consensus about the impacts and relations of the universal emotions in the engagement. Although the measurement of engagement based on facial expressions has been explored by a few researchers, their findings can be quite controversial [19].

Aiming to contribute within this scenario, we here investigate if there is a correlation between emotions recognized by FER and engagement. The choice for this technique considers its effectiveness, already explored by previous studies [3,20,22], as well as the ease of its use without major impacts on the user's environment or setup. Since the engagement has different interpretations and measurement approaches, we present two studies: the first one, using emotional and engagement data provided by the Affdex SDK during the use of serious games; and the second one, concerning emotional data collected during the of use two games, with the engagement obtained by a self-assessment questionnaire.

2 Emotion Recognition

Just as engagement, understanding human emotions can be a complex task, since the literature presents different interpretations of emotional aspects. In this sense, few approaches to the classification of emotions are known [14], and the most used are the discrete approach proposed by Darwin [10] and the dimensional approach proposed by Wundt [35]. While Darwin [10] understands emotions as discrete (or modular), and represented by terms such as joy, sadness and disgust, for example, Wundt [35] classifies emotions using dimensions, such as pleasant/unpleasant and low/high intensity. In the Computer Science context, researches involving emotions consider both discrete and dimensional approaches [3].

In most cases, choosing an approach depends on the emotion recognition technique used. In facial expressions analysis, for example, it is usual to adopt the discrete approach [32,33]. This is because studies that investigate the expression of emotions on the face consider the discrete emotions approach [15].

Facial expressions are recognizable using at least two techniques: facial electromyography (fEMG), which uses sensors coupled to the user's face, and image processing. In this study, we consider only the latter, since it only needs the use of a camera and software to process the images. Usually, software that recognize facial expressions can use at least two approaches.

The first one is to analyze facial landmarks directly. Facial landmarks are fiducial facial key points used in Computer Vision to extract and identify components of the face [34]. DLib, for example, a common library used to extract facial landmarks, recognizes 68 points in the human face. Considering these facial landmarks and previously labelled image datasets, it is possible to train machine learning algorithms to recognize facial expressions.

The second approach uses a coding system about muscle movements. In this scope, the FACS (Facial Action Coding System) is commonly adopted. FACS was proposed by Ekman and Friesen [15] to measure all visible facial behavior by analyzing muscle movements and their components, which receive the name of Action Units (AUs) [15,16]. FACS contains the definition of 44 AUs, each one identified by a number. The analysis of movements of the AUs and their intensities allows mapping facial expressions to emotions through Emotional FACS (EMFACS) [17]. The emotion of joy, for example, involves AU6 (orbicularis oculi muscle) and AU12 (zygomaticus major muscle). Figure 1 represents neutral and facial expressions, with facial landmarks processed using DLib. From the neutral to the joy facial expression, it is possible to observe that the second case involves cheek and lip corners rising.

3 Related Works

Although facial expressions have traditionally been used to recognize basic or universal emotions (anger, disgust, fear, joy, sadness and surprise), only few works have investigated their use for recognizing engagement. In a literature review about the measurement of engagement, Dewan, Murshed and Lin [11] indicated that only recently have FACS received attention for engagement recognition. In this review, the authors present some studies that investigated the recognition of discrete emotions associated with engagement in learning, such as "boredom", "confusion" and "frustration" [11]. The authors identified no studies considering engagement as an emotion, but some authors related engagement to the combination of other emotional states, such as boredom and delight. However, even because these studies are relatively recent, there is not consensus about the findings. For example: in [23], the AUs related to confusion were AU1, AU4, AU7, and AU12. In [18], this emotion can be identified by AU4 and AU7. Finally, in a more recent work, confusion was associated with AU45, AU1, and AU4 [7].

In [9], researchers proposed FaceEngage, an engagement estimator that analyzes the facial expressions in gaming videos obtained from YouTube. Considering that engagement annotation is challenging both for computer engineers and psychologists, the authors analyzed the game events in the videos to classify if a user was active or not in the game. The authors extracted the eyes and the head motion as features, and trained Machine Learning algorithms. Despite the positive results, with an accuracy of 83.8%, the authors mentioned as further work the development of a Likert-scale engagement measurement tool, to enhance the analysis of engagement in videos initially classified as "uncertainty".

Outside the FACS context, Nezami et al. [26] explored the use of deep learning to recognize user's engagement through facial expressions. The authors collected a dataset containing about 20 h of students interacting with an educational virtual environment. To classify the users engagement, Nezami et al. [26] considered two annotation steps, embracing the behavioral and emotional dimensions of engagement. The annotations were performed by Psychology students, who classified engagement in the behavioral dimension (on-task, off-task, cannot decide) and in the emotional dimension (satisfied, confused, bored, cannot decide). Engagement was defined by mixing both dimensions labels. The results indicated that the approach proposed by the authors was more effective in recognizing non-engaged users, with accuracy of 60%.

Although these works show promising results, highlighting the possibility of analyzing users' engagement through their facial expressions, this field of study

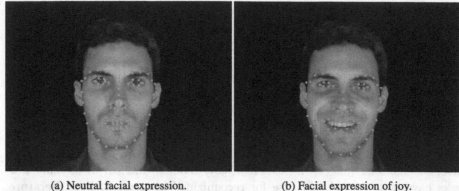

(a) Neutral facial expression.   (b) Facial expression of joy.

Fig. 1. Facial expressions with facial landmarks processed using the Dlib library. The facial expression of joy, compared to the neutral facial expression, involves raising the cheek and the lip corners. Images from FacesDB dataset [24].

still has great open challenges. A relation between universal discrete emotions and user engagement, for example, was not addressed by these articles.

4   Methods

Given the challenging scenario about the automatic measurement of engagement and the feasibility of recognizing emotions by facial expressions, this paper analyzes if discrete emotions can indicate players' engagement in games. To offer a broader perspective about this topic, we describe two studies using different scenarios. The first study was based on data collected during the use of a serious game for motor rehabilitation, while the second study comprised two entertainment games. Considering these scenarios, our approach allows identifying whether there is any relation between emotions and engagement, even under different conditions, which could define the later using knowledge about the former. With both studies, we aimed to answer the following research questions (RQs):

– RQ1: Is there a relation between discrete emotions and users' engagement?
– RQ2: Can users experience different emotions when they are engaged and when they are not engaged?

We present the studies and how these questions are answered in each as follows.

4.1   Study 1: Emotions and Engagement Analyzed by Software

In this first study, we analyze if there is a relation between discrete emotions and engagement when both are measured by software. For this, we use a previously collected dataset, which includes emotion and engagement records measured by software during the use of a serious game.

Software. Developed by Affectiva, the Affdex SDK is an emotion recognition software that analyzes the user's facial expressions considering FACS [1]. For each frame processed, in addition to the discrete categorization of seven emotions (joy, contempt, fear, disgust, anger, surprise and sadness), this software offers indices for dimensional affective states, such as valence and engagement [1]. This feature is a differential of *Affdex*, since most similar applications focus on the recognition of the six universal emotions.

The Affectiva website describes that engagement is "a measure of facial muscle activation that illustrates the subject's expressiveness" [1]. It is calculated from the weighted sum of some AUs, having a variable index from 0 to 100, where 0 indicates no engagement and 100 represents total engagement. The weight attributed to each AU in the calculation of engagement is not described by the company. However, a study published by Kapoor and Picard [21] indicates the relation between some AUs and engagement. Although it is not possible to state that the engagement analysis adopted by Affdex is based on this study, there is a great similarity with the mentioned AUs in the Affectiva website.

Dataset. EasyAffecta Dataset is a dataset of emotional data collected during a longitudinal experimental evaluation with 11 individuals (approved by the Ethics Committee of the School of Arts, Sciences and Humanities of the University of São Paulo). This dataset comprises more than one million records of emotional states obtained with *Affdex SDK* during the use of a serious game with four exercises in a motor rehabilitation process, encompassing about 33 h of data collection. In addition to the percentages of seven discrete emotions, each record also includes the engagement and valence indices. An important feature of this dataset is that the individuals' facial expressions were not stimulated. Therefore, they tend to represent a situation closer to everyday life.

Data Analysis. Considering the data from the EasyAffecta Dataset, the following indices were calculated to answer the questions RQ1 and RQ2: i) the Pearson correlation between emotions and engagement; ii) the average intensity of each emotion when users were engaged and when they were not engaged; and iii) the analysis of emotional intensity (AEI) that comprises, for each emotion, the percentage of records in which it was the most intense. At this point, we should highlight that for each frame, the ER software provides a probability index for each emotion. The AEI analysis focuses on the peaks, indicating the percentage of frames in which that emotion has the highest probability. The threshold to split the records between engaged and non-engaged is the engagement average of all players. The results are presented and discussed in Sect. 5.

4.2 Study 2: Emotions Analyzed by Software, and Engagement Self-assessed by Users

Complementing the aforementioned approach, the second study consists of a hybrid analysis, with discrete emotions recognized by software being compared to the engagement self-assessed by the users. This analysis involved the preparation of a specific experimental evaluation with users, which is described below.

Evaluation Design. Figure 2 presents an overview of the experimental evaluation, approved by the Ethics Committee of School of Arts, Sciences and Humanities of the University of São Paulo. A web platform was developed to conduct the experiment. When accessing the platform, the user found a text informing the invitation to participate in the experiment. Accepting the invitation, the user was redirected to a screen containing the Informed Consent Form. Agreeing to the term, the user made a registration and then was presented with the activities to be performed during the experiment. The stages of the experiment involved: activating the camera; interacting with two games and, after using each, self-evaluate the engagement using a questionnaire. In the last phase, we asked users to leave free text comments to researchers on their perceptions when participating in the experiment. The last phase was not mandatory.

Fig. 2. Overview of the experimental evaluation.

Games. During the experimental evaluation, the volunteers can interact with two games, as shown in Fig. 3. The first one is based on "Color Switch Replica", a project available on GitHub [4]. In this game, illustrated in Fig. 3a, there is a small circle with gravity in the center of the screen. There is also a greater and spinning circle around it drawn in different colors. The player should click on the screen to move up the small circle. However, when moving up, the player should take care to prevent the small circle from colliding with the part of the greater circle that has another color.

The second game consists of a game developed by the authors, based on the classic Memory Game, in which the player should find a pair of cards, as shown in Fig. 3b. Both games were customized to communicate with the experimental platform created for this evaluation. Volunteers were asked to play each game as many times as wanted.

(a) Screenshot of the Color Switch Replica.   (b) Screenshot of the Memory Game.

Fig. 3. Screenshots of the games used in this experimental evaluation.

Self-assessment Engagement. To assess the user engagement, we chose the short form of User Engagement Scale (UES) [28], which contains 12 items with statements about the experience of using software. For each statement, the volunteer should classify his/her agreement in a Likert scale, from 1 to 5. Besides a global engagement measure, UES also provides information about four dimensions of engagement: aesthetic appeal (AE), focused attention (FA), perceived usability (PU), and reward (RW) [28]. Table 1 shows the items that composes this scale. Following the instructions described in [28], the items order was randomized in each application of the UES.

Table 1. Items that composes the short form of UES.

Dimension	Item
FA-1	I lost myself in this experience
FA-2	The time I spent using this game just slipped away
FA-3	I was absorbed in this experience
PU-1	I felt frustrated while using this game
PU-2	I found this game confusing to use
PU-3	Using this game was taxing
AE-1	This game was attractive
AE-2	This game was aesthetically appealing
AE-3	This game appealed to my senses
RW-1	Using this game was worthwhile
RW-2	My experience was rewarding
RW-3	I felt interested in this experience

Facial Expressions. Unlike the first study, we chose to use another facial expression recognition software. Face-api.js is an open-source software that recognizes facial expressions, but does not provide engagement levels as Affdex SDK does. For each processed frame, this software offers the probability of the presence of each one of these facial expressions: neutral, anger, disgust, fear, joy, sadness, and surprise. In addition to its open source feature, which allows its adoption without financial impact, the accuracy of *Face-api.js* in recognizing emotions was investigated in [2]. Besides the aforementioned advantages, the fact that this tool works in the browser without the need to install components was the main factor that contributed to its choice. The emotional data generated was stored in a database.

Participants. The volunteers were invited by e-mail and by using social networks. In general, 37 volunteers concluded all the steps. In this scope, 12 are female and 25 are male. No volunteer declared not to identify with one of these binary genres. The average age of the volunteers was about 34 years. Then 80 activities were recorded, 39 for the Memory Game and 41 for the Color Game. The term "activity" is used to define the process that involves the use of a game, with the subsequent completion of the UES. Two volunteers participated in the experiment more than once, which justifies the greater number of computed activities. Additionally, 107876 records of emotional states were stored, encompassing about 5 h of data collection.

Data Analysis. Similarly to the first study, to answer question RQ1 we considered the Pearson correlation between the engagement measured by UES with the average intensity of each emotional state, both computed for each activity. To answer RQ2, we analyzed the average intensity of each emotional state when users were engaged and when they were not engaged. In this case, since two games were addressed in the experiment, the analysis was separated for each game. Also similarly to the previous experiment, the AEI was also computed, indicating, for each emotion, the percentage of records in that emotion was the most intense.

For these last two analyses, two thresholds were calculated, which consist of: i) the average engagement of all players in activities related to the Memory Game (MG); and ii) the average engagement of all players in activities related to the Color Switch Replica (CSR). The results are presented and discussed in Sect. 5.

5   Results and Discussion

We next present the results and discussions from the two studies aforementioned. In the first study (described in Sect. 4.1), which comprises emotions and engagement measured by software in a rehabilitation scenario, we observed that: i) players did not experience all the discrete emotions while using the game; ii) there was great variability in the engagement average of the players; iii) only facial expression of joy had a moderate correlation with engagement; and iv) when players are engaged, they do not necessarily feel different emotions from when they are not engaged. This discussion will be detailed in Sect. 5.1.

Concerning the second study (described in Sect. 4.2), which mixed emotions measured by software and engagement measured using a questionnaire in entertainment games, we can point out that: i) similarly to the previous study, players did not experience all the discrete emotions when playing the games; ii) players themselves indicate high levels of engagement by filling the questionnaire; iii) for both games, no emotion has a moderate correlation with engagement; and iv) again, similarly to the previous study, there was not a difference between the emotions experienced when users are engaged or not. The discussion will be presented in Sect. 5.2.

5.1   Study 1: Emotions and Engagement Analyzed by Software

Overview. Figure 4 shows the distribution of each facial expression of emotion in the dataset. In general, there is a greater density of records with low intensity (in the range of 0 to 20%). Only the facial expressions of joy, contempt and disgust showed significant densities at high intensity (in the range of 80 to 100%).

These data can indicate that users may not experience all seven facial expressions of emotions while using games, and reaffirm that people do not necessarily express emotions all the time, as mentioned by Paul Ekman [13]. In the context of games, this aspect may be relevant, since the facial expression of an emotion tends to indicate a reaction to an event of the game - which arouses an emotion in the user.

Concerning engagement, Fig. 5 shows an overview about the engagement levels experienced by users in this dataset, considering the minimum, the maximum, the median and the first and third quartiles of each volunteer's engagement. Aiming to improve the understanding, the data were sorted by the median value. This figure indicates that there was a great variation in the engagement of the participants, which had low indexes. A great part of the volunteers (77%) showed median engagement under the average, as indicated by the red line.

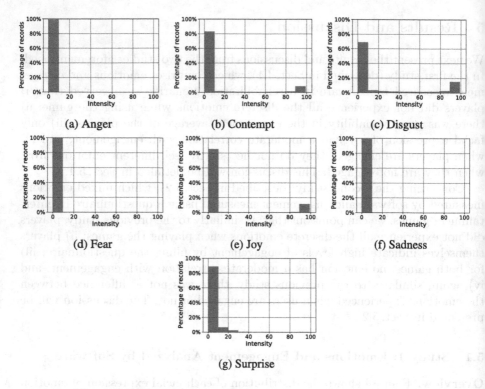

Fig. 4. Distribution of emotional states in the first experiment.

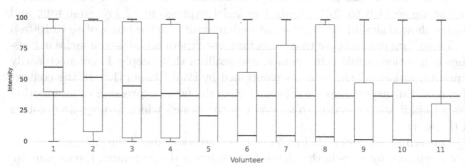

Fig. 5. Overview about user's engagement in the first experiment.

Emotions Intensity and Engagement. The correlation between discrete facial expression of emotions and engagement in the scope of EasyAffecta Dataset is shown in Table 2. The main finding is that the facial expression of joy had a moderate correlation ($\rho = 0.6$) with engagement. When considering the AUs involved in engagement described in [21], this correlation is expected, since the AUs referring to the emotional state of joy, AU6 and AU12, are positive indicators of engagement. Even moderate, this correlation can reinforce a common feelıng that, if the user is experiencing joy or a positive emotion, he/she is engaged ın the task.

Table 2. Correlation between engagement and discrete emotions.

Emotion	Anger	Contempt	Disgust	Fear	Joy	Sadness	Surprise
Correlation (ρ)	0.09	−0.05	0.19	0.08	0.6	0.06	0.32

Complementarily, although it presented a weak correlation ($\rho = 0.32$), the facial expression of surprise is also an expected correlation, considering that some of its action units (AUs 1,2 and 5) are considered positive indicators of engagement by Kapoor and Picard [21]. Since the emotion of surprise indicates a reaction to an unexpected event, its correlation with engagement is likely, indicating that the user was probably paying attention to the games.

Finally, the facial expression of disgust had a weak correlation with engagement ($\rho = 0.19$). However, this is an unexpected positive correlation, considering that AUs 9 and 15, which make up this facial expression together with AU16, are presented as negative indicators of engagement [21]. We can next observe, respectively, the following facial expressions of emotions: anger ($\rho = 0.09$), fear ($\rho = 0.08$) and sadness ($\rho = 0.06$), all with low indices.

Emotions Experienced. Another observed aspect, related with the RQ2 question, aims to identify whether the volunteers experienced facial expression of emotions while they were engaged differently from when they were not engaged. Figure 6 presents a comparative analysis of the average and AEI in the two engagement situations.

Considering the average of the intensity, Fig. 6a reveals that, while the volunteers were engaged in the task, they mainly experienced four emotional states: joy, disgust, contempt and surprise. When users were not engaged, the facial expressions of joy and surprise had a very low intensity average. Only the facial expression of contempt showed a higher intensity average in not engaged situations.

In turn, although it looks similar to Fig. 6a, Fig. 6b reveals an important fact regarding the facial expression of disgust. Although this facial expression of emotion had a higher average of intensity when users were engaged, it was not necessarily the predominant emotion most of the time. Figure 6b shows, in reality, that there is a greater number of records of the facial expression of disgust with higher intensity in situations of non-engagement. This conflicting result can suggest that the duration of the facial expression of emotion in higher intensities may be a factor that impacts engagement.

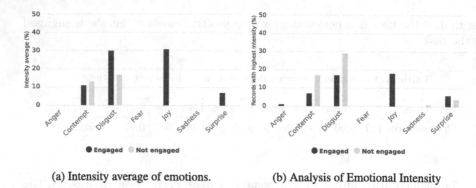

(a) Intensity average of emotions.   (b) Analysis of Emotional Intensity

Fig. 6. Facial expressions of emotions experienced by users.

5.2   Study 2: Emotions Measured by Software and Engagement Measured by Self-assessment

Overview. The distribution of each facial expression of emotion in the dataset obtained in this experiment is shown in Fig. 7. Similarly to the previous experiment, there was a greater density of facial expression of emotions with records in low intensity (0 to 20%). Besides the neutral facial expression, only the facial expressions of joy and sadness got significant densities at high intensity (in the range of 80 to 100%). Although the facial expressions of anger and surprise had high intensity emotional records, a minor volume of data is related with these records.

The data shows that not all universal facial expressions of emotions were experienced by the users; likewise, users will not necessarily facially express an emotion all the time. This fact is even more evident, since the software used recognizes neutral facial expression.

Figure 8 shows the engagement obtained by the volunteer's self-assessment in this experimental evaluation, showing the minimum, the maximum, the median and the first and third quartiles of engagement for each volunteer. To enhance the understanding, the data were sorted by the median value. Users' engagement in activities was high. As indicated by the figure, the rates of most users exceed the average engagement, indicated by the red line.

Emotion Intensity and Engagement. The correlation between the average intensity of facial expression of emotions experienced by players and the engagement shown in Table 3 reveal a remarkable variation in this metric from one game to another. Despite this variation, facial expression of emotion did not have a strong correlation with the engagement measured by UES in either of the cases. In a way, a low correlation between these indices can be expected, since it involves two different approaches to analyze the player's experience, and relating them is a complex task [25].

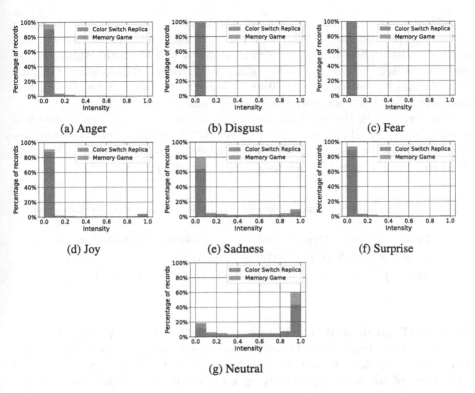

Fig. 7. Distribution of emotional states in the second experiment. In each histogram, the darker blue color indicates the overlap of registers from the two games.

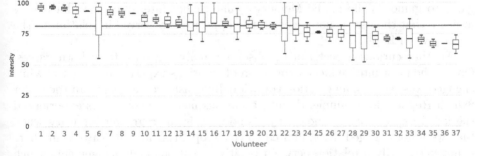

Fig. 8. Overview about user's engagement in the second experiment.

In this experiment, the highest positive index identified indicates correlation of $\rho = 0.22$ of the facial expression of joy with engagement when users were playing the Memory Game. In this game, joy was the only facial expression of emotion with a positive correlation with engagement. Curiously, this facial expression had a negative correlation ($\rho = -0.05$) with engagement in the Color Switch Replica.

Still regarding the differences, while the facial expression of fear showed a negative correlation ($\rho = -0.28$) with engagement in the Memory Game, this facial expression showed a positive correlation ($\rho = 0.15$) with engagement in the Color Switch Replica. Also in the latter game, the facial expression of disgust showed a similar correlation ($\rho = 0.18$). However, the facial expressions of fear and disgust had lower intensities, with their values usually equal to zero.

The variation in the correlation from one game to another can be justified by the difference in the context of the games. While the Memory Game requires less agility from the user, the Color Switch Replica demands constant agility and attention, which may have made users tenser, albeit engaged.

Table 3. Correlation between engagement and discrete emotions for each game.

Emotion	Anger	Disgust	Fear	Joy	Sadness	Surprise	Neutral
CSR (ρ)	−0.25	0.18	0.15	−0.05	0.06	0.04	−0.02
MG (ρ)	−0.03	0	−0.28	0.22	0	−0.12	0

Emotions Experienced. Figure 9 shows the average intensity of facial expression of emotions experienced by users when using the two games, also as the AEI (metric explained in Sect. 4). This analysis allows us to identify the facial expressions of emotions experienced by users when engaged and not engaged. As described in Sect. 4, the data were grouped into two categories, engaged (E) and non-engaged (NE).

Figure 9 enriches the discussion by reinforcing that the results vary from game to game. While in the Memory Game higher intensities of sadness may indicate that the user is not engaged, the opposite is observed in relation to the Color Switch Replica.

Another curious aspect can be observed analyzing data from both games. One of the most intense facial expression of emotions experienced by users while engaged was sadness, an emotion traditionally considered negative. In the Color Switch Replica, for example, there is a curious fact: the volunteers experienced the facial expressions of emotions joy and surprise at a greater intensity when they were not engaged. Even limited to this scope, this fact indicates that there is not necessarily a relation between positive emotions and engagement, which is often suggested or expected.

No significant differences were found in the metrics of medium intensity and AEI. In this case, this may be due to a characteristic of the software used. The software Face-api.js does not recognize that more than one facial expression of emotion can happen simultaneously with maximum intensity, as occurs in Affdex. For this reason, in most cases, when an emotion is identified by Face-api.js, this emotion tends to be the most intense at that moment.

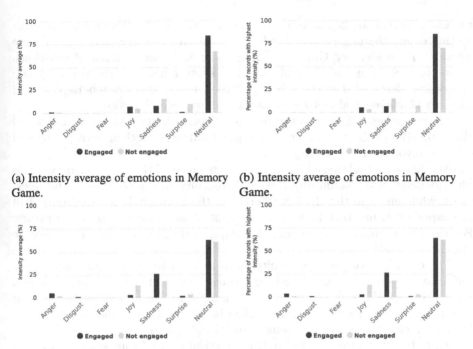

(a) Intensity average of emotions in Memory Game.

(b) Intensity average of emotions in Memory Game.

(c) Intensity average of emotions in Color Switch Replica.

(d) Analysis of Emotional Intensity for Color Switch Replica.

Fig. 9. Facial expressions of emotions experienced by users in both games.

Comments from Volunteers. In the last stage of the experiment, the volunteers were asked to write their suggestions, criticisms or considerations. Only 10 volunteers wrote their considerations. In general, the comments involve the users' opinions about the game based on the Color Switch Replica and considerations about the questionnaire.

Concerning the game, some volunteers considered the game complex to use and, in some cases, expressed their preference for the Memory Game. One volunteer wrote that he/she "was a little upset with the first game (Color Switch Replica) for not being able to keep the ball going up", and "really liked it (Memory Game), because it was much more interesting". In fact, the data collected reinforce the preference of this volunteer: while in Color Switch Replica the engagement was 2.75, the engagement was 4.33 in the Memory Game. Regarding facial expressions of emotions, in the Color Switch Replica, the most frequent facial expressions identified were joy and anger (besides the neutral facial expression), while in the Memory Game the neutral facial expression and the facial expression of joy were identified.

The Color Switch Replica attracted another volunteer, who wrote: "In the Color Switch Replica I had more difficulty, but it is challenging and holds my attention; I want to overcome at each restart". Although this volunteer played the Color Switch Replica more than once, which tends to reinforce the interest in this game, the engagement levels obtained on both occasions (4.17) were inferior to the Memory Game (5). Regarding facial expressions of emotions, in one play of Color Switch Replica, this volunteer has only the neutral facial expression identified. For the other activities, from Color Switch Replica and Memory Game, neutral facial expression and joy were identified.

These comments from the volunteers reinforce the fact that the individual characteristics of the players can have a great influence on their perceptions and on their involvement with the game.

Another aspect addressed in the comments involved the engagement analysis questionnaire. Some volunteers reported difficulty in understanding the questions, while one said that he felt interest in the games only for the context of the experiment, but that he would not want to use such games in the future. For this last volunteer, the writing of the question did not make this difference clear.

The considerations of the volunteers in relation to the questionnaire is an important aspect to be considered for the assessment of engagement. Although the UES is widely used and validated, the difficulty in understanding certain statements in the questionnaire identified in our study may indicate the need for better clarification of the items. Additionally, this is already a challenge known in the literature [11]. In further investigations, it is interesting to assess whether simpler metrics, such as "like" or "don't like", can offer users a better understanding when evaluating their experiences.

5.3   Overall Analysis

In the first study, the evaluation indicated a correlation between facial expressions of discrete emotions, especially joy and surprise, with engagement. However, some emotions – such as fear and sadness – were little experienced by the volunteers. Therefore, the correlation of these facial expressions of emotions with engagement may not have been identified. Additionally, an important observation regarding this study is that the data collection occurred in a process of motor rehabilitation, with the game used reproducing real rehabilitation tasks. Since the motor rehabilitation tasks can result in pain or physical discomfort in patients, this may also have influenced the users' facial expressions and, consequently, the correlation of facial expressions of emotions with engagement.

Although our findings in the first study did not fully agree with that stated in [21], it was possible to confirm some promises about facial expressions of discrete emotions and engagement using the Affdex SDK. At this point, we can conclude that the facial expressions of emotions of joy and surprise can be considered indicative – even if slight – that the user is engaged in the task.

However, the second study improved this discussion, indicating that the correlation of engagement with facial expressions of discrete emotions is variable to the context and the design of the game. The great difference regarding the correlation presented in the games of the second study and the game of the first study is a factor that deserves to be highlighted, suggesting that there is no universal relation between facial expressions of emotions and engagement.

Another contribution from the second study is that there is not necessarily a relation between positive emotions and engagement (which can be understood in the first study). Interestingly, the facial expressions of emotions identified when users were engaged at using Color Switch Replica encompass emotions usually considered to be negative. These findings reinforce the discussion presented by Bopp, Mekler and Opwis [5], who observed that negative affect can be related with a positive experience in games. Similarly to movies, games can arouse emotions in players that are considered negative, but the arousal of these emotions in the player/viewer can be an indication that the user is involved with the multimedia content.

As already discussed the facial expression of fear was rarely identified in both studies. Some facial expressions of emotions, such as disgust and anger, were identified in one study, but not in the other. Although these emotions were not widely experienced, they can play an important role in engagement depending on the context of the game.

In general, the volunteers' engagement levels in the second study were higher than in the first study. This difference is understandable and justified for two reasons: i) first, the volunteers from the first study were in physiotherapy sessions, while the volunteers from the second study participated in the research freely; and ii) the metrics used to measure engagement are considerably different, which justifies the wide variation in this metric.

Although the results of our studies are not conclusive, the facts discussed here make the analysis of the relation between facial expressions of discrete emotions and engagement even more challenging. The differences identified in the relation of engagement and facial expressions of discrete emotions depend on the goal and the characteristics of each game.

In a game for motor rehabilitation, for example, it is important to motivate the player to carry out the activities – which may not occur with such intensity in traditional games. These aspects certainly influence the player's reaction to the events of the game. In addition, motor rehabilitation patients, for example, tend to deal with pain and motor difficulties, unlike typical users of entertainment games. Therefore, it is essential that the characteristics of each game are considered when investigating the correlation between engagement and emotions.

6   Final Remarks

Although there are several techniques for evaluating user's engagement, most of them are focused on face-to-face evaluations, with a high degree of involvement of specialists in the collection and analysis of data. In order to contribute to this scenario, we here investigated if facial expressions of discrete emotions can indicate player's engagement. Our findings from two studies involving the use of three games and involving different contexts initially revealed that users do not experience universal emotions constantly. Although it seems strange, this is in agreement with the literature of the area and, in the case of games, it can indicate an emotional reaction of the user to specific events of the game.

Both studies indicated that the correlation between discrete emotions identified by facial expressions and engagement is weak. In the first experiment, joy and surprise could be considered positive indicators of engagement. In the second experiment, although joy also showed a positive correlation with engagement in the Memory Game, this emotion has a negative correlation with engagement in the Color Switch Replica.

Another important finding in this article is that there is not necessarily a relation between positive emotions and engagement, as evidenced in the aforementioned case of Color Switch Replica. In other words, our findings indicated that there is not necessarily a global relation of emotions or group emotions with engagement, which can be used or exchanged to different types of games.

Finally, even though the results of this study do not provide an equation for calculating engagement from facial expressions, for example, our findings reinforce the need for further investigation in this regard, also including the use of other techniques for analyzing the player's engagement in conjunction with facial expressions. In future work, we intend to explore the correlation of engagement with discrete emotions and other metrics extracted from non-invasive methods, such as gaze and game logs. Additionally, this should involve the use of Machine Learning techniques to identify possible correlations between these data, also including a temporal analysis considering the use of the game at different moments.

Acknowledgments. This study was financed in part by the Coordenação de Aperfeiçoamento de Pessoal de Nível Superior – Brasil (CAPES) – Finance Code 001; Brazilian National Council of Scientific and Technological Development (CNPq) - grant 309030/2019-6); São Paulo Research Foundation (FAPESP) – National Institute of Science and Technology – Medicine Assisted by Scientific Computing (INCT-MACC) – grant 2014/50889-7; PIBIC/CNPq/USP - grant 160013/2020-8), and PUB program of Provost for Undergraduate affairs of Universidade de São Paulo (USP).

References

1. Affectiva. Emotion AI 101: All About Emotion Detection and Affectiva's Emotion Metrics, August 2020
2. Aranha, R.V., Casaes, A.B., Nunes, F.L.S.: Influence of environmental conditions in the performance of open-source software for facial expression recognition. In: Proceedings of the 19th Brazilian Symposium on Human Factors in Computing Systems. ACM, October 2020
3. Aranha, R.V., Correa, C.G., Nunes, F.L.S.: Adapting software with affective computing: a systematic review. IEEE Trans. Affect. Comput. 1 (2019)
4. Oussama Bonnor. Color switch replica - github, January 2020
5. Bopp, J.A., Mekler, E.D., Opwis, K.: Negative emotion, positive experience? In: Proceedings of the 2016 CHI Conference on Human Factors in Computing Systems. ACM, May 2016

6. Borges, J.B., Juy, C.L., De Andrade Matos, I.S., Silveira, P.V.A., De Gois Ribeiro Darin, T.: Player experience evaluation: which instrument should i use? J. Interact. Syst. 11(1), 74–91 (2020)
7. Bosch, N.: Detecting student engagement: human versus machine. In: Proceedings of the 2016 Conference on User Modeling Adaptation and Personalization, UMAP 2016, pp. 317–320. Association for Computing Machinery, New York, NY, USA (2016)
8. Brockmyer, J.H., Fox, C.M., Curtiss, K.A., McBroom, E., Burkhart, K.M., Pidruzny, J.N.: The development of the game engagement questionnaire: a measure of engagement in video game-playing. J. Exp. Soc. Psychol. 45(4), 624–634 (2009)
9. Chen, X., Niu, L., Veeraraghavan, A., Sabharwal, A.: FaceEngage: robust estimation of gameplay engagement from user-contributed (YouTube) videos. IEEE Trans. Affect. Comput. 1 (2019)
10. Darwin, C.: The expression of the emotions in man and animals. Oxford University Press, USA (1998)
11. Dewan, M.A.A., Murshed, M., Lin, F.: Engagement detection in online learning: a review. Smart Learn. Environ. 6(1), 1–20 (2019)
12. Doherty, K., Doherty, G.: Engagement in HCI. ACM Comput. Surv. 51(5), 1–39 (2019)
13. Ekman, P.: Emotions Revealed: Understanding Faces and Feelings. A Phoenix paperback, Phoenix (2004)
14. Ekman, P.: What scientists who study emotion agree about. Perspect. Psychol. Sci. 11(1), 31–34 (2016)
15. Ekman, P., Friesen, W.V.: Measuring facial movement. Environ. Psychol. Nonverbal Behav. 1(1), 56–75 (1976)
16. Ekman, P., Oster, H.: Facial expressions of emotion. Annu. Rev. Psychol. 30(1), 527–554 (1979)
17. Ekman, P., Rosenberg, E.L.: What the Face RevealsBasic and Applied Studies of Spontaneous Expression using the Facial Action Coding System (FACS). Oxford University Press, April 2005
18. Grafsgaard, J.F., Wiggins, J.B., Boyer, K.E., Wiebe, E.N., Lester, J.C.: Automatically recognizing facial indicators of frustration: a learning-centric analysis. In: 2013 Humaine Association Conference on Affective Computing and Intelligent Interaction, pp. 159–165 (2013)
19. Hookham, G., Nesbitt, K.: A systematic review of the definition and measurement of engagement in serious games. In: Proceedings of the Australasian Computer Science Week Multiconference, ACSW 2019. Association for Computing Machinery, New York, NY, USA (2019)
20. Huang, Y., Chen, F., Lv, S., Wang, X.: Facial expression recognition: a survey. Symmetry, 11(10) (2019)
21. Kapoor, A., Mota, S., Picard, R.W.: Towards a learning companion that recognizes affect. In: Proceedings from Emotional and Intelligent II: The Tangled Knot of Social Cognition, AAAI Fall Symposium, number 543 in 1, pp. 2–4 (2001)
22. Li, S., Deng, W.: Deep facial expression recognition: a survey. IEEE Trans. Affect. Comput. 1 (2020)
23. McDaniel, B., D'Mello, S., King, B., Chipman, P., Tapp, K., Graesser, A.: Facial features for affective state detection in learning environments. In: Proceedings of the Annual Meeting of the Cognitive Science Society (2007)
24. Mena-Chalco, J., Marcondes, R., Velho, L.: Banco de dados de faces 3d: Impaface3d. Technical report, IMPA - VISGRAF Laboratory (2008)

25. Nacke, L.E.: Introduction to biometric measures for Games User Research. Oxford University Press, March 2018

26. Nezami, O.M., Dras, M., Hamey, L., Richards, D., Wan, S., Paris, C.: Automatic recognition of student engagement using deep learning and facial expression. In: Machine Learning and Knowledge Discovery in Databases, pp. 273–289. Springer International Publishing (2020)

27. Noldus. Facial expression recognition software — FaceReader, June 2020

28. O'Brien, H.L., Cairns, P., Hall, M.: A practical approach to measuring user engagement with the refined user engagement scale (UES) and new UES short form. Int. J. Hum. Comput. Stud. **112**, 28–39 (2018)

29. O'Brien, H.L., Toms, E.G.: The development and evaluation of a survey to measure user engagement. J. Am. Soc. Inform. Sci. Technol. **61**(1), 50–69 (2009)

30. Robinson, R., Wiley, K., Rezaeivahdati, A., Klarkowski, M., Mandryk, R.L.: let's get physiological, physiological!. In: Proceedings of the Annual Symposium on Computer-Human Interaction in Play. ACM, November 2020

31. Sharek, D., Wiebe, E.: Measuring video game engagement through the cognitive and affective dimensions. Simul. Gaming **45**(4–5), 569–592 (2014)

32. Stöckli, S., Schulte-Mecklenbeck, M., Borer, S., Samson, A.C.: Facial expression analysis with AFFDEX and FACET: a validation study. Behav. Res. Methods **50**(4), 1446–1460 (2017). https://doi.org/10.3758/s13428-017-0996-1

33. Vallverdú, J. (ed.): Handbook of Research on Synthesizing Human Emotion in Intelligent Systems and Robotics. IGI Global (2015)

34. Yue, W., Ji, Q.: Facial landmark detection: a literature survey. Int. J. Comput. Vis. **127**(2), 115–142 (2018)

35. Wilhelm Wundt. Emotions. Grundriss der Psychologie, **13** (1896)

Explore Data, Enjoy Yourself - KUbism, A Playful Approach to Data Exploration

Bruno Cardoso[1](✉), Neil Cohn[1], Frederik Truyen[2], and Koenraad Brosens[2]

[1] Department of Communication and Cognition, University of Tilburg, Tilburg, The Netherlands
{bruno.cardoso,n.cohn}@tilburguniversity.edu
[2] Faculty of Arts, KU Leuven, Leuven, Belgium
{fred.truyen,koen.brosens}@kuleuven.be

Abstract. The increasing relevance of information in today's world has grown the challenge of accessible data exploration. Most existing approaches are primarily utilitarian, where the motivation for exploration remains mostly extrinsic, correlated to the value of the outcome. In light of our natural drives for exploration, we argue that data exploration can be made more rewarding and enjoyable via interfaces that leverage the intrinsic motivations of users. To that end, we present KUbism, a prototype emphasizing the hedonic value of data exploration through a playful interface built with elements of Minecraft gameplay. Implemented as a Terasology module, KUbism invites users to explore data in voxel worlds populated with data blocks. We conducted a user study (n = 41) to validate our approach in both hedonic and utilitarian dimensions. Our results demonstrate that KUbism allows effective data exploration while arousing curiosity and joy, thereby reinforcing the extrinsic value of data exploration with intrinsic rewards.

Keywords: Data exploration interfaces · Playfulness · Gameplay · User study

1 Introduction

In a world where information is progressively more digital, it is paramount to empower diverse people, with varying levels of technological expertise and divergent interests, to explore that information effectively [1]. We can find many different tools and approaches in the literature focusing on different aspects of data exploration, like steering the user towards important "areas" of datasets [2], or leveraging the visual capabilities of users to foster data comprehension [3] (see Sect. 2.1 for examples). Notwithstanding the flexibility and potential of these approaches [4], they often have a considerable learning curve [5] and require a degree of domain knowledge that may pose difficulties for less experienced users [6–10]. Furthermore, most of these approaches remain utilitarian in nature, meaning the rewards of the exploration correlate primarily with the value of the

Electronic supplementary material The online version of this chapter (https://doi.org/10.1007/978-3-030-85613-7_4) contains supplementary material, which is available to authorized users.

C. Ardito et al. (Eds.): INTERACT 2021, LNCS 12934, pp. 43–64, 2021.
https://doi.org/10.1007/978-3-030-85613-7_4

outcomes and less with the experience of exploration itself. In light of how naturally people engage in intrinsically motivated exploratory behavior [10–13], we believe that additional value can be found in promoting the intrinsic rewards of the experience offered by data exploration tools, making them more enjoyable, playful and fulfilling of users' needs in a more comprehensive manner [13].

The approach of fluid interaction [14] is well aligned with this point of view. As proposed by Elmqvist et al. [14], fluid interfaces are designed to leverage the psychological concept of flow [15] – an elusive concept that, in short, refers to a mental state of total immersion in an activity. Placing special emphasis on the interaction with the data, fluid interfaces adhere to principles like the promotion of flow [15], support of direct manipulation [16] and minimization of the gulfs of action [17].

In this line of reasoning, we posit that the complex and intrinsically rewarding experience of gameplaying may prove to be an interesting approach to build truly fluid interfaces for data exploration that are playful, immersive, useful and enjoyable.

To the best of our knowledge this concept has not yet been the focus of significant research, but several reasons motivate its value. First, both data exploration [4] and gameplay can be motivated by curiosity [18, 19], an intrinsically motivating factor that suggests that a synergy may be found in combining the two activities. Second, playing fosters the cognitive processes involved in learning [20] – which often motivates data exploration. Third, videogames are known to create high levels of immersion and devotion, and they appeal to broad and diverse audiences [21, 22]. Therefore, datasets made available for exploration in interfaces that harness the playfulness of videogames have the potential of becoming more appealing to the general public. In other words, the self-rewarding nature of gameplay may draw people without special interest in given datasets to explore them, if only because of the enjoyable experience. Even people already interested in the data may find additional value in the intrinsically rewarding form of exploration we are proposing. Fourth, the approachability of videogames may empower people of varying data analysis experience to contribute to noteworthy findings. Indeed, these observations align with Elmqvist et al.'s argument that fluid interfaces for data visualization are, "in many respects, similar to computer games" [14].

Given the exploratory nature of our proposal, we developed KUbism, a prototype platform that aims to let users explore data via an interface built as an extension to the gameplay of Minecraft [23]. It was implemented as a Terasology [24] module, a Java game engine inspired by Minecraft. There are several reasons why the gameplay of Minecraft is well suited to our hypothesis of playful data exploration. First, as an open world, sandbox game, Minecraft's gameplay is hinged on exploration and free gameplay. It offers players expansive worlds to explore without the limitations of linear storylines or predefined goals and a considerable degree of creative freedom to experiment with gameplay [25, 26]. We expect that Minecraft's curiosity-arousing gameplay may predispose, or prime, users towards exploring the data. Second, the voxel worlds that make for one of the most distinctive features of Minecraft's gameplay can be considered tridimensional canvases on which all sorts of immersive data visualizations can be drawn with blocks (see Fig. 1 for simple examples, or [27] for a more complex one). Finally, we draw on another of Minecraft's most distinctive aspects, arbitrary structure building, as a metaphor for data manipulation. For example, by representing information elements (e.g., words) as blocks, structures built with such blocks can represent collections of those elements (e.g., bags-of-words or sentences depending on attributing meaning to the positioning of our hypothetical word blocks).

In line with these observations, KUbism represents information as a special type of block in the game world, and users are empowered to explore that information via in-game tools and game mechanics. Because it is based on Minecraft's first-person gameplay, KUbism's interface is immersive by design: both users (through the avatars) and data (through the blocks) become actors in the game world. Data blocks interact with one another and share information when attached together. By allowing these blocks to be "mined", structures built with them acquire additional meaning – walls and houses become more than barriers or shelters: they become in-game datasets. Furthermore, players have a number of functional blocks at their disposal that allow them to query those datasets. By providing these tools, and allowing players to ask questions and get answers without leaving the game world, Minecraft's gameplay becomes a de facto interface between the data and the user.

Fig. 1. Data representations in voxel worlds. Left: a representation of our study's demographics: (a) one gray block for each of our 41 participants; (b) a vertical bar chart for participant gender (yellow for females); (c and d) horizontal bar charts for participant area of expertise (yellow for females; top: humanities; middle: science and technology; bottom: middle school). Right: a world generated from a two-dimensional Gaussian function, exhibiting the characteristic bell curve. (Color figure online)

We validated out approach by conducting a user study with 41 participants that allowed us to assess use patterns and subjective user experience in two complementary perspectives – as a utilitarian and a hedonic-motivation system. Prior work [28] has shown that KUbism could help art historians gain a sense of situational awareness while conducting their research. In contrast, the present work explores the human-computer interactions of KUbism, ensuring our findings can extrapolate relevantly to the HCI community. The contributions of the work presented herein are: (1) we describe our approach of gameplay-embedded data exploration fluid interfaces; (2) we present KUbism, our proof-of-concept platform; and (3) we present and analyze the results of our user study, drawing conclusions in favor of future research.

2 Related Work

2.1 Data Exploration and Fluid Interaction

Given the growing importance of data in today's world, the research community has already proposed a number of promising approaches for data exploration, concentrating on different facets of this challenge. AIDE [2], for instance, is an interactive data exploration framework that steers users towards interesting areas of the data, while predicting queries that would retrieve relevant information. Another interesting approach is Queriosity [7], an automated and personalized data exploration system that, instead of just retrieving data by request, aims to discover what is interesting in datasets and offer those insights to users. We can also find many approaches based in visualization, aiming to leverage users' proficiency for processing visual information. Perhaps the best known examples are interactive environments like Tableau [29], that enable users to design visualizations while replacing code-writing with resources such as visual grammars and data pipelines. While highly configurable, the process of specifying visualizations in these platforms requires a degree of knowledge and experience that may impact the experience of new users. Addressing that challenge, we can find proposals like SeeDB [30], a visualization recommendation engine that, given a subset of data to be studied, suggests the visualizations ranked the most useful. Inspired by the *small multiples* paradigm, Elzen and Wijk's [8] approach offers multiple simultaneous perspectives over a dataset based on smaller, easier to understand, visualizations.

Placing interaction design at the forefront, fluid interfaces [14] offer a different perspective over data visualization which is closely related to our work. While acknowledging the elusiveness of the concept of *flow*, Elmqvist et al. [14] proposed fluid interfaces for information visualization to be characterized by one or more of the following properties: (1) promotion of flow [15]; (2) support of direct manipulation [16]; and (3) minimization of the gulfs of action [17]. We can find many proposals in the literature that recognize the value of offering an experience that helps users stay immersed in the current activity and not be distracted by the user interface (i.e., *in the flow*) [1, 14]. For instance, ImAxes [31] is an interactive multidimensional visualization tool that relies on the arrangement of data axes to create collections of data visualizations in immersive, virtual spaces. Keshif [5] proposes an easy-to-use platform for exploring tabular data by summarizing it, aggregating records by value and visualizing aggregate aspects of the data according to the type of the data. Vizdom [1], the front end of the Northstar system [1], is a data exploration environment designed for pen-and-touch interfaces that relies on prompt feedback and approximate results to offer fast response times to users.

Though there are many similarities between KUbism and the approaches mentioned in this section – especially those that offer fluid experiences to users – perhaps the main distinction to be made lies in the utilitarian/hedonic continuum. Even though some of these examples do emphasize the intrinsic rewards offered by their systems, they are fundamentally utilitarian, with the value of the exploration effort positively correlated to the value of the retrieved information. By contrast, KUbism's data exploration experience is embedded in the gameplay of Minecraft and that makes our approach rather unique. It is as much a utilitarian-motivation system as a hedonic-motivation one. Users can use the elements of KUbism to query the dataset from within Minecraft worlds; they can just play classical Minecraft bearing no mind to the information contained in KUbism's blocks; or they can do both and use KUbism elements to add further meaning to elements of Minecraft's gameplay, like building structures that double as datasets (anecdotally, one of our study participants daydreamed of building a "temple with columns composed of blocks of data").

It is also interesting to note the conceptual analogy between KUbism and tangible interfaces, which have been studied to enhance the experience of interacting with digital information like programming languages [32] or bar charts [33]. KUbism's data exploration interface actually builds on a sort of tangibility "by proxy" – both users (via the avatars) and the data (via the data blocks) co-exist and are agents in the same space (the game world), while abiding to the same set of rules (the game mechanics). From the user's perspective, avatars are arguably as tangible as the data: they share the same world. This is very much what happens with tangible interfaces, where digital information is given physical form (avatars) so as to share the (real) world with users.

2.2 Exploration in Videogames

Many videogames maintain exploration as a core gameplay activity [34]. For instance, exploration is one of No Man's Sky [35]'s gameplay pillars. No Man's Sky offers an open virtual universe including over 18 quintillion procedurally generated planets, including unique biomes. Allowing for multiplayer gameplay, the game informs players of unique discoveries they made. A companion website allows players to share interesting in-game discoveries with the player community. Similarly, Elite Dangerous [36] is a space-flight simulation game that allows players to explore a realistic 1:1 scale representation of the Milky Way. The game world contains some 400 billion-star systems and circa 150,000 are modeled after real astronomical data, complete with planets and moons that rotate and orbit in real time. How well this game appeals to players' drives for exploration is well illustrated by its (at the time of writing) 38,241-subscriber Reddit community [37] of explorers. In a different approach, Planetarium [38] is a "planet generator with creatures and secrets" that invites players to "discover" planets generated out of textual seeds (the planet names). Although it is possible to change parameters like planet temperature or land/water ratio and thereby change the aspect of the planets, the most original form of exploration in Planetarium lies in discovering planet names, an endeavor with its own community of name-sharing enthusiasts [39].

Although these examples illustrate how some videogames are using the allure of exploration and player's curiosity to keep them engaged, we found only one other example in the literature exploring the use of videogames to enhance the experience of exploring data: Onto-Frogger [40, 41]. Using elements of the classic game Frogger [42], Onto-Frogger focuses on communicating the emergent semantic structures of datasets to users, in a way that is both understandable and enjoyable. While both Onto-Frogger and KUbism offer users an interface to data exploration based on videogames, there are also some notable differences. For instance, Onto-Frogger is focused on exploring the structure of graph-based data repositories whereas our approach emphasizes the exploration of the data itself. Also, Onto-Frogger is, for all effects, a videogame by itself; a reimagination of Frogger's gameplay to allow players to learn about the structure of graph-based data repositories. KUbism, in turn, is an extension to Minecraft's gameplay.

It does not require the removal or repurposing of any of the existing gameplay elements; instead, it extends Minecraft with an interface for interacting with data.

2.3 Minecraft in Research

Minecraft is a multiplayer, open world, sandbox game [43] whose default gameplay invites players to explore procedurally generated worlds of blocks that can be picked up and placed in order to build arbitrarily complex structures. It was inspired by Infiniminer [44], a 2009 independently created videogame that laid the foundations of the well-known Minecraft game mechanics, including the procedural generation of worlds composed of blocks that players can pick up and place. More than just a successful means of entertainment, Minecraft's gameplay lends a flexible medium that has been used in research, while keeping true to its intrinsically motivating playful nature [19, 45–47]. Examples come from fields as diverse as education [46, 48–50], health [51], art [52], productivity and planning [53], creative experimentation [54] and technology [55–57], among many others (see Rey et al.'s work for a more complete review [46]). Emphasizing the creative potential of this game, OPERAcraft [54] is a Minecraft-based arts and technology education platform that promotes live performances combining gaming, telematics, machinima and opera. As highlighted above, applications of Minecraft for purposes other than entertainment are diverse and plentiful. However, with the exception of MetaboCraft [27] where Minecraft structures are used to visualize metabolomics information, to our knowledge KUbism is the first application of a Minecraft-like game engine to data exploration.

3 KUbism

3.1 Implementation and Architecture

Although the mechanics and overall look-and-feel of KUbism are akin to Minecraft's, we implemented our platform as an extension to Terasology [24]. The Terasology project started in 2011 as an LWJGL-based[1] Minecraft demo before later developers guided it to its current state. Terasology is an open source, Minecraft-like, voxel-based game engine implemented in Java. It is a community effort, developed and maintained by software developers, designers, game testers, graphic artists and musicians [58]. KUbism was implemented in Java as a Terasology module – an independent modular container for code and assets, including game systems, logic and content, with restricted access to the core Terasology engine.

Architecturally, the KUbism prototype was developed as a desktop application that communicates with a database server, acting as a client in a standard client-server architecture. This way, KUbism stands as an interface between the user and the data contained in a remote database (see Sect. 4.1).

---

[1] LightWeight Java Game Library (https://www.lwjgl.org).

3.2 Data Source Format

KUbism assumes its supporting data to be modeled after the Entity-Relationship (ER) model [59], and therefore to be formatted as a graph of nodes (entities) and vertices between them (relations). Given the ER model's more "natural" view over data [59], the mapping of data elements (entities) to game elements (blocks) in KUbism becomes more straightforward, facilitating user understanding and reasoning about the underlying data model (see Sect. 4.1). True to the ER model, KUbism entities and relations have attributes that characterize them.

3.3 A Gameplay-Based Interface to Data Exploration

KUbism may be understood as a mapping between elements of the domain of data exploration to the domain of gameplay. As such, the entities and relationships of a data source must have a representation in the game world that allows users to interact with them, as well as the necessary tools to navigate the graph of data.

As "things that can be distinctly identified" [59], entities are represented in the game world as a special type of block, the *entity block* (Fig. 2, a), which can contain one or more entities of the same type.

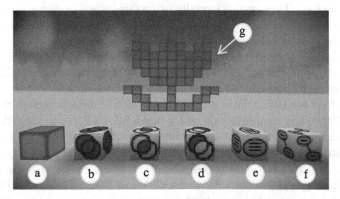

Fig. 2. KUbism's data exploration tools: (a) entity block; (b) set union block; (c) set intersection block; (d) set difference block; (e) entity filter block; (f) relation filter block; and (g) an entity structure, composed of many attached entity blocks sharing the same entities. (Color figure online)

Users can interact with these blocks in the same way they would with other Minecraft blocks: they can be activated, picked up, carried, and placed anywhere in the world. Entities are shared between attached entity blocks, thereby allowing players to create in-game datasets with any shape or format by attaching entity blocks together. We designate groups of attached *entity blocks* sharing a common set of entities as *entity structures*, playing on both their in-game block structure aspect, and the role they play for data exploration as datasets (Fig. 2, g).

In turn, because relationships are "associations between entities" [59], their operationalization in KUbism is less straightforward. As the existence of relationships depends upon the existence of the related entities, their manifestation in the game world does not have the same independent and individual "presence" as that of entities. As such, players are only able to explore relationships by attaching a dedicated functional block, the *relation filter block* (Fig. 2, f) to entity blocks (Fig. 2, a) or structures (Fig. 2, g) containing related entities.

We now present the full list of blocks that comprise KUbism's data exploration interface. For the sake of simplicity, in the following examples we will refer to a hypothetical and minimalist data source composed of (1) one type of entity, *person*, with a single property, *name*; and (2) one relationship, *parenthood*, which assigns the roles of *parent* and *child* to related entities. Finally, assume there are only three entities in the data source: "Lenny" and his parents "Mom" and "Dad".

Entity Block (Fig. 2, a). The red entity blocks act as containers for one or more entities of the same type. Activating an entity block allows the player to see the entities it contains – a popup window will display the entities in a list. Entities are shared, without repetitions, between entity blocks attached together (entity structures). Imagine two entity blocks, EB_1 and EB_2, such that EB_1 = {Lenny, Mom} and EB_2 = {Lenny, Dad}. Attaching these two blocks together would result in a 2-block entity structure containing the entities of both blocks without repetitions, i.e., {Lenny, Mom, Dad}.

Set Union, Intersection and Difference Blocks (Fig. 2, b, c and d). These blocks implement the three basic operations of the algebra of sets, the union ($\cup$), intersection ($\cap$) and difference ($\backslash$). They operate virtually in the same way: once attached to different structures they will produce a new entity block containing the entities resulting from the application of the corresponding operation to the structures' entities. For EB_1 and EB_2, that would mean a new entity block containing {Lenny, Mom, Dad} for the set union, or just {Lenny} for the intersection. In turn, because the set difference operation is not commutative by convention, the set difference block is configurable – when activated, it will display a form requesting the user to indicate which of the attached structures is the "main" one. Depending respectively on which block EB_1 or EB_2 was set as the "main", that would mean a new entity block containing either {Mom} or {Dad}.

Entity Filter Block (Fig. 2, e). This block operates like a filter, retrieving all entities of an attached structure that meet specified criteria. Users can express the criteria as predicates using a syntax similar to the where clause of SQL, in a window that pops up when the block is activated. E.g., to extract the entity named "Lenny" from the structure {Lenny, Mom, Dad}, we could attach an entity filter block to said structure and write an expression like person.name = 'Lenny' (where the "person.name" notation states the type and property of the entities we are interested in). Since there is only one matching entity, we would obtain a new entity block for {Lenny}.

Relation Filter Block (Fig. 2, f). This block works like the previous one but, instead of properties, the entities are filtered according to the role they play in relationships. If we wanted to find the parents of the entity Lenny, we could attach one of these blocks to a pair of structures, S_1 = {Lenny, Mom, Dad} and S_2 = {Lenny}, configure it to focus on the *parenthood* relation between the entities of S_1 and S_2, set the former as *parents* and the latter as *children*, and thus obtain a new entity block containing {Mom, Dad}.

4 Methods

4.1 Experiment Data

The data we used in our user tests comes from Project Cornelia's database [60], a data repository containing archival historical data about the 17th-century creative communities of Brussels and Antwerp [60]. Because the Cornelia database contains over 30 types of entities and many more relations, and since our study is focused on KUbism as an interface between users and datasets, we needed to minimize the potential inadvertent effects brought by factors such as data complexity. As such, to keep our model simple yet complete enough for the purposes of our study, we limited the data model to two types of entity, *actor* and *place*, and two relations, *parenthood* and *baptism*.

To provide some context, the actors in the Cornelia database correspond to people mentioned in historical records like painters, gold-beaters, stained-glass makers and their respective families, while the places stand for locations mentioned in said archives. Regarding the relationships between these entities, parenthood is a relation between two actors (*parent* and *child*), and baptism is a relation between an actor and the place where they were baptized (*baptized* and the *place of baptism*).

Communication between KUbism and the Cornelia database was implemented via the latter's API, so all queries built by our participants ran against a live database.

4.2 Experiment World

Because KUbism's interface is built as an extension to Terasology's default gameplay, our participants could engage in a range of playful activities instead of the data exploration required by our study, like exploring the world or mining. We thus needed to constrain our virtual world so as to keep participants focused in our experiment instead of just playing. Therefore, we devised a very simple world, featuring only a sky, and an endless flat ground (Fig. 3).

Fig. 3. The Experiment World. This was the setting of our study, featuring (a) the study block used to guide participants through the study tasks and (b and c) two column-shaped entity structures containing a block for each entity of type *place* (b) and *actor* (c).

We arranged the entities of our simple data model in two columns in this rather dull world, conveniently at hand for participants to interact with (Fig. 3, b). We also included a study block (Fig. 3, a) in the experiment world that guided participants through our study from within the game world. When participants activated this block, a popup window would be displayed with varying content: before starting the study, it presented participants with a demographic questionnaire; during the session, the block would either present users with the current task (Table 1) or verify their answers; finally, after the last task participants were asked to complete two questionnaires intended to assess their subjective experience with KUbism (see Sect. 4.4). Note that this block is a resource of our experiment and not part of KUbism's data exploration interface.

4.3 Study Design

Our study sessions followed a task-based protocol requiring participants to perform 7 tasks involving different aspects of our interface (see Table 1).

Table 1. The 7 challenges of our task-based user study, along with possible solutions.

Task 1. Find all actors named "Marcus"

1. Attach an entity filter block to the structure of actors;
2. Activate the block with the condition actor.name = 'Marcus'

Task 2. Find all actors with surname "Auwercx"

1. Attach an entity filter block to the structure of actors;
2. Activate the block with the condition actor.surname = 'Auwercx'

Task 3. Find all actors with first name "Marcus" or surname "Auwercx"

1. Attach a union block to the blocks produced in tasks 1 and 2;
2. Activate the union block

Task 4. Find all actors named "Marcus Auwercx"

1. Attach an intersection block to the blocks produced in tasks 1 and 2;
2. Activate the intersection block

Task 5. Find all actors named "Marcus" without the "Auwercx" surname

1. Attach a difference block to the blocks produced in tasks 1 and 2;
2. Activate the difference block, setting the block of Task 1 as the main block

Task 6. Who were the children of actor Marcus Auwercx?

1. Attach a relation filter block to the structure of actors;
2. Attach the entity block produced in Task 3 to the relation filter block;
3. Activate the block focusing on the parenthood relation between the entities in the Task 3 block (parents) and those in the structure of actors (children)

Task 7. Where were the children of actor Marcus Auwercx baptized?

1. Attach a relation filter block to the structure of places;
2. Attach the entity block produced in Task 6 to the relation filter block;
3. Activate block focusing on the baptism relation between the entities in the block of Task 6 (baptized) and those in the structure of places (places of baptism)

Since KUbism's data source is a graph (see Sect. 3.2), we designed these tasks based on Lee et al.'s graph visualization taxonomy [61]. In that sense, all tasks involved the retrieval of values, tasks 1 and 2 required filtering entities by attribute value; tasks 3, 4 and 5 assessed the use of set operations; and tasks 6 and 7 focused on node adjacency, i.e., the retrieval of entities related to other entities.

Before starting the experiment, we asked participants to read a short document explaining the ideas behind KUbism (data exploration via gameplay embedded inter-faces), the KUbism world (data is represented by blocks and can be explored via other blocks), and the controls. After reading the document, we invited participants to have a first-hand experience with KUbism, try the controls freely, and ask any questions. Although we did not impose restrictions on how long this first experience lasted, it generally took less than a couple of minutes. Because most of our participants did not report playing videogames frequently (see Sect. 5.1), this phase served as a "crash course" that allowed them to gain familiarity with the controls. To start the experiment, we informed participants that they had to activate the study block (Fig. 3, a) whenever they felt ready. Upon activation, the study block presented participants with a questionnaire intended to gather demographic data, like date of birth, gender, education level, and gameplay frequency. Once the demographic questionnaire was answered, participants were presented with the first task of the study. Each of the seven tasks was formulated as a "challenge", a question about the entities or the relationships in the experiment's data model. All tasks followed the step sequence below:

1. Participants activated the study block;
2. The study block presented participants with a popup displaying the current challenge (see preceding list);
3. Participants proceeded to execute operations on data freely, following whatever course of action they felt appropriate, until obtaining an entity block with the entities, they thought to be the answer to the challenge;
4. Participants placed the response block on top of the study block; the response was verified automatically:

   a. If it was incorrect, participants were informed and asked to try again (step 3);
   b. Otherwise, participants were either informed of their success and presented with the next challenge (step 2), or the experiment would end if this was the final challenge.

In order to complement our understanding of the user experience, KUbism automatically kept a log of participant actions inside the game, like block-placing or activation, that we analyzed through process mining procedures.

4.4 Subjective Experience Evaluation

After completing all tasks we asked participants to answer two questionnaires to assess their overall user experience with the system: the well-known System Usability Scale (SUS), which is widely used and has become an industry standard [62] and the more recently proposed Hedonic-Motivation System Adoption Model (HMSAM) [18]. The

SUS is a technology agnostic model for assessing system usability composed of 10 5-point Likert items. The SUS scale ranges from 0 to 100, with higher scores indicating generally more usable systems. In turn, the HMSAM is a more recent proposal aimed at evaluating hedonism-oriented systems such as videogames, and focuses on the inherent factors influencing said systems. To that end, the HMSAM models user experience based on eight constructs (definitions in [18, 63]): *joy*; *control*; *focused immersion*; *temporal dissociation*; *curiosity*; *perceived ease of use*; *perceived usefulness*; and finally *behavioral intention to use*.

Given that KUbism aims to enhance data exploration via gameplay, we applied both the SUS and HMSAM questionnaires to assess both the utilitarian and the hedonic facets of KUbism, to draw a more complete picture of the overall user experience.

5   Results

Our study took place in the second semester of 2018, in a quiet room at the university, with only the presence of the participant and an observer.

5.1   Demographics

Participants were recruited via direct invitation and snowball sampling, resulting from communications through our university's student and departmental mailing lists. Participation was voluntary and not compensated. This procedure yielded a total of 41 participants (19 male, 22 female; mean age: 29, range: 14 to 58). Participant's education range included middle school (1), undergraduates (15), Bachelor's (3), Master's (12) and Ph.D (10). Other than the middle-schooler participant, 26 reported studying Humanities (e.g., Cultural Studies and Art History) and 14 Science and Technology (e.g., Computer Science and Biology). On a 5-point scale (0 – "never" to 5 – "daily"), reported gameplay frequency was: 17 participants "never" played videogames, 11 played "rarely", 3 played "monthly", 6 did so "weekly" and 4 participants played "daily". With the exception of 3, none of the participants had previous contact with the data source we used in our study (see Sect. 4.1). All participants gave their informed consent, and express consent was also given by the parents of our middle-school participant.

Participant Groups – Player vs. Non-player. Given the relevance of videogames to our research, we divided the study participants in "Player" and "Non-Player' groups to control for the effect of gameplaying habits in the experience with our tool. Participants reporting "daily", "weekly" or "monthly" playing habits were considered "Players" ($n = 13$), and the rest, who "rarely" or "never" played videogames, were considered "Non-Players" ($n = 28$).

5.2   Task Time

All of our participants completed the 7 tasks of our study successfully, though time taken varied considerably. From the start of the first task to the completion of the final one, each testing session took an average of 886 s (00:14:46). The shortest session took 170 s

(00:02:50) and the longest a total of 1992 s (00:33:12). Figure 4 and Table 2 provide an overview of the time taken for each task, across participants, and for the Player and Non-Player groups.

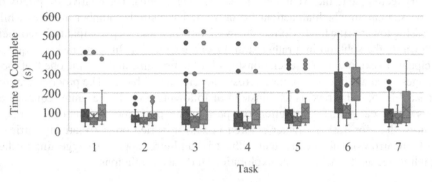

Fig. 4. Boxplots depicting the times for each of the 7 tasks of our study, for all participants (■), and the Player (■) and Non-Player (■) groups.

A Friedman test was run to understand the differences between the task times, across all participants (Table 2, first line). Pairwise comparisons were performed with a Bonferroni correction for multiple comparisons, yielding statistically significantly differences $\chi^2(6) = 79.251, p < .0005$. Post hoc analysis revealed those differences to be between tasks 1 and 4 ($p = 0.32$), and between the times of task 6 and all the other tasks' ($p < .0005$ for all comparisons; refer to Table 2 for the median times).

Table 2. Minimum, median and maximum task times, in seconds, for each of the 7 challenges, across participants (n = 41) and for the Player (n = 13) and Non-Player (n = 28) groups. Table cell format: minimum-**median**-maximum.

Task	1	2	3	4	5	6	7
All	23-**76**-411	22-**59**-175	6-**59**-517	9-**41**-454	14-**55**-367	27-**172**-508	21-**61**-366
Player	23-**49**-411	22-**47**-95	6-**47**-298	9-**23**-76	14-**49**-208	27-**92**-347	21-**46**-135
Non-player	36-**84**-376	28-**65**-175	12-**62**-517	14-**59**-454	30-**63**-367	73-**275**-508	28-**68**-366

To explore the effects of playing videogames frequently on task execution time, we ran a Mann-Whitney U test on the times of each task comparing the Player and Non-Player groups (Table 2, second and third lines). We found statistically significant differences in the times of task 1 (Player mean rank = 14.93 vs. Non-Player mean rank = 24.15; U = 274, z = 2.338, p = .019), task 4 (13.50 vs. 24.89; U = 294, z = 2.888, p = .004) and task 6 (13.57 vs. 24.85; U = 293, z = 2.859, p = .004).

5.3 Task Activity

Process mining procedures can bring insight into the way users interact with systems. To understand the first contact of our participants with KUbism we applied a process discovery technique to the event logs of Tasks 1 (Fig. 5, left). The relative simplicity of the process map, in which all actions occur a relatively similar number of times while progressing towards the final "Correct Answer" box, reveals that participants found their way towards the solution in a rather straightforward manner. In turn, Task 6 required participants to explore database relationships for the first time and was the one that took the longest median time to complete across participants (Table 2). The process map for this task (Fig. 5, right) reveals that, instead of following roughly the same sequence of actions while searching for a solution, our participants performed a more diverse range of actions than for Task 1 (lighter colored boxes) in varied order (relatively intricate web of thin arrows). This is consistent with a trial-and-error approach suggesting further research is needed to facilitate the exploration of database relations.

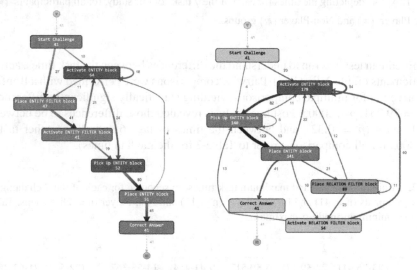

Fig. 5. Process Mining Map for the event logs of tasks 1 (left) and 6 (right), for all participants, showing the most frequent events and transitions. Transition frequency is indicated by the boxes' background darkness and thickness of the arrows. (Color figure online)

It is also worth noting that there is a considerable number of consecutive repetitions of the "Activated Entity" action, meaning that participants repeatedly activated entity blocks to see the entities contained therein. Given that (1) the most straightforward solution for Task 6 involved reusing the entity block previously used to complete Task 3; (2) participants generally did not destroy the entity blocks as they progressed through the tasks; and (3) the only way to see the contents of entity blocks is by activating them, this finding likely reflects our participants searching for the entity block of Task 3.

Another insightful perspective over the many ways our participants used KUbism can be found in the way they left the world after the last task (Fig. 6). Some participants were methodical, keeping the blocks with the answers to previous tasks in a systematized way, easy to find and reuse in following tasks (Fig. 6, left). Others adopted a more ad hoc approach, focusing on solving the tasks one at a time (Fig. 6, right). Ultimately, all were able to complete the tasks, evidencing that our platform is flexible enough for participants to experiment with data and find their own way to explore the data.

Fig. 6. Screenshots of the study world after two different participants completed the study. Some participants were methodical and organized (left), others found their answers in a more ad hoc approach (right). Ultimately, all participants completed the seven tasks of our study.

5.4 Subjective Experience Evaluation

As previously mentioned, we asked our participants to answer two experience evaluation questionnaires after the testing sessions, the SUS and the HMSAM (Sect. 4.4). These results are illustrated of these two assessments are illustrated in Fig. 7, for all participants and the "Player" and "Non-Player" groups.

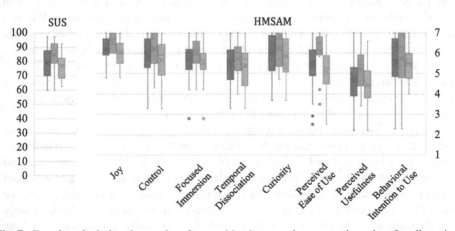

Fig. 7. Boxplots depicting the results of two subjective experience questionnaires for all participants (■), and the Player (■) and Non-Player (■) groups: (left) the System Usability Scale (SUS, 0–100 scale) and (right) the Hedonic-Motivation System Adoption Model (HMSAM, 8 dimensions, 1–7 scale).

The median SUS score was 80 (min: 60, max: 97.5) across participants, 87.5 (min: 60, max: 97.5) for the Player group and 77.5 (min: 62.5, max: 92.5) for the Non-Player group. We ran a Mann-Whitney U test on the results of the two groups revealing a statistically significant difference in their SUS scores (Player mean rank = 28 vs. Non-Player mean rank = 17.75; U = 273, z = 2.559, p = .011).

The HMSAM results may be found in Table 2, again for all participants and the Player and Non-Player groups. To understand the difference in the subjective experience of the two groups, we ran a Mann-Whitney U test on the scores of each HMSAM construct. These tests revealed differences between the two groups in three of the eight dimensions: joy (27 vs. 18.21; U = 260, z = 2.207, p = .027), control (26.58 vs. 18.41.; U = 254.5, z = 2.038, p = .042) and perceived ease of use (29.81 vs. 16.91; U = 296.5, z = 3.212, p = .001).

6 Discussion

In this work we propose KUbism, a data exploration interface embedded in Minecraft's gameplay. Through our user testing we showed that people can use our tool to successfully explore data while having an enjoyable experience. This supports the overall viability of our vision of data exploration interfaces embedded in gameplay.

All participants successfully completed all tasks of the study, indicating that people can effectively use KUbism to explore data and find answers. This observation becomes even more important in light of our participants' heterogeneity (see Sect. 5.1), showing that our approach is accessible and flexible enough to allow people of diverse backgrounds and experience to explore data effectively. This is further corroborated by the process maps of tasks 1 and 6 (Fig. 5) that illustrate the many different, sometimes unique, ways our participants devised to complete the study tasks (Fig. 6).

The analysis of the task execution times for all participants also emphasizes the overall accessibility of our approach: with the exception of tasks 1 and 6, the median time of completion was approximately 1 min for all tasks (Table 2, first row). It is also insightful that Task 6 took significantly longer to complete than all the other tasks, but the following Task 7, which also involved exploring relationships between entities, did not. With the exception of the relationship involved, both tasks were similar in all aspects. This suggests that there is a narrow learning curve involved in the exploration of relationships that is quickly overcome. In other words, exploring relationships becomes as straightforward as exploring entities after the first time.

Comparing task times between groups, the Player group had systematically lower median times for all tasks than the Non-Player group, but this was only statistically significant for tasks 1, 4 and 6. To help position this finding: (1) Task 1 was the first time participants interacted with KUbism without supervision, so it was a first contact scenario with the novelty that entails; (2) Task 4 was generally the quickest for everyone and, with the exception of the used block (*set intersection* instead of *set union*), the steps were the same as in the preceding Task 3 (Table 1); and finally, (3) the longest-taking Task 6 was the first time participants had to explore a relationship. In light of these observations, the increased familiarity of users with gameplaying experience seems to make them grasp new mechanics faster, but this difference tends to become less evident after the first contact with said mechanics.

Regarding the assessments of subjective experience, the overall scores for both the SUS and the HMSAM questionnaires are encouraging. The median SUS score of 80 obtained across participants placed KUbism's general usability between "good" and "excellent" [64] for our experiment, and this is also the case for the median SUS scores for the Player (87.5) and Non-Player groups (77.5). The statistical difference between these groups, however, suggests that people with more frequent gaming habits tend to perceive KUbism's usability more positively.

In turn, all eight HMSAM dimensions also received high median scores across all participants, with the constructs of joy and curiosity receiving the highest scores (6.2 and 6, respectively). The joy construct refers to the hedonic quality of the interaction experience (see Sect. 4.4), and curiosity is a known motivation of exploratory behavior. We consider this observation to be a particularly positive result since one of our main goals is to enhance the intrinsically motivating factors of data exploration, making it not only a useful activity but also a positive and exciting experience.

Higher scores for HMSAM's joy, control and ease of use found for the Player group indicate that they generally felt more in control of the interaction and had a more pleasurable overall experience than Non-Players. This observation is in line with the higher SUS usability score also found for this group, and sheds some light on the rationale. Indeed, the relatively higher appeal that KUbism seems to have for people with more frequent gameplaying habits appears to be linked to factors related to *control* and *ease of use*. Given the influence that *control* seems to have in the overall user experience [18, 62, 63], it is reasonable to conclude that better gaming skills lead to a more pleasurable experience with our interface. Interestingly, the remaining constructs of HMSAM, namely *focused immersion, temporal dissociation, perceived usefulness, behavioral intention to use* and – more importantly for our study – *curiosity*, did not yield statistically significant differences between the two groups. This indicates that playing habits did not appear to influence these dimensions strongly – which were all rated highly. In light of the alignment between these dimensions and factors of flow [14] like *transformation of time, sense of control, intrinsically rewarding interaction, concentration* and *loss of self-consciousness*, we have reasons to believe that the experience of KUbism does indeed promote user flow, the main concept behind fluid interaction.

Though KUbism is a proof-of-concept, these encouraging results support that gameplay offers an interesting stage for data exploration. All participants were able to explore our study's data and enjoyed doing so, meaning that neither the utilitarian value of data exploration nor the hedonic rewards of gameplay were lost in our hybrid platform. That is the promise of our approach: an accessible, self-rewarding, fun, and compelling way to find valuable information – playful data in a literal sense.

7 Conclusions and Future Work

Our work yielded evidence supporting the value of gameplay as a promising stage for building effective and playful interfaces for data exploration, leveraging both the utilitarian aspects of data exploration and the immersive, self-reinforcing nature of gameplay. All participants of our study successfully completed all study tasks while evaluating the experience positively. Overall, our approach scored highly in HMSAM's curiosity and joy. This is an encouraging finding as curiosity is a well-known motivator of exploratory behavior, and joy is a known predictor of behavioral intention to use [18]. Furthermore, in light of the diversity of our participants' backgrounds and the lack of familiarity most had with the study's dataset, the relatively low time taken to complete the study tasks and the several different paths participants devised to find their answers are also important evidence towards the overall accessibility of our approach.

The novelty of KUbism warranted a conservative approach to the design of our study. Specifically, a controlled, task-based design allowed us to focus on each of our platform features one at a time. Following these initial results, a less restricted study should be considered, with participants being allowed to explore a data world without limitations or predefined goals. Such study is bound to yield a rich set of data and enable us to acquire a broader perspective on the way people experience KUbism's open-ended, sandbox approach to data exploration, which could include, for instance, affective dimensions [65].

Ultimately, KUbism is but a first approach towards data exploration intertwined with gameplay, and many possibilities for further research lie ahead. For instance, multiplayer gameplay modes could offer great potential, especially if paired with persistent worlds. Rather than just exploring the results of procedurally generated worlds for fun, like what happens with many titles nowadays, we can imagine scenarios in education where communities of students explore relevant datasets together. If needed, minigames could be used to frame the exploration efforts – e.g., the task-based experiment of the study we present in this paper may be considered a minigame where players seek to answer questions in order to advance through the game.

On another perspective, we built the KUbism data exploration interface focusing mainly on structure building and block interactivity. However, another promise of our approach lies in the generation of worlds informed by the underlying data. As suggested in Fig. 1, there is clear potential for further research along this line. We can imagine whole worlds built in ways that reflect the dataset in some form or another, using pertinent aspects of the data as seeds for procedural generation. E.g., taking the term "seed" literally, a family's genealogical data could be used to generate trees of blocks with growth patterns hinting at important aspects of the data, like branch quantity and length to indicate the amount and lifespan of descendants. While observing such a tree would convey interesting information about a given family, a whole genealogy database could generate a forest for players to explore and learn about populations. On a different take, just like we used a Gaussian function to generate the terrain in Fig. 1, we could also use functions fitted to data points to create worlds with unique and meaningful features – e.g., wave-shaped mountains for skewed data distributions. Ultimately, the challenge of generating meaningful worlds, alluring yet useful, will be about finding the right balance between gameplay and data exploration, learning and fun.

References

1. Kraska, T.: Northstar: an interactive data science system. Proc. VLDB Endow. **11**, 2150–2164 (2018). https://doi.org/10.14778/3229863.3240493
2. Dimitriadou, K., Papaemmanouil, O., Diao, Y.: Explore-by-example: an automatic query steering framework for interactive data exploration. In: Proceedings of the 2014 ACM SIG-MOD International Conference on Management of Data (2014). https://doi.org/10.1145/258 8555.2610523
3. Ferreira de Oliveira, M.C., Levkowitz, H.: From visual data exploration to visual data mining: a survey. IEEE Trans. Vis. Comput. Graph. (2003). https://doi.org/10.1109/TVCG.2003.120 7445
4. Yalçin, M.A., Elmqvist, N., Bederson, B.B.: Cognitive stages in visual data exploration. In: Proceedings of the Sixth Workshop on Beyond Time and Errors on Novel Evaluation Methods for Visualization, pp. 86–95 (2016). https://doi.org/10.1145/2993901.2993902
5. Yalçin, M.A., Elmqvist, N., Bederson, B.B.: Keshif: rapid and expressive tabular data exploration for novices. IEEE Trans. Vis. Comput. Graph. (2018). https://doi.org/10.1109/TVCG. 2017.2723393
6. Mayr, E., Federico, P., Miksch, S., Schreder, G., Smuc, M., Windhager, F.: Visualization of cultural heritage data for casual users. IEEE VIS Work. Vis. Digit. Humanit. (2016). https:// doi.org/10.1109/TVCG.2016.2598468
7. Wasay, A., Athanassoulis, M., Idreos, S.: Queriosity: automated data exploration. In: Proceedings of 2015 IEEE International Congress on Big Data, BigData Congress 2015, pp. 716–719 (2015). https://doi.org/10.1109/BigDataCongress.2015.116
8. Van Den Elzen, S., Van Wijk, J.J.: Small multiples, large singles: a new approach for visual data exploration. Comput. Graph. Forum. (2013). https://doi.org/10.1111/cgf.12106
9. Wongsuphasawat, K., et al.: Voyager 2: augmenting visual analysis with partial view specifications. In: Conference on Human Factors in Computing Systems - Proceedings (2017).https:// doi.org/10.1145/3025453.3025768
10. Idreos, S., Papaemmanouil, O., Chaudhuri, S.: Overview of data exploration techniques. In: Proceedings of the ACM SIGMOD International Conference on Management of Data (2015).https://doi.org/10.1145/2723372.2731084
11. Maddi, S.R., Hoover, M., Kobasa, S.C.: Alienation and exploratory behavior. J. Pers. Soc. Psychol. (1982). https://doi.org/10.1037/0022-3514.42.5.884
12. Loewenstein, G.: The psychology of curiosity: a review and reinterpretation. Psychol. Bull. (1994). https://doi.org/10.1037//0033-2909.116.1.75
13. Korhonen, H., Montola, M., Arrasvuori, J.: Understanding playful user experience through digital games. In: International Conference on Designing Pleasurable Products and Interfaces, pp. 274–285 (2009)
14. Elmqvist, N., et al.: Fluid interaction for information visualization. Inf. Vis. **10**, 327–340 (2011). https://doi.org/10.1177/1473871611413180
15. Csikszentmihalyi, M.: Flow: The Psychology of Optimal Experience. Harper & Row, New York (1990)
16. Hutchins, E.L., Hollan, J.D., Norman, D.A.: Direct manipulation interfaces. Hum. Comput. Interact. (1985). https://doi.org/10.1207/s15327051hci0104_2
17. Norman, D.A., Draper, S.W.: User centered system design: new perspectives on human-computer interaction. Am. J. Psychol. **101**, 148–151 (1988). https://doi.org/10.2307/1422802
18. Lowry, P.B., Gaskin, J.E., Twyman, N.W., Hammer, B., Roberts, T.L.: Taking "fun and games" seriously: proposing the hedonic-motivation system adoption model (HMSAM). J. Assoc. Inf. Syst. **14**, 617–671 (2013). https://doi.org/10.17705/1jais.00347

19. Mayes, D.K., Cotton, J.E.: Measuring engagement in video games: a questionnaire. In: Proceedings of the Human Factors and Ergonomics Society 45th Annual Meeting, pp. 692–696 (2012). https://doi.org/10.1177/154193120104500704
20. Steinkuehler, C., Squire, K.: Videogames and Learning. The Cambridge Handbook of the Learning Sciences, 2nd edn (2014). https://doi.org/10.1017/CBO9781139519526.023
21. Jegers, K.: Pervasive game flow: understanding player enjoyment in pervasive gaming. Comput. Entertain. **5**, 9es (2007)
22. Entertainment Software Association: 2020 Essential Facts About the Video Game Industry. https://www.theesa.com/esa-research/2020-essential-facts-about-the-video-game-industry/. Accessed 25 Aug 2020
23. Persson, M.: Minecraft. Game [Windows], 18 November 2011. Mojang, Stockholm, Sweden (2011)
24. Glatzel, B., Kireev, A., Praestholm, R.: Terasology. Game [Windows]. Open-source, community-based development and maintenance (2011)
25. Min, W., Mott, B., Rowe, J., Liu, B., Lester, J.: Player goal recognition in open-world digital games with long short-term memory networks. In: IJCAI International Joint Conference on Artificial Intelligence (2016)
26. Tavinor, G.: The Art of Videogames (2009). https://doi.org/10.1002/9781444310177
27. Megalios, A., Daly, R., Burgess, K.: MetaboCraft: building a Minecraft plugin for metabolomics. Bioinformatics (2018). https://doi.org/10.1093/bioinformatics/bty102
28. Brosens, K., Cardoso, B., Truyen, F.: Slow Digital Art History and KUbism. The Routledge Companion to Digital Humanities and Art History (2020)
29. Stolte, C., Tang, D., Hanrahan, P.: Polaris: a system for query, analysis, and visualization of multidimensional relational databases. IEEE Trans. Vis. Comput. Graph. **8**, 52–65 (2002). https://doi.org/10.1109/2945.981851
30. Vartak, M., Rahman, S., Madden, S., Parameswaran, A., Polyzotis, N.: SeeDB: efficient data-driven visualization recommendations to support visual analytics. In: Proceedings of the VLDB Endowment International Conference on Very Large Data Bases (2015). https://doi.org/10.14778/2831360.2831371
31. Cordeil, M., Cunningham, A., Dwyer, T., Thomas, B.H., Marriott, K.: ImAxes: immersive axes as embodied affordances for interactive multivariate data visualisation. In: UIST 2017 – Proceedings of the 30th Annual ACM Symposium User Interface Software Technology, pp. 71–83 (2017). https://doi.org/10.1145/3126594.3126613
32. Horn, M.S., Crouser, R.J., Bers, M.U.: Tangible interaction and learning: the case for a hybrid approach. Pers. Ubiquit. Comput. **16**, 379–389 (2012). https://doi.org/10.1007/s00779-011-0404-2
33. Taher, F., et al.: Exploring interactions with physically dynamic bar charts. In: Conference on Human Factors in Computing Systems - Proceedings (2015).https://doi.org/10.1145/2702123.2702604
34. Heaven, D.: The gamers who only want to explore virtual worlds. https://www.newscientist.com/article/dn27946-buttonmasher-the-gamers-who-only-want-to-explore-virtual-worlds/. Accessed 15 Mar 2019
35. Hello Games: No Man's Sky. Game [Windows]. Hello Games, Guildford, England (2016)
36. Frontier Developments: Elite Dangerous. Game [Windows], 16 December 2014. Frontier Developments, Cambridge, England (2014)
37. r/eliteexplorers. https://www.reddit.com/r/EliteExplorers. Accessed 28 Aug 2020
38. Linssen, D.: Planetarium. Game [Windows], May 2015. (2015)
39. r/planetarium. https://www.reddit.com/r/planetarium/. Accessed 14 Mar 2019
40. Kallergi, A., Verbeek, F.J.: Onto-frogger: the making of. In: Proceedings of the 6th Nordic Conference on Human-Computer Interaction: Extending Boundaries (NordiCHI 2010), pp. 691–694. ACM, New York (2010). https://doi.org/10.1145/1868914.1869006

41. Kallergi, A., Verbeek, F.J.: Video games for collection exploration: games for and out of data repositories. In: Proceedings of the 14th International Academic MindTrek Conference: Envisioning Future Media Environments - MindTrek 2010, pp. 143–146 (2010). https://doi.org/10.1145/1930488.1930518
42. Konami: Frogger. Game [Arcade], 5 June 1981. Sega, Tokyo, Japan (1981)
43. Ekaputra, G., Lim, C., Eng, K.I.: Minecraft: a game as an education and scientific learning tool. In: Information Systems International Conference (2013)
44. Barth, Z.: Infiniminer. Game [Windows], April 2009. Zachtronics, Washington, USA (2009)
45. Malone, T.W.: Toward a theory of intrinsically motivating instruction. Cogn. Sci. (1981). https://doi.org/10.1016/S0364-0213(81)80017-1
46. Nebel, S., Schneider, S., Rey, G.D.: Mining learning and crafting scientific experiments: a literature review on the use of Minecraft in education and research. J. Educ. Technol. Soc. 19, 355 (2016)
47. Shneiderman, B.: Designing for fun: how can we design user interfaces to be more fun? Interactions (2004)
48. Schifter, C.C., Cipollone, M.: Constructivism vs constructionism: implications for Minecraft and classroom implementation. In: Isaías, P., Spector, JMichael, Ifenthaler, D., Sampson, D.G. (eds.) E-Learning Systems, Environments and Approaches, pp. 213–227. Springer, Cham (2015). https://doi.org/10.1007/978-3-319-05825-2_15
49. Bebbington, S., Vellino, A.: Can playing Minecraft improve teenagers' information literacy? J. Inf. Lit. (2015). https://doi.org/10.11645/9.2.2029
50. West, D.M., Bleiberg, J.: Education technology success stories (2013).https://doi.org/10.1097/MEG.0b013e32833bce39
51. Villani, D., Carissoli, C., Triberti, S., Marchetti, A., Gilli, G., Riva, G.: Videogames for emotion regulation: a systematic review (2018).https://doi.org/10.1089/g4h.2017.0108
52. Styles, E.B.: Tate worlds: art and artifacts reimagined in Minecraft. Adv. Archaeol. Pract. (2016). https://doi.org/10.7183/2326-3768.4.3.410
53. Saito, D., Takebayashi, A., Yamaura, T.: Minecraft-based preparatory training for software development project. In: IEEE International Professional Communication Conference (2015).https://doi.org/10.1109/IPCC.2014.7020393
54. Bukvic, I., Cahoon, C., Wyatt, A., Cowden, T., Dredger, K.: OPERAcraft: blurring the lines between real and virtual. In: Proceedings ICMC SMC 2014 (2014)
55. Johnson, M., Hofmann, K., Hutton, T., Bignell, D.: The Malmo platform for artificial intelligence experimentation. In: IJCAI International Joint Conference on Artificial Intelligence (2016)
56. Alstad, T., et al.: Minecraft computer game performance analysis and network traffic emulation by a custom bot. In: Proceedings of the 2015 Science and Information Conference, SAI 2015 (2015). https://doi.org/10.1109/SAI.2015.7237149
57. Bayliss, J.D.: Teaching game AI through Minecraft mods. In: 4th International IEEE Consumer Electronic Society - Games Innovation Conference, IGiC 2012 (2012). https://doi.org/10.1109/IGIC.2012.6329841
58. What is Terasology. https://github.com/MovingBlocks/Terasology/wiki/What-is-Terasology. Accessed 18 Mar 2019
59. Chen, P.P.-S.: The entity-relationship model: toward a unified view of data. ACM Trans. Database Syst. 1, 9–36 (1976). https://doi.org/10.1145/320434.320440
60. Project Cornelia. https://projectcornelia.be/. Accessed 10 June 2021
61. Lee, B., Plaisant, C., Parr, C.S., Fekete, J.-D., Henry, N.: Task taxonomy for graph visualization. In: Proceedings of the 2006 AVI Workshop on BEyond Time and Errors: Novel Evaluation Methods for Information Visualization, pp. 1–5. Association for Computing Machinery (2006). https://doi.org/10.1145/1168149.1168168

62. Brooke, J.: SUS - a quick and dirty usability scale. Usability Eval. Ind. **189**, 4–7 (1996)
63. Agarwal, R., Karahanna, E.: Time flies when you're having fun: cognitive absorption and beliefs about information technology usage. MIS Q. (2006). https://doi.org/10.2307/3250951
64. Bangor, A., Kortum, P., Miller, J.: Determining what individual SUS scores mean: adding an adjective rating scale. J. Usability Stud. **4**, 114–123 (2009)
65. Cardoso, B., Santos, O., Romão, T.: On sounder ground: CAAT, a viable widget for affective reaction assessment. In: Proceedings of the 28th Annual ACM Symposium on User Interface Software & Technology (UIST 2015), pp. 501–510. ACM, New York (2015). https://doi.org/10.1145/2807442.2807465

Goalkeeper: A Zero-Sum Exergame for Motivating Physical Activity

Evangelos Niforatos[1,3](✉), Camilla Tran[2], Ilias Pappas[3,4], and Michail Giannakos[3]

[1] TU Delft, Delft, The Netherlands
e.niforatos@tudelft.nl
[2] Sogeti, Oslo, Norway
[3] NTNU, Trondheim, Norway
{evangelos.niforatos,ilpappas,michailg}@ntnu.no
[4] University of Agder, Kristiansand, Norway
ilias.pappas@uia.no

Abstract. Incentives and peer competition have so far been employed independently for increasing physical activity. In this paper, we introduce Goalkeeper, a mobile application that utilizes deposit contracts for motivating physical activity in group settings. Goalkeeper enables one to set up a physical exercise challenge with a group of peers that deposit a fixed amount of money for participating. If a peer fails to complete the challenge, Goalkeeper redistributes their deposit to those who managed to complete it (i.e., zero-sum game). We evaluated the potential of Goalkeeper in increasing physical activity with a total of 50 participants over the course of 2 months. Our findings suggest that deposit contracts induce a loss-aversion bias, that in combination with peer competition, is effective in increasing exercise motivation. Ultimately, we generate a set of design principles for exergames that utilize deposit contracts for increasing physical activity in group settings.

Keywords: Physical activity · Motivation · Exercise contracts · Peer competition · Zero-sum game

1 Introduction

Modern sedentary lifestyle has been identified as one of the leading causes of preventable death worldwide. Prolonged physical inactivity has been linked to cardiovascular diseases, type 2 diabetes, depression, and even some types of cancer [62]. In fact, cardiovascular diseases were the leading cause of death in the United States, accounting for more than 900,000 deaths in 2016 with a considerable number linked to low levels of physical activity [52]. Traditionally, adopting a healthier lifestyle by promoting physical exercise has been deemed the remedy for the aforementioned health risks [68]. This has sparked a great interest in creating and developing a plethora of wearable devices, mobile applications, and websites that

C. Ardito et al. (Eds.): INTERACT 2021, LNCS 12934, pp. 65–86, 2021.
https://doi.org/10.1007/978-3-030-85613-7_5

Fig. 1. The User Interface of the Goalkeeper mobile app with the main functionalities of: (a) setting up a challenge, (b) keeping track of a challenge, and (c) viewing leaderboard and amount invested in the current challenge.

can track one's physical activity and motivate one to exercise more. As a result, the sales of fitness-tracking enabled devices (e.g., Fitbit, Garmin Fitness, Apple Watch, etc.) has skyrocketed. However, medical studies have shown that the long-term health benefits of fitness trackers are rather limited [10,25]. In fact, mobile health researchers, practitioners, and system developers still struggle to identify strategies for retaining users well after the fitness trackers' novelty has worn off [41]. Prominent HCI research has identified the lack of goal setting as the primary culprit for discontinued use of fitness trackers [18,47]. Here, we posit that peer pressure and loss aversion can be combined for increasing the motivation to exercise.

Peer pressure through social networking has been considered an affordable alternative to increasing physical exercise motivation [43]. While social networks were still in their infancy, Toscos et al., proposed the use of a "cell phone" application for motivating teenage girls to exercise by leveraging on their desire to stay connected with their peers [61]. Nowadays, the idea of using social networking to promote physical exercise is well-received. Skriloff et al., developed an asynchronous-play social game platform that they claim fills the gap in motivation left by fitness trackers [55]. Gui et al., aimed at the same gap by developing WeRun, a plugin for a social networking service for sharing fitness data among peers [19]. WeRun was found to sustain participants' interest in fitness tracking and exercise motivation. Kaos et al., investigated the social play dimension of exergaming in 6-week trials [27]. They found that people who engage in group play have superior adherence to people who primarily play alone. Generally, "social validation" is considered the main driver for human behaviour [15]. Thus, approaches that utilize peer pressure are particularly effective in increasing exercise motivation.

"**Loss aversion**," introduced by Tversky and Kahneman [26], is a prominent theory in the field of Behavioral Economics that can also be pivotal in increasing exercise motivation. The loss aversion theory describes the strong reluctance to give away a bestowed utility. A direct implication of loss aversion is that the loss of utility linked to a valued good is greater than the utility gain linked with receiving it [63]. The simplest explanation of the loss aversion theory is the two following scenarios of a coin toss: In (a) heads will make you lose 100€ and tails will make you win 200€. Conversely in (b), heads will make you lose 200€ and tails will make you win 100€. Scenario (a) appears attractive, since the potential gains outweigh possible losses. However, in scenario (b), loss aversion manifests, resulting in a person to less likely flip the coin. Innately, humans are more aversive to losses than attracted to gains–"*losses loom larger than gains* [63]."

In practice, Goalkeeper implements the loss aversion theory by the formation of deposit contracts that require one to deposit a specific amount of money to participate in a physical exercise challenge. On one hand, we expect that the requirement for investing a deposit from one's own funds—forming a deposit contract—will greatly strengthen commitment to a physical exercise challenge (i.e., adherence). On the other hand, this commitment can only be further bolstered by peer competition, and the possibility of one benefiting from a peer's failure to complete a challenge. In essence, Goalkeeper is a zero-sum game: In the field of game theory, zero-sum game is a situation in which each participant's gain or loss of utility is exactly balanced by the losses or gains of the utility of the other participants [9]. Thus, Goalkeeper displays a significant potential for motivating physical activity, without utilizing additional hardware apart from a typical smartphone. In this paper, we present findings from testing Goalkeeper with 50 participants in a study with a total duration of 2 months. Based on our findings, we elicit a set of design principles for exergames that utilized deposit contracts for increasing physical activity in group settings.

2 Related Work

A systematic literature review by Texeira et al., elucidated the factors that inhibit motivation in physical activity by examining a total of 66 relevant studies published until 2011 [59]. Drawing on the self-determination theory, the authors differentiate between intrinsic and extrinsic types of physical exercise motivation. As such, when one is intrinsically motivated, they experience enjoyment, personal accomplishment, and excitement [31]. Conversely, when one is extrinsically motivated, they are typically outcome-driven, by aiming for a tangible or social reward, or by avoiding disapproval (i.e., social validation by peer pressure). The literature review by Teixeira et al., highlights the role of developing self-regulation via autonomous forms of extrinsic or intrinsic motivation [59]. In fact, high autonomous motivation is linked with sustaining exercise behaviors over time (i.e., high adherence). Typically, exergames employ a form of gamification (e.g., achievements, leaderboards, points, etc.) following design guidelines for the representation of physical activity data with the aim to boost intrinsic and extrinsic motivation [29].

Prior studies in literature propose the idea of turning exercise into an indoor game with the use of Virtual Reality (VR) or Augmented Reality (AR) headsets, Microsoft Kinect, or other devices, thus coining the term "exergames [42]." For example, Ganesan and Anthony came up with an early prototype game that used Microsoft Kinect for tracking the movement of elderly people in order to help them be more active [17]. Bolt et al., designed a VR cycling based game that utilizes the Oculus Rift VR headset, a stationary bicycle and Microsoft Kinect to detect when a user performs the move of throwing a newspaper into neighbourhood mailboxes [8]. Hagen et al., designed an online multiplayer exergame where one controls a tank by pedaling on a stationary bicycle [20]. Players compete with each other in a "capture the flag" arena game. In the same guise, Ijaz et al. designed VR-Rides, an exergame platform that uses and the HTC VIVE VR headset and a stationary bicycle for enabling one to navigate in a safe virtual environment comprised of Google Street View imagery [24]. ExerCube utilizes a cube immersive environment that tracks and surrounds a player with 3 video-walls [40]. The walls serve both as projection screens and a haptic interface for energetic bodily interactions with the aim to enhance personal training. Fitnamo is another exergame that utilizes Google Glass for providing entertaining exercise routines and encouraging a user to be active [46]. Undoubtedly, exergames is an effective way to motivate physical activity. However, with the exception of Pokémon GO[1] and the like, exergames often require expensive equipment that is also likely to be cumbersome to wear or use, while they are mostly played indoors. Moreover, the habit-forming nature of exergames is under-explored. In other words, there is a lack of evidence that exergames can instil an exercise habit that can be sustained in the long-term [28]. Thus, there is a need for new types of applications that will stimulate users' motivation to exercise, while keeping some of the game design aspects which make the experience more fun or engaging in the long-run.

2.1 Gamifying Physical Activity: The Case of Pokémon GO

When it was first launched in 2016, Pokémon GO was deemed by many the pinnacle of exergaming [34,49,66]. Pokémon Go is an AR mobile game developed and published by Niantic in collaboration with The Pokémon Company for iOS and Android devices. It uses the mobile device GPS to locate, capture, combat, and train virtual creatures (Pokémons), called Pokémon, which appear embedded in the player's real world. Pokémon GO utilizes a combined effect of intrinsic and extrinsic motivation, attributed to collecting Pokémons and combating other users, respectively. Indeed, Pokémon GO has been found to increase walking activity of previously idle users [34], it promotes cross-generational play [49], and it may help engage young adults suffering from severe social withdrawal [58]. Conversely, Pokémon GO has led to accidents during playing and driving or cycling, walking without paying attention, and has been linked to trespassing [66]. Most importantly however, a recent systematic literature review showed

---

[1] https://pokemongolive.com/en/.

that despite the fact that Pokémon GO yields a statistically significant increase in the number of daily steps, the increase is clinically modest [28]. Plus, longer follow-up study periods are required for reliably assessing if Pokémon GO can promote physical activity over longer periods [28]. In other words, the health benefits associated with playing Pokémon GO were moderate and questionable in the long-run.

2.2 Deposit Contracts and Physical Activity Motivation

Some exergames may introduce storytelling to engage users in physical activity (e.g., Zombies, Run!² and Step Ahead³), whereas others focus on goal-setting (e.g., Runkeeper⁴) and financial incentives (e.g., StepCity [67]). A special category of financial exergames are those that employ deposit contracts. To boost one's self-discipline, one may commit to goals by voluntarily accepting deadlines with consequences [57]. Deposit contracts are pre-commitment strategies that force one's future self to certain behaviors [60]. In the field of Behavioral Economics, deposit contracts have been extensively utilized for helping one achieve self-defined goals in a certain period [16,36]. Deposit contracts utilize monetary incentives funded by one's own money, invested in completing a (personal) goal. In case one fails to achieve the goal, one loses the deposited amount.

So far, numerous studies have investigated how financial incentives can motivate people to reduce alcohol consumption [45,70], reduce tobacco use [23], improve their nutrition [39], and increase their physical activity levels [51]. However, this work focuses on how deposit contracts (and peer competition) increase physical activity. A study by Burns and Rothman compares different types of financial incentives in how they affect walking behavior [12]. The study had a sample size of 153 participants, randomly assigned in four groups with different incentive conditions. Participants in the deposit contract group were told that they had a bank account with $50 deposited, and that over the next five weeks they would lose money from their bank account each week if the goal was not met. Interestingly, the observed effect on walking did not differ across different incentive conditions. Deposit contracts were not more effective than cash rewards in increasing the frequency or likelihood of meeting a walking goal. However, exploratory analyses indicated that the perceived value of the incentive was associated with walking behavior over time. Lesser et al., examined how deposit contracts could help one to lose weight by utilizing a website that employs deposit contracts as a motivation factor [36]. The participants made individual deposit contracts and they were free to deposit as much money as they wished. The amount of deposit, period, and the weekly weight-loss goal could be decided by themselves. After setting the goal, the participants could select from four types of contract that would be activated if they failed: anti-charity—money goes to a charity/organization opposite to what the individual

---

² https://zombiesrungame.com/.
³ https://www.astepaheadchallenge.com/.
⁴ https://runkeeper.com/cms/.

supports, charity—money goes to a general charity fund, friend—money goes to participants' designated "friend," and no deposit—no money invested at all. The outcome of this study was that the type of contract and size had a moderate effect on keeping up with a goal, but individuals that used deposit contracts appear to lose weight. Notably, Behavioral Economics suggest that anti-charity is the most effective motivator, with "no deposit" as the least effective. The conclusion was that voluntary use of commitment contracts may assist weight loss [36].

Deposit contracts have been utilized by several commercial applications and services (e.g., sticKK.com, SPAR!, and waybetter.com). Despite the fact that deposit contracts is a well-received strategy for motivating behavioral change, both scientifically and commercially, there is a lack of studies that inquire into the effect of deposit contracts in closed social groups. As we have seen, some studies bring evidence forward about the effect the deposit amount bears on motivation. However, there is little research on how people experience pursuing a goal or if their behavior changes during this challenge. In this work, we look into how deposit contracts can be utilized as an effective goal-setting strategy using a mobile application called Goalkeeper (see Fig. 1). Goalkeeper has similar rules as Waybetter's applications, but instead of the term "games" it uses the term "challenges", while it only focuses on motivating physical activity within user-made, closed social groups. Notably, social groups in this study are groups of people that are friends or acquaintances—we refer to both types of relationships as "peers."

2.3   Is Goalkeeper Betting?

Goalkeeper's challenges are neither defined nor described as betting, gambling, or lottery, even though they involve depositing, earning, or losing money. On one hand, according to the Oxford Dictionary of English [56], the definition of the term *"betting"* is *"The action of gambling money on the outcome of a race, game, or other unpredictable event."* Also, the definition for the term *"lottery"* is *"A means of raising money by selling numbered tickets and giving prizes to the holders of numbers drawn at random."* On the other hand, the definition of *"deposit contract"* is *"an agreement between a financial institution and its customer,"* according to US Law[5]. The Norwegian Gaming Authority[6] declared that **Goalkeeper is neither a betting nor a lottery game, since every participant has a chance to get their money back**. Goalkeeper's challenges have no unpredictable outcomes, except for the cases of sickness or death. Nevertheless, in this study we will not take sickness or death into account, but we will not call Goalkeeper a betting or a lottery game, since the Norwegian law does not define the concept as such. However, the questionnaires, used in this study, include question items about betting to investigate if the participants have joined a commitment with money before, and the term "bet" is used in the system as

---

[5] https://definitions.uslegal.com/d/deposit-contract/.

[6] https://lottstift.no/en/the-gaming-and-foundation-authority/.

"Place your bets" when supplying the deposit money (see Fig. 1). Furthermore, a feature is under development that can refund people due to sickness, and it will be available in a future version of Goalkeeper. In conclusion, we will use the terms "investing" and *"deposit contract"* when referring to Goalkeeper.

3 The Goalkeeper App

The Goalkeeper's functionality is essentially implemented on 3 Application Programming Interfaces (APIs), namely Facebook API, Vipps API, and Strava API. Goalkeeper utilizes Facebook API login and befriend functionalities for authentication and presenting a peer with an exercise challenge. Vipps API is then used for safely collecting (and returning) the deposits from all the peers who accepted the exercise challenge, in the form of mobile payments. The Strava API is tasked with monitoring the physical activity of each peer participating in the exercise challenge for the entire duration of the challenge. From a mobile user's perspective, the Goalkeeper supports the following primary actions: (1) create a challenge by setting a start and an end date—a challenge should last at least for a week, (2) decide how many exercise days (sessions) the participants should complete during each week, (3) set the amount of the deposit each participant should pay for joining in, (4) invite peers to join the challenge before the challenge can start. Typically, 150 min of moderate exercise intensity per week is recommended for adults of 18–64 years old. However, for motivating people to start exercising, we "lowered the bar" to an exercise duration of at least 30 minutes for a session to count towards completing a challenge. In its current version, Goalkeeper approves any variant of physical activity, such as walking, running, yoga, and others, as long as they last for more than 30 minutes per session. Upon the end of an exercise challenge, Goalkeeper returns the deposited amount back to each participant who successfully completed the challenge. In the event a participant fails to complete the exercise challenge, their deposit is distributed evenly among the other participants who completed the challenge. In the unlikely event all participants fail to complete the exercise challenge, Goalkeeper returns to everyone their deposits (i.e., zero-sum game [9]).

4 Study

Drawing on the loss aversion theory [63], and prior literature on physical exercise motivation and exergames, we hypothesize that the requirement for a monetary incentive, invested by the participants themselves (i.e., deposit contract), will result in motivating them to complete an exercise challenge. In turn, we anticipate an increase in the overall physical activity levels of our participants. Bearing in mind the limitations of previous studies, we seek to answer the following research questions (RQs):

RQ1: **Are deposit contracts an effective strategy for motivating physical activity on a mobile application?** Prior studies have investigated the introduction of financial incentives for reducing alcohol consumption [45], marijuana [70], and tobacco use [23], improving nutrition [39], and increasing physical activity [12,51]. However, our work differs in that it proposes the idea of utilizing one's own funds as a financial incentive for one to exercise. In fact, one is further convinced to invest in an exercise challenge by the possibility of profiting in case one's peers fail to complete the same challenge. Thus, we expect that the potential of profiting, with the inherent risk of losing one's own money, will motivate our participants to commit to an exercise challenge, and increase their physical activity levels. However, we do expect a higher success rate in the 2-week challenge as opposed to the 6-week one, simply due to the increased period of commitment required in the 6-week challenge.

RQ2: **How do group dynamics motivate physical activity when deposit contracts are involved?** Peer competition is a well-known way for increasing physical activity [69]. For example, online social networks have been found to increase social activity [71], and promote weight loss [33]. However, the interplay between group dynamics and deposit contracts remains under-explored, particularly in user-made, closed group settings. Besides striving for reclaiming one's invested deposit, we expect that participating in an exercise challenge with a group of peers will greatly bolster competition leading to an overall increase in physical activity for all the members of the group.

RQ3: **How does user profile characteristics influence how participants exercised with Goalkeeper?** Apart from the bodily benefits, physical exercise is highly beneficial for one's emotional state, inducing positive emotions [7], and reducing negative emotions such as stress [54]. In fact, post-exercise positive emotions play a central role in continuing exercising [21]. Thus, we expect Goalkeeper will be associated with inducing positive emotions, reflected on challenge outcome, and invested deposit amounts. We also expect age, and particularly gender, to have a bearing on challenge outcome and deposit amount, given that males engage in risk-taking behaviors more frequently than females do [14].

4.1   Participants and Groups

We recruited a total of 50 healthy and **adult** participants from the premises of NTNU in Norway. We specifically opted for recruiting participants that know each other, and would form exercise groups based on friendship, or at least acquaintance. Typically, students, as young adults, are technology enthusiasts, and thus more curious to try out a novel mobile application such as Goalkeeper. Two participants (1 male and 1 female) dropped out before the actual exercise challenges commence due to not being able to keep up with a schedule of 3 exercise days per week. **The remaining 48 participants were equally split between the two genders** ($N = 24$ females). All participants were students with the majority falling under the 20–24 years age group ($N = 37$ or 75.5%), followed by the 25–29 age group (N = 10 or 20.4%), and the 30–34 age group (N = 1 or 2%). Participants selected, within their respective groups, the duration of the exercise challenge in which they would participate by choosing between the 2-week (N = 21 or 43.8%) and the 6-week challenge (N = 27 or 56.3%). Next, the participants selected, within their respective groups, the amount of money they would deposit in each challenge opting in for 0 (N = 14 or 29.2%), 150 (N = 19 or 39.6%), or 500 Kr (Krone) (N = 15 or 31.3%). In general, **participants were free to organize themselves in groups based on the duration of the challenge, the amount deposited, and personal acquaintance—thus of relatively similar socioeconomic background** [11]. This produced a total of 12 groups whose size ranged from 3 peers (N = 6 or 36.7%) to 6 peers (N = 2 or 25%). Participants formed all-female groups (N = 5 or 41.7%), all-male groups (N = 4 or 33.3%), or mixed-gender groups (N = 3 or 25%). Upon the completion of the study, each participant was rewarded with a 75 Kr gift card that could be spent in the cafeteria of the University. The reward was intentionally kept significantly smaller than the contract deposits that involved money (150 and 500 Kr).

4.2 Procedure and Measures

Before commencing with the user trials, we had obtained the necessary ethical approval from the National Ethical Board. During the onboarding of our participants, we asked for their informed consent about collecting and analyzing their personal and physical activity data, as well as their questionnaire responses. **We were explicit about the fact that the study does not involve betting, but it requires investing one's money that may be lost.** In particular, we clarified that in the event one fails to complete an exercise challenge, one's deposit is lost and cannot be retrieved. In the current version of the Goalkeeper app, this stands even when one fails to complete an exercise challenge due to illness. All participants belonging to the same group mutually agreed to participate in exercise challenges of predefined duration (2 or 6 weeks) and predefined deposit (0, 150, and 500 Kr), as previously mentioned. For investigating participants' habits, attitude, motivation, and behavior before, during, and after using Goalkeeper app, we employed a series of established measures and methods. One week before the exercise challenges commenced, we administered our first questionnaire comprised of items that target attitude (ATT) [2], exercise motivation (MOT) [44], exercise habits (HAB) [65], and value (VAL) **about participants' relationship with money** [35]. At the start of the 2nd and 3rd week for the 2-week and 6-week challenges, respectively, we administered the second questionnaire. This questionnaire included the previously mentioned MOT and HAB items, as well as continuance intentions for system use (CIU) [6], network exposure (NET) [37], positive (POS) and negative (NEG) emotions [50], exercising with peers (EXE) [53], reciprocal benefits (REB) [22], recognition from peers (REC) [38], subjective norms (SUB) [64], word-of-mouth intentions (WOM) [30], behavioral intention (BEH) and perceived behavioral control (PEB) [65]. We administered the third questionnaire two weeks after a challenge had ended, and it encompassed only factual follow-up question items, such

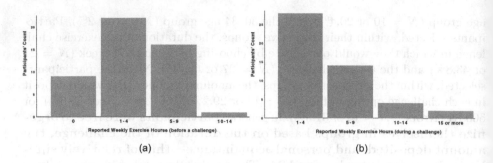

(a)   (b)

Fig. 2. Reported exercise hours (a) before committing to an exercise challenge with Goalkeeper, and (b) during pursuing an exercise challenge. Participants reported exercising significantly more frequently during an exercise challenge set with Goalkeeper app.

as inquiring whether the participants had exercised or not. All questionnaires were administered electronically, and almost all items were statements to which one could respond by indicating one's level of agreement in a Likert-scale from 1 ("strongly disagree") to 7 ("strongly agree"). We also collected information about participants' demographics, profiles, and challenge outcome (win or loss).

5   Results

For deciding on our statistical methods, we first perform all the necessary pretests, such as Shapiro-Wilk tests of normality and Levene's tests of homogeneity of variance. Here, we omit the pre-tests for the sake of brevity. Due to dealing with non-normally distributed data (e.g., dichotomous, categorical, and ordinal variables), we resort to non-parametric tests such as Wilcoxon signed-ranks tests and Pearson chi-square tests of independence. For pinpointing any significant differences after a chi-square test on categorical variables of more than two levels, we perform post-hoc pairwise tests using the adjusted standardized residuals, and an adjusted p value (i.e., Bonferroni method) [3]. Due to lack of space, we mainly opted for presenting results that help us answer our RQs.

5.1   Deposit Contracts and Physical Exercise Motivation (RQ1)

First, we investigated if the introduction of the Goalkeeper app had a positive impact on our participants' exercise frequency when comparing to that of before using the app. From the outset, a Wilcoxon signed-ranks test displayed a significant difference in the reported weekly exercise hours before ($Mdn = 1$–4 h) and during ($Mdn = 5$–9 h) a challenge set with Goalkeeper ($Z = -2.558, p < .05$). This indicates that **participants reported exercising significantly more hours per week when pursuing a challenge with Goalkeeper, as opposed to their normal working-out schedule** (RQ1), as shown in Fig. 2. Next, we inquired into whether the deposit amount

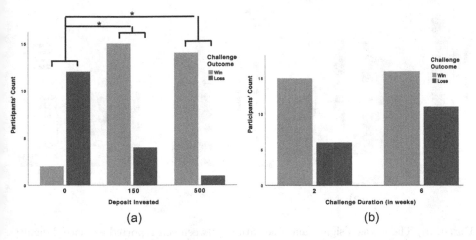

Fig. 3. Number of challenge outcomes in wins and losses in relation to (a) amount of deposit invested, and (b) exercise challenge duration.

invested in a challenge played any role in completing a challenge. A Pearson chi-square test of independence was performed to determine whether there is an association between the amount invested and challenge outcome. The test displayed a significant association between deposit and challenge outcome $(x^2(2) = 22.619, p < .001, V = .686)$. A series of pairwise chi-square tests of goodness of fit were performed to determine whether participants completed the challenges in equal numbers among the 3 distinct money groups (i.e., 0, 150, and 500 kr). The analyses displayed a significant difference in successful outcomes between groups that bet 0 $(N = 2)$ and 150 kr $(N = 15)$ $(x^2(1) = 9.941, p < .01)$, groups that invested 0 $(N = 2)$ and 500 kr $(N = 14)$ $(x^2(1) = 9, p < .01)$, but no significant difference in success rates of groups that invested 150 and 500 kr $(x^2(1) = .034, p = .853)$ (see Fig. 3a). **These results indicate that users who invested money in a workout challenge using Goalkeeper were significantly more probable to complete it, as opposed to those who did not invest any money** (RQ1). Similarly, a Pearson chi-square test of independence was performed to investigate if there is an association between the duration of the challenge and its outcome. However, the test displayed no significant association between the duration of a challenge and its outcome $(x^2(1) = .765, p = .382, V = -.126)$ (see Fig. 3b). **This indicates that the duration of the challenge did not play a significant role in completing a challenge** (RQ1).

A series of tests next aimed at investigating perceived motivation in relation to committing to a challenge, and investing a deposit in a challenge. A Pearson chi-square test of independence displayed a significant association between self-reported motivation due to using Goalkeeper (*"I think that participating in a Goalkeeper challenge improves my motivation to exercise."*) and reported exercise hours per week $(x^2(18) = 38.368, p < .01, V = .516)$. Inter-

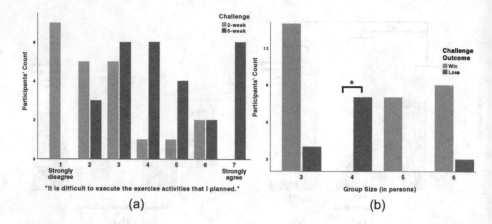

Fig. 4. (a) There was a significant association between self-reported exercise difficulty and challenge duration. (b) Group size played a significant role in challenge outcome for 4-person groups simply because all 4-person groups invested no money as deposits.

estingly, self-reported challenge difficulty (*"It is difficult to execute the exercise activities that I planned."*) was not associated with challenge outcome ($x^2(6) = 2.283, p = .892, V = .218$), but it was significantly associated with challenge duration ($x^2(6) = 18.501, p < .01, V = .621$) (see Fig. 4a). Nevertheless, **having a deposit contract was reported as a significant factor for convincing one to complete a challenge.** Indeed, a Pearson chi-square test of independence revealed a significant association between self-reported determination (*"I felt the money gave me motivation not to fail."*) and challenge outcome ($x^2(6) = 12.770, p < .05, V = .516$). Post-hoc pairwise comparison tests using the Bonferroni correction revealed no significant differences among the different Likert-scores. Next, we also inquired into whether the challenge outcome played a significant role in participants' self-reported motivation to continue exercise after a challenge was completed. However, a Pearson chi-square test of independence displayed no significant association between self-reported future motivation to exercise (*"I am motivated to continue exercise after the challenge."*) and challenge outcome ($x^2(6) = 4.640, p = .461, V = .311$). These findings highlight that **deposit contracts are an effective strategy for motivating physical activity via a mobile application such as Goalkeeper** (RQ1).

5.2   Group Dynamics and Peer Competition (RQ2)

In this subsection, we investigate whether group characteristics played an important role in pursuing a physical exercise challenge with Goalkeeper. At first, a Pearson-chi square test of independence demonstrated a significant association between group size and challenge outcome ($x^2(3) = 17.567, p < .01, V = .605$). Interestingly, post-hoc pairwise tests using the Bonferroni correction revealed a significant difference in the challenge outcome for 4-person groups (0 wins,

8 losses, $p < .001$) (see Fig. 4b). When we had a closer look into why the two 4-person groups had no wins, we found out that both groups were all-female groups that invested 0 kr as a deposit. Having classified our groups into 3 main categories based on participants' genders that comprised them (i.e., all-male, all-female, and mixed), we investigated if group gender had an effect on challenge outcome. However, a Pearson-chi square test of independence displayed no significant association between group gender and challenge outcome ($x^2(2) = 5.749, p = .056, V = .346$). Interestingly, a Pearson-chi square test of independence revealed a significant difference for group gender in the amount of deposit invested ($x^2(4) = 13.452, p < .01, V = .374$). Post-hoc pairwise tests using the Bonferroni correction revealed a significant difference in the number of participants belonging to all-female groups ($N = 8$) and the number of participants belonging to mixed groups ($N = 0$) that invested 0 kr as a deposit ($p < .001$). This indicates that **groups that included participants of both genders were more likely to use deposit contracts investing actual money, as opposed to female-only groups** (RQ2).

Next, we investigated a series of self-reported measures on how group collaboration influenced challenge outcome. In particular, a Pearson chi-square test of independence displayed no significant association between self-reported degree of peer cooperation in exercise (*"My friends exercised with me."* | $Mdn = 2$) and outcome challenge ($x^2(6) = 4.833, p = .565, V = .317$). Similarly, there was no significant association between self-reported degree of reminding to exercise by peers (*"My friends gave me helpful reminders to exercise."* | $Mdn = 5$) ($x^2(6) = 9.699, p = .138, V = .450$), self-reported peer encouragement (*"My friends gave me encouragement to stick with my exercise program."* | $Mdn = 3$) ($x^2(6) = 7.328, p = .292, V = .391$), and self-reported peer-schedule flexibility (*"My friends changed their schedule so we could exercise together."* | $Mdn = 3$) ($x^2(6) = 6.063, p = .416, V = .355$) with challenge outcome. However, we were able to unveil a significant association between self-reported willingness to enlist more peers (*"I want more friends to join the challenge to increase the pot."* | $Mdn = 4$) for maximizing returns ($x^2(6) = 12.624, p < .05, V = .513$). These findings showcase that **participants that belonged to the same group did not collaborate in the course of an exercise challenge** (RQ2).

5.3 User Profile Effects (RQ3)

Here, we investigated if certain aspects of our participants' profiles (e.g., age, gender, habits, personality traits, and feelings) bear an effect on deposit amount, challenge duration, and challenge outcome. A Mann-Whitney U test displayed a significant difference in the median amount deposited by each gender ($U = -2.754, p < .01$). In particular, **male participants invested in a challenge significantly greater amounts** ($M = 291.67, SE = 41.120$) **than females did** ($M = 139.58, SE = 36.487$). However, **gender did not play a substantial role in completing a challenge**. In particular, a Pearson-chi square test of independence displayed no significant association between gender and challenge outcome ($x^2(1) = 2.277, p = .131, V = .218$). Interestingly, age appears to bear

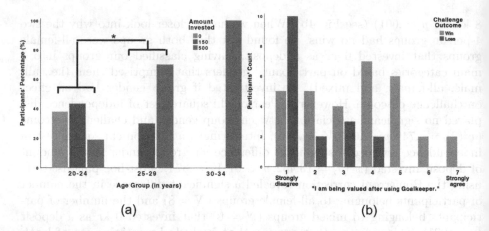

Fig. 5. (a) We unveiled a significant difference between the deposit amounts invested in an exercise challenge by 20–24 and 25–29 age groups. (b) There was a significant association between self-reported self-value and challenge outcome.

an effect on deposit amounts invested by different age groups. A Kruskal-Wallis H test revealed a significant difference in the amounts deposited by each age group ($x^2(2) = 11.742, p < .05$) for the age groups of 20–24 ($Mdn = 150$), 25–29 ($Mdn = 500$), and 30–34 ($Mdn = 500$) (see Fig. 5a). After excluding the 30–34 age group for low occurrence ($N = 1$), a follow-up Mann-Whitney U test displayed a significant difference in the median invested amounts between 20–24 ($Mdn = 150$) and 25–29 ($Mdn = 500$) age groups ($U = 69.500, p < .01$). However, age appears to have no bearing on successfully completing an exercise challenge ($x^2(2) = .771, p = .680, V = .127$). In sum, **gender and age displayed a significant impact on deposit amount, but not on challenge outcome** (RQ3).

For investigating if prior exercising habits and schedules influenced challenge outcome, we performed a Pearson chi-square test of independence. The analysis displayed no significant association between prior exercising and challenge outcome ($x^2(1) = .440, p = .507, V = .096$). This indicates that people who exercise regularly did not have an advantage over those who did not in winning a challenge. Similarly, self-reported competitiveness (*"I think I am competitive."*) exhibited no significant association with challenge outcome ($x^2(5) = 2.392, p = .793, V = .223$). Also, prior self-reported betting experience (*"I have previously joined a bet with money."*) did not display any significant association with the amount of the deposit invested in an exercise challenge via the Goalkeeper ($x^2(2) = .027, p = .987, V = .096$). These findings indicate that **prior exercising habits and betting experience did not affect substantially challenge outcome and deposit amount** (RQ3).

However, self-reported positive feelings displayed strong associations with challenge outcome. For example, a Pearson chi-square test of independence unveiled a significant association between self-reported "warm feeling" (*"I have a warm feeling after using Goalkeeper.*") and challenge outcome $(x^2(6) = 12.624, p < .05, V = .096)$. Similarly, self-reported self-value (*"I am being valued after using Goalkeeper."*) was also found significantly associated with challenge outcome $(x^2(6) = 12.886, p < .05, V = .518)$ (see Fig. 5b). Interestingly, investigating self-reported negative feelings revealed no significant associations to challenge outcomes. In particular, two Pearson chi-square tests of independence revealed no significant associations between self-reported bad mood (*"I am in a bad mood after using Goalkeeper."*) $(x^2(4) = 5.852, p = .211, V = .349)$, and self-reported anger levels (*"I feel angry after using Goalkeeper."*) $(x^2(5) = 3.788, p = .580, V = .281)$. These findings suggest that **Goalkeeper was more frequently associated with positive than negative feelings** (RQ3).

6 Discussion

Beyond the immense benefits of physical activity for the human body, adopting an active lifestyle could help save billions of euros in health care costs in the years to come. According to a report from the World Health Organization (WHO) in the EU Region, for a European country of 10 million people, of whom half are insufficiently active, the overall incurred health cost is estimated to be 910€ million per year [48]. Nowadays, health insurance companies are increasingly introducing policies that encourage people to stay active (e.g., TK-App). We believe exergames that involve financial incentives to increase physical activity can inherently contribute more in the health and well-being economy, when compared to typical gamification approaches (e.g., points, achievements). This paper highlights the potential of deposit contracts and peer competition in increasing physical exercise motivation. By drawing on our findings, we elicit design principles for exergames that involve financial incentives.

6.1 Embrace Risk and Design for the Long-Run

Overall, deposit contracts as monetary incentives proved to significantly increase physical activity for our participants. In fact, the median reported exercise duration before using Goalkeeper was between 1 to 4 h per week. While pursuing an exercise challenge with Goalkeeper, participants reported a median of 5 to 9 exercise duration per week. Interestingly, when having a look at challenge outcome, in relation to the amount of the deposit invested in a challenge, we observe a significantly higher success rate for participants who invested 150 kr as opposed to those who invested 0 kr. This indicates that participants who invested money in an exercise challenge using Goalkeeper were significantly more dedicated to completing it, compared to those who did not invest any money at all (RQ1). These findings are directly inline with prior findings in literature, where monetary incentives were found to support weight-loss [36] and motivate physical activity [1,4,12,51]. Interestingly, one would expect that a challenge of a longer duration would display substantially lower completion rates than a challenge of a shorter duration (RQ1). Contrary to our expectations, the success rate of the 2-week challenge did not differ significantly from the success rate of the 6-week challenge, despite the fact that the 6-week challenge lasted 3 times longer. However, challenge duration was not associated with challenge outcome. **This possibly demonstrates that deposit contracts is an effective way to keep people committed to exercise challenges over long periods.** This finding should be noted as it indicates that deposit contracts, and Goalkeeper, bear substantial potential to promote the formation of healthy habits. In fact, 21 days is believed to be the threshold for forming a new habit, with others raising the threshold to 66 days [32]. Although, we did a followup interview with our participants 2 weeks after a challenge had concluded, we will need to investigate exercise habits over longer periods to reliably claim that Goalkeeper forms strong exercising habits. However, we found a significant association between self-reported motivation and exercise duration per week. Moreover, we detected a significant association between reported determination to complete a challenge and challenge outcome. This suggests that by further manipulating the deposit amount and the challenge duration, Goalkeeper could be instrumental in forming exercising habits. **Thus, loss aversion theory may serve as a driver of positive behavioral change when sufficiently long periods are involved.**

6.2   Design for Peer Competition in Zero-Sum Exergame Settings

Recent studies in literature report only moderate effects for deposit contracts in increasing one's motivation to exercise when one's own assets are not involved [12, 36]. Even so, the very nature of loss aversion theory is counter-intuitive in our approach in the first place. **From the outset, loss aversion per se should discourage one from unnecessarily jeopardizing one's own assets for no clear financial benefit** [63]. Enabling loss aversion was the reason for a rather low monetary incentive (75 kr) to participate in the study. In fact, the incentive amount pales in comparison to the amounts invested from participants' own money (150 and 500 kr). Thus, we have a reason to believe that deposit contracts did not single-handedly improve our participants' motivation to exercise. In other words, we believe that our participants did not simply exercise just to take their money back. Instead, we think that **peer pressure generated by peer competition played a substantial role, not only in completing a challenge, but also in mitigating barriers to entry (i.e., investing money).**

On one hand, we discovered that participants who belonged to groups which did not invest any money in an exercise challenge were significantly less probable to complete it, as opposed to groups which did (see RQ1). On the other hand, when having a look at measures that characterize self-reported collaboration in a group (e.g., exercise together), we detected no association with challenge outcome. In fact, participants reported relatively low cooperation, if any, during the course of an exercise challenge (RQ2). We believe this can be explained by our participants treating a Goalkeeper challenge as a zero-sum game—in a way it actually is. However, **zero-sum games should involve gain or loss of utility to effectively motivate physical exercise.**

6.3   Design for the Group and the Individual

Interestingly, when having a look at participants' profiles and characteristics, we were able to unveil additional effects. For example, we found that gender played a significant role in deposit amount, with male participants investing on average 292 kr as opposed to 140 for females (RQ3). We ascribe this finding to males typically displaying a risk-taking behavior more frequently than females do [14]. Age also had a significant impact on deposit amount, with the age group of 20–24 years depositing 150 kr for an exercise challenge, as opposed to the age group of 25–29 years that deposited 500 kr (RQ3). This finding is also aligned with prior evidence in literature, where income appears positively correlated with age [13]. However, neither gender nor age displayed a significant effect on challenge outcome. Moreover, one would assume that someone who exercises regularly bears an advantage over someone who does not, when it comes to completing an exercise challenge. However, we did not find any effect of prior exercising habits on deposit amount or challenge outcome. A plausible explanation for this is that we set a rather low difficulty threshold (i.e., 3 exercise sessions per week of at least 30 min each) for one's physique to play a substantial role in deposit amount or challenge outcome. All in all, **exergames that utilize own financial incentives in group settings should implement group decision policies on the intensity, type, and duration of the exercise challenge, as well as the amount invested.**

Interestingly, prior experience with betting or lottery games was neither associated with deposit amount nor challenge outcome. This possibly indicates that **participants did not perceive Goalkeeper as a betting game.** Finally, we were surprised to discover that Goalkeeper was only linked to inducing positive feelings, as reported by our participants. On one hand, challenge outcome was associated with participants reporting exhibiting a "warm feeling," and feeling valued. On the other hand, we did not find any association between challenge outcome and the emotion of anger, or bad mood. A plausible explanation is that our participants perceived Goalkeeper as part of their exercise routine (RQ3). Exercising is generally associated with positive emotions [7], and reduced stress [54]. **Positive emotions related to physical exercise may reinforce the adoption of an exergame, leading to the formation of an exercise habit** [5].

6.4   Limitations

As young adults, we assume our participants were innately keen on technology and novel applications. Being also students, we expect that our participants had ample time to pursue an exercise challenge with the Goalkeeper app. Thus, physical challenge completion rates for older age groups may have been lower. However, Goalkeeper supports setting challenges that even people who do not originally exercise can complete. In fact, for this study we already set a lower exercise threshold than the recommended 150 min of moderate exercise per week. For simplicity, we employed pre-made challenges that did not distinguish between different types of physical activity (e.g., cycling, running, etc.) or different levels of exercise intensity (e.g., walking vs. running). Nevertheless, Goalkeeper, via the Strava API, can detect and identify different exercise types and intensity levels, and thus support highly customized challenges. Our participants organized themselves in groups freely based on friendship, and thus we do not expect significant socioeconomic disparities within groups [11]. We acknowledge that our findings generalize in the context of a northern European country, and sample populations from different cultural and socioeconomic backgrounds might affect our results. Even so, Goalkeeper enables peers to set physical exercise challenges with deposit contracts of any amount and in any currency. Moreover, we did not account for the event a participant failed to complete a challenge due to illness. Currently, a feature is developed that enables one to report illness on Goalkeeper and reclaim one's deposit. Finally, although we have evidence that Goalkeeper may facilitate the habit formation of exercising regularly, we will still need to investigate this over substantially longer periods than that of 6 weeks.

7   Conclusion and Future Work

Lack of physical activity is not only considered the prime culprit for a range of preventable causes of death across the globe, but it has also been associated with substantial health costs for the state. As a result, increasing and sustaining exercise motivation has been in the spotlight for a range of related research fields, including HCI. However, numerous existing solutions adopt highly sophisticated approaches that often involve the use of expensive hardware and bulky equipment, restricted by default to indoor settings, or reporting clinically modest results. In this work, we introduced Goalkeeper, a mobile application that fosters exercise motivation by the interplay between deposit contracts and peer competition. Our results showcase that participants who invested money in a physical exercise challenge using Goalkeeper were significantly more dedicated to completing it, while challenge duration appeared of secondary importance. Thus, peer competition and loss aversion provide a "carrot-and-stick" approach to effectively increasing physical exercise motivation. In future work, we will investigate exercise motivation for Goalkeeper over substantially longer periods. All in all, we believe exergames that employ one's own financial incentives in group settings bear a significant potential to advance the formation of strong physical exercise habits that in turn promote a healthier lifestyle.

References

1. Acland, D., Levy, M.R.: Naiveté, projection bias, and habit formation in gym attendance. Manag. Sci. **61**(1), 146–160 (2015)
2. Ajzen, I., et al.: The theory of planned behavior. Organ. Behav. Hum. Decis. Process. **50**(2), 179–211 (1991)
3. Beasley, T.M., Schumacker, R.E.: Multiple regression approach to analyzing contingency tables: post hoc and planned comparison procedures. J. Exp. Educ. **64**(1), 79–93 (1995)

4. Berg, C.J., Stratton, E., Giblin, J., Esiashvili, N., Mertens, A.: Pilot results of an online intervention targeting health promoting behaviors among young adult cancer survivors. Psychooncology **23**(10), 1196 (2014)
5. Bexheti, A., Fedosov, A., Findahl, J., Langheinrich, M., Niforatos, E.: Re-live the moment: visualizing run experiences to motivate future exercises. In: Proceedings of the 17th International Conference on Human-Computer Interaction with Mobile Devices and Services Adjunct, pp. 986–993 (2015)
6. Bhattacherjee, A.: Understanding information systems continuance: an expectation-confirmation model. MIS Q. pp. 351–370 (2001)
7. Biddle, S.J.: Emotion, mood and physical activity. In: Physical Activity and Psychological Well-being, pp. 75–97. Routledge (2003)
8. Bolton, J., Lambert, M., Lirette, D., Unsworth, B.: PaperDude: a virtual reality cycling exergame. In: CHI'14 Extended Abstracts on Human Factors in Computing Systems, pp. 475–478 (2014)
9. Bowles, S.: Microeconomics: Behavior, Institutions, and Evolution. Princeton University Press, Princeton (2009)
10. Bravata, D.M., et al.: Using pedometers to increase physical activity and improve health: a systematic review. JAMA **298**(19), 2296–2304 (2007)
11. Brown, B.B., Klute, C.: Friendships, cliques, and crowds (2003)
12. Burns, R.J., Rothman, A.J.: Comparing types of financial incentives to promote walking: an experimental test. Appl. Psychol. Health Well Being **10**(2), 193–214 (2018)
13. Charles, K.K., Hurst, E.: The correlation of wealth across generations. J. Polit. Econ. **111**(6), 1155–1182 (2003)
14. Charness, G., Gneezy, U.: Strong evidence for gender differences in risk taking. J. Econ. Behav. Organ. **83**(1), 50–58 (2012)
15. Cialdini, R.B.: The science of persuasion. Sci. Am. **284**(2), 76–81 (2001)
16. Costa, D.F., Carvalho, F.D.M., Moreira, B.C.D.M.: Behavioral economics and behavioral finance: a bibliometric analysis of the scientific fields. J. Econ. Surv. **33**(1), 3–24 (2019)
17. Ganesan, S., Anthony, L.: Using the kinect to encourage older adults to exercise: a prototype. In: CHI'12 Extended Abstracts on Human Factors in Computing Systems, pp. 2297–2302 (2012)
18. Gouveia, R., Karapanos, E., Hassenzahl, M.: How do we engage with activity trackers?: a longitudinal study of habito. In: Proceedings of the 2015 ACM International Joint Conference on Pervasive and Ubiquitous Computing, pp. 1305–1316. ACM (2015)
19. Gui, X., Chen, Y., Caldeira, C., Xiao, D., Chen, Y.: When fitness meets social networks: Investigating fitness tracking and social practices on werun. In: Proceedings of the 2017 CHI Conference on Human Factors in Computing Systems, pp. 1647–1659 (2017)
20. Hagen, K., Chorianopoulos, K., Wang, A.I., Jaccheri, L., Weie, S.: Gameplay as exercise. In: Proceedings of the 2016 CHI Conference Extended Abstracts on Human Factors in Computing Systems, pp. 1872–1878 (2016)
21. Helfer, S.G., Elhai, J.D., Geers, A.L.: Affect and exercise: positive affective expectations can increase post-exercise mood and exercise intentions. Ann. Behav. Med. **49**(2), 269–279 (2015)
22. Hsu, C.L., Lin, J.C.C.: Acceptance of blog usage: the roles of technology acceptance, social influence and knowledge sharing motivation. Inf. Manag. **45**(1), 65–74 (2008)

23. Ierfino, D., Mantzari, E., Hirst, J., Jones, T., Aveyard, P., Marteau, T.M.: Financial incentives for smoking cessation in pregnancy: a single-arm intervention study assessing cessation and gaming. Addiction 110(4), 680–688 (2015)

24. Ijaz, K., Wang, Y., Ahmadpour, N., Calvo, R.A.: Immersive VR exergames for health and wellbeing. In: Extended Abstracts of the 2019 CHI Conference on Human Factors in Computing Systems, pp. 1–4 (2019)

25. Jakicic, J.M., et al.: Effect of wearable technology combined with a lifestyle intervention on long-term weight loss: the idea randomized clinical trial. JAMA 316(11), 1161–1171 (2016)

26. Kahneman, D., Tversky, A.: Prospect theory: an analysis of decision under risk. In: Handbook of the Fundamentals of Financial Decision Making: Part I, pp. 99–127. World Scientific (2013)

27. Kaos, M.D., Rhodes, R.E., Hämäläinen, P., Graham, T.N.: Social play in an exergame: how the need to belong predicts adherence. In: Proceedings of the 2019 CHI Conference on Human Factors in Computing Systems, pp. 1–13 (2019)

28. Khamzina, M., Parab, K.V., An, R., Bullard, T., Grigsby-Toussaint, D.S.: Impact of pokémon go on physical activity: a systematic review and meta-analysis. Am. J. Prev. Med. 58(2), 270–282 (2020)

29. Khot, R.A., Hjorth, L., Mueller, F.: Shelfie: a framework for designing material representations of physical activity data. ACM Trans. Comput.-Human Interact. (TOCHI) 27(3), 1–52 (2020)

30. Kim, S.S., Son, J.Y.: Out of dedication or constraint? A dual model of post-adoption phenomena and its empirical test in the context of online services. MIS Q. 49–70 (2009)

31. Deci, E.L.: Intrinsic motivation. New York, NY, US (1975)

32. Lally, P., Gardner, B.: Promoting habit formation. Health Psychol. Rev. 7(sup1), S137–S158 (2013)

33. Leahey, T.M., Kumar, R., Weinberg, B.M., Wing, R.R.: Teammates and social influence affect weight loss outcomes in a team-based weight loss competition. Obesity 20(7), 1413–1418 (2012)

34. LeBlanc, A.G., Chaput, J.P.: Pokémon go: a game changer for the physical inactivity crisis? Prev. Med. 101, 235–237 (2017)

35. Lesieur, H.R., Blume, S.B.: The south oaks gambling screen (SOGS): a new instrument for the identification of pathological gamblers. Am. J. Psychiatry 144(9), 1 (1987)

36. Lesser, L.I., Thompson, C.A., Luft, H.S.: Association between monetary deposits and weight loss in online commitment contracts. Am. J. Health Promot. 32(1), 198–204 (2018)

37. Lin, C.P., Bhattacherjee, A.: Elucidating individual intention to use interactive information technologies: the role of network externalities. Int. J. Electron. Commer. 13(1), 85–108 (2008)

38. Lin, C.P., Bhattacherjee, A.: Extending technology usage models to interactive hedonic technologies: a theoretical model and empirical test. Inf. Syst. J. 20(2), 163–181 (2010)

39. Loewenstein, G., Price, J., Volpp, K.: Habit formation in children: evidence from incentives for healthy eating. J. Health Econ. 45, 47–54 (2016)

40. Martin-Niedecken, A.L., Rogers, K., Turmo Vidal, L., Mekler, E.D., Márquez Segura, E.: Exercube vs. personal trainer: evaluating a holistic, immersive, and adaptive fitness game setup. In: Proceedings of the 2019 CHI Conference on Human Factors in Computing Systems, pp. 1–15 (2019)

41. Molina, M.D., Sundar, S.S.: Can mobile apps motivate fitness tracking? A study of technological affordances and workout behaviors. Health Commun. **35**(1), 65–74 (2020)
42. Mueller, F., et al.: Designing sports: a framework for exertion games. In: Proceedings of the SIGCHI Conference on Human Factors in Computing Systems, pp. 2651–2660 (2011)
43. Mueller, F., Gibbs, M.R., Vetere, F.: Design influence on social play in distributed exertion games. In: Proceedings of the SIGCHI Conference on Human Factors in Computing Systems, pp. 1539–1548 (2009)
44. Mullan, E., Markland, D., Ingledew, D.K.: A graded conceptualisation of self-determination in the regulation of exercise behaviour: development of a measure using confirmatory factor analytic procedures. Personality Individ. Differ. **23**(5), 745–752 (1997)
45. Murphy, J.G.: A randomized controlled trial of a behavioral economic supplement to brief motivational interventions for college drinking. J. Consult. Clin. Psychol. **80**(5), 876 (2012)
46. Nguyen, E., Modak, T., Dias, E., Yu, Y., Huang, L.: Fitnamo: using bodydata to encourage exercise through google glass^{TM}. In: CHI'14 Extended Abstracts on Human Factors in Computing Systems, pp. 239–244 (2014)
47. Niess, J., Woźniak, P.W.: Supporting meaningful personal fitness: The tracker goal evolution model. In: Proceedings of the 2018 CHI Conference on Human Factors in Computing Systems, pp. 1–12 (2018)
48. World Health Organization, et al.: Physical activity strategy for the who European region 2016–2025 (2016)
49. Paavilainen, J., Korhonen, H., Alha, K., Stenros, J., Koskinen, E., Mayra, F.: The pokémon go experience: a location-based augmented reality mobile game goes mainstream. In: Proceedings of the 2017 CHI Conference on Human Factors in Computing Systems, pp. 2493–2498 (2017)
50. Pappas, I.O., Kourouthanassis, P.E., Giannakos, M.N., Chrissikopoulos, V.: Shiny happy people buying: the role of emotions on personalized e-shopping. Electron. Mark. **24**(3), 193–206 (2014). https://doi.org/10.1007/s12525-014-0153-y
51. Patel, M.S., Asch, D.A., Volpp, K.G.: Framing financial incentives to increase physical activity among overweight and obese adults. Ann. Intern. Med. **165**(8), 600 (2016)
52. Roth, G.A., et al.: The burden of cardiovascular diseases among us states, 1990–2016. JAMA Cardiol. **3**(5), 375–389 (2018)
53. Sallis, J.F., Grossman, R.M., Pinski, R.B., Patterson, T.L., Nader, P.R.: The development of scales to measure social support for diet and exercise behaviors. Prev. Med. **16**(6), 825–836 (1987)
54. Schlicht, W.: Does physical exercise reduce anxious emotions? A meta-analysis. Anxiety Stress Coping **6**(4), 275–288 (1994)
55. Skriloff, S.J.G., Gonzalez, D.C., Christensen, K.C., Bentley, L.J., Mortensen, C.V.: Fitplay games: increasing exercise motivation through asynchronous social gaming. In: Proceedings of the 2016 CHI Conference Extended Abstracts on Human Factors in Computing Systems, pp. 164–167 (2016)
56. Stevenson, A.: Oxford Dictionary of English. Oxford University Press, Oxford (2010)
57. van der Swaluw, K., et al.: Physical activity after commitment lotteries: examining long-term results in a cluster randomized trial. J. Behav. Med. **41**(4), 483–493 (2018). https://doi.org/10.1007/s10865-018-9915-x

58. Tateno, M., Skokauskas, N., Kato, T.A., Teo, A.R., Guerrero, A.P.: New game software (Pokémon go) may help youth with severe social withdrawal, hikikomori. Psychiatry Res. **246**, 848 (2016)
59. Teixeira, P.J., Carraça, E.V., Markland, D., Silva, M.N., Ryan, R.M.: Exercise, physical activity, and self-determination theory: a systematic review. Int. J. Behav. Nutr. Phys. Act. **9**(1), 78 (2012)
60. Thaler, R.H., Shefrin, H.M.: An economic theory of self-control. J. Polit. Econ. **89**(2), 392–406 (1981)
61. Toscos, T., Faber, A., An, S., Gandhi, M.P.: Chick clique: persuasive technology to motivate teenage girls to exercise. In: CHI'06 Extended Abstracts on Human Factors in Computing Systems, pp. 1873–1878 (2006)
62. Tremblay, M.S., Colley, R.C., Saunders, T.J., Healy, G.N., Owen, N.: Physiological and health implications of a sedentary lifestyle. Appl. Physiol. Nutr. Metab. **35**(6), 725–740 (2010)
63. Tversky, A., Kahneman, D.: Loss aversion in riskless choice: a reference-dependent model. Q. J. Econ. **106**(4), 1039–1061 (1991)
64. Venkatesh, V., Morris, M.G., Davis, G.B., Davis, F.D.: User acceptance of information technology: toward a unified view. MIS Q. 425–478 (2003)
65. Verplanken, B., Melkevik, O.: Predicting habit: The case of physical exercise. Psychol. Sport Exerc. **9**(1), 15–26 (2008)
66. Wagner-Greene, V.R., Wotring, A.J., Castor, T., Kruger, J., Mortemore, S., Dake, J.A.: Pokémon go: healthy or harmful? Am. J. Public Health **107**(1), 35 (2017)
67. Walsh, G., Golbeck, J.: StepCity: a preliminary investigation of a personal informatics-based social game on behavior change. In: CHI'14 Extended Abstracts on Human Factors in Computing Systems, pp. 2371–2376 (2014)
68. Warburton, D.E., Nicol, C.W., Bredin, S.S.: Health benefits of physical activity: the evidence. CMAJ **174**(6), 801–809 (2006)
69. Weiss, M.R., Stuntz, C.P.: A little friendly competition: Peer relationships and psychosocial development in youth sport and physical activity contexts (2004)
70. Yurasek, A.M., Dennhardt, A.A., Murphy, J.G.: A randomized controlled trial of a behavioral economic intervention for alcohol and marijuana use. Exp. Clin. Psychopharmacol. **23**(5), 332 (2015)
71. Zhang, J., Brackbill, D., Yang, S., Becker, J., Herbert, N., Centola, D.: Support or competition? How online social networks increase physical activity: a randomized controlled trial. Prev. Med. Rep. **4**, 453–458 (2016)

Graph-Based Method for the Interpretation of User Activities in Serious Games

Iwona Grabska-Gradzińska(iD) and Jan K. Argasiński(✉)(iD)

Institute of Applied Computer Science, Faculty of Physics, Astronomy and Applied
Computer Science, Jagiellonian University, Kraków, Poland
{iwona.grabska,jan.argasinski}@uj.edu.pl

Abstract. Computer-based training systems are of growing importance
nowadays. Demand for remote skill and knowledge validating solutions is
higher than ever before. Serious games provide safe and replayable conditions for teaching and practice. The main issue with education founded
on serious games paradigm is the evaluation of the players. Virtual environments allow for various activities that are hard to grasp and quantify
automatically. Gameplay log files are usually filled with an excess of trivial activities that don't provide vital information about user's skills or
knowledge in the relevant domain. In this paper, the authors propose
a novel method for classification and interpretation of user activities in
computer-based training systems. The innovation of the presented idea
lies in the combination of layered graphs data structures, and Bayesian
inference about the user's skills and knowledge.

Keywords: Layered graphs · Serious games · Training evaluation ·
Educational assessment

1 Introduction: Player Evaluation in Serious Games

Serious games are usually defined after the classic book of Clark C. Abt as having
"an explicit and carefully thought-out educational purpose and (...) not intended
to be played primarily for amusement" [1]. Most of the modern computer based
serious games are training or educational applications [16]. The main problem
with regard to educational games is the assessment. Like in any other scholarly
context the information about learners' progress is crucial for evaluating the
entire projects. Fortunately, the educational progress of users can be viewed in
part in terms of the player's progress in the game. The games have "naturally"
built-in progress tracking systems such as points, achievements, character levels
etc. They also allow detailed logging of user activity.

Nowadays - not only due to the global crisis caused by the COVID-19 pandemic started in 2020 - there is a growing interest in remote training. More
and more companies, training centers and schools are forced to work on-line.

C. Ardito et al. (Eds.): INTERACT 2021, LNCS 12934, pp. 87–96, 2021.
https://doi.org/10.1007/978-3-030-85613-7_6

Regardless of the future epidemiological situation, this trend will in all likelihood increase. From the point of view of designers and creators of serious games, this means the need to introduce more and more sophisticated methods of evaluation and the need to automate this process. Generally, procedural assessment based on mechanics is an idea to strengthen one of the most important added values in serious games - the potential variety of scenarios that go hand in hand with the repeatability of the assessment. Procedural story and/or world generation is widely used in entertainment, education and reasoning [7–12].

At this point, attention should also be paid to the distinction between the assessment and evaluation. As authors of [2] indicate - assessment is a formative, diagnostic and process-oriented activity, while evaluation is more often summative, judgmental and product oriented. Nevertheless, the common areas of these two ways of looking at educational progress include the fact that they are data-intensive, utilizing measures, and user-oriented.

In the case of computer games, the players' behaviors observed in the game are in fact activations of mechanics implemented by the designers. We define mechanics after M. Sicart as "methods invoked by agents to interact with the game states" [3]. The player - within the system - cannot do anything that would not be mechanics (although there is a problem of *subversive play* - exploiting *bugs* and *glitches* [4]). This means that for the purposes of evaluating educational progress in serious games, we can treat mechanics as observables - from their applications and parameters (timing, sequence, speed, context) we can obtain some information about the knowledge, skills, abilities or attitudes of players [13]. Such a framework - combining the ECD *(Evidence Centered Design)* paradigm [5] with the MDA *(Mechanics, Dynamics, Aesthetics)* model [6] is proposed by authors of [4]. In our proposal, mechanics applied in the contexts will constitute the basis for updating the values of evaluation variables.

The spheres of designer's responsibility are grouped into two separate entities here simply called *the game* and *the educational robot*:

> However, the domain content and learning theories, the pedagogy, and the learning profile have a common context representing serious sides which can be grouped into one entity called an educational robot; on the other hand, all game aspects will be represented in one entity called a game. The educational robot and the game should exchange data or information; the game knows what the learner/player is doing, and by communicating relevant information (learner traces) to the educational robot, the last one knows what the player has done, and by analyzing learner's traces a decision is communicated back to the game (pedagogical order) to be applied such as repeating the same level (...) [14]

In our, presented below, concept – instead of the *communication protocol* between the layers of the system, we propose that the competences of the *educational robot* should be implemented by a properly structured game system, and that the progress in the student's profile is tracked with the use of variables represented in the graph system, which also describes the player's possible mechanics with their context. In this way, the system architecture is significantly reduced while maintaining full designer's control over the application and with the possibility of procedural content generation, e.g. as repetitions with variants required for accurate testing and predictions [15].

2   Bayesian Knowledge Tracing

Bayesian Knowledge Tracing (BKT) is a well established algorithm for modeling learners educational progress [19]. BKT is a proven solution for the estimation of student proficiency and the effectiveness of the educational process [30]. Due to its probabilistic construction, it is suitable for prediction and use in [29] recommending systems. A natural development of this solution is its use in intelligent systems, [28] also those based on deep learning [27].

An important element of the solution presented in this article is the use of before-mentioned idea. According to the Bayes Theorem (1), the likelihood of event A under the condition of B: $p(A/B)$ is equal to likelihood of event B under A: $p(B/A)$ multiplied by probability of observing event A: $p(A)$ under condition of B: $p(B)$ [22].

$$p(A/B) = \frac{p(B/A)p(A)}{p(B)} \tag{1}$$

Therefore marginal probability of B: $p(B)$ is equal to sum of joint probability $p(A,B)$ over all possible values of the other variables (in this case a represents particular value of A, (2):

$$p(B) = \sum_{a \in A} p(B, a) \tag{2}$$

The proposed method of constructing evaluation in serious games is based on the idea of Bayesian Knowledge Tracing [18–20] often used in Intelligent Tutoring Systems [21]. These systems can be described as based on the following modules: Student, Tutor, Domain and Interface - just like in the case of before-mentioned educational *robot architecture*, created for the needs of thinking about serious games. For us, the most interesting activity is to model the Student module and the context in which he/she is thrown (game world, *diegesis*). According to [21], the Student module can be considered as a quantitative representation of the recorded behavior of the application user. There are many ways to express the actions performed in the context of a certain domain. We propose a *game*-related view through the prism of mechanics, described by the structure of layered graphs.

In the light of classical Bayesian Knowledge Tracing theory (as described e.g. in [17,19]), the key parameters are:

– $p(L_0)$ - probability that the student u has the skill k from an external source (it can be estimated, for example, using the initial knowledge test);

- $p(T)$ - probability of transfer of knowledge about the student's state from *unknown* to *known* after the occurrence of a situation enabling its application;
- $p(G)$ - probability of correct execution of the action despite the lack of the skill ("by accident", "guess");
- $p(S)$ - probability of making a mistake despite having the appropriate skill ("accidental mistake", "slip").

The initial situation is illustrated by Eq. (3). Equations (4) and (5) are used to calculate $p(L)$ in the following steps in the case of observed *(obs)* correctly (4) and incorrectly (5) performed operations. At the end (6) and (7) are used to update the probability that student u will apply k correctly when given the opportunity.

$$p(L_1)_u^k = p(L_0)^k \tag{3}$$

$$p(L_{t+1}|obs = correct)_u^k = \frac{p(L_t)_u^k \cdot (1 - p(S)^k)}{p(L_t)_u^k - (1 - p(S)^k) + (1 - p(L_t)_u^k) \cdot p(G)^k} \tag{4}$$

$$p(L_{t+1}|obs = wrong)_u^k = \frac{p(L_t)_u^k \cdot p(S)^k}{p(L_t)_u^k \cdot p(S)^k + (1 - p(L_t)_u^k) \cdot (1 - p(G)^k)} \tag{5}$$

$$p(L_{t+1})_u^k = p(L_{t+1}/obs)_u^k + (1 - p(L_{t+1}/obs)_u^k) \cdot p(T)^k \tag{6}$$

$$p(C_{t+1})_u^k = p(L_t)_u^k \cdot (1 - p(S)^k) + (1 - p(L_t)_u^k) \cdot p(G)^k \tag{7}$$

The dynamics of the described situation is presented in the Fig. 1 below where K stands for the *knowledge* node, and Q for the *quiz* node (or - in our case - *quest* node).

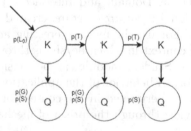

Fig. 1. The standard Bayesian knowledge tracing model (after [23])

3   Layered Graphs in the Description of Gameplay

Players' behaviours and decisions are closely connected with game mechanics and interactive game elements available at the moment of decision. Both for player actions analysis and game design verification, it is useful to represent the gameplay in the formal way. Graphs are very efficient and flexible mechanisms for modelling the system dependencies and user-evoked changes [24]. Moreover, layered graphs are very useful for describing particular points within the story [25]. It is due to the fact that the states of the world elements are divided into separate layers, and graph edges correspond to different dependencies of the system according to the layer type of connected nodes. The formal definition is described in [26].

In presented system the model of a game consists of two separate graphs: a graph model of the world state and a graph model of the gameplay. The graph model of the game world (the World State Graph) is layered and hierarchical. The four layers: layer of locations, layer of characters, layer of items or layer of narrative elements represent objects of the given world. Connections between objects are represented by edges, e.g. the edge between item and character means ownership, the edge between location and location means passage. Node attributes represent object properties. Most player's decisions are influenced by his surroundings: location, elements placed there, as well as his own belongings and attributes. That is why a specific graph structure is assigned - a sheaf subgraph. This structure is most often used in graph operations, called productions. The schematic view of world graph with the division into layers is presented in the Fig. 2.

3.1   User Decision as Graph Production

The events which change the game world, evoked by the player as well as external factors, can be easily represented as graph rules, also known as productions. A production is a pair of graphs called the left-hand side and the right-hand side of the production. The player action is possible if there is in the world graph subgraph identical with the left-side of the production and is implemented as replacing the right side of the production and its embedment.

The structure of the vertex information and relations between vertices in JSON format is shown below.

```
"L_Side": {  "Locations": [ {"Name": "Accident scene",
"Attributes": { }, "Characters":
[ { "Name": "Hero",  "Items": [ { "Id":"Phone"} ] },
{ "Name": "Victim","Attributes": { "Conscious": 0},
"Characters": [ ], "Items": [ { "Id":"Id card"}] } ],
"Items": [ ], "Connections": [ { "Destination":
"Emergency service","Attributes": { "Type":"Phone call" } } ] }
{ "Name": "Emergency service", "Connections":
[ { "Destination": "Accident scene"} ] } ] }
```

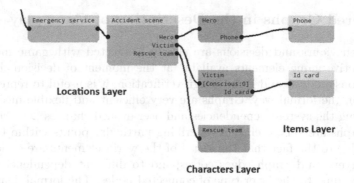

Fig. 2. Implementation of world state graph in the Godot game engine.

Application of the production to a given World State Graph causes replacement of the nodes of the left-hand side by the nodes of the right-hand side and their embedment in the World State Graph. The first step of applying the production is to match, i.e., to fit the left-hand side to the World State Graph. A successful fit means that there is a subgraph in the WSG which is equal to the left-hand side graph.

3.2 Gameplay Graph

The sequence of players action is one of the most important elements of player evaluation. Possible sequences of available productions are used to describe the designed scenarios. The initial state of the world graph allows for these sequences to be generated by player or by testers (manually or semi-automatically, using graph matching functions). The graph of the all possible sequences give us the model of gameplay.

4   Applying Graph-Based Method for the Interpretation of User Activities in Serious Games

The example shown below concerns the application supporting the CPR training for OSH (Occupational Safety and Health) courses for employees and helps to evaluate the user's competences after the training. The system is implemented in Godot engine 3.2.3 and graph information is stored in JSON format.

The application of the proposed idea in which we combine the concept of using layer graphs to describe the course of a serious game with the Bayesian Knowledge Tracking method is presented below. A fragment of a serious game is described, in which the protagonist (*the player*) has to undertake a rescue action, taking into account the knowledge and skills related to performing CPR *(cardiopulmonary resuscitation)* (Fig. 3). The following graph productions describe possible actions and their results. In particular, the red node denotes the death

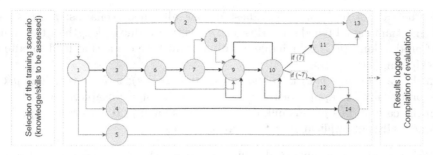

Fig. 3. Gameplay graph describing simple CPR scenario in educational serious game

of the injured person and the green one - the success of the rescue operation. The scene (*quest*) starts at the gray node marked with the number (1).

Description of the Nodes: (1) The accident happens; (2) Another actor takes over initiative; (3) Player checks victim's breath; (4) Player engages in idle activity (e.g. plays games on their cellphone, ignoring victim); (5) Player falls into despair (consequently ceasing the aid); (6) Player checks victim's pulse; (7) Player calls an ambulance by the phone; (8) Player takes instructions from the dispatch; (9) Player delivers rescue breath; (10) Push hard, push fast...; (11) Arrival of the medical assistance; (12) Loss of strength; (13) Patient is saved; (14) Patient dies.

In the challenge presented above, the following production series are possible:

(a) 1-3-2-13 (success)
(b) 1-3-6-7-9-10-11-13 (success)
(c) 1-3-6-7-8-9-10-11-13 (success)
(d) 1-3-6-9-10-12-14 (defeat)
(e) 1-4-14 (defeat)
(f) 1-5-14 (defeat)

It's worth noting that the scenario 1-3-6-9-10-11-13 is impossible. If an ambulance is not called (7), help will not arrive in time and the action will end in failure (14).

Now we can apply Bayesian Knowledge Tracing methods to provide means for interpreting various outcomes. For the purposes of this example, we will not build a matrix with weights assigned to particular nodes since it would require the expertise of a domain specialist and conducting tests. We will limit ourselves to showing some dependencies in terms of parameters previously defined as interesting for us. Thus we can conclude that:

- in the case of (a) - $p(L)$ remains unknown; $p(T)$ is very low; $p(G)$ is unknown; $p(S)$ is unknown;
- in the case of (b) - $p(L)$ is the greatest among all scenarios; $p(T)$ is highest among all scenarios; $p(G)$ is very low due to length of the chain of productions; $p(S)$ is not applicable;
- in the case of (c) - $p(L)$ is lower than in (b) but higher than in other cases; $p(T)$ is lower than in (b) but higher than in other cases; $p(G)$ is very low due to length of the chain of productions; $p(S)$ is not applicable;

- in the case of (d) - $p(L)$ is highest among all failed scenarios; $p(T)$ is the highest among all failed scenarios; $p(S)$ is very low due to length of the chain of productions; $p(G)$ is high due to only one mistake made that lead to failure (skipping (7));
- in the case of (e) - $p(L)$ is unknown (attitude is low); $p(T)$ is very low; $p(G)$ is practically not applicable; $p(S)$ is very much not applicable;
- in the case of (f) - $p(L)$ is unknown (ability is low); $p(T)$ is very low; $p(G)$ is practically not applicable; $p(S)$ is not applicable;

Writing the correct numerical values (multipliers) to the above general statements will automate the process of assessing the probability $p(C)$ - that a given skill will be correctly applied in the next test case. Of course, it is essential to test knowledge, skills, abilities and attitudes many times in different contexts. But the very construction of a serious game based on a generator in the form of a layered graph makes it easier and enables it. In the Sect. 3.1 the example of a JSON code was presented to describe a test situation followed by the example of implementation in a game engine (Fig. 2). Innovation of the presented idea is also in the ability to represent user's contextual information in the form of gameplay reports generated after the simulation. Graphs and probabilities provide an effective generalized language of communicating the user's skills, knowledge and abilities in a varied context. In proposed solution input block visible on the left side of the Fig. 3 represents the moment of selection of the context of simulation; output block represents the process of writing contextualized data into a generalized database from which the further compilation of the results is possible.

5   Conclusion

The article above presents a way to describe the structure of a serious game using layer graphs. Furthermore, it describes a method proposed for combining mechanics with a statistical measure, which is used to evaluate the educational progress of the player. Of course, there are many possible vectors for further development of the concept above - one can mention such issues as the automation of metrics construction, various possible strategies of the user's model fitting - including predictions in the scope of the application's operation. There is also the question of whether is it possible to estimate $p(S)$ - *slip*, and $p(G)$ - *guess* using the context [18]. The next step of the presented system development is to propose the same narrative structure but with the different production sequences to evaluate different fields of the skills and knowledge for different types of users.

As shown above, the graph based system of representation of important game objects and events can be effectively and profitably used to support computer based educational evaluation tools.

References

1. Abt, C.C.: Serious Games. Viking Press (1970)
2. Daoudi, I., Tranvouez, E., Chebil, R., Espinasse, B., Chaari, W.L.: Learners' assessment and evaluation in serious games: approaches and techniques review. In: Dokas, I.M., Bellamine-Ben Saoud, N., Dugdale, J., Díaz, P. (eds.) ISCRAM-med 2017. LNBIP, vol. 301, pp. 147–153. Springer, Cham (2017). https://doi.org/10.1007/978-3-319-67633-3_12
3. Sicart, M.: Defining game mechanics. Game Stud. Int. J. Comput. Game Res. **8** (2008)
4. Aarseth, E.: I fought the law: transgressive play and the implied player. In: Segal, N., Koleva, D. (eds.) From Literature to Cultural Literacy, pp. 180–188. Palgrave Macmillan, London (2014). https://doi.org/10.1057/9781137429704_13
5. Mislevy, R.J., Almond, R.G., Lukas, J.F.: A brief introduction to evidence-centered design (CSE report 632). Center for Research on Evaluation, Standards, and Student Testing, CA (2004)
6. Winn, B.: The Design, Play, and Experience Framework, Hershey (2009)
7. Compton, K., Filstrup, B., Mateas, M.: Tracery: approachable story grammar authoring for casual users. In: Papers from Seventh Intelligent Narrative Technologies Workshop (INT 07), pp. 63–67 (2014)
8. Compton, K., Kybartas, B., Mateas, M.: Tracery: an author-focused generative text tool. In: Schoenau-Fog, H., Bruni, L.E., Louchart, S., Baceviciute, S. (eds.) ICIDS 2015. LNCS, vol. 9445, pp. 154–161. Springer, Cham (2015). https://doi.org/10.1007/978-3-319-27036-4_14
9. Grinblat, J., Bucklew, C.B.: Subverting historical cause & effect: generation of mythic biographies in Caves of Qud. In: Proceedings of the 12th International Conference on the Foundations of Digital Games (FDG 2017), Article 76, pp. 1–7. Association for Computing Machinery, New York (2017). https://doi.org/10.1145/3102071.3110574
10. Grinblat, J., Bucklew, C.B.: Warm rocks for cold lizards: generating meaningful quests in Caves of Qud. In: Experimental AI in Games Workshop (AIIDE 2020) (2020)
11. Adams, T.: Secret identities in dwarf fortress. In: Proceedings Experimental AI in Games (AIIDE 2017), pp. 22–25 (2017)
12. Tarn Adams, T.: Simulation principles from Dwarf Fortress. In: Game AI Pro 2: Collected Wisdom of Game AI Professionals, pp. 519–521. CRC Press (2015)
13. Argasinski, J.K., Wegrzyn, P.: Affective patterns in serious games. Futur. Gener. Comput. Syst. (2018). https://doi.org/10.1016/j.future.2018.06.013
14. Mestadi, W., Nafil, K., Touahni, R., Messoussi, R.: An assessment of serious games technology: toward an architecture for serious games design. Int. J. Comput. Games Technol. **2018**, 1–16 (2018). https://doi.org/10.1155/2018/9834565
15. Alonso-Fernández, C., Martínez-Ortiz, I., Caballero, R., Freire, M., Fernández-Manjón, B.: Predicting students' knowledge after playing a serious game based on learning analytics data: a case study. J. Comput. Assisted Learn. (2019). https://doi.org/10.1111/jcal.12405
16. Djaouti, D., Alvarez, J., Jessel, J.-P., Rampnoux, O.: Origins of serious games. In: Ma, M., Oikonomou, A., Jain, L.C. (eds.) Serious Games and Edutainment Applications, pp. 25–43. Springer, London (2011). https://doi.org/10.1007/978-1-4471-2161-9_3

17. Orun, A., Seker, H.: Development of a computer game-based framework for cognitive behaviour identification by using Bayesian inference methods. Comput. Hum. Behav. **28**(4), 1332–1341 (2012). https://doi.org/10.1016/j.chb.2012.02.017

18. Pelánek, R.: Bayesian knowledge tracing, logistic models, and beyond: an overview of learner modeling techniques. User Model. User-Adap. Inter. **27**(3–5), 313–350 (2017). https://doi.org/10.1007/s11257-017-9193-2

19. Yudelson, M.V., Koedinger, K.R., Gordon, G.J.: Individualized Bayesian knowledge tracing models. In: Lane, H.C., Yacef, K., Mostow, J., Pavlik, P. (eds.) AIED 2013. LNCS (LNAI), vol. 7926, pp. 171–180. Springer, Heidelberg (2013). https://doi.org/10.1007/978-3-642-39112-5_18

20. Baker, R.S.J., Corbett, A.T., Aleven, V.: More accurate student modeling through contextual estimation of slip and guess probabilities in Bayesian knowledge tracing. In: Woolf, B.P., Aïmeur, E., Nkambou, R., Lajoie, S. (eds.) ITS 2008. LNCS, vol. 5091, pp. 406–415. Springer, Heidelberg (2008). https://doi.org/10.1007/978-3-540-69132-7_44

21. Manrique, R., López, C., Leon, E.: Student modeling via Bayesian knowledge tracing: a case study (2014). https://doi.org/10.13140/RG.2.1.3646.4167

22. Englebienne, G.: Bayesian methods for the analysis of human behaviour. In: Salah, A., Gevers, T. (eds.) Computer Analysis of Human Behavior, pp. 3–20. Springer, London (2011). https://doi.org/10.1007/978-0-85729-994-9_1

23. Pardos, Z.A., Heffernan, N.T.: KT-IDEM: introducing item difficulty to the knowledge tracing model. In: Konstan, J.A., Conejo, R., Marzo, J.L., Oliver, N. (eds.) UMAP 2011. LNCS, vol. 6787, pp. 243–254. Springer, Heidelberg (2011). https://doi.org/10.1007/978-3-642-22362-4_21

24. Slusarczyk, G.: Graph-based representation of design properties in creating building floorplans. Comput. Aided Des. **95**, 24–39 (2018). https://doi.org/10.1016/j.cad.2017.09.004

25. Grabska-Gradzińska, I., Grabska, E., Nowak, L., Palacz, W.: Towards automatic generation of storyline aided by collaborative creative design. In: Luo, Y. (ed.) CDVE 2020. LNCS, vol. 12341, pp. 47–56. Springer, Cham (2020). https://doi.org/10.1007/978-3-030-60816-3_6

26. Grabska-Gradzińska, I., Nowak, L., Grabska, E.: Automatic story generation based on graph model using Godot engine. In: Rutkowski, L., Scherer, R., Korytkowski, M., Pedrycz, W., Tadeusiewicz, R., Zurada, J.M. (eds.) ICAISC 2020. LNCS (LNAI), vol. 12415, pp. 397–405. Springer, Cham (2020). https://doi.org/10.1007/978-3-030-61401-0_37

27. Gervet, T., Koedinger, K., Schneider, J., Mitchell, T.: When is deep learning the best approach to knowledge tracing? J. Educ. Data Min. **12**(3), 31–54 (2020). https://doi.org/10.5281/zenodo.414361

28. Minn, S.: BKT-LSTM: efficient student modeling for knowledge tracing and student performance prediction. arXiv preprint arXiv:2012.12218 (2020)

29. Zhao, J., Bhatt, S., Thille, C., Zimmaro, D., Gattani, N.: Interpretable personalized knowledge tracing and next learning activity recommendation. In: Proceedings of the Seventh ACM Conference on Learning@ Scale, pp. 325-328 (2020)

30. Corbett, A.T., Anderson, J.R.: Knowledge tracing: modeling the acquisition of procedural knowledge. User Model. User-Adap. Inter. **4**(4), 253–278 (1995)

Improving Student Experience and Learning Performance with Traditional Instructional Methods and New Digital Media

Pamela Andrade[(✉)] and Effie L.-C. Law[(✉)]

University of Leicester, Leicester, UK
{pyas2,lcl9}@le.ac.uk
https://le.ac.uk/informatics

Abstract. Studies in Technology-enhanced learning (TEL) involve different instructional media and methods to understand their effects on two main outcomes: learning performance and user experience. This paper investigated the impact of three gamification elements (point, badge, leaderboard) integrated into an educational software application on these outcomes. To expand the scope of the related work focusing on the Higher Education learners, our study targeted secondary school students. Results from 74 participants, who were divided into four groups (one non-gamified and three gamified), showed that the group receiving badges had a more positive user experience and that learning gain was observed in all groups.

Keywords: Gamification · Education · User experience · Learning performance · Secondary schools · Points · Badges · Leaderboards

1 Introduction

Several well-established pedagogical practices have been implemented in educational software in recent years to enable positive user experience (UX) and learning gain. Among others, pedagogical theories such as Flipped Classroom, Inquiry-Based Learning, and Learning by Questioning have shown to be beneficial to improve learning performance. Based on the findings of our literature review, we decided to ground this study in the *Learning by Questioning* approach. However, a serious drawback of using any of such powerful pedagogical strategies for the design and development of educational software is that they do not sustain student attention, as they can be sometimes perceived by students as difficult or tiresome. An unfortunate consequence is that many students lose interest in completing a task, or altogether quit their interaction with the educational software, jeopardizing their opportunity to learn. To counteract this

© IFIP International Federation for Information Processing 2021
Published by Springer Nature Switzerland AG 2021
C. Ardito et al. (Eds.): INTERACT 2021, LNCS 12934, pp. 97–106, 2021.
https://doi.org/10.1007/978-3-030-85613-7_7

possible effect, we suggest the implementation of engagement strategies to maintain student interest in using the educational software. In particular, we study which specific gamification elements can potentiate UX and learning gain.

According to the related literature in Human-Computer Interaction (HCI), further research in this specific topic could help improve the understanding of which gamification elements would better enhance user perceptions of the interactive software. Likewise, concerning TEL, the related literature attests the need to select appropriate pedagogical methods if the objective is to boost learning gain. Therefore, based on the findings identified in previous studies as described in the sections below (see Sect. 2), an important contribution of this research is to compare individual user interface (UI) design elements in an educational application, with the goal to analyse which of these elements make a significant difference on the students' overall experience and learning performance. In addition, this study aims to investigate student perceptions of the instructional media selected for the purposes of this research, to analyse how this selection influence the learning experience of students in secondary schools.

Our reason for choosing this particular target group is simple: plenty has been studied in the field of gamified educational technologies, but most of the research has focused on the effects in Higher or Distance Education only [8,15]. Another weakness identified in previous research is the limited breadth of contexts in which instructional media and methods have been studied, with the most common topics being different from those parts of secondary school curricula. Therefore, our work contributes to the understanding of how instructional media and methods can improve the learning experience and performance of adolescent students, by using three gamification elements to teach physics as part of an online lesson.

2   Related Work

The activity planned for this study (Sect. 3.2) used attractive instructional media (Sect. 2.1) to analyse how this makes an impact on student performance and UX. On the other hand, the software developed for this research (Sect. 3.1) used engaging instructional methods (Sect. 2.2) with the same aim.

2.1   Instructional Media

An important reason why similar research has studied the effects of instructional media in TEL, is due to the expectation that its implementation could help improve learning performance and user experience [4]. In general, instructional *media* refers to materials and devices used to deliver instructions online [13].

Numerous scientific websites and resources are nowadays available on the Internet, giving the web the potential to become a favourable environment for complex learning [6]. In this context, multimedia tools can help students to make the transition from a passive participation to a more responsible and self-aware instruction. Although self-exploration and experimentation is encouraged, online resources still need to be carefully selected and organized by teachers so students do not waste cognitive efforts of trying to find or figure out which ones fit best for a particular topic. Additionally, instructional media and virtual interactions are being used in modern times to encourage students to use logical reasoning to gain a deeper understanding of a topic. In this particular study, the design of the learning activity (Sect. 3.2) included multimedia such as illustrations, animations, and interactive experiments to encourage students to focus on learning through instructional media.

Nonetheless, although some studies have shown that multimedia instruction is an effective method to complement science lessons [12] (in some cases even exceeding the results from many traditional pedagogical strategies), sometimes using multimedia by itself does not guarantee improved learning performance and real understanding [9,13]. A combination of online scientific resources and other procedures (e.g. opinion exchange, group work, interactive exercises) could help to better balance critical thinking and collaborative knowledge formation.

2.2 Instructional Methods

Instructional *methods* refer to the techniques used to enhance cognitive processing in learners [13], which can include many types of pedagogical strategies that teachers—or software applications in this case—implement in the classroom to help students to learn the course material.

Although recent studies have pointed out the necessity of better instructional *methods* rather than focusing on instructional *media* to foster learning gain [13], findings remain inconclusive about the benefits with regard to UX. Hence, we have been motivated to explore to what extent using *Learning by Questioning* and *Gamification*—which are traditional instructional methods—can utilize the potential of the new instructional media—interactive educational software—to encourage positive experience and learning gain.

Gamification aims to create more enjoyable experiences by adding a recreational element to the interaction between students and technology [7]. In consequence, gamified software support and motivate students to perform tasks (such as questioning) promoted by the engaging nature of a gameful experience. Previous research suggests that game design elements at a surface level can be more easily manipulated independently of one another [2,15]. Thus, badges, points, and leaderboards were selected for the software development (Sect. 3.1) to address the limited experimental analyses of individual game design elements and comparisons of groups thereof [11,15].

3 Design of the Experiment

3.1 Software Development

To study how instructional methods (Sect. 2.2) can influence UX and learning performance, three UI design elements were implemented in Go-Lab[1]. The gam-

---

[1] Go-Lab (https://golabz.eu) is an educational platform that enables the creation and distribution of interactive online lessons.

ification elements badges, points, and leaderboards were implemented as plugins or *apps* that can be selected by teachers to add to their online lessons. The teacher view allowed the user to assign or revoke rewards by selecting students in a class from a dropdown menu (Fig. 3). Teachers were also able to configure various features in the app, including a selection of prizes and languages (see the gear icon at the bottom right corner of Fig. 3). The student view was restricted to visualizing the learning activity and any available rewards (Fig. 1 and Fig. 2).

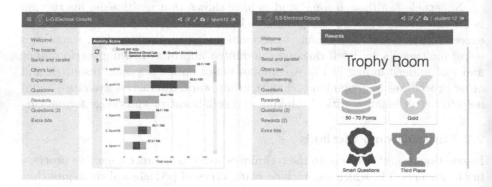

Fig. 1. Student view of leaderboards   **Fig. 2.** Student view of badges & points

3.2   The Learning Activity

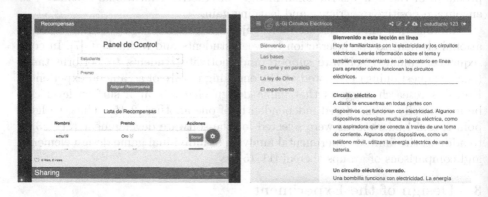

Fig. 3. Teacher view of the app   **Fig. 4.** Initial view of the online lesson

Following the work of [1], an online lesson aligned with the appropriate curricula was selected from the Go-Lab repository. The online lesson was designed with various types of instructional media (Sect. 2.1) and covered the physics topic of

Electric Circuits. Moving along the phases of the learning activity (see the side navigation menu, Fig. 4) students learned about current, tension, power, serial and parallel circuits, and Ohm's law. The lesson was assembled with textual information and several pieces of multimedia content. Also, interactive experiments were available for students to practice the concepts they had learned.

4 Methodology

This empirical study was approved by the Research Ethics Committee of the University of Leicester. Participants worked individually during this experiment, which took place with the school's facilities for two sessions. A researcher and a science teacher were present during the experiment to monitor the process, but did not offer any unsolicited help. There were four software versions under evaluation in this study (non-gamified [NG], gamified with points [GP], gamified with badges [GB], and gamified with leaderboards [GL]).

4.1 Hypotheses and Instruments

Two main **null hypotheses** were formulated for this study:

H1: There are no significant differences in the learning performance of secondary school students among the NG, GP, GB, and GL groups.

H2: There are no significant differences in the students' experience in terms of their perceptions of software usability, user engagement and motivation among the NG, GP, GB, and GL groups.

Several data collection methods and instruments were used to test the null hypotheses. To analyse **learning performance** identical pre- and post-knowledge tests were designed with questions closely related to the physics lesson part of the experimental session (Sect. 3.2). The homegrown knowledge tests comprised 12 multiple-choice questions, with a single possible correct answer. To analyse **user experience** various standardised scales measuring student perceptions of software usability, user engagement, and motivation were used: the System Usability Scale SUS [3], the User Engagement Scale Short-Form UES-SF (5-point Likert Scale) [14], and the Situational Motivation Scale SIMS (7-point Likert Scale) [10]. These standardised scales were selected due to their proven psychometric properties and their ease of administration. Additionally, a demographic questionnaire was used and a group discussion was held to provide insights into the habits, preferences, and background of participants in this sample. Note that SUS and UES-SF (subscale – usability) were used to assess the reliability of the participants' responses.

4.2 Procedure and Participants

A public school in the Basque Country in the northwest of Spain was involved in this study. A public school in Spain refers to education that is funded by the state and is free of charge. Students had access to good scientific and technological facilities in the school. A total of 74 students participated in the experiment.

Each class was allocated to one of the four groups (NG, GL, GP, GB) randomly. The first of the two sessions started with students filling in a demographic questionnaire, after which students interacted with the same online physics lesson (Sect. 3.2). Then, participants were asked to: complete a knowledge test, create questions based on the lesson's content, and complete the SIMS questionnaire. Following a schedule set by the participants' school, students had a 24–48 h break. Over the break, a researcher and the teacher of each participating class evaluated the quality of the questions created by students to award them prizes (points, badges, leaderboards) accordingly.

During the second session, participants were presented with results of their efforts in the form of the gamification element under evaluation in their respective groups (non-gamified interfaces showed no gamification element). Afterwards, participants had the opportunity to create a second set of questions and they completed once again the SIMS questionnaire and the knowledge test. All students then filled in the SUS and UES-SF. To conclude the session, each class gave feedback through a moderated discussion.

5   Results

In total, six data collection methods and instruments were used in this experiment to test our two null hypotheses (see Sect. 4.1). The main results of this analysis are discussed in the sections below.

5.1   Demographic Data

The average age of the 74 students participating in this study was 14.56 ($SD = 0.94$); 36 participants were male, 33 were female, and 5 people preferred not to specify their gender. Participants rated their IT skills on a scale 1–10 with a mean score of 7.41 ($SD = 1.22$).

5.2   Learning Performance

Data were normally distributed in all groups for the scores of the pre-test and the post-test used in this study (Table 1). Parametric tests were therefore used to investigate the null hypothesis H1. The Cronbach alpha for the knowledge tests was 0.771, implying that the reliability of the knowledge test was acceptable.

Students achieved a pre-test mean of 7.05 ($SD = 1.86$) out of 12 possible points and a mean of 8.12 ($SD = 1.99$) in the post-test. Significant differences were found in the learning performance over all the four groups using a paired sample t-test ($t(73) = -7.028, p < 0.000$)).

When comparing the two knowledge tests, a significant improvement was found on the knowledge tests scores of the non-gamified group [NG] ($t(20) = -2.014, p = 0.009$)). Likewise, students receiving points [GP], badges [GB], and

Table 1. Results of the knowledge tests classified per group ([N] = Sample Size, [A] = Average, [SD] = Standard Deviation, [Dif.] = Difference)

Group	N	Pre-Test(A)	SD	Post-Test(A)	SD	Dif.
NG	21	8.00	2.00	8.62	2.16	+0.62
GL	17	6.82	1.56	8.12	1.69	+1.30
GB	18	7.11	1.94	8.67	2.08	+1.56
GP	18	6.11	1.41	7.00	1.57	+0.89

leaderboards [GL] showed significant learning gains (GP[$t(17) = -3.332, p = 0.004$)], GB[$t(17) = -4.177, p = 0.001$)], GL[$t(16) = -3.801, p = 0.002$)]); all with a medium to large effect size (GP[$r = 0.29$, Cohen's $d = 0.596$], GB[$r = 0.36$, Cohen's $d = 0.776$], GL[$r = 0.37$, Cohen's $d = 0.799$]). Given this statistical analysis, the **null hypothesis H1** was **rejected**. Significant differences were found in the learning performance between the two knowledge tests.

5.3   User Experience

Three standardised questionnaires were used to assess UX in this study. Data were normally distributed in all scores of the SUS, UES-SF, and SIMS (Table 2). Parametric tests were therefore used to investigate the null hypothesis H2. Note that not all students answered all the questionnaires. Cronbach alphas for the three instruments are 0.769, 0.676 and 0.505, respectively. The range of 0.7 to 0.8 was acceptable, but 0.5 was rather poor; it implied that SIMS might not be the best instrument to be used in this context.

Table 2. Quantitative UX results classified per group ([N] = Sample Size, [A] = Average, [SD] = Standard Deviation, [Dif.] = Difference)

Group	N	SUS(A)	SD	N	UES-SF(A)	SD	N	SIMS1(A)	SIMS2(A)	Dif.
NG	21	61.67	15.15	21	3.01	0.66	18	4.55	4.67	+0.12
GL	16	66.00	10.51	16	2.82	0.31	15	4.17	4.22	+0.05
GB	18	67.36	22.04	18	3.37	0.72	18	4.10	4.12	+0.02
GP	17	61.33	9.90	18	3.25	0.34	15	4.00	4.04	+0.04

A one-way ANOVA showed non-significant differences among the groups ($F(3, 68) = 1.240$, $p = 0.302$) on the student perception of software usability (SUS). Likewise, a paired sample t test showed non-significant differences between the students' motivation before and after the intervention as measured by the SIMS questionnaire ($t(65) = -1.001, p = 0.320$). Nevertheless, a one-way ANOVA revealed significant differences among the groups on the self-reported perception of user engagement as measured by the UES-SF ($F(3, 71) = 1.582$,

$p = 0.039$). Results of Tukey post-hoc tests revealed that the badges [GB] showed a significant difference on the UES-SF scores compared to the non-gamified groups [NG] ($p = 0.032$) with a medium effect size ($r = 0.25$, Cohen's $d = 0.521$). In addition, a Pearson correlation coefficient was computed with the SUS and UES-SF results to assess the reliability of the participants' responses regarding usability and a positive correlation was found between the two variables ($r = 0.625, n = 72, p < 0.001$). Given these results, the **null hypothesis H2** was **partially rejected**.

6   Discussion

Contrary to the findings of several similar studies [15,16], results of this experiment supported those of [1,5], which found that badges were the gamification element with the most significant influence on user experience and learning gains.

However, the empirical results of this study suggested that the design of the gamified elements could have been improved. Firstly, one should ensure the uniformity of the assessment criteria for determining the rewards to be granted. Secondly, by enhancing the design of the gamification elements to appeal visually to the students, using appropriate positioning, size, and animation for this effect.

To trigger a comparison of different instructional media and methods that could influence learning performance and UX, this study expanded on the work of [1] by selecting students from the same age group, following the same methodological procedure, but from a different background (i.e. country and native language). Hence, future work should involve a cross-cultural analysis of these results with the aim to identify differences and similarities between behavioural patterns of students in varied socio-cultural and educational settings (e.g., private vs public education, developed vs developing countries, etc.).

Although our intention was to compare the benefits and drawbacks of instructional media and instructional methods, it is possible that the results of this study could have been influenced by external validity threats such as the *multiple treatment interference* as the same subjects were using a combination of multimedia content, gamified strategies, and questioning-based software, making it difficult to discern the effects of each in this particular sample. Also, by the different waiting time students had between sessions, which was decided entirely by the participating school depending on their available timings. Furthermore, the low reliability of SIMS suggested that an alternative instrument could have been used, and it might explain the non-significant difference in motivation between the two sessions.

7   Conclusion

Granted the appropriate selection of instructional media, we argue that the use of instructional methods is crucial for positively influencing learning performance and UX. Results of this study suggested that both *media* and *methods* could positively influence learning performance, whereas only instructional *methods* had an impact on (the quantitative analysis of) UX.

Further research is necessary to understand the contextual characteristics that could lead to these effects. Analysing implications from cross-cultural data on a larger scale would be the first step.

References

1. Andrade, P., Law, E.L.C., Farah, J.C., Gillet, D.: Evaluating the effects of introducing three gamification elements in STEM educational software for secondary schools. In: 32nd Australian Conference on Human-Computer Interaction, pp. 220–232 (2020)
2. Bedwell, W.L., Pavlas, D., Heyne, K., Lazzara, E.H., Salas, E.: Toward a taxonomy linking game attributes to learning: an empirical study. Simul. Gaming **43**(6), 729–760 (2012)
3. Brooke, J.: SUS: a 'quick and dirty' usability scale. In: Jordan, P.W., Thomas, B., McClelland, I.L., Weerdmeester, B.A. (eds.) Usability Evaluation in Industry, chap. 21, pp. 189–194. Taylor & Francis, London (1996)
4. Clark, R.E.: Learning from Media: Arguments, Analysis, and Evidence. IAP, Greenwich (2001)
5. Denny, P.: The effect of virtual achievements on student engagement. In: Proceedings of the SIGCHI Conference on Human Factors in Computing Systems, pp. 763–772. ACM, New York (2013)
6. DeSchryver, M., Spiro, R.J.: New forms of deep learning on the web: meeting the challenge of cognitive load in conditions of unfettered exploration in online multimedia environments. In: Web Technologies: Concepts, Methodologies, Tools, and Applications, pp. 2563–2581. IGI Global (2010)
7. Deterding, S., Björk, S.L., Nacke, L.E., Dixon, D., Lawley, E.: Designing gamification: creating gameful and playful experiences. In: CHI'2013 Extended Abstracts on Human Factors in Computing Systems, pp. 3263–3266 (2013)
8. Dichev, C., Dicheva, D.: Gamifying education: what is known, what is believed and what remains uncertain: a critical review. Int. J. Educ. Technol. High. Educ. **14**(1), 9 (2017)
9. Greenfield, P.M.: Technology and informal education: what is taught, what is learned. Science **323**(5910), 69–71 (2009)
10. Guay, F., Vallerand, R.J., Blanchard, C.: On the assessment of situational intrinsic and extrinsic motivation: the situational motivation scale (SIMS). Motiv. Emot. **24**(3), 175–213 (2000). https://doi.org/10.1023/A:1005614228250
11. Hamari, J., Koivisto, J., Sarsa, H.: Does gamification work?—A literature review of empirical studies on gamification. In: Proceedings of the 47th Hawaii International Conference on System Sciences, pp. 3025–3034. IEEE (2014). https://doi.org/10.1109/HICSS.2014.377
12. Jamison, D., Suppes, P., Wells, S.: The effectiveness of alternative instructional media: a survey. Rev. Educ. Res. **44**(1), 1–67 (1974)
13. Mayer, R.E.: The promise of multimedia learning: using the same instructional design methods across different media. Learn. Instr. **13**(2), 125–139 (2003)
14. O'Brien, H.L., Cairns, P., Hall, M.: A practical approach to measuring user engagement with the refined user engagement scale (UES) and new UES short form. Int. J. Hum. Comput. Stud. **112**, 28–39 (2018). https://doi.org/10.1016/j.ijhcs.2018.01.004

15. Sailer, M., Homner, L.: The gamification of learning: a meta-analysis. Educ. Psychol. Rev. **32**(1), 77–112 (2019). https://doi.org/10.1007/s10648-019-09498-w
16. Seaborn, K., Pennefather, P., Fels, D.I.: Reimagining leaderboards: towards gamifying competency models through social game mechanics. In: Proceedings of the First International Conference on Gameful Design, Research, and Applications, pp. 107–110 (2013)

JoyFlick: Japanese Text Entry Using Dual Joysticks for Flick Input Users

Kaisei Yokoyama[✉], Rei Takakura, and Buntarou Shizuki

University of Tsukuba, Tsukuba, Ibaraki, Japan
{kyokoyama,takakura,shizuki}@iplab.cs.tsukuba.ac.jp

Abstract. We show JoyFlick: A Japanese text entry method on game consoles with dual joysticks for flick-input users. To reduce the learning cost, the procedure of JoyFlick is designed based on a flick-input, which is a Japanese text entry method that approximately 80% of young Japanese people use daily on smartphones. The user using JoyFlick is able to enter a Japanese basic phonetic character with two joystick operations. In addition, JoyFlick's widgets spend a little amount of real estate on a screen, making it easy for developers to allocate space for other content. We conducted user studies that compared the performance of JoyFlick with a *Kana* syllabary keyboard, the de-facto standard for the Japanese text entry method on game consoles. The results showed the followings: (1) after training employing 28 phrases (289 characters, mean entry time = 373 s), the flick-input users using JoyFlick can enter texts faster than using the *Kana* syllabary keyboard; (2) the flick-input users can enter text using JoyFlick 1.53-fold faster (60.1 CPM) than the *Kana* syllabary keyboard (39.2 CPM) after one-week training in which the users enter texts less than 140 (M = 135) characters per day. These results show that JoyFlick provides a fast and easy Japanese text entry method to the flick-input users using the game controllers and yet spends a little amount of real estate on a screen.

Keywords: Game controller · Dual-joystick input · Circular keyboard layout

1 Introduction

Many people have game consoles. The game console users often enjoy text chat on games and share game clips on SNS. In addition, games involving several people are popular [8,9]; participants communicate via text or voice. In such games, users use voice chat or text chat. The use of voice chat is noisy for people around the user limiting the situations in which it can be used. Text chat

Electronic supplementary material The online version of this chapter (https://doi.org/10.1007/978-3-030-85613-7_8) contains supplementary material, which is available to authorized users.

C. Ardito et al. (Eds.): INTERACT 2021, LNCS 12934, pp. 107–125, 2021.
https://doi.org/10.1007/978-3-030-85613-7_8

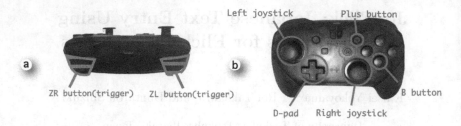

Fig. 1. Views of game controller (Nintendo Switch Pro Controller [16]). (a) Front view. (b) Top view.

is quieter than voice chat, although the text entry speed is slower. For these reasons, rapid text entry methods are required on game consoles.

Using a physical QWERTY keyboard is not always a good way for all game console users. To use a physical QWERTY keyboard, the users need to connect hardware keyboards to the game console. In addition, a physical keyboard is an extra device for game consoles. Thus, the user needs to pay extra costs for installation. On the other hand, the user can save these costs by using a soft keyboard: the user can enter texts using only the game controller (e.g., Fig. 1).

A *Kana* syllabary keyboard is the most popular soft keyboard for Japanese text entry on game consoles. The *Kana* syllabary keyboard has more than 50 keys and 1 cursor. After the user moves the cursor over keys to the desired key, the user pushes the button on the game controller to enter the character. The *Kana* syllabary keyboard has the advantage that any Japanese can understand how to use it at a glance since the *Kana* syllabary keyboard is designed based on a Japanese syllabary chart, which any Japanese learned in elementary school. However, it is difficult to manage many keys with a single cursor, as if a user uses a QWERTY keyboard with only one finger. In addition, since the *Kana* syllabary keyboard has many keys, it occupies almost half of the small game console screen. In such a case, we consider that the keyboard could hinder the user experience.

We built a new Japanese soft keyboard called JoyFlick. In order to become a new option for Japanese text entry on game consoles, JoyFlick was designed to meet the following requirements.

Simple entry: With a *Kana* syllabary keyboard, the user moves the cursor to the desired key to enter a character. The relative position of the cursor and the desired key determine the required operations. In most cases, entering a character contains "button-bashing" or long press and then opportune release. If the user can enter texts without these slow operations, the user can enter texts faster.

Low learning cost: Many users have been used to enter texts using a *Kana* syllabary keyboard. If the learning cost is lower, more users will use not *Kana* syllabary keyboard but JoyFlick.

Small widget: The size of the keyboard should be reduced to that of a *Kana* syllabary keyboard so that the screen is not covered as much as possible.

JoyFlick adopts dual joysticks for text entry. Most modern game controllers have two joysticks (like Fig. 1). In addition, most of the Japanese alphabet (*kana*) consists of 2 elements (consonant and vowel). Therefore, we mapped one joystick to consonant and the other joystick to vowel. The combination of two selected keys determines the character. JoyFlick adopts the key layout based on flick-input, which approximately 80% of young Japanese people use daily on the smartphone [12]. In addition, JoyFlick has only 15 keys; thus JoyFlick's widget can be smaller than the *Kana* syllabary keyboard.

The four main contributions of this research are:

- We designed a novel Japanese text entry method called JoyFlick using dual joysticks on the game controller.
- We showed that the text entry speed of the flick-input users using JoyFlick exceeds that of a *Kana* syllabary keyboard after 28 phrases of entry by user studies.
- We showed that the flick-input users can enter text using JoyFlick 1.53-fold faster (60.1 CPM) than *Kana* syllabary keyboard (39.2 CPM) after one-week training in which the users entered texts less than 140 (M = 135) characters per day by user studies.
- We showed that the learning cost of JoyFlick for flick-input users is less than the *Kana* syllabary keyboard by user studies.

2   Japanese Writing System

Consonants (Left chart)

	A	K	S	T	N	H	M	Y	R	W	
a	あ	か	さ	た	な	は	ま	や	ら	わ	
i	い	き	し	ち	に	ひ	み		り		
u	う	く	す	つ	ぬ	ふ	む	ゆ	る		
e	え	け	せ	て	ね	へ	め		れ		ん
o	お	こ	そ	と	の	ほ	も	よ	ろ	を	ー

Consonants (Right chart)

	Voiced letter				P-sound	Small letter		
	K*(G)	S*(Z)	T*(D)	H*(B)	H**(P)	A-	Y-	T-
a	が	ざ	だ	ば	ぱ	ぁ	ゃ	
i	ぎ	じ	ぢ	び	ぴ	ぃ		
u	ぐ	ず	づ	ぶ	ぷ	ぅ	ゅ	っ
e	げ	ぜ	で	べ	ぺ	ぇ		
o	ご	ぞ	ど	ぼ	ぽ	ぉ	ょ	

Fig. 2. Japanese syllabary charts. (Left) Basic letters only. (Right) Voiced letters, the P-sound, and small letters.

This section introduces the basis of Japanese text entry and the Japanese writing system [5]. Japanese text can be transcribed with *kana* and *kanji*. *Kana* are phonograms and *kanji* are ideograms derived from Chinese letters. Each *kanji* letter has (a) phonetic value(s) written using *kana* character(s). In most Japanese text entry systems, the user enters *kana* characters first. Then, the system displays candidates consisted of *kanji* character(s) and *kana* character(s) on the basis of the entered *kana* character(s), since there are multiple candidates because the relationship between *kana*(s) and *kanji* is many-to-many. The user selects the desired candidate to enter the required words that consist of *kana* characters and kanji letters (*kana-kanji* conversion).

Kana letters can be transcribed into one to three (M = 1.8) alphabetical letters following the Japanese syllabary chart (Fig. 2). Most basic *kana* letters ("Basic letter" in Fig. 2 left) consist of consonants and vowels (e.g., 'と' consists of 't' and 'o': 't' as the consonant and 'o' as the vowel). Some basic *kana* letters can be converted into the special *kana* letters by adding a symbol (e.g., 'と' can be converted into 'ど' by adding '*' as a symbol). In other words, the special *kana* letters consist of consonants, vowels, and symbols (e.g., 'ど' consists of 't', 'o', and '*', Fig. 2 right).

3 Related Work

Our work relates to the work on phonetics-based *kana* input (particularly, flick-input), text entry with a game controller, and the hybrid of both.

3.1 Phonetics-Based *Kana* Input

Since JoyFlick is a phonetic based *kana* input method, we describe popular methods in the same category used on personal computers, smartphones, and game consoles.

QWERTY. Japanese speakers usually use a QWERTY keyboard for *kana* input on personal computers. Some of them use a QWERTY keyboard on mobile devices.

A hardware QWERTY keyboard can be connected to game consoles such as Nintendo Switch [15] and PlayStation 4 [20] for *kana* input. However, it is not always a good way for all users due to the following reasons. First, these consoles are not sold with a keyboard; thus, the user needs to purchase a keyboard to use it on a game console. Second, the user must switch from the controller to the keyboard to enter text. Moreover, the user's posture and position are restricted to where the keyboard is placed. Third, young Japanese people are not very good at typing on a QWERTY keyboard [11]. For these reasons, Japanese people commonly use only the game controller to enter text with a soft keyboard.

Fig. 3. View of the *Kana* syllabary keyboard.

Syllabary. Nowadays, the typical text entry method for game controllers is an onscreen selection keyboard [21,22]. The user moves a cursor to the desired key using a joystick or a directional pad (D-pad) and then presses the key using a button. For English text entry, a QWERTY or alphabetical key layout is commonly used [10].

Similarly, an onscreen selection keyboard for Japanese text entry, whose the key layout looks similar to the syllabary chart (Fig. 2), is used. In this paper, we term this "*Kana* syllabary keyboard" (e.g., Fig. 3). Most Japanese can understand how to use it at the glance because an onscreen selection keyboard displays all characters users can input and because a *Kana* syllabary keyboard looks similar to the syllabary chart that anyone who has learned the Japanese language knows, which allows Japanese users to quickly recognize where the desired key is.

Although the above design of a *Kana* syllabary keyboard achieves low learning cost, the design can hinder the user experience. Since a *Kana* syllabary keyboard has more than 50 keys and the user manages any keys with a single cursor, text entry with the keyboard can be cumbersome because large distances have to be traversed between some keys. Moreover, the keyboard occupies almost half of the screen in some cases since it needs to display many keys.

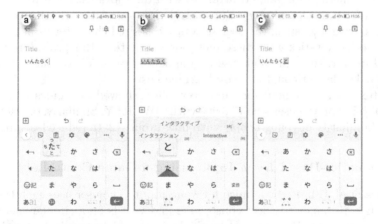

Fig. 4. Process of flick-input. (a) Pressing the 'た' key will provide feedback on characters that can be input by tapping or flicking the 'た' key. (b) Flicking the 'た' key downwards will input (c) "と".

Flick Input. Flick-input is one of the input methods widely used in touchscreen-equipped mobile devices [5]. Approximately 80% of young Japanese people use flick-input [12]. Flick-input has a 3 × 4 key layout, similar to the 3 × 4 key layout of old mobile phones. It adopts four-directional flick operations, which takes advantage of the characteristics of touchscreens and allows for gesture input. The user can perform five kinds of inputs for each key: tapping the key or flicking in four directions from the center of the key (left, up, right, or down).

With this design, the user can easily enter a basic *kana* letter by tapping or flicking a key once. For example, by flicking the 'た' key downwards, the user can enter "と" (Fig. 4). Converting a basic *kana* letter to a special *kana* letter requires flicking or tapping the '*' key. For example, flicking the 'た' key downwards and then tapping the '*' key once enter "ど".

Flick-Based Methods. Many techniques are aimed at improving flick input.

Blossom [17,18] supports *kana* input using flick operation on the soft QWERTY keyboard. After pressing the desired key to select the consonant, the user flicks the key to select the vowel. By contrast, JoyFlick's key layout is based on flick-input, not QWERTY.

A method proposed by Ikawa and Miyashita [7] and No-Look Flick [5] adopt flick operations for selecting both consonant and vowel on devices with touchscreens. We extend this approach to dual joysticks.

3.2   Text Entry with a Game Controller

Some text entry techniques for game controllers has been developed. Pizza-Text [24] is an English text entry using dual joysticks. TwoStick [10] is also a text entry method for game controllers with dual joysticks, which is designed to be used for English and many European languages. After selecting a group of characters using a joystick, the user selects the desired character from the group using the other joystick with these methods. We extend this procedure to *kana* input. Moreover, these methods use unique key layouts. We considered that an unfamiliar key layout could increase learning cost.

The text entry technique for game controllers showed by Sandes and Aubert et al. [19] relies on the user's familiarity with QWERTY. Similarly, our keyboard uses the familiarity of young people with flick-input [12] to reduce learning costs.

3.3   Phonetics-Based *Kana* Input using a Game Controller

Nakamura et al. [14] used two mice for *kana* input. The user uses each trackball of mice in both hands to select consonants and vowels on a circular menu. The key layout is unique. By contrast, JoyFlick uses joysticks to select slices instead of trackballs.

EGConvert [13] is a *kana* input method using dual joysticks. Two rings that surround a circle share a central point (Fig. 5). Both rings have eight slices. The outer ring, accessed using the left joystick, contains the consonant menu. The inner ring, accessed using the right joystick, contains the vowel menu. The ring arrangement reduces the size of widget, although it may increase the cognitive load on the user to map the left and right joysticks to the outer and inner rings [6]. In addition, the key layout is unique.

Fig. 5. View of the EGConvert when the user selects 'と' (T-o).

These methods use their original key layouts that should be unfamiliar to most users. By contrast, JoyFlick adopts the key layout of flick-input used by approximately 80% of young Japanese to reduce the user's learning cost.

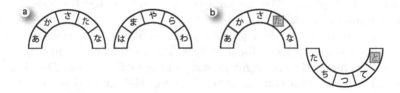

Fig. 6. Views of IToNe (a) when both sticks are in the neutral position and (b) when the user selects the 'と' (T-o) key.

IToNe [6] is also a *kana* input method using dual joysticks. The left and right half-rings are mapped to the left and right joysticks (Fig. 6). The user tilts one joystick upward to select a consonant and the other joystick downward to select a vowel. The inputs may be in either order. IToNe's key layout is based on the Japanese syllabary chart while JoyFlick's one is based on flick-input. In addition, IToNe's key layout has 5 duplications; that is, each of the 5 vowels has a corresponding key in both left and right bottom half rings. Since reducing these duplications make the slices larger, JoyFlick's key layout has no duplications.

4   JoyFlick

JoyFlick is a novel Japanese text entry method for game controllers. Approximately 80% of young Japanese uses flick-input; thus, JoyFlick adopts the flick-input key layout to save the user's learning costs. All keys can be selected in one operation. Specifically, to enter a basic *kana* character, the user selects two keys.

4.1   Key Layout

JoyFlick adopts a flick-input key layout modified for dual joysticks (Fig. 7). We consider that our key layout enables the flick-input user to save the learning

Left component   Right component

Fig. 7. JoyFlick's widget in the neutral position (both sticks) and descriptions.

costs. As described in Sect. 2, a combination of consonant and vowel determines a basic *kana* letter. Therefore, the consonant selected by one operation and the vowel selected by one operation derives the character. There are 10 consonants and 5 vowels in Japanese. We use joysticks to select the key because a joystick has a rich input vocabulary.

To treat the keys with dual joysticks, we modified flick-input's key layout. Figure 7 shows the key layout for JoyFlick. The right component and the left component are mapped to the right joystick and the left joystick. The right component corresponds to the consonant key layout of flick-input (Fig. 4c). However, the 'わ' key's position is different from the original: the 'わ' key is subscripted at the right of the 'な' key. This design gives the user the affordance, telling that the key can be selected with push-in. The left component corresponds to the vowel key layout of flick-input (Fig. 4a). In addition, no elevation angle of the joystick is used for key selection to reduce the required accuracy of operation for the user.

The consonant key layout has more keys than the vowel key layout; thus, the user needs to operate more precisely the former than the latter. We thus mapped the consonant key layout to the right joystick because most people are right-handed.

Special letters are entered by converting basic *kana* letters. JoyFlick adopts the ZR or ZL buttons for the conversion. This design allows the user to quickly convert a character to its special character by keeping their thumbs touching each joystick.

The user pushes the B button to backspace. It is the same button layout as the *Kana* syllabary keyboard to save the user's learning cost.

4.2   Entry Method

A *kana* character is entered in two operations. First, the user tilts or presses the right joystick to select the desired consonant. Second, the user tilts or pushes the left joystick to select the desired vowel. When the left joystick returns to neutral, the character is entered. The neutral position of the left joystick corresponds to "*no vowel*"; the neutral position of the right joystick to the consonant 'な' (N). The push-in of the right joystick corresponds to the consonant 'わ' (W) and

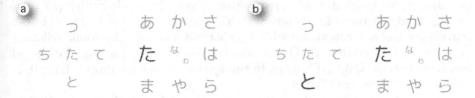

Fig. 8. JoyFlick's widget (a) when the user selects the 'た' key and (b) when the user selects the 'た' and 'お' keys to enter "と" (T-o).

the push-in of the left joystick corresponds to the vowel 'あ' (a). When a key is selected, the game controller briefly vibrates to give the user tactile feedback to notify the user that a key is selected. The user can enter a special *kana* character by pushing the ZR or ZL button after entering a basic character. For example, pushing the ZR or ZL button one or more times will convert "つ " (T-u) to "づ" (T*-u), "っ" (T~-u), and "つ" (T-u). The user backspaces by pushing the B button.

For example, to enter the character "と" (T-o), the user first selects the consonant 'た' (T) by tilting the right joystick to the left (Fig. 8a). After that, the user selects the vowel 'お' (o) (in other words, now the user selects the character "と" (T-o)) by tilting the left joystick down (Fig. 8b). In the end, the user enters "と" (T-o) by releasing the left joystick.

4.3 Design Features

As a new option of Japanese text entry on game consoles, JoyFlick has the following features:

Simple entry: A basic *kana* character is entered in two operations.
Low learning cost: JoyFlick's key layout is based on the key layout of flick-input used by approximately 80% of young Japanese people.
Small widget: Although a *Kana* syllabary keyboard has more than 50 keys, JoyFlick has only 15 keys except for modifier keys. Thus, the size of JoyFlick's widget is less than half of a *Kana* syllabary keyboard.

5 User Study 1

We initially compared the performance of JoyFlick beginners to that of a *Kana* syllabary keyboard (the de-facto standard for Japanese text entry on game consoles).

5.1 Participants

We enrolled 24 native Japanese speakers (19–25 years old, M = 21.8, SD = 1.19). 2 participants were female. 1 participant was left-handed, 23 were right-handed, and none have ambidexterity. 23 participants have a Nintendo Switch [15]. The average total play time of Nintendo Switch is 1.23×10^3 h (SD $= 1.19 \times 10^3$ h). No participant had any experience with JoyFlick; all had used the *Kana* syllabary keyboard of Nintendo Switch. On the smartphone, 18 participants use flick-input and the others use QWERTY daily. In this section, we call the former TARGET-USERS and the latter OTHERS.

12 participants joined the study online using Discord [2] as a COVID-19 precaution and the others came to our laboratory (and were thus offline).

5.2 Apparatus

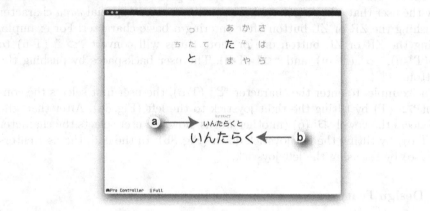

Fig. 9. Display during the tests. In this example, the participant was instructed to enter "いんたらくと" ("INTERACT") (a) and "いんたらぐ" ("INTERAC") has been entered (b). During the trainings, the text explaining how to complete the entry was additionally showed.

We developed a prototype system (Fig. 9), which runs on macOS and Windows 10, in Rust using joycon-rs [23]. We implemented JoyFlick and a *Kana* syllabary keyboard in the system. A Nintendo Switch Pro Controller [16] (Fig. 1) served as the input device, which was connected to the participants' computer via Bluetooth. We distributed the prototype system to the online participants.

5.3 Task

Displayed phrases were transcribed. Entry was completed by pushing the Plus button (Fig. 1). All participants were instructed to enter the text as quickly and accurately as possible. The participants could use the B button to correct errors, although this was not compulsory.

5.4   Procedure

Each participant completed two sessions of text transcription. One session was for JoyFlick and the other was for the *Kana* syllabary keyboard. Each session consisted of training and test. We counterbalanced the session and phrase orders to neutralize any effects of learning and fatigue.

We first explained the purpose of the study. We then used a questionnaire to gather participant demographics. Before each session, we explained how to use the relevant keyboard. All participants then transcribed all phrases, which consisted of basic and special *kana* characters and the "prolonged sound" character marks ("—"). We prepared 28 phrases with 289 characters for training and 24 phrases with 167 characters for test. In total, each participant was required to enter the following amount of characters:

$$2\,\text{sessions} \times (289\,\text{characters} + 167\,\text{characters}) = 912\,\text{characters}.$$

All participants completed two sessions within 1 h.

5.5   Results and Analysis

We measured the text entry speed and accuracy. Characters per Minute (CPM) was used as the metric of text entry speed because Japanese text is not written with a space between words. Total Error Rate (Total ER) and Minimum String Distance Error Rate (MSD ER) [1] were used as the metric of text entry accuracy. The methods tested (2 levels) and daily *kana* entry methods into smartphones (2 levels: TARGET-USERS and OTHERS) were the independent variables. The dependent variables were CPM, Total ER, and MSD ER. We used a two-way ANOVA test followed by the post-hoc analysis using Tukey's HSD test for CPM. Since Shapiro-Wilk tests showed that Total ER and MSD ER had no normality, we used Steel-Dwass tests for Total ER and MSD ER. Only the test data were analyzed.

Online vs. Offline. No statistically significant differences were shown in CPM (Welch's t-test), Total ER (Wilcoxon-Mann-Whitney test), and MSD ER (Wilcoxon-Mann-Whitney test) between online and offline participants.

Speed. The text entry speeds are shown in Fig. 10, 11 and 12. During the tests, the text entry speeds were 42.8 CPM (SD = 8.98 CPM) in JoyFlick and 37.2 CPM (SD = 5.96 CPM) in *Kana* syllabary keyboard; the difference was statistically significant ($p < 0.05, F_{1,44} = 10.4, \eta^2 = 0.166$). Statistically significant differences were shown between TARGET-USERS and OTHERS in JoyFlick ($p < 0.05, d = 1.16$) and JoyFlick and the *Kana* syllabary keyboard in TARGET-USERS ($p < 0.05, d = 1.20$).

JoyFlick was faster than the *Kana* syllabary keyboard for most phrases (Fig. 10). TARGET-USERS' curve attained 40 CPM in 15 phrases, whereas OTHERS' curve could not attain 40 CPM in the test (Fig. 11).

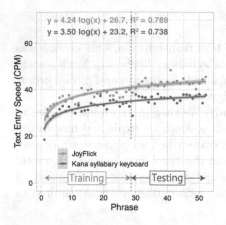

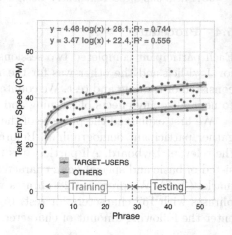

Fig. 10. Average text entry speeds using JoyFlick and *Kana* syllabary keyboard. The gray bands show 95% confidence interval.

Fig. 11. Average JoyFlick text entry speeds of TARGET-USERS and OTHERS. The gray bands show 95% confidence interval.

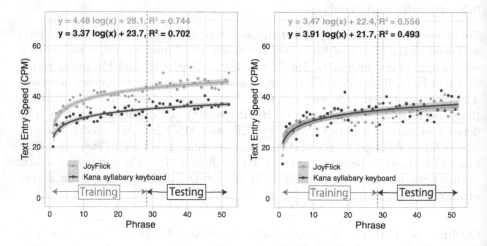

Fig. 12. Average text entry speeds using JoyFlick and *Kana* syllabary keyboard of (left) TARGET-USERS and (right) OTHERS. The gray bands show 95% confidence interval.

Accuracy. The Total ERs were 8.22% (SD = 3.90%) in JoyFlick and 5.29% (SD = 7.75%) in the *Kana* syllabary keyboard for the tests. Statistically significant difference ($p < 0.05, d = 0.315$) was shown between TARGET-USERS using JoyFlick (8.22%, SD = 3.46%) and TARGET-USERS using the *Kana* syllabary keyboard (6.05%, SD = 8.83%). The difference between TARGET-USERS using JoyFlick and OTHERS using the *Kana* syllabary keyboard (3.02%, SD = 1.63%) was also statistically significant ($p < 0.05, d = 1.60$). The MSD ERs were 0.648% (SD = 0.965%) in JoyFlick and 0.749% (SD = 0.955%) in the *Kana* syllabary keyboard. The MSD ER differences were not significant. We observed that JoyFlick's Total ER tended to be higher than the *Kana* syllabary keyboard and that JoyFlick's MSD ER tended to be lower than the *Kana* syllabary keyboard.

Table 1. The correlation coefficients between total play time; and the CPM, Total ER, and MSD ER.

		CPM	Total ER	MSD ER
JoyFlick	TARGET-USERS	0.321	−0.415	−0.041
	OTHERS	0.480	0.036	−0.583
Kana syllabary keyboard	TARGET-USERS	0.155	0.009	−0.183
	OTHERS	−0.256	0.023	−0.473

Total Play Time. The correlation coefficients between the total play time of Nintendo Switch; and the CPM, Total ER, and MSD ER are listed in Table 1.

5.6 Discussion

Speed. The results showed that TARGET-USERS, even with little experience, were faster in JoyFlick than the *Kana* syllabary keyboard. In addition, the results showed that the learning cost of JoyFlick for TARGET-USERS is less than for OTHERS: TARGET-USERS learned JoyFlick very quickly.

Accuracy. The results of MSD ER showed that the text transcripted using JoyFlick was as accurate as using the *Kana* syllabary keyboard. The Total ER and MSD ER suggested that JoyFlick was more error-prone; however, mistakes were easily corrected by backspacing.

Total Play Time. Overall, the correlations between the total play time and the other metrics were weak, suggesting that the effect of total play time on performance was minimal.

6 User Study 2

Participants used JoyFlick and the *kana* syllabary keyboard daily for 7 days.

6.1   Participants

We enrolled 15 native Japanese speakers (20–25 years old, M = 21.9, SD = 1.28). All participants were male. 1 participant was left-handed, 14 were right-handed, and none have ambidexterity. All participants owned a Nintendo Switch [15]. The average total play time of Nintendo Switch was 1.52×10^3 h (SD = 1.39×10^3 h). All participants had been enrolled in the User Study 1. On the smartphone, 11 participants used flick-input and 4 used QWERTY daily. In this section, we call the former TARGET-USERS and the latter OTHERS.

6.2   Apparatus, Task, and Procedure

The apparatus, task, and procedure were as described above with the following exceptions:

- All participants completed 1 session daily; both JoyFlick and the *Kana* syllabary keyboard were tested; the order of text entry methods was randomly determined.
- We prepared the phrase set that includes 60 phrases with 451 characters for the test.
- All participants entered approximately 18 phrases (i.e., 135 characters) for each method.
- All participants engaged in 1 session once daily for 7 consecutive days.
- After the last session, all participants completed questionnaires about preference.
- In total, each participant was required to enter approximately the following amount of characters:

$$7 \text{ sessions} \times 2 \text{ methods} \times 135 \text{ characters} = 1890 \text{ characters}.$$

All participants completed a session within 15 min.

6.3   Results and Analysis

The analysis was as described above with the following exceptions:

- The methods tested (2 levels), the daily *kana* entry methods into smartphones (2 levels: TARGET-USERS and OTHERS), and the number of sessions (7) were the independent variables.
- The main effects were tested via a three-way repeated measures ANOVA for CPM.
- Since Shapiro-Wilk tests showed that Total ER and MSD ER had no normality, we tested Total ER and MSD ER of the last sessions using Steel-Dwass tests.

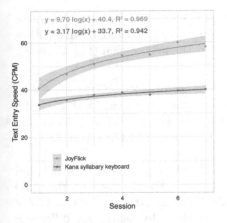

Fig. 13. Average text entry speeds for JoyFlick and *Kana* syllabary keyboard. The gray bands show 95% confidence interval.

Fig. 14. Average JoyFlick text entry speeds of TARGET-USERS and OTHERS. The gray bands show 95% confidence interval.

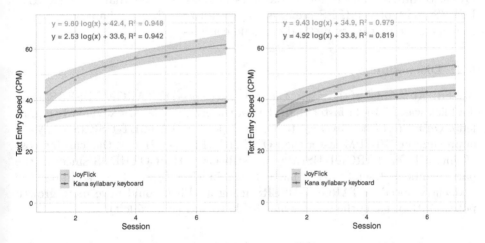

Fig. 15. Average text entry speeds for JoyFlick and *Kana* syllabary keyboard of (left) TARGET-USERS and (right) OTHERS. The gray bands show 95% confidence interval.

Speed. The text entry speeds are shown in Fig. 13, 15 and 15. The main effect of sessions was statistically significant ($p < 0.005, F_{1,189} = 118, \eta^2 = 0.102$). A statistically significant difference was evident between JoyFlick and the *Kana* syllabary keyboard ($p < 0.005, d = 7.11$). During the last test, the average text entry speeds of TARGET-USERS were 60.1 CPM (SD = 11.8 CPM) in JoyFlick and 39.2 CPM (SD = 7.45 CPM) in the *Kana* syllabary keyboard. Statistically significant differences were evident between TARGET-USERS and OTHERS in JoyFlick ($p < 0.005, d = 0.624$) and between JoyFlick and the *Kana* syllabary keyboard of TARGET-USERS ($p < 0.005, d = 2.03$).

At the last test, the text entry speed in JoyFlick was 1.45-fold faster than the *Kana* syllabary keyboard (Fig. 13). The text entry speed of OTHERS in JoyFlick overtook that in the *Kana* syllabary keyboard at the first session (Fig. 15 right).

Accuracy. During the last test, the Total ERs were 11.2% (SD = 6.49%) in JoyFlick and 2.53% (SD = 12.2%) in *Kana* syllabary keyboard. A statistically significant difference was shown between JoyFlick (11.3%, SD = 7.53%) and the *Kana* syllabary keyboard (2.35%, SD = 1.15%) in TARGET-USERS ($p < 0.005, d = 1.60$).

For the first test, the MSD ERs were 2.82% (SD = 1.13%) in JoyFlick and 2.11% (SD = 3.30%) in the *Kana* syllabary keyboard. For the last test, the MSD ERs were 1.13% (SD = 8.31×10^{-1}%) in JoyFlick and 0.244% (SD = 3.57×10^{-1}%) in the *Kana* syllabary keyboard. A statistically significant difference was shown between JoyFlick (1.15%, SD = 0.705%) and the *Kana* syllabary keyboard (0.265%, SD = 0.368%) in TARGET-USERS ($p < 0.05, d = 1.51$).

Questionnaire. The result of the questionnaire showed that all TARGET-USERS and 2 of OTHERS preferred JoyFlick to the *Kana* syllabary keyboard as a Japanese text entry method on game consoles.

6.4   Discussion

Speed. At the end of the study, the text entry speed of TARGET-USERS using JoyFlick was 1.53-fold faster than that of the *Kana* syllabary keyboard (Fig. 15 left). On all tests, the average text entry speed of TARGET-USERS is always approximately 10 CPM faster than OTHERS (Fig. 14). Hence, the learning cost of JoyFlick for TARGET-USERS was still lower than OTHERS since all the participants in User Study 2 participated in User Study 1. In addition, the text entry speed of TARGET-USERS using JoyFlick could have more growth potential than using the *Kana* syllabary keyboard (Fig. 15 left).

Accuracy. Although the MSD and Total ERs of JoyFlick tended to be higher than those of the *Kana* syllabary keyboard, neither error level would be fatal. During the last test, almost all JoyFlick entry errors were corrected (MSD ER 1.13%). In addition, since the CPM includes the correction time, the results showed that JoyFlick was faster than the *Kana* syllabary keyboard, even with corrections. We consider that the increased speed (53.3% for TARGET-USERS and 25.0% for OTHERS) outweighs the reduced accuracy (Total ER = 8.64% and MSD ER = 0.886%).

Questionnaire. TARGET-USERS preferred JoyFlick. OTHERS stated that they would likely to use JoyFlick, which is consistent with the result where the text entry speed of OTHERS in JoyFlick was faster than the *Kana* syllabary keyboard even at the first session.

7   Discussion and Future Work

7.1   Input Method Editor

While our two user studies showed that JoyFlick has a good text entry performance, incorporating Input Method Editor (IME) into JoyFlick could further improve performance. Japanese text contains several kinds of characters (e.g., *kana*, *kanji*, numbers, symbols, and emoji). The user uses IME, which is a part of an input method, to convert *kana* characters to other kinds of characters. Moreover, a contemporary IME has a feature of autocorrection so that some *kana* entry errors are tolerable. Therefore, IME could compensate for lower accuracy in text entry with JoyFlick. Therefore, evaluating the performance of JoyFlick and the *Kana* syllabary keyboard with IME by user studies is our important future work to examine the feasibility of JoyFlick.

7.2   User-Defined Key

8 participants of User Study 1 found it difficult to push in the joysticks. 3 participants of User Study 1 suggested that the functions of the left and right joysticks should be swapped. 1 participant of the study suggested user-defined keys would be valuable (this is common in shooting games [3,4]). Therefore, user-defined key mapping might improve user experience.

7.3   Other Contexts

JoyFlick was designed for Japanese text entry on game consoles; it could be useful in other contexts. For example, JoyFlick could be used for text entry in virtual reality. While an English text entry method for virtual reality using dual joysticks already exists [24], evaluating the performance using JoyFlick in virtual reality by user studies is left for our future work.

7.4   Combination of JoyFlick and *Kana* Syllabary Keyboard

Since JoyFlick and the *Kana* syllabary keyboard have their strengths, it would be desirable that both are implemented on game consoles. The former would be better when speed is required (e.g., text chat and posting entries of more than two phrases). The latter would be better when accuracy is essential (e.g., SSID and password entry and entering a short phrase such as a name). However, frequent switching between methods increases the cost of text entry. We conjecture that the user chooses a method based on the context of text entry. Presetting the appropriate method for each text entry beforehand could save the cost of switching between different methods.

8   Conclusion

We presented a Japanese text entry method on game consoles with dual joysticks for flick-input users, which we call JoyFlick. We designed JoyFlick so that a basic *kana* character is entered in two operations of joysticks. In addition, we adopted the key layout based on that of flick-input used by approximately 80% of young Japanese people to lower the learning cost. Furthermore, JoyFlick has only 15 keys except for modifier keys; thus, JoyFlick occupies the screen space less than half of a *Kana* syllabary keyboard (the de-facto standard for Japanese text entry on game consoles). Our user studies showed that (1) text entry using JoyFlick became faster than the *Kana* syllabary keyboard after training using only 28 phrases; (2) JoyFlick users entered text 1.53-fold faster (60.1 CPM) than the *Kana* syllabary keyboard (39.2 CPM) after one week of training (entry of fewer than 140 characters/day). These results suggest that JoyFlick is a fast, easy, and unobtrusive Japanese text entry method on game consoles.

References

1. Arif, A.S., Stüerzlinger, W.: Analysis of text entry performance metrics. In: 2009 IEEE Toronto International Conference Science and Technology for Humanity, TIC-STH '09, pp. 100–105 (2009). https://doi.org/10.1109/TIC-STH.2009. 5444533
2. Discord Inc.: Discord—Your Place to Talk and Hang Out. https://discord.com/. Accessed 27 Jan 2021
3. Electronic Arts Inc.: Apex Legends - The Next Evolution of Battle Royale - Free on Playstation® Xbox, and PC. https://www.ea.com/games/apex-legends. Accessed 27 Jan 2021
4. Fortnite—Free-to-Play Cross-Platform Game - Fortnite: Epic Games, Inc. https:// www.epicgames.com/fortnite/. Accessed 27 Jan 2021
5. Fukatsu, Y., Shizuki, B., Tanaka, J.: No-look flick: single-handed and eyes-free japanese text input system on touch screens of mobile devices. In: Proceedings of the 15th International Conference on Human-Computer Interaction with Mobile Devices and Services, MobileHCI 2013, pp. 161–170. Association for Computing Machinery, New York (2013). https://doi.org/10.1145/2493190.2493243
6. Go, K., Konishi, H., Matsuura, Y.: IToNe: a Japanese text input method for a dual joystick game controller. In: Proceedings of CHI '08 Extended Abstracts on Human Factors in Computing Systems, CHI EA 2008, pp. 3141–3146 (2008). https://doi. org/10.1145/1358628.1358821
7. Ikawa, Y., Miyashita, H.: "Direction Only" flick-input method for shorthand with eyes-free. In: Proceedings of Interaction 2013, pp. 651–656 (2013). http://www. interaction-ipsj.org/archives/paper2013/data/Interaction2013/interactive/data/ pdf/3EXB-22.pdf
8. Innersloth: Among Us for Nintendo Switch - Nintendo Game Details. https://www. nintendo.com/games/detail/among-us-switch/. Accessed 27 Jan 2021
9. Innersloth: Among Us on Steam. https://store.steampowered.com/app/945360/ Among_Us/. Accessed 27 Jan 2021
10. Költringer, T., Isokoski, P., Grechenig, T.: TwoStick: writing with a game controller, pp. 103–110 (2007). https://doi.org/10.1145/1268517.1268536

11. Kojima, K.: On the information literacy of the net generation in the BYOD era. J. Nagoya Gakuin University. Soc. Sci. **52**(3), 45–57 (2016). https://doi.org/10. 15012/00000619. (in Japanese)
12. Nagasawa, N.: How Japanese university students type on smartphone and PC. Comput. Educ. 67–72 (2017). https://doi.org/10.14949/konpyutariyoukyouiku.43. 67. (in Japanese)
13. Nakamura, K.: Character input control method, program, record media and character input device (2002). https://patents.google.com/patent/JP2002268818A/
14. Nakamura, S., Tsukamoto, M., Shojiro, N.: A text input method using the double-mouse for wearable computing environments. Technical report, IPSJ SIG Technical Report (1999). https://ipsj.ixsq.nii.ac.jp/ej/index.php?active_action=repository_view_main_item_detail&page_id=13&block_id=8&item_id=37112&item_no=1
15. Nintendo: Nintendo Switch™ Family – Official Site. https://www.nintendo.com/ switch/. Accessed 27 Jan 2021
16. Nintendo: Pro Controller. https://store.nintendo.com/pro-controller.html. Accessed 27 Jan 2021
17. Sakurai, Y.: keroxp/Blossom-iOS: SoftwareKeyboard for iOS. https://github.com/ keroxp/Blossom-ios. Accessed 27 Jan 2021
18. Sakurai, Y., Masui, T.: Blossom - Flick-based Japanese Input System on QWERTY keyboard. Technical report, IPSJ (2013). http://id.nii.ac.jp/1001/00094712/
19. Sandnes, F.E., Aubert, A.: Bimanual text entry using game controllers: relying on users' spatial familiarity with QWERTY. Interact. Comput. **19**(2), 140–150 (2007). https://doi.org/10.1016/j.intcom.2006.08.003. HCI Issues in Computer Games
20. Sony Interactive Entertainment LLC: PS4—Incredible games, non-stop entertainment—PlayStation. https://www.playstation.com/en-us/ps4/. Accessed 27 Jan 2021
21. Wilson, A.D., Agrawala, M.: Text entry using a dual joystick game controller. In: Proceedings of the SIGCHI Conference on Human Factors in Computing Systems, CHI '06, pp. 475–478. Association for Computing Machinery, New York (2006). https://doi.org/10.1145/1124772.1124844
22. Wobbrock, J.O., Myers, B.A., Aung, H.H.: Writing with a joystick: a comparison of date stamp, selection keyboard, and EdgeWrite. In: Proceedings of Graphics Interface 2004, pp. 1–8. Canadian Human-Computer Communications Society, Waterloo (2004)
23. Yokoyama, K.: KaiseiYokoyama/joycon-rs: Joy-Con library for Rust. https:// github.com/KaiseiYokoyama/joycon-rs. Accessed 27 Jan 2021
24. Yu, D., Fan, K., Zhang, H., Monteiro, D., Xu, W., Liang, H.: PizzaText: text entry for virtual reality systems using dual thumbsticks. IEEE Trans. Vis. Comput. Graph. **24**(11), 2927–2935 (2018). https://doi.org/10.1109/TVCG.2018.2868581

MuseFlow: Facilitating Mind-Wandering Through Video Games

Juan F. Olaya-Figueroa$^{(\boxtimes)}$ (iD), Younes Lakhnati$^{(\boxtimes)}$, and Jens Gerken$^{(\boxtimes)}$

Human-Computer Interaction Group, Westphalian University of Applied Sciences, Neidenburger Str. 43, 45897 Gelsenkirchen, Germany
{juan.olaya,younes.lakhnati,jens.gerken}@w-hs.de

Abstract. Mind-wandering, i.e., letting the mind drift away from the task at hand, is mostly seen as a state of mind to avoid, as it may negatively impact the current task. However, evidence in cognitive science shows that mind-wandering can also positively affect creativity and problem-solving. Still, there is a lack of technological solutions to facilitate and utilize mind-wandering in such a specific way. In this short paper, we present MuseFlow, a video game designed to facilitate mind-wandering deliberately. Our study shows that MuseFlow induces mind-wandering significantly more often compared to a demanding game condition while maintaining the players' motivation to play and succeed in the game.

Keywords: Mind-wandering · Creativity · Problem-solving · Game mechanics · Video game · Creativity support tools · Serious games

1 Introduction and Motivation

Creativity is the ability to generate novel and useful ideas, for example as a means to solve problems with unusual solutions [5,38]. Likewise, creativity is a valuable asset when attempting to solve individual and social issues [4]. There are some analog techniques to unlock it such as outdoor walking [17] or sleeping [35], both activities which try to involve the mind in task-unrelated thoughts. Such task-unrelated thoughts, often referred to as mind-wandering or daydreaming [27], are a mental phenomenon in which attention is reallocated from the task at hand to unrelated-thoughts without leaving the task [2,29], this is the opposite construct of Flow [8] or Mindfulness [24], since both practices are associated with being completely immersed in the process of the current activity that concerns us. Among others, Baird et al. [3] were able to show strong indications for a positive direct connection between mind-wandering and creativity. They furthermore found that the effect of mind-wandering is larger when invoked through an

This research is funded by Ministry of Economic Affairs, Innovation, Digitalisation and Energy, North-Rhine Westphalia, Germany (MWIDE NRW).

C. Ardito et al. (Eds.): INTERACT 2021, LNCS 12934, pp. 126–135, 2021.
https://doi.org/10.1007/978-3-030-85613-7_9

undemanding task compared to a demanding task or even compared to resting. Seli et al. showed that people can modulate their mind-wandering during an undemanding task as long as they can anticipate the upcoming challenges [21].

In this paper, we present the first results of a research endeavour, which aims at transferring these research insights into a usable everyday tool. As such, we developed MuseFlow, a video game that aims at facilitating mind-wandering using undemanding game mechanics while keeping the participants still engaged. In this short paper, we present the Museflow game design based on game mechanics we identified as potentially undemanding. We conducted a study to investigate if MuseFlow induces mind-wandering significantly more often compared to a demanding game condition, while not negatively affecting the players' motivation to play and succeed in the game.

2   Related Work

2.1   Mind-Wandering

Mind-wandering also known as task-unrelated thought [29], self-generated thought [1], stimulus-unrelated thought [32], absent-mindedness [7] or daydreaming [26] is a cognitive phenomenon in which the attention is assigned to inner thoughts while performing an external task. Evidence indicates that mind-wandering is present between 30 and 50% of our waking life [12]. In the literature there are some hypotheses about *how* mind-wandering occurs. One of the most featured is the Meta-Awareness Hypothesis, which proposes that mind-wandering is the result of a temporal dissociation of meta-awareness, i.e., a lack of monitoring one's mind, which can happen even during tasks that one regards as important [20]. Although there is no definitive explanation about *why* mind-wandering happens, there are some factors that can affect the occurrence of mind-wandering, such as: tiredness [36], task difficulty [22] and working memory capacity [12].

2.2   Incubation Effect

The incubation effect refers to putting an unsolved problem aside for a period of time and returning to it later, making it easier to find a solution to it [9,37]. In a meta-analytic review, Sio et al. found a greater positive incubation effect when people perform an undemanding task during the incubation interval than when people are involved in resting or in demanding tasks [28].

One example of the relation between the incubation effect and mind-wandering is the study "Inspired by Distraction: Mind Wandering Facilitates Creative Incubation" of Baird et al. [3]. In this study, the authors used the creativity task called Unusual Uses Task (UUT) [11] to measure divergent thinking. In this task, the participants had to provide as many unusual uses as possible for an everyday object, like a pencil, for two minutes. Then, they immediately had to put it aside for twelve minutes. During this incubation interval, participants had to carry out one of the following conditions: perform a demanding task, perform an undemanding task, or sit quietly while taking a break. When the incubation interval finished, the participants went back to the same UUT problem and worked again for two minutes. The study showed that the group who performed the undemanding task exhibited the highest improvement rate in the postincubation, suggesting that mind-wandering caused by the undemanding task facilitates creative thinking.

3   MuseFlow Game Design

MuseFlow is a video game deliberately designed to facilitate mind-wandering and keep the players motivated. In this game, the player moves a ball horizontally across the moving bars. The game is over when the player gets a flag after crossing multiple platforms towards the right (see Fig. 1). The following are the four main game mechanics that define MuseFlow:

- Predictability and Segmented Interaction: Seli et al. demonstrated that people could modulate their mind-wandering during an undemanding task, especially when the upcoming challenges can be anticipated. Indeed, in that study it was shown that participants pressed a button and then were able to continue mind-wandering in the order of seconds, due to the anticipation signal of a timer [21]. In MuseFlow, the bars move up and down periodically with a constant speed, it makes the players wait and anticipate the right moment to press the button and jump to the next bar (Fig. 1A).
- Absence of competition: Although competing against other players and getting more assets during a video game are essential parts of a video game [19], some of them do not use these properties. For instance, Proteus [10], Playne [25] and Journey [33] use the progression and exploration of virtual worlds to engage the players. We defined MuseFlow as a non-competitive single player experience. The scorecard on the top right only shows the number of crossed platforms.
- Absence of a failure: Similarly, penalties such as going back to the beginning of the level or decreasing the amount of health of the main avatar are common punishments after making mistakes gaming. There are also video games such as The Longing [23], Dear Esther [34] and Pause [6,18] that lack these failure properties. For example, in The Longing the avatar should cross between rooms and waits until the king awakens without any risk of failure or any penalty. In MuseFlow, there is no risk of failure during the game; even when the ball falls in a gap (e.g. Fig. 1C), immediately the system restart the ball on the previous bar without any penalty
- Simple controls: This concept is related to the fact that mind-wandering is associated with a low level of task difficulty [21] and with the tendency of mind-wandering when performing a practiced task [15]. For this purpose, we limit MuseFlow to use only the left and right arrows to play the game.
- Visual Appearance: MuseFlow uses a minimalist and geometric aesthetics with a black background in order to avoid extra stimuli.

Overall, the game should be an undemanding experience that can induce mind-wandering in the player while still keeping them motivated. In order to study this, we developed a second version of the game as a demanding condition. This included two fundamental changes:

- Increased Game Speed: In the demanding condition platforms moved on average 5.3 times faster. This resulted in less waiting time as well as requiring more attention in order not to miss a platform.
- Increased Challenges: Gaps between platforms were introduced that required players to precisely find the point in motion when to move the ball towards the next platform so it does not fall in the gap.

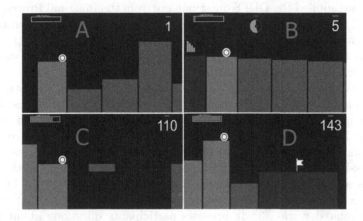

Fig. 1. The game prototype. The player character is represented by the white ball. The rectangular bars are the platforms that move up and down - traversed platforms turn red. A composite image of four game screenshots. The game looks like this: A black background with grey bars in the foreground that represent the platforms - it looks like a bar chart. A white ball is positioned on the leftmost platform. There is a game progress bar at the top left and a Score counter in the top right. 4A: Shows the start of the game with the ball sitting on the first platform. 4B: On the far left, there is an Orange stair symbol which represents the Stair power-up. The white ball is past the power-up and in front of it, the bars have taken on a down-ward stair structure. 4C: The ball is waiting in front of a gap. A floating platform is coming from the right. 4D: On the far right there is the final platform colored in blue with a white flag on top of it.

4 Study Method and Design

To evaluate if and how the MuseFlow game would be able to facilitate mind-wandering, we conducted a remote study with 36 participants (13 female, 23 male). The 2020 Covid-19 pandemic led to the decision to run the study remotely and not in a lab. We used the online platform Survey Circle [31] to recruit participants. The age ranged from 20–44 years old, with one participant being older than 60 and the median age group being 25–29 years. Most participants were from central Europe. We did not request further details from participants to follow the GDPR principle of data economy. We applied a between-subjects design with the type of game (Undemanding, Demanding) as independent variable. We decided against a within-subjects design as this would include a game learning experience. Being more familiar with the game could, in turn, increase the chance for mind-wandering, independent of the experimental condition.

4.1 Dependent Variables and Measures

- Daydreaming Frequency Scale (DDFS): In order to measure the general mind-wandering propensity of our participant sample and based on existing literature [3], we applied the DDFS questionnaire from the Imaginal Process Inventory (IPI) [27,30]. The DDFS produces a score between 12 (low propensity) and 60 (high propensity).
- Thought Probes: A Thought Probe is a typical measure of mind-wandering activity adapted from the literature [13,14,16,21], we prompted the user during the game with a pop-up question "Just now, where was your attention?" with a 6-point scale from "on task" (1) to "off task" (6). For scores above 3, this Thought Probe was tagged as a mind-wandering episode. Overall, five Thought Probes were distributed evenly across the game experience.
- From the Dundee Stress State Questionnaire (DSSQ) - TUT: we applied the Task-irrelevant Interference from part 4 (Thinking Content) of the DSSQ, which is also referred to as task-unrelated thinking (TUT) in the literature. This is a retrospective measure for mind-wandering activity that was also used in related work [3]. It presents participants questions about specific examples of off-task thoughts. We wanted to understand if MuseFlow would also induce longer-lasting off-task thoughts that participants would still be aware of after playing the game. The DSSQ-TUT produces a score between 8 (no task-unrelated thinking) and 40 (high task-unrelated thinking).
- From the Dundee Stress State Questionnaire (DSSQ) - Motivation: This part from the DSSQ (with sub-scales for Intrinsic and Success Motivation) was used as a measure to analyze how engaged participants were in playing the game. The DSSQ-Motivation scales each produce a score between 7 (low motivation) and 35 (high motivation). The results should indicate if there is a difference in motivation between MuseFlow and the demanding game condition, i.e. if the undemanding game characteristics had a negative impact on the overall motivation.
- Missed Opportunities: To check if our two game versions did indeed differ in terms of demand, we logged the number of times a participant could have moved on to the next platform but hesitated or oversaw that opportunity. This number should consequently be higher for the Demanding condition of the game, which moves much faster.

4.2   Procedure

Participants were randomly and evenly assigned to one of the conditions, based on the internal ID they received on the SoSci Survey platform. After filling out the consent form and the demographic questionnaire, participants were politely asked turn off their mobile phones and not engage in any activities outside the game. A short description explained the controls of the game and the overall goal as moving the ball towards the right until a flag signals the end of the game. Following that, the participants would play the game until completion (ca. 10 min). During that time, at five separate set intervals, the game would be paused and a Thought Probe would pop-up with a 6-point scale, asking the participant whether their current thoughts were "on task" (1) or "off task" (6) [14]. Upon answering, the dialogue would close and the game would resume. Before the start of the experiment, the participants were not made aware of the interruption through Thought Probes. When the participant reached the flag, the game ended and participants would be forwarded to the two DSSQ scales, followed by the DDFS (ca. 9 min). The overall duration was around 19 min.

5   Results and Discussion

As our data, while being of metric scale, was mostly not normally distributed, we decided to analyze it through the means of non-parametric test statistics.

First, we take a look at the DDFS results to understand the mind-wandering propensity in our participant sample. The descriptive data shows that mind-wandering propensity is slightly above average (40, DDFS range: 12–60) but similar for both groups (Undemanding $m = 39.39; SD = 10.80; Md = 40$ and Demanding $m = 40.22; SD = 10.87; Md = 44$). Accordingly, the Mann-Whitney-U does not show any significant differences ($z = -0.143; p = 0.887; N = 36$).

Looking at the number of missed opportunities, participants on average missed many more opportunities during the Demanding condition of the game (see Table 1). This difference is statistically significant as shown by the Mann-Whitney-U test ($z = -4.619; p < 0.001; N = 36$). As a result, we can conclude that our goal of creating a demanding version of MuseFlow was successful.

Next, the DSSQ motivation scales (range 7–35) tell us that the two experimental groups did not significantly differ in terms of their intrinsic and success motivation to play the game (see Table 1). Accordingly, these results suggest that the mind-wandering characteristics of the Undemanding MuseFlow game did not reduce motivation to play the game.

Addressing our main research question, whether the game design was able to induce mind-wandering episodes in participants, we have two different measures. Starting with the Thought Probes, we counted the number of mind-wandering episodes for each participants. As such, we regarded each probe with a *score* > 3 on the $6 - point - scale$. Only Probes 2–5 were taken into account as Probe 1 was meant to get participants accustomed to this type of measurement. The descriptive data suggests that the Undemanding condition ($m = 1.72$ episodes)

Table 1. The average and mean scores for the DSSQ Motivation and TUT scale, Missed Opportunities and the average and median number of mind-wandering episodes per participant (Thought Probes).

DSSQ-motivation and missed opportunities					
Condition	Measure	n	Mean	Median	SD
Undemanding	Missed Opp.	18	1.17	0.00	4.22
	DSSQ Intrinsic Mot	18	18.89	19.50	4.13
	DSSQ Success Mot	18	18.89	17.00	5.80
	DSSQ-TUT	18	14.89	15.00	5.03
	Thought Probes	18	1.72	1.00	1.60
Demanding	Missed Opp.	18	15.33	13.50	9.16
	DSSQ Intrinsic Mot	18	20.33	21.50	3.29
	DSSQ Success Mot	18	17.78	16.00	7.13
	DSSQ-TUT	18	14.83	13.50	3.03
	Thought Probes	18	0.44	0.00	1.04

led to more mind-wandering episodes compared to the Demanding condition ($m = 0.44$ episodes; Table 1). Accordingly, the Mann-Whitney-U test shows a significant difference between the conditions ($z = -0.291; p = 0.04; N = 36$). The histogram shows that 14 participants in the demanding condition did not report any mind-wandering episodes at all and only 1 participant experienced 3 or 4 mind-wandering episodes compared to 7 in the MuseFlow undemanding condition (see Fig. 2).

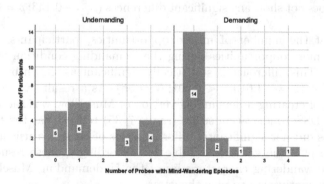

Fig. 2. The distribution and frequency of mind-Wandering episodes across the two conditions

The Thinking Content Scale of the DSSQ (DSSQ-TUT: range 8–40) does not show any significant differences between the groups (Mann-Whitney-U test: $p = 0.89$). Descriptive data shows that both conditions seemed to induce the same and relatively low amount of such long-lasting task-unrelated thoughts (Table 1). We conclude that the MuseFlow game is currently not capable to induce the type of task-unrelated thoughts that participants can later attribute to coherent thoughts and ideas.

6 Limitations

As an exploratory research into a new field, we would see most limitations as inspiration for future research. For example the inconclusive results regarding the amount of mind-wandering activity between the Thought Probes and the DSSQ-TUT scale hints that there are different levels of mind-wandering and it may be important to better understand how to evoke which level. As a remote study, we were not fully in control of any external factors that may have influenced our results. We designed the study as a rather short and concise experience to limit such effects. Future research should still aim to replicate these results in a lab environment and with larger sample sizes to increase statistical power.

7 Conclusion and Future Work

Inspired by the research of Baird et al. [3], who suggests mind-wandering can be beneficial for creative problem solving, we designed MuseFlow, a game that is deliberately designed to facilitate mind-wandering. In our study, we compared MuseFlow to a more demanding version of the game. Our results show that MuseFlow was indeed able to induce significantly more mind-wandering episodes compared to the demanding condition without showing a decrease in participants' motivation to play the game. However, the mind-wandering episodes measured through Thought Probes are not reflected in the retrospective DSSQ-TUT measurement. We conclude that these mind-wandering episodes are therefore rather short and volatile. This can be attributed to the game design, which allowed participants only to briefly abstain from the task, not allowing for more coherent off-task thinking and long term mind-wandering. We are not aware of existing research that would allow to make inferences regarding what kind of mind-wandering is necessary to facilitate problem solving and creativity. Therefore, these results require more research regarding the nature of mind-wandering episodes.

Overall, this work is a first step to better understand this relatively new field of research by investigating the processes and interaction mechanics which might induce mind-wandering. Our future work will in particular focus on analyzing the impact on creative problem solving that can be achieved through such game experiences. For that, we will also elaborate the game design, for example by increasing the motivational aspects, and the influence of different game mechanics on mind-wandering. The MuseFlow code is available as Open Source[1] and we invite interested researchers to contribute to this endeavor.

---

[1] MuseFlow repository: https://github.com/JuanOlaya/MuseFlow.

References

1. Andrews-Hanna, J.R., Reidler, J.S., Huang, C., Buckner, R.L.: Evidence for the default network's role in spontaneous cognition. J. Neurophysiol. **104**(1), 322–335 (2010). https://doi.org/10.1152/jn.00830.2009
2. Antrobus, J.S., Singer, J.L., Goldstein, S., Fortgang, M.: Mindwandering and cognitive structure. Trans. N. Y. Acad. Sci. **32**(2), 242–252 (1970). https://doi.org/10.1111/j.2164-0947.1970.tb02056.x
3. Baird, B., Smallwood, J., Mrazek, M.D., Kam, J.W.Y., Franklin, M.S., Schooler, J.W.: Inspired by distraction: mind wandering facilitates creative incubation. Psychol. Sci. **23**(10), 1117–1122 (2012). https://doi.org/10.1177/0956797612446024
4. Barbot, B., Besançon, M., Lubart, T.: Creative potential in educational settings: its nature, measure, and nurture. Education 3–13 **43**(4), 371–381 (2015). https://doi.org/10.1080/03004279.2015.1020643
5. Boden, M.A.: Dimensions of Creativity. MIT Press, Cambridge (1994). https://doi.org/10.7551/mitpress/2437.001.0001. First mit press papterback edition
6. Cheng, P., Lucero, A., Buur, J.: PAUSE: exploring mindful touch interaction on smartphones (2016)
7. Cheyne, J.A., Carriere, J.S.A., Smilek, D.: Absent-mindedness: lapses of conscious awareness and everyday cognitive failures. Conscious. Cogn. **15**(3), 578–592 (2006). https://doi.org/10.1016/j.concog.2005.11.009
8. Csikszentmihalyi, M., Csikzentmihaly, M.: Flow: The Psychology of Optimal Experience, vol. 1990. Harper & Row New York (1990)
9. Dobson, C., Christoff, K.: Productive mind wandering in design practice. In: Creativity and the Wandering Mind, pp. 271–281. Elsevier (2020)
10. Key, E., Kanaga, D.: Proteus. Game [Steam], January 2013
11. Guilford, J.P.: The nature of human intelligence (1967)
12. Kane, M.J., Brown, L.H., McVay, J.C., Silvia, P.J., Myin-Germeys, I., Kwapil, T.R.: For whom the mind wanders, and when: an experience-sampling study of working memory and executive control in daily life. Psychol. Sci. **18**(7), 614–621 (2007). https://doi.org/10.1111/j.1467-9280.2007.01948.x
13. Laflamme, P., Seli, P., Smilek, D.: Validating a visual version of the metronome response task. Behav. Res. Methods **50**(4), 1503–1514 (2018). https://doi.org/10.3758/s13428-018-1020-0
14. Levinson, D.B., Smallwood, J., Davidson, R.J.: The persistence of thought: evidence for a role of working memory in the maintenance of task-unrelated thinking. Psychol. Sci. **23**(4), 375–380 (2012). https://doi.org/10.1177/0956797611431465
15. Mason, M.F., Norton, M.I., van Horn, J.D., Wegner, D.M., Grafton, S.T., Macrae, C.N.: Wandering minds: the default network and stimulus-independent thought. Science (New York N.Y.) **315**(5810), 393–395 (2007). https://doi.org/10.1126/science.1131295
16. Morrison, A.B., Goolsarran, M., Rogers, S.L., Jha, A.P.: Taming a wandering attention: short-form mindfulness training in student cohorts. Front. Hum. Neurosci. **7**, 897 (2014). https://doi.org/10.3389/fnhum.2013.00897
17. Oppezzo, M., Schwartz, D.L.: Give your ideas some legs: the positive effect of walking on creative thinking. J. Exp. Psychol. Learn. Mem. Cogn. **40**(4), 1142–1152 (2014). https://doi.org/10.1037/a0036577
18. PauseAble: Pause. [Mobile app] (2015)
19. Rouse, R., Ogden, S.: Game design: Theory & practice. Wordware Game Developer's Library, Wordware Publ., Plano (2005)

20. Schooler, J.W.: Re-representing consciousness: dissociations between experience and meta-consciousness. Trends Cogn. Sci. **6**(8), 339–344 (2002). https://doi.org/ 10.1016/S1364-6613(02)01949-6
21. Seli, P., Carriere, J.S.A., Wammes, J.D., Risko, E.F., Schacter, D.L., Smilek, D.: On the clock: evidence for the rapid and strategic modulation of mind wandering. Psychol. Sci. **29**(8), 1247–1256 (2018). https://doi.org/10.1177/0956797618761039
22. Seli, P., Konishi, M., Risko, E.F., Smilek, D.: The role of task difficulty in theoretical accounts of mind wandering. Conscious. Cogn. **65**, 255–262 (2018). https:// doi.org/10.1016/j.concog.2018.08.005
23. Seufz, S.: The Longing. Game [Steam], March 2020
24. Shapiro, S.L., Carlson, L.E., Astin, J.A., Freedman, B.: Mechanisms of mindfulness. J. Clin. Psychol. **62**(3), 373–386 (2006)
25. Shrikumar, K.: PLAYNE: the meditation game. Game [Steam], June 2018
26. Singer, J.L.: Daydreaming: an introduction to the experimental study of inner experience (1966)
27. Singer, J.L., Antrobus, J.S.: Daydreaming, imaginal processes, and personality: a normative study (1972)
28. Sio, U.N., Ormerod, T.C.: Does incubation enhance problem solving? A meta-analytic review. Psychol. Bull. **135**(1), 94–120 (2009). https://doi.org/10.1037/ a0014212
29. Smallwood, J., Schooler, J.W.: The restless mind. Psychol. Bull. **132**(6), 946–958 (2006). https://doi.org/10.1037/0033-2909.132.6.946
30. Stawarczyk, D., Majerus, S., van der Linden, M., D'Argembeau, A.: Using the daydreaming frequency scale to investigate the relationships between mind-wandering, psychological well-being, and present-moment awareness. Front. Psychol. **3**, 363 (2012). https://doi.org/10.3389/fpsyg.2012.00363
31. SurveyCircle: The largest community for online research (2020). https://www. surveycircle.com/
32. Teasdale, J.D., et al.: Stimulus-independent thought depends on central executive resources. Mem. Cogn. **23**(5), 551–559 (1995). https://doi.org/10.3758/bf03197257
33. Thatgamecompany, Santa Monica Studio: Journey. Game [PlayStation 3], March 2012. Directed by Jenova Chen
34. The Chinese Room, Robert Briscoe: Dear Esther. Game [Steam], February 2012
35. Wagner, U., Gais, S., Haider, H., Verleger, R., Born, J.: Sleep inspires insight. Nature **427**(6972), 352–355 (2004). https://doi.org/10.1038/nature02223
36. Walker, H.E., Trick, L.M.: Mind-wandering while driving: the impact of fatigue, task length, and sustained attention abilities. Transp. Res. F: Traffic Psychol. Behav. **59**, 81–97 (2018). https://doi.org/10.1016/j.trf.2018.08.009
37. Wallas, G.: The art of thought (1926)
38. Woolley, J.D., Bunce, L., Boerger, E.A.: Relations between imagination and creativity. In: Creativity and the Wandering Mind, pp. 181–203. Elsevier (2020)

Gesture Interaction

Fingerprint Scroll: Comparison of Touchless and Touch-Based Scroll Navigation Methods

Saurabh Garg$^{(\boxtimes)}$ and Scott Mackenzie$^{(\boxtimes)}$

York University, Toronto, ON M3J 1P3, Canada
mack@cse.yorku.ca

Abstract. We conducted a user study comparing the efficiency and speed of three scroll navigation methods for touch-screen mobile devices: Tap Scroll (the traditional touch-based method), Kinetic Scroll (a touch-based gestural method), and Fingerprint Scroll (our newly introduced hybrid method). The study involved 12 participants and employed a Google *Pixel* device. The accuracy results for Fingerprint Scroll were higher, with an average accuracy of 97.6% compared to 96.3% for Tap Scroll and 88.7% for Kinetic Scroll. The completion time for Fingerprint Scroll was 2.43 times longer than that for Kinetic Scroll and 2.32 times longer than for Tap Scroll. Despite the long completion times, participants showed a preference for Fingerprint Scroll because of ease-of-use, high accuracy, and interruption-free vision while reading ebooks. The latter is a significant issue for Kinetic and Tap Scroll because gestures are touch-based and hence the display view is obscured. Participants did not value the higher speed of navigation using Kinetic Scroll over Fingerprint Scroll for web browsing.

Keywords: Fingerprint scroll · Fingerprint sensor · Scroll navigation · Scroll method · Mobile interaction · Hybrid interaction · Human - computer interaction

1 Introduction

Mobile devices such as tablets, phones, handhelds, or personal digital assistants (PDAs), provide easy and convenient access to information at the tap of your finger virtually anywhere and anytime. However, the small screen and limited input capabilities impact the user experience with these devices. This is additionally muddled by the very idea of these gadgets – versatility and mobility. Mobile phones are frequently utilized in dynamic and busy environments, for example, while walking, running, standing, etc. This makes designing interaction techniques for mobile phones difficult and challenging. The classical techniques used on a desktop computer may not be always accurate.

© IFIP International Federation for Information Processing 2021
Published by Springer Nature Switzerland AG 2021
C. Ardito et al. (Eds.): INTERACT 2021, LNCS 12934, pp. 139–150, 2021.
https://doi.org/10.1007/978-3-030-85613-7_10

1.1   Input Styles for Mobile Devices

A significant challenge with mobile devices is providing appropriate input that is easy to use and can accurately work on tasks. Numerous tasks such as target selection, text entry, or navigating user interfaces are challenging. Broadly speaking, input styles can be classified into three categories: software, hardware, and hybrid. Hardware-based input methods utilize physical components on the device. Software-based input methods are built inside real applications such as touch software buttons or scrollbars. Hybrid-based input methods combine the approaches from software and hardware input techniques.

Hardware-Based Input. Most mobile phones have hardware components and accessories to provide different kinds of inputs. For example, physical buttons can be programmed as a "home" button or a "mode" button suitable for different purposes depending on the context. Hence, the button is not fixed absolutely but changes based on the current perspective of the screen. Another example is a scroll wheel for navigating a document vertically. In 1996, Rekimoto introduced the idea of navigating using the device itself and added a sensor that would detect device tilt and rotation when the user moved the device [16]. Figure 1 demonstrates the use of tilt for navigating a map. The utilization of tilt for navigation and selection tasks [1–3,6,7] and text input on mobile devices [13,20] has been explored extensively. Researchers have combined tilt with other external inputs like buttons [13,19], gestures, and other sensors [9]. A key advantage of hardware-based input interactions is that they can provide single-handed interaction. NaviPoint [9] and ScrollPad [4] are other examples of hardware-based inputs.

Software-Based Input. Software-based input ordinarily utilizes a stylus or finger on a touch-sensitive display. For general navigation in smartphones, the most common strategy uses scrollbars that are created in software. Even though this technique is familiar to most users, it has limitations on the desktop [22]. Using the same technique on a mobile device is challenging. A study by Smith and schraefel [18] identified three ways of user interaction with scrollbars and potential challenges with each. Figure 2 illustrates the operation of a scrollbar. Users can drag the handle of the scrollbar by maintaining constant pressure on the button of the mouse. This might result in skipping important parts caused by users unintentionally or letting go of the thumb and skipping the desired parts of the document. Due to smaller screen sizes, this problem can become even more critical on mobile devices. Secondly, users can click on the arrow buttons at each end of the scrollbar to move the document. But, this can be slow and tiring. Users can also click positions on the scrollbar to jump to a particular segment of the document. But, this can be disorienting [3,22] and the problem is compounded on smaller screens. Scrollbars require the user to draw their attention from the document to a software-designed scrollbar which may require additional cognitive effort and motor resources. Also, scrollbars restrict movement to a single direction (i.e., horizontal or vertical).

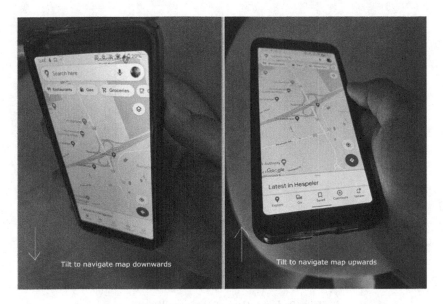

Fig. 1. Navigation of map by tilting a display.

Another software-based method for navigation on a mobile device is tap-and-drag. This technique requires the user to tap anywhere on the screen with a stylus and drag in the display area in any direction. This is a familiar interaction for desktop users. Johnson [8] compared different drag techniques with edge navigation on a touch screen and found that users were faster and had a preference for drag to navigate. One major disadvantage of using dragging is that it is not suitable for documents containing many selection targets. Also, dragging is limited by the size of the screen as users can only drag in increments of screen size [10]. Research has also studied the use of touch gestures on mobile devices. For example, Harrison et al. [6] used finger gestures to mimic flipping pages in a digital document. The advantage of software-based input is that it is built into the application itself and can use paradigms similar to a desktop application. The main drawback is that these interactions often require the use of both hands. Sometimes users prefer to hold a device with one hand while the other hand interacts with the device to avoid missing targets.

Hybrid-Based Input. Hybrid methods for scrolling combine external hardware-based input with software-based input. Usually, this involves using the hand to hold the mobile device while navigating displayed information (e.g., tilt) and using the freehand to make selections. Peephole displays [21] utilize a spatially-aware device that is moved to reveal different parts of an information space while making selections with a stylus. Eslambolchilar and Murray-Smith [2] and Eslambolchilar et al. [3] coupled an SDAZ (speed-dependent automatic

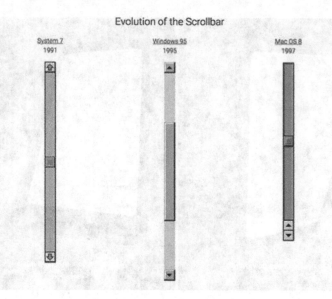

Fig. 2. Evolution of the scrollbar.

zooming) system with tilt to navigate and scroll through information while using a stylus for selection.

Interaction techniques for mobile devices all face the common challenge of needing to be used while the user is mobile. In general, it is hard for users to navigate and select items while mobile, regardless of the input method they are using. Research has shown that tactile [15] or audio feedback [3,14] can improve users' accuracy and efficiency when performing navigation and selection tasks.

We introduce a new method called Fingerprint Scroll that utilizes a hybrid approach using an external hardware fingerprint sensor placed on a mobile device. In most devices, it exists on the rear of a mobile device. It does not block the user's view of the display while in use. Swiping up on the sensor scrolls up the page and swiping down on the sensor scrolls down the page. For comparison, we will also include two other methods for scroll navigation. Kinetic Scroll utilizes swipe gestures on the screen to navigate and scroll. Tap Scroll is another method that uses on-screen taps over arrow buttons to scroll in the desired direction.

In this paper, we evaluate and compare the performances of touch-based and touch-less scroll navigation methods. We compare the three scroll methods mentioned above. The results obtained are presented after that.

2   Related Work

Table 1 summarizes the results from four papers where user studies were performed utilizing scroll navigation methods.

Table 1. Summary of results from four papers where user studies were performed utilizing scroll navigation methods.

1st author	Type	n	Notes
Smith [18]	Touch	8	Radial Scroll performs better than traditional methods on short scroll target acquisition
MacKay [10]	Touch	18	The techniques of touch-n-go and tap-and-drag outperformed the traditional scrollbar technique for the simple navigation tasks
Moscovich [11]	Touch	10	The virtual scroll ring is a tenable scrolling alternative. This is especially true when most scrolling actions are expected to be longer than half a page
Oakley [12]	Touchless	12	User performance using the position-based input was good and provided promise, and allowed us to select optimum parameters for position-based list navigation

n = number of participants

Smith [18] assessed a scroll navigation method called *radial scroll*, which was effective for variable fast document scrolling for touch screen devices. He also anticipates improving radial scrolling by presenting distant headings and giving the user the ability to change aspects of the scrolling mid-scroll, such as switching between per-line verses per-page scrolling.

MacKay [10] compared software-based navigation techniques with the new *touch-n-go* approach on a mobile device. In terms of preference, users found *touch-n-go* easier than the *scrollbar* and *tap-and-drag* methods during multiple levels of mobility. Participants achieved better performance while sitting but were considerably slower while walking for all of the navigation techniques.

Moscovich [11] assessed the virtual scroll ring as a tenable scrolling alternative. This was especially true when scrolling is longer than half a page. In the case of smaller than a half-page, extra care should be taken to ensure that enough data is collected for a robust estimate of the circle. Since the virtual scroll ring scrolls the view smoothly in increments as small as one pixel, it allows users to read the text while they scroll.

Oakley [12] believed position-based input mapping had considerable potential. One reason is that users can learn to reach specific list items, which in turn, may lead to an open loop interaction, where an item can be selected with confidence without explicitly requiring feedback from the system. It would also be interesting to look at the implications of using this input technique with nested menu systems, where multiple selections are made to reach a single goal. In conclusion, the author believed that interfaces based around motion input and vibrotactile output have an important role in next-generation mobile interaction techniques.

3   Methodology

A user study was conducted to compare the three scroll navigation methods. The goal was to compare the three scroll methods in terms of quantitative measures, user preference, and ease of use.

3.1   Participants

Twelve participants were recruited remotely from different universities across Canada. Six were male, six were female. Ages ranged from 22 to 26 years. All participants were comfortable with using smartphones. All were right-handed and sat during testing. Participants were constrained to use only a single hand. They had prior experience of using the Kinetic Scroll method but no prior experience in using Tap Scroll or Fingerprint Scroll method. Participants were compensated $20 for their assistance.

3.2   Apparatus

The experiment was conducted on Google *Pixel 3a* running the Android 11.0 operating system. The device has a 5.6-in. OLED display with a resolution of 2220×1080 pixels and a density of 441 PPI. The weight of the device is 147 g.

The software was developed in Java using the Android SDK in the Android Studio. This experimental application was developed specifically for this research. Three scroll methods were implemented. The application begins with a configuration activity that prompts the user to select the participant code and other experimental parameters, like input method, session code, group code (for counterbalancing). Once configured, the user presses the SUBMIT button to initiate the testing process. The main activity contains a scrolling user interface. See Fig. 3.

3.3   Procedure

Participants were informed and explained the purpose of the user study. They were requested to keep the Internet switched on during the entire experiment. Participants watched a video explaining the interaction methods and did some practice trials. They were asked to use just one hand for all interactions. Arm support was not allowed. With this brief introduction, testing began. Participants completed five blocks for each method. A block consists of five trials. A participant took about 15–20 min to complete the experiment. The data were stored in a remote database in Google *Firebase* and analyzed later for results and meaningful insights. After testing was complete, the user was prompted with a questionnaire to gather feedback regarding the preference of scroll methods. Participants were asked the following questions -

– How many hours do you use a smartphone per day?
– Do you regularly use a smartphone?

Fig. 3. Main activity for the scroll navigation application

- Do you browse the web on a smartphone?
- Do you read books on your smartphone?
- Which method would you prefer for web browsing?
- Which method would you prefer for reading books?
- Overall preference of method on a scale of 1 (Least likely) to 5 (most likely) for scroll method?

3.4 Design

The experiment was a 3 × 5 within-subjects design with the following independent variables and levels:

- Scroll Method: Kinetic Scroll, Tap Scroll, Fingerprint Scroll
- Block Code: 1, 2, 3, 4, 5

Each participant completed five blocks of five trials for each scroll method. As such, the total number of trials was 12 Participants × 3 Scroll Methods × 5 Blocks × 5 Trials = 900.

Participants were counterbalanced using a Latin square method. The application grouped the participants into three groups using a group code assigned to every participant. Each group tested in a specific sequence of scroll methods. The dependent variables were completion time (s) and error rate (%). The duration of the experiments was roughly one hour per participant.

4   Results and Discussion

All trials were completed successfully. The data were later imported into a spreadsheet tool where summaries of various measures were calculated and charts were created. The analysis of variance[1] test was performed using the GoStats[2] application.

4.1   Completion Time

The grand mean for completion time was 13.62 s. From Fig. 4, we observe that Tap Scroll took 4.71% more time to complete a similar trial than Kinetic Scroll. The completion time of Fingerprint Scroll was 2.43 times longer than that of Kinetic Scroll and 2.32 times longer than Tap Scroll.

The effect of the group on completion time was not statistically significant ($F_{2,9} = 0.494$, ns), thus indicating that counterbalancing had the desired effect of offsetting order effects. The effect of scrolling method on completion time was statistically significant ($F_{2,18} = 1099.3$, $p < .0001$). The Scrolling Method × Group interaction effect was not statistically significant, however ($F_{4,18} = 0.357$, ns). A Fisher LSD post hoc pairwise comparison test indicated a significant difference between the Fingerprint Scroll method and each of the Kinetic Scroll and Tap Scroll methods ($p < .05$).

The effect of block on completion time was statistically significant ($F_{4,36} = 4243.7$, $p < .0001$). The Block × Group interaction effect was not statistically significant ($F_{8,36} = 0.241$, ns). The Scrolling Method × Block interaction effect was statistically significant ($F_{8,72} = 375.2$, $p < .0001$).

4.2   Error Percentage

Errors were logged when a user fails to do a task correctly. For example, the task can be "go to page 6 and come back to page 1". If the user goes to a different page than instructed, it counts as an error. Error percentage is the percentage of total such error cases with respect to total cases. The effect of group on error percentage was not statistically significant ($F_{2,9} = 0.150$, ns). The effect of scrolling method on error percentage was statistically significant ($F_{2,18} = 73.50$, $p < .0001$). The scrolling method × group interaction effect was also not statistically significant ($F_{4,18} = 0.288$, ns). The Fisher LSD pairwise comparison

---

[1] A parametric analysis of variance was used even though the data did not meet the underlying distribution assumptions. There are a few reasons for this. The dependent variables were all ratio-scale user performance measurements, as opposed to measurements on an interval or ordinal scale. So, a parametric test, which is intended for ratio-scale data, is the natural test to use. Notably, as well, using the parametric analysis of variance avoids the inevitable loss of information that occurs when ratio-scale data are down-graded to ranks for a non-parametric test. Finally, the parametric analysis of variance is known to be robust to violations in the underlying distribution assumptions [5, 17].

[2] http://www.yorku.ca/mack/GoStats/.

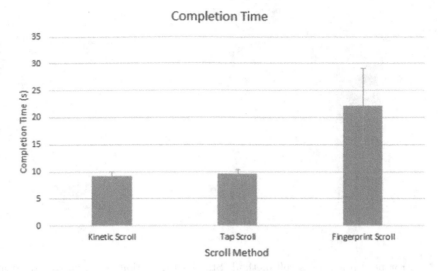

Fig. 4. Completion time by scroll method. Standard deviation is shown as red error bars.

test revealed a significant difference between the Kinetic Scroll method and each of the Tap Scroll and Fingerprint Scroll methods ($p < .05$).

The error percentage differences between different methods can also be talked about in terms of accuracy. More error percentage leads to lower accuracy.

From the graph in Fig. 5, The accuracy results for fingerprint scroll were higher, with an average accuracy of 97.6% compared to 96.3% for tap scroll and 88.67% for Kinetic Scroll.

4.3 Participant Feedback

In the post-experiment questionnaire, participants were asked their preference of the scroll navigation method on a scale of 1 (least likely) to 5 (most likely), and their answers were recorded. Using a Friedman test, the differences in opinion were statistically significant ($\chi^2 = 15.54$, $p = .0004$). The standard deviation for the preference rating of the kinetic scroll, tap scroll, fingerprint scroll was recorded as 0.37, 0.58, and 0.62. Using a post hoc test, it was also observed that all three pairwise comparisons were statistically significant. See Table 2.

Most participants stated that they found kinetic scroll frustrating to use while reading ebooks since it blocks the view and creates a bad user experience. Most preferred using Fingerprint Scroll as it does not block the vision and they do not consider the speed that important for a majority of tasks like reading ebooks or web browsing. One participant noted:

Fingerprint Scroll is great as I read a lot of books on my phone during commuting. I don't want to see the finger coming in my way of vision all the time.

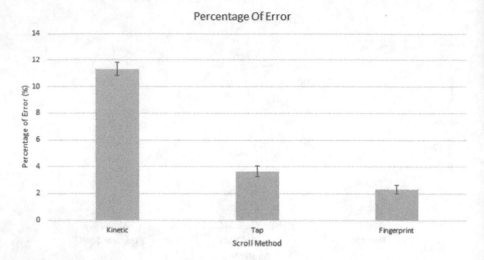

Fig. 5. Error percentage by scroll method. Standard deviation is shown as red error bars.

Overall participants praised Fingerprint scrolling and Kinetic Scroll in a majority for various usage. The average rating for Fingerprint Scroll, Tap Scroll, and Kinetic scroll was 4.3, 3, and 4.1 on a scale of 1–5.

Table 2. Post-hoc pairwise comparison test of scroll methods.

Comparison	Difference	Significance
Kinetic vs *Tap*	$abs(2.708 - 1.125) > 0.422$	Significant
Kinetic vs *Fingerprint*	$abs(2.708 - 2.167) > 0.422$	Significant
Tap vs *Fingerprint*	$abs(1.125 - 2.167) > 0.422$	Significant

5   Conclusion

A user study was conducted comparing the performance of three scroll navigation methods. The results indicated higher accuracy for our newly introduced method (Fingerprint Scroll) compared to two alternatives. The accuracy for fingerprint scroll was higher, with an average accuracy of 97.6% compared to 96.3% for tap scroll and 88.67% for Kinetic Scroll. The completion time was relatively long for Fingerprint Scroll compared to other traditional alternatives like Kinetic Scroll. Overall participants gave a favorable and preferential rating for Fingerprint Scroll for ebook reading and web browsing over mobile devices.

References

1. Bartlett, J.F.: Rock'n'scroll is here to stay. IEEE Comput. Graphics Appl. **20**(3), 40–45 (2000)
2. Eslambolchilar, P., Murray-Smith, R.: Tilt-based automatic zooming and scaling in mobile devices – a state-space implementation. In: Brewster, S., Dunlop, M. (eds.) Mobile HCI 2004. LNCS, vol. 3160, pp. 120–131. Springer, Heidelberg (2004). https://doi.org/10.1007/978-3-540-28637-0_11
3. Eslambolchilar, P., Williamson, J., Murray-Smith, R.: Multimodal feedback for tilt controlled speed dependent automatic zooming. In: Proceedings of Annual ACM Symposium on User Interface Software and Technology - UIST 2004. ACM, New York (2004)
4. Fallman, D., Lund, A., Wiberg, M.: Scrollpad: tangible scrolling with mobile devices. In: Proceedings of the 37th Annual Hawaii International Conference on System Sciences, p. 6. IEEE, New York (2004)
5. Glass, G.V., Hopkins, K.D.: Statistical Methods in Education and Psychology, 3rd edn. Prentice-Hall, Englewood Cliffs (2008)
6. Harrison, B.L., Fishkin, K.P., Gujar, A., Mochon, C., Want, R.: Squeeze me, hold me, tilt me! An exploration of manipulative user interfaces. In: Proceedings of the ACM SIGCHI Conference on Human Factors in Computing Systems - CHI 1998, pp. 17–24. ACM, New York (1998)
7. Igarashi, T., Hinckley, K.: Speed-dependent automatic zooming for browsing large documents. In: Proceedings of the 13th Annual ACM Symposium on User Interface Software and Technology - UIST 2000, pp. 139–148. ACM, New York (2000)
8. Johnson, J.A.: A comparison of user interfaces for panning on a touch-controlled display. In: Proceedings of the ACM SIGCHI Conference on Human Factors in Computing Systems - CHI 1995, pp. 218–225. ACM, New York (1995)
9. Kawachiya, K., Ishikawa, H.: NaviPoint: an input device for mobile information browsing. In: Proceedings of the ACM SIGCHI Conference on Human Factors in Computing Systems - CHI 1998, pp. 1–8. ACM, New York (1998)
10. MacKay, B., Dearman, D., Inkpen, K., Watters, C.: Walk'n scroll: a comparison of software-based navigation techniques for different levels of mobility. In: Proceedings of the 7th International Conference on Human-Computer Interaction with Mobile Devices & Services, pp. 183–190. ACM, New York (2005)
11. Moscovich, T., Hughes, J.F.: Navigating documents with the virtual scroll ring. In: Proceedings of the 17th Annual ACM Symposium on User Interface Software and Technology - UIST 2004, pp. 57–60. ACM, New York (2004)
12. Oakley, I., O'Modhrain, S.: Tilt to scroll: evaluating a motion based vibrotactile mobile interface. In: First Joint Eurohaptics Conference and Symposium on Haptic Interfaces for Virtual Environment and Teleoperator Systems. World Haptics Conference, pp. 40–49. IEEE, New York (2005)
13. Partridge, K., Chatterjee, S., Sazawal, V., Borriello, G., Want, R.: TiltType: accelerometer-supported text entry for very small devices. In: Proceedings of the 15th Annual ACM Symposium on User Interface Software and Technology - UIST 2002, pp. 201–204. ACM, New York (2002)
14. Pirhonen, A., Brewster, S., Holguin, C.: Gestural and audio metaphors as a means of control for mobile devices. In: Proceedings of the ACM SIGCHI Conference on Human Factors in Computing Systems - CHI 2002, pp. 291–298. ACM, New York (2002)

15. Poupyrev, I., Rekimoto, J., Maruyama, S.: TouchEngine: a tactile display for hand-held devices. In: Proceedings of Extended Abstracts of the ACM SIGCHI Conference on Human Factors in Computing Systems - CHI EA 2002, pp. 644–645. ACM, New York (2002)
16. Rekimoto, J.: Tilting operations for small screen interfaces. In: Proceedings of the 9th Annual ACM Symposium on User Interface Software and Technology - UIST 1996, pp. 167–168. ACM, New York (1996)
17. Sheskin, D.: Handbook of Parametric and Non-parametric Statistical Procedures, 5th edn. CRC Press, Boca Raton (2011)
18. Smith, G.M., schraefel, m.: The radial scroll tool: scrolling support for stylus-or touch-based document navigation. In: Proceedings of the 17th Annual ACM Symposium on User Interface Software and Technology - UIST 2004, pp. 53–56 (2004)
19. Weberg, L., Brange, T., Hansson, Å.W.: A piece of butter on the PDA display. In: Proceedings of the Extended Abstracts of the ACM SIGCHI Converene on Human Factors in Computing Systems - CHI EA 2001, pp. 435–436. ACM, New York (2001)
20. Wigdor, D., Balakrishnan, R.: Tilttext: using tilt for text input to mobile phones. In: Proceedings of the 16th Annual ACM Symposium on User Interface Software and Technology - UIST 2003, pp. 81–90. ACM, New York (2003)
21. Yee, K.P.: Peephole displays: pen interaction on spatially aware handheld computers. In: Proceedings of the ACM SIGCHI Conference on Human Factors in Computing System - CHI 2003, pp. 1–8. ACM, New York (2003)
22. Zhai, S., Smith, B.A., Selker, T.: Improving browsing performance: a study of four input devices for scrolling and pointing tasks. In: Howard, S., Hammond, J., Lindgaard, G. (eds.) Human-Computer Interaction INTERACT '97. ITIFIP, pp. 286–293. Springer, Boston (1997). https://doi.org/10.1007/978-0-387-35175-9_48

Gesture Interaction in Virtual Reality

A Low-Cost Machine Learning System and a Qualitative Assessment of Effectiveness of Selected Gestures vs. Gaze and Controller Interaction

Cloe Huesser[1] ⓘ, Simon Schubiger[2] ⓘ, and Arzu Çöltekin[1(✉)] ⓘ

[1] Institute of Interactive Technologies, University of Applied Sciences and Arts Northwestern Switzerland, Brugg-Windisch, Switzerland
{cloe.huesser,arzu.coltekin}@fhnw.ch
[2] Esri Inc., Zurich R&D, Zurich, Switzerland
sschubiger@esri.com

Abstract. We explore gestures as interaction methods in virtual reality (VR). We detect hand and body gestures using human pose estimation based on off-the-shelf optical camera images using machine learning, and obtain reliable gesture recognition without additional sensors. We then employ an avatar to prompt users to learn and use gestures to communicate. Finally, to understand how well gestures serve as interaction methods, we compare the studied gesture-based interaction methods with baseline common interaction modalities in VR (controllers, gaze interaction) in a pilot study including usability testing.

Keywords: Gestures · VR · Interaction · Usability

1 Introduction

The overarching goal of this project is to enable interactions in VR through gestures in affordable, efficient, and effective ways. This idea is not new, in fact the question of using gestures for human-computer interaction (HCI) is one of the persistent challenges in VR research, *e.g.,* already in 1999, Weissmann and Solomon presented a gesture recognition approach based on data gloves and neural networks [1]. Some gestures have also been examined from various human-centric perspectives, *e.g.,* object manipulation effectiveness [2], intuitiveness [3], or usability [4]. With recent popularization of VR and other extended reality (XR) devices, it became (even more) evident that much work is needed to create seamless interactions between humans and XR systems [*e.g.,* 5, 6] where standard interaction approaches do not work well [7], and speech interaction lacks privacy and feel intrusive when the user is not alone [8]. Thus, gestures have a lot of potential in VR interaction [8]. However, their development and adaptation have been hindered by several factors, *e.g.,* without dedicated devices interactions are imprecise; or they lack usability, learnability and/or intuitiveness. Here we re-examine a set of gestures, as recent developments in machine learning yielded promising results for employing off-the-shelf, ubiquitous cameras (webcams, smartphone cameras) with

© IFIP International Federation for Information Processing 2021
Published by Springer Nature Switzerland AG 2021
C. Ardito et al. (Eds.): INTERACT 2021, LNCS 12934, pp. 151–160, 2021.
https://doi.org/10.1007/978-3-030-85613-7_11

decent accuracy [9]. Specifically, we select a set of gesture candidates, and use a webcam (as an addition to VR hardware) to detect and employ gestures for user interaction, and explore an avatar that can mirror the user to improve learnability of gestures. Finally, we report the results from a pilot user study to better understand the usability of our prototype implementations as well as initial subjective user experience with the gestures we implemented.

2   Methods

Gesture Selection. Based on literature [*e.g.,* 10, 11] and introspection, we identified commonly used human gestures as candidates for interaction in VR. We differentiated gestures that can be tracked in the headset *vs.* using an external webcam (Table 1).

Computational Approach. For the VR headset (Samsung HMD Odyssey), we used built-in solutions whereas for the webcam gesture recognition, we reviewed optical motion tracking and machine learning (ML) solutions for tracking users' hands and head. Subsequently, we developed an ML-system to detect gestures in the live feed of a webcam (Logitech, c922 Pro Stream Webcam). We then examined human pose estimation approaches, specifically on 2D color images [14–16] and selected OpenPose [15] due to its wide distribution and the quality of documentation. Thus, we implemented our gesture tracking algorithm using OpenPose 1.5.1 for 2D images directly from the webcam. An example outcome is shown in Fig. 1.

Fig. 1. OpenPose human pose detection with image (left), without image (right).

We constructed a 1750-image dataset for the gestures, and an evaluation dataset with 10 images for each gesture class for testing the ML solution. Images of each gesture from the view of OpenPose were manually classified. To minimize false predictions, we also created three *non-gesture* classes, *i.e.,* no human visible, no gesture present, user handling headset. To improve the ML performance, we augmented the training data set by flipping all images, thus doubling their number. To classify the images, we created a convolutional neural network with Keras/TensorFlow 2.0 [17]. The network consists of three Conv2D layers with max pooling and a dropout layer. In the end, the data is flattened and reduced to the number of classes with a dense layer and softmax activation [18]. OpenPose receives and processes the images, and returns a color image with the human key points, which is stored in an image folder (Fig. 2).

Fig. 2. Depiction of ML-pipeline.

Table 1. Overview of gesture candidates included in the study.

Name	Action	Meaning	Interactions	Tracking
a)	**Gestures that can be tracked with a VR headset**			
nodding	lift / lower head	yes	answer to direct yes/no question	headset sensors
head shake	turn head left to right	no	answer to direct yes/no question	headset sensors
head tilt	pause head tilted	thinking / not sure	show help / explanation	headset sensors
chin point	move chin into direction of something	selecting	select object in front direction	headset sensors
wandering look	move head / not focusing on one point	uninterested	skip intro / info / help	headset sensors
b)	**Gestures that can be tracked with an external webcam**			
shrugging	lift shoulders (and arms)	i don't know	repeat tutorial / intro, skip question	continuous / motion /position camera
beckoning	move hand far to near (more than once)	nearer / bigger	zoom in, choose something	continuous / motion
stop	move hand near to far, then stop	stop / pause	stop an action, pause	one picture / position camera
face cover	move hand / hands before eyes	shocked, feeling uncomfortable	pause	one picture / position camera
hands up	raise both hands open above the head	giving up	giving up	one picture / position camera
hand raise	raise one hand open, or only the index finger stretched over head	volunteer or want to say something	question	one picture / position camera
pointing	point with open hand or stretched index finger	indicates direction	choose, go in one direction	needs testing one picture / position camera
drink	drinking movement pretending to hold glass	drink	using resources pause	needs testing one picture / position camera
t-sign	one hand horizontal, the other vertical underneath	time-out	pause	one picture camera

The prediction file loads in the neural network model, acquires the last pose image from OpenPose, and predicts a class for it. A server gets created at runtime and a REP socket is bound to "tcp://*:5555". The REP socket type acts as a service for clients, receiving requests and replying to the client. When the socket receives a message from a client, it sends the classification of the last image back. Once the ML model and the pipeline was functional, we implemented an avatar that can mirror the users' gestures using tools from Unity3D, MakeHuman, Mixamo, OpenPose, and others.

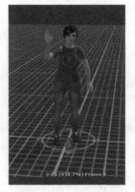

Fig. 3. Waving avatar animation in Unity (right).

User Study. We conducted a usability test to evaluate our prototypes, and have a first assessment of user experience with the gestures listed in Table 1. Our three independent variables were *interaction with gestures*, traditional VR interaction *with* and *without controllers* (*i.e.*, gaze). Our dependent variables were *task completion rate, task time, SUS score* [12] and subjective feedback on *overall experience, 'naturalness' of interactions, consistency of the interactions with real-world, perceived intuitiveness, satisfaction, effectiveness,* and *fun* (reported selectively in this paper due to page limits).

Participants. We collected qualitative feedback throughout prototype development (n = 2), and recruited 6 participants (4 women, 2 men, age range 28–69) for the user study (reportedly, after six participants no new usability problems are detected [13]). We excluded participants younger than 18 for consent reasons, and 'VR power users' to remove possible bias.

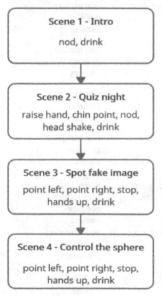

Fig. 4. User study overview.

Materials. Gesture prototypes (Table 1) and the avatar (Fig. 3) were developed as described in previous sections. We then generated scenarios (Fig. 4) that require the use of the selected gestures, and VR scenes to facilitate these scenarios (not shown here due to page limits) using the tools mentioned in earlier sections. We collected demographic information (*e.g.,* age, gender, education) with a self-generated digital questionnaire, and controlled for potentially confounding variables (*e.g.,* VR/gaming experience).

Procedure. We followed an identical protocol and strict hygiene measures with all participants (due to the covid-19 pandemic). At the experiment site, participants signed an informed consent form, filled in the demographic questionnaire, and practiced the gestures with the avatar prototype for a fixed amount of time (the avatar was included in the study to train the users for the gestures, also see Table 2, 'Start'). Then, participants moved on to solve the same tasks three times: Once with gestures, once with controllers and once with gaze interaction (without controllers). Specific experiment tasks are shown in Table 2. We rotated the order of interaction methods to counterbalance for a possible learning effect.

Table 2. Overview tasks for the user study, including the descriptions of the tasks.

#	Task	Gesture	Gaze	Controller
Start: The avatar welcomes the participant, instructs them to act as naturally as possible, informs on the available interaction possibilities, and asks if they are ready to start.				
Task 0	Indicate that they need a break	Drink *	Gaze on pause	Click on pause with trigger
Task 1	Indicate that they are ready to start	Nod	Gaze on start button	Click on start with trigger
Quiz night (true/false): The participant is challenged with a couple of fun trivia yes/no questions. Right answers give 50 points, false give -50 points, no answer no points.				
Task 2	Select if the answer is true, false or indicate that they don't know the answer. Goal is a high score	Nod, head shake, shoulder shrug	Gaze on yes, no, or no answer button	Click on yes, no or no answer button with trigger
Fake or not (select): Participant is challenged to select two images and asked to identify which one is fake. S/he has the option to raise the hand for help/a joker. 50 points for right selection -50 for wrong, the joker reduces possible points to 25.				
Task 3	Select the fake image	Chin point	Gaze on image	Click on image with trigger
Task 4	Ask for a tip	Raise hand	Gaze on help button	Click on tip button with trigger
Task 5	Confirm selection of image	Nod, head shake	Gaze on yes or no, button	Click on yes, or no button with trigger
Command the rolling sphere: A sphere rolls from side to side over an indicated stop point. The closer the sphere stopped to the middle, the more points were won.				
Task 6	Stop the sphere as close to a certain point as possible	Stop	Gaze on stop button	Click on stop button with trigger
Task 7	Select direction in which the sphere should start again	Point direction	Gaze on direction button	Click on direction button with trigger
Task 8	Give up placement of sphere	Hands up	Gaze on finish button	Click on finish button with trigger

* We did not ask participants to perform this task in all scenes, but it is *performable* in all of them.

Once the tasks were completed, participants filled in the SUS questionnaire(s), answered numerous subjective rating questions using a 5-point Likert scale, and open-ended interview questions. SUS is a standardized questionnaire with a balanced positive and negative statements [12], and we worded the rest of the questions also as neutral as possible to avoid priming or biasing the participants.

3 Results

ML for Gesture Recognition. As mentioned earlier, to evaluate the ML model, we used a separate dataset (each class containing 10 images) that the model has not seen before. Figure 5 shows the model's accuracy and loss during the training over 60 epochs. Train model classified the images, and we created a confusion matrix with the results (Fig. 6). The confusion matrix shows, for example, *no_human*, *pointing_left* and *pointing_right* images were never wrongly classified, but the *t-sign* was classified as *pointing_left* in majority of the cases.

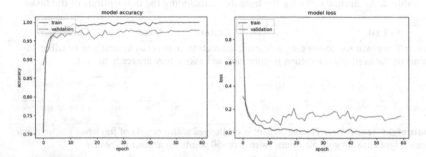

Fig. 5. Model accuracy (right) and model loss (left) during training.

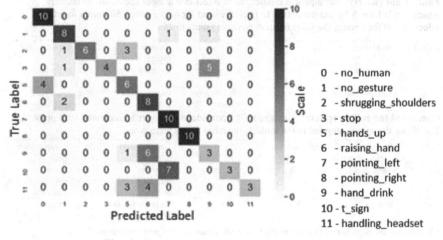

Fig. 6. Confusion matrix for gesture recognition.

Usability Study and Pilot Experiment. The overall feedback from the usability test was positive. The average SUS score is 78.75 out of 100. Since everything above 68 is considered 'usable' [12], this is good feedback. All participants successfully completed all tasks in all three conditions (controller, gaze, gesture). There was some variance in how long the users took to finish their tasks, as can be seen in Fig. 7.

Most of the subjective ratings in the general feedback were also positive. The participants overall liked the general concept of using gestures for interaction in several dimensions (Fig. 8). One participant voted either neutral or somewhat negative in all conditions, whereas the rest of them were positive or very positive.

In a broader question ('how would you evaluate your experience with gestures/gaze/controller?'), the interaction with the controller was overall rated better (2×

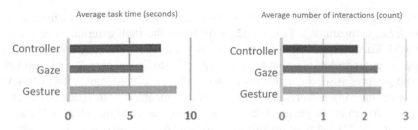

Fig. 7. Overall average task time (left) and number of interactions (right) per interaction method.

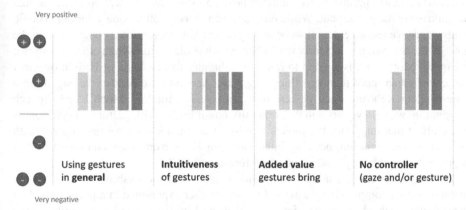

Fig. 8. General subjective feedback from the questionnaire. Each bar shows one participant. The question is presented as a 5-point Likert scale ranging from "very negative" to "very positive".

very positive, 1× positive, 1× neutral) than the gestures (5× positive, 1× neutral), whereas gaze received somewhat mixed reviews (2× very positive, 3× positive, 1× negative). Questions on realism and authenticity led to overall similar results. In sum, the overall rating for gestures is quite positive (also as shown in Fig. 8). At more specific level, the pointing and the hands up gestures had some negative ratings, whereas the other individual gestures were all positively rated. In the qualitative interviews, we gained some interesting insights, where participants also made positive remarks overall. However, we also observed that accidental triggering of actions frustrated the participants, and when interacting with the avatar, the delay between performing an action and seeing the action performed on an avatar seems to be irritating. On a tangential note, participants with no previous VR experience were very much fascinated by it ("wow" factor is anecdotally confirmed yet again).

4 Discussion and Conclusions

We set out to examine various commonly-used gestures in human-human interactions as interaction methods in VR, a core HCI problem one can study taking computational (recognition, tracking) as well as human-centered perspectives. As a computational contribution, our ML-based gesture recognition software prototype functions reasonably well, *i.e.,* comparable to [19, 21, 22], with an off-the-shelf external webcam, when the network learns from 2D images. Gestures that are *not* about hand-tracking, such as nodding, shrugging, chin-pointing are not frequently studied, especially in combination with hand gestures as we did in this paper. While there is considerable effort in tracking and recognizing hand gestures these are often accompanied with specialized sensors [*e.g.,* 20]. Webcam based gesture recognition efforts, methodologically similar to ours do exist [*e.g.,* 21, 22], but they are also often focused on hand-gestures, for example, for sign language recognition [*e.g.,* 23]. Because tracking more parts of the body (in addition to hands) increases precision, we included head and shoulders, as well as an avatar that was mirroring the participant. While our approach works well uniquely for our specific setup where we use an external webcam to support VR interactions, comparable to the state-of-the-art systems, it clearly works better with some gestures than others (as shown in Fig. 6). More work is needed to remove ambiguity from a hand or body movement that could mean more than one thing (*e.g.,* user handling the headset vs. signaling a command) in webcam-based gesture tracking research for VR. Much like in speech recognition, we believe this will be eventually possible also with gesture recognition. A future effort that integrates the modes of gesture communication we investigated with face/emotion recognition, possibly intention recognition from gaze data might further improve the 'vocabulary' and range of gesture-based HCI.

As a human-centered design contribution, we tested the usability of our gesture prototypes, and comparatively assessed the initial user experience in a pilot study. Our participants received the gesture interactions overall positive/promising, similar to the earlier studies conducted on different gesture types and combinations in different VR environments [*e.g.,* 2–4]. Using gestures is still an experimental mode of interaction in VR. We believe more precision in tracking and recognition, further design considerations/testing, and importantly, contextualization of the gesture use, and user training are necessary. Based on the developments in these areas, gestures *can* become a main mode of interaction (such as it is in sign language), or at least a secondary supporting mode of interaction (such as it is in nonverbal body language humans constantly use). The avatar experience in this study was not precisely positive mainly due to system delays, however the approach (*i.e.,* an avatar as a virtual guide/teacher/trainer) seems very promising [24] and may lead to interesting applications such as—among many—a recent paper titled 'Everybody Dance Now' [25] where pose detection is used to lead/motivate/teach somebody else dance. As a tangential observation we also noted that gaze-based interaction receives mixed reactions at this point, and it would be important to keep testing this mode of interaction on its own as well a complimentary modality.

In summary, we believe gestures will remain important not only in VR but in the future of all XR interactions, and our findings suggest that usability as well as user acceptance is on its way after some more testing/training/tweaking. Our observations from the user study presented in this paper should be taken as preliminary insights due to low number of participants, and reduced trials (both of which were necessary to respect the limitations introduced by the global pandemic at the time of the study). A future controlled laboratory experiment is being planned with more participants and more trials/comparisons which will help us confirm some of the hypotheses generated based on this exploratory study.

References

1. Weissmann, J., Salomon, R.: Gesture recognition for virtual reality applications using data gloves and neural networks. In: Proceedings of the International Joint Conference on Neural Networks, vol. 3, pp. 2043–2046. IEEE (1999)
2. Lin, W., Du, L., Harris-Adamson, C., Barr, A., Rempel, D.: Design of hand gestures for manipulating objects in virtual reality. In: Kurosu, Masaaki (ed.) HCI 2017. LNCS, vol. 10271, pp. 584–592. Springer, Cham (2017). https://doi.org/10.1007/978-3-319-58071-5_44
3. Frey, G., Jurkschat, A., Korkut, S., Lutz, J., Dornberger, R.: Iintuitive hand gestures for the interaction with information visualizations in virtual reality. In: Tom Dieck, M.C., Jung, T. (eds.) Augmented Reality and Virtual Reality: The Power of AR and VR for Business, pp. 261–273. Springer International Publishing, Cham (2019)
4. Cabral, M.C., Morimoto, C.H., Zuffo, M.K.: On the usability of gesture interfaces in virtual reality environments. In: Proceedings of the 2005 Latin American Conference on Human-Computer Interaction - CLIHC 2005, pp. 100–108. ACM Press, New York (2005)
5. Çöltekin, A., et al.: Geospatial information visualization and extended reality displays. In: Guo, Huadong, Goodchild, Michael F., Annoni, Alessandro (eds.) Manual of Digital Earth, pp. 229–277. Springer, Singapore (2020). https://doi.org/10.1007/978-981-32-9915-3_7
6. Çöltekin, A., et al.: Extended reality in spatial sciences: a review of research challenges and future directions. ISPRS Int. J. Geo Inf. **9**(7), 439 (2020)
7. Çöltekin, A., Hempel, J., Brychtova, A., Giannopoulos, I., Stellmach, S., Dachselt, R.: Gaze and feet as additional input modalities for interaction with geospatial interfaces. ISPRS Ann. Photogramm. Remote Sens. Spat. Inf. Sci. **III-2**, 113–120 (2016)
8. Maloney, D., Freeman, G., Wohn, D.Y.: Talking without a voice. In: Proceedings of the ACM Human-Computer Interaction, vol. 4, pp. 1–25 (2020)
9. Valliappan, N., et al.: Accelerating eye movement research via accurate and affordable smartphone eye tracking. Nat. Commun. **11**, 4553 (2020)
10. Morris, D.: Bodytalk: A World Guide to Gestures. Jonathan Cape, London (1994)
11. Pease, A.: Body Language: How to Read Others' Thoughts by Their Gestures. Sheldon Press, London (1988)
12. Brooke, J.: SUS - a quick and dirty usability scale usability and context. In: Jordan, P.W., Thomas, B., McClelland, I.L., Weerdmeester, B. (eds.) Usability Evaluation in Industry, pp. 189–196 (1996)
13. Nielsen, J.: How many test users in a usability study? https://www.nngroup.com/articles/how-many-test-users/. Accessed 10 June 2021
14. Oved, D.: Real-time human pose estimation in the browser with TensorFlow.js I by TensorFlow I TensorFlow I Medium. https://medium.com/tensorflow/real-time-human-pose-estimation-in-the-browser-with-tensorflow-js-7dd0bc881cd5. Accessed 10 June 2021
15. Cao, Z., Hidalgo, G., Simon, T., Wei, S.-E., Sheikh, Y.: OpenPose: realtime multi-person 2D pose estimation using part affinity fields. IEEE Trans. Pattern Anal. Mach. Intell. **43**, 172–186 (2018)
16. Bazarevsky, V., Grishchenko, I., Raveendran, K., Zhu, T., Zhang, F., Grundmann, M.: BlazePose: on-device real-time body pose tracking. arXiv (2020)
17. Abadi, M., et al.: TensorFlow: a system for large-scale machine learning. In: Proceedings of the 12th USENIX Symposium on Operating Systems Design and Implementation, OSDI 2016 (2016)

18. Shanmugamani, R.: Deep learning for computer vision: expert techniques to train advanced neural networks using TensorFlow and Keras. Birmingham Mumbai: Packt (2018)

19. Ahlawat, S., Batra, V., Banerjee, S., Saha, J., Garg, A.: Hand gesture recognition using convolutional neural network. In: Bhattacharyya, S., Hassanien, A.E., Gupta, D., Khanna, A., Pan, I. (eds.) International Conference on Innovative Computing and Communications. LNNS, vol. 56, pp. 179–186. Springer, Singapore (2019). https://doi.org/10.1007/978-981-13-2354-6_20

20. Hayashi, E., et al.: RadarNet: efficient gesture recognition technique utilizing a miniature radar sensor. In: Proceedings of the 2021 CHI Conference on Human Factors in Computing Systems, pp. 1–14 (2021)

21. Golash, R., Jain, Y.K.: Trajectory-based cognitive recognition of dynamic hand gestures from webcam videos. Int. J. Eng. Res. Technol. 13(6), 1432–1440 (2020). ISSN 0974-3154

22. Agrawal, M., Ainapure, R., Agrawal, S., Bhosale, S., Desai, S.: Models for hand gesture recognition using deep learning. In: 2020 IEEE 5th International Conference on Computing Communication and Automation (ICCCA), pp. 589–594. IEEE (2020)

23. Bendarkar, D., Somase, P., Rebari, P., Paturkar, R., Khan, A.: Web based recognition and translation of American sign language with CNN and RNN. International Association of Online Engineering (2021). https://www.learntechlib.org/p/218958/

24. Khan, O., Ahmed, I., Cottingham, J., Rahhal, M., Arvanitis, T.N., Elliott, M.T.: Timing and correction of stepping movements with a virtual reality avatar. PlosOne 15(2), e0229641 (2020)

25. Chan, C., Ginosar, S., Zhou, T., Efros, A.: Everybody dance now. In: 2019 IEEE/CVF International Conference on Computer Vision (ICCV), Seoul, Korea (South), October 2019, pp. 5932–5941 (2019)

Sticking Out Like a Non-dominant Thumb

Handedness and Fitts' Throughput for Touch-Based Mobile Interfaces

Maulashree Shanbhag[1]([✉]) [iD], Anirudha Joshi[2] [iD], and Bijoy Singh Kochar[3] [iD]

[1] Indian Institute of Technology, Mumbai, India
[2] Industrial Design Centre, IIT Bombay, Mumbai, India
[3] London, UK

Abstract. In this paper we present our study ($n = 30$) to gauge the effect of hand-dominance on Fitts' throughput through four test cases—forefingers and thumbs of dominant and non-dominant hands in tapping tasks for touch-based mobile interfaces. We set out with the expectation that throughput for a dominant digit would exceed that for the corresponding digit of the other hand. We reveal that this was followed in the case of right-handed users for both forefingers and thumbs, and in case of forefingers for all users. Right-handed users had higher throughput for dominant digits (mean = 5.608) than non-dominant digits (mean = 4.736). All users had higher throughput for dominant forefingers (mean = 6.081) than non-dominant forefingers (mean = 5.436). However, surprisingly, left-handed users showed a higher throughput for non-dominant thumbs (mean = 6.078) than dominant thumbs (mean = 5.721). Throughputs of forefingers and thumbs were not significantly different for any groups.

Keywords: Handedness · Fitts' Law · Touch input

1 Introduction

While left-handed individuals are a minority (reported numbers ranging from 8–15%) and being left-handed is not exactly a handicap, it is often for this reason that the specific needs of this user group are overlooked and they find themselves at a disadvantage while using daily objects designed with the majority in mind, such as cutting with scissors, unscrewing lids, sharpening pencils and so on. In the case of digital devices, too, it is commonly assumed that left-handed usage would just mirror that of the vast majority i.e., the right-handed population. With handheld mobile devices becoming our way of connecting with the world, it becomes necessary to question this assumption and to make our designs more inclusive to handedness. The first step to this would be to identify the difference, if any, in user performance.

Fitts [10] proposed a relation between amplitude, duration and variability of motor response, which is better known today as Fitts' Law. Different forms of Fitts' equation have been accepted as well as discussed [7] since. There exists no benchmark data nor standard prescribed method readily available to compare the performance of left- and

© IFIP International Federation for Information Processing 2021
Published by Springer Nature Switzerland AG 2021
C. Ardito et al. (Eds.): INTERACT 2021, LNCS 12934, pp. 161–181, 2021.
https://doi.org/10.1007/978-3-030-85613-7_12

right-handed individuals in touch-based Fitts' tasks. Similarly, there seemed to be no means to comment on whether there exists a sizable difference between the performance of a digit of the dominant hand and that of the corresponding one of the non-dominant hand.

The purpose of this paper is to explore Fitts' Law as applicable for touch-based interfaces through the lens of laterality and hand-dominance. We take Fitts' Law as a given and adopt the form prescribed by MacKenzie [21] to calculate Fitts' Throughput (measured in bits/s) for a series of simple point-and-touch tasks which are then compared and analyzed from the perspective of handedness of the subjects. These are studied bearing in mind two common input configurations based on the primary interacting digit - forefingers and thumbs.

Through this paper, we make three specific contributions. Firstly, we compare and provide benchmark data about relative performances of right- and left-handed people with their dominant and non-dominant forefingers and thumbs for common tapping tasks. Secondly, we reveal that on the whole right-handed users are more accurate and precise than left-handed users and yet the left-handed users have higher throughput than right-handed users. Thirdly, we reveal a surprising finding about the better performance of the non-dominant thumb of left-handed users. This exploratory study could form the basis of argument for better personalization for left- and right-handed users, especially with the consideration that the performance effects are asymmetric. It can set the stage for further work wherever there arises a question of whether left-handed users are at any major disadvantage or need separate consideration. While several studies [17, 21, 24, 25, 29] have been carried out in the domain of tapping tasks on mobile touch devices, these have exclusively recruited right-handed participants, often with an apparently inherent assumption that a laterally flipped interface would exhibit similar results for left-handed users. So also, studies on Back of Device (BoD) interactions [16], handedness detection [20] have recruited only right-handed participants. Our study argues in favor of more inclusive recruitment and perhaps revisiting some of these studies through the lens of handedness.

2   Background

2.1   Hand Usage in Touch Input

In mobile phones designed for portable handheld usage, a single-handed/monomanual grip (see Fig. 1) is used fairly commonly when tapping the screen [14, 15]. When using a single hand, front of screen input on a mobile device is generally limited to thumb tapping, where the motor performance of the thumb has been found to vary across configurations and target positions on the screen for a Fitts' based task [29]. The other common configuration for phone usage is bimanual, where one hand supports the phone and a digit of the other hand (usually the forefinger) is used for touch-based input (see Fig. 1).

Fig. 1. Single-handed grip with thumb used for input, and two-handed grip with forefinger used for input

2.2 Fitts' Law and Throughput

The law originally proposed by Fitts [10] may be framed as follows, given time (T) to complete the movement to a target is a linear function of the Index of Difficulty (ID):

$$T = a + b\,ID \tag{1}$$

Here, a and b are arrived upon through empirical measurement, while the Index of Difficulty is a function of target distance (D) and target width (W):

$$ID = \log_2\left(\frac{2D}{W}\right) \tag{2}$$

This has been discussed and modified since [28] to the form:

$$ID = \log_2\left(\frac{D}{W} + 1\right) \tag{3}$$

This [21] formulation for Fitts' throughput for touch-based target selection accounts for amplitude of movement, movement time and accuracy in a single term. This form describes Fitts' throughput (TP) as the ratio of effective index of difficulty (ID_e) measured in bits, to movement time (MT) measured in seconds:

$$TP = \frac{ID_e}{MT} \tag{4}$$

Here, MT is measured empirically while ID_e expands as follows, given that A_e corresponds to the effective movement amplitude and W_e corresponds to effective target width:

$$ID_e = \log_2\left(\frac{A_e}{W_e} + 1\right) \tag{5}$$

The value of Fitts' Throughput varied based on the kind of hardware setup and interaction used. However, for a particular device, input technique, and a given set of tasks, throughput may be compared through direct subtraction.

Fitts law has been researched extensively by various people, and especially in the context of touchscreens. For example, FFitts law [2] proposes a dual distribution hypothesis to interpret the distribution of endpoints considering fat-finger input. The authors suggest a relative component controlled by the speed-accuracy trade-off of the performer, and an absolute component independent of the performer's desire of following the specified task precision which cannot be controlled by the speed-accuracy trade-off. While this [2] formulation could be used as an alternative, the work does not make explicit the method to calculate throughput. To the best of our knowledge, the most recent paper specifying method to calculate Fitts' throughput is MacKenzie [21]. As our goal was not to investigate which model gives the most reliable throughput, but rather how do different digits of differently handed people affect the throughput, for this limited scope we adopted this [21] formulation for our study.

2.3 Laterality and Handedness in HCI

While the human exterior appears to be bilaterally symmetrical, the left and the right sides are differentiated through laterality or sidedness. Laterality manifests in terms of preferential usage or relatively better performance of one of the bilateral counterparts. Despite its seemingly binary nature, there are arguments in favor of a continuous distribution that takes into account the degree of laterality and not just directionality [22]. Attempts have been made to measure different manifestations such as handedness, footedness, earedness, eyedness [5], etc. Of these, handedness is a widely studied manifestation and of our specific interest. It is commonly gauged through self-reporting on the basis of questionnaires consisting commonly carried out day to day activities [1, 23], the merits of which have subsequently been discussed [4, 30].

We found the Edinburgh Handedness Inventory (EHI) [23] to be the most interesting method to determine handedness as it comments on the degree of laterality and not just directionality. It takes into account hand dominance for activities such as writing, drawing, throwing things, and so on. It scores individuals in a range of -100 to 100. Individuals with scores below -28 are considered to be left-handed, while those with scores above 40 are considered to be right-handed. Individuals with scores between $-$ 28 and 40 form the 'middle decile' and cannot be conclusively said to have a preferred hand. Formulated in 1971, the EHI includes several daily activities but does not cover touch screens or mice. However, it continues to be used commonly as a means to establish handedness and is thereby relevant to our study. We could also argue that because EHI is independent of most current-day computing tasks, in some sense it provides an assessment of a person's handedness that is independent of the influences of technology use. This argument gathers importance given our results, as we discuss below.

Existing work takes into account the effect of handedness in HCI, such as comparing touchscreens and touchpads in flight-control interfaces [18], or attempts to design specifically left-hand controlled configurations, such as for games [6]. Cursorless pointing has been studied from the perspective of laterality in terms of handedness as well as ocular dominance [26].

A study carried out from the perspective of finger movement pointed out that there are differences in the way motor areas of the brain are functionally organized in right- and left-handed people [27]. Performance on touchscreen mobile phones has been studied 'in the wild' [13] as well as in controlled conditions [19]. Work on one-handed thumb tapping on mobile devices [25] mentions the lack of a study on handedness. Despite the popularity of touchscreen mobile devices, we did not find extensive studies that compare handedness on touchscreens. Effect of hand use has been studied for one-handed BoD interactions [9]. The closest investigation into handedness on touchscreens that we came across [3] was carried out with only four participants. This work attempted to compare the index of difficulty between left- and right-handed individuals through a Flutter-based prototype. However, we did not come across studies that specifically consider differential performance caused by handedness in terms of Fitts' throughput for tapping tasks on touch-based mobile interfaces.

3   Study

We looked at two commonly used configurations for touch-based interaction in particular: double-handed forefinger (index finger) and one-handed thumb. The study is exploratory and designed to be within-subject, where dominant hand performance of an individual would be compared with their own non-dominant hand performance for corresponding configurations. Users were recruited on the basis of self-reporting (later verified via EHI) and were treated the same for the purpose of data collection i.e., they were not separated into groups. Once collected, readings were separated on the basis of hand dominance for the purpose of analysis, which formed the between-subject aspect of the study.

3.1   Experiment

Study Design. We conducted a mixed design study, with hand-dominance as a between-subject independent variable, and counterbalanced finger configuration—dominant hand forefinger (DF), non-dominant hand forefinger (NF), dominant hand thumb (DT), and non-dominant hand thumb (NT), (see Fig. 2), as the within-subject independent variable. In the cases involving input using the thumb, a single-handed grip was used, while for input using the forefinger, a double-handed grip was used (see Fig. 1).

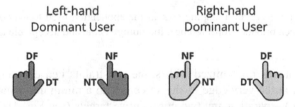

Fig. 2. Dominant hand forefinger (DF), non-dominant hand forefinger (NF), dominant hand thumb (DT), and non-dominant hand thumb (NT) for left- and right-handed users respectively

Our primary dependent variable was Fitts' throughput, while we also measured errors and speed as additional dependent variables. The handedness was initially determined based on self-reporting, but we did use the EHI to verify the self-reports. We did not consider the users who turned out to be ambidextrous i.e., those in the middle decile with EHI scores between -28 and 40.

Apparatus. The study was conducted using an Android application (developed in-house) running on a single touch-screen smartphone device[1]. There was no screen guard or external cover on the phone which could add to bulk or reduce sensitivity of the screen. The app logged metrics such as the cartesian coordinates of subsequent touches, the time elapsed between them, and the location at which the touch target spawned. The data exported from the app was processed and analyzed using a Python3 script and spreadsheet tools.

The touch targets were high contrast (black on white background) to avoid visual difficulty/unwanted confounding effects, and circular, to prevent any external influence of directionality (see Fig. 3). The center of each target was marked by crosshairs to promote accuracy.

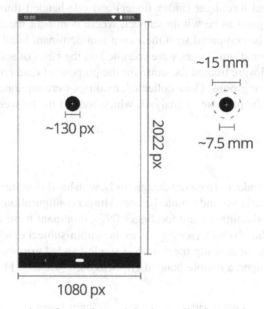

Fig. 3. A sample screenshot of a tapping task in the application used to evaluate throughputs. Dimensions have been provided for reference, including visible and acceptable target sizes

Target position was randomized with some constraints i.e., ensuring that a target would not appear at the very edge of the screen, with a minimum distance of 130 px ($\approx$ one target size) separating any two consecutive targets (see Fig. 4). The minimum distance between spawned targets was ~1.49 cm (260 px), the maximum was ~11.41 cm (1981 px), while the mean distance between targets was ~4.64 cm (806 px) with sd = 2.113 cm (367 px). Target size was kept constant as a controlled variable, with visible diameter fixed at 12% of display width (~7.5 mm). Targets smaller than that have been found to have higher error rates [21]. Our choice of target width was driven by the need for

---

[1] Google Pixel 3a - weight: 147 g, dimensions: 151.3 × 70.1 × 8.2 mm (5.96 × 2.76 × 0.32 in.), display size (measured diagonally): 142.2 mm (5.6 in.), display resolution: 1080 × 2220 pixels, pixel density: 441 PPI.

it to be ergonomically large enough to touch (7–10 mm) [11], with the visible area being small enough to encourage precision. We considered the touches within a concentric circle of diameter of 36% of the display width (~390 px ≈ 22.5 mm) as intentional, and ignored any touches outside of this region, regarding these as unintended touches, probably caused by some other part of the hand coming in contact with the screen, such as the base of the palm touching the screen while extending thumb, etc. (see Fig. 5).

0	0	0	0	0	0	0	0	0	0	0	0
0	49	52	52	56	50	51	63	55	46	41	0
0	52	41	68	51	61	42	53	60	52	51	0
0	75	64	62	58	49	47	53	52	58	60	0
0	46	57	49	60	60	47	53	48	60	68	0
0	53	49	48	52	46	49	55	55	68	37	0
0	61	49	50	64	53	59	46	57	50	55	0
0	58	50	47	70	56	62	66	60	63	53	0
0	54	57	55	46	53	56	43	49	75	66	0
0	41	50	53	65	46	67	60	58	62	36	0
0	53	63	47	48	44	49	52	61	61	57	0
0	53	57	51	50	50	65	61	62	59	42	0
0	41	51	63	52	44	43	50	66	58	43	0
0	50	63	63	42	52	50	62	51	48	42	0
0	55	47	62	40	65	58	48	62	49	44	0
0	59	62	47	55	49	49	58	74	44	52	0
0	47	41	58	61	49	56	49	65	60	58	0
0	60	60	55	60	39	39	55	50	56	44	0
0	52	58	44	45	64	56	55	52	59	57	0
0	55	68	49	56	62	62	57	53	50	48	0
0	63	49	58	53	45	63	48	52	52	50	0
0	0	0	0	0	0	0	0	0	0	0	0

Fig. 4. Distribution of target count (total: 10,800) if phone screen were bucketed into even cells

We note that the targets were randomly spawned, and they turned out with a reasonably even distribution, except at the very edges of the screen.

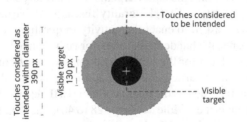

Fig. 5. Target visible to user (130 px ≈ 7.5 mm), region where touches are considered to be intentional (enclosed by dotted line, 390 px ≈ 22.5 mm), and the touches on the rest of the screen ignored as unintentional (outside the bounds of the dotted line)

Participants. Participants were recruited locally in the Thane-Mumbai region, India (aged 18–60 years). The stipulation was that participants were regular users of a touch-screen phone, and had been for at least a month. During recruitment, participants were asked to self-identify as left- or right-handed. While self-reporting handedness, potential participants were also asked in particular which hand they preferred for input on mobile touchscreens, being clearly told that preference was a matter of their choice (see Table 1). It was decided not to take a representative sample of the population in terms of handedness distribution, as the proportion of left-handed participants would be lower. Instead, there was balanced recruitment (equal number) of self-reported left- and right-handed participants to ensure enough data could be gathered for both groups, although they were not treated any differently during data collection. Participants with severe or uncorrected visual or hand-eye coordination issues were excluded from the study. While carrying out the study, it was ensured that the participants were not injured or inconvenienced in a way which could affect or bias their motor movement.

Table 1. Breakdown of participants as per self-reported preference of hand usage (A—Left hand preferred, B—Mostly prefer left hand, but at times use right, C—No particular preference, D—Mostly prefer right hand, but at times use left, E—Right hand preferred) and gender

	A	B	C	D	E	Total
Female	5	3	0	3	3	13
Male	6	2	1	2	7	19
Total	11	5	1	5	10	32

Upon being recruited for the study, participants were initially asked to respond to the Edinburgh Handedness Inventory (EHI) Laterality Test as available on brainmapping.org [8]. If in doubt, they were asked to enact the activity in question in order to help them answer. Of the participants, the handedness index for right-handed ones varied from 50 to 95 with a median of 80 and for the left-handed ones varied from −30 to −95 with a median of −65. Initially, 32 participants were administered the EHI Test, of which 2 had to be excluded from the study as the results of their EHI Test were inconclusive as to handedness, placing them in the middle decile (−28 to 40). The 2 participants (1 female, 1 male) excluded from the final study had reported "mostly prefer left hand but at times use right" and "no particular preference" respectively. The remaining 30 participants (see Table 2), mean age 33.5 years (SD = 11.23), were included in the final study and their EHI Indices conformed with their self-reported handedness.

Procedure. Each participant was asked to sit comfortably on a chair for the duration of the experiment, with no direct glare on the mobile screen. The task was explained to the participants, and they were told the order in which they would be carrying out the four cases (DF, NF, DT, NT) which was ordered across participants such that no consecutive test cases would require the use of the same hand for tapping, to prevent any fatigue effects. The conditions were order-balanced through Latin square for each group of users. For each test case a participant would undergo 3 consecutive sequences

Table 2. Breakdown of participants as per handedness and gender after excluding the two participants whose EHI results placed them in the middle decile

	Left-handed	Right-handed	Total
Female	7	5	12
Male	8	10	18
Total	15	15	30

of 30 touch targets (appearing one after the other on the screen) across which we later calculated mean throughput. Successive sequences were separated by a minimum of 45 s rest period. This gave a total of 3 sequences × 30 touch targets × 4 test cases i.e., 360 targeted touches for each user, and 360 × 30 users i.e., 10,800 total touch tasks in the study.

A screenshot of the target was shown while explaining the task, and the display brightness was adjusted to the participant's comfort. By default, this was kept at ~75% of maximum. Of the 30 participants, 4 chose to increase it slightly while 2 chose to decrease it. They were asked to tap as close to the center of the tapping target using the finger corresponding to the test case. When a touch was registered, the next target would appear elsewhere on the screen without any programmed delay. The participants were asked to touch the targets as quickly and accurately as possible. They were told that if their finger were slightly off a target, it was OK, and that they should try to keep going as quickly and accurately as possible. We calculated throughput over a sequence of targets i.e. 'serial target clicking' where each trial begins at the selection point of the previous trial. Thereby for a sequence of 30 consecutive targets (serial target clicking [21] tasks), we have 29 data points contributing to the overall throughput. As we were not studying discrete tasks, there was no assigned 'home' position for the input finger.

For the test cases requiring the use of a thumb (DT, NT) for tapping, the participants were asked to hold the phone in the corresponding hand, while the trials with the fore-finger (DF, NF) needed the phone to be held in the other hand. We asked the users not to use any other part of their body/any external support for the phone, and to adjust to a comfortable grip before starting a trial sequence.

3.2 Results

We took the mean of 3 sequences of each test case to get corresponding throughput. As discussed earlier, we had to exclude two of the thirty-two initial participants, giving us overall n = 30 (see Tables 3, 4 and 5) (Figs. 6 and 7).

Table 3. Overall throughputs (bits/s) for the different cases (DF—Dominant Forefinger, NF—Non-Dominant Forefinger, DT—Dominant Thumb, NT—Non-Dominant Thumb)

	Mean	N	SD	95% CI from	95% CI to
Overall DF	6.081	30	1.365	5.592	6.569
Overall NF	5.436	30	1.479	4.907	5.965
Overall DT	5.572	30	1.458	5.050	6.093
Overall NT	5.328	30	1.624	4.747	5.909
Overall D (DF, DT)	5.826	30	1.312	5.357	6.296
Overall N (NF, NT)	5.382	30	1.457	4.861	5.903
Overall F (DF, NF)	5.758	30	1.376	5.266	6.251
Overall T (DT, NT)	5.450	30	1.434	4.937	5.963
Overall (DF, NF, DT, NT)	5.604	30	1.328	5.129	6.079

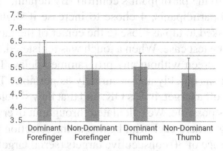

Fig. 6. Overall comparison between throughputs (error bars for 95% CI)

We validated our data by graphing for Fitts' Law (MT v/s ID_e) and found that it follows (see Fig. 8) with a performance front [12].

We performed a 4 × 2 mixed ANOVA with Finger as a within-subject factor with four levels (dominant forefinger, non-dominant forefinger, dominant thumb and non-dominant thumb), Handedness as the between subject factor with two levels (left-handed and right-handed), and with Age as a covariate (as we suspect that the dexterity, and throughput varies with age).

Tests of between-subjects effects showed that there were significant effects of Age ($F = 15.625$, $p = 0.001$), but Handedness did not have a significant effect ($F = 2.747$, $p = 0.109$). We checked the studentized residuals, and found that one left-handed user was an outlier in each of the four fingers ($t = -2.66$ to -3.24 for the different fingers, critical t for 14 degrees of freedom = 2.145). Hence, we removed this outlier and ran the above ANOVA again.

Table 4. Throughputs (bits/s) for the different cases (DF—Dominant Forefinger, NF—Non-Dominant Forefinger, DT—Dominant Thumb, NT—Non-Dominant Thumb) for right-handed participants

	Mean	N	SD	95% CI from	95% CI to
Right-handed DF	5.792	15	1.390	5.089	6.496
Right-handed NF	4.894	15	1.146	4.314	5.474
Right-handed DT	5.423	15	1.561	4.633	6.213
Right-handed NT	4.577	15	1.381	3.879	5.276
Right-handed D (DF, DT)	5.608	15	1.365	4.917	6.298
Right-handed N (NF, NT)	4.736	15	1.101	4.178	5.293
Right-handed F (DF, NF)	5.343	15	1.219	4.726	5.960
Right-handed T (DT, NT)	5.000	15	1.378	4.303	5.697
Right-handed Overall (DF, NF, DT, NT)	5.172	15	1.173	4.578	5.765

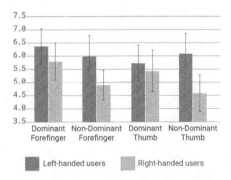

Fig. 7. Comparing throughputs across left and right-handed individuals (error bars for 95% CI)

After removal of the outlier, tests of between-subjects effects showed that there were significant effects of both Age (F = 12.526, p = 0.002) and Handedness (F = 7.568, p = 0.011). After accounting for age, left-handed users had significantly higher Fitts' Throughput (mean 6.193, N = 14, standard error = 0.234, 95% CI lower bound = 5.712, higher bound = 6.673) than the right-handed users (mean = 5.289, N = 15, standard error = 0.226, 95% CI lower bound = 4.825, higher bound = 5.753) evaluated at Age = 33. The 95% CI for the difference varies from 0.229 to 1.579 in favor of the left-handed users. Thus, the left-handed users gave higher Fitts' throughput than right-handed users.

Tests of within-subjects effects showed that there was a significant interaction between Finger and Handedness (F = 3.731, p = 0.015). This is perhaps explained by the fact that the non-dominant thumb of left-handed users (i.e. their right thumb) showed higher mean Fitts' throughput than all the other three thumb conditions (their own dominant thumb, and both left and right thumbs of right-handed users).

Table 5. Throughputs (bits/s) for the different cases (DF—Dominant Forefinger, NF—Non-Dominant Forefinger, DT—Dominant Thumb, NT—Non-Dominant Thumb) for left-handed participants

	Mean	N	SD	95% CI from	95% CI to
Left-handed DF	6.369	15	1.324	5.700	7.039
Left-handed NF	5.978	15	1.608	5.164	6.792
Left-handed DT	5.721	15	1.384	5.020	6.421
Left-handed NT	6.078	15	1.532	5.303	6.854
Left-handed D (DF, DT)	6.045	15	1.265	5.405	6.685
Left-handed N (NF, NT)	6.028	15	1.512	5.263	6.794
Left-handed F (DF, NF)	6.174	15	1.439	5.446	6.902
Left-handed T (DT, NT)	5.900	15	1.387	5.197	6.602
Left-handed Overall (DF, NF, DT, NT)	6.037	15	1.369	5.344	6.730

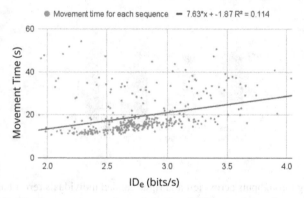

Fig. 8. Plotting movement time v/s index of difficulty for each sequence

Overall, Finger was not a significant factor by itself in the omnibus ANOVA, though post-hoc tests using the Bonferroni correction revealed that the dominant forefinger gave slightly higher throughput (mean = 6.204, N = 29, standard error = 0.196, 95% CI lower bound = 5.801, higher bound = 6.606) than the non-dominant forefinger (mean = 5.588, N = 29, standard error = 0.179, 95% CI lower bound = 5.220, higher bound = 5.955) and the non-dominant thumb (mean = 5.458, N = 29, standard error = 0.222, 95% CI lower bound = 5.001, higher bound = 5.915). The throughput of the dominant thumb (mean = 5.714, N = 29, standard error = 0.205, 95% CI lower bound = 5.293, higher bound = 6.135) did not differ from any of the other conditions.

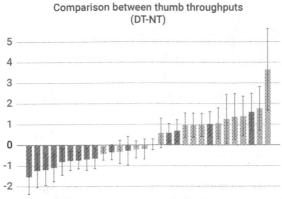

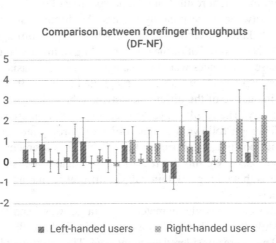

■ Left-handed users   ▨ Right-handed users

Fig. 9. Comparison of (dominant to non-dominant) thumb throughputs and forefinger throughputs for corresponding participants, where yellow (dotted) indicates right-handed and blue (lined) indicates left-handed users with error bars denoting ±1 SD. The results have been arranged in an increasing order as per DT-NT. (Color figure online)

Table 6. Overall percentage erroneous touches and their adjusted Wald 95% confidence intervals

	Error%	Adjusted Wald 95% CI from	Adjusted Wald 95% CI to
Overall DF	2.26	1.69	2.83
Overall NF	2.37	1.79	2.95
Overall DT	2.30	1.72	2.87
Overall NT	3.63	2.92	4.34
Overall D (DF, DT)	2.28	1.88	2.68

(*continued*)

Table 6. (*continued*)

	Error%	Adjusted Wald 95% CI from	Adjusted Wald 95% CI to
Overall N (NF, NT)	3.00	2.54	3.46
Overall F (DF, NF)	2.31	1.91	2.72
Overall T (DT, NT)	2.96	2.51	3.42
Overall (DF, NF, DT, NT)	2.64	2.34	2.94

There was no significant interaction between Finger and Age.

However, another important result from the perspective of our study was the within-subject comparison between corresponding fingers. As throughput comparison might be carried out through direct differences [21], we subtracted the throughput of the non-dominant finger (NF, NT) from that of the corresponding dominant finger (DF, DT) for each participant. These differences were then categorized on the basis of handedness as 'left' (blue, lined) or 'right' (yellow, dotted), and plotted (see Fig. 9).

The graphs are indicative of the difference between throughputs of DF and NF and DT and NT respectively. The results have been arranged in an increasing order as per DT-NT. The DF-NF graph follows the same order of participants. It was found that DF-NF was primarily positive, as expected, but DT-NT was segmented largely across left and right-handed users. We did not record the physical dimensions of fingers, as our argument here was that taking a within-subject difference in readings would nullify anthropometric effects.

As mentioned above, the visible diameter of the target was fixed at 12% of display width (~7.5 mm) while the touches within a concentric circle of diameter 36% of the display width (~390 px) were considered as intentional. Those within 24% of the display width (~260 px, ~15 mm) were accepted as correct touches. Touches within a concentric circle of diameter of 36% of the display width (~390 px) were considered to be erroneous as they were intended to land on the target but were clearly off. Any touches outside of this region were ignored as unintended touches.

By this definition, we found that the errors (clearly missed intentional touches) were generally quite low. Overall, 285 of the 10,800 touches, or 2.64% (adjusted Wald 95% confidence interval from 2.34% to 2.94%), were erroneous. The non-dominant forefingers of the right-handed users were the most accurate (10 errors out of 1,350, 0.74%, CI 0.24% to 1.24%), followed by the dominant forefingers of the right-handed users (12 errors out of 1,350, 0.89%, CI 0.35% to 1.43%). The non-dominant forefingers of the left-handed users and the non-dominant thumb of the right-handed users were the least accurate (54 errors each out of 1,350, 4.00%, CI 2.94% to 5.06%) (see Tables 6, 7 and 8 for the descriptive statistics of other combinations).

Table 7. Percentage erroneous touches and their adjusted Wald 95% confidence intervals for right-handed participants

	Error%	Adjusted Wald 95% CI from	Adjusted Wald 95% CI to
Right-handed DF	0.89	0.35	1.43
Right-handed NF	0.74	0.24	1.24
Right-handed DT	1.63	0.93	2.33
Right-handed NT	4.00	2.94	5.06
Right-handed D (DF, DT)	1.26	0.83	1.69
Right-handed N (NF, NT)	2.37	1.79	2.95
Right-handed F (DF, NF)	0.81	0.46	1.17
Right-handed T (DT, NT)	2.81	2.18	3.45
Right-handed Overall (DF, NF, DT, NT)	1.81	1.46	2.47

Table 8. Percentage erroneous touches and their adjusted Wald 95% confidence intervals for left-handed participants

	Error%	Adjusted Wald 95% CI from	Adjusted Wald 95% CI to
Left-handed DF	3.63	2.62	4.64
Left-handed NF	4.00	2.94	5.06
Left-handed DT	2.96	2.04	3.89
Left-handed NT	3.26	2.29	4.22
Left-handed D (DF, DT)	3.30	2.62	3.98
Left-handed N (NF, NT)	3.63	2.92	4.34
Left-handed F (DF, NF)	3.81	3.09	4.54
Left-handed T (DT, NT)	3.11	2.45	3.77
Left-handed Overall(DF, NF, DT, NT)	3.46	2.97	3.95

We also plotted scatter plots of the touches that were considered accurate by the above definition. On the whole, the right handers seem to be more accurate and precise than the left handers (see Fig. 10).

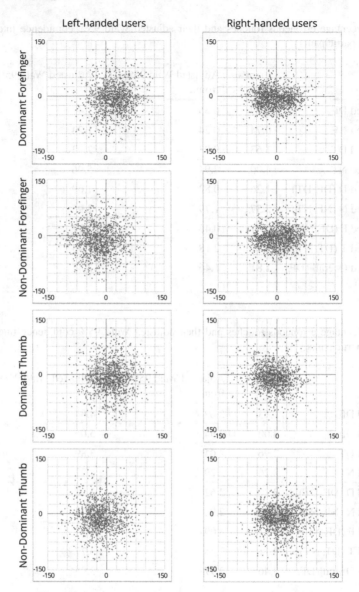

Fig. 10. Scatter plots of touches for different combinations

We summarized these distributions numerically with mean difference in the X and Y axes and their standard deviations (see Table 9). We can see that all mean differences in the Y axis are negative, indicating that most people hit just below the intended point. On the other hand, all mean differences of the digits of the right hands tend to overshoot slightly to the left of the intended target, and conversely for the fingers of the left hand.

Table 9. Distribution of touches for the different cases (DF—Dominant Forefinger, NF—Non-Dominant Forefinger, DT—Dominant Thumb, NT—Non-Dominant Thumb) for right-handed and left-handed participants respectively

	Mean diff x	SD diff x	Mean diff y	SD diff y
Right-handed DF	−1.7	37.1	−5.4	27.9
Right-handed NF	4.0	37.2	−5.2	28.0
Right-handed DT	−8.4	36.7	−8.5	35.5
Right-handed NT	9.6	39.2	−12.9	34.8
Left-handed DF	19.8	37.2	−7.0	39.1
Left-handed NF	−16.1	41.6	−11.6	40.1
Left-handed DT	11.0	36.8	−7.3	41.8
Left-handed NT	−12.3	40.1	−9.5	40.4
Right-handed DF	−1.7	37.1	−5.4	27.9

4   Discussion

The hypothesis in our study was that the throughput of the dominant finger would be higher than the corresponding non-dominant finger for both thumb and forefinger for all users. The forefinger throughputs conformed to this for both right- and left-handed participants. It was also followed in the case of thumbs for the right-handed participants. Surprisingly, though, left-handed participants had higher throughput with their non-dominant thumb compared to their dominant thumb.

4.1   Thumb Performance of Left-Handed Participants

One might question if there's also a concept such as 'fingeredness' which transcends beyond mere hand laterality but looks at the preference as well as efficiency of use of each individual digit in light of the digital world. The high throughput for the DF case for all users seems particularly compelling for such an argument. The choice of using forefingers might be said to demonstrate intent, unlike engaging only one hand for phone usage.

The comparison between DT and NT of left-handed users, however, clearly deviated from our expectation of a positive return. A point to be noted here is that 'dominant' and 'non-dominant' labels were assigned on the basis of initial self-reporting of handedness by the subject and verified by the EHI.

In the scenario where both hands are available for use, there is a natural tendency to use the preferred (dominant) hand for touch input. A possible explanation of the surprising better performance of the non-dominant thumb of the left-handed users is that the user interfaces of touch-screen devices are biased in favor of right-handed users for thumb use. This will provide incentive and practice to the left-handed users to use their right i.e. non-dominant thumb more frequently. Another possible explanation could be that the difference in performance is a result of inherent neurobiological differences in left- and right-handed individuals such as functional organization of motor areas in the brain [27].

By and large, the throughput of left-handed users was found to be higher than that of right-handed users, which could be the cumulative result of intrinsic proficiency combined with years of conditioning over a lifetime.

The result of our study leads us to question the notion of handedness from the perspective of handheld touch-based devices. What exactly is "handedness" and do we need to redefine it? As we discussed above, established handedness inventories are old, and do not consider the day-to-day activities of today's age—such as using touchscreen phones, computer trackpads and so on. With writing or drawing no longer being the main activity requiring high levels of hand dexterity, should such inventories take into account the activities from the modern context—such as using touchscreen phones and computer trackpads?

5 Conclusion

Through our paper we studied the Fitts' throughput for 4 test cases – dominant forefinger, non-dominant forefinger, dominant thumb and non-dominant thumb within-subject for 30 participants, and compared these results from the perspective of handedness. We found that the throughput for the dominant finger was higher than that of the corresponding non-dominant finger for a series of tapping tasks on a handheld touchscreen device. However, an exception to this was the performance of left-hand dominant users, for whom the throughput of the non-dominant (right) thumb was found to be better than that of the dominant (left) thumb. We also reveal that right-hand dominant users, when using their non-dominant (left) thumbs for tapping on a handheld touchscreen device perform the poorest (with the least mean Fitts' throughput). We also found that right-handed users were more accurate and precise than left-handed users.

We believe that taking our observations into consideration could potentially strengthen the design of relevant interfaces and improve inclusivity for both left- and right-handed individuals. While there is potential to bring some benefits especially in frequent tasks such as text input or gaming, additional research would be required to assess the benefits and the costs. We acknowledge the difficulties posed by tailoring the interface to multiple intersections of users in real-life projects. Further work will be required to establish standards related to design for handedness on touchscreens.

The major limitation of our study is that the conditions in which it was carried out may not encompass all the contexts in which touchscreen devices may be used in real life. Varying target widths, landscape vs. portrait modes, screen sizes, screen resolutions, display brightness and contrast, device weight, touch sensitivity, screen glare, different visual appearances of touch targets, and urgency of tasks might impact users' performance. We understand that the grips prescribed by us in the study are not exhaustive and there may be other more preferred or familiar configurations for certain users, and further work may be carried out to investigate the effect of grips on Fitts' throughput. In real life, users would not always be seated in ideal lab conditions and work may be carried out to confirm the applicability of our results with greater external validity.

While our choice to spawn targets at random destinations with varying amplitudes provides additional external validity to the study – in real life settings, targets could be anywhere on the screen and at any amplitude – further experiments may be conducted with our motivation incorporating multiple target widths, using a standardised task, or fixing amplitude over a sequence and the results could be compared. The study design choice of using a constant target width may have an effect on the error rate observed, while random spawning positions may explain a small reduction in throughput (among other factors such as age) due to the additional time a user might spend looking for the next target. The study could be repeated using other formulations of Fitts' Law such as FFitts [2], and these results could be compared.

Further, tapping, though common, is only one type of action that a user might be engaged in. Relationship between laterality and dexterity of other tasks, such as sliding, flicking, pinching and expanding need to be investigated in future.

Our study does not take into account factors such as the impact of gender, education, cultural background or ethnicity on performance. The study was carried out in a fairly localized sample group (technologically adept individuals from the Thane-Mumbai region), and repeating the study in a different geolocation with a more diverse sample might yield different results. For the purpose of collecting sufficient data for both left and right-handed participants, we recruited an equal number of these, which is not representative of the population at large. It is not obvious how this choice might have affected the outcomes. Our study does not delve into the anthropometric aspect, and there could be further work where empirical relations may be drawn between the dimensions of the thumb or finger and the performance in the task, or while taking into account the peculiar nature of movement of the human thumb and the limitations of its reach or range of extension. The directionality of movement might also play a role and further work would be required to determine this.

We believe that the clear asymmetry revealed through our work in the interaction by left- and right-hand dominant users warrants for incorporating handedness into future work in HCI. These could include revisiting several existing HCI studies that have been conducted with right-hand dominant participants which have implicitly assumed a laterally symmetric response. Our work points to possible areas of future research that could be explored, viz. intent-driven tasks such as text input or gaming controls, which might also include two-handed operation, specific grip configurations, etc. There might be exploration into questioning handedness indices and revising them to include contemporary activities on digital interfaces. The work could form a background for personalization and optimization of interfaces based on laterality. Our current work does not establish causality or reasoning behind the results observed, and there exist opportunities for further work to be carried out in this area. For this paper, we only took into account the users who have used a touch-based device regularly for at least a month. It could be interesting to study if similar results are observed by repeating the experiment in the case of users completely new to touchscreen usage, and perhaps thereby free of the biases arising thereof.

References

1. Annett, M.: A classification of hand preference by association analysis. Br. J. Psychol. **61**, 303–321 (1970). https://doi.org/10.1111/j.2044-8295.1970.tb01248.x
2. Bi, X., Li, Y., Zhai, S.: FFitts law: modeling finger touch with Fitts' law. In: 2013 CHI Conference on Human Factors in Computing Systems, pp. 1363–1372 (2013). https://doi.org/10.1145/2470654.2466180
3. Brush, K., et al.: Index of difficulty measurement for handedness with biometric authentication. In: Stephanidis, C., Antona, M. (eds.) HCII 2019. CCIS, vol. 1088, pp. 413–423. Springer, Cham (2019). https://doi.org/10.1007/978-3-030-30712-7_51
4. Chapman, L.J., Chapman, J.P.: The measurement of handedness. Brain Cogn. **6**(2), 175–183 (1987). https://doi.org/10.1016/0278-2626(87)90118-7
5. Coren, S.: The lateral preference inventory for measurement of handedness, footedness, eyedness, and earedness: norms for young adults. Bull. Psychon. Soc. **31**(1), 1–3 (1993). https://doi.org/10.3758/BF03334122
6. Crotte, A.M., Hepting, D.H., Roshchina, A.: Left-handed control configuration for side-scrolling games. In: Extended Abstracts of the 2019 CHI Conference on Human Factors in Computing Systems, pp. LBW1622. ACM (2019). https://doi.org/10.1145/3290607.3312777
7. Drewes, H.: Only one Fitts' law formula please! In: CHI 2010 Extended Abstracts on Human Factors in Computing Systems, pp. 2813–2822. ACM (2010). https://doi.org/10.1145/1753846.1753867
8. Edinburgh Handedness Inventory. http://www.brainmapping.org/shared/Edinburgh.php. Accessed 2020
9. Fan, Z., Coutrix, C.: Impact of hand used on one-handed back-of-device performance. In: Proceedings of the ACM on Human-Computer Interaction 4, pp. 1–19. ISS (2020). https://doi.org/10.1145/3427316
10. Fitts, P.M.: The information capacity of the human motor system in controlling the amplitude of movement. J. Exp. Psychol. **47**(6), 381 (1954). https://doi.org/10.1037//0096-3445.121.3.262
11. Google Material Design Guidelines. https://material.io/design/usability/accessibility.html#layout-typography. Accessed 2020
12. Gori, J., Rioul, O., Guiard, Y., Beaudouin-Lafon, M.: The perils of confounding factors: how Fitts' law experiments can lead to false conclusions. In: Proceedings of the 2018 CHI Conference on Human Factors in Computing Systems, pp. 1–10. ACM (2018). https://doi.org/10.1145/3173574.3173770f
13. Henze, N., Boll, S.: It does not Fitts my data! Analysing large amounts of mobile touch data. In: Campos, P., Graham, N., Jorge, J., Nunes, N., Palanque, P., Winckler, M. (eds.) INTERACT 2011. LNCS, vol. 6949, pp. 564–567. Springer, Heidelberg (2011). https://doi.org/10.1007/978-3-642-23768-3_83
14. Hoober, S.: How do users really hold mobile devices? https://www.uxmatters.com/mt/archives/2013/02/how-do-users-really-hold-mobile-devices.php. Accessed 2020
15. Kim, I., Hyeon, J.J.: Performance comparisons between thumb-based and finger-based input on a small touch-screen under realistic variability. Int. J. Hum. Comput. Interact. **31**(11), 746–760 (2015). https://doi.org/10.1080/10447318.2015.1045241
16. Le, H.V., Mayer, S., Wolf, K., Henze, N.: Finger placement and hand grasp during smartphone interaction. In: Proceedings of the 2016 CHI Conference Extended Abstracts on Human Factors in Computing systems, pp. 2576–2584. https://doi.org/10.1145/2851581.2892462

17. Lehmann, F., Kipp, M.: How to hold your phone when tapping: a comparative study of performance, precision, and errors. In: Proceedings of the 2018 ACM International Conference on Interactive Surfaces and Spaces, pp. 115–127. ACM (2018). https://doi.org/10.1145/327 9778.3279791

18. Lewis, R.: The effect of handedness on use of touch screen versus touch pad. In: Proceedings of the 5th International Conference on Application and Theory of Automation in Command and Control Systems, pp. 115–120. ACM (2015). https://doi.org/10.1145/2899361.2899373

19. Ljubic, S., Glavinic, V., Kukec, M.: Finger-based pointing performance on mobile touchscreen devices: Fitts' law fits. In: Antona, M., Stephanidis, C. (eds.) UAHCI 2015. LNCS, vol. 9175, pp. 318–329. Springer, Cham (2015). https://doi.org/10.1007/978-3-319-20678-3_31

20. Löchtefeld, M., Schardt, P., Krüger, A., Boring, S.: Detecting users handedness for ergonomic adaptation of mobile user inrfaces. In: Proceedings of the 14th International Conference on Mobile and Ubiquitous Multimedia, pp. 245–249 (2015). https://doi.org/10.1145/2836041. 2836066

21. Scott MacKenzie, I.: Fitts' throughput and the remarkable case of touch-based target selection. In: Kurosu, M. (ed.) HCI 2015. LNCS, vol. 9170, pp. 238–249. Springer, Cham (2015). https://doi.org/10.1007/978-3-319-20916-6_23

22. McManus, I.C.: The interpretation of laterality. Cortex 19(2), 187–214 (1983)

23. Oldfield, R.C.: The assessment and analysis of handedness: the Edinburgh inventory. Neuropsychologia 9(1), 97–113 (1971). https://doi.org/10.1016/0028-3932(71)90067-4

24. Parhi, P., Karlson, A.K., Bederson, B.B.: Target size study for one-handed thumb use on small touchscreen devices. In: Proceedings of the 8th Conference on Human-Computer Interaction with Mobile Devices and Services, pp. 203–210. ACM (2006). https://doi.org/10.1145/115 2215.1152260

25. Perry, K.B., Hourcade, J.P.: Evaluating one handed thumb tapping on mobile touchscreen devices. In: Proceedings of Graphics Interface 2008, pp. 57–64. Canadian Information Processing Society (2008). https://doi.org/10.5555/1375714.1375725

26. Plaumann, K., Weing, M., Winkler, C., Müller, M., Rukzio, E.: Towards accurate cursorless pointing: the effects of ocular dominance and handedness. Pers. Ubiquit. Comput. 22(4), 633–646 (2017). https://doi.org/10.1007/s00779-017-1100-7

27. Solodkin, A., Hlustik, P., Noll, D.C., Small, S.L.: Lateralization of motor circuits and handedness during finger movements. Eur. J. Neurol. 8(5), 425–434 (2001). https://doi.org/10.1046/j.1468-1331.2001.00242.x

28. Soukoreff, R.W., MacKenzie, I.S.: Towards a standard for pointing device evaluation, on perspectives on 27 years of Fitts' law research in HCI. Int. J. Hum. Comput. Stud. 61(6), 751–789 (2004)

29. Trudeau, M.B., Young, J.G., Jindrich, D.L., Dennerlein, J.T.: Thumb motor performance varies with thumb and wrist posture during single-handed mobile phone use. J. Biomech. 45(14), 2349–2354 (2012). https://doi.org/10.1016/j.jbiomech.2012.07.012

30. Williams, S.M.: Handedness inventories: Edinburgh versus Annett. Neuropsychology 5(1), 43 (1991). https://doi.org/10.1037/0894-4105.5.1.43

The Effect of Rhythm in Mid-air Gestures on the User Experience in Virtual Reality

Vincent Reynaert[1]([✉]), Florent Berthaut[1], Yosra Rekik[2], and Laurent Grisoni[1]

[1] Univ. Lille, UMR 9189 CRIStAL, 59000 Lille, France
{vincent.reynaert,florent.berthaut,laurent.grisoni}@univ-lille.fr
[2] Univ. Polytechnique Hauts-de-France, LAMIH, CNRS, UMR 8201,
59313 Valenciennes, France
yosra.rekik@uphf.fr

Abstract. In this work, we examine the effect of mid-air gesture rhythm on user experience in Virtual Reality. In particular, we investigate gesture regularity, speed and highlighting with a sound guide. We measure the effect of these components on the perceived fatigue, presence, difficulty, success and helpfulness. Our findings indicate that an irregular and slow rhythm leads to a lower arm fatigue. We also find that such an irregular rhythm could increase the user perceived difficulty of the task and the absence of a sound guide could decrease the sense of presence.

Keywords: Virtual Reality · Mid-air gestures · Muscular fatigue · Presence · Rhythm · Sound guide · User experience

1 Introduction

VR headsets have become increasingly ubiquitous, with VR applications that support long period VR experience like immersive cinematographic content, video games or creative applications. A major feature of VR applications is their ability to enable users to directly manipulate information with their hands through mid-air gestures. However, interacting through mid-air gestures during a long period of time can affect the perceived arm fatigue due to the "gorilla-arm effect" [2,10] which can eventually lead to physical injury and consequently can deteriorate the user experience. Thus, designing gestures for a VR application can prove a challenging task. The current practice of mid-air gestures design and VR applications has outlined several guidelines to assist practitioners in this regard [6,10,20]. Researchers have also reported users preferences in arm position [2,4,8,10] and provided specific insight on how alternative gesture sets should be designed [10] to reduce fatigue. Different arm fatigue measures have been also proposed to characterize the gorilla-arm effect including subjective ones (like Borg [1], NASA-TLX [9] or Likert ratings) and quantitative ones like the "Consumed Endurance" metric [10].

© IFIP International Federation for Information Processing 2021
Published by Springer Nature Switzerland AG 2021
C. Ardito et al. (Eds.): INTERACT 2021, LNCS 12934, pp. 182–191, 2021.
https://doi.org/10.1007/978-3-030-85613-7_13

Aside from understanding how to measure such fatigue, it is also important to investigate approaches to diminish it. Remarkably, perceived fatigue has been shown to be affected by music, especially when synchronised with the user's movements. For example, Szmedra et al. [18] demonstrated that listening to music while running decreases perceived muscular fatigue. Williams et al. [21] showed that generative music with a rhythm synchronised to the cadence of runners can improve their performance but also decrease their perceived effort. However, and despite that rhythm and audio have been proved useful to reduce fatigue in real scenarios, no study have examined the effect of gesture rhythm on user experience during mid-air gestures in VR, in particular of components of rhythm such as regularity, speed and highlighting using sound guides. Previous work on rhythm in gestural and 3D interfaces have focused on uses other than fatigue reduction.

In most interactive systems, users have full control over application automata execution, through the time that interaction events are generated. In VR and for some specific use-cases, it is occasionally possible that some time constrains may exist, e.g., with timers for gaze-based selection or (standard or serious) games. For interaction situations in which it is reasonable to have the application influence the rate at which user is interacting, and in order to explore approaches to control perceived interaction fatigue, gestural rhythm is one of the promising exploration roads, as advocated by Costello [12]. For example, Mueller et al. [14] proposed to "Help players identify rhythm in their movements", and to acknowledge the rhythm in a sequence of gestures. Rhythm has been also used as a way to input commands through sequences of tapping gestures [7] or with micro-gestures performed at a given tempo [5] or for target selection by following trajectories at a given speed with mid-air gestures [3,19]. In 3D User Interfaces, sound guides were primarily investigated to help visually impaired users find targets in a 3D environment [13,15].

In this context, among other fundamental questions, one can for instance ask the following: Does imposing a rhythm in the production of the gesture have an effect on the fatigue? What causes articulation difficulty and what triggers perceived fatigue? How does gesture speed affect the user experience? Is there a link between the regularity of the speed and the perceived fatigue? Do sound guides helps users in increasing the perceived presence?

We argue that rhythm in mid-air gestures is an important factor for improving the user experience in VR applications, including perceived fatigue and presence, that has been little explored so far and, consequently, is little understood. In this paper, we conducted an experiment to examine the effect of rhythm (in terms of speed, regularity and highlighting using a sound guide) in mid-air gestures on the user experience in VR and we provide the community with some insight on this phenomenon. We used a pointing task where the participants were asked to follow a target moving to a predefined rhythm in the presence or not of a sound guide.

Table 1. Questions employed to elicit user experience. For the fatigue we used the Borg CR10 [1] and for the remainder questions, we used a 7-points Likert-scale question (strongly disagree to strongly agree).

Label	Question
Post. Fatigue	How tiring did you find this task? (Borg CR10)
Presence	Average result of the Adaptation/Immersion presence questionnaire [16]
Difficulty	How difficult did you find this task?
Success	How successful did you feel in performing the task?
Liveliness	How lively did you find the rhythm?
Helpfulness	How much did the sound help you in following the target?

2   Experiment

We conducted an experiment to measure the effect of rhythm during mid-air pointing task in VR on user experience in terms of user perceived fatigue, presence, difficulty, success and helpfulness.

Participants. 15 participants (12 males, 3 females) volunteered to take part in our experiment. They were aged between 18 and 45 years ($mean = 28.4, s.d = 6.8$). Thirteen participants were right handed and two were left handed. Two participants considered themselves as experts in understanding the rhythm, seven as proficient, three as intermediate and three as novices. Five participants defined themselves as VR experts, three participants used it frequently, six others occasionally and the last one had never tested it.

Due to the COVID-19 pandemic, part of this experiment was done remotely with seven participants who owned a VR headset. They were recruited via mailing-lists and forums. These participants downloaded the experiment software which was a Godot application build for SteamVR and Oculus Quest. Then, they performed the task while videoconferencing with one of the authors. The remainder eight participants carried out the experiment in our laboratory and used the SteamVR version. We follow all necessary sanitary precautions, in particular cleaning the equipment before and after use. The headsets used by the participants were: 2 × Oculus Quest 2, 1 × Oculus Quest 1, 1 × Oculus Rift S, 2 × HTC Vive Pro and 8 × Valve Index in the lab.

Design. The experiment used a 2 × 2 × 2 × 5 within-subjects design for the factors: *regularity*, *speed*, *sound* and *time period*. The *regularity* of the rhythm of the target's displacement covers two conditions: *regular* (there is no change in speed) and *irregular* (speed is randomly reduced by 0%, 5%, 10%, 25%, 50%, but never increased in order to avoid higher speeds). We chose a random variation to prevent any learning of changes in speed that participants might develop. The *speed* of the target to follow covers two conditions: *slow* (1 s = 4 beats = 1 trajectory, *speed* = 1 m/s) and *fast* (700 ms = 4 beats = 1 trajectory, *speed* = 1.4 m/s).

Fig. 1. Experimental setup. Left: Seated participant with VR headset. Center: what they saw, i.e. the moving Borg CR10 scale on the left and the spherical cursor and cylindrical target with its trajectory. Right: Borg Scale Panel

The *sound* played at the same rhythm as the target displacement covers two conditions: *playing* (audio feedback is used to highlight the rhythm, consisting in four sounds played per trajectory, one at each beat) and *muted* (no audio feedback). The *time period* corresponds to a re-sampling of the task in five successive periods of time: 30–60, 60–90, 90–120, 120–150, 150–180 s. We voluntarily removed the first period of time 0–30 from our analysis to reduce the bias in speed and accuracy when starting to follow the target at the beginning of the task.

Task. We use a pointing task in which participants had to keep a spherical cursor inside a cylindrical target moving on the XY plane in front of them. The trajectory of the target was shown as a trail behind the target, moving towards the user. The target the participant had to follow was a cylinder with a *radius* = 25 cm and a *height* = 10 cm. The controller was represented by a sphere of *radius* = 5 cm. In addition, the target was constrained in a circle whose center was located at $(x = 0\,cm, y = 100\,cm, z = -46\,cm)$ and with *radius* = 50 cm. The result is depicted in Fig. 1 and in a short video (download or watch).

Procedure. At the beginning of the experiment, participants signed an informed consent agreement. Participants were then instructed to seat on a chair without armrest and to make sure to have a clear area in front of them in order to avoid risk of collisions when interacting with the application. All participants then put their VR headset on. Distant participants were instructed to calibrate as accurately as possible the ground and the center of their VR headset so that the interaction area was the same for all. When participants opened the virtual environment, the task was explained to them both orally and with a text on a virtual panel. Participants then filled a brief demographic questionnaire.

The experiment started with a training phase composed of one training block before moving to the experimental phase composed of eight blocks. In both phases, participants were instructed to follow the target as accurately as possible with their dominant hand. In parallel they had to use their non-dominant hand to report their perceived arm fatigue on the Borg scale by using the joystick on the controller. This scale was displayed on a panel that appeared every 15 s on the left side of the interaction area and slowly moved out of the field of view of participants while fading out, in order to remind participants to provide ratings regularly.

After each trial participants had to complete a questionnaire composed of the Adaptation/Immersion part of the presence questionnaire [16] with additional questions on their final level of fatigue and on their perception of the task. Table 1 provides the list of corresponding questions. At the end of the questionnaire, participants were instructed to rest as much as possible in order to reduce the effect of accumulated fatigue. Participants then reported their initial level of fatigue for the following trial. During tasks, we also recorded the hand and target positions, in order to retrieve the distance to the target.

The training phase was designed so that participants familiarize themselves with the task without creating a learning or order effect. Therefore, all participants performed a first trial in a condition which was not part of the ones we wanted to compare. More specifically, in this training phase, we alternated each 8 beats (2 trajectories) between *sound playing* and *sound muted* conditions, we set a medium *speed* (850 ms = 4 beats = 1 trajectory) and the *regularity* was *regular*. This allowed participants to understand the relation between their movements and the imposed rhythm and the sound, and to get used to reporting their level of fatigue on the Borg scale.

In the experiment phase, participants then successively performed eight blocks (2 *regularity*× 2 *speed*× 2 *sound*). The order of the 8 blocks was counterbalanced across participants through a balanced latin square, in order to avoid an order effect on fatigue or engagement. For each block, participants completed the six periods of time for a total of 180 s. After each block, participants took a break. The experiment took around one hour.

3   Results

In this section, we present the results for the performances and the questionnaire. A Shapiro-Wilk normality test [17] showed that the data was not normal for all the measures of performance ($.39 < W < .93$ and $p < .0001$), consequently, we used the ARTool [11,22] test to perform an ANOVA on non-parametric data, followed by post-hoc ART-Contrast for statistically significant main effects or interactions. In addition, as the answers to the questionnaire correspond to ordinal data, the same ARTool method was applied. In the following, we report significant results.

3.1   User Performances

We measured the following depending variables: the *perceived arm fatigue* (evolution of the fatigue on the Borg CR10 scale during the task), the *distance to target* (distance between the hand and the target) and the *accuracy* (ratio of time spent in the target). Figure 2 shows bar-plots of all conditions for results with statistically significant differences.

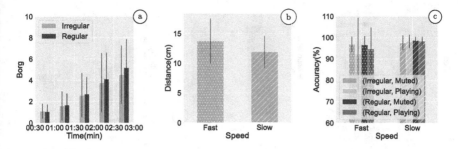

Fig. 2. Results for each of the dependent measures: (a) Average level of arm fatigue by *regularity* and *time period*, (b) Average distance between hand and target by *speed* and (c) Average accuracy by *regularity*, *sound* and *speed*.

During Task Fatigue. There were significant main effects of *regularity* ($F_{1,546} = 13.21$, $p < .0001$) and *time period* ($F_{1,546} = 181.34$, $p < .0001$) on *fatigue*. Post-hoc tests showed that *regular* tasks were rated significantly more fatiguing than *irregular* ones ($p = .0003$). We also found that the perceived fatigue increased significantly across increasing period of time ($p < .001$).

Distance to Target. There was a significant main effect of *speed* ($F_{1,546} = 94.52, p < .0001$) on *the distance of the hand to the target*. Post-hoc tests revealed that *fast speed* increased significantly the distance between the hand and the target than when using *slow speed* ($p < .0001$).

Accuracy. There were significant main effects of *regularity* ($F_{1,546} = 7.49$, $p = .0064$) and *speed* ($F_{1,546} = 45.91$, $p < .0001$) on *accuracy* with significant *regularity* × *speed* ($F_{1,546} = 4.66$, $p = .0313$), *speed* × *sound* ($F_{1,546} = 4.29$, $p = .0388$), *regularity* × *speed* × *sound* ($F_{1,546} = 8.15$, $p = .0045$) interactions. Post-hoc tests revealed that when using either *regular regularity* in *sound muted* or *irregular regularity* in *sound playing*, *fast speed* was significantly less accurate than *slow speed* ($p < .05$). However, the accuracy remained high in all cases (min $= 92.26\%$, max $= 98.62\%$).

3.2 Questionnaire

Figure 3 shows bar-plots of all conditions for questions with statistically significant differences.

Post-task Fatigue. There were significant main effects of *speed* ($F(1, 98) = 12.91, p = .0005$) and *sound* ($F(1, 98) = 5.96, p = .0165$) on *fatigue*. Post-hoc tests revealed that both the *fast speed* and the *sound playing* significantly implied more perceived fatigue than respectively the *slow speed* and the *sound muted* ($p < .05$).

Presence. There was significant main effect of *sound* ($F(1, 98) = 7.30$, $p = .0081$) on *presence*. Post-hoc tests revealed that the *sound playing* implied a significantly greater sense of presence than the *sound muted* ($p < .05$).

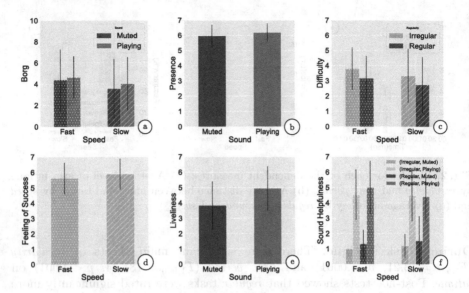

Fig. 3. Results for each of the dependent measures: (a) Average level of arm fatigue at the end of tasks by *sound* and *speed*, (b) Average sense of presence by *sound*, (c) Average perceived difficulty by *regularity* and *speed*, (d) Average feeling of success by *speed*, (e) Average liveliness by *sound* and (f) Average feeling of helpfulness of the sound by *regularity*, *speed* and *sound*.

Difficulty. There were significant main effects of *regularity* ($F(1, 98) = 11.93$, $p = .0008$) and *speed* ($F(1, 98) = 6.05$, $p = .0157$) on difficulty. Post-hoc test revealed that the *irregular regularity* conditions were rated significantly more difficult than the *regular* ones ($p < .001$). In addition, the *fast speed* was rated, significantly more difficult than the *slow speed* ($p < .05$).

Feeling of Success. There was a significant main effect of *speed* ($F(1, 98) = 4.96$, $p = .0282$) on *feeling of success*. Post-hoc tests showed the *slow* speed increased significantly the feeling of the success than *fast* speed ($p < .05$).

Liveliness. There was a significant main effect of *sound* ($F(1, 98) = 30.72$, $p < .0001$) on *liveliness*. Post-hoc revealed that the *sound playing* helped participants feel the rhythm and made it more lively than the *sound muted* ($p < .0001$).

Sound Helpfulness. There was a significant main effect of *sound* ($F(1, 98) = 221.76$, $p < .0001$) on *sound helpfulness* with significant *regularity* × *sound* ($F(1, 98) = 7.09$, $p = .0091$) and *sound* × *speed* ($F(1, 98) = 4.48$, $p = .0369$) interactions. Post-hoc tests revealed that for both *regular* and *irregular regularity*, *sound playing* was perceived as helping target following when compared with *sound muted* ($p < .0001$). We also found that for both *fast* and *slow speed*, *sound playing* was perceived as helping target following when compared with *sound muted* ($p < .0001$).

3.3 Discussion of Experiment Results

Effect of the *sound*. In terms of perceived fatigue, our findings indicate that the *sound* does not have an impact during the task. However and contrarily to related work [18,21], after tasks, we found an increase in perceived fatigue when the *sound* was played. These findings could be explained by a greater sense of presence and liveliness in *sound playing*. However, only one participant explicitly confirmed this. Five other participants found that they were more concentrated on their arm fatigue during *sound muted* and consequently they felt more fatigued. In addition, even if the *sound playing* is perceived helpful to follow the target, it did not seem to impact the perception of success or difficulty of tasks. These results seem to contradict previous research in which music helped increase the endurance [21]. However, we used basic sounds which only served to highlight the target displacement and could therefore reinforce the perception of effort, compared to more complex music which might instead "mask" the effort.

Effect of the *speed*. In terms of perceived fatigue, as for the *sound*, participants felt an impact of the *speed* only after the task but unsurprisingly a *fast speed* implied more fatigue than a *slow* one. However, during interviews at least five participants felt that the *slow speed* was more fatiguing that the *fast* because it was less "fun". The *fast speed* also had a bad impact on the distance between the hand and target and on the accuracy (although it remained high). In the same way, *fast speed* increased the perception of difficulty and decreased the feeling of success. In other words, the *fast speed* had a negative impact on users performances and on their perceived arm fatigue.

Effect of the *regularity*. In terms of perceived fatigue, contrarily to speed and sound, we found that the *regularity* has an impact during the task but not after, with the *irregular* condition being less fatiguing than the *regular* one. This difference in terms of fatigue could be explained by the slower average speed induced by the irregularity. However, the *irregular* condition also seemed to increase the perceived difficulty, which would not be the case if the difference in *regularity* was only a difference in speed. In addition, three participants suggested that the in the *irregular* condition was funnier and more engaging and therefore that they were less focused on the fatigue.

4 Conclusion

Through an experiment, we explored how the rhythm of mid-air gestures impacted the user experience in Virtual Reality. We found that, if the aim is to reduce fatigue, the use of *irregular* and *slow* gestures without a *sound* highlighting the gesture speed may be an interesting choice. However, our results also suggest that the absence of *sound* reduces the sense of presence and liveliness. Our experiment suffers from some limitations which could be lifted in future studies. A first bias may come from the lack of diversity in participants' gender and from the remote and therefore little controlled conditions of the experiment.

Our results should be refined with more participants and by looking at the impact of gender, level of VR expertise and dominant hands. As pointed out earlier, we observed differences with related work on the effect of the sound on perceived fatigue. Future work should investigate the role of sound/music complexity and the effect of mapping the sound with either the wanted trajectory or the user's gesture. While our results suggest a large effect of the *speed* and *regularity* on the user experience, variations on these parameters should be investigated, such as slower and faster speeds and patterns in irregular rhythms. We believe that our results are applicable beyond VR, in mid-air interactions where the temporality of gestures is controlled or when a long-term use is frequent, such as games or creative applications. In particular, rehabilitation exercises require series of repetitive movements whose rhythm could be adjusted to control fatigue.

References

1. Borg, G.: Borg's Perceived Exertion and Pain Scales. Borg's Perceived Exertion and Pain Scales, p. viii, 104. Human Kinetics, Champaign (1998)
2. Boring, S., Jurmu, M., Butz, A.: Scroll, tilt or move it: using mobile phones to continuously control pointers on large public displays. In: Proceedings of the 21st Annual Conference of the Australian Computer-Human Interaction Special Interest Group: Design: Open 24/7, pp. 161–168 (2009)
3. Carter, M., Velloso, E., Downs, J., Sellen, A., O'Hara, K., Vetere, F.: PathSync: multi-user gestural interaction with touchless rhythmic path mimicry. In: Proceedings of the 2016 CHI Conference on Human Factors in Computing Systems, pp. 3415–3427 (2016)
4. Cockburn, A., Quinn, P., Gutwin, C., Ramos, G., Looser, J.: Air pointing: design and evaluation of spatial target acquisition with and without visual feedback. Int. J. Hum. Comput. Stud. **69**(6), 401–414 (2011)
5. Freeman, E., Griffiths, G., Brewster, S.A.: Rhythmic micro-gestures: discreet interaction on-the-go. In: Proceedings of the 19th ACM International Conference on Multimodal Interaction, pp. 115–119 (2017)
6. Fuller, J.R., Lomond, K.V., Fung, J., Côté, J.N.: Posture-movement changes following repetitive motion-induced shoulder muscle fatigue. J. Electromyogr. Kinesiol. **19**(6), 1043–1052 (2009)
7. Ghomi, E., Faure, G., Huot, S., Chapuis, O., Beaudouin-Lafon, M.: Using rhythmic patterns as an input method. In: Proceedings of the SIGCHI Conference on Human Factors in Computing Systems, pp. 1253–1262 (2012)
8. Harrison, C., Ramamurthy, S., Hudson, S.E.: On-body interaction: armed and dangerous. In: Proceedings of the Sixth International Conference on Tangible, Embedded and Embodied Interaction, pp. 69–76 (2012)
9. Hart, S.G., Staveland, L.E.: Development of NASA-TLX (task load index): results of empirical and theoretical research. In: Advances in Psychology, vol. 52, pp. 139–183. Elsevier (1988)
10. Hincapié-Ramos, J.D., Guo, X., Moghadasian, P., Irani, P.: Consumed endurance: a metric to quantify arm fatigue of mid-air interactions. In: Proceedings of the 32nd Annual ACM Conference on Human Factors in Computing Systems, pp. 1063–1072. ACM (2014)
11. Kay, M., Wobbrock, J.O.: Package 'artool' (2020)

12. Mary Costello, B.: Paying attention to rhythm in HCI: some thoughts on methods. In: 32nd Australian Conference on Human-Computer Interaction, pp. 471–480 (2020)
13. Mereu, S.W., Kazman, R.: Audio enhanced 3D interfaces for visually impaired users. ACM SIGCAPH Comput. Phys. Handicap. **57**, 10–15 (1997)
14. Mueller, F., Isbister, K.: Movement-based game guidelines. In: Proceedings of the SIGCHI Conference on Human Factors in Computing Systems, pp. 2191–2200 (2014)
15. Sánchez, J., Sáenz, M.: 3D sound interactive environments for problem solving. In: Proceedings of the 7th International ACM SIGACCESS Conference on Computers and Accessibility, pp. 173–179 (2005)
16. Schneider, D.K.: Presence Questionnaire (PQ) - EduTech Wiki, July 2019. http://edutechwiki.unige.ch/en/Presence/Presence_Questionnaire_(PQ)
17. Shapiro, S.S., Wilk, M.B.: An analysis of variance test for normality (complete samples). Biometrika **52**(3/4), 591–611 (1965)
18. Szmedra, L., Bacharach, D.: Effect of music on perceived exertion, plasma lactate, norepinephrine and cardiovascular hemodynamics during treadmill running. Int. J. Sports Med. **19**(1), 32–37 (1998)
19. Velloso, E., Carter, M., Newn, J., Esteves, A., Clarke, C., Gellersen, H.: Motion correlation: selecting objects by matching their movement. ACM Trans. Comput. Hum. Interact. (TOCHI) **24**(3), 1–35 (2017)
20. Wang, H.: How will different control/display ratios influence muscle fatigue and game experience in virtual reality games? (2016)
21. Williams, D.A., Fazenda, B., Williamson, V.J., Fazekas, G.: Biophysiologically synchronous computer generated music improves performance and reduces perceived effort in trail runners. In: Michon, R., Schroeder, F. (eds.) Proceedings of the International Conference on New Interfaces for Musical Expression, pp. 531–536. Birmingham City University, Birmingham, July 2020. https://www.nime.org/proceedings/2020/nime2020_paper102.pdf
22. Wobbrock, J., Findlater, L., Gergle, D., Higgins, J.: The aligned rank transform for nonparametric factorial analyses using only ANOVA procedures. In: Proceedings of the SIGCHI Conference on Human Factors in Computing Systems (2011)

User-defined Bend Gesture Completion Strategies for Discrete and Continuous Inputs

Pranjal Protim Borah[1]([✉]), Keyur Sorathia[1], and Sayan Sarcar[2]

[1] EI Lab, IIT Guwahati, Guwahati, India
keyur@iitg.ac.in
[2] University of Tsukuba, Tsukuba, Japan

Abstract. Bend gesture-based input on a flexible device requires a distinct indication of gesture completion. Existing research commonly used threshold-based strategies for discrete input, whereas releasing the bend is used to confirm continuous input. However, the simplest form of these strategies does not allow the rejection of unwanted or unintended input and bi-directional manipulation of the output parameter before confirming continuous input. This work aims to identify user-defined gesture completion strategies with the potential to overcome these drawbacks. Ten blind or low vision (BLV) and fifteen sighted students participated in the study. We identified four and three unique strategies for discrete and continuous inputs, respectively. We believe the reported implications and recommendations with potential application scenarios will help researchers and interaction designers take advantage of these strategies.

Keywords: Gesture completion strategy · Bend gesture · Accessibility

1 Introduction and Background

A flexible electronic device allows input interaction through manipulation of the physical form factor of the device [12,18,21]. Researchers have explored and investigated bend gestures on flexible devices [3,10,12,29] and found these interactions to be feasible, effective, and enjoyable [26]. The bend gestures are also studied with BLV users [6,7] and found to be easy to learn and perform [8].

Bend gestures are naturally associated with bending the flexible device at different locations and in two directions (upward and downward) [15,20,21,29]. This act of performing the bend on a flexible device (Fig. 1) is dynamic in nature. Usually, a dynamic gesture involves three stages: start, update, and end stages [25]. For bend gestures, the initial neutral or relaxed state (Fig. 1a) before bending the device is commonly the start stage [16,26], and the gradual bending is the update stage. For continuous input, this gradual bend is detected by the system, and respectively the output parameter value changes until the end-stage indicate the gesture's completion to confirm a value. For discrete input, the end-stage is

© IFIP International Federation for Information Processing 2021
Published by Springer Nature Switzerland AG 2021
C. Ardito et al. (Eds.): INTERACT 2021, LNCS 12934, pp. 192–202, 2021.
https://doi.org/10.1007/978-3-030-85613-7_14

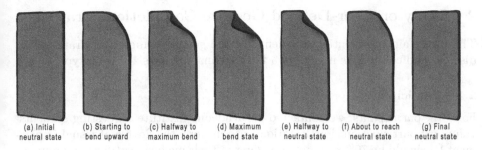

(a) Initial neutral state   (b) Starting to bend upward   (c) Halfway to maximum bend   (d) Maximum bend state   (e) Halfway to neutral state   (f) About to reach neutral state   (g) Final neutral state

Fig. 1. Different intermediate states while bending a flexible device.

detected by the system, and accordingly, the discrete output action is triggered. Although the end-stage plays a vital role in completing the gestures, based on our understanding, the existing research provides evidence of implementing gesture completion strategies that depend on reaching or crossing predefined thresholds [5,10,16,17,22,26,27,30,31] to provide discrete input and releasing the bend to confirm continuous input [16,26].

The major drawback of using only a threshold-based strategy in its simplest form is the lack of freedom to reject unwanted or unintended input as reaching or crossing the threshold triggers the output action immediately. Identifying a common threshold for different user groups also becomes challenging due to diverse manual dexterity and user expertise. On the contrary, a smaller threshold to support a wide range of user groups may adversely affect spurious input rejection. This indicates that applying only a threshold-based gesture completion strategy is insufficient. Similarly, for confirming continuous input, the simplest form of gesture completion on releasing the bend also has certain drawbacks. As soon as the bend is released (or starts to move back), the respective value for the most recent degree of bend gets confirmed for the output parameter. As a result, only uni-directional (either increase or decrease) manipulation of the output parameter is allowed before confirming a value. For instance, if an output parameter value increases on bending upward, the user will have the freedom to only increase (but not decrease) the value before confirming one. Since all bend gestures end up confirming a value on releasing the bend, this strategy also does not allow the rejection of unwanted or unintended input. This indicates that a controlled study that investigates bend gesture completion strategies is necessary to overcome these drawbacks. However, to the best of our knowledge, no prior research has investigated user-defined bend gesture completion strategies.

As both BLV and sighted users can perform these bend gestures, the involvement of both the user groups will allow the interaction designers to draw more accessible and inclusive design decisions. The smartphones being the most commonly used and carried digital devices by BLV users [14], we conducted this study on a flexible smartphone-sized mock-up prototype. We identified four and three strategies for discrete and continuous inputs, respectively.

2   Study on User-Defined Gesture Completion Strategies

This study aims to identify user-defined bend gesture completion strategies for discrete and continuous inputs on a flexible smartphone-sized prototype.

2.1   Participants

For BLV participants, we contacted an academic institute requesting students' voluntary participation. Participation criteria were: the degree of visual impairment [1] should be 70% or more according to their medical certificates, no upper limb disorder, and minimum 3 years of experience using smartphones through screen reader (Google TalkBack). Ten students (8 male, 2 female, and 3 left-handed) with a degree of visual impairment 100% (except one has 80%) between the ages of 18–22 years (Mean = 19.4, SD = 1.58) participated in the study. For the sighted group, we asked first-year university students for their voluntary participation. The participation criteria were: minimum 3 years of experience using smartphones and no upper limb disorder. Fifteen students (9 male, 6 female, and 3 left-handed) between the ages of 18–25 years (Mean = 20.73, SD = 2.49) participated in the study. We have taken prior consent from all participants and followed the ethics of conducting research on human subjects.

2.2   Apparatus

We conducted the study with a flexible smartphone-sized mock-up prototype (154 mm × 74 mm × 6 mm) measuring 6.7 in. at the diagonal. The prototype comprises a flexible 3D printed internal structure (thickness 1 mm, shore 95A) sandwiched between two silicon layers (shore 25A) for higher flexibility [16,19].

2.3   Task

We asked the participants to assume interacting with a flexible smartphone in two scenarios and propose bend gesture completion strategies to confirm discrete and continuous inputs. We selected the following scenarios, which are familiar to users, distinguishable as discrete and continuous inputs, and also been studied with bend gestures [2,20,26]. To reduce the effort in learning and performing bend gestures, we selected only the corners and asked them to perform bend gestures towards upward and downward directions. No external feedback was provided as the gestures' ends (completions) were proposed by the participants.

Scenario-1: This scenario was to provide discrete input to open a file or application. We asked the participant to assume that a selected file or application will open as soon as the participant indicates the completion of the bend gesture.

Scenario-2: This scenario was to provide continuous input to change the volume. We asked the participant to assume that the volume changes with respect to the degree of bend and the current value will be confirmed for the volume parameter as soon as the participant indicates the completion of the gesture.

2.4   Procedure

We conducted the study in a controlled environment. Before conducting the study, we organized two separate training sessions (one week before and immediately preceding the study) to help the participants effectively familiarize themselves with bend gestures to utilize the full potential of the device's flexibility and to reduce the effect of prior experience [23]. In the first training session, we demonstrated (by holding BLV participants' hands) the bend gestures at the corners, while one hand was holding the device and another hand was bending the corners towards upward and downward directions. Then the participants practiced the gestures under the moderator's observation and assistance (if required) until they found themselves ready. We followed the same procedure for the second training session before introducing the participants to the concept of gesture completion strategy. Irrespective of participants' prior knowledge, we explained the need and role of gesture completion strategies for discrete and continuous inputs by referring to the scenarios. We introduced them to the threshold-based strategy for discrete input and releasing the bend gesture for continuous input and explained their drawbacks. This was done to help the participants propose new strategies that can overcome the drawbacks.

We referred to each gesture by combining the names of the location (corner) and direction as a pair [3] for example, "Top-Right-Corner Bend-Upward". First, we asked the participants to perform bend gestures at one corner (for both directions) to provide discrete input (Scenario-1). Then we asked the participants to explore a set of gesture completion strategies that are intuitive [3,4,11], easy to perform, and do not involve other input modalities such as touch or voice. The exact process was repeated for the remaining corners, where we asked the participants to perform the previously explored strategies and explore new strategies. Then participants performed the final set of strategies for each location and direction. They finally proposed a sequence of preferences (maximum three) that are intuitive, easy to perform, and can overcome the drawbacks of existing strategies. After they proposed the strategies, we asked them to share their experience regarding confidence during input, scope of one-handed interaction, and potential application. Then we repeated this process for continuous input (Scenario-2). We randomized the sequence of scenarios and corners.

3   Results and Discussion

The BLV and sighted participant groups proposed a total of 42 strategies (26 for discrete and 16 for continuous inputs) and 75 strategies (44 for discrete and 31 for continuous inputs), respectively. The demonstrations and the verbal descriptions of the strategies enabled us to identify the functionally similar strategies. Finally, we identified four unique strategies (D1, D2, D3, and D4) for discrete input and three unique strategies (C1, C2, and C3) for continuous input (Table 1). We calculated the total number of participants from both BLV and sighted groups who reported the strategies as their first, second, and third preferences and presented in Table 1 as the sum of the two groups (Number of BLV participants + Number of sighted participants = Total). These preferences are based on intuitiveness, ease of performance, and the ability to overcome the drawbacks of existing strategies. The majority of the BLV participants reported the On-Hold strategies (D1 and C1) as their first preferences for discrete (80%) and continuous (88.89%) inputs. The majority of the sighted participants reported the On-Release strategy (D2) and the On-Hold strategy (C1) as their first preferences for discrete (76.92%) and continuous (66.67%) inputs, respectively.

Table 1. The unique strategies proposed by BLV and sighted participants.

Strategy codes	Strategy names	Input types	Preferences of (BLV + sighted) participants			Total count out of 25 (10 + 15)
			First preference	Second preference	Third preference	
D1	On-Hold	Discrete	8 + 2 = 10	1 + 10 = 11	1 + 2 = 3	10 + 14 = 24
D2	On-Release	Discrete	2 + 10 = 12	3 + 2 = 5	0 + 1 = 1	5 + 13 = 18
D3	On-Relax	Discrete	0 + 2 = 2	1 + 1 = 2	4 + 6 = 10	5 + 9 = 14
D4	On-Double-Bend	Discrete	0 + 1 = 1	5 + 2 = 7	1 + 5 = 6	6 + 8 = 14
C1	On-Hold	Continuous	8 + 10 = 18	1 + 4 = 5	0 + 1 = 1	9 + 15 = 24
C2	On-Second-Bend	Continuous	2 + 3 = 5	4 + 2 = 6	0 + 2 = 2	6 + 7 = 13
C3	On-Quick-Relax	Continuous	0 + 2 = 2	0 + 6 = 6	1 + 1 = 2	1 + 9 = 10

During the analysis of participants' verbal feedback, we noticed that confidence during input was a major deciding factor for the BLV group. Since they solely relied on tactile and kinesthetic perception, their preferences were inclined towards strategies (D1, D4, C1, and C2) that not only allow them to continue the grip on the device, also offer rejection mechanisms. The grip on the bent location allowed participants to perceive the innate tactile and kinesthetic feedback of bend gestures. In contrast, the ease of performing the strategies was often a major deciding factor for the sighted participants during discrete input. However, during continuous input, the confidence during input was a major deciding factor due to the difficulty in measuring the degree of bend only through visual perception. The continuous grip on the bent location offered them higher confidence. We also noticed that participants often refer to their prior experience with button and touch-based [13,24,28] interactions. Considering legacy-inspired interactions to be easily guessable and learnable [23,32], we believe these strategies can help touchscreen users easily adapt to bend gestures of flexible devices.

We also noticed participants' inconsistency in performing degrees of bend, especially a few participants who performed very small degrees of bend for discrete inputs. This may result in unintended input, hence leading to poor user experience. We believe using a bend angle-based activation threshold [22] in combination with the proposed input strategies can address this issue. Crossing the activation threshold does not trigger actions rather confirms the current bend as a valid bend and informs the user to go ahead with the proposed strategies.

3.1 Gesture Completion Strategies for Discrete Input

Gesture Completion On-Hold (D1): This strategy indicates the bend gesture's completion on holding the bend in the same state (without any change in the degree of bend) for a predefined interval of time (hold-time). As soon as the predefined interval ends, the associated action gets triggered. As a result, this strategy offers the freedom to reject unwanted or unintended input by avoiding the hold-time. However, this hold-time does not allow quick input. Although the hold-time between 1–1.5 s was preferred by the majority of the BLV (70%) and sighted (64%) participants, further investigation is required to identify one or multiple appropriate values. According to both participant groups, this strategy can be applied during one-handed interaction. The higher confidence during input reported by the BLV participants resulted in maximum BLV participants under the first preference (D1 row in Table 1). In contrast, the associated hold-time resulted in maximum sighted participants under the second preference. One BLV participant said, "When I bend, I can feel the device all the time, I will not hold this bend unless I am confident about the action". Literature [28] also discussed a similar touch input strategy of Android devices.

Gesture Completion On-Release (D2): This strategy indicates the completion of a bend gesture on releasing the bend. As soon as the bend is released (or starts to move back), the associated action gets triggered. As a result, it allows the user to decide the precise moment of discrete input. However, this strategy alone does not offer the freedom to reject unwanted or unintended input. According to both participant groups, this strategy can be applied during one-handed interaction. The ease of performing the strategy and its intuitiveness resulted in maximum sighted participants under the first preference (D2 row in Table 1). In contrast, the reduced confidence during input reported by the BLV participants and the lack of rejection mechanism resulted in a lower (less than or equal to 50%) number of proposals by this group. One sighted participant mentioned, "It is easier than threshold-based strategy in terms of reduced cognitive load as I don't have to focus on bending the device to trigger an action". Literature also reported similar strategies for touch [24] and bend gesture-based [9] input.

Gesture Completion On-Relax (D3): This strategy indicates the bend gesture's completion on reaching the final neutral state (Fig. 1g) after releasing the bend. As soon as the bent location reaches the final relaxed or neutral state, the associated action gets triggered. Although this strategy alone does not offer the freedom to reject unwanted or unintended input, according to the participants, bending the device in the opposite direction (without stopping at the neutral state) can serve the purpose. However, they also reported that the application of this strategy would be difficult during one-handed interaction due to the rejection mechanism. The less intuitive rejection mechanism at the cost of more effort resulted in maximum sighted participants under the third preference (D3 row in Table 1). In contrast, the reduced confidence during input reported by the BLV participants and the less intuitive rejection mechanism resulted in a lower number of proposals by this group. A similar strategy was reported in the literature [18] to provide bend input during bi-manual interaction.

Gesture Completion On-Double-Bend (D4): This strategy indicates the bend gesture's completion on quickly performing double (two identical) bend gestures with the same location and direction. After performing the first bend gesture, the user quickly starts the second bend gesture, and as soon as the second bend gesture reaches the previous gesture's maximum degree of bend, the associated action gets triggered. As a result, this strategy offers the freedom to reject unwanted or unintended input by avoiding the repeated bend. According to both participant groups, this strategy can be applied during one-handed interaction. The higher confidence during input at the cost of more effort reported by the BLV participants resulted in maximum BLV participants under the second preference (D4 row in Table 1). In contrast, the additional effort required to perform repeated bends resulted in maximum sighted participants under the third preference. Kane et al. [13] reported a similar strategy for touch input.

3.2   Gesture Completion Strategies for Continuous Input

For continuous input, a user starts a bend gesture, and based on the degree of bend, the output parameter value increases or decreases. This manipulation of the parameter is temporary until the user confirms a respective value for a degree of bend by indicating the gesture's completion at that degree of bend.

Gesture Completion On-Hold (C1): This strategy indicates the bend gesture's completion on holding the bend in the same state (without any change in the degree of bend) for a predefined interval of time (hold-time). As soon as the predefined interval ends, the respective value for the degree of bend gets confirmed. As a result, this strategy allows the rejection of unwanted or unintended input and bi-directional manipulation of the output parameter before confirming a final value. However, this hold-time does not allow quick input. Since, unlike discrete input, a user has to try the manipulated value before confirming it, the majority of the BLV (78%) and sighted (60%) participants preferred a higher hold-time between 1.5–2 s. According to the participants, this strategy can be applied during one-handed interaction. The higher confidence during input reported by both groups and the ability to overcome the drawbacks resulted in maximum participants under the first preference (C1 row in Table 1).

Gesture Completion On-Second-Bend (C2): This strategy indicates the currently performing bend gesture's completion on performing a second bend gesture at a different location. When a user is manipulating the output parameter by performing a bend gesture, as soon as the user decides to confirm the respective value for a degree of bend, the user performs a second bend gesture at a different location to confirm the value. As a result, this strategy allows rejection of unwanted or unintended input, user-decided precise moment of input, and bi-directional manipulation of the output parameter before confirming a final value. Bi-manual interaction is required for this strategy. Despite the higher confidence during input reported by both participant groups, the bi-manual interaction and associated effort resulted in maximum BLV participants under the second preference and the lack of intuitiveness resulted in a lower number of proposals by the sighted group (C2 row in Table 1). Kane et al. [13] reported a similar touch input strategy (Second-Finger Tap) for BLV users.

Gesture Completion On-Quick-Relax (C3): This strategy indicates the completion of the bend gesture on reaching the final neutral or relaxed state (Fig. 1g) quickly. As soon as the user decides to confirm the respective value for a degree of bend, the user allows the bent location to quickly reach its final relaxed state (freely or manually) without any intermediate delay. Quickly reaching the neutral state acts as confirmation. As a result, this strategy allows bi-directional manipulation of the output parameter before confirming a final value. According to the participants, the rejection of unwanted or unintended input can be achieved by slowly moving the bent location back to its relaxed state, which could be difficult during one-handed interaction. We believe implementing this strategy will require sophisticated hardware support and pattern recognition algorithms. The less intuitive rejection mechanism with reduced confidence resulted in maximum sighted participants under the second preference (C3 row in Table 1). In contrast, the lack of intuitiveness and reduced confidence resulted in a lower number of proposals by BLV participants.

4   Implications and Recommendations

For Both BLV and Sighted Users: On-Hold (D1), On-Double-Bend (D4), On-Hold (C1), and On-Second-Bend (C2) strategies are the most appropriate while designing for both BLV and sighted users and eyes-free interaction by sighted users, as these strategies offer higher confidence during input.

For Quick Input: On-Release (D2), On-Relax (D3), and On-Double-Bend (D4) strategies are appropriate for quick discrete input. While On-Release (D2) strategy is more suitable when a precise moment of input is demanded (for example, pause audio at a specific moment on the timeline). During continuous input, On-Second-Bend (C2) strategy is more suitable for quick input during bi-manual interaction (for example, change volume and content zooming).

Discrete Input for Critical Actions: On-Hold (D1) and On-Double-Bend (D4) strategies are appropriate for critical actions, where triggering the action can lead to significant or irreversible changes in the outcome (for example, close an application and delete a file). On-Hold (D1) is also suitable for shortcuts and input without shaking the device (for example, start camera and capture image).

Multiple Actions with the Same Bend Gesture: Mapping multiple actions to the same bend gesture can reduce frequent re-gripping. This can be achieved by mapping different actions to different discrete input strategies of the same bend gesture. Multiple actions can also be mapped with different hold-times of On-Hold (D1) strategy and different degrees of bend of On-Release (D2) and On-Relax (D3) strategies. Also, two related actions can be mapped with the update-stage and end-stage (completion strategy) of the same gesture.

5   Conclusion

This work aims to identify user-defined bend gesture completion strategies for discrete and continuous inputs on a flexible smartphone-sized device. Ten BLV and fifteen sighted participants proposed a total of 117 strategies. We identified four unique strategies (On-Hold, On-Release, On-Relax, and On-Double-Bend) for discrete and three unique strategies (On-Hold, On-Second-Bend, and On-Quick-Relax) for continuous inputs. We noticed that the participants' prior turn is a major source of inspiration, which in turn may help users quickly adapt to bend gestures. We believe the proposed strategies can be applied to other sizes of flat flexible devices. However, further investigation to compare the strategies and explore the effect of device size may produce promising results.

References

1. Guidelines for assessment of disabilities under RPwD act. 2016 notified (2018). http://www.egazette.nic.in/WriteReadData/2018/181788.pdf. Accessed 12 Apr 2020
2. Ahmaniemi, T.T., Kildal, J., Haveri, M.: What is a device bend gesture really good for? In: Proceedings of the SIGCHI Conference on Human Factors in Computing Systems, pp. 3503–3512 (2014)
3. Borah, P.P., Sorathia, K.: Natural and intuitive deformation gestures for one-handed landscape mode interaction. In: Proceedings of the Thirteenth International Conference on Tangible, Embedded, and Embodied Interaction, pp. 229–236 (2019)
4. Byrd, N.: Intuitive and reflective responses in philosophy. University of Colorado (2014)
5. Daliri, F., Girouard, A.: Visual feedforward guides for performing bend gestures on deformable prototypes. In: Graphics Interface, pp. 209–216 (2016)
6. Ernst, M., Girouard, A.: Bending blindly: exploring bend gestures for the blind. In: Proceedings of the 2016 CHI Conference Extended Abstracts on Human Factors in Computing Systems, pp. 2088–2096 (2016)
7. Ernst, M., Girouard, A.: Exploring haptics for learning bend gestures for the blind. In: Proceedings of the 2016 CHI Conference Extended Abstracts on Human Factors in Computing Systems, pp. 2097–2104 (2016)
8. Ernst, M., Swan, T., Cheung, V., Girouard, A.: Typhlex: exploring deformable input for blind users controlling a mobile screen reader. IEEE Pervasive Comput. 16(4), 28–35 (2017)

9. Gallant, D.T., Seniuk, A.G., Vertegaal, R.: Towards more paper-like input: flexible input devices for foldable interaction styles. In: Proceedings of the 21st Annual ACM Symposium on User Interface Software and Technology, pp. 283–286 (2008)
10. Girouard, A., Lo, J., Riyadh, M., Daliri, F., Eady, A.K., Pasquero, J.: One-handed bend interactions with deformable smartphones. In: Proceedings of the 33rd Annual ACM Conference on Human Factors in Computing Systems, pp. 1509–1518 (2015)
11. Grandhi, S.A., Joue, G., Mittelberg, I.: Understanding naturalness and intuitive-ness in gesture production: insights for touchless gestural interfaces. In: Proceedings of the SIGCHI Conference on Human Factors in Computing Systems, pp. 821–824 (2011)
12. Harrison, B.L., Fishkin, K.P., Gujar, A., Mochon, C., Want, R.: Squeeze me, hold me, tilt me! an exploration of manipulative user interfaces. In: Proceedings of the SIGCHI Conference on Human Factors in Computing Systems, pp. 17–24 (1998)
13. Kane, S.K., Bigham, J.P., Wobbrock, J.O.: Slide rule: making mobile touch screens accessible to blind people using multi-touch interaction techniques. In: Proceed-ings of the 10th International ACM SIGACCESS Conference on Computers and Accessibility, pp. 73–80 (2008)
14. Kane, S.K., Jayant, C., Wobbrock, J.O., Ladner, R.E.: Freedom to roam: a study of mobile device adoption and accessibility for people with visual and motor dis-abilities. In: Proceedings of the 11th International ACM SIGACCESS Conference on Computers and Accessibility, pp. 115–122 (2009)
15. Khalilbeigi, M., Lissermann, R., Kleine, W., Steimle, J.: Foldme: interacting with double-sided foldable displays. In: Proceedings of the Sixth International Confer-ence on Tangible, Embedded and Embodied Interaction, pp. 33–40 (2012)
16. Kildal, J.: Interacting with deformable user interfaces: effect of material stiffness and type of deformation gesture. In: Magnusson, C., Szymczak, D., Brewster, S. (eds.) HAID 2012. LNCS, vol. 7468, pp. 71–80. Springer, Heidelberg (2012). https://doi.org/10.1007/978-3-642-32796-4_8
17. Kildal, J., Boberg, M.: Feel the action: dynamic tactile cues in the interaction with deformable UIs. In: CHI 2013 Extended Abstracts on Human Factors in Computing Systems, pp. 1563–1568 (2013)
18. Kildal, J., Paasovaara, S., Aaltonen, V.: Kinetic device: designing interactions with a deformable mobile interface. In: CHI 2012 Extended Abstracts on Human Factors in Computing Systems, pp. 1871–1876 (2012)
19. Kildal, J., Wilson, G.: Feeling it: the roles of stiffness, deformation range and feedback in the control of deformable UI. In: Proceedings of the 14th ACM Inter-national Conference on Multimodal Interaction, pp. 393–400 (2012)
20. Lahey, B., Girouard, A., Burleson, W., Vertegaal, R.: PaperPhone: understanding the use of bend gestures in mobile devices with flexible electronic paper displays. In: Proceedings of the SIGCHI Conference on Human Factors in Computing Systems, pp. 1303–1312 (2011)
21. Lee, S.S., et al.: How users manipulate deformable displays as input devices. In: Proceedings of the SIGCHI Conference on Human Factors in Computing Systems, pp. 1647–1656 (2010)
22. Lo, J., Girouard, A.: Bendy: exploring mobile gaming with flexible devices. In: Proceedings of the Eleventh International Conference on Tangible, Embedded, and Embodied Interaction, pp. 163–172 (2017)
23. Morris, M.R., et al.: Reducing legacy bias in gesture elicitation studies. Interactions 21(3), 40–45 (2014)

24. Potter, R.L., Weldon, L.J., Shneiderman, B.: Improving the accuracy of touch screens: an experimental evaluation of three strategies. In: Proceedings of the SIGCHI Conference on Human Factors in Computing Systems, pp. 27–32 (1988)
25. Ramamoorthy, A., Vaswani, N., Chaudhury, S., Banerjee, S.: Recognition of dynamic hand gestures. Pattern Recogn. **36**(9), 2069–2081 (2003)
26. Schwesig, C., Poupyrev, I., Mori, E.: Gummi: a bendable computer. In: Proceedings of the SIGCHI Conference on Human Factors in Computing Systems, pp. 263–270 (2004)
27. Tajika, T., Yonezawa, T., Mitsunaga, N.: Intuitive page-turning interface of e-books on flexible e-paper based on user studies. In: Proceedings of the 16th ACM International Conference on Multimedia, pp. 793–796 (2008)
28. Trewin, S., Swart, C., Pettick, D.: Physical accessibility of touchscreen smart-phones. In: Proceedings of the 15th International ACM SIGACCESS Conference on Computers and Accessibility, pp. 1–8 (2013)
29. Warren, K., Lo, J., Vadgama, V., Girouard, A.: Bending the rules: bend gesture classification for flexible displays. In: Proceedings of the SIGCHI Conference on Human Factors in Computing Systems, pp. 607–610 (2013)
30. Watanabe, J., Mochizuki, A., Horry, Y.: Booksheet: bendable device for browsing content using the metaphor of leafing through the pages. In: Proceedings of the 10th International Conference on Ubiquitous Computing, pp. 360–369 (2008)
31. Wightman, D., Ginn, T., Vertegaal, R.: BendFlip: examining input techniques for electronic book readers with flexible form factors. In: Campos, P., Graham, N., Jorge, J., Nunes, N., Palanque, P., Winckler, M. (eds.) INTERACT 2011. LNCS, vol. 6948, pp. 117–133. Springer, Heidelberg (2011). https://doi.org/10.1007/978-3-642-23765-2_9
32. Wobbrock, J.O., Aung, H.H., Rothrock, B., Myers, B.A.: Maximizing the guess-ability of symbolic input. In: CHI 2005 Extended Abstracts on Human Factors in Computing Systems, pp. 1869–1872 (2005)

Human-Centered AI

Consumer Needs and Design Practices for Trusted Social Commerce Platforms

Aisha Ahmed AlArfaj[1,2](✉) and Ellis Solaiman[2](✉)

[1] College of Computer and Information Sciences, Princess Nourah Bint Abdulrahman University, Riyadh, Saudi Arabia
aiaalarfaj@pnu.edu.sa
[2] School of Computing, Newcastle University, Newcastle Upon Tyne, UK
ellis.solaiman@newcastle.ac.uk

Abstract. Due to the increased popularity of social networking platforms, a new form of electronic commerce (e-commerce) has emerged, namely social commerce (s-commerce). This research examines trust mechanisms based on the buyers' perspectives in Saudi Arabia and how social platforms can be better designed to enhance trust. Two studies were conducted to achieve the aims: co-design workshops undertaken to develop and finalize design recommendations, and the second comprised a critique of the mock-up to evaluate the recommendations. These two studies helped validate the results of previous studies conducted to understand the current use of s-commerce platforms. In this paper, critical features for such platforms are identified and design preferences are explored (e.g., news feed and explore). This paper can help inform the design of s-commerce, especially with regard to social and trust aspects. For example, the features related to family and friends, such as friends' verifications, reviews and profiles, have a crucial impact on enhancing trust within social commerce platforms.

Keywords: E-commerce · Social commerce · Social media · Trust · Social features · Social influence · Instagram

1 Introduction

Over the last few years, electronic commerce (e-commerce) has changed remarkably. With the extensive use and increasing popularity of social networking platforms, social commerce (s-commerce) has emerged, first introduced as a concept in 2005 by Yahoo [1]. S-commerce refers to a new e-commerce business model driven by the use of social media platforms to conduct commercial activities [2]. A distinction can be made between e-commerce (e.g. Amazon) and s-commerce (e.g. Facebook) as the former entails one-way activity, whereas the latter enables interactions between sellers and buyers, as well as interactions between members and communities [3]. Many people rely on their friends' opinions and recommendations before buying a product, which makes the purchase process a social experience [4].

C. Ardito et al. (Eds.): INTERACT 2021, LNCS 12934, pp. 205–226, 2021.
https://doi.org/10.1007/978-3-030-85613-7_15

Consumers in many countries, such as the Kingdom of Saudi Arabia (KSA), Kuwait, Egypt [5], Indonesia [6], and Malaysia [7], are increasingly using social media platforms like Instagram to buy and sell products and services. Using social networks for conducting e-commerce has become popular, even though social networking platforms lack e-commerce tools. People need to trust the platform, find what they need, and communicate with the buyer/seller to conduct commercial transactions.

In the field of human-computer interaction (HCI), some studies have explored user behaviours in social media applications [3, 8, 9]. Most current studies have investigated the use of Facebook. There is a clear need to investigate different social media platforms and to conduct research in non-Western countries [3, 9]. Although various features of s-commerce have been identified in previous research, they have not been studied in depth [3]. Moreover, with the growth in s-commerce, using social media to engage in business transactions, it has become necessary to understand user behaviours and routines to tailor the design of s-commerce platforms. The challenges facing users should be identified, especially concerning trust, which remains one of the issues requiring further study, especially in different contexts. Therefore, this study focused on the KSA context, examining consumers' current use of s-commerce platforms and how to design such platforms to better meet their needs and enhance their trust. The research question addressed in this study was as follows: RQ1. What are the features that can create or enhance trust between sellers and buyers on social commerce platforms?

To answer this question, two studies were undertaken: Co-design and critique workshops were conducted to investigate the use of s-commerce features and their effect on trust and presented after the background. The data from these workshops were analyzed focusing on how to improve trust. Both social and commercial features were identified. Moreover, four main categories of features were shown to enhance trust, related to sellers, the App, previous customers, and family and friends, which are described in the discussion section. This research paper makes the following contributions:

- It investigates the features and factors that affect trust in s-commerce platforms.
- It discusses design implications and considerations for s-commerce platforms.

2 Background

Social media is widely used to socialize and share information, and more recently has begun to be used for conducting commercial activities. The use of social aspects for business transactions has created a new form of e-commerce called s-commerce [3]. This is defined in various ways as it encompasses many disciplines, such as psychology, marketing, and computer science. It can be defined as a subset of e-commerce that includes the use of social media to help in conducting commercial activities and transactions [10]. The use of social media enables consumers to share their shopping information [1]. Therefore, it is used to support consumers, allowing them to contribute and interact, thus assisting businesses, mainly due to the popularity of social networks [10].

Several studies have discussed the importance of including social features together with commercial functions [2, 11]. Consumers' intention to buy on s-commerce platforms can be affected positively by both social and technical factors [12]. Huang and

Benyoucef (2017) found that purchase decision-making can be influenced by the design of s-commerce [13]. In e-commerce platforms, designing for trust is increasingly gaining attention in the HCI field [3, 9]. In particular, trust is one of the essential factors that can affect online shopping [14]. Therefore, features that create trust are needed on these platforms [15]. Previous studies investigated how to create trust between peers in some applications such as Etsy and Airbnb [15–17]. Despite lacking the traditional e-commerce tools that assist commercial activities, social media platforms are being used to conduct business transactions [9]. Importantly, some features are available on social media that can initiate trust [12]. For example, a study found that a sale group in Facebook established trust by sharing membership within a close group [9].

Various features might initiate or enhance trust in online shopping platforms [1, 9, 15]. The user profile is one such feature that can foster trust [1], helping consumers share their experiences with others [13]. A tool adopted by businesses is direct communication [15], as an online social presence that gives a sense of direct human contact can influence trust [18]. Furthermore, sellers can enhance their social presence through the amount of information they provide [19].

Information that cannot be manipulated by sellers (e.g. third-party verification and reputation-based systems) is also essential to establish trust, an aspect that is related to warranting theory [20, 21]. A previous studies found that the provision of verification by an App can positively affect trust, such as that found on Airbnb [17]. In the KSA, the government has launched an initiative called "Maroof," a form of third-party authentication that ensures sellers' data are correct based on verification of their national ID; this has been found to increase consumers' purchase intention [22].

Information provided by previous customers has been found to be one of the main factors helping consumers identify trustworthy sellers [3, 9]. Ratings, reviews, and relationships with other customers can reduce uncertainty and develop familiarity [23]. It is considered more trustworthy than information provided by sellers [14, 24, 25]. Information about the reviewers can help consumers assess the reviewers' credibility [26], by reviews by peers are more important to consumers than those by strangers [27]. As well as reviews, photographs of products posted by reviewers support consumers in making a purchase decision as they are more credible than sellers' images of products and indicate that the customers have tried the product [28].

Family and friends are trusted sources for consumers [29], and features associated with them, such as highlighting friends' reviews, can enhance trust [2]. Previous studies have suggested including social approval features, such as enabling the sharing of purchase activities with friends, as these can positively influence the consumer purchase decision [30]. In China, 50% of consumers tend to rely on their friends' suggestions and recommendations to make a purchase decision [4].

Users should be encouraged to use social features and interact with the public or friends and family. Previous studies have recommended including rewards for customers who make purchase recommendations [31]. Moreover, a study in China found that consumers tend to share their shopping information more if there are economic rewards, such as discounts [27]. Privacy also plays a significant role in sharing activities, and thus it has been proposed that consumers should be given options for privacy settings to choose what information they share and with whom [12].

In Saudi Arabia, s-commerce use has rapidly grown [22, 32]. It has been used by women entrepreneurs to sell and present their products such as handmade and customized products. Previous studies examine the use of social media applications by entrepreneurs to conduct commercial activities such as marketing strategy [33] and how to interact with and attract customers [34]. Other studies focus on factors that positively associate with behavioral intentions such as social support, and social commerce constructs [35, 36], as well as factors that influence the adoption of social commerce [37]. There are very few studies that investigate factors that have an effect on consumer trust. Examples of such studies include [22], which looks at factors such as Social Media Influencers (SMIs), Key Opinion Leaders (KOLs), and consumer feedback. Another interesting work [38] demonstrates how trust mediates the relationship between social support and social commerce intentions. However, in general, we have found that research work into the identification of mechanisms that enhance trust in online social commerce through design is currently insufficient. The aim of this paper is to fill this important gap.

3   Methods

A qualitative approach was employed [38], comprising co-design workshops [39] and critique design workshops [40]. To recruit participants for the two studies, a message was sent through social networks. The message included a brief description of the research, the workshop aims, and a link to a Google form to register. The Google form including an information sheet and a consent form. Those interested in participating could open the form and complete it, providing details such as name, nationality, whether they used s-commerce, whether they used e-commerce, and their contact details. The workshops took place either in meeting rooms or cafés. All the participants (buyers) were Saudi females. The target audience for the workshops was female consumers with experience of using s-commerce and/or e-commerce, i.e., current users, as well as potential users.

The co-design workshops were held in February 2019 and the critique design workshops were conducted in December 2019. Most of the participants had university-level education – either a bachelor's or postgraduate degree. The range of income was less than SAR 5,000 to SAR 20,000. We purposely recruited participants covering a wide range of ages and occupations and with different experience of ecommerce and s-commerce so the results would be more generalisable to the general population, not a specific demographic or user case.

3.1   Study One

Co-design workshops can be used to direct future design directions [40, 41], and in this study, inspired by previous research [41, 42], were conducted to identify improvements that could be made to the existing s-commerce site (Instagram), used as an example, to enhance trust. There were 10 participants in total, all female for reasons of culture as it was not possible to conduct workshops with male participants as cross-gender communication and interactions in Saudi Arabia should be mediated by guardians/chaperones and due to gender segregation [43]. The first workshop involved four participants, while the second and third workshops involved three. The two-hour workshops comprised four activities with a break in the middle.

The first activity entailed welcoming the participants and having them complete the survey and consent form. In the second, they discussed their current use of s-commerce and e-commerce, the extent to which they trusted platforms, and issues concerning trust. The third activity involved examining existing online shopping applications. For this activity, participants were provided with cards that included screenshots of interfaces for two applications, Amazon and Instagram. The key reason for choosing these was that they are widely used and highly preferred applications in the KSA [44]. The workshops included key questions inspired by those suggested in previous research for co-design workshops [40]. The participants were first asked to check the Instagram screenshots and discuss what they currently liked/did not like about the application, and what they would change. They then undertook the same process with the Amazon screenshots. The fourth and final activity entailed discussing and sorting the social features and commercial functions they considered essential to conduct a commercial transaction using cards with items identified through a review of previous studies. The participants were asked to categorize them as essential, very important, and less important. (See Fig. 1, 2 & 3 for workshop photographs).

Fig. 1. Second activity in the co-design workshop

Fig. 2. Checking the screenshots and writing notes

Fig. 3. Card sorting in the co-design workshop

3.2 Study Two

Critique workshops were conducted to assess and review a mock-up, and to finalize the design recommendations (considerations). These workshops aimed to evaluate the existing idea rather than suggesting new ideas [40], and to establish how participants interacted with the mock-up. The mock-up was a clickable Smartphone prototype designed using Adobe XD software based on the findings of the prior investigations (co-design workshops and previous studies [32, 34]). Three two-hour workshops were conducted and each included 5–6 participants (16 in total).

In conducting the workshops, a design critique technique was followed [40]. The mock-up was presented to the groups as a pre-installed prototype using laptops, iPads, and mobile phones. The interface was also available as a printed version, enabling the participants to make notes and write comments on them. The workshops started with a brief explanation of the project, stating that the design was in its first stage and could easily be changed to allow them to feel free to critique. It was primarily about evaluating the concepts. The participants were asked to write reviews on cards coded in three colors: things you like, e.g., I like that I can see popular products (green); things not clear, e.g., tell me more about placing an order (yellow); things you suggest adding, e.g., have you thought about including owner accounts under their shop account (pink)?

The workshops were structured based on the functionalities of the mock-up: (i) browsing and exploring; (ii) searching; (iii) checking the seller's profile; (iv) checking the product page; (v) writing reviews and the reward system; (vi) sharing with others; (vii) placing an order. For each function, participants were asked to navigate and write their comments on the relevant critique cards. Then, the participants discussed their comments and how/why the design did/did not satisfy a user need, together with their suggestions for improving the design. The participants were encouraged to focus on the features and functionalities of the prototype rather than the representation and graphical interface. (See Fig. 4. for the workshop photographs).

Fig. 4. Evaluation workshops

The data from the workshops, the participants' notes, and images of the card sorting were collated. All the workshop sessions were audio-recorded and professionally transcribed. The data were analyzed inductively, adopting a realist approach using thematic analysis, i.e., reporting the experiences of the participants (their realities and meanings) [45]. All the qualitative data collected were coded in ATLAS.ti. First, the transcripts were read line by line to become familiar with the data and to develop initial ideas. Open coding was then conducted before grouping the codes, merging similar codes, and finally categorizing them under themes [33]. The research team discussed the codes and themes and agreed on them.

4 Findings

4.1 News Feeds and Browsing (Social and Commercial Features and Functions – Ease and Difficulty)

The inclusion of social content on s-commerce platforms was one of the motivations discussed by participants fostering engagement. Having a platform that included social content, such as recipes posted by others, influencers' posts, and so on, would motivate participants to use and buy from the platform as this would keep them up to date. For example, P8 said "I love the idea that I can view the social news and feeds, and also can shop. It is also easy because it is clearly divided, so I can choose what I am looking for." They believed that by combining both social and commercial aspects, for example, showing them nearby shops, popular products, and friends' products, the purchase decision would become easier and faster as these features could enhance trust.

Those involved in the first and second critique workshops loved the idea of mixing social media with shopping activities. They wanted to see social news and feeds, and be able to find or view products and buy them at the same time. P2 reported "I love the idea that I can do everything on one app – there is a shopping aspect and a social aspect." However, those in the third workshop suggested having a social/commercial application that focused more on shopping, with the social side of the platform being mostly related to the shopping activities. As P11 said, "I want to have a social shopping experience, so I want to have a shopping application with my friends where we can share and see what they like and include only businesses and my friends."

Participants greatly liked having different options for placing an order, for example, placing an order automatically without the need to communicate with the sellers, which would save time and be easier. They also liked having payment options that they could choose from. They believed that they could trust cash on delivery, but having various trusted payment methods would ease the process because they would not always have cash. They particularly liked being able to use Apple Pay as it is faster than other methods and cand be trusted. As P6 remarked, "I love that I can choose to pay by Apple Pay because I have stopped carrying cash with me."

Although participants liked being able to place orders automatically, they said that they also needed other means of doing so, namely by communicating directly with the seller, and by sending the order to friends or family to place it for them. Some participants felt that sometimes they would want to communicate directly with the seller to check details about the product, or because it was easier. Moreover, participants mentioned that some older people or those who do not trust automatic ordering might prefer to place an order by sending messages and communicating directly with the sellers. As P10 noted, "Some people insist on having direct communication with the seller and ordering by sending a message, especially elderly people, or if they want to ask something before ordering. Some people do not like to place an order automatically as they do not trust the technical aspects; they just trust dealing directly with people."

Participants also liked being able to place orders through family and friends, and they thought this was an important feature. Participants mentioned that they often had difficulties ordering for their family and friends because they had to get a screenshot sent to them and then order it. Their family and friends did this mostly because they were not sure if they should trust a particular shop, or they did not want to have any communication with the sellers or drivers when they delivered the products. As P14 remarked, "My friends and my family always ask me to order for them, so I think this feature is important for me. So, instead of searching for what they want, I will ask them to send me their order and then I will do the transaction because they do not trust placing the order themselves. They usually tell me what they want and I search and read the reviews and decide if I can trust buying from that seller or not. Sometimes, they do not want to communicate with the sellers, so they ask me to order what they want."

4.2 Searching and Exploring

The participants found the exploring and browsing features useful in helping them choose a product and make a purchase decision. They mentioned that the ability to view popular products, those currently trending, and those being bought by many people could enhance trust. They believed that such products were becoming popular because the people who had bought and tried them liked them and recommended them to their friends and family, and thus they became popular. P14 said "I always want to see what the trending products are now and which shops sell them. This will really save my time and I can find what I want faster." Participants mentioned that they really liked being able to explore what their friends and friends of friends had bought. They believed that this would help them to find trustworthy shops as they trusted their friends. As P8 put it, "I love that I can see what my friends have bought because then I can trust the shop because my friends have bought from it."

Moreover, participants confirmed that the filter in the search was an essential element, helping them to enhance their trust as they could choose to see only what was trusted by their friends or just to view products from verified shops. Participants provided examples of the essential elements in the filters: nearby, price, verified by, and top reviews. As P12 said, "I like that I can filter the results of my search by choosing what my friends bought or choosing the price."

4.3 Sellers' Practices

The participants described sellers' practices as one of the main factors affecting their trust. Sellers' practices include the provision of information and detail in their profiles, and the ways in which they communicate. Participants reported the value of having more information, such as their location, policies, product types, payment methods, and contact details; these would enhance trust and help with the purchase decision. However, they debated whether the sellers would add all their information or not. Therefore, participants suggested encouraging sellers to add full information. As P8 commented, "...from the trust perspective, I think it is really important to find out more information about sellers. So, having sellers' profiles with full details would lead to greater trust. I think the app should force sellers to fill in all the details." Moreover, the participants suggested that some of the sellers' information should be verified by the platform to provide greater trust. As P13 noted, "I like to find information about the sellers, but not only written by them; there should be information that is verified by the app."

In addition, participants discussed the importance of having verification icons on the sellers' profiles to enhance trust. These icons would be verified by the app, by friends, and by Maroof. As P1 commented, "I like the verification icons on sellers' profiles because they can increase my trust, especially as there can be three different icons, for Maroof, the app, and friends. All of these can affect my trust." Participants discussed the need for government control to enhance trust between buyers and sellers, specifically by asking sellers to register with Maroof. They also proposed that government control should not just be about taking details, but also checking the quality of products. For example, it should be verified that food being sold is clean and complies with standards. As P2 commented, "Sellers' accounts should be linked directly to Maroof and verified by the government. Also, sellers should be monitored to assure quality."

Participants also expressed how the means of communication with sellers affected their trust. They believed that direct communication (instant messaging) on the s-commerce platform was very advantageous. It helped them find out any more details they were looking for, as well as the sellers' responses giving them comfort and a sense of trust. If sellers did not respond directly, the participants might not purchase from them. As P2 commented, "I sent a message to the seller to ask a question, but I did not get any response and so I decided not to buy from that seller."

4.4 Product Information

Participants believed that the products page was more useful when it included all the details and information needed, mainly when it contained information provided by the seller, app, and previous customers. The participants articulated the importance of having the price on the product page as this assured them that the price was fixed and the seller was not playing them. They thought one of the main issues with Instagram was that the price was not made available and they needed to send a private message to ask the seller, who they did not trust, for a price, and then it took time to get a response. For this reason, participants suggested encouraging sellers to add their prices. For example, P14 stated "I do not trust sellers who do not include prices because I think they manipulate them. So, I suggest making sellers include the prices of all the products."

The statistics showing the number of purchases and returns were also discussed by participants. Those in one of the critique workshops mentioned that they did not think they needed statistics for purchases. They believed that this information was essential for the sellers. They thought that they could find out if people did not like the product and had returned it through reviews. As P1 remarked, "I love that the reviews have the verified purchase feature so I can trust that for sure they tried the product and there is no need for the return numbers or information because it could be written in the reviews." However, the participants in the other two workshops thought having the purchase and return numbers would help in the purchase decision. If there were many returns with reasons given, they would change their mind and would not buy the product. However, if the number of purchases was very high, they might trust the product and buy it. As P6 commented, "I would like to see the number of returns and the reasons to help me to choose whether to buy or not. For example, if the reason is that she thinks it is too sweet, it is ok with me, I like sweet things and I will buy it."

Images of products can help consumers make a purchase decision. The participants mentioned that they liked seeing many images of the same product. These images could be from different angles, have an item such as a mobile next to the product to show its size, and should be professional and clear. However, they wanted to have real photographs, not images doctored using filters. P10 remarked "I like to see photos of the products that are high quality and clear, but a natural photo, not with filters." Another suggestion was to add multiple photographs to show the product. Having plenty of photographs and videos would enhance trust and encourage them to purchase the product.

Participants discussed the option of having "similar products" from different sellers and "frequently bought together" on the product page, features that are currently available on Amazon can enhance their trust. Similar products help users to compare prices and view other options, similar to those they are seeking. As P1 commented, "I like to see similar products because I can compare prices and see other options." The "frequently bought together" feature also helps consumers make a purchase decision as it shows which products they might need to buy with the original product. The participants discussed the importance of these features as sometimes consumers do not know which other items they might need to buy with what they have chosen. For example, P6 remarked "I bought a printer, but I was not sure what ink to buy with it, and this feature helped me identify the right one."

4.5 Reviews and Feedback

On Instagram, the participants mentioned that the number of followers was one of the features that helped enhance their trust as a review mechanism. However, they were concerned that there was a chance that sellers bought the number of followers and faked it. Therefore, they checked the comments under the posts, which might contain previous customers' opinions. For example, P9 recounted "From my experience, the number of followers is not enough to gain trust because you might buy a product from an account but not follow it, so this does not mean that nobody buys from them. Maybe it is helpful to check the number but also check the comments."

However, on Amazon there is a review system that includes reviews from previous customers. Participants mentioned that the review system was one of the most critical factors that affected their trust. Some participants wanted to be sure that the reviews were not fake or from people who knew the sellers and just wanted to help them. They considered that the verified purchase feature might help them feel that the reviews were real. As P7 noted, "I like that you cannot add a review unless you have a verified purchase to be sure it is not fake." Participants mentioned that reviews may also help them with their purchase decision, especially in terms of gaining more details about the products. As P6 said, "Customers' reviews are really important. I changed my mind based on a customer's experience, which was in a review, because usually customers can mention the drawbacks of a product."

A couple of participants (n = 2) mentioned that they would like to see information about the reviewers for two reasons: (i) they may have the same interests, so they would want to see what the reviewer bought; (ii) to be sure that the reviewer was not fake. For example, P10 said "I would like to be able to access the profile to be able to know if we share the same interests in terms of what products they bought. For example, if they had a kid the same age as my son, I could check what toys they bought for their son." P5 added "…having access to the reviewer's profile and checking the reviews on the profile can help ensure that this review is trustworthy."

Participants liked the feature enabling them to see photos from customers because they were more genuine than other images. They believed that they could verify that the seller was trustworthy if the photos from customers and sellers matched. As noted by P10, "The photos taken by the customers will be reassuring and show whether the seller's photos are real or not."

Two groups mentioned that they liked the feature enabling them to ask previous customers about a product, or to be asked about products by new customers. Participants thought this provided greater reliability and they could trust the answers that they got from previous customers. As P4 noted, "I love the idea of having the ability to ask previous customers because they are more trustworthy."

4.6 Writing Reviews' Issues and Motivations

The participants discussed an issue with the review system in the KSA specifically, namely reviews with few details or no reviews at all. Foreign reviews tend to be more helpful and more detailed than Arabic reviews. The participants mentioned that generally few people in the KSA write reviews and sometimes not at all. The participants explored their experiences of writing reviews. Most of the participants (n = 7) said that they did not write reviews for various reasons, such as not being excited about sharing their experience. In particular, most people said they did not like to write, were busy, or had no inclination to do so. However, some of the participants (n = 3) mentioned that they were encouraged to write reviews on global websites, such as Amazon, because they saw many other people did so. As P10 explained, "I became keen on writing reviews like those from other countries because I wanted other people to have the benefit of my experience. I would have liked to find reviews from Arabian purchasers, but usually I just found foreigners' reviews."

Moreover, the participants discussed their motivations for writing reviews. As noted, people could be incentivized to share their experiences by seeing others sharing theirs. Sometimes people would forget to provide a review, but receiving a reminder email would prompt them to do so. However, P8 said "I hate receiving it by email. I think I should just receive the reminder in the app. Or have an option in the app to choose to receive reminders by email or not." Another suggestion was having optional questions to rate with stars instead of writing a review because it is easier and quicker; it would even remind the reviewer to rate specific details about the product that the reviewer might forget to write about. As P9 explained, "It is easier for the reviewer to rate specific details instead of writing a review, for example rating the size and the quality of materials. Also, it is important that the questions are optional."

Having a reward system would also motivate users to add a review. The reward should be financial, such as a 5% off, free delivery, and/or coupons. As P6 remarked, "I love the reward system; I think it would really encourage me to leave a review and collect points to receive offers." Participants expressed their concern about who was giving the reward: Was it from the app or the sellers? As P5 noted, "…ok, I get it. So, when I collect points, I may have free delivery. But the rewards, will they be from the sellers or the platform?" They believed that it should be from the app, as the buyers would have a variety of options for rewards.

Finally, privacy aspects can also affect whether customers write a review or not. The participants considered that when they reviewed a product, they should be able to choose to show their account or hide it. On Instagram, writing a comment as a review will be linked to the reviewer's profile, so people may opt out to protect their privacy. In particular, they were afraid that if they wrote a bad review, other people would attack them and say they were destroying the seller's business. All the participants were concerned about privacy. They liked having the option to share what they wanted and have different levels of privacy: only for them, only their friends, or public. As P7 commented, "I love the feature that lets me choose if I share with others or keep it private for me, especially that there is the option to share or not next to each product. So, I can choose what to show depending on the product."

4.7 Family and Friends

Family and friends depend on each other and they were one of the main ways of identifying and trusting Instagram accounts or e-commerce websites. As already noted, they can place orders for one another, for instance due to trust issues. As P10 remarked, "A lot of my friends and family send me the picture of the product that they want to order and ask me to buy it for them because they trust me more."

Moreover, participants mentioned that they might need their friends' or family's opinion to buy something. As P6 said, "I send them a message to check this product and say what they think, whether it is nice." Participants also liked the option to check their friends' profiles and see the shops that their friends trusted, the products that they bought or reviewed, and their wish list. P7 said "I shared my wish list with my friends and family when I was pregnant. So, they knew what I really wanted and needed."

The participants stated that they liked sharing good experiences with their friends and family, and receiving recommendations from them, as these helped them identify trusted sites they could buy from. For example, P10 stated "I have tried vitamins for hair growth, and I found that they really helped my hair to be heathier. So, I sent the information to my friends." Therefore, when designing an s-commerce platform, family and friends should be considered, adding social features that would encourage them to share their experiences and thus enhance users' trust.

5 Discussion

5.1 Mixing and Simplifying Social and Commercial Features and Functions

As pointed out in previous research, people's views of social media and e-commerce have changed with the introduction of commercial functionality on social media [1, 5]. Various studies have explored the importance of providing social features with commercial functions [2, 11]. However, there is still much room for improvement, and appropriate social and commercial features should be specified to make it possible to conduct transactions efficiently and effectively. The findings show that integrating commercial functions with social features can ease the use of s-commerce and enhance trust, helping users make a purchase decision (see Table 1 for preferences for features), as also recommended by a previous study [46].

Among the features preferred by the participants was a news feed (timeline) and explorer. The participants liked being able to monitor up-to-date social content and see new products without searching for them. Previous research on the use of Facebook commerce noted that buyers like to see products on the news feed without the need to check the group sale profile [9]. Moreover, browsing on s-commerce platforms improves accessibility to shops [47].

The findings demonstrate that participants like showing both popular products and those purchased by their friends in small preview within the social feeds, and this might increase intention to buy the products. These findings are in line with a previous study indicating that when many customers purchase products and they become popular, yet more consumers are then attracted [48]. Another study demonstrated that social approval is a critical mechanism in fostering consumer preferences and encouraging purchases based on what is accepted by the majority of other consumers in the community [30]. Some participants from one of the critique workshops mentioned that they wished to have an app that was primarily commerce-based, but "tweaked" to contain a social dimension, similar to Etsy [15]. However, those in the other workshops argued that the platform with both social and commercial news and posts was preferable because they might find something they liked while looking at the social news feed.

The findings show that the s-commerce app (Instagram) lacked a sophisticated search engine, which means it is more challenging to search for a product and may lead to confusion for consumers. This point was also raised by a previous study on Facebook [9]. Having a sophisticated search engine showing the preferences of friends and previous customers with filters is one of the main elements easing the purchase process, helping consumers find what they are looking, fostering trust, and providing support in making a purchase decision. It has been suggested that integrating the search engine with social media could aid the search process [25].

According to the participants, two essential features in terms of enhancing trust currently available on Amazon are "similar products" and "frequently bought together." These help in comparing prices and finding the right match for the product. This corroborates research demonstrating that these features can affect consumer behaviors [49], and provide a means of comparison to ease the purchase decision [50].

The participants mentioned that placing an order on Instagram currently entails sending a private message to the seller. A previous study has shown that this is also how orders are placed using Facebook [8, 9]. The participants wanted to have the choice to place orders automatically, saving time when everything about the product was clear, or through messaging, enabling them to ask for details or customize the product. The latter option tends to be particularly critical for older people in fostering confidence. A previous study suggested allowing consumers to place an order by direct message [51].

The participants preferred paying cash on delivery as they felt this was more trustworthy, reflecting the findings of previous studies in Indonesia [52] and China [53]. However, they liked being able to choose from various trusted payment methods because they

Table 1. Preferences for features on both s-commerce and e-commerce sites with suggestions for enhancement

Feature(s)	Details	Benefit(s)
Home page (news feed)	Include posts by the user's network/Include popular products	Being up to date with social news and products/Enhance trust
Explore	Posts related to user's interests	Being up to date with social news and products
Filter	Location, price, verified shops, etc.	Easier/enhance trust
Payment options	Choose from a list for payment methods	Enhance trust if cash on delivery is an option/Easier
Seller's profile	Information from sellers (e.g., location, payment methods, exchange and refund policy)	Enhance trust/Help in purchase decision/(sellers' profiles should be public & should have a rating)
Photographs posted by sellers	Adding multiple photographs/Clear photograph/Different angles/Photograph without filters	Enhance trust/Help in purchase decision
Similar products	Compare prices	Enhance trust/Find options
Frequently bought together	Show products frequently bought with that chosen by the user	Enhance trust/find the right product
Product page	Full details about the product/depend on the sellers	Full details enhance trust/Cannot trust without the price
Direct messaging with sellers	Being able to communicate directly with the seller	Enhance trust/place an order easily/seek more product details
Verifications	Government (e.g., Maroof)/Third party	Enhance trust
Purchase history statistics	Number of purchases & returns	Enhance trust
Reviews	Number of reviews (followers)/Rating/Review details (comments)/Reviewer profile/Verified purchase	Help in purchase decision/Enhance trust
Seller's rating	Rating sellers, not just the products	Enhance trust

(continued)

Table 1. (*continued*)

Feature(s)	Details	Benefit(s)
Photographs and videos by customers	Photographs taken and posted by previous customers	Enhance trust
Reviewer's profile	Check the reviewer's profile	Enhance trust (not fake)
Reward system	Give points or offers as a reward for reviewers	Motivate users to review
Individual's profile	Being able to communicate and share	Enhance trust
Following network	Having a connection/Being able to follow accounts (individuals and sellers)	Trust their friends and who their friends recommend/being up to date with what their post
Direct messages with family and friends	Being able to send direct messages to friends	Share products they like/ask about product/ask for opinion
Privacy options	Being able to choose what to share and at what level	Motivate customers to share

would not always have cash. They were excited to see Apple Pay as an option because it is easy and faster than transferring money, as also suggested by a previous study [54].

5.2 Trust Activities and Mechanisms

This study examined the social features and commercial functions that can initiate and increase trust. These features and functions are related to sellers, the platform, previous customers, and family and friends. The design of a platform can influence consumers' trust, which is a critical factor that affects the purchase decision [19]. Therefore, trust should be a concern when designing an s-commerce platform.

Sellers as a Source of Information. The findings reveal the importance of the seller profile, direct instant messaging, and product page as these features can increase the perception of social presence, which enhances trust. These results are consistent with previous research, arguing that social presence has a strong influence on trust, especially the sense of human worth and communication [18, 32, 34]. Previous studies found that social presence features built and improved trust in China [11] and Canada [55]. The participants felt that the more information they had, the greater their trust in the seller. A previous study of Facebook found that profiles can help provide consumers gain a sense of the human being selling the product [9], and showing more information can increase social presence [19]. Moreover, previous studies have shown that posting a profile and disclosing substantial information could affect trust [17, 56]. Buyers at least needed to know information under main categories, such as location, exchange and refund policies, and payment methods. This is consistent with prior research, which found that the provision of information can help develop trust [17].

The findings show that the ways in which sellers communicate and the speed of response to consumers can affect trust, as also found by a previous study [57]. Furthermore, communication is vital in helping consumers obtain sufficient detail about products [10]. Participants like to see all details and images of the product as these can foster trust. A previous study found these features as essential [52], and both the quality of information [2] and quality of images [57] can develop trust. Therefore, sellers should be obliged to provide key information that is accurate. Also, they should be encouraged to disclose ample information [56].

The App as a Source of Information. The study findings highlight the need for warranty cues on sellers' profiles, such as product statistics about purchases, including the number of returns and reasons (displayed under the product on the product page), and verification icons (shown as icons next to the account name). These can all affect consumer trust, consistent with earlier research regarding warranting theory, which indicates that information sellers cannot manipulate is more trustworthy and informative than information provided freely [21]. Statistics on the product page can also enhance trust, as mentioned by the participants, but it is necessary to show the reason for returns.

Both Amazon and Instagram currently provide some verifications, which the participants said they could trust. In our mock-up, the icons reflected verification from the platform, friends and family, and Maroof. It was clear that the participants trusted shops with these verification icons. These findings are consistent with previous studies on the sharing economy (Airbnb [17]), referring to the positive effect of platform verification provided by the app on trust. A previous study has also shown that Maroof verification can increase consumers' purchase intentions [22, 32, 34]. Indeed, the participants suggested that registration with Maroof should be mandatory.

Previous Customers as a Source of Information. Based on the discussions among participants, information provided by previous customers critically affects their trust. Features representing such information are ratings, reviews, numbers of reviews, photographs, popular products, and the number of followers. Consumers judge the trustworthiness of sellers by checking the features related to previous customers [32, 57, 58].

Previous studies have suggested that having greater numbers of followers enhances trust [32, 34, 58]. Comments can be considered reviews on Instagram, but the participants had concerns that sellers could delete negative comments. Therefore, they suggested implementing a reputation system for s-commerce platforms, as also proposed by a previous study on using Facebook for commerce [8].

In agreement with previous research [2], the reputation system played a positive role in generating consumers' trust. Moreover, based on the findings, reviews with photographs taken by customers can help consumers trust a seller and make a purchase decision. This result is consistent with previous studies on Airbnb and Couchsurfing, which found that profiles with ratings and reviews were among the essential features helping hosts establish trust [17, 59].

The findings show that obtaining information regarding the product from previous consumers with purchase experience can improve consumer trust, as also found by a previous study [18]. Reviews may add information on aspects and details not provided by the seller. Previous studies have shown similar findings, indicating that customers' reviews include information about the product that can be considered more trustworthy [14] as it reflects the reality of the product experience [25]. This finding is in line with previous research discussing the elements that make a review more trustworthy [28], and examining verified purchases [1]. Furthermore, there are concerns about fake reviews. The findings show that there are elements that may help ensure that reviews are not fake, namely "verified purchase," friends' reviews, photographs posted by customers, reviewers' profiles, and questions and answers (Q&A).

The "verified purchase" icon can show that the person writing the review has actually bought the product. This trust mechanism was introduced to ensure that only a buyer of the product could write a review [1]. Such reviews can increase credibility [60]. Furthermore, a few participants checked the reviewers' profiles after seeing their comments on Instagram to ensure that they were trustworthy (not fake), or to see if they shared the same interests. A previous study suggested providing additional information about the reviewers to help consumers assess the reviewers' credibility [26].

Based on the findings, photographs posted by customers are viewed as credible and can give the sense that the seller is trustworthy, enabling consumers to see what the product really looks like, as also found by a previous study [28]. Photographs taken by customers also provide a sense that the customer has really tried the product [28].

Also, enabling consumers to ask previous customers questions is regarded as a source of trust. Amazon has implemented the Q&A feature in terms of fulfilling a social role to help consumers obtain valuable information from previous customers [49].

Family and Friends as a Source of Information. The findings show that family and friends are essential in terms of their influence on trust and the purchase decision, in line with previous studies [29, 32, 34]. A previous study of Facebook found that consumers could also be influenced by people sharing the same interests as their friends within their network [46]. They play five main roles: sharing their shopping experiences, sharing trusted shops, giving opinions and advice, sharing their reviews, and placing orders.

Profiles are among the social features that can assist consumers in sharing their previous experience [13]. The participants liked being able to explore what their friends and family had bought and trusted sites. Furthermore, sharing purchased products and trusted shops helped friends make a purchase decision, feeling assured that the seller was trustworthy. These findings are consistent with previous research suggesting the inclusion of social approval features and mechanisms to enhance consumer willingness to purchase the product [30]. Furthermore, the participants might even trust shops trusted by friends of friends, as also found by previous research [61].

Moreover, the platform should provide users with conversational channels through which they can send messages to their friends and ask their opinions. The findings are consistent with previous research showing that friends' advice influences consumer intention [10]. One study found that 50% of Chinese consumers rely on suggestions from their friends and relatives to make a purchase decision [4].

Consumers found that the reviews from peers were the most important [27] and they could rely on them [2]. In line with the findings, previous research has found that the level of trust in reviews differs depending on who writes them, with trust in those by friends being higher than those written by strangers [17, 29].

Placing an order through friends or family was an exciting feature for the participants, and one they viewed essential for those not confident about placing an order themselves. This feature would make it easier to identify what their family or friends wanted and order for them, as was common practice for some.

Motivations for Customers to Interact Socially. The findings reveal the importance of social features and how they can enhance trust, but without customer engagement there is no use for these social features. A previous study found that social media tools encourage users to participate and foster contribution [3]. The customers' social interactions can reduce uncertainty and develop familiarity [23]. Therefore, it is essential to encourage customers to use these social features. The results indicate that several factors might increase consumer engagement and interaction.

Reminders to Post Reviews. Participants mentioned that reminders might motivate them to write a review. A previous study found that Amazon used email reminders asking customers to rate and review products [49]. However, consumers should only receive one reminder as more would be frustrating. Also participants have been found to want control over whether they receive reminders or not [15]. The participants also liked getting a reminder as a message from sellers because they believed that the seller cared and want to know their opinion.

Rating Based on Points/Features/Questions. People in the KSA generally do not like writing reviews, but would rather rate specific points or respond to questions indicating why they would give a specific rating for quality, delivery, and so on. Previous studies have shown that helpful reviews require responses of a minimum length and ask reviewers to upload photographs [28]. However, the findings show that the reviews should not include mandatory questions, or have compulsory elements, as consumers may give up and not leave a review at all.

Privacy. Privacy was a concern for the participants. A previous study conducted in the KSA found that the participants had privacy concerns, and would not share information concerning their personal lives or views with strangers, revealing the importance of the ability to manage their privacy [62]. Participants liked having three levels of privacy settings that they could choose from: only for me, only friends, the public. Such privacy options could encourage buyers to write a review or upload a photograph because there is a fear that writing a negative review might have negative consequences. In particular, the participants wanted their friends to see their reviews, but not the public. This reflects the findings of a previous study that concluded users should be provided with privacy settings that would allow them to leave anonymous reviews or control who could see their ratings [12].

Reward System. It seemed that privacy concerns could be mitigated by giving rewards, as well as allowing consumers to decide what to share and with whom. A previous study conducted in China found the same concern regarding privacy, but that it could be mitigated by providing economic rewards [27]. The findings show that participants liked the reward system and considered it would encourage them to leave reviews. It appears that the participants were not interested in gamification or badges. They mostly discussed economic (financial) rewards, preferring open offers from the platform, rather than those attached to a specific shop. Therefore, the reward system is among the essential elements that should be considered when designing s-commerce platforms, as also recommended by a previous study [31, 34].

6 Conclusion

This paper has provided an in-depth exploration of the use of social features and commercial functions for conducting business transactions online, specifically in terms of engendering trust in s-commerce platforms. The findings confirm that s-commerce platforms should include both traditional trust mechanisms, such as third-party verification and reviews, and social trust mechanisms, such as profiles and communication channels. In addition, it is essential to provide options for privacy settings enabling users to choose what to share and with whom. Finally, previous customers' interactions play a crucial role in potential consumers' intention to buy and purchase decisions. Therefore, s-commerce platforms should include elements that encourage such interactions, such as reward systems.

Future studies might be undertaken to identify what may motivate consumers to share and engage in s-commerce platforms to a greater extent across different cultures. Many prior studies have been conducted with samples of university students and future studies should target more diverse groups of participants to enable generalization.

References

1. Curty, R.G., Zhang, P.: Social commerce: looking back and forward. In: The American Society for Information Science and Technology (ASIST), New Orleans, LA, USA, pp. 1–10 (2011)
2. Kim, S., Park, H.: Effects of various characteristics of social commerce (s-commerce) on consumers' trust and trust performance. Int. J. Inf. Manag. 33, 318–332 (2013)
3. Huang, Z., Benyoucef, M.: From e-commerce to social commerce: a close look at design features. Electron. Commer. Res. Appl. 12, 246–259 (2013)
4. Liu, H., Chu, H., Huang, Q., Chen, X.: Enhancing the flow experience of consumers in China through interpersonal interaction in social commerce. Comput. Hum. Behav. 58, 306–314 (2016)
5. Gibreel, O., AlOtaibi, D.A., Altmann, J.: Social commerce development in emerging markets. Electron. Commer. Res. Appl. 27, 152–162 (2018)
6. Algi, A., Irwansyah: Consumer trust and intention to buy in Indonesia Instagram stores. In: International Conference on Information Technology Information System Electrical Engineering, pp. 199–203 (2018)
7. Jalaldeen, M., Razi, M., Izzuddin, M., Tamrin, M.: Social commerce behavior among university students in Malaysia. In: International Conference on Computer Informatics, pp. 350–355 (2017)
8. Evans, H.I., et al.: Facebook in Venezuela: understanding solidarity economies in low-trust environments. In: Conference on Human Factors in Computing Systems, pp. 1–12 (2018)

9. Moser, C., Resnick, P., Schoenebeck, S.: Community commerce: facilitating trust in mom-to-mom sale groups on Facebook. In: Conference on Human Factors in Computing Systems (2017)
10. Liang, T.-P., Ho, Y.-T., Li, Y.-W., Turban, E.: What drives social commerce: the role of social support and relationship quality. Int. J. Electron. Commer. **16**, 69–90 (2011)
11. Huang, Z., Yoon, S.Y., Benyoucef, M.: Adding social features to e-commerce. In: 2012 Proceedings of the Conference on Information System Applied Research, pp. 1–11 (2012)
12. Hajli, N., Wang, Y., Tajvidi, M., Hajli, M.S.: People, technologies, and organizations interactions in a social commerce era. IEEE Trans. Eng. Manag. **64**, 594–604 (2017)
13. Huang, Z., Benyoucef, M.: The effects of social commerce design on consumer purchase decision-making: An empirical study. Electron. Commer. Res. Appl. **25**, 40–58 (2017)
14. Al-Adwan, A.S., Kokash, H.: The driving forces of facebook social commerce. J. Theor. Appl. Electron. Commer. Res. **14**, 15–32 (2019)
15. Gheitasy, A., Abdelnour-Nocera, J., Nardi, B.: Socio-technical gaps in online collaborative consumption (OCC): an example of the Etsy community. In: International Conference on Design Communication, pp. 1–9 (2015)
16. Lee, D., Hyun, W., Ryu, J., Lee, W.J., Rhee, W., Suh, B.: An analysis of social features associated with room sales of Airbnb. In: ACM Conference on Companion Computer Supported Cooperative Work Social Computing, pp. 219–222 (2015)
17. Finley, K.: Trust in the Sharing Economy: An Exploratory Study (2012)
18. Sharma, S., Menard, P., Mutchler, L.A.: Who to trust? Applying trust to social commerce. J. Comput. Inf. Syst. **59**, 32–42 (2019)
19. Gefen, D., Straub, D.: Managing user trust in B2C e-Services. e-Service J. **2**, 7–24 (2003)
20. Sanders, W.S.: Testing the application of warranting theory to online third party marketplaces: the effects of information uniqueness and product type. In: International Conference on Social Media Society, pp. 1–7 (2016)
21. Walther, J.B., Parks, M.R.: Cues filtered out, cues filtered in: computer-mediated communication and relationships. Handb. Interpers. Commun. 529–563 (2002)
22. Alotaibi, T.S., Alkhathlan, A.A., Alzeer, S.S.: Instagram shopping in Saudi Arabia: what influences consumer trust and purchase decisions? Int. J. Adv. Comput. Sci. Appl. **10**, 605–613 (2019)
23. Li, C.Y.: How social commerce constructs influence customers' social shopping intention? An empirical study of a social commerce website. Technol. Forecast. Soc. Change **144**, 282–294 (2017)
24. Zhang, J., Ip, R.K.F.: E-commerce advertising in social networking sites and implications for social commerce. In: Pacific Asia Conference on Information System, pp. 1–10 (2015)
25. Hajli, N., Sims, J., Zadeh, A.H., Richard, M.-O.: A social commerce investigation of the role of trust in a social networking site on purchase intentions. J. Bus. Res. **71**, 133–141 (2016)
26. Filieri, R., Hofacker, C.F., Alguezaui, S.: What makes information in online consumer reviews diagnostic over time? The role of review relevancy, factuality, currency, source credibility and ranking score. Comput. Human Behav. **80**, 122–131 (2018)
27. Li, M., Zhang, J., Liu, Z., Johnson, G.I.: An experimental study of Chinese shopping related sharing behaviors. In: Kotzé, P., Marsden, G., Lindgaard, G., Wesson, J., Winckler, M. (eds.) INTERACT 2013. LNCS, vol. 8119, pp. 608–615. Springer, Heidelberg (2013). https://doi.org/10.1007/978-3-642-40477-1_39
28. Filieri, R., Raguseo, E., Vitari, C.: When are extreme ratings more helpful? Empirical evidence on the moderating effects of review characteristics and product type. Comput. Human Behav. **88**, 134–142 (2018)
29. Bai, Y., Yao, Z., Dou, Y.-F.: Effect of social commerce factors on user purchase behavior: an empirical investigation from renren.com. Int. J. Inf. Manag. **35**, 538–550 (2015)

30. Xu, F., Han, Z., Piao, J., Li, Y.: "I think you'll like it": modelling the online purchase behavior in social e-commerce. Proc. ACM Hum.-Comput. Interact. **3** (2019)

31. Osatuyi, B., Turel, O.: Social motivation for the use of social technologies: an empirical examination of social commerce site users. Internet Res. **29**, 24–45 (2019)

32. AlArfaj, A.A., Solaiman, E., Marshall, L.: "Why would you buy from a stranger?" Understanding Saudi Citizens' motivations and challenges in social commerce. In: Lamas, D., Loizides, F., Nacke, L., Petrie, H., Winckler, M., Zaphiris, P. (eds.) INTERACT 2019. LNCS, vol. 11747, pp. 711–732. Springer, Cham (2019). https://doi.org/10.1007/978-3-030-29384-0_43

33. Alghamdi, E., Reilly, D.: Social media based business in Saudi Arabia. In: Dalhousie University Computer Science In-House Conference (DCSI), pp. 2012–2014 (2013)

34. AlArfaj, A.A., Solaiman, E.: Investigating commercial capabilities and trust in social media applications for entrepreneurs. In: Proceedings of the ACM C&T Conference (C&T'19), p. 11 (2019)

35. Sheikh, Z., Islam, T., Rana, S., Hameed, Z., Saeed, U.: Acceptance of social commerce framework in Saudi Arabia. Telemat. Informat. **34**, 1693–1708 (2017). https://doi.org/10.1016/j.tele.2017.08.003

36. Makki, E., Chang, L.: Understanding the effects of social media and mobile usage on e-commerce : an exploratory study in Saudi Arabia. Int. Manag. Rev. **11**, 98–110 (2015)

37. Abed, S.S., Dwivedi, Y.K., Williams, M.D.: Consumers' perceptions of social commerce adoption in Saudi Arabia. In: Janssen, M., et al. (eds.) I3E 2015. LNCS, vol. 9373, pp. 133–143. Springer, Cham (2015). https://doi.org/10.1007/978-3-319-25013-7_11

38. Zimmerman, J., Forlizzi, J., Evenson, S., Zimmerman, J., Forlizzi, J., Evenson, S.: Research through design as a method for interaction design research in HCI design research in HCI. In: Proceedings of the SIGCHI Conference on Human Factors Computing System, pp. 493–502 (2007)

39. Sanders, E.B.-N., Jan Stappers, P.: Co-creation and the new landscapes of design. In: Design: Critical and Primary Sources, pp. 1–16 (2017)

40. Tomitsch, M., et al.: Design. Think. Make. Break. Repeat. A Handbook of Methods. BIS Publishers (2018)

41. Steen, M., Manschot, M., Koning, N.D.: Benefits of co-design in service design projects. Int. J. Des. **5**, 53–60 (2011)

42. Dillahunt, T.R., Malone, A.R.: The promise of the sharing economy among disadvantaged communities. In: Proceedings of the 33rd Annual ACM Conference on Human Factors Computing System - CHI 2015, pp. 2285–2294 (2015)

43. Nassir, S., Leong, T.W.: Traversing boundaries: understanding the experiences of ageing Saudis. In: Proceedings of the 2017 CHI Conference on Human Factors Computing System, pp. 6386–6397 (2017)

44. Alam, M., Elaasi, S.: A study on consumer perception towards E-shopping in KSA. Int. J. Bus. **11**, 202–210 (2016)

45. Braun, V., Clarke, V.: Using thematic analysis in psychology. Qual. Res. Psychol. **3**, 77–101 (2006)

46. Xu, Y., Lee, M.J.: Shopping as a social activity: understanding people's categorical item sharing preferences on social networks. In: CEUR Workshop Proceedings (2018)

47. Stephen, A.T., Toubia, O.: Deriving value from social commerce networks. J. Mark. Res. **47**, 215–228 (2010)

48. Noh, M., Lee, K., Kim, S., Garrison, G.: Effects of collectivism on actual s-commerce use and the moderating effect of price consciousness. J. Electron. Commer. Res. **14**, 244–260 (2013)

49. Adaji, I., Vassileva, J.: Evaluating personalization and persuasion in e-commerce. In: Proceedings of the Personalization in Persuasive Technology, vol. 1582, pp. 107–113 (2016)

50. Andriadi, K., Fitriani, W.R., Hidayanto, A.N., Sandhyaduhita, P.I., Samik-Ibrahim, R.M.: Analysis of factors influencing consumer intention to buy in s-commerce business. In: International Conference on Data Science and Information Technology, pp. 64–70 (2019)
51. Todri, V., Adamopoulos, P.: Social commerce: an empirical examination of the antecedents and consequences of commerce in social network platforms. In: International Conference on Information Systems, pp. 1–18 (2014)
52. Syuhada, A.A., Gambett, W.: Online marketplace for Indonesian micro small and medium enterprises based on social media. Procedia Technol. 11, 446–454 (2013)
53. Yoldas, S.: A Research about Buying Behaviours of Online Customers, Comparison of Turkey with UK (2012)
54. Liébana-Cabanillas, F., Muñoz-Leiva, F., Sánchez-Fernández, J.: A global approach to the analysis of user behavior in mobile payment systems in the new electronic environment. Serv. Bus. 12(1), 25–64 (2017). https://doi.org/10.1007/s11628-017-0336-7
55. Hassanein, K., Head, M.: Manipulating perceived social presence through the web interface and its impact on attitude towards online shopping. Int. J. Hum. Comput. Stud. 65, 689–708 (2007)
56. Ma, X., Hancock, J.T., Lim Mingjie, K., Naaman, M.: Self-disclosure and perceived trustworthiness of Airbnb host profiles. In: Proceedings of the 2017 ACM Conference on Computer Supported Cooperative Work and Social Computing (CSCW 2017), pp. 2397–2409. ACM, New York (2017)
57. Rafinda, A., Suroso, A., Rafinda, A., Purwaningtyas, P.: Formative variables of trustworthiness on Instagram online sellers. Performance 25, 1–7 (2018)
58. Din, S.M., Ramli, R., Bakar, A.A.: A review on trust factors affecting purchase intention on Instagram. In: 2018 IEEE Conference on Application, Information and Network Security, pp. 49–53 (2019)
59. Decrop, A., Del Chiappa, G., Mallargé, J., Zidda, P.: "Couchsurfing has made me a better person and the world a better place": the transformative power of collaborative tourism experiences. J. Travel Tour. Mark. 35, 57–72 (2018)
60. Wan, Y.: The Matthew effect in social commerce: the case of online review helpfulness. Electron. Mark. 25, 313–324 (2015)
61. Chaube, V., Kavanaugh, A.L., Pérez-Quiñones, M.A.: Leveraging social networks to embed trust in rideshare programs. In: Hawaii International Conference on System Sciences, pp. 1–8 (2010)
62. Abokhodair, N., Vieweg, S.: Privacy & social media in the context of the Arab gulf. In: Designing Interactive Systems, pp. 672–683 (2016)

DeepVANet: A Deep End-to-End Network for Multi-modal Emotion Recognition

Yuhao Zhang[1], Md Zakir Hossain[1,2] (ID), and Shafin Rahman[3(✉)] (ID)

[1] The Australian National University, Canberra, ACT 2601, Australia
{yuhao.zhang,zakir.hossain}@anu.edu.au
[2] CSIRO Agriculture and Food, Black Mountain, Canberra, ACT 2601, Australia
[3] North South University, Dhaka, Bangladesh
shafin.rahman@northsouth.edu

Abstract. Human facial expressions and bio-signals (e.g., electroencephalogram and electrocardiogram) play a vital role in emotion recognition. Recent approaches employ both vision-based and bio-sensing data to design multi-modal recognition systems. However, these approaches require tremendous domain-specific knowledge, complex pre-processing steps and fail to take full advantage of the end-to-end nature of deep learning techniques. This paper proposes a deep end-to-end framework, DeepVANet, for multi-modal valence-arousal-based emotion recognition that applies deep learning methods to extract face appearance features and bio-sensing features. We use convolutional long short-term memory (ConvLSTM) techniques in face appearance feature extraction to capture spatial and temporal information from face image sequences. Unlike conventional time or frequency domain features (e.g., spectral power and average signal intensity), we use a 1D convolutional neural network (Conv1D) to learn bio-sensing features automatically. In experiments, we evaluate our method using DEAP and MAHNOB-HCI datasets. Our proposed multi-modal framework successfully outperforms both single- and multi-modal methods achieving superior performance compared to state-of-the-art approaches and reaches as high as 99.22% correctness.

Keywords: Emotion recognition · Deep learning · Physiological signals

1 Introduction

Emotion is an important mental state of human beings and dominates people's attitudes and behaviors. Recently, emotion recognition has become a popular research topic due to its wide applications in the medical, education, and gaming

Electronic supplementary material The online version of this chapter (https://doi.org/10.1007/978-3-030-85613-7_16) contains supplementary material, which is available to authorized users.

fields [5,35]. In particular, existing works predominantly investigate two modalities of data for the emotion recognition task. *Firstly*, vision-based data, i.e., face image/video, widely dominates emotion recognition research. Facial expressions can reflect human's emotions directly, and they are easy to capture by cameras. State-of-the-art studies have successfully explored both hand-crafted and deep learning methods to extract these kinds of facial expression features [16]. Hand-crafted methods include facial specific methods based on facial landmarks (angle and distance of landmark pairs) [8,37] and other effective general visual feature extraction methods such as Local Binary Pattern (LBP) [10] and Histogram of Gradients (HoG) [20,34]. Deep learning methods, particularly convolutional neural network (CNN) and its variations, have shown their powerful visual data processing ability in facial emotion recognition tasks [21]. Especially for facial image sequences or videos, 3D CNN [9], recurrent convolutional neural network (RCNN) [14,23] and ConvLSTM [11] perform well in spatial and temporal facial expression feature extraction. *Secondly*, physiological/bio-sensing signals, i.e., electroencephalogram (EEG), electrocardiogram (ECG), and galvanic skin response (GSR) data are used to extract discriminative information of human emotions [27,31]. Compared to facial expressions, physiological signals are more instinctive and uncontrolled. So, they can reflect the real emotions more accurately. Methods use hand-crafted features like power spectral density (PSD) from different frequency bands, conditional cross-entropy, and statistical features to extract discriminative information [18]. However, due to inconsistency across hardware, the necessity of expert pre-processing, and the expensive nature of bio-sensing data, there is not enough work on deep learning strategies.

Apart from single modality (either bio-sensing or vision) approaches, some multi-modal affective computing efforts have been proposed and shown advantages in emotion recognition accuracy [25,28,38]. Single modal features have their respective strength in some aspects. Thus, their fusion can take advantage of their strengths by generating comprehensive and salient multi-modal features. While dealing with multi-modal data, current literature does not utilize the full benefit of deep learning (e.g. complicated data pre-processing). This paper investigates an end-to-end approach to address the emotion recognition task using both modalities. Human emotional states can be represented qualitatively (discrete model) [6] or quantitatively (dimensional model) [24]. Discrete models generally classifies emotions into six basic types: happiness, sadness, anger, surprise, disgust, and fear. The dimensional model represents emotions in a multidimensional space, such as valence-arousal space, which is more flexible and represents a broader range of emotions. This study focuses on emotion recognition in valence-arousal space using multi-modal data (vision-based and bio-sensing).

Limitation of Prior Works: We identify several issues in existing works of the valence-arousal model of emotion classification: *(a)* Although some models used deep learning in vision pipeline, they failed to incorporate the same on bio-sensing data [12]. *(b)* Some models pre-processed raw bio-sensing signals to 2D-frames (e.g. EEG heatmap of PSD bands) to extract CNN features [13,28,36].

(c) Other models usually extracted individual modal features separately and then applied a decision-level fusion on them [12,25]. All the mentioned issues hamper the end-to-end nature of deep learning.

This paper proposes a deep end-to-end network, DeepVANet, to recognize humans emotions using both face videos and physiological signals by extracting vision-based and bio-sensing features, respectively. At the vision pipeline, we use a Convolutional Recurrent Neural Network (CRNN) based on convolutional long short-term memory (ConvLSTM) as face appearance feature extractor to obtain spatio-temporal information from face videos [26]. Similarly, we use Conv1D neural network at the bio-sensing pipeline instead of traditional hand-crafted time/frequency-based extraction methods. Later, we employ a fusion pipeline to fuse both modality features enriching the feature quality for better classification. Our fusion pipeline supports both feature- and decision-level fusion strategies. Different modal features are concatenated together then pass through some fully-connected (FC) classifier layers to predict the valence/arousal label for feature-level fusion. In contrast, for decision-level fusion, FC sub-classifiers accept single modal features and output predict scores separately. Then, adaptive boosting techniques are employed to yield the final emotion label. Our method combines all steps while maintaining the end-to-end nature of the work. We present experimental results on DEAP [17] and MAHNOB-HCI [29] datasets demonstrating new state-of-the-art results on multi-modal emotion recognition. In summary, the main contributions of our work are: *(1)* To the best of our knowledge, we propose the first end-to-end deep network for multi-modal (face and bio-sensing) valance-arousal-based emotion recognition. *(2)* Instead of the traditional use of hand-crafted features, we fuse Conv1D based bio-sensing and CRNN/ConvLSTM based vision feature to learn a rich feature representation jointly for emotion classification. *(3)* We perform extensive experiments on two well-known datasets achieving state-of-the-art performance: 98.56/98.18% and 99.19/99.22% (valence/arousal) on DEAP and MAHNOB-HCI, respectively.

2 Multi-modal Emotion Recognition

Problem Formulation: Suppose, for ith facial emotion video frames, $F_i = \langle I_t | 1 \ldots n_i \rangle$ where, I_t represents tth image frame, we collect bio-sensing signals, $B_i = \langle e_t | 1 \ldots m_i \rangle$, where, e_t represent tth data point. n_i and m_i are the length of the video and physiological signal, respectively. For ith instance the ground-truth annotation is y_i which can be valence or arousal value. We train an end-to-end parameterized model, $\mathcal{F}_\theta$ using a set of tuples $\{\langle (F_i, B_i), y_i \rangle : i \in [0, T]\}, y_i \in [0, 1]$, where T is the total number of instances in the dataset, $y_i = 0$ represents low valence/arousal, high valence/arousal otherwise. During inference, given a test video and physiological signal pair (F_j, B_j) as input, $\mathcal{F}_\theta$ predicts $\hat{y}_j$ which approximates ground-truth annotation y_j as follows: $\hat{y}_j = \mathcal{F}_\theta((F_j, B_j); \Theta)$.

2.1   Architecture

Our proposed DeepVANet for VA based emotion recognition has three blocks: Face Appearance, Bio-sensing Data, and Classification Pipelines (Fig. 1).

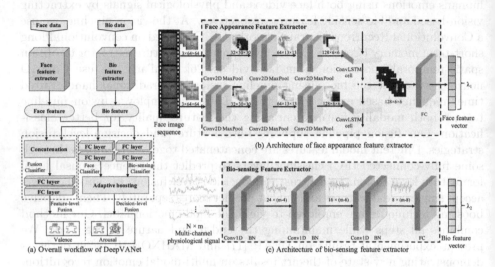

Fig. 1. Our proposed DeepVANet for Valance and Arousal based emotion recognition; FC and BN stand for fully connected layer and batch normalisation respectively.

Face Appearance Pipeline: We deploy 3-layer CNN (pretrained on AFEW-VA dataset [19]) at the top of our face appearance feature extractor to capture high-level spatial information. The inputs of the face appearance feature extractor are face image sequences (with size of 64×64). Each sample F_i has the shape of $n \times 3 \times 64 \times 64$, where n denotes the sequence length and 3 represents the number of RGB channels. The kernel number of three convolutional layers are 32, 64, and 128, respectively, where all the kernels have the same size of 3×3. Each layer is followed by a ReLu activator and a 3×3 max pooling. So, through a series of 2D convolutional and max-pooling operations, the CNN layers output the feature maps F' with the shape of $n \times 128 \times 6 \times 6$. Facial expressions are dynamic and evolve during the video containing temporal patterns. We extract face expression information in both spatial and temporal dimensions using a ConvLSTM [26]. For each timestep t, input gate i_t, forget gate f_t, cell gate g_t and output gate o_t are defined as $i_t = \sigma(W_{xi} * F'_t + W_{hi} * h_{t-1} + b_i)$, $f_t = \sigma(W_{xf} * F'_t + W_{hf} * h_{t-1} + b_f)$, $g_t = \tanh(W_{xg} * F'_t + W_{hg} * h_{t-1} + b_g)$ and $o_t = \sigma(W_{xo} * F'_t + W_{ho} * h_{t-1} + b_o)$; cell state c_t and hidden state h_t are defined as $c_t = f_t \odot c_{t-1} + i_t \odot g_t$ and $h_t = o_t \odot \tanh(c_t)$, where $\odot$ and $*$ demote the Hadamard product and 2D convolutional operator. A followed FC layer accepts the final hidden state and outputs the face appearance features which is a $1 \times \lambda_1$ vector $f_{face} = (a_1, a_2, ..., a_{\lambda_1})$.

Bio-sensing Data Pipeline: Instead of traditional time or frequency domain methods, we use deep learning methods to extract bio-sensing features automatically. To extract high-level bio-sensing features, we apply a multi-layer CNN architecture consisting of three 1D convolutional layers and a fully connected layer [32]. Each convolutional layer is followed by a batch normalization layer and a ReLu activator, and the last fully connected layer is deployed for further feature extraction and flattening. The inputs to the bio-sensing data pipeline are multi-channel physiological signals (concatenate EEG and peripheral physiological signals over channel dimension). For each bio-sensing input instance B_i with the shape of $c_{bio} \times m$, where c_{bio} and m represent the channel number and signal length respectively, the forward propagation in our bio feature extractor is shown as follows. Firstly, B_i flows into three-layer 1D CNN. The kernel sizes of three 1D CNN layers are 5, 3, 3, respectively. We choose to decrease output channel numbers for CNN layers 24, 16, and 8, to reduce the bio-sensing feature size and computation complexity. So, the output of convolutional layers is in the shape of $8 \times (m - 8)$, where m denotes the signal length. Then it is put into a FC layer and flattened into a $1 \times \lambda_2$ bio feature vector $f_{bio} = (b_1, b_2, \ldots, b_{\lambda_2})$.

Classification Pipeline: The classification pipeline predicts a score for valence or arousal. For each instance, we have ground-truth $\hat{y} \in \{0, 1\}$ to represent the emotion label (valence or arousal), where 0 and 1 represent low and high, respectively. Here, we investigate two kinds of fusion methods (feature-level and decision-level fusion) to make full use of different modalities. For *feature-level fusion*, face appearance feature f_{face} and bio feature f_{bio} are concatenated to generate a multi-modal feature vector $f_{multi} = f_{face} \oplus f_{bio}$, which is fed into the fusion classifier containing a two-layer fully-connected neural network. Using different value for λ_1 and λ_2, we can set different feature size combinations and explore the contribution of each single modality. For *decision-level fusion*, we use Adaptive Boosting (AdaBoost) [7,12]. The face and bio-sensing features are used to train two sub-classifiers separately. The sub-classifier network is the same as the fusion classifier. Each sub-classifier yields a predicted score S_i, which are used together to calculate a fusion score S_{fusion} using the Adaboost to get the proper weights of each sub-classifier. Generally, the sub-classifier having the less predict error holds the higher weight in calculating the fusion score. Training samples are also given the weights which influence their contribution to the error. The sample weights are initialized uniformly. The weight decreases if the sample is predicted correctly and increases otherwise. After finishing all training iterations, we can get the sub-classifier weights and calculate the fusion score.

2.2 Training and Inference

We use binary cross-entropy as a loss function for both feature- and decision-level fusion cases. Considering $\mathcal{N}, \mathbf{y}$ and S_i as the training batch size, target emotion label and predicted score, respectively, the loss is calculated as:

$$Loss = -\frac{1}{\mathcal{N}} \sum_{i=1}^{\mathcal{N}} (\mathbf{y}_i \cdot \ln S_i + (1 - \mathbf{y}_i) \cdot \ln (1 - S_i))$$

During inference, we forward test video, $\boldsymbol{F}_j$ and physiological signal, $\boldsymbol{B}_j$ to our proposed network, obtain score S_{fusion} and use the following formula for final prediction, $\hat{\mathbf{y}}$.

$$\hat{\mathbf{y}} = \begin{cases} High, & S_{fusion} > 0.5 \\ Low, & S_{fusion} \leq 0.5 \end{cases}$$

3   Experiment

Dataset: Two public multi-modal emotion datasets, namely DEAP, MAHNOB-HCI are used to evaluate our network separately. A brief statistics about the dataset is shown in Table 1.

Table 1. Statistics of the datasets used in this work

Criterion	DEAP	MAHNOB-HCI
Dataset size	22 subjects × 40 trials	27 subjects × 20 trials
Stimulus duration	60 s	49.7–117 s
Modality	Vision, EEG, Peripheral	Vision, EEG, Peripheral
Used bio signals	EEG, EOG, EMG, GSR, Respiration belt, Plethy-smograph, Temperature	EEG, ECG, GSR, Respiration belt, Temperature
Labels	Continuous valence and arousal from 1 to 9	Discrete valence and arousal of integers from 1 to 9

Experimental Evaluation: In line with the previous works [12,28], we divide valence and arousal into 'High'/'Low' using value = 5 as the threshold. We notice that physiological signals vary significantly across subjects [2,17,36], and this inter-subject difference affects the emotion recognition accuracy while predicting valence and arousal across people. Therefore, similar to the past works [2,36], we train and evaluate our model for every single subject (called per-subject experiment) to improve the recognition performance. In addition to the per-subject experiment, we also conduct inter-subject experiments. Here, all subjects' data is used to train and test one model aiming to evaluate our proposed network's generalization ability. For both per- and inter-subject experiments, we run 10-fold cross-validation and take the average testing accuracy as the model performance metric. Besides our multi-modal network, we also evaluate two single modalities, face and bio-sensing, separately. Furthermore, EEG and peripheral physiological signals are used separately in bio-sensing modality experiments.

Validation Strategy: We have two hyper-parameters in our model: the face feature dimension λ_1 and the bio-sensing feature dimension λ_2. For both hyper-parameter cases, we choose a set of candidates $\{16, 32, 64, 128, 256\}$, and perform a grid search to determine the best hyper-parameter. We use the mean recognition accuracy of valence and arousal as validation metric, and 16 and 64 are chosen as the face appearance feature and bio-sensing feature size.

Implementation Details[1]: To overcome the limited data size for deep learning, we divide each trial into 1-second length segments as proposed in [36]. We extract frames from face videos 5 Hz for vision-based data and perform face detection [3], cropping, and alignment on each frame. These face images are resized to 64×64 resolution and normalized within the interval $[0, 1]$ before feeding into our model. For bio-sensing data, we perform average reference, 4–45 Hz bandpass filter, and artifact removal using EEGLab [4] on 32-channel EEG signals. Both EEG and peripheral signals are downsampled 128 Hz and concatenated together along with channel dimension. For each segment, we apply the baseline removal on bio-sensing signals by subtracting the mean of 3-second pre-trial data [36]. We use the Adam algorithm [15] as the optimizer during training. The batch size, numbers of training epochs, and learning rate for all face-, bio-, and multi-modal are 64, 50, and 10^{-3}, respectively. We implement our work with the *Pytorch* framework using a single Nvidia V100 GPU.

3.1 Quantitative Results

Overall Result: Table 2 reports the inter- and per-subject experiment results of proposed DeepVANet on DEAP and MAHNOB-HCI datasets. We choose [17, 29] as baseline methods and consider some studies applying deep learning for comparison. These studies used the same binary VA labels as this paper. Some notable observations are: *(1)* Multi-modal methods [12,18,28] achieved better accuracy than single model methods [17,29] which justifies the significance of fusion strategy on face images and physiological signals. *(2)* Some deep learning-based approaches[1,2,36] get an accuracy above 90% by only using EEG signals. This is because the deep learning-based (LSTM) EEG features are more discriminative than handcrafted features. *(3)* We notice that the per-subject experiment result is better than the inter-subject experiment because the bio-sensing data variance across subjects impacts emotion recognition performance. However, our DeepVANet also performs well in inter-subject experiments and shows a good generalization ability to predict emotion for different people. *(4)* Overall, our feature-level fusion approach achieves the highest average recognition accuracy of 98.56%/98.18% and 99.19%/99.22% on DEAP and MAHNOB-HCI datasets, respectively, and surpasses the previous methods by a considerable margin. This

---

[1] Code and evaluation are available at: https://github.com/geekdanielz/DeepVANet.

Table 2. Overall results of VA based emotion recognition. Both inter-subject and per-subject experiment results are reported. For accuracy (%), valence at left and arousal at right.

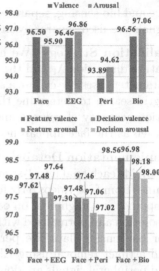

Fig. 2. Ablation study results (recognition accuracy %) for DEAP dataset

Data	Study	Modalities	Accuracy
DEAP	Inter-subject experiments		
	Siddharth et al. [28]	Face, EEG, Peripheral	79.52/78.34
	Tang et al. [30]	EEG, Peripheral	83.82/83.23
	This work	Face, EEG, Peripheral	**95.56/95.33**
	Per-subject experiments		
	Keoltra et al. [17]	EEG, Peripheral	62.70/62.00
	Huang et al. [12]	Face, EEG	80.30/74.23
	Liu et al. [22]	EEG, Peripheral	85.20/80.50
	Alhagry et al. [1]	EEG	85.65/85.45
	Yang et al. [36]	EEG	90.80/91.03
	Anubhav et al. [2]	EEG	94.69/93.13
	This work	Face, EEG, Peripheral	**98.56/98.18**
MAHNOB	Inter-subject experiments		
	Soleymani et al. [29]	EEG, Peripheral	57.00/52.40
	Wiem and Lachiri [33]	EEG, Peripheral	68.75/64.23
	Siddharth et al. [28]	Face, EEG, Peripheral	85.49/82.93
	This work	Face, EEG, Peripheral	**96.82/97.79**
	Per-subject experiments		
	Keolstra et al. [18]	Face, EEG	74.00/70.00
	Huang et al. [12]	Face, EEG	75.21/75.63
	This work	Face, EEG, Peripheral	**99.19/99.22**

success is a result of utilizing advanced deep learning-based feature extraction for bio-sensing data.

Ablation Study: To explore the emotion recognition performance of different modalities, we test our approach using both single- and multi-modal input on DEAP dataset. From the results in Fig. 2, we find that: *(1)* EEG features are more salient than peripheral features, and bio-sensing modality (EEG+Peripheral) performs better than individual EEG and peripheral modality. *(2)* multi-modality outperforms all the single modalities, which demonstrates the effectiveness of our feature- and decision-level fusion strategies. *(3)* feature-level fusion method performs better than decision-level fusion in most cases. We believe it is because we only have two sub-classifiers in our approach, limiting the effectiveness of the decision-level fusion based on AdaBoost.

3.2 Qualitative Visualization

We use t-SNE to reduce the feature dimension into 2D space and visualize different modal features in Fig. 3. We find that the HIGH and the LOW class features successfully form two rough clusters in 2D space. Notably, for the fusion modal, two clusters are separated more clearly. It also demonstrates that our multi-modal features are salient and discriminative.

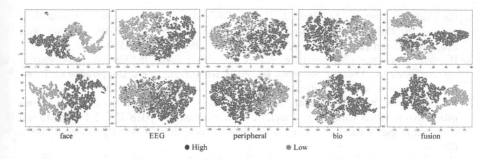

Fig. 3. 2D t-SNE visualization of features extracted from subject 1 of DEAP dataset; top and bottom rows represent valence and arousal, respectively.

4 Conclusion

In this paper, we propose a deep end-to-end network, DeepVANet, for multi-modal emotion recognition. The network accepts face image sequences and bio-sensing signals (e.g., EEG, EOG, ECG, GSR etc.) as input and yields valence-arousal labels for emotion recognition. We adopt ConvLSTM and Conv1D to extract face appearance and bio-sensing computing features, respectively, demonstrating a significant advantage in the valance-arousal emotion recognition model. Furthermore, we evaluate our method with per-subject and inter-subjects experiments. For both strategies, the experiments' results show that our end-to-end network outperforms previous studies and establishes new state-of-the-art performance on DEAP and MAHNOB-HCI datasets.

References

1. Alhagry, S., Fahmy, A.A., El-Khoribi, R.A.: Emotion recognition based on EEG using LSTM recurrent neural network. Emotion 8(10), 355–358 (2017)
2. Anubhav, Nath, D., Singh, M., Sethia, D., Kalra, D., Indu, S.: An efficient approach to EEG-based emotion recognition using LSTM network. In: IEEE International Colloquium on Signal Processing & Its Applications (CSPA), pp. 88–92 (2020)
3. Bulat, A., Tzimiropoulos, G.: How far are we from solving the 2d & 3d face alignment problem? (and a dataset of 230,000 3d facial landmarks). In: International Conference on Computer Vision (2017)
4. Delorme, A., Makeig, S.: EEGLAB: an open source toolbox for analysis of single-trial EEG dynamics including independent component analysis. J. Neurosci. Methods 134(1), 9–21 (2004)
5. Dzedzickis, A., Kaklauskas, A., Bucinskas, V.: Human emotion recognition: review of sensors and methods. Sensors 20(3), 592 (2020)
6. Ekman, P.: Are there basic emotions? Psychol. Rev. 99, 550–553 (1992)
7. Freund, Y., Schapire, R.E., et al.: Experiments with a new boosting algorithm. In: ICML, vol. 96, pp. 148–156 (1996)
8. Ghimire, D., Lee, J.: Geometric feature-based facial expression recognition in image sequences using multi-class adaboost and support vector machines. Sensors 13(6), 7714–7734 (2013)

9. Haddad, J., Lezoray, O., Hamel, P.: 3D-CNN for facial emotion recognition in videos. In: Bebis, G., et al. (eds.) ISVC 2020. LNCS, vol. 12510, pp. 298–309. Springer, Cham (2020). https://doi.org/10.1007/978-3-030-64559-5_23

10. Happy, S., George, A., Routray, A.: A real time facial expression classification system using local binary patterns. In: 2012 4th International Conference on Intelligent Human Computer Interaction (IHCI), pp. 1–5. IEEE (2012)

11. Huang, J., Li, Y., Tao, J., Lian, Z., Yi, J.: End-to-end continuous emotion recognition from video using 3D ConvLSTM networks. In: 2018 IEEE International Conference on Acoustics, Speech and Signal Processing (ICASSP), pp. 6837–6841 (2018)

12. Huang, Y., Yang, J., Liu, S., Pan, J.: Combining facial expressions and electroencephalography to enhance emotion recognition. Future Internet 11(5), 105 (2019)

13. Jinliang, G., Fang, F., Wang, W., Ren, F.: EEG emotion recognition based on granger causality and CapsNet neural network. In: International Conference on Cloud Computing and Intelligence Systems (CCIS), pp. 47–52 (2018)

14. Kahou, S.E., Michalski, V., Konda, K., Memisevic, R., Pal, C.: Recurrent neural networks for emotion recognition in video. In: Proceedings of the 2015 ACM on International Conference on Multimodal Interaction, pp. 467–474 (2015)

15. Kingma, D.P., Ba, J.L.: Adam: a method for stochastic optimization. arXiv preprint arXiv:1412.6980 (2014)

16. Ko, B.C.: A brief review of facial emotion recognition based on visual information. Sensors 18(2), 401 (2018)

17. Koelstra, S., et al.: DEAP: a database for emotion analysis using physiological signals. IEEE Trans. Affect. Comput. 3(1), 18–31 (2012)

18. Koelstra, S., Patras, I.: Fusion of facial expressions and EEG for implicit affective tagging. Image Vis. Comput. 31(2), 164–174 (2013)

19. Kossaifi, J., Tzimiropoulos, G., Todorovic, S., Pantic, M.: AFEW-VA database for valence and arousal estimation in-the-wild. Image Vis. Comput. 65, 23–36 (2017)

20. Kumar, P., Happy, S., Routray, A.: A real-time robust facial expression recognition system using HOG features. In: 2016 International Conference on Computing, Analytics and Security Trends (CAST), pp. 289–293. IEEE (2016)

21. Lee, J., Kim, S., Kim, S., Park, J., Sohn, K.: Context-aware emotion recognition networks. In: Proceedings of the IEEE/CVF International Conference on Computer Vision, pp. 10143–10152 (2019)

22. Liu, W., Zheng, W.-L., Lu, B.-L.: Emotion recognition using multimodal deep learning. In: Hirose, A., Ozawa, S., Doya, K., Ikeda, K., Lee, M., Liu, D. (eds.) ICONIP 2016. LNCS, vol. 9948, pp. 521–529. Springer, Cham (2016). https://doi.org/10.1007/978-3-319-46672-9_58

23. Nie, W., Ren, M., Nie, J., Zhao, S.: C-GCN: correlation based graph convolutional network for audio-video emotion recognition. IEEE Trans. Multimed. 1 (2020)

24. Panoulas, K.J., Hadjileontiadis, L.J., Panas, S.M.: Brain-computer interface (BCI): types, processing perspectives and applications. In: Tsihrintzis, G.A., Jain, L.C. (eds.) Multimedia Services in Intelligent Environments. Smart Innovation, Systems and Technologies, vol. 3, pp. 299–321. Springer, Heidelberg (2010). https://doi.org/10.1007/978-3-642-13396-1_14

25. Salama, E.S., El-Khoribi, R.A., Shoman, M.E., Shalaby, M.A.W.: A 3D-convolutional neural network framework with ensemble learning techniques for multi-modal emotion recognition. Egypt. Inform. J. 22, 167–176 (2020)

26. Shi, X., Chen, Z., Wang, H., Yeung, D.Y., Wong, W.K., Woo, W.C.: Convolutional LSTM network: a machine learning approach for precipitation nowcasting. In: Advances in Neural Information Processing Systems, vol. 28, pp. 802–810 (2015)

27. Shu, L., et al.: A review of emotion recognition using physiological signals. Sensors **18**(7), 2074 (2018)

28. Siddharth, J., T.P., Sejnowski, T.J.: Utilizing deep learning towards multi-modal bio-sensing and vision-based affective computing. IEEE Trans. Affect. Comput. (2019)

29. Soleymani, M., Lichtenauer, J., Pun, T., Pantic, M.: A multimodal database for affect recognition and implicit tagging. IEEE Trans. Affect. Comput. **3**(1), 42–55 (2012)

30. Tang, H., Liu, W., Zheng, W.L., Lu, B.L.: Multimodal emotion recognition using deep neural networks. In: Liu, D., Xie, S., Li, Y., Zhao, D., El-Alfy, E.S. (eds.) ICONIP 2017. LNCS, vol. 10637, pp. 811–819. Springer, Cham (2017). https://doi.org/10.1007/978-3-319-70093-9_86

31. Torres, E.P., Torres, E.A., Hernandez-Alvarez, M., Yoo, S.G.: EEG-based BCI emotion recognition: a survey. Sensors **20**(18), 5083 (2020)

32. Ullah, I., Hussain, M., Aboalsamh, H., et al.: An automated system for epilepsy detection using EEG brain signals based on deep learning approach. Expert Syst. Appl. **107**, 61–71 (2018)

33. Wiem, M.B.H., Lachiri, Z.: Emotion classification in arousal valence model using MAHNOB-HCI database. Int. J. Adv. Comput. Sci. Appl. **8**(3), 1–6 (2017)

34. Yan, J., Zheng, W., Xu, Q., Lu, G., Li, H., Wang, B.: Sparse kernel reduced-rank regression for bimodal emotion recognition from facial expression and speech. IEEE Trans. Multimed. **18**(7), 1319–1329 (2016)

35. Yang, Y., Hossain, M.Z., Gedeon, T., Rahman, S.: RealSmileNet: a deep end-to-end network for spontaneous and posed smile recognition. In: Ishikawa, H., Liu, C.-L., Pajdla, T., Shi, J. (eds.) ACCV 2020. LNCS, vol. 12626, pp. 21–37. Springer, Cham (2021). https://doi.org/10.1007/978-3-030-69541-5_2

36. Yang, Y., Wu, Q., Qiu, M., Wang, Y., Chen, X.: Emotion recognition from multi-channel EEG through parallel convolutional recurrent neural network. In: 2018 International Joint Conference on Neural Networks (IJCNN), pp. 1–7. IEEE (2018)

37. Zeng, Z., et al.: Audio-visual affect recognition. IEEE Trans. Multimed. **9**(2), 424–428 (2007)

38. Zhang, H.: Expression-EEG based collaborative multimodal emotion recognition using deep autoencoder. IEEE Access **8**, 164130–164143 (2020)

Detection of Subtle Stress Episodes During UX Evaluation: Assessing the Performance of the WESAD Bio-Signals Dataset

Alexandros Liapis[1,2(✉)], Evanthia Faliagka[1], Christos Katsanos[3], Christos Antonopoulos[1], and Nikolaos Voros[1]

[1] Department of Electrical and Computer Engineering, University of Peloponnese, Patras, Greece
{a.liapis,e.faliagka}@esda-lab.gr, {ch.antonop,voros}@uop.gr
[2] School of Science and Technology, Hellenic Open University, Patras, Greece
[3] Department of Informatics, Aristotle University of Thessaloniki, Thessaloniki, Greece
ckatsanos@csd.auth.gr

Abstract. Stress is a highly subjective condition and may largely vary in different contexts. Bio-signals have been widely used by researchers and practitioners to monitor stress levels. Consequently, various bio-signals datasets for stress recognition have been recorded. The most of publicly available physiological datasets have been emotionally annotated in a context where users have been exposed to intense stressors, such as movie clips, songs, major hardware/software failures, image datasets, and gaming. However, it remains unexplored how effectively such datasets can be used in different contexts. This paper investigates the performance of the publicly available dataset named WESAD (Wearable Stress and Affect Detection) in the context of UX evaluation. More specifically, skin conductance signal from WESAD was used to train four machine learning classifiers. Regarding the binary classification problem (stress vs. no stress), models' accuracy was rather high (at least 91.1%). However, it was found that their effectiveness in assessing stress in the context of UX was rather poor when a new bio-signals dataset was used.

Keywords: Stress detection · UX evaluation · Bio-signals · Electrodermal activity

1 Introduction

The combined research efforts of various fields, such as Human-Computer Interaction, Ubiquitous Computing, Ambient Intelligence and Internet of Things, have substantially increased the interest on affective qualities of software products [1]. User eXperience (UX) emerged as a research field allowing HCI researchers and practitioners to better understand users' interaction experiences by using tools and techniques beyond traditional user interaction metrics [2]. As a term, UX encompasses aspects such as usability,

© IFIP International Federation for Information Processing 2021
Published by Springer Nature Switzerland AG 2021
C. Ardito et al. (Eds.): INTERACT 2021, LNCS 12934, pp. 238–247, 2021.
https://doi.org/10.1007/978-3-030-85613-7_17

usefulness, aesthetics and emotions [3]. UX design often begins before the product is even in the user's hands. Designing and developing for UX requires a deep understanding of how users feel during their interaction with a system or a product [4].

Emotional aspects of UX can be measured by using a variety of approaches, such as post-questionnaires, interviews and observation. However, these methods have been criticized as time consuming and prone to subjectivity [5]. Alternatively, modalities such as facial expression [6], speech tone [7] and touchscreen patterns analysis [8, 9] have been proposed to minimize any subjectivity effect. Towards the same direction, bio-signals monitoring (e.g., heart rate, respiration, skin conductance) is also an approach that has been adopted by researchers in the context of UX evaluation [10].

In UX evaluation of interactive environments, one is mostly interested in the identification of system flaws [11]. A system or a product with flaws can cause undesirable activations of users' physiology widely referred as "*fight or flight*" event or stress [12].

Skin Conductivity (SC), also known as Galvanic Skin Response (GSR), is one of the most well-studied psychophysiological markers of the functioning of people's Autonomic Nervous System. The evolution of appealing wearables [13] has further transformed SC into a popular measurement allowing experiments to take place in more ecologically valid settings [14] at a relatively low cost [15]. SC signal characteristics, such as peak height and instantaneous peak rate, are reliable indicators of stress level of a user. In [16] an extensive summary of SC research in relation to stress is presented.

There is a large number of publicly available physiological datasets [17–19] for stress research that have been emotionally annotated in a context where users have been exposed to intense stressors (e.g., movie clips, songs, major hardware/software failures, image datasets, and gaming). Although such approaches are able to create stress prediction models with rather high classification accuracy, it remains questionable if they could be effectively used in capturing subtle stress responses, which are mostly expected in UX evaluation studies [20].

This paper investigates the performance of such a dataset in the context of UX evaluation. To the best of our knowledge, this is the first paper to do so. More specifically SC signals of 15 users from the publicly available physiological dataset named WESAD (Wearable Stress and Affect Detection [21]) were used in order to train four machine learning classifiers (L-SVM, C, SCM, Q-SVM and sTree). Next, a publicly[1] available emotionally annotated bio-signals dataset, made available by Liapis et al. [22], was considered as the ground truth dataset in order to evaluate the performance of the aforementioned classifiers in stress detection in the context of UX evaluation. This ground truth dataset consists of SC segments that have been emotionally annotated by users' valence-arousal ratings. Such self-reported periods indicate usability issues confronted while they were interacting with a web-based platform during a UX evaluation study. Using users' self-reporting as ground truth is a common practice in UX research [23, 24].

---

[1] https://www.researchgate.net/publication/350855591_EDA_Dataset_in_UX_Context.rar.

2 Description of Datasets

2.1 WESAD Dataset

WESAD [21] is a publicly available multimodal physiological dataset for wearable stress and affect detection. It includes the following physiological signals: blood volume pulse (BVP), electrocardiogram (ECG), electrodermal activity (EDA), electromyogram (EMG), respiration (RESP), body temperature (TEMP), and three axis acceleration (ACC). The bio-signals were recorded during a lab study in which 15 participants with a mean age of 27.5 years (SD = 2.4) were exposed in three different affective states: neutral, stress, and amusement. The Trier Social Stress Test (TSST) was employed by the researchers in order to elicit stress. Regarding the binary classification problem (stress vs. non-stress), a classification accuracy of up to 93% was reported when all physiological signals participated in the training process. Classification was also conducted by using only EDA data. In this case, the accuracy was 80%.

Effective identification of an emotional state requires the recording of adequate bio-signals, under well-organized experimental conditions (field or lab) by using the appropriate sensing equipment. However, the number of recorded signals affects the number of sensors that are required. On the contrary, Liu et al. [25] used a single bio-signal in order to create a more practical, unobtrusive and comfortable wearable system for stress detection. In particular, the SC signal along with Linear Discriminant Analysis (LDA) were used in order to discriminate three stress levels: low, medium and high. A classification accuracy of 81.82% was achieved. In addition, Jussilla et al. [26] proposed an effective stress management bio-sensor named "smart ring". Smart ring measures EDA from the palmar side of the wearers. Such approaches might be a better tradeoff between recognition performance and computational load, which in turn could be a promising line of research for the development of practical personal stress monitors. These studies are our rationale to use only SC in the present study.

Despite the high classification accuracy in both approaches (all signals vs. EDA), WESAD authors indicate that "results should be interpreted with caution due to the limitations of WESAD, regarding the number of subjects and the lack of age and gender diversity". Furthermore, the authors invite the research community to consider their dataset for algorithm development and benchmarking, which is an objective of this paper.

2.2 Ground Truth Dataset

In the section, we present the ground truth dataset that was used to assess the stress detection mechanisms created from the WESAD dataset. More specifically, the ground-truth dataset consists of SC segments that have been emotionally annotated by users' self-reported valence-arousal ratings. Such periods indicate usability issues confronted while users were interacting with a platform during a UX evaluation study [22].

More specifically the aforementioned study involved 30 participants (13 female), aged between 18 and 45 (Mean = 32.1, SD = 7.1) who were asked to complete a set of interaction tasks in a web-based service while their SC signal was recorded. At the end of each user testing session each participant was involved in a retrospective think aloud (RTA) protocol in order to report any usability issues (UIs) that she/he confronted while performing the interaction tasks. For each one of his/her retrospectively reported UIs, the participant was asked to provide: a) the duration of the confronted UI and b) an emotional rating, using the emotional scale of Valence (from 1 to 9)–Arousal (from 1 to 9). Overall, a number of 113 emotionally annotated UIs were reported. For each annotated UI there is an associated segment of SC signal that constitutes the ground truth bio-signals dataset that are used in the present study to test the classifiers created from the WESAD dataset.

3   Classifiers Creation: Training Process and Results

Non-Specific Skin Conductance Responses (NS-SCRs) from the SC signals included in the WESAD dataset were used as the training dataset for the development of the stress classifiers. The use of intensive sub-periods that might appear within an emotional period can probably contribute to the final assessment of the experienced emotion (i.e., feeling stressed, happy, angry etc.). In terms of stress detection, intensive sub-periods could be interpreted as NS-SCRs within a stress session. A validated software named PhysiOBS [22, 27], freely available, was used to detect and extract NS-SCRs.

For each SC signal in the WESAD dataset, we used only the signal part that is associated with the stress sessions (TSST) as already mentioned in Sect. 2.1. The detected significant NS-SCRs segments within each TSST session were used as the stress class and the rest parts of the TSST session were used as the non-stress class (see Fig. 1). This specific dataset creation approach has been also applied in [28].

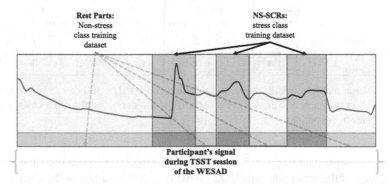

Fig. 1. An example of the dataset creation process. From each SC signal in the WESAD dataset we extract NS-SCRs and use them as the stress class. The rest parts of the session constitute the non-stress class.

More specifically, the NS-SCRs extraction process consists of the following steps. Initially, the SC signals were smoothed using Hann function and then normalized as proposed in [29]. Subsequently, we used the signal amplitude from which we extracted 21 features as proposed in [30]. Next, the extracted features were provided as input to the selected machine learning algorithms aiming to differentiate the two emotional states (stress vs non-stress). A 5-fold cross-validation training was applied in all classification methods. Overall, the training dataset consisted of 380 cases; 165 in the class stress (NS-SCRs) and 215 in the class non-stress (signal rest parts). As proposed in [16], NS-SCR's segments with duration larger or equal to 4 s from NS-SCR's initial deflection to peak were considered; a rule also applied in [31].

Regarding the binary problem (stress vs non-stress), Table 1 presents the obtained performance metric for each trained classifier. All classifiers achieved high accuracies (at least 91%). The best classification result was achieved by the sTree classifier (95.8%). These results indicate that our applied training method improved the classification results compared to the 80% accuracy reported by [21] when using only the SC signal. Furthermore, the confusion matrix (see Fig. 2) presents details about the correctly classified cases per trained model.

Table 1. Performance for each classifier (F1 score was also calculated). The F1-score is an important metric when there are imbalanced classes as in our case.

	Precision	Recall	Accuracy	F1-score
C-SVM	89,7%	89,7%	**91,1%**	89,7%
L-SVM	92,6%	91,5%	**93,2%**	92,1%
Q-SVM	92,4%	88,5%	**91,8%**	90,4%
sTree	96,3%	93,9%	**95,8%**	95,1%

		Predicted Classes / model						
		C-SVM		L-SVM		Q-SVM		sTree	
		Stress	No Stress	Stress	No Stress	Stress	No Stress	Stress	No Stress
True Class	Stress	148	17	151	14	146	19	155	10
	No Stress	17	198	12	203	12	203	6	209

Fig. 2. Confusion matrix. Overall, the training dataset consisted of 380 cases; 165 in the class stress and 215 in the class no-stress. Green parts show the correctly classified cases for each classifier. (Color figure online)

The plot of sensitivity versus 1-Specifity is called Receiver Operating Characteristic (ROC) curve and the area under this ROC curve is called Area Under the Curve (AUC) (see Fig. 3). Both ROC and AUC are effective measures of accuracy. This curve plays a central role in evaluating diagnostic ability of tests to discriminate the true state of subjects. In our case, the AUC can be interpreted as the probability that a randomly chosen stress signal is rated or ranked as more likely to be stress than a randomly chosen non-stress signal. All classifiers achieved high AUC (at least 94%). The best AUC result was achieved by the L-SVM classifier (98%).

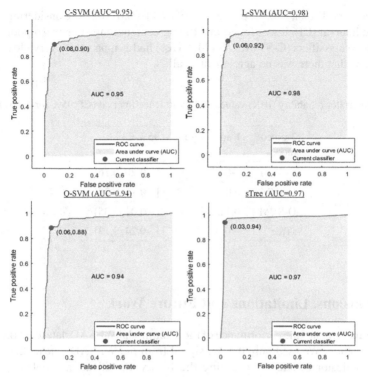

Fig. 3. Receiver operating characteristic (ROC) curve and area under the curve (AUC) performance for each trained model. Red dot in each plot shows classifiers' optimal performance between true positive rate (TPR) and false positive rate (FPR).

4   Evaluation of Classifiers

In Sect. 3 we presented the training process and the results of four classifiers. To this end, the SC signals from the publicly available dataset named WESAD were used. In order to measure the performance of the created models we used an existing UX bio-signals dataset (see Sect. 2.2). More specifically, the test dataset consists of 113 emotionally annotated (according to VA ratings) user-reported SC segments. Kappa coefficient [32] metric was used to quantify the agreement between users' emotional ratings and created classifiers. Agreement among raters ranges from -1 to 1. Values near or below zero suggest that the agreement is probably attributable to chance. On the contrary, the higher the positive value of Kappa is, the higher the agreement is.

Any SC segment with Valence lower than 5 and Arousal greater than 5 was assigned as stress and the rest SC segments as non-stress [29, 33]. Next, the 113 SC segments, were used as an input to the trained classifiers. For each segment each classifier returned the classification result (1 = stress, 2 = non-stress). The returned values of the stress models were compared with participants' self-reported stress ratings that constitutes our ground truth dataset. Table 2 presents the interrater reliability for each classifier. According to the levels of agreement presented in [34], the Q-SVM achieved a non-significant slight agreement; Kappa $= 0.17$, $p > 0.05$, 95% CI $[-0.01, 0.35]$. Considering the 95% confidence interval (CI), it was found that the agreement ranged between poor and fair. The rest three classifiers (C-SVM, L-SVM, sTree) had Kappa values very close to zero, which means that there was no agreement at all.

Table 2. Interrater reliability (IRR) values and confidence interval (CI) 95% for each classifier.

Trained model	Kappa value	95% CI
C-SVM	−0.02	[−0.20, 0.16]
L-SVM	0.02	[−0,16, 0,20]
Q-SVM	0.17	[−0.01, 0.35]
sTree	−0.06	[−0.24, 0.13]

5   Conclusions, Limitations and Future Work

This paper investigates the performance of the multimodal WESAD dataset in the context of UX evaluation. We used only the SC signal from the WESAD dataset because it is a reliable indicator of stress. Regarding the binary classification problem (stress vs non-stress) accuracy of up to 95.8% was reached.

An existing bio-signals dataset, which consists of SC segments, was used as the ground truth dataset in order to assess the performance of the stress classifiers in the context of UX evaluation. In contrast with the training dataset (WESAD), the ground truth dataset was recorded during a UX evaluation study, a context that could cause subtle emotional reaction. More specifically, the ground truth dataset represents users' self-reported periods of usability issues confronted while they were interacting with a web-based platform. We assessed the performance of the stress classifiers by conducting an interrater reliability analysis using the Kappa coefficient. The higher interrater reliability was found for Q-SVM but it was still non-statistically significant and poor-to-fair; Kappa $= 0.17$, $p > 0.05$. The aforementioned level of agreement is quite lower than the one presented in [22]. In the latter the same ground truth dataset was used. The reported interrater reliability was found to be statistically significant and fair-to-moderate; Kappa $= 0.35$, $p < 0.001$. This is probably explained by the fact that in [22] the stress classifier was assessed against the ground truth dataset which was trained with bio-signals that had been recorded while users performed typical HCI tasks [35].

In this study we assessed the classifiers performance by using only skin conductance. Such an approach aims to maximize practicality by reducing the number of sensors while maintaining accuracy in high levels. Although classification results of the trained models were high, future efforts could consider more bio-signals and different combinations of them in the context of optimal balance vs efficiency. Furthermore, this study serves as a first proof of concept by investigating if a dataset emotionally annotated in a context where users have been exposed to intense stressors can indeed be used effectively in a different context (i.e., UX evaluation). In the next steps of our work more participants and additional datasets will be included to further increase objectivity and accuracy of presented results. Additional approaches such as subject dependent training along with more in-depth analysis techniques such as deep learning should also be investigated. Creating more flexible stress assessment mechanism analysis combining bio-signals dataset from various contexts could be also a challenge for future work.

Overall, the preliminary results presented in this paper reveal that performance of the available bio-signal datasets in various contexts should be carefully taken into consideration. Although the one size fits all approach is not suggested, this study provides some interesting insights on the generalizability of the bio-signals datasets.

Acknowledgments. This research has been co-financed by the European Union and Greek national funds through the Operational Program Competitiveness, Entrepreneurship and Innovation, under the call RESEARCH CREATE INNOVATE (project code: T2EΔK-02159 PLan-V).

References

1. Sarsenbayeva, Z., et al.: Does smartphone use drive our emotions or vice versa? A causal analysis. In: Proceedings of the 2020 CHI Conference on Human Factors in Computing Systems, New York, pp. 1–15. Association for Computing Machinery (2020). https://doi.org/10.1145/3313831.3376163
2. Remy, C., et al.: Evaluation beyond usability: validating sustainable HCI research. In: Proceedings of the 2018 CHI Conference on Human Factors in Computing Systems, ACM, New York, pp. 216:1–216:14 (2018). https://doi.org/10.1145/3173574.3173790
3. Silvennoinen, J.M., Jokinen, J.P.P.: Aesthetic appeal and visual usability in four icon design eras. In: Proceedings of the 2016 CHI Conference on Human Factors in Computing Systems, pp. 4390–4400. Association for Computing Machinery, San Jose, California, USA (2016). https://doi.org/10.1145/2858036.2858462
4. Díaz-Oreiro, I., López, G., Quesada, L., Guerrero, L.A.: Standardized questionnaires for user experience evaluation: a systematic literature review. Proceedings **31**, 14 (2019). https://doi.org/10.3390/proceedings2019031014
5. Marshall, C., Rossman, G.B.: Designing Qualitative Research. Sage Publications, London (2014)
6. Tarnowski, P., Kołodziej, M., Majkowski, A., Rak, R.J.: Emotion recognition using facial expressions. Procedia Comput. Sci. **108**, 1175–1184 (2017)
7. Mao, Q., Dong, M., Huang, Z., Zhan, Y.: Learning salient features for speech emotion recognition using convolutional neural networks. IEEE Trans. Multimedia **16**, 2203–2213 (2014)
8. Tikadar, S., Bhattacharya, S.: A novel method to build and validate an affective state prediction model from touch-typing. In: Lamas, D., Loizides, F., Nacke, L., Petrie, H., Winckler, M., Zaphiris, P. (eds.) INTERACT 2019. LNCS, vol. 11749, pp. 99–119. Springer, Cham (2019). https://doi.org/10.1007/978-3-030-29390-1_6
9. Tikadar, S., Kazipeta, S., Ganji, C., Bhattacharya, S.: A minimalist approach for identifying affective states for mobile interaction design. In: Bernhaupt, R., Dalvi, G., Joshi, A., Balkrishan, D.K., O'Neill, J., Winckler, M. (eds.) INTERACT 2017. LNCS, vol. 10513, pp. 3–12. Springer, Cham (2017). https://doi.org/10.1007/978-3-319-67744-6_1
10. Maier, M., Marouane, C., Elsner, D.: DeepFlow: detecting optimal user experience from physiological data using deep neural networks. In: Proceedings of the 18th International Conference on Autonomous Agents and Multiagent Systems, Montreal QC, Canada, pp. 2108–2110. International Foundation for Autonomous Agents and Multiagent Systems (2019)

11. Lazar, J., Feng, J.H., Hochheiser, H.: Research Methods in Human-Computer Interaction. Wiley, Hoboken (2010)
12. Hernandez, J., Paredes, P., Roseway, A., Czerwinski, M.: Under pressure: sensing stress of computer users. In: Proceedings of the SIGCHI Conference on Human Factors in Computing Systems, ACM, New York, pp. 51–60 (2014). https://doi.org/10.1145/2556288.2557165
13. Lee, H., Kleinsmith, A.: Public speaking anxiety in a real classroom: towards developing a reflection system. In: Extended Abstracts of the 2019 CHI Conference on Human Factors in Computing Systems, Glasgow, Scotland, UK, pp. 1–6. Association for Computing Machinery (2019). https://doi.org/10.1145/3290607.3312875
14. Betella, A., et al.: Inference of human affective states from psychophysiological measurements extracted under ecologically valid conditions. Front. Neurosci. **8**, 286 (2014)
15. Cowley, B., et al.: The psychophysiology primer: a guide to methods and a broad review with a focus on human–computer interaction. Found. Trends® Hum.–Comput. Interact. **9**, 151–308 (2016)
16. Boucsein, W.: Electrodermal Activity. Springer, US (2012). https://doi.org/10.1007/978-1-4614-1126-0
17. Koelstra, S., et al.: DEAP: a database for emotion analysis; using physiological signals. IEEE Trans. Affect. Comput. **3**, 18–31 (2012). https://doi.org/10.1109/T-AFFC.2011.15
18. Koldijk, S., Sappelli, M., Verberne, S., Neerincx, M.A., Kraaij, W.: The SWELL knowledge work dataset for stress and user modeling research. In: Proceedings of the 16th International Conference on Multimodal Interaction, ACM, New York, pp. 291–298 (2014). https://doi.org/10.1145/2663204.2663257
19. Subramanian, R., Wache, J., Abadi, M.K., Vieriu, R.L., Winkler, S., Sebe, N.: ASCERTAIN: emotion and personality recognition using commercial sensors. IEEE Trans. Affect. Comput. **9**, 147–160 (2018). https://doi.org/10.1109/TAFFC.2016.2625250
20. Alberdi, A., Aztiria, A., Basarab, A.: Towards an automatic early stress recognition system for office environments based on multimodal measurements: a review. J. Biomed. Inform. **59**, 49–75 (2016)
21. Schmidt, P., Reiss, A., Duerichen, R., Marberger, C., Van Laerhoven, K.: Introducing WESAD, a multimodal dataset for wearable stress and affect detection. In: Proceedings of the 20th ACM International Conference on Multimodal Interaction, ACM, New York, pp. 400–408 (2018). https://doi.org/10.1145/3242969.3242985
22. Liapis, A., Katsanos, C., Karousos, N., Xenos, M., Orphanoudakis, T.: User experience evaluation: a validation study of a tool-based approach for automatic stress detection using physiological signals. Int. J. Hum.-Comput. Interact. **37**, 470–483 (2021). https://doi.org/10.1080/10447318.2020.1825205
23. Pakarinen, T., Pietilä, J., Nieminen, H.: Prediction of self-perceived stress and arousal based on electrodermal activity*. In: 2019 41st Annual International Conference of the IEEE Engineering in Medicine and Biology Society (EMBC), pp. 2191–2195 (2019). https://doi.org/10.1109/EMBC.2019.8857621
24. Bruun, A.: It's not complicated: a study of non-specialists analyzing GSR sensor data to detect UX related events. In: Proceedings of the 10th Nordic Conference on Human-Computer Interaction, ACM, Oslo, Norway, pp. 170–183 (2018). https://doi.org/10.1145/3240167.3240183
25. Liu, Y., Du, S.: Psychological stress level detection based on electrodermal activity. Behav. Brain Res. **341**, 50–53 (2018). https://doi.org/10.1016/j.bbr.2017.12.021
26. Jussila, J., Venho, N., Salonius, H., Moilanen, J., Liukkonen, J., Rinnetmäki, M.: Towards ecosystem for research and development of electrodermal activity applications. In: Proceedings of the 22nd International Academic Mindtrek Conference, Tampere, Finland, pp. 79–87. Association for Computing Machinery (2018). https://doi.org/10.1145/3275116.3275141

27. Liapis, A., Karousos, N., Katsanos, C., Xenos, M.: Evaluating user's emotional experience in HCI: the PhysiOBS approach. In: Kurosu, M. (ed.) HCI 2014. LNCS, vol. 8511, pp. 758–767. Springer, Cham (2014). https://doi.org/10.1007/978-3-319-07230-2_72
28. Liapis, A., Katsanos, C., Karousos, N., Xenos, M., Orphanoudakis, T.: UDSP+: stress detection based on user-reported emotional ratings and wearable skin conductance sensor. In: Adjunct Proceedings of the 2019 ACM International Joint Conference on Pervasive and Ubiquitous Computing and Proceedings of the 2019 ACM International Symposium on Wearable Computers, ACM, New York, pp. 125–128 (2019). https://doi.org/10.1145/3341162.3343831
29. Mandryk, R.L., Atkins, M.S.: A fuzzy physiological approach for continuously modeling emotion during interaction with play technologies. Int. J. Hum Comput Stud. **65**, 329–347 (2007). https://doi.org/10.1016/j.ijhcs.2006.11.011
30. Healey, J., Picard, R.: Detecting stress during real-world driving tasks using physiological sensors. IEEE Trans. Intell. Transp. Syst. **6**, 156–166 (2005). https://doi.org/10.1109/TITS.2005.848368
31. Bruun, A., Law, E.L.-C., Heintz, M., Alkly, L.H.A.: Understanding the relationship between frustration and the severity of usability problems: what can psychophysiological data (not) tell us? In: Proceedings of the 2016 CHI Conference on Human Factors in Computing Systems, ACM, New York, pp. 3975–3987 (2016). https://doi.org/10.1145/2858036.2858511
32. Cohen, J.: A coefficient of agreement for nominal scales. Educ. Psychol. Measur. **20**, 37–46 (1960). https://doi.org/10.1177/001316446002000104
33. Liapis, A., Katsanos, C., Sotiropoulos, D.G., Karousos, N., Xenos, M.: Stress in interactive applications: analysis of the valence-arousal space based on physiological signals and self-reported data. Multimedia Tools Appl. **76**(4), 5051–5071 (2016). https://doi.org/10.1007/s11042-016-3637-2
34. Landis, J.R., Koch, G.G.: The measurement of observer agreement for categorical data. Biometrics **33**, 159–174 (1977)
35. Liapis, A., Katsanos, C., Sotiropoulos, D., Xenos, M., Karousos, N.: Recognizing emotions in human computer interaction: studying stress using skin conductance. In: Abascal, J., Barbosa, S., Fetter, M., Gross, T., Palanque, P., Winckler, M. (eds.) INTERACT 2015. LNCS, vol. 9296, pp. 255–262. Springer, Cham (2015). https://doi.org/10.1007/978-3-319-22701-6_18

Emotion Elicitation with Stimuli Datasets in Automatic Affect Recognition Studies – Umbrella Review

Paweł Jemioło[1]([⊠])(ORCID), Dawid Storman[2,3](ORCID), Barbara Giżycka[1](ORCID), and Antoni Ligęza[1](ORCID)

[1] AGH University of Science and Technology, al. A. Mickiewicza 30, 30-059 Krakow, Poland
{pawljmlo,bgizycka,ligeza}@agh.edu.pl
[2] Department of Hygiene and Dietetics, Systematic Reviews Unit, Jagiellonian University Medical College, Krakow, Poland
dawid.storman@doctoral.uj.edu.pl
[3] Department of Adult Psychiatry, University Hospital, Krakow, Poland

Abstract. Affect Recognition has become a relevant research field in Artificial Intelligence development. Nevertheless, its progress is impeded by poor methodological conduct in psychology, computer science, and, consequently, affective computing. We address this issue by providing a rigorous overview of Emotion Elicitation utilising stimuli datasets in Affect Recognition studies. We identified relevant trials by exploring five electronic databases and other sources. Eligible studies were those reviews identified through the title, abstract and full text, which aimed to include subjects who underwent Emotion Elicitation in laboratory conditions with passive stimuli presentation for Automatic Affect Recognition. Two independent reviewers were involved in each step in the process of identification of eligible studies. The discussion resolved any discrepancies. 16 of 1308 references met the inclusion criteria. The 16 papers reviewed 271 primary studies, in which 3515 participants were examined. We found out that datasets containing video, music, and pictures stimuli are most widely explored, while researchers should focus more on these incorporating audio excerpts. Five of the most frequently analysed emotions are: sadness, anger, happiness, fear and joyfulness. The Elicitation Effectiveness and techniques towards emotion assessment, are not reported by the review authors. We also provide conclusions about the lack of studies concerning Deep Learning methods. All of the included studies were of *Critically low* quality. Much of the critical information is missing in the reviewed papers, and therefore a comprehensive view on this research area is disturbingly hard to claim.

Keywords: Umbrella review · Dataset · Stimuli · Emotion elicitation · Automatic affect recognition · Affective computing

C. Ardito et al. (Eds.): INTERACT 2021, LNCS 12934, pp. 248–269, 2021.
https://doi.org/10.1007/978-3-030-85613-7_18

1   Introduction

For several decades now, combined efforts in the field of Affective Computing and Artificial Intelligence have been proving to facilitate our day-to-day activities. Although Affective Computing aims to enhance our lives with emotionally intelligent technologies, many promising ideas and designs are still confined in research laboratories. Since its advent in the 1990s [51], Affective Computing has been promoting an approach that emphasises three areas of research in Human-Computer Interaction: Emotion Recognition, emotional data interpretation, and affective computer or system behaviour.

Affective data can come in different formats and from various levels, ranging from physiological to behavioural. Physiological data encompasses all of the body biological signals [23,68], while behavioural cues related to changes in one's emotional state comprise information conveyed by, e.g., facial expressions [2] and gestures [30]. To develop a system capable of handling this kind of information, more so a system equipped with Artificial Intelligence technology, it is fundamental to implement it with an emotion classification model [15]. Although such models can be trained with data harvested from people's everyday activities, such as cameras, GPS data, or the recordings of wearable technologies, in this paper, we focus on Emotion Elicitation performed in the laboratory setting studies because due to controlled conditions (such as limiting the influence of confounders, strict protocol), we obtain more accurate results. One of the essential steps in an experimental protocol for developing Emotion Recognition models is Emotion Elicitation, employing affect-inducing stimuli presentation. Type of the stimuli can affect not only participants emotions [14,75] but also Emotion Recognition efficiency [74]. The stimuli used in the experiments can either be prepared by the study author or be selected from one of the several available stimuli datasets.

The contemporary methodology of affective experiments is placed in a difficult situation. For at least a decade, the field of psychology has been suffering from a so-called replicability crisis [70], which refers to ongoing difficulties with the reproduction of scientific studies, rooted in poor methodological conduct and lack of robustness in scientific method descriptions in papers. Although the problem stems from social sciences and medicine, other areas – including Affective Computing – are severely affected by it as well. The persistent need for well-proven and meticulously verified solutions is reflected in the demand for Meta-Analyses and Systematic Reviews, which was our motivation for this work.

This paper aims at providing an Umbrella Review of the current state of Emotion Elicitation with stimuli datasets (comprised of at least two elements) by analysing recent reviews on the topic. We concentrate on Automatic Affect Recognition, meaning that the emotional responses are detected and recognised by an artificial system. We also analyse the methodological discrepancies between the reviews included in this Umbrella Review.

The rest of the paper is organised as follows. In Sect. 2, we provide the context for our work by a brief description of Emotion Recognition and Affect Elicitation, as well as a brief outline of several currently available emotional stimuli datasets.

Section 3 specifies the characteristics of Systematic Reviews, emphasising the importance of using reviews to develop consistent research methodologies. In Sect. 4, we precisely outline the procedure of how our Umbrella Review was conducted. In Sect. 5, we put forward the results of our overview analysis, and in Sect. 6, we discuss them. The paper ends with Sect. 7, where we provide general conclusions and suggestions for future works.

2   Affective Experiments Outline

After deciding on a theoretical approach, Emotion Recognition researchers may proceed to the experiment planning and design phase. Usually, the standard protocol involves a series of steps, including the experiment itself (stimuli presentation and experimental task), following data pre-processing, feature extraction, classification or regression, and finally validation (see Fig. 1). This paper focuses on the first (excluding the design phase) step of the Emotion Recognition, meaning the stimuli set preparation and choice.

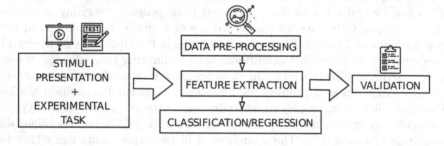

Fig. 1. An illustration of an experimental procedure for Emotion Recognition.

For reliable results of recognising emotions through automatic detection and identification, solid knowledge background in emotion theory is of great importance [67]. Unfortunately, for more than 150 years of scientific studies on this topic, researchers still cannot agree on one approach to the subject. However, in most modern experiments, it is possible to notice a distinctive contrast concerning the theoretical background.

2.1   Emotion Theories

Researchers may adopt one of the numerous theories of emotion for studies on emotion, developed throughout decades of psychological research. The vast range of available approaches includes, among others, a so-called *discreet* and *continuous* stance on emotions. In the discreet emotion theories, each of human emotions (usually including basic, i.e. happiness, sadness, anger, surprise, disgust, and fear) is a category of its own, having features and behaviours that are specific just for them, and which are triggered by a specific neural circuit in the brain [17,47]. As for the continuous approach, emotional states are interpreted on a scale of level of arousal (from high to low intensity of emotion) and valence (from positive to negative) [54], sometimes with an additional dimension of dominance (from top to slight degree of feeling of being in control) [45].

2.2   Emotion Elicitation

To collect data on emotional states, a researcher needs proper tools for evoking affective responses in the study participant. Emotions can be induced in either an active or a passive manner [33]. The active approach engages the study participant to interact with the experimental setup (e.g., video games [49]) or a passive manner, where the stimuli are presented in a way that does not require any action from the participant. The passive materials include images [12,34,36,40,43], emotion-evoking videos [13,38,56], sounds [6], and music tracks [63].

Many static picture databases contain photographs of human facial expressions [1,16,37,42]. While selecting a proper dataset for an experimental procedure, one needs to focus on the stimuli quantity and length (in the case of video and audio databases). These features tend to vary among different databases. These characteristics need to be controlled to ensure that a specific emotion is effectively elicited in each subject, regardless of individual variations. In turn, an effective elicitation enables the generalization of results.

2.3   Emotional Datasets

The study authors are free to identify the stimuli that will best serve the aims of their experiments. Nonetheless, it is often convenient to use one of the publicly available affective stimuli datasets. The specific structure of each database may vary from one to another, but they comprise a collection of stimuli in general. Usually, those include pictures/photographs, audio tracks, or videos, which are adequately annotated or labelled concerning their content and specific emotion designed to induce. For example, the affective annotations are provided in terms of valence and arousal scores [34,36] or basic emotion labels [1,16,37,42] (or distributions of labels [50]), acquired through analysing the ratings performed by the subjects in initial studies during database development. Although the databases should be validated and standardised for research purposes to eliminate the possibility of incurring any uncontrolled variables, some do not meet this requirement. Several of the stimuli sets are listed and briefly described below.

- IAPS (International Affective Picture System) [36] is one of, if not *the*, most often used sets of standardised, emotionally evocative pictures. It includes 1192 images of various aspects of human experience, i.e., people, architecture, everyday objects, animals, landscapes, and unpleasant sightings such as mutilated bodies.
- IADS (International Affective Digitised Sounds) [8] is an IAPS counterpart for the auditory modality. Its latest version [7] consists of 167 sounds that one can encounter in their daily life, such as sounds of nature, people talking, laughing, etc. Each sound has a duration of precisely 6 s. Recently, Yang et al. [71] has proposed a revised and extended version of this set, called IADS-E.

- ANEW (Affective Norms for English Words) [6] is a collection of 1034 English words developed for emotion research. Other language adaptations of ANEW are also present, including, e.g., German [58] or Spanish [53].
- GAPED (Geneva Affective Picture Database) [12], with 730 pictures, was created to increase the availability of visual, emotional stimuli. The picture categories are strictly specified in terms of their negative (spiders, snakes, scenes of moral and legal norms violation), positive (human and animal babies, nature sceneries), and neutral (inanimate objects) content.
- NAPS (Nencki Affective Picture System) [43] attempts to provide the largest (to date) database of visual stimuli, with 1356 high-quality photographs of 5 categories: people, faces, animals, objects, and landscapes, annotated by mostly European population. Each picture physical properties are also provided with valence, arousal ratings, and approach-avoidance ratings (luminance, contrast, entropy).
- OASIS (Open Affective Standardised Image Set) [34] is an open-access online database of 900 colour images of various themes, described with valence and arousal normative ratings. The distinctive features of this collection are that it allows for free research use and has been assembled using online sources, unlike databases restricted by copyrights, such as IAPS images.
- CAPS (Chinese Affective Picture System) [40] is an answer to the need for a culturally accurate affective stimuli database, in this case, for the Chinese.
- POFA (Pictures of Facial Affect) [16] is (dating to 1993) presumably one of the oldest affective datasets. It consists of 110 black and white photographs of facial expressions of six basic emotions.
- LIRIS-ACCEDE (the Annotated Creative Commons Emotional DatabasE) [13] is a public database of 9800 video excerpts shared under Creative Commons licenses and annotated along affective dimensions of valence and arousal.

With the above examples being only a few from the variety of existing databases, researchers have a sound number of Emotion Elicitation tools from which they can choose. The question of which of these are used most often and how exactly they are applied to Emotion Recognition studies was one of our motivations for developing this review.

2.4 Emotion Elicitation Effectiveness

Another factor that motivated us to conduct this research was determining what emotions are exactly elicited in the studies and the effectiveness of different elicitation databases. One needs to remember that many features may affect the process of emotion induction in individuals. The personality [35] is one of them, and the mood [11] is the other. Due to this, the emotions that participants of the experiment experience could be different than assumed while designing the protocol (see the beginning of Sect. 2).

It is thus necessary to examine the effectiveness of the Emotion Elicitation process. It can be measured using Detection Theory metrics [21], e.g. accuracy.

Additionally, one must remember that emotional labels can be gathered using different methods. There is, for example, a standardised tool called SAM (Self-Assessment Manikin) [5]. Experimenters or other non-related people may also assure labels. What is more, one can also easily calculate the agreement between mentioned methods [11].

3   Reviews

Due to the rapidly increasing number of primary studies, the need to analyse and synthesise them grew [52].

Particularly in medicine, where clinical decisions should be based on credible data, this need to develop data identifying and synthesis methods in an unbiased, rigorous, and transparent approach is present. These are the basis for conducting Systematic Reviews, distinguishing them from traditional reviews.

The quality of Systematic Reviews depends mainly on the extent to which the methods are used to minimise the risk of error and bias while conducting a review [3]. The standards for producing high-quality Systematic Reviews are supposed to support best practices in publishing scientific studies. They indicate how to include appropriate sections and information in authors' manuscripts that can be understood by the readers or replicated by the researchers. Some organizations provide them, e.g., Cochrane Collaboration (health care), Campbell Collaboration (social, behavioural, and educational areas) or EQUATOR Network (Enhancing the Quality and Transparency of Health Research), which is an international collaboration that promotes quality and consistency in research publications [18]. These organizations publish their guidelines for conducting different types of reviews [24] and provide reporting tools [39, 46].

In Systematic Review, the fundamental research unit included in the synthesis is a primary study, e.g., cross-sectional, observational, experimental. Due to the growing popularity of secondary studies and an enormous number of published papers, it is impossible to follow their results. Due to this and the need to collect evidence in reduced timeframes, tertiary studies methodology (Umbrella Reviews, also known as Meta-review, Overview) was developed. The defining feature of Umbrella Review is considering a Systematic Review as the first and often the only study type for inclusion [52, 62]. Because the methodology of Systematic Reviews is not well-grounded in Artificial Intelligence, and there are only a few papers published as a Systematic Review, we decided to include all types of reviews in our article to collect as much interesting data as possible.

4   Materials and Methods

4.1   Protocol, Search Strategies, Inclusion Criteria

First, we conducted a pre-search before April 2020 to determine if any interesting papers could be eligible for our study. A protocol has been published [28] on the Open Science Framework (OSF) platform on 07 June 2020 before the data extraction stage. Electronic databases (MEDLINE Ovid, EMBASE, Web of Science, dblp, Cochrane Library), IEEE library, and preprint database arXiv were initially searched from inception to 09 May 2020 using predefined search strategies.

We included both free-text terms, such as *review, overview, dataset,* and MESH terms. We combined: 'dataset.ti, ab. or (video* or picture* or photo* or stimuli or audio or sound*).ti,ab' and 'exp emotions/or (emotion*).ti,ab.' and 'exp Recognition, Psychology/or (recogni* or classif* or regres* or clusteriz* or discriminat*).ti,ab.' and '(facial expression* or body movement* or gesture* or speech or behavio?r* or eye gaze or eye movement* or physiological or ECG or electrocardiograph* or EDA or electrodermal activity or GSR or galvanic skin response or EEG or electroencephalograph* or BVP or blood volume pressure* or HR or HRV or heart rate* or EMG or electromyograph* or temperature*).ti,ab.'

Search strategies are provided on the OSF [28] in Appendix 1. Language restrictions were imposed. We restricted to papers written in English and Polish.

Eligible studies were reviews including at least 50% healthy adult ($\geq$18 years old) subjects who underwent Emotion Elicitation in laboratory conditions with passive stimuli presentation for Automatic Affect Recognition. We did not exclude those reviews that omit the information about age, health and number of the subjects, and the setting. All the records containing information about post-conference books were excluded. However, the aforementioned does not apply to conference publications themselves.

4.2   Screening, Data Extraction, Quality Assessment

Identified references were checked for duplications using Endnote (Clarivate Analytics ®). We screened titles and abstracts using Rayyan software [48]. Then, full texts of included papers were assessed for meeting our eligibility criteria. Using a pre-specified extraction form, we extracted data from included articles. Following published protocol with research questions [28], we were particularly interested in the type of stimuli, their number and length, emotions – how they were elicitated and measured in primary studies and emotions. We also extracted information about the standardization, validation, and public availability of the datasets. We also focused on setting and Emotion Recognition procedures, e.g., pre-processing, features, algorithms, and validation process. Besides, we collected the necessary information about the population and bibliometric data. All the mentioned stages (identification, screening, eligibility assessment, and extraction) of conducting Systematic Reviews were done independently (PJ and BG).

Quality assessment was also done independently in pairs (partly by PJ and BG and partly by PJ and DS). QASR [27] tool was applied for quality assessment. It is based on a well-known method developed for healthcare, i.e., A Critical Appraisal Tool for Systematic Reviews (AMSTAR 2) [59]. This adapted instrument contains several generic domains about conducting Systematic Review, e.g., registration of protocol, comprehensive literature searching, reproducible and transparent assessment of included articles, or declaring funding and conflict of interest.

Pilot exercises preceded each phase (screening, full-text assessment, extraction, or quality assessment) of the presented Umbrella Review. These exercises were aimed at improving the common understanding of criteria. We worked separately on a material sample until achieving a 90% agreement. We resolved any conflicts through discussion and consensus.

4.3 Analysis

We analysed bibliographic and other most essential characteristics of included studies descriptively. We prepared a qualitative summary concerning the number of primary studies, population, outcomes (Emotion Elicitation in Automatic Affect Recognition), datasets, experimental procedures (Automatic Affect Recognition), and quality of reviews.

Additionally, we planned on conducting a quantitative analysis. However, due to insufficient reporting and poor quality, we could not conduct a planned statistical synthesis. The numbers and calculations are based on these reviews that report on specific factors for all primary studies, except interesting outcomes – data regarding them we extracted from primary studies.

5 Results

5.1 Study Selection

Primary electronic databases searches yielded a total of 869 references to screen after duplicates were removed. Of these, 54 full texts were obtained and screened. Altogether 16 studies [4,9,10,19,22,29,32,44,55,57,60,61,64–66,73] were included for qualitative synthesis.

The study flow is presented in Fig. 2. Our reporting is consistent with PRISMA guidelines [39,46]. Lists of included and excluded studies (with reasons) and full details are available online on the OSF platform [28] in Appendices 2, 3, and 4, respectively. The spreadsheet forms are also available from authors on request.

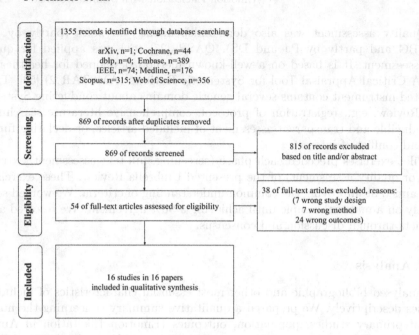

Fig. 2. Preferred reporting items for systematic reviews and meta-analyses (PRISMA) study flow diagram.

5.2 Characteristics of Included Studies

Table 1 presents the essential characteristics of the included trials. 14 (87.5%) included studies [4,9,10,19,22,32,44,55,57,60,61,64,66,73] were published after 2017. The included reviews were based on 530 primary studies and 271 interesting papers (mean: 83.33 and 16.94, respectively). However, 10 (62.5%) of considered reviews [4,9,10,29,44,57,60,61,65,66] did not provide explicit information about the number of analysed papers.

There were at least 3515 participants altogether in included trials. Sample sizes ranged from 47 [73] to 1634 [55] subjects. 6 (37.5%) articles [10,22,29,44,57, 61] report on the number of participants only in part of the primary studies, and 2 (12.5%) publications [60,64] did not contain such information at all. Similarly, 12 (75%) included papers [4,9,10,19,29,44,60,61,64–66,73] did not report on the age of subjects, and 11 (68.75%) trials [4,10,19,22,29,57,60,61,64,73] on sex or gender. The rest provided only partial information.

Synthetic results regarding datasets are presented in Table 2. Studies utilising video (adverts, movies excerpts), music (different genres), and audio (sounds of nature, people talking, laughing) datasets were reported in 15 (93.5%) [4,9,10,19, 22,29,32,44,55,57,61,64–66,73], 12 (75%) [4,10,19,22,29,32,44,55,61,64–66], and 7 (43.75%) [4,19,22,32,55,61,64] included reviews. Publications focused on papers using datasets containing only facial expressions were provided by 3 (18.75%) works [32,55,64], while 12 (75%) reviews [4,9,10,19,29,32,44,55,57,

Table 1. Most essential characteristics of the included studies.

Review ID	Included studies		Population			QASR [27]^f
	Total^a	Analysed^b	Total^c	Age^d	Gender^e	
[22]	100	39	PI	PI	NR	5/3
[57]	U	6	PI	PI	NR	7/5
[61]	U	25	PI	NR	NR	7/5
[66]	U	22	526	NR	PI	6/4
[9]	U	4	112	NR	PI	8/5
[19]	62	19	702	NR	NR	7/4
[73]	40	2	47	NR	NR	8/5
[65]	U	8	245	NR	PI	8/5
[29]	U	10	PI	NR	NR	8/5
[10]	U	6	PI	NR	NR	8/5
[55]	137	45	1634	PI	PI	7/4
[64]	60	57	NR	NR	NR	5/3
[60]	U	2	NR	NR	NR	7/5
[44]	U	10	PI	NR	PI	7/4
[32]	131	4	92	PI	PI	7/5
[4]	U	12	157	NR	NR	8/5

PI – Partial Information (provided only for some primary studies);
U – Unclear; NR – Not Reported.
^{a} Total number of studies included by a review.
^{b} Total number of interesting studies in this review.
^{c} Total number of the subjects.
^{d} Age of the subjects.
^{e} Gender of the subjects.
^{f} QASR results: number of flaws/number of critical flaws.

60, 61, 64] attached information about datasets which comprise various pictures (architecture, landscapes, and unpleasant sightings such as mutilated bodies).

Moreover, 4 (25%) studies [29, 44, 55, 65] analysed references incorporating other types of datasets, i.e., multimodal, 3D photorealistic models, and emotional narratives (text). The reviews did not explain what *multimodal* in this context means. 2 (12.5%) studies [22, 64] employed own incoherent classification. To name it, authors did not differentiate photo and face or music, audio and video dataset. We, therefore, cannot assign their primary references accordingly and excluded them from the analysis.

It should be noted that the length of stimuli was based on only 2 (12.5%) reviews for video [9, 57] and music [55, 66] datasets (containing 5 and 25 primary studies respectively), and 1 (6.25%) in terms of audio [55] (4 primary articles). 8 (50%) interesting trials [19, 22, 29, 32, 44, 60, 61, 64] did not contain information

Table 2. Emotion elicitation datasets.

Type of stimuli		Mean (range)
No. of datasets used in primary studies		
Total		17.38 (2–65)
	Video	6.13 (0—34)
	Music	3.07 (0–21)
	Audio[b]	1.07 (0–8)
	Face	0.33 (0–4)
	Picture	3.20 (0–18)
	Other	0.31 (0–2)
Length[a]of stimuli used in primary studies [seconds]		
Total		129.03 (2–600)
	Video	63.75 (15–393)
	Music	157.08 (2–600)
	Audio[b]	19.00 (6–30)

[a] Calculated only for primary studies with length provided.
[b] Sounds other than music.

about the number of stimuli in datasets, while 7 (43.75%) [4,9,10,55,57,65,66] described it only for some of the included studies.

Finally, 1 (6.25%) work [73] analysed such data in full (2 primary studies). According to it, the number of elements in datasets varied from 15 to 40.

Additionally, we checked which publicly available datasets were reported in the reviews (Fig. 3). There were 10 datasets utilised in Emotion Elicitation for Automatic Affect Recognition. However, 6 of them were mentioned only by exactly 1 (6.25%) review [55]. Validation of datasets was partly checked by authors of 2 (12.5%) reviews [55,57], while only 1 (6.25%) study [4] partly focused on the availability of standardised instructions.

Regarding the outcomes, we focused on emotions elicited with stimuli datasets. There were 132 different states reported in the reviews. We found out that some of them overlap themselves, and that is why we merged them into the same categories, e.g. *relaxed*, *relax*, *relaxation* and *relaxing* fell into the same group. After this processing, we got 101 separate affective states.

The most common discrete emotions evoked in the studies included in 16 analysed reviews are presented in Fig. 4. On the other hand, some researchers focused on dimensional emotions. 78.23% of included papers concerned discrete states, while only 9.59% was connected with dimensional ones; the rest did not report the nature of elicited emotions.

We also wanted to establish the most popular tools used for emotion assessment. However, the reviews provided information only about 4 out of 271 studies, two of them used SAM [5], and the other 2 utilised the questionnaire, but the name was not provided.

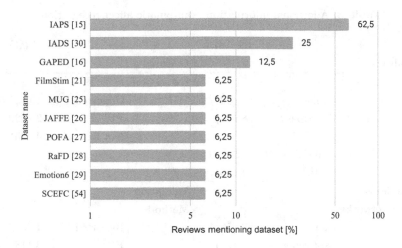

Fig. 3. Reviews with primary studies utilising publicly available datasets, log. scale.

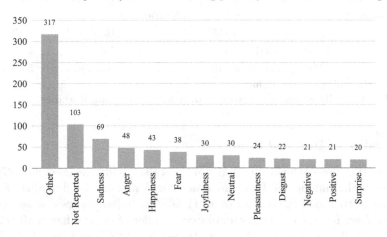

Fig. 4. Discrete emotional states evoked among included primary studies.

Only Sarma and Barma [55] provided information about the protocol of emotion elicitation with the indication of SAM assessment. On the other hand, they derived only 57.78% of included studies. All of them asked participants about emotions after each stimulus.

The remaining results concerning the Automatic Affect Recognition procedure are presented in Table 3. All the reviews focused only on physiological or behavioural modalities (or both). The setting was partly provided by 5 (31.25%) trails [32, 44, 55, 57, 61]. 13 (81.25%) of included studies [4, 9, 10, 19, 22, 29, 32, 44, 57, 60, 61, 65, 66] analysed multiple recognition methods.

Table 3. Additional information – automatic affect recognition.

		N (%)			N (%)
Modalities			Features		
No.			Extraction		
	Single	8 (50)		Reported	10 (63.5)
	Multiple	8 (50)		PR[b]	2 (12.5)
Type				Not Reported	4 (25)
	Physiological	12 (75)			
	Both[a]	4 (25)			
AI methods			Validation		
Neural networks			Methods		
	Reported	9 (56.25)		Reported	1 (6.25)
	Not reported	4 (25)		PR[b]	3 (18.75)
	Not applicable	3 (18.75)		Not reported	12 (75)
Deep learning			Metrics		
	Reported	4 (25)		Reported	6 (37.5)
	Not reported	9 (56)		PR[b]	5 (31.25)
	Not applicable	3 (19)		Not reported	5 (31.25)

[a] Both – Physiological and Behavioral.
[b] [2] PR – Partially Reported – provided only for some primary studies.

5.3   Quality of Included Studies

Following the pre-specified method for overall quality assessment [27], we summed up the number of *Flaws* in crucial and non-crucial domains (Fig. 5). According to this tool, the quality of all (100%) included papers was assessed as *Critically Low*. Regarding the accumulated number of critical flaws, 10 (62.5%) works [4, 9, 10, 29, 32, 57, 60, 61, 65, 73] contained 5, 4 (25%) articles [19, 44, 55, 66] – 4, and 2 (12.5%) reviews [22, 64] – 3.

The QASR items that most of the included references failed to meet were the following: 3 (independent screening), 4 (extraction process), 5 (justification for excluded studies), 6 (assessment of the Risk of Bias in individual studies), 7 (incorporating Risk of Bias when interpreting results).

The 8th criterion (financial issues) was the only one that was met by almost all reviews. All (100%) analysed studies reported on funding, and 15 (93.75%) [4, 9, 10, 19, 22, 29, 32, 44, 55, 60, 61, 64–66, 73] provided exact information about funding type.

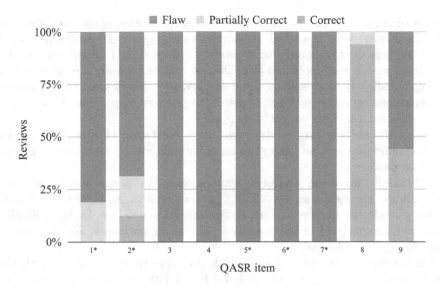

Fig. 5. Percentage of reviews with a given number of critical flaws; * means crucial items.

6   Discussion

6.1   Summary, Quality and Potential Biases in Results

Our overview aimed at analysing Emotion Elicitation with Stimuli Datasets in Automatic Affect Recognition. 16 reviews were included for a thorough qualitative analysis. Using VOSviewer [69] (tool enabling visualisation and frequency assessment of words in examined records), we visualised the most common words among the early 822 (see Fig. 6) and final 16 (see Fig. 7) references. The use of VOSviewer confirmed that the included works belong to the area we were interested in this review.

We found that authors most willingly analyse video, picture, and music datasets (see Table 2). However, the last type was overestimated (modal: 1), as 1 included work [66] focused on musical stimulation of the subjects. Its authors described 21 sets, while others provided less than 7 in their overview. Described video and music datasets contained excerpts of various lengths. It did not apply to audio stimuli, which were shorter than 30 s. Included reviews mentioned 10 publicly available datasets (see Fig. 3) utilised by primary studies. The number of elements within a particular set of stimuli varied from 15 to 40. It should be noted, though, that this range was based on one review [73]. Additionally, we reveal that only 4 (25%) reviews [10, 19, 57, 61] analyse Deep Learning methods, while 12 (75%) [4, 9, 22, 29, 32, 44, 55, 60, 64–66, 73] did not report on validation methods used in primary studies (see Table 3). Similarly, only 4 (25%) of the reviews [10, 44, 57, 73] included works focused on behaviour.

Regarding the outcomes, the authors focus on positive, negative and neutral emotions. In one-seventh of primary studies, the information about the types of evoked emotions was not provided. There were over 100 different names and variants of emotions. Two types of approaches to emotion elicitation (discrete and dimensional) were identified. Researchers more often choose the first approach. The four most explored discrete states correspond to Ekman's model [16], i.e. sadness, anger, happiness and fear. Disgust and surprise are also present but investigated slightly more seldom. Interestingly, researchers seem to distinguish more emotional granularity when it comes to positive states than Ekman, i.e. pleasantness, and joyfulness next to happiness.

Due to the authors skip information about elicitation effectiveness, assessment tools and protocol, and therefore unambiguous conclusions regarding them cannot be made.

Additionally, all of the interesting studies comprised a vast amount of other shortcomings. For example, 10 (62.5%) reviews [4,9,10,29,44,57,60,61,65,66] did not provide the number of included primary studies (see Table 1). Similar applies to characteristics of the examined population, outcomes, and Automatic Affect Recognition process.

What is more, there were several methodological issues connected with the reviews. 4 out of 9 domains were violated by all (100%) studies. According to the QASR tool [27], the overall quality is *Critically Low* for all the reviews.

We, therefore, reckon that our findings should be interpreted with great care. The results say more about the issues concerning the current state of the art reviews than the relationships within Automatic Affect Recognition.

6.2   Suggestions

As for outcomes, we suggest that researchers should specify unequivocal emotion nomenclature. We encourage scientists to explore dimensional emotions often as

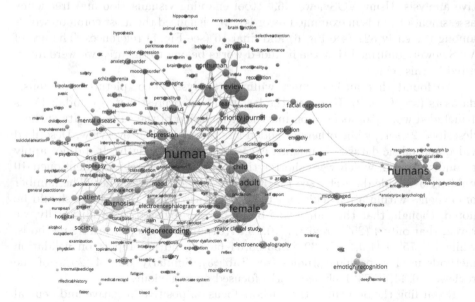

Fig. 6. Most common words among early 882 studies.

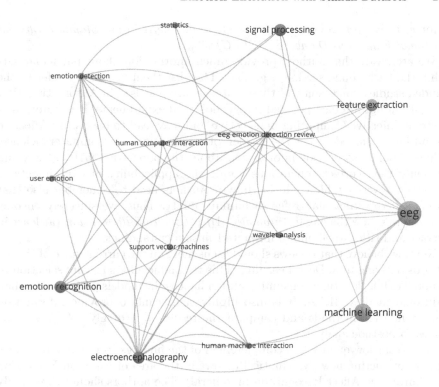

Fig. 7. Most common words among final 16 studies.

they provide an alternative insight into the nature of affective states. What is essential, the authors of the reviews and primary studies ought to conduct and report on Emotion Elicitation effectiveness measurements. The same applies to assessment tools and protocol of the Emotion Elicitation experiments.

Regarding the datasets, we encourage authors to focus more on works utilising facial expressions and audio datasets. More effort should be put on other modalities, e.g., 3D models or emotional narratives. Authors ought to also explore the stimuli generated using Artificial Intelligence methods such as GANs (Generative Adversarial Networks [20]). They may be used when generating stimuli, e.g. pictures, videos, audio, and video games [26] or even signals, e.g. physiological if the data is missing [41]. Additionally, we also believe that researchers should pay attention to sound stimuli length as using more extended excerpts seems an unaddressed issue. We also encourage the reviewers and authors of primary studies to include works containing various publicly available datasets, e.g., [12,13,36,63].

What is more, authors should not confuse stimuli datasets with databases containing physiological signals, e.g., in [55]. Of course, such sets are reused in recognition processes but serve as a benchmark, not a tool for inducing affect. It can be confusing and misleading for scientists who want to utilise specific stimuli in their Emotion Elicitation experiments. Additionally, authors of the reviews should more carefully report on the names of publicly available datasets. For example, *Film Clip* provided in [55] needs to be referred to as *Standard Chinese Emotional Film Clips Database (SCEFC)* [38].

We are aware that authors provide much information about particular sets within the background section, e.g., [55]. They list them but do not refer to the included studies. Since some of these datasets are not used in Automatic Affect Recognition but are incorporated in psychological experiments, it is uninformative from Affective Computing perspective and may lead to biases. As Affective Computing is embedded on the border of Psychology and Computer Science, authors should also provide information about the population [51], i.e., sex and age. Only then correct conclusions about the applicability of experiments in this area to everyday life could be drawn. Authors need to remember also that *Emotion Recognition* may refer to human ability. Thus, we sincerely encourage authors to use the name *Automatic Affect/Emotion Recognition* (at least in abstract and title) to eliminate unwanted misunderstandings.

Next, we believe that reviews should focus more on the current state of the art methods deriving from Deep Learning. This technique allows feature selection to be more flexible, less time-consuming and enhances the models performance than traditional models [31,72]. It is also highly significant to provide information about validation methods and compare the results accordingly [24]. The same applies to posthoc analyses.

Due to the low quality and completeness of the findings mentioned above, we suggest conducting new Systematic Reviews in the area of Emotion Elicitation (and Automatic Affect Recognition in general). The authors should thoroughly report the utilised methodology with compliance to PRISMA guidelines [39,46], publish the protocol, and provide synthetic results.

We encourage the authors to provide all the mentioned information as it helps determine whether the issue is addressed in primary studies or whether there is an unaddressed gap in current research. Such a methodological approach can lead to a reduction in resource and time-wasting [24]. Due to the growing number of works in Affective Computing, we reckon that upcoming reviews should focus on particular modalities, i.e., physiological and behavioural, or even better divided into individual signals, e.g., facial expressions, electroencephalography, cardiovascular. The last one is especially relevant due to the growing popularity of wearable devices able to measure such signals.

Following Cochrane guidelines for Systematic Reviews [24,25], in this Section, we also wanted to address differences and similarities with Umbrella Reviews on the congruent subject. Using Endnote (Claritive Analytics ®), we have chosen 277 studies from 822 selected first. We obtained them by applying search in title and abstracts with keywords specific for Umbrella Reviews, e.g., *Overview, Meta-review*. However, none of the studies selected this way was connected with Affect Elicitation, Emotion Recognition, Affective Computing, Human-Computer Interaction, Artificial Intelligence, or Computer Science.

6.3   Limitations and Strengths

To the best of our knowledge, we are one of the first authors to provide Umbrella Review in the field of Emotion Elicitation (if not in the whole Affective Computing). This study strengths include the publication of protocol and incorporating solid methodological background for all we present here. It enabled us to synthesise the results in a comprehensive, unbiased, rigorous, and transparent way [52]. Despite the page limit, we share all the information gathered in the process of preparing this research via OSF [28], which is a platform for sharing research data with permanent DOI and funding secured for years from now. We also proposed a method for quality assessment (QASR [27]) – it can be incorporated as a checklist for other researchers or reviewers.

On the other hand, the proposed tool is not validated and standardised. Our assessment should thus be regarded as preliminary. However, the tool is an interpretation of AMSTAR 2 [59], which is respected and widely used among reviewers. We also did not search grey literature, and we omit the references to the whole post-conference books. Next, we imposed language limitations on the included publications. However, based on this criterion, we excluded only one paper. Finally, we did not check on the overlapping of interesting works. Nonetheless, following Cochrane guidelines [24], when one wants to *present and describe the current body of Systematic Review evidence on a topic, it may be appropriate to include the results of all relevant Systematic Reviews, regardless of topic overlap.*

7   Conclusions and Future Work

This overview aimed at gathering knowledge about the Emotion Elicitation with Stimuli Datasets in Automatic Affect Recognition experiments.

We found out that authors prefer discrete over-dimensional emotions. However, the nomenclature of affective states is still undeveloped. Review authors do not report on techniques that enable researchers assessment of emotional state. Its effectiveness is also neglected.

Datasets containing video, music, and pictures are most widely explored, while researchers should focus more on these incorporating audio excerpts. We also reveal that authors need to put more effort into analysing Deep Learning methods and incorporating more modalities, e.g. cardiovascular signals, into the process of classification of emotion.

However, considering the *Critically low* quality of studies included in the review, we believe that there is still a place for a comprehensive Systematic Review in discussed area. We suggest that authors follow the strict methodology and use a common language to avoid resource and time-wasting.

We are now working on providing a thorough analysis, including all these remarks. Next, we want to explore active Emotion Elicitation in Affective Computing and focus more on non-laboratory emotion examination. Additionally, we want to validate and standardise the QASR [27] tool utilised in this review.

Author   contributions. Paweł Jemioło (PJ) – all listed stages. Barbara Giżycka (BG) – conceptualization, investigation, validation, writing. Dawid Storman (DS) – conceptualization, formal analysis, investigation, methodology, supervision, writing. Antoni Ligęza (AL) – supervision.

Conflict of Interest. Authors declare that they have no conflict of interest.

Funding Sources. Current work is supported by AGH UST grants.

References

1. Aifanti, N., Papachristou, C., Delopoulos, A.: The mug facial expression database. In: 11th International Workshop on Image Analysis for Multimedia Interactive Services WIAMIS 10, pp. 1–4. IEEE (2010)
2. Anderson, K., McOwan, P.W.: A real-time automated system for the recognition of human facial expressions. IEEE Trans. Syst. Man Cybern. Part B (Cybern.) **36**(1), 96–105 (2006)
3. Aromataris, E., Munn, Z.: Chapter 1: JBI systematic reviews. Joanna Briggs Institute Reviewer's Manual. The Joanna Briggs Institute (2017)
4. Baghdadi, A., Aribi, Y., Alimi, A.M.: A survey of methods and performances for EEG-based emotion recognition. In: Abraham, A., Haqiq, A., Alimi, A.M., Mezzour, G., Rokbani, N., Muda, A.K. (eds.) HIS 2016. AISC, vol. 552, pp. 164–174. Springer, Cham (2017). https://doi.org/10.1007/978-3-319-52941-7_17
5. Bradley, M.M., Lang, P.J.: Measuring emotion: the self-assessment manikin and the semantic differential. J. Behav. Ther. Exp. Psychiatry **25**(1), 49–59 (1994)
6. Bradley, M.M., Lang, P.J.: Affective norms for English words: Instruction manual and affective ratings. Technical report, The center for research in psychophysiology (1999)
7. Bradley, M.M., Lang, P.J.: The international affective digitized sounds (IADS-2): affective ratings of sounds and instruction manual. University of Florida, Gainesville, FL, Technical report B-3 (2007)
8. Bradley, M., Lang, P.: International affective digitized sounds: stimuli, instruction manual and affective ratings. Center for Research in Psychophysiology (1999)
9. Chen, J., Mehmood, R.: A critical review on state-of-the-art EEG-based emotion datasets. In: Proceedings of the International Conference on Advanced Information Science and System, pp. 1–5 (2019)
10. Christensen, L.R., Abdullah, M.A.: EEG emotion detection review. In: 2018 IEEE Conference on Computational Intelligence in Bioinformatics and Computational Biology (CIBCB), pp. 1–7. IEEE (2018)
11. Correa, J.A.M., Abadi, M.K., Sebe, N., Patras, I.: Amigos: a dataset for affect, personality and mood research on individuals and groups. IEEE Trans. Affect. Comput. **12**, 479–493 (2018)
12. Dan-Glauser, E.S., Scherer, K.R.: The Geneva affective picture database (GAPED): a new 730-picture database focusing on valence and normative significance. Behav. Res. Methods **43**(2), 468 (2011)
13. Dellandréa, E., Huigsloot, M., Chen, L., Baveye, Y., Xiao, Z., Sjöberg, M.: Predicting the emotional impact of movies. ACM SIGMM Rec. **10**, 1–7 (2018)
14. Dhaka, S., Kashyap, N.: Explicit emotion regulation: comparing emotion inducing stimuli. Psychol. Thought **10**(2), 303–314 (2017)
15. D'Mello, S., Kappas, A., Gratch, J.: The affective computing approach to affect measurement. Emot. Rev. **10**(2), 174–183 (2018)
16. Ekman, P.: Pictures of Facial Affect. Consulting Psychologists Press (1976)
17. Ekman, P., et al.: Universals and cultural differences in the judgments of facial expressions of emotion. J. Pers. Soc. Psychol. **53**(4), 712 (1987)

18. EQUATOR: Enhancing the quality and transparency of health research (2014). https://equator-network.org
19. García-Martínez, B., Martinez-Rodrigo, A., Alcaraz, R., Fernández-Caballero, A.: A review on nonlinear methods using electroencephalographic recordings for emotion recognition. IEEE Trans. Affect. Comput. (2019)
20. Goodfellow, I.J., et al.: Generative adversarial networks. arXiv preprint arXiv:1406.2661 (2014)
21. Green, D.M., Swets, J.A., et al.: Signal Detection Theory and Psychophysics, vol. 1. Wiley, New York (1966)
22. Hamada, M., Zaidan, B., Zaidan, A.: A systematic review for human EEG brain signals based emotion classification, feature extraction, brain condition, group comparison. J. Med. Syst. 42(9), 162 (2018)
23. Hamdi, H., Richard, P., Suteau, A., Allain, P.: Emotion assessment for affective computing based on physiological responses. In: 2012 IEEE International Conference on Fuzzy Systems, pp. 1–8. IEEE (2012)
24. Higgins, J., et al.: Methodological expectations of cochrane intervention reviews. Cochrane 6, London (2019)
25. Higgins, J.P., Thomas, J., Chandler, J., et al.: Cochrane Handbook for Systematic Reviews of Interventions. Wiley, Hoboken (2019)
26. Jemioło, P., Giżycka, B., Nalepa, G.J.: Prototypes of arcade games enabling affective interaction. In: Rutkowski, L., Scherer, R., Korytkowski, M., Pedrycz, W., Tadeusiewicz, R., Zurada, J.M. (eds.) ICAISC 2019. LNCS (LNAI), vol. 11509, pp. 553–563. Springer, Cham (2019). https://doi.org/10.1007/978-3-030-20915-5_49
27. Jemioło, P., Storman, D.: Quality assessment of systematic reviews (QASR), June 2020. https://osf.io/dhtw3/
28. Jemioło, P., Giżycka, B., Storman, D.: Datasets for affect elicitation in emotion recognition (2020). https://osf.io/vdbqg/
29. Jerritta, S., Murugappan, M., Nagarajan, R., Wan, K.: Physiological signals based human emotion recognition: a review. In: 2011 IEEE 7th International Colloquium on Signal Processing and its Applications, pp. 410–415. IEEE (2011)
30. Kapur, A., Kapur, A., Virji-Babul, N., Tzanetakis, G., Driessen, P.F.: Gesture-based affective computing on motion capture data. In: Tao, J., Tan, T., Picard, R.W. (eds.) ACII 2005. LNCS, vol. 3784, pp. 1–7. Springer, Heidelberg (2005). https://doi.org/10.1007/11573548_1
31. Khalil, R.A., Jones, E., Babar, M.I., Jan, T., Zafar, M.H., Alhussain, T.: Speech emotion recognition using deep learning techniques: a review. IEEE Access 7, 117327–117345 (2019)
32. Khosla, A., Khandnor, P., Chand, T.: A comparative analysis of signal processing and classification methods for different applications based on EEG signals. Biocybern. Biomed. Eng. 40, 649–690 (2020)
33. Kory, J.M., D'Mello, S.K.: Affect elicitation for affective computing. In: The Oxford Handbook of Affective Computing, p. 371 (2015)
34. Kurdi, B., Lozano, S., Banaji, M.R.: Introducing the open affective standardized image set (OASIS). Behav. Res. Methods 49(2), 457–470 (2017)
35. Kutt, K., et al.: BIRAFFE: bio-reactions and faces for emotion-based personalization. CEUR Workshop Proceedings (2019)
36. Lang, P.J., Bradley, M.M., Cuthbert, B.N., et al.: International affective picture system (IAPS): technical manual and affective ratings. NIMH Cent. Study Emot. Attent. 1, 39–58 (1997)

37. Langner, O., Dotsch, R., Bijlstra, G., Wigboldus, D.H., Hawk, S.T., Van Knippenberg, A.: Presentation and validation of the radboud faces database. Cogn. Emot. **24**(8), 1377–1388 (2010)
38. Liang, Y., Hsieh, S., Weng, C., Sun, C.: Taiwan corpora of Chinese emotions and relevant psychophysiological data - standard Chinese emotional film clips database. Chin. J. Psychol. **55**(4), 597–617 (2013)
39. Liberati, A., et al.: The PRISMA statement for reporting systematic and meta-analyses of studies that evaluate interventions. PLoS Med. **6**(7), 1–28 (2009)
40. Lu, B., Hui, M., Yu-Xia, H.: The development of native Chinese affective picture system - a pretest in 46 college students. Chin. Ment. Health J. (2005)
41. Luo, Y., Cai, X., Zhang, Y., Xu, J., Yuan, X.: Multivariate time series imputation with generative adversarial networks. In: Proceedings of the 32nd International Conference on Neural Information Processing Systems, pp. 1603–1614 (2018)
42. Lyons, M.J., Akamatsu, S., Kamachi, M., Gyoba, J., Budynek, J.: The Japanese female facial expression (JAFFE) database. In: Proceedings of Third International Conference on Automatic Face and Gesture Recognition, pp. 14–16 (1998)
43. Marchewka, A., Żurawski, Ł, Jednoróg, K., Grabowska, A.: The nencki affective picture system: introduction to a novel, standardized, wide-range, high-quality, realistic picture database. Behav. Res. Methods **46**(2), 596–610 (2014)
44. Maria, E., Matthias, L., Sten, H.: Emotion recognition from physiological signal analysis: a review. Notes Theor. Comput. Sci. **343**, 35–55 (2019)
45. Mehrabian, A.: Pleasure-arousal-dominance: a general framework for describing and measuring individual differences in temperament. Curr. Psychol. **14**(4), 261–292 (1996)
46. Moher, D., Liberati, A., Tetzlaff, J., Altman, D.G.: Prisma 2009 flow diagram. PRISMA statement **6**, 97 (2009)
47. Moors, A.: Theories of emotion causation: a review. Cogn. Emot. **23**(4), 625–662 (2009)
48. Ouzzani, M., Hammady, H., Fedorowicz, Z., Elmagarmid, A.: Rayyan–a web and mobile app for systematic reviews. Syst. Control Found. Appl. **5**(1), 210 (2016)
49. Pallavicini, F., Ferrari, A., Pepe, A., Garcea, G., Zanacchi, A., Mantovani, F.: Effectiveness of virtual reality survival horror games for the emotional elicitation: preliminary insights using resident evil 7: biohazard. In: Antona, M., Stephanidis, C. (eds.) UAHCI 2018. LNCS, vol. 10908, pp. 87–101. Springer, Cham (2018). https://doi.org/10.1007/978-3-319-92052-8_8
50. Peng, K.C., Chen, T., Sadovnik, A., Gallagher, A.C.: A mixed bag of emotions: model, predict, and transfer emotion distributions. In: Proceedings of the IEEE conference on computer vision and pattern recognition, pp. 860–868 (2015)
51. Picard, R.W.: Affective Computing. MIT Press, Cambridge (1997)
52. Pollock, M., Fernandes, R.M., Becker, L.A., Pieper, D., Hartling, L.: Chapter V: overviews of reviews. Cochrane Handb. Syst. Rev. Intervent. Version **6** (2018)
53. Redondo, J., Fraga, I., Padrón, I., Comesaña, M.: The Spanish adaptation of anew. Behav. Res. Methods **39**(3), 600–605 (2007)
54. Russell, J.A., Barrett, L.F.: Core affect, prototypical emotional episodes, and other things called emotion: dissecting the elephant. J. Pers. Soc. Psychol. **76**(5), 805 (1999)
55. Sarma, P., Barma, S.: Review on stimuli presentation for affect analysis based on EEG. IEEE Access **8**, 51991–52009 (2020)
56. Schaefer, A., Nils, F., Sanchez, X., Philippot, P.: Assessing the effectiveness of a large database of emotion-eliciting films: a new tool for emotion researchers. Cogn. Emot. **24**(7), 1153–1172 (2010)

57. Schmidt, P., Reiss, A., Dürichen, R., Laerhoven, K.V.: Wearable-based affect recognition - a review. Sensors **19**, 4079 (2019)
58. Schmidtke, D.S., Schröder, T., Jacobs, A.M., Conrad, M.: ANGST: affective norms for German sentiment terms, derived from the affective norms for English words. Behav. Res. Methods **46**(4), 1108–1118 (2014)
59. Shea, B.J., et al.: AMSTAR 2: a critical appraisal tool for systematic reviews that include randomised or non-randomised studies of healthcare interventions, or both. bmj **358**, j4008 (2017)
60. Shoumy, N.J., Ang, L.M., Seng, K.P., et al.: Multimodal big data affective analytics: a comprehensive survey using text, audio, visual and physiological signals. J. Netw. Comput. Appl. **149**, 102447 (2020)
61. Shu, L., et al.: A review of emotion recognition using physiological signals. Sensors **18**(7), 2074 (2018)
62. Smith, V., Devane, D., Begley, C.M., Clarke, M.: Methodology in conducting a systematic review of systematic reviews of healthcare interventions. BMC Med. Res. Methodol. **11**(1), 15 (2011)
63. Soleymani, M., Aljanaki, A., Yang, Y.: DEAM: MediaEval database for emotional analysis in music (2016)
64. Spezialetti, M., Cinque, L., Tavares, J.M.R., Placidi, G.: Towards EEG-based BCI driven by emotions for addressing BCI-illiteracy: a meta-analytic review. Behav. Inf. Technol. **37**(8), 855–871 (2018)
65. Szwoch, W.: Using physiological signals for emotion recognition. In: International Conference on Human System Interactions (HSI), pp. 556–561. IEEE (2013)
66. Tandle, A.L., Joshi, M.S., Dharmadhikari, A.S., Jaiswal, S.V.: Mental state and emotion detection from musically stimulated EEG. Brain Inf. **5**(2), 14 (2018)
67. Thanapattheerakul, T., Mao, K., Amoranto, J., Chan, J.H.: Emotion in a century: A review of emotion recognition. In: Proceedings of the 10th International Conference on Advances in Information Technology, pp. 1–8 (2018)
68. Valenza, G., Citi, L., Lanata, A., Scilingo, E.P., Barbieri, R.: A nonlinear heartbeat dynamics model approach for personalized emotion recognition. In: 2013 35th Annual International Conference of the IEEE Engineering in Medicine and Biology Society (EMBC), pp. 2579–2582. IEEE (2013)
69. Van Eck, N., Waltman, L.: Software survey: VOSviewer, a computer program for bibliometric mapping. Scientometrics **84**(2), 523–538 (2010)
70. Witkowski, T.: Is the glass half empty or half full? Latest results in the replication crisis in psychology. Skept. Inq. **43**(2), 5–6 (2019)
71. Yang, W., et al.: Affective auditory stimulus database: an expanded version of the international affective digitized sounds (IADS-E). Behav. Res. Methods **50**(4), 1415–1429 (2018)
72. Zhang, Q., Chen, X., Zhan, Q., Yang, T., Xia, S.: Respiration-based emotion recognition with deep learning. Comput. Ind. **92**, 84–90 (2017)
73. Zhao, Y., Zhao, W., Jin, C., Chen, Z.: A review on EEG based emotion classification. In: 2019 IEEE 4th Advanced Information Technology, Electronic and Automation Control Conference (IAEAC), vol. 1, pp. 1959–1963. IEEE (2019)
74. Zhou, F., Qu, X., Jiao, J., Helander, M.G.: Emotion prediction from physiological signals: a comparison study between visual and auditory elicitors. Interact. Comput. **26**(3), 285–302 (2014)
75. Zupan, B., Babbage, D.R.: Film clips and narrative text as subjective emotion elicitation techniques. J. Soc. Psychol. **157**(2), 194–210 (2017)

Detecting Emotions Through Machine Learning for Automatic UX Evaluation

Giuseppe Desolda(✉), Andrea Esposito, Rosa Lanzilotti, and Maria F. Costabile

Computer Science Department, University of Bari Aldo Moro, Bari, Italy
{giuseppe.desolda,andrea.esposito,rosa.lanzilotti,
maria.costabile}@uniba.it

Abstract. Although User eXperience (UX) is widely acknowledged as an important aspect of software products, its evaluation is often neglected during the development of most software products, primarily because developers think that it is resource-demanding and complain about the fact that is scarcely automated. Various attempts have been made to develop tools that support and automate the execution of tests with users. This paper is about an ongoing research work that exploits Machine Learning (ML) for automatic UX evaluation, specifically for understanding users' emotions by analyzing the log data of the users' interactions with websites. The approach described aims at overcoming some limitations of existing proposals based on ML.

Keywords: Usability · User eXperience · Automatic UX evaluation

1 Introduction

User eXperience (UX) has become an increasingly important aspect of software products. It extends the more traditional quality of usability, focused primarily on ease of learning and ease of use. Standard ISO 9241-11:1988 defines UX as *a person's perceptions and responses resulting from the use and/or anticipated use of a product, system or service*. Other definitions are available in the literature (e.g., [15]). Designing for UX is much more than designing for the traditional attributes of usability. UX also refers to attributes related to people feelings and emotions, such as pleasure, fun, surprise, intimacy, joy; it focuses on beautiful (harmonious, clear), emotional (affectionate, lovable), stimulating (intellectual, motivational), and also on tactile (smooth, soft), acoustic (rhythmic, melodious).

Some main reasons why usability and UX are still neglected during the development of most software products is that developers think that usability and UX evaluations are resource-demanding and require specific expertise because they are scarcely automated [19, 31]. In order to foster more attention on usability and UX, the automation of evaluation tests, performed remotely, could be a solution due to its great potential of reducing costs. Remote usability testing was defined around the mid-'90s to limit some usability testing drawbacks [21]; it refers to user testing performed by evaluators who

C. Ardito et al. (Eds.): INTERACT 2021, LNCS 12934, pp. 270–279, 2021.
https://doi.org/10.1007/978-3-030-85613-7_19

are in different physical locations from the participants and might operate at different times [10]. Software tools for remote testing were developed to allow participants to test systems from their locations, at times when it is convenient for them. The tools automatically gathered and stored data about the tests. Examples of more recent tools are Userlytics [27], Loop11 [16], eGLU-Box PA [9]; while complete automation is still far from possible, these tools take great advantage of current technology and provide more useful features with respect to the tools of the '90s. For example, eGLU-Box PA also allows the detection of issues concerning UX, called "UX smells" (in a similar fashion to the commonly known expression "code smells"), using visualization techniques that show the paths followed by participants to carry out tasks on websites during a test [4].

Since emotions are important elements of UX, some authors are looking for ways of identifying users' emotions by analyzing the users' interaction with the system (e.g., mouse movements) through machine learning (ML) algorithms [3, 5, 12, 20, 29, 32]. These proposals are not mature enough due to several limitations, such as 1) the proposed models are often trained on datasets that are too small, contain data collected in controlled environments (thus with low ecological validity), and the emotions are self-reported by the users; 2) there is not a comparison of different ML algorithms and no clear indication on the most suitable one for this kind of task is provided; 3) the prediction provided by the ML algorithm is always in relation to long timespan, thus making impossible to understand users' emotions during intermediate moments.

This paper presents an ongoing research work that exploits ML for emotion detection, with the aim to overcome the above limitations. It provides the following contributions. First, a dataset of users' emotions and interaction logs of real users that interact with real websites "in the wild" for 30 days is built. Second, the results of the comparison of the four ML algorithms mainly used for detecting emotions are provided. Third, the resulting classification models can predict users' emotions moment by moment during the users' interaction. The paper is organized as follows. Section 2 discusses the rationale and background of our research. Section 3 illustrates how the dataset was built, and Sect. 4 presents the comparison of four ML algorithms to predict emotions felt by users interacting with websites. Section 5 provides the conclusions and highlights future works.

2 Background and Related Work

UX integrates the usability concept by emphasizing more subjective feelings. A valuable UX increases user satisfaction: an aesthetically pleasing interface, which is easily navigable and presents updated and trustable content, heavily increases user satisfaction [30].

Various evaluation techniques have been proposed (see, e.g., [14, 22]). One of the most successful is user testing, it is considered the most complete form of evaluation because it assesses usability and UX through samples of real users [18]. However, it is often perceived as impractical mainly because it is very resource-demanding [2]; for small companies/organizations, the cost of recruiting users and expert evaluators and transporting them to different locations can be prohibitive [26, 31]. Various approaches for semi-automating user testing have been proposed. The tools for remote user testing developed about 20 years ago (e.g., [7]) used the technology available at that time, which was limited. Technology advances in recent years have opened up new scenarios. Nowadays, it is possible to realize web applications with functions for screen recording, user-interaction tracking, access to peripheral devices, such as webcams and microphones to capture the face and speech of the participants during user tests. The tools developed in the last five years (e.g., [16, 28]) provide several features to better support automatic testing and to collect much more qualitative data that may help discover further usability issues. The main limitation is that it is impossible to keep track of the actual test reliability: users may choose to "rush" the test or may be influenced by the testing environment (this is an issue that also affects "classic" methods), thereby distorting the final results. Finally, while reducing the costs with respect to conducting the tests in-house, the costs are still higher than fully automatic evaluations.

To move toward automatic UX evaluation, some research works exploit ML algorithms to build models that, starting from interaction logs, predict the emotions felt by users. For each user interface the users interact with, or for each task the users perform, these models return the score of each emotion. However, these solutions still have room for improvement. For example, the datasets used to train the models are built during in-lab sessions but, as it is widely known, user interaction in the lab is biased [23], thus the resulting models are also biased. Other datasets are built during the execution of a limited number of tasks or on a specific model [1, 3, 5, 12, 29], thus reducing the generalizability of the predictions. In some cases, users are asked about their emotions at the end of a task or after a long time span (e.g., n minutes) [1, 5, 12, 20, 32] by using a Likert scale [1] or a SAM (Self-Assessment Manikin) scale [12]. This determines a strong limitation caused by the so-called *peak–end rule* [6]: it is a psychological behavior of people that judge an experience depending on how they felt during its peak (the most intense point) and at the end, rather than based on the total sum or average of every moment of the experience. Thus, these datasets cannot be representative of the overall users' emotions since users tend to recall the last part of the interaction and/or the pick. Another limitation regards the data pre-processing since datasets used until now are not further refined, excluding simple filters [29] or aggregation in time frames [1]. Finally, to the best of our knowledge, no previous works aim at predicting users' emotions at a lower granularity, i.e., at predicting emotions every second. This low-level prediction helps evaluators in understanding users' emotions not only during the visit of a webpage or during a task execution but, more deeply, it permits identifying emotions felt by users during the interaction with specific elements of the webpages. In this way, it is possible to understand, for instance, if UI elements like a menu, video, widget, etc., determine positive or negative emotions.

3   Construction of in-the-Wild Dataset

With the objective of overcoming some of the limitations identified in the literature, this paper presents an ongoing research work to provide researchers, practitioners, and companies with a software tool for the automatic detection of emotions. This tool, which is still under development, consists of 1) a JavaScript snippet to be integrated into the pages of a website, and 2) a dashboard to analyze users' emotions. In particular, the snippet asynchronously tracks the user's interactions (mouse movements and keyboard press) and sends them to a web server. The dashboard reports for each webpage the results of an ML model applied to the logs of all the users that visited that page, to predict their average emotions. Figure 1 reports an example of a prototype of the dashboard that visualizes a heatmap depicting the emotion, joy in this example, the users felt while interacting with the webpage. This heatmap indicates in red the web pages elements with high emotion values, while in blue elements with low values. On the right side, there is a legend and a radio-box menu to change the emotion visualized in the heatmap. It is worth noticing that some users might feel emotions not related to the specific website but caused by external factors (e.g., mood, tiring, etc.). However, the final values computed by the ML models and visualized on the heatmap are an average of emotions of hundreds, thousand or more users, thus possible wrong values are mitigated or cancelled by the sample size.

Fig. 1. Example of heatmap showing an emotion intensity on a webpage.

At the current stage of our research, we are focusing on two activities related to the construction of the prediction model: 1) the creation of a significant dataset overcoming the limitations identified in the literature, and 2) the comparison of different ML methods for classification. We built a new dataset according to the following requirements:

1. *Data are collected in the wild*, i.e., while users naturally interact with any website for any kind of activity, without any restriction. In this way, the models trained on these data better reflect the real user behavior and emotions.
2. *Data are collected with low granularity*, possibly every a few seconds. This low-level sampling enables the emotion prediction moment by moment, in order to understand users' emotions while interacting with specific website elements (e.g., a menu, a label) instead of more high-level predictions that simply indicate users' emotions during the interaction with a webpage or during task execution, as it occurs in [5, 29].
3. *Data are collected transparently.* Interaction tracking must be transparent to users. Similarly, users should not be asked to stop their activity to declare their emotions, as required in [1, 5, 12, 20, 32].
4. *Emotions are automatically computed by analyzing the user's facial expressions.* Facial expression analysis avoids both the use of intrusive hardware for emotion

detection (e.g. brain-computer-interfaces devices [32]) and to stop users during the test to ask them to declare their emotions. In addition, this analysis is more precise than self-declared emotions, which also suffers from the peak-end rule problem.

5. *Participants' data anonymization is guaranteed.* This is required for ethical issues. It also fosters participant recruiting.

We recruited 12 volunteers of different ages (mean age 32.3) and gender (6 women). They were asked to install for 30 days on their browser (Chrome or Firefox was required) a plugin we purposely developed. This plugin records, every 2 s, a picture from the webcam that frames the user's face as well as mouse and keyboard logs (to avoid a keylogger effect, the plugin only records the type of key pressed, i.e., number, letter, special character). This data was anonymously sent, through an SSL connection, to a web server where a Node.js module manages them. Every time this module receives the data, it invokes the Affdex SDK [17] to translate the picture into a set of pairs [emotion-value], according to the EMFACS (Emotional Facial Action Coding System) model which identifies seven emotions: Anger, Contempt, Disgust, Joy, Fear, Sadness, and Surprise [8]. It is worth remarking that recent advances in computer visions and Deep Learning make visual emotion recognition, and in particular the Affdex tool, as reliable as human coding [24, 25], as well as precise like more advanced and invasive instruments as facial electromyography [13]. Then, the Node.js module permanently discards the picture and then associates the emotions to the user logs. The result is an *interaction object* stored in a MongoDB database that describes what the user was doing and his/her emotions in the sampling moment. At the end of the 30 days, around 3 GB of data on the users' interactions on 473 websites were stored.

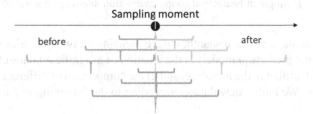

Fig. 2. Three-time windows of different lengths (25/50/100 ms) were computed before (green), after (orange), and before and after (blue) each sampled moment. Nine-time windows are associated with each interaction object. (Color figure online)

A preprocessing phase was performed before using the dataset with the ML algorithms. First, since the emotion values returned by Affdex SDK range from 0 to 100, in line with previous works we discretized such values in three classes [1, 5, 12, 20, 32], i.e., low (from 0 to 33), medium (from 34 to 66), and high (from 67 to 100). Then, each interaction object was extended by computing further metrics, namely mouse speed, acceleration, and direction. In addition, metrics measuring three-time windows of variable length (25/50/100 ms) were calculated before, after, and before and after the sampling moment (see Fig. 2). A total of 9 windows were computed and each of them contains: average speed among all axes, average number of clicks per second, average idle time, average number of mouse movements per second, average number per second of mouse's trajectory changes, URL change rate, number of website changes, average number of key pressed per second per type. In the end, each interaction object contains the interaction log in the sampling moments, the 7 emotion values, and the 9-time windows, each one characterized by additional features. The final dataset contains 527853 interaction objects characterized by 549 features. An example of a resulting interaction object described in JSON format is reported at this link https://bit.ly/3s3BvmL.

4 Comparison of Learning Algorithms for User's Emotions Classification

In the literature, there are no comparisons between ML algorithms for emotion prediction starting from users' interactions. Moreover, there is no comparison among the best sets of features (related to keyboard and mouse usage) to predict emotions. For this reason, we compared different learning algorithms, in particular, all the ones already used in previous works, i.e., binary decision trees, random forests, AdaBoost, and Multi-Layered Perceptron. To select the best set of features for each kind of model, a forward feature selection algorithm was applied.

The training phase poses an important problem related to the required computational time and resources. For each type of learning algorithm, we built 7 models (one for each emotion). For each of these 7 models, we trained 9 models, each one related to the different time windows. This led to the computation of a total of 252 models (4 learning algorithms × 7 emotions × 9-time windows). The k-fold cross-validation used to evaluate the models' performance (with k = 10) and the feature selection algorithm further amplify this problem, leading to the computation of thousands of intermediate models.

The model computation were performed by writing a Python 3 script that uses *SciKit-Learn* for model computation and *MLxtend* library for the feature selection algorithm. The computation was performed on an HPC cluster machine provided by our University. This is equipped with CentOS 7.6 – 64bit, and it has up to 400 physical cores (800 considering hyperthreading), each with 4 GB of RAM. For this computation, only 8 cores were used (the allocation of more cores required too much time). To make possible the computation of all the combinations of the models in a reasonable amount of time, we empirically established that no more than 0.1% of the dataset could be used. To deal with the "class imbalance problem" [11], a stratified sampling was applied, so that each class was represented by a similar number of examples (463 objects for each class of each emotion). The entire computation lasted 35 h and 43 min.

As reported in Fig. 3a, random forest and binary decision trees perform better than AdaBoost, and Multi-Layered Perceptron. Looking at the results aggregated for the time windows (25/50/100 and after/before/full), no relevant difference seems to exists by varying the time frame's width (Fig. 3b), while "after" window seems determining better results (Fig. 3c).

A more focused analysis was performed by inspecting the performance of each ML algorithm according to the seven emotions. As reported in Fig. 4, it is evident that, in general, emotions like sadness, anger, fear, disgust and surprise are predicted with higher

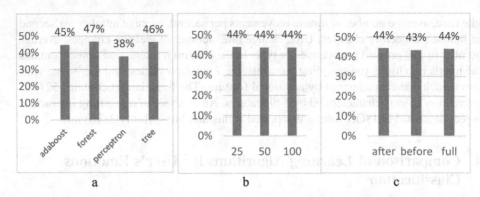

Fig. 3. Average accuracies of the four ML algorithms (a), the average accuracy of all the algorithms aggregated by time windows length (b) and time windows position (c).

accuracy (in all cases, outperforming a random classifier that should have an accuracy of 33%); joy is instead predicted with a medium accuracy (around 40% in all cases), while contempt has lower accuracy in all cases (around 34%). At this link https://bit.ly/3yUtrcF, it is available an Excel file reporting the details of the performance of all the models, as well as a set of visualization we built for our analysis.

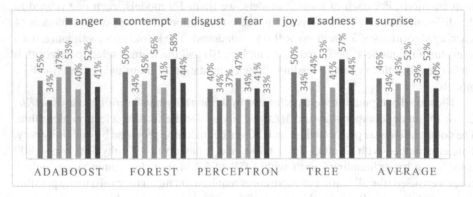

Fig. 4. Average accuracies of the four ML algorithms detailed for each emotion.

The results obtained at the end of the entire ML algorithm training process are promising. Regarding the emotion's prediction, it emerged that two algorithms, namely random forest and binary decision trees, on average, outperform AdaBoost, and Multi-Layered Perceptron. The limitations of the predictive models both in the accuracy levels can be explained by remembering that only a very small and random portion of the dataset (0.1%) was actually used.

Another interesting result comes from the time windows. For some algorithms, wider windows seem more informative and useful in creating more accurate models. The position of the window (before, after, before and after) does not seem the same. It would be interesting to compute more time windows in a wider time span to assess their effect on model accuracy, even considering the entire dataset extended with further data.

It seems that various algorithms perform better in different emotions (e.g.: random forest outperforms AdaBoost in predicting fear, but the contrary is true for disgust).

5 Conclusion and Future Works

The research work presented in this paper is about a full-automatic evaluation of UX. A tool that, starting from the user interaction logs of websites, detects users' emotions by exploiting ML algorithms is illustrated. Even if it is in an embryonic stage, it has great potential: the predictive models described can be easily embedded in a script to be provided to web developers so that, once inserted in a web page, collects users' interactions with the page and infers their emotions. This permits a page-by-page and point-by-point reconstruction of users' emotions, for example by using heatmaps.

As future work, we are going to complete the development of the software tool for the automatic detection of emotions. The average accuracy of ML algorithms like random forest and binary decision trees seem adequate and promising for this goal. However, a more accurate predictive model would be desirable: this could be obtained by either increasing the number of samples used in the training phase (the limitation to the 0.1% was only introduced to avoid a too long execution time) and by increasing the number of participants in the data-collection phase (thus expanding it "horizontally"). At the end of this research project, this dataset will be shared to foster similar studies. In addition, the spectrum of algorithms that have been compared may be broadened by including other classification algorithms like Support Vector Machines and k-Nearest Neighbors. Finally, models will be trained on emotions stratified in 5 and 7 classes, as proposed by SAM questionnaire. This could allow us a more detailed prediction. However, more classes will lower the prediction accuracy, but this will help us to establish a fair compromise between accuracy and detail of the prediction.

Acknowledgment. This work is partially supported by the Italian Ministry of University and Research (MIUR) under grant PRIN 2017 "EMPATHY: EMpowering People in deAling with internet of THings ecosYstems.".

References

1. Alibasa, M.J., Calvo, R.A.: Supporting mood introspection from digital footprints. In: Proceedings of the International Conference on Affective Computing and Intelligent Interaction (ACII 2019). IEEE (2019)
2. Ardito, C., et al.: Usability evaluation: a survey of software development organizations. In: Proceedings of the International Conference on Software Engineering and Knowledge Engineering (SEKE 2011). Knowledge Systems Institute, Skokie, Illinois, pp. 282–287 (2011)
3. Atterer, R., Wnuk, M., Schmidt, A.: Knowing the user's every move. In: Proceedings of the International Conference on World Wide Web (WWW 2006). ACM (2006)
4. Buono, P., Caivano, D., Costabile, M.F., Desolda, G., Lanzilotti, R.: Towards the detection of UX smells: the support of visualizations. IEEE Access **8**, 6901–6914 (2020)

5. Constantine, L., et al.: A framework for emotion recognition from human computer interaction in natural setting. In: Proceedings of the Conference on Knowledge Discovery and Data Mining (KDD 2016). ACM (2016)
6. Do, A.M., Rupert, A.V., Wolford, G.: Evaluations of pleasurable experiences: the peak-end rule. Psychon. Bull. Rev. 15(1), 96–98 (2008)
7. Edmonds, A.: Uzilla: a new tool for web usability testing. Behav. Res. Methods Instrum. Comput. 35(2), 194–201 (2003)
8. Ekman, R.: What the Face Reveals: Basic and Applied Studies of Spontaneous Expression Using the Facial Action Coding System (FACS). Oxford University Press, USA (1997)
9. Federici, S., et al.: A chatbot solution for eGLU-Box Pro: the usability evaluation platform for Italian public administrations. In: Kurosu, M. (ed.) HCII 2021. LNCS, vol. 12762, pp. 268–279. Springer, Cham (2021). https://doi.org/10.1007/978-3-030-78462-1_20
10. Hartson, H.R., Castillo, J.C., Kelso, J., Neale, W.C.: Remote evaluation: the network as an extension of the usability laboratory. In: Proceedings of the International Conference on Human Factors in Computing Systems (CHI 1996). ACM, pp. 228–235 (1996)
11. Japkowicz, N., Stephen, S.: The class imbalance problem: a systematic study. Intell. Data Anal. 6, 429–449 (2002)
12. Khan, I.A., Brinkman, W.-P., Hierons, R.M.: Towards a computer interaction-based mood measurement instrument. In: Proceedings of the Annual Workshop of the Psychology of Programming Interest Group (PPIG 2008). ACM (2008)
13. Kulke, L., Feyerabend, D., Schacht, A.: A comparison of the affectiva iMotions facial expression analysis software with EMG for identifying facial expressions of emotion. Front. Psychol. 11(329) (2020)
14. Lanzilotti, R., Ardito, C., Costabile, M.F., Angeli, A.D.: Do patterns help novice evaluators? A comparative study. Int. J. Hum.-Comput. Stud. 69(1–2), 52–69 (2011)
15. Law, E.L.-C., Roto, V., Hassenzahl, M., Vermeeren, A.P.O.S., Kort, J.: Understanding, scoping and defining user experience: a survey approach. In: Proceedings of the Conference on Human Factors in Computing Systems (CHI 2009). ACM, pp. 719–728 (2009)
16. Loop11.: Online user testing made easy I loop11. https://www.loop11.com/. Accessed 7 April 2021
17. McDuff, D., Mahmoud, A., Mavadati, M., Amr, M., Turcot, J., Kaliouby, R.E.: AFFDEX SDK: a cross-platform real-time multi-face expression recognition toolkit. In: Proceedings of the Conference on Human Factors in Computing Systems - Extended Abstracts (CHI 2016). ACM, pp. 3723–3726 (2016)
18. Rubin, J., Chisnell, D.: Handbook of Usability Testing: How to Plan, Design and Conduct Effective Tests. Wiley, Indianapolis (2008)
19. Russo, P., Lanzilotti, R., Costabile, M.F., Pettit, C.J.: Towards satisfying practitioners in using planning support systems. Comput. Environ. Urban Syst. 67, 9–20 (2018)
20. Salmeron-Majadas, S., Santos, O.C., Boticario, J.G.: An evaluation of mouse and keyboard interaction indicators towards non-intrusive and low cost affective modeling in an educational context. Procedia Comput. Sci. 35, 691–700 (2014)
21. Scholtz, J.: Usability evaluation. National Institute of Standards and Technology, 1 (2004)
22. Shneiderman, B.: Software Psychology: Human Factors in Computer and Information Systems (Winthrop Computer Systems Series). Winthrop Publishers, Cambridge (1980)
23. Sonderegger, A., Sauer, J.: The influence of laboratory set-up in usability tests: effects on user performance, subjective ratings and physiological measures. Ergonomics 52(11), 1350–1361 (2009)
24. Stöckli, S., Schulte-Mecklenbeck, M., Borer, S., Samson, A.C.: Facial expression analysis with AFFDEX and FACET: a validation study. Behav. Res. Methods 50(4), 1446–1460 (2017). https://doi.org/10.3758/s13428-017-0996-1

25. Taggart, R.W., Dressler, M., Kumar, P., Khan, S., Coppola, J.F.: Determining emotions via facial expression analysis software. In: Proceedings of the Student-Faculty Research Day (CSIS). Pace University (2016)
26. Thompson, K.E., Rozanski, E.P., Haake, A.R.: Here, there, anywhere: remote usability testing that works. In: Proceedings of the Conference on Information Technology Education (ITE 2004). ACM, pp. 132–137 (2004)
27. Userlytics.: Remote user testing platform | userlytics. https://www.userlytics.com/. Accessed 7 April 2021
28. UserTesting.: UserTesting: the human insight platform. https://www.usertesting.com/. Accessed 7 April 2021
29. Vea, L., Rodrigo, M.M.: Modeling negative affect detector of novice programming students using keyboard dynamics and mouse behavior. In: Numao, M., Theeramunkong, T., Supnithi, T., Ketcham, M., Hnoohom, N., Pramkeaw, P. (eds.) PRICAI 2016. LNCS (LNAI), vol. 10004, pp. 127–138. Springer, Cham (2017). https://doi.org/10.1007/978-3-319-60675-0_11
30. Zahidi, Z., Lim, Y.P., Woods, P.C.: Understanding the user experience (UX) factors that influence user satisfaction in digital culture heritage online collections for non-expert users. In: Proceedings of the Science and Information Conference (SAI 2014), pp. 57–63. IEEE (2014)
31. Zaina, L.A.M., Sharp, H., Barroca, L.: UX information in the daily work of an agile team: a distributed cognition analysis. Int. J. Hum.-Comput. Stud. **147**, 102574 (2021)
32. Zimmermann, P., Guttormsen, S., Danuser, B., Gomez, P.: Affective computing—a rationale for measuring mood with mouse and keyboard. Int. J. Occup. Saf. Ergon. **9**(4), 539–551 (2003)

Helping Professionals Select Persona Interview Questions Using Natural Language Processing

Joni Salminen[1,2](✉), Kamal Chhirang[3], Soon-gyo Jung[1], and Bernard J. Jansen[1]

[1] Qatar Computing Research Institute, Hamad Bin Khalifa University, Doha, Qatar
jsalminen@hbku.edu.qa
[2] Turku School of Economics at the University of Turku, Turku, Finland
[3] Fulda University of Applied Sciences, Fulda, Germany

Abstract. Personas are often created based on user interviews. Yet, researchers rarely make their interview questions publicly available or justify how they were chosen. We manually extract 276 interview questions and categorize them into 10 themes, making this list publicly available for researchers and practitioners. We also demonstrate an approach of using natural language processing to assist in selecting persona interview questions for a given use case.

Keywords: Personas · Information design · Interview questions

1 Introduction

A persona is a fictitious person describing a real user or customer segment [1]. Personas are presented as profiles containing key information about a particular user segment, such as goals, needs, and wants [2]. Personas are used for multiple purposes, such as communicating information about the users within teams [3], aligning preconceptions with reality [4], and to better understand user needs for requirements engineering [5].

The approaches to persona creation include qualitative [6], quantitative (including algorithmic or data-driven personas [7–9]), and mixed methods [10]. Most often, personas are created using qualitative methods [6, 10]. In such cases, the data is collected via ethnographic means, field studies, or interviews [6]. Out of all of these, interviews are often preferred because they can be easily implemented.

After the persona creators have decided their methodological approach (e.g., qualitative) and data collection means (e.g., interviews), they typically consider what information the persona profile contains. This selection process is referred to as persona information design [11], defined as selection of information elements (attributes, characteristics) that the finalized persona profiles will communicate to their users. Ideally, the persona information design process is driven by the information needs of the eventual persona users, such as software developers, designers, and business managers.

Persona information design deals with the fundamental question of what information personas should contain. As personas are often created based on user interviews [6, 12], practitioners frequently ask for a comprehensive list of persona interview questions.

© IFIP International Federation for Information Processing 2021
Published by Springer Nature Switzerland AG 2021
C. Ardito et al. (Eds.): INTERACT 2021, LNCS 12934, pp. 280–290, 2021.
https://doi.org/10.1007/978-3-030-85613-7_20

In this research, we offer a meta-synthesis of common persona interview questions, identified from top-ranking search results on Google. The results offer 276 interview questions categorized into 10 themes. We provide suggestions on how researchers and practitioners can select the appropriate questions for their particular persona use case.

Our contribution addresses the challenge in HCI, and in the field of personas, that designers often have too many interview questions to choose from. Our data collection shows that, even when using a limited number of nine sources, one ends up with a list of more than two-hundred possible questions. This excessive variety and dimensionality of potential interview questions results in a daunting paradox of choice for those creating personas, especially to those that are less inexperienced, such as students and novices, with the method and, therefore, less certain of what questions to include in their user interviews. As such, our contribution offers help and guidance for researchers and practitioners dealing with the challenge of persona information design.

2 Related Literature

Persona design is discussed in several textbooks [1, 2, 6, 10]. All of these sources mention interviews as a form of data collection for persona creation. According to Google Scholar, "persona information design" is explicitly mentioned by three studies: [9, 11, 13]. These studies briefly mention the concept, defining it as the choice of what information to include in the persona profiles (regardless of the source of data).

The generic persona creation process, when using interviews, is as follows [6]:

Use case definition → Persona information design → Interview question selection → Conducting interview → Analyzing the results → Creating the persona profiles

First, one defines the use case that gives motivation and explains why personas are needed (e.g., "we need to improve employee satisfaction and believe that using personas to understand our employees would be useful"). Second, the information design of the personas is defined – what do we want to know about the people the personas portray? (e.g., employee pain points, their life situation, their decision making). This will result in the identification of various information elements to include in the personas. Then, we operationalize these information elements by creating a list of interview questions. This is followed by the interviews, the transcription and analysis of the results, and the creation (write-up) of the persona profiles [6].

Reviewing past works reveals a consistent pattern wherein researchers have constructed personas based on user interviews but have not disclosed their interview questions. For instance, in their work to understand users for product design, DiMicco and Mann [14] created three personas from interviews but there was no mention of the questions used. On similar lines, Gao et al. [15], Chang et al. [16], Falk et al. [17], Antle [18], and Sharbatdar et al. [19] conducted studies to understand medical prenatal care users, language learners, decision makers in the oil and gas industry, children, and transportation management practitioners, respectively, and created several personas but there was no mention of the interview questions applied.

Therefore, a consistent pattern in prior works is that researchers rarely disclose the interview questions which were used to collect data for making personas. Not only does this make replication of their studies difficult, but also leaves practitioners with a gap of knowledge, as academic sources do not explicitly recommend specific interview questions. Our study addresses this issue by proposing a systematic approach of identifying persona interview questions.

3 Methodology

3.1 Data Collection

We searched Google to identify lists of persona interview questions. A search using "persona interview questions" yields 13,900 results in Google (29,100,000 results without brackets). We chose six sources based on (a) high rank in Google and (b) extensiveness of the list of questions. We then manually collected all the questions from each source website and stored them in a spreadsheet. This yielded 350 questions. These were manually screened to remove duplicates, i.e., asking the same question twice. In total, 74 (21.1%) duplicates were found and removed. After the screening process, 276 questions remained. The original and the final list of questions after applying the screening criteria have been made available in the Supplementary Material[1].

3.2 Classifying the Questions

The remaining 276 questions were classified under ten themes (see Table 1). A theme taxonomy was created based on abduction, i.e., a qualitative technique which involves using both pre-existing knowledge and also analyzing the emerging properties of the data [20]. In our case, we made use of (a) the authors' pre-existing knowledge of persona information content, and (b) the emerging communalities in the question material.

In this process, one of the researchers created the themes and categorized the questions under these themes. The other two researchers independently commented on the validity and definitions given by the first researcher for each theme. In Table 1, we present the different themes which emerged during our analysis along with a short description of the theme. At this stage, the definitions became more precise, e.g., 'Life Situation' was described as day-to-day life of the users. Themes **I** (Marketing Team) and **J** (Sales Team) could be seen as subthemes of **D** (Work Life). However, since the questions of these sub-themes were very specific to their respective professions, we decided to represent them as separate themes as well in the current work.

Since personas are widely used in different fields such as sales, marketing, and e-commerce [21–25], the themes in Table 1 reflect the questions which can be used in these different fields for creating personas specific to the fields. Thus, our work can have a wide impact on not just design practice but also other professions.

---

[1] https://www.dropbox.com/s/uwshanbm674a5ui/supporting%20material_INTERACT.xlsx?dl=0.

Table 1. Themes for the interview questions.

ID	Theme	This theme contains questions about...	N (%)
A	Demographics	The most basic questions that form the basis of the persona, such as age, gender, family size, income, occupation, race, religion, education, and so on	9 (3.3%)
B	Life Situation	The general day-to-day life of the users. As well as offering insights into their personality, these questions reveal what products and services users are likely to be interested in and what would be useful to them	79 (28.6%)
C	School Life	The lives of users during their school days. What subjects did they take, what extracurricular activities they participated in, what kind of school they attended and so on	18 (6.5%)
D	Work Life	The users' working life such as their current job, position, career goals, obstacles, and solutions in their job	72 (26.1%)
E	Decision Making	The users' process of making decisions. This involves, e.g., goals to be achieved, problem awareness, evaluation of options, decision-making styles, and post-decision behavior	20 (7.2%)
F	Information Sources	The channels users obtain information from. Do they go online, prefer to learn in-person, or rely on newspapers and magazines? If they are online learners, do they visit social networks? Google? Which sources do they trust the most -- friends, family, coworkers, or industry experts?	20 (7.2%)
G	Consumer Habits	The habits and preferences of the users when buying products and making other consumption choices	36 (13.0%)
H	Pain Points	The problems faced by the users and how organizations can see and find solutions to these problems	11 (4.0%)
I	Marketing Team	Information related to the work of marketing team members	7 (2.5%)
J	Sales Team	Information related to the work of sales team members	4 (1.4%)
NOTE: N indicates the number of questions in the theme			N = 276

3.3 Clustering the Questions

The number of questions in Table 1 seem excessive – it does not appear realistic to ask 79 questions from a user relating to their life situation. Therefore, we need to trim down the list. This was accomplished by setting a maximum number of questions to ask under each theme. This way, the total number of questions will not exceed the maximum number multiplied by the number of themes selected for a specific use case.

We set the maximum to five questions. For example, if five themes were selected, the maximum number of questions would be $5 \times 5 = 25$ questions, which is reasonable number of questions for a user interview [26, 27].

Next, we will need to decide how to choose the representative five questions from each theme. For this study, we opted for using Natural Language Processing (NLP). Specifically, we used *Roberta-Large*[2], a transformer-based model. In brief, the transformer enables us to transform the questions into numerical format in a 1024-dimensional space where each dimension describes a position in the vector space relative to other questions. The NLP model computes the semantic similarity between each question under each theme – the meaning of two questions is similar when the numerical distance is low, and dissimilar when the distance is high [28].

To avoid a situation in which the very similar questions would appear among the Top-5 questions of a theme, we apply clustering on the word embeddings given by the transformer model. By creating five clusters from each theme (apart from 'Sales Information,' which only contains four questions, all of which will be selected), we can ensure that the chosen questions are separate from the other questions.

4   Results

4.1   Use Case Definition

In this part, we address the question, *"How to use the themes to select the final interview questions?"*. For this, we created three fictitious scenarios to demonstrate how the themes can be used for persona information design:

- **Scenario 1:** A startup company wants to develop a software product for enterprise users. (Use case: *product development*)
- **Scenario 2:** A corporation wants to understand how their salespeople work and how to help them in their daily work. (Use case: *employee support*)
- **Scenario 3:** Marketers want to understand their potential target market in order to better market products for them. (Use case: *marketing*)

We selected the themes for each scenario (see Table 2) by considering the typical information needs of stakeholders facing the decision-making scenario. For the first scenario, as the target users are enterprise users, 'Work Life' is a relevant theme. Other relevant themes include 'Decision Making' and 'Pain Points,' as these themes help to understand the target users' needs and thinking. For the second scenario, important themes are 'Life Situation' (provides background information about the persons), 'Work Life' (informs about how they see their work role), 'Pain Points' (what concerns they have), and 'Sales Team' (specific questions about the sales profession). For the third scenario, the chosen themes include 'Demographics' (important for a marketing use

---

[2] https://huggingface.co/roberta-large.

cases), 'Decision Making' (to understand how the target market thinks), 'Information Sources' (to understand where they get their information from), and 'Consumer Habits' (to understand consumer behavior). Since the first scenario has three themes, the number of questions will be $3 \times 5 = 15$. The second scenario has four themes, so the number of questions will be $4 \times 5 = 20$. The third scenario also has four themes, but 'Sales Team' only contains four questions, so there will be a total of 19 questions.

Table 2. Identification of interview question themes based on the example use case scenarios.

	Scenario 1	Scenario 2	Scenario 3
Demographics			x
Life situation		x	
School life			
Work life	x	x	
Decision making	x		x
Information Sources			x
Consumer habits			x
Pain points	x	x	
Marketing team			
Sales team		x	

4.2   The Final Questions

Table 3 shows the final questions for the three persona scenarios. As described in Sect. 3.3, a representative question was selected from each selected them based on the similarity scores obtained using NLP. The similarity scores for each question are provided in the Supplementary Material[3].

Some fine-tuning was conducted for the final presentation. The questions that referred to 'they' instead of 'you' were changed to 'you' for consistency (e.g., "What job are they currently doing?" $\rightarrow$ "What job are you currently doing?"). If the top question in a theme was a follow-up from another question, we skipped it and selected the question with the next highest similarity score. We also skipped personal and potentially sensitive questions regarding income ("How much are they worth?", "How much do they earn?") and religion ("Were you raised in a religious household? If yes, which religion were you raised under?") as not everyone might be comfortable in answering these. Since Cluster 4 of 'Life Situation' only contained questions about religion, we chose instead two questions from the largest cluster (Cluster 3).

---

[3] https://www.dropbox.com/s/uwshanbm674a5ui/supporting%20material_INTERACT.xlsx?dl=0.

Table 3. Questions inferred by mapping persona information themes with scenarios and then using NLP to infer representative questions from each theme.

Scenario 1	Scenario 2	Scenario 3
Work Life	Life Situation	Demographics
What job are you currently doing? What is a typical workday like for you? What's important to you and what's driving the change? What kind of customer or user information do you need? How often do you buy high ticket items? (for work)	Tell us about your family life What hobbies (if any) do you have? Do you regularly go on vacations? What type of indulgent or luxurious purchases do you make? Do you tend to break or follow rules?	What is your name? Are you male or female? Which city were you born in? What is your current occupation? What is your income?
Decision Making	Work Life	Decision Making
What are the goals you're trying to achieve? Who do you consult with and trust for advice and information? What is your decision-making process when planning on buying [your product/service]? (If a customer) Why did you choose [your company] over another company? (If not a customer) Why did you choose X Company over us? What is most important to you when selecting a vendor?	What job are you currently doing? What is a typical workday like for you? What's important to you and what's driving the change? What kind of customer or user information do you need? How often do you buy high ticket items? (for work)	What are the goals you're trying to achieve? Who do you consult with and trust for advice and information? What is your decision-making process when planning on buying [your product/service]? (If a customer) Why did you choose [your company] over another company? (If not a customer) Why did you choose X Company over us? What is most important to you when selecting a vendor?
Pain Points	Pain Points	Information Sources
What is the most frustrating part of your day? What is the worst customer service experience you've ever had? What do you enjoy most? What makes you nervous? What is your least favorite part of your job?	What is the most frustrating part of your day? What is the worst customer service experience you've ever had? What do you enjoy most? What makes you nervous? What is your least favorite part of your job?	How adept are you at using technology? Do you use any social media websites? Which search engine do you use the most? What's your process for finding something online? Who do you ask for product/service recommendations? What websites or publications do you read regularly?

(continued)

Table 3. (*continued*)

Scenario 1	Scenario 2	Scenario 3
	Sales Team	Consumer Habits
	What types of customers do you typically meet? Why do different types of customers typically make a purchase? What reasons do customers cite for selecting your business over a competitor? What are the most common objections you hear?	Think back on a recent purchase. How did you research the purchase? What factors were most important to you in evaluating your options? What doubts did you have? Did anyone help you make the final decision? What's your preferred method of communication? Emailing, texting, using an app (such as WhatsApp), or do you prefer to pick up the phone? Do you shop online? Are you willing to make the purchase by alternative means, or is there only one means by which you are happy or able to buy? What could we do to reach more people just like you?

4.3 Evaluation and Guidance for Application

Even though we have tried to be exhaustive in the questions for each scenario, some questions may or may not make sense to all researchers. For instance, Question 5 (the high-ticket item) does not seem directly relevant in Scenario 1, but other questions do seem to make sense. For Scenario 3, the two first questions can be considered optional, as this information may either not be pertinent (name) or can be observed in the interview situation (gender). Overall, a best practice is to conduct a manual 'sanity check' for the questions before conducting the interviews. This is because an "AI-generated" approach that uses algorithms might miss specific contextual and cultural nuances important for a given use case [29, 30].

5 Discussion

5.1 Research Contribution

The current work can help both practitioners and researchers to find inspiration and justification when creating or selecting their persona interview questions. Make all the questions – original, deduplicated, and final lists – publicly available. We hope this inspires others to make their interview questions more transparent, and to build upon this effort to support the research community.

Based on the use case, persona creators can select different combinations of persona information themes. For example, picking A+B+F (see IDs in Table 1) that combines demographics, life situation, and information sources might yield very different personas than E+H (decision making and pain points). By combining the different themes, one can create alternative "lenses" of user understanding. Future development could include an online tool that recommends persona interview questions based on the user's selection of themes. Currently, the same can be accomplished by sorting the spreadsheet provided in the Supplementary Material[4] for theme and cluster, and then selecting the questions with the highest similarity score.

5.2   Limitations, Future Research, and Theorization

Whilst we focus on three persona scenarios, there are many more use cases for personas where the approach we suggested could be tested. Moreover, it would be interesting to see other researchers' take on how to organize the themes into original persona types. In this regard, one idea we offer is the concept of *instrumental* and *intrinsic* personas. It can be said that when personas are instrumental, they contain information for a specific goal. While this is compatible with Cooper's idea of goal-oriented design [1], there are other, alternative ways of seeing personas, most prominently the idea that personas are immersive portrayals of users that have value in unexpected ways.

Therefore, the question of "what is a complete persona profile?" can be addressed in different ways – the goal-oriented approach postulate that a persona profile is complete when it contains all the necessary information that the persona user needs [13]. In turn, the intrinsic view postulates that defining the user's information needs a prior may not be feasible or even possible, resulting in either the presumption that "completeness" is impossible, or at least it is understood much more broadly than one may think.

Finally, the persona technique may benefit from different data sources [31] and interviews are only one type of data. Therefore, creating personas using only interviews may not result in representative personas.

6   Conclusion

Interviews are a popular data collection technique for persona creation. Literature offers little guidance on what questions to include when interviewing users. In turn, the blogosphere offers hundreds, if not thousands of possible questions. Those that are new to personas, are therefore pinned between too little and too much information. We demonstrated an approach of collecting a large base of questions, manually categorizing them to themes, and then applying NLP techniques to create a manageable list of questions that corresponds to specific use cases. This approach can be applied by researchers and practitioners alike when choosing interview questions for persona creation.

References

1. Cooper, A.: The Inmates are Running the Asylum: Why High Tech Products Drive Us Crazy and How to Restore the Sanity. Sams - Pearson Education, Indianapolis, IN (1999)

---

[4] ibid.

2. Adlin, T., Pruitt, J.: The Essential Persona Lifecycle: Your Guide to Building and Using Personas. Morgan Kaufmann Publishers Inc., San Francisco (2010)
3. Friess, E.: Personas and decision making in the design process: an ethnographic case study. In: Proceedings of the SIGCHI Conference on Human Factors in Computing Systems, pp. 1209–1218 (2012)
4. Nielsen, L., Jung, S., An, J., Salminen, J., Kwak, H., Jansen, B.J.: Who are your users?: comparing media professionals' preconception of users to data-driven personas. In: Proceedings of the 29th Australian Conference on Computer-Human Interaction, Brisbane, Queensland, Australia, pp. 602–606. ACM (2017). https://doi.org/10.1145/3152771.3156178
5. Aoyama, M.: Persona-scenario-goal methodology for user-centered requirements engineering. In: Proceedings of the 15th IEEE International Requirements Engineering Conference (RE 2007), Delhi, India, pp. 185–194 (2007). https://doi.org/10.1109/RE.2007.50
6. Nielsen, L.: Personas - User Focused Design. Springer, New York (2019)
7. An, J., Kwak, H., Salminen, J., Jung, S., Jansen, B.J.: Imaginary people representing real numbers: generating personas from online social media data. ACM Trans. Web (TWEB) 12, 27 (2018). https://doi.org/10.1145/3265986
8. McGinn, J.J., Kotamraju, N.: Data-driven persona development. In: Proceedings of the SIGCHI Conference on Human Factors in Computing Systems, Florence, Italy, pp. 1521–1524. ACM (2008). https://doi.org/10.1145/1357054.1357292
9. Salminen, J., Guan, K., Jung, S., Chowdhury, S.A., Jansen, B.J.: A literature review of quantitative persona creation. In: Proceedings of the 2020 CHI Conference on Human Factors in Computing Systems, CHI 2020, Honolulu, Hawaii, USA, pp. 1–14. ACM (2020). https://doi.org/10.1145/3313831.3376502
10. Mulder, S., Yaar, Z.: The User is Always Right: A Practical Guide to Creating and Using Personas for the Web. New Riders (2006)
11. Salminen, J., Guan, K., Nielsen, L., Jung, S.-G., Jansen, B.J.: A template for data-driven personas: analyzing 31 quantitatively oriented persona profiles. In: Yamamoto, S., Mori, H. (eds.) HCII 2020. LNCS, vol. 12184, pp. 125–144. Springer, Cham (2020). https://doi.org/10.1007/978-3-030-50020-7_8
12. Nielsen, L., Hansen, K.S., Stage, J., Billestrup, J.: A template for design personas: analysis of 47 persona descriptions from danish industries and organizations. Int. J. Sociotechnol. Knowl. Dev. 7, 45–61 (2015). https://doi.org/10.4018/ijskd.2015010104
13. Salminen, J., Santos, J.M., Kwak, H., An, J., Jung, S., Jansen, B.J.: Persona perception scale: development and exploratory validation of an instrument for evaluating individuals' perceptions of personas. Int. J. Hum Comput Stud. 141, 102437 (2020). https://doi.org/10.1016/j.ijhcs.2020.102437
14. DiMicco, J.M., Mann, N.: User research to inform product design: turning failure into small successes. In: Proceedings of the 2016 CHI Conference Extended Abstracts on Human Factors in Computing Systems, pp. 872–879 (2016)
15. Gao, Y., Li, X., Lin, Y.-H., Liu, X., Pang, L.: Nuwa: enhancing the pregnancy experience for expectant parents. In: Proceedings of the Extended Abstracts of the 32nd Annual ACM Conference on Human Factors in Computing Systems - CHI EA 2014, Toronto, Ontario, Canada, pp. 257–262. ACM Press (2014). https://doi.org/10.1145/2559206.2580928
16. Chang, Y.-J., Li, L., Chou, S.-H., Liu, M.-C., Ruan, S.: Xpress: crowdsourcing native speakers to learn colloquial expressions in a second language. In: Extended Abstracts on Human Factors in Computing Systems, CHI 2013, pp. 2555–2560 (2013)
17. Falk, K., Kamara, A.K., Braathen, E.P., Helle, K., Moe, P.T., Kokkula, S.: Digitizing the maintenance documentation; a system of systems in oil and gas industry. In: 2020 IEEE 15th International Conference of System of Systems Engineering (SoSE), pp. 493–500. IEEE (2020)

18. Antle, A.: Supporting children's emotional expression and exploration in online environments. In: Proceedings of the 2004 Conference on Interaction Design and Children: Building a Community, pp. 97–104 (2004)

19. Sharbatdar, N., Lamine, Y., Milord, B., Morency, C., Cheng, J.: Capturing the practices, challenges, and needs of transportation decision-makers. In: Extended Abstracts of the 2020 CHI Conference on Human Factors in Computing Systems, pp. 1–7 (2020)

20. Richardson, R., Kramer, E.H.: Abduction as the type of inference that characterizes the development of a grounded theory. Qual. Res. **6**, 497–513 (2006)

21. Al-Qirim, N.: Personas of e-commerce adoption in small businesses in New Zealand. J. Electron. Commer. Organ. (JECO) **4**, 18–45 (2006)

22. Duda, S.: Personas—who owns them. In: von Gizycki, V., Elias, C.A. (eds.) Omnichannel Branding: Digitalisierung als Basis erlebnis- und beziehungsorientierter Markenführung, pp. 173–191. Springer, Wiesbaden (2018). https://doi.org/10.1007/978-3-658-21450-0_8

23. Li, K., Deolalikar, V., Pradhan, N.: Mining lifestyle personas at scale in e-commerce. In: 2015 IEEE International Conference on Big Data (Big Data), pp. 1254–1261. IEEE (2015)

24. Salminen, J., Jansen, B.J., An, J., Kwak, H., Jung, S.: Are personas done? Evaluating their usefulness in the age of digital analytics. Persona Stud. **4**, 47–65 (2018). https://doi.org/10.21153/psj2018vol4no2art737

25. Thoma, V., Williams, B.: Developing and validating personas in e-commerce: a heuristic approach. In: Gross, T., et al. (eds.) INTERACT 2009. LNCS, vol. 5727, pp. 524–527. Springer, Heidelberg (2009). https://doi.org/10.1007/978-3-642-03658-3_56

26. Baker, S.E., Edwards, R.: How Many Qualitative Interviews is Enough. National Centre for Research Methods, UK (2012)

27. Bolderston, A.: Conducting a research interview. J. Med. Imaging Radiat. Sci. **43**, 66–76 (2012). https://doi.org/10.1016/j.jmir.2011.12.002

28. Mikolov, T., Sutskever, I., Chen, K., Corrado, G.S., Dean, J.: Distributed representations of words and phrases and their compositionality. In: Burges, C.J.C., Bottou, L., Welling, M., Ghahramani, Z., Weinberger, K.Q. (eds.) Advances in Neural Information Processing Systems 26, pp. 3111–3119. Curran Associates, Inc. (2013)

29. Amershi, S., et al.: Guidelines for human-AI interaction. In: Proceedings of the 2019 CHI Conference on Human Factors in Computing Systems, pp. 1–13 (2019)

30. Kocielnik, R., Amershi, S., Bennett, P.N.: Will you accept an imperfect AI? Exploring designs for adjusting end-user expectations of AI systems. In: Proceedings of the 2019 CHI Conference on Human Factors in Computing Systems, pp. 1–14 (2019)

31. Jansen, B., Salminen, J., Jung, S., Guan, K.: Data-Driven Personas. Morgan & Claypool Publishers (2021)

ML Classification of Car Parking with Implicit Interaction on the Driver's Smartphone

Enrico Bassetti, Alessio Luciani, and Emanuele Panizzi$^{(\boxtimes)}$

Department of Computer Science, Sapienza University of Rome, Rome, Italy
{bassetti,panizzi}@di.uniroma1.it, luciani.1797637@studenti.uniroma1.it

Abstract. On-street parking places parallel to the curb have variable lengths, depending on the size of the car that emptied the place. Thus, a Smart Parking system should publish such places only to drivers whose car is shorter than the available parking length. We developed a crowd-sourced Smart Parking app, based on implicit interaction, intending to publish an available parking spot only to drivers whose car can fit the existing place. This app detects the type of parking (parallel vs angle or perpendicular) using machine learning on the driver's smartphone and considers the length of the cars involved.

Keywords: Smartphone · Parking · Sensing · Implicit interaction · Machine learning · Curb · Parallel · Angle parking · Smart city · Context aware

1 Introduction

Finding an on-street parking place is a problem, especially in big cities. Cars cruising for parking constitute 30% of urban traffic [7] and contribute significantly to air pollution. The average search time for parking is 8 min [10], which causes driver frustration.

Smart Parking solutions try to overcome this problem by providing the driver with information about the available parking spots' exact location. Unfortunately, this approach is sensitive to the quality of the information provided, and users may abandon the Smart Parking system if the information is incorrect.

In this work, we focus on one possible misinformation, i.e. the on the size of the parking place. In particular, we refer to parking places that are not delimited in length by marks on the ground, like the on-street parking places marked by a continuous line parallel to the curb (Fig. 1 top). These places have variable length, as it depends on the length of the car parked there before. For this reason, before providing a driver with the information of an available place, it should be evaluated if the place is suitable for the driver's car, as it will not host a car longer than the car which made the parking available.

© IFIP International Federation for Information Processing 2021
Published by Springer Nature Switzerland AG 2021
C. Ardito et al. (Eds.): INTERACT 2021, LNCS 12934, pp. 291–299, 2021.
https://doi.org/10.1007/978-3-030-85613-7_21

Fig. 1. Parking place types: parallel (top), angle (bottom left), perpendicular (bottom right)

If the Smart Parking system provides a driver with the wrong parking spot information, the driver will discover it only by driving to that place. This mistake prolongs cruising and reduces the Smart Parking system's perceived reliability, wasting the effort made. The more frequently these mistakes happen, the less the service is attractive and valuable, leading to user abandonment.

We refer to the crowd-sourced type of Smart Parking systems [4]. Data about the available parking spaces are collected on the drivers' smartphones, possibly using the smartphone's sensors, without any local physical infrastructures.

We approach evaluating the suitability of an on-street parking place for a given car by collecting and processing all the necessary data on the drivers' smartphones and then providing the Smart Parking server with more accurate information about available parking spaces to be published.

In the following sections, after reporting about related work, we describe the mobile app that we developed to collect and process the relevant information to perform available parking evaluation: we describe the driver's interaction with the app, which is both explicit and implicit; we then describe the app architecture and the smartphone sensors we used to allow for implicit interaction; we describe the machine learning model we trained for the evaluation of the parking type and, finally, we report on the results of a test we ran on 540 parking manoeuvres. We conclude with known limitations and ongoing and future work.

2   Related Work

Among the different Smart Parking solutions [4], we focus on crowdsourced Smart Parking systems. We tackled parking information quality and particularly the parking size evaluation in on-street parallel car parks. We did not find papers about this specific problem in the literature. Nevertheless, many inspiring works are available about crowdsourcing for Smart Parking systems and the use of a smartphone for this purpose.

Smartphone sensors have proved quite useful for solving car parking-related issues. Nandugudi et al. use crowdsourced park-unpark events from smartphone sensors to create an estimation of park availability [6]. Soubam et al. [11] use a hybrid approach (accelerometer + WiFi) to spot parking events. Cervantes et al. [3] and Castignani et al. [2] both address the car maneuvering detection using smartphone accelerometer, though not related to parking. Kim et al. [5] exploit IoT sensors, such as wireless beacons and NFC readers, in combination with mobile applications. Wahlström et al. leverage accelerometer and gyroscope samplings to cluster the possible positions of the smartphone in the vehicle [12]. Although we draw from these papers the idea of classifying car motion and smartphone position through smartphone sensors, we exploit sensor data using implicit interaction to address a problem not previously encountered in the literature. Furthermore, we experiment with a different ML approach (i.e. supervised learning).

3   User Interaction

We developed a mobile app to collect relevant data about cars and car parks. We also developed a Smart Parking service to which the app connects to get information about available car parks and to provide information when the driver leaves a parking place.

The driver can add their car to the app, providing some primary data, including car length. Once added, a car is associated with the car Bluetooth (generally available in the car radio or In-Vehicle Information System – IVIS).

The app tracks Bluetooth connections and disconnections to the IVIS when the driver enters and exits the car. Each disconnection is considered a parking operation, and the app records the smartphone GPS position. Each connection to the IVIS is, on the other hand, tracked as an unparking operation, and the app reports to the Smart Parking service an available parking place at the previously recorded location. This interaction is implicit, and in fact, it does not require user intervention, avoiding user fatigue and enhancing reliability on the information gathering. We monitor GPS speed after connection to confirm the unparking event. We call the *giver* a driver who unparked their car and is leaving a place.

The other main interaction in our app is explicit and corresponds to searching for an available parking place. We call the *taker* a driver who is looking for parking. The Smart Parking service provides only available places suitable for the taker's car size, if any. To do this, the giver and taker apps send four pieces of information to the Smart Parking server:

1. giver's GPS position
2. giver's car length
3. giver's parking type (see below)
4. taker's car length

In fact, as described, the GPS location alone is not sufficient for the reporting of an available parking place. The place's size determines the possibility of parking the car: most of the time, the place width is large enough for any car model, while the place length may vary if strips do not delimit it. Generally, strips delimit the length and width of angle and perpendicular parking places (Fig. 1, bottom-left and bottom-right). On the other hand, parallel places are often delimited only in width, using a stripe parallel to the curb.

Thus, the type of parking of the giver (*parallel* vs *angle* or *perpendicular* [13]) is essential information (along with the length of both cars) to decide if the taker's car can be parked in the place just made available by the giver. Thus, the Smart Parking service will provide a giver's availability information only to takers whose car fits the place size[1].

The app detects the parking type automatically when the driver parks the car through a machine learning algorithm running on the mobile phone. Here the interaction is again implicit. To train the supervised machine learning model, we recorded the smartphone sensors data during parking, and then we asked the driver to label their parking. We used a simple explicit interaction after parking: an actionable notification appears on the driver's smartphone a few seconds after Bluetooth disconnection, asking to select one of the three types of parking.

4   Architecture and ML Model

To classify the parking in the three categories (angle, parallel, and perpendicular) using implicit interaction, we first trained a machine learning model using data collected from the smartphone sensors. After that, we deployed the ML model in the mobile app to run it every time the user parks their car.

Three drivers collaborated with us in collecting data for the model training, exploiting the implicit interaction that we designed. The app recorded the sensor data about their car parking automatically. They only had to report the type of parking by selecting an answer to the automatic notification they received after each parking. The dataset thus collected is composed of 540 parking samples that we doubled by mirroring the manoeuvres.

The app collects smartphone sensor data from the beginning to the end of the trip, using the framework in [8], and store them in a circular buffer that contains 2048 samples. The app collects samples at a rate 10 Hz, i.e. every 100 ms. At parking time, the buffer contains the last 204 s of trip data.

The data collected in the samples are the timestamp, the acceleration on the X, Y, and Z axes, the rotation rate on the three axes, the car speed, and the heading, i.e. the angle that the device forms with the geographical north.

The smartphone we used is an iPhone XS running iOS 13.

The collected samples are processed to clean up sensor signals from noise and spikes and remove any part of the trip after the parking manoeuvre. After normalization, we generated new samples by mirroring the collected parking manoeuvres longitudinally to obtain 540×2 samples to feed the ML model.

---

[1] We do not address the parking space reservation problem, which is ongoing work.

4.1   Trimming

First, we use gyroscope samples to detect if the smartphone is in an idle position in the car or is taken in the user's hands [12]. We observed that the smartphone's rotation rate is relatively stable when positioned in the car (it only undergoes some small fluctuations). However, it reaches high peaks when the smartphone is manually moved (for example, when the driver gets off the car). After doing some tests, we established a threshold of 85°/s, and we remove the final samples of all sensors from the first gyroscope peak to the end of the sample set.

Secondly, we trim the initial interval and leave only the last 30 s of data. We determined it as the average time for parking by visually analysing a subset of the parking samples that we collected.

4.2   Heading Normalization

The heading is the first feature for the ML model (Fig. 2).

All the heading values undergo a normalization process to have the last sample always oriented at 180°. We do this because we want to train the model about manoeuvres independently from the actual car orientation. Also, heading values are allowed to go over degree bounds (0° and 360°) to indicate complete rotations. The final result is a signal as shown in Fig. 3.

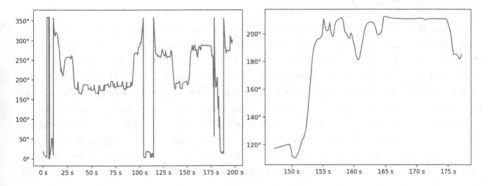

Fig. 2. Raw heading samples   **Fig. 3.** Final heading signal

Once finished with the heading normalization, we compute a new feature column as the difference between the current heading value and the previous one for every sample. This data is helpful since it resembles the angular velocity on the horizontal plane.

4.3   Acceleration and Rotation Rate

The mobile framework that we use automatically removes the gravity component from the accelerometer data and the gyroscope data's bias. However, generally, the smartphone's axes are not aligned with the car's ones. So we shift and rotate acceleration and rotation rate data in order to match the least-squares plane [9] with the horizontal plane (Fig. 4). Thus, obtained values are similar to what we could collect if the smartphone were positioned horizontally in the car.

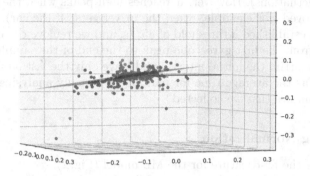

Fig. 4. 3D distribution of acceleration points. The least squares plane is drawn in blue (side view) - values are in m/s^2 (Color figure online)

4.4   Model Creation

The classifier we use is the Create ML "Tabular" classifier [1], based on tree ensemble techniques, which does not need an extensive data set size. We chose it as we have not collected a sufficient number of parking samples yet; thus, we decided to opt for shallow learning. As an ensemble method, it provides good generalization capabilities even with little data. Due to the lack of data, we could not sufficiently train a more sequence-aware model (e.g. an RNN). Therefore, we handcrafted some features that the tree ensemble could interpret as time-related. To do this, we split the total sampling time frame into five contiguous intervals and computed the difference of the heading value between the extremes of those five intervals. This way, those five features formed a sort of temporal sequence of events. We compute other features on the entire time frame (e.g. the acceleration mean). The final feature vector is eventually ready to be input into the classifier (Fig. 5).

5   Results and Limitations

We trained two versions of the model. In the first version, we defined the three classes described previously. The model needs to distinguish angle and perpendicular parking motions, although it is not relevant for our case. Results are encouraging, although there is confusion between parallel and angle classes (Fig. 7. However, this model's overall accuracy is 71.42% over three classes (see Table 1).

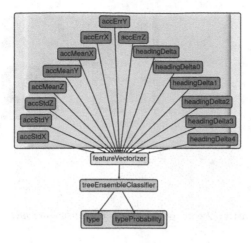

Fig. 5. Tree ensemble classifier model - generated by `coremltools` library by Apple[TM]

Table 1. Results obtained with CreateML Tabular classifier (tree ensemble). The dataset was enhanced using generated data mirroring the samples

Input		Result - accuracy	
Samples	Classes	Training	Validation
540 * 2	Angle parallel	93.30%	85.99%
540 * 2	Angle parallel perpendicular	92.41%	71.42%

The second version simplifies the first one: we group angle and perpendicular parking samples since they make little difference in our case. The latter model's overall accuracy is higher since it is a binary classification, and it reaches 85.99% with significantly reduced confusion between classes (Fig. 6).

The described approach comes with an obvious limitation since it only relies on data from the smartphone's sensors. The aid of external sensors (e.g. car and street-based sensors) would help reach a better accuracy. Additionally, the collected data is manually labelled, and this can have lead to accuracy problems.

For instance, our users may have sometimes postponed labelling to a later moment, then forgetting the type of manoeuvre they did. Another possible error is that they may have had difficulties distinguishing a perpendicular and an angle parking. Last but not least, they may have tapped the wrong button inadvertently in the actionable notification. Therefore the training set can contain some wrongly labelled samples.

In case the user moves the smartphone during the parking manoeuvre, the data collection will be invalidated, as it would have a low probability of belonging to be classified correctly. During training, we assumed that drivers did not move the smartphone during parking, as we instructed them so.

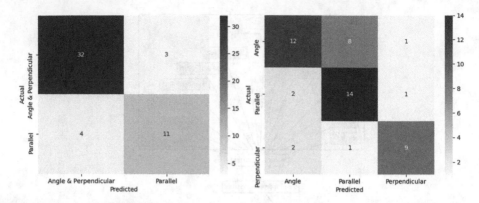

Fig. 6. Confusion matrix (2 categories)　**Fig. 7.** Confusion matrix (3 categories)

6　Conclusions and Ongoing Work

Our application proved very effective in collecting parking data on the driver's smartphone and can detect parallel vs angle or perpendicular parking type, with an acceptable accuracy of 86%. We obtained this binary classification grouping angle and perpendicular samples in a single class. For our use case of crowd-sourced information for Smart Parking systems, it is unnecessary to distinguish between these two parking types. However complete classification in the three parking types yielded an accuracy value of 71.

Our app's interface successfully exploits implicit interaction to detect parking manoeuvres and unparking actions without the user's need to open the app and interact with it explicitly. Users can perform other tasks in an explicit-interaction style, like adding a car, looking for any available parking spaces, and labelling the parking type for our machine learning model training.

Currently, our collected dataset of parking manoeuvres does not allow us to train a model with our desired accuracy (95% or greater, as opposed to the current 71%–86% for the validation and testing sets). We plan to add more contributors to the data collection process and start filling the dataset at a higher rate. We will then test other neural network architectures designed for motion activity data that could handle time-series samples and, therefore, automatically extract information from the sequence of timestamp-indexed feature vectors (e.g. a recurrent unit).

Acknowledgements. This work was partially supported by the MIUR grant "Dipartimenti di eccellenza 2018–2022" and by the grant "Progetti di Ateneo 2019" of Sapienza University.

References

1. Apple: Create ML tabular classifier. https://developer.apple.com/documentation/createml/mlclassifier
2. Castignani, G., Derrmann, T., Frank, R., Engel, T.: Smartphone-based adaptive driving maneuver detection: a large-scale evaluation study. IEEE Trans. Intell. Transp. Syst. **18**(9), 2330–2339 (2017)
3. Cervantes-Villanueva, J., Carrillo-Zapata, D., Terroso-Saenz, F., Valdes-Vela, M., Skarmeta, A.F.: Vehicle maneuver detection with accelerometer-based classification. Sensors **16**(10), 1618 (2016)
4. Diaz Ogás, M.G., Fabregat, R., Aciar, S.: Survey of smart parking systems. Appl. Sci. **10**(11) (2020). https://doi.org/10.3390/app10113872. https://www.mdpi.com/2076-3417/10/11/3872
5. Kim, D., Park, S., Lee, S., Roh, B.: In: IoT platform based smart parking navigation system with shortest route and anti-collision. In: 2018 18th International Symposium on Communications and Information Technologies (ISCIT), pp. 433–437. IEEE (2018)
6. Nandugudi, A., Ki, T., Nuessle, C., Challen, G.: PocketParker: pocketsourcing parking lot availability. In: Proceedings of the 2014 ACM International Joint Conference on Pervasive and Ubiquitous Computing, UbiComp 2014, pp. 963–973. Association for Computing Machinery, New York (2014). https://doi.org/10.1145/2632048.2632098
7. Nawaz, S., Efstratiou, C., Mascolo, C.: Parksense: a smartphone based sensing system for on-street parking. In: Proceedings of the 19th Annual International Conference on Mobile Computing & Networking, MobiCom 2013, pp. 75–86. Association for Computing Machinery, New York (2013). https://doi.org/10.1145/2500423.2500438
8. Panizzi, E., Calvitti, D.: A framework to enhance the user experience of car mobile applications. In: Proceedings of the 20th International Conference on Human-Computer Interaction with Mobile Devices and Services Adjunct, MobileHCI 2018, pp. 245–252. Association for Computing Machinery, New York (2018). https://doi.org/10.1145/3236112.3236146
9. Romero, L., Garcia, M., Suárez, C.: A tutorial on the total least squares method for fitting a straight line and a plane. Rev. Cien. Ingeniería Inst. Tecnol. Superior Coatzacoalcos **1**, 167–173 (2014)
10. Shoup, D.: Cruising for parking. Access Mag. **1**(30), 16–23 (2007)
11. Soubam, S., Banerjee, D., Naik, V., Chakraborty, D.: Bluepark: tracking parking and un-parking events in indoor garages . In: Proceedings of the 17th International Conference on Distributed Computing and Networking, ICDCN 2016. Association for Computing Machinery, New York (2016). https://doi.org/10.1145/2833312.2833458
12. Wahlström, J., Skog, I., Händel, P., Bradley, B., Madden, S., Balakrishnan, H.: Smartphone placement within vehicles. IEEE Trans. Intell. Transp. Syst. **21**(2), 669–679 (2020)
13. Yousif, S., Purnawan, S.: On-street parking: effects on traffic congestion. Traffic Eng. + Control **40**(9), 424–7 (1999)

ObjectivAIze: Measuring Performance and Biases in Augmented Business Decision Systems

Thomas Baudel[1]([✉])[iD], Manon Verbockhaven[1,2], Victoire Cousergue[1,3,4], Guillaume Roy[1,5], and Rida Laarach[1,6]

[1] France Lab, IBM, Orsay, France
baudelth@fr.ibm.com
[2] ENSAE, Palaiseau, France
[3] Université Paris-Dauphine, Paris, France
[4] Mines ParisTech, Paris, France
[5] ENSAI, Rennes, France
[6] Telecom ParisTech, Palaiseau, France

Abstract. Business process management organizes flows of information and decisions in large organizations. These systems now integrate algorithmic decision aids leveraging machine learning: each time a stakeholder needs to make a decision, such as a purchase, a quote, or hiring someone, the software leverages the inputs and outcomes of similar past decisions to provide guidance, as a recommendation. If the confidence is high, the process may be automated. Otherwise, it may still help provide consistency in the decisions. Yet, we may question how these aids affect task performance. Can we measure an improvement? Can hidden biases influence decision makers negatively? What is the impact of various presentation options? To address those issues, we propose metrics of performance, automation bias and resistance. We validated those measures with an online study. Our aim is to instrument those systems to secure their benefits. In a first experiment, we study effective collaboration. Faced with a decision, subjects alone have a success rate of 72%; Aided by a recommender that has a 75% success rate, their success rate reaches 76%. The human-system collaboration had thus a greater success rate than each taken alone. However, we noted a complacency/authority bias that degraded the quality of decisions by 5% when the recommender was wrong. This suggests that any lingering algorithmic bias may be amplified by decision aids. In a second experiment, we evaluated the effectiveness of 5 presentation variants in reducing complacency bias. We found that optional presentation increases subjects' resistance to wrong recommendations. We intend to leverage these findings to guide the design of human-algorithm collaboration in financial compliance alert filtering.

Keywords: Business decision systems · Decision theory · Cognitive biases

Electronic supplementary material The online version of this chapter (https://doi.org/10.1007/978-3-030-85613-7_22) contains supplementary material, which is available to authorized users.

1 Introduction

For the past 20 years, Business Process Management (BPM) [29, 51] has streamlined processes and operational decision-making in large enterprises, transforming work organization. BPM organizes information flows, from input events such as a purchase order or a hiring request, through chains of stakeholders involved in various parts of the process, to reach some outcome. In a nutshell, a BPM system allows programming an enterprise like one would a robot.

Because all inputs and operational decisions are stored, recent improvements involve applying machine learning techniques on past inputs and outcomes, to automate decision processes or to assist decision makers by providing suggestions on the likely outcome of each decision, assuming similar causes produce similar effects [37, 49]. This technology ought to be largely beneficial, reinforcing the consistency of decisions and improving productivity, enabling "extended cognition", or "active externalism" as described by Chalmers [14], or as envisioned as "Human-Centered AI" by Schneiderman [50]. Now, augmenting decision processes is not without risks. There is a large institutional community focusing on the area of AI Ethics, that stresses the requirements of fairness, transparency, explainability, accountability [28]... In particular, the prevention of algorithmic biases is a major concern [40], which needs to be addressed by technology [6], best practices [3] and regulations [35]. There is less institutional visibility on the changes to work practices and human decision-making these tools introduce. Cognitive biases induced by decision support systems are largely studied, identifying patterns such as automation and complacency biases [5] or, on the contrary, algorithm aversion [9] and decision fatigue [4, 27] when higher productivity is expected. There is less work directly applicable to the context of business decision-making, in our present situation, where decision aids can be provided as a generic, system-level feature, regardless of their relevance for the task being performed by the human agent.

To ensure this type of assistance can be safely and profitably incorporated in business decision support systems, we first narrow down the type of tasks we are interested in augmenting, and the type of aids we wish to evaluate. Then, we review the literature to guide our designs. We present a performance and cognitive biases evaluation model, as a set of metrics that can be evaluated empirically for various kinds of decision aids and tasks. We conduct a study to evaluate the ability of our model to measure performance and biases. Finally, we propose a methodology to incorporate bias measurement and compensation in business decision support systems, to ensure they provide their expected benefits with minimal inconvenience.

2 Augmented Business Decision Making

A business process is modeled in a flowchart. In this model, decision steps take as input some information, leverage external information, such as regulations or resource constraints, presumably only known to the decision maker, to advance the process through a predetermined set of possible outcomes. The type of decision tasks we investigate are constrained, leave little room for creativity and presumably rely on a combination of explicit rules and heuristics.

When the decision logic can be formally expressed, decisions can be automated deterministically, via deduction [10]. When sufficiently robust heuristics are available, scoring methods or more sophisticated algorithms may automate the decision via induction, with an escalation process to handle exceptions. Finally, many operational business decisions involve complex tradeoffs, which, we assume, involve so many factors that automation is for now out of question. In these cases, a decision aid fed with previous decisions and possibly external data sources, such as revenue targets for the team and staffing statistics, may provide information that can be useful, for instance to a manager who considers granting a hiring request.

More formally, we are interested in measuring, and possibly improve, the effects decision aids may have in the following circumstances:

- Some information regarding a case is available and is assumed to be reliable.
- A choice, among a predefined set of alternatives, needs to be made.
- The choice is partly constrained by explicit constraints (regulations, resource limitations…)
- Some contextual information, exact or probabilistic, explicit or intuitive, is available to the decision maker (e.g. guidelines & priorities regarding the business context). Those allow the decision maker to form an *internal decision model,* which is a non-explicited procedure a priori followed consistently by the decision maker.
- Other information is known only by the system, such as a history of cases.
- There is a best possible choice, but it may not be knowable in advance, if ever, for a given case.
- It is possible to provide, a posteriori, exact or approximate measures of which choices tend to perform better for which types of cases, for instance as an actuarial report. These measures can be used to create a *computable decision model.*

Numerous business situations implemented with BPM match this description, ranging from the mundane, such as a purchase decision, to more serious decisions such as hiring someone, granting a loan or selecting the winner of a bid, finally to morally heavy situations like deciding of a prison sentence [47]. Still, much decision-making activity, such as medical diagnostic or investment decisions, allow more creativity in choice-making and falls outside the scope of our work. What matters in our circumstances is that no algorithm may deliver a choice with 100% accuracy. An algorithm may be better than humans in general, but there is no substitute for human judgment and liability, when it is not possible, even a posteriori, to know if a particular decision was the right one.

A variety of decision aids can be automatically provided to users in this context, which we categorize, inspired from Miller's description of explanations [39]:

- Attributes deemed most important in the decision (inputs)
- Scoring (computed by deterministic rules, deduction)
- Comparable cases and their outcomes (nearest neighbors, induction)
- Decision tree branch and weights (probabilistic deduction).
- Counterfactuals (abduction).

While there may be more types of decision aids, these cover the use cases we have reviewed in the literature that can be implemented generically, without specific tuning for the decision task, for instance creating a custom visualization. Finally, the presentation of these decision aids may influence their usage. They may be provided as plain recommendations, inciting the user to follow them, or available only on request, after a delay, or even after the decision has been made, as a verification step.

Our goal is to assess if decision aids improve the decision-making process, moving it towards a definition of rational decision-making suitable to our context. For now, we focus on performance metrics:

- Can we provide a methodology to measure decision-making performance in our contexts of use?
- Can the combination of human and algorithmic aids outperform both the human and the algorithm taken alone? How can we reach this stage of human-machine "collaboration"?
- Machine learning biases are a major concern. Even if this human-machine collaboration is an improvement, it seems inevitable that underlying algorithmic biases may taint decisions. Various cognitive biases may interfere. Can we identify and separate those to design correction strategies targeted at each of them?

To address those questions, we propose a model, as a set of metrics, to define performance, various biases and resistance, and carry an experimental study on a simple decision task meeting our requirements to assess the capacity of the model to discriminate various presentations modes. The aim is to generalize this study in our contexts and provide continuous monitoring of decision tasks and decision aids. But before, we must acknowledge that there is a large body of literature addressing similar issues, which has guided our research.

3 Related Work

3.1 Decision Theory

Understanding decision-making is a full research area in psychology. For a start, there are several positions regarding the notion of "correct" decision. For Rational Decision Theory, a rational choice maximizes an expected utility function [26, p. 237]. Non rational theories [23] consider effects such as risk aversion or naturalistic viewpoints. Ultimately, these approaches can be reconciled when assumptions are clearly stated [30]. We take mostly a Rational Decision Theory standpoint: simple hypotheses are acceptable in our context. We also assume good will: the decision maker and the decision stakeholders (the company) share the same utility. Under stress, pressure, or poor motivation, we may find a divergence, which leads to a complacency bias or decision fatigue [4]. Within decision theory, our work falls into the area of judge-advisor systems [8]. Although much of the literature in this area is focused on human advisors, we retain the importance of advice presentation on the decision outcomes [36].

A major lesson of Decision Theory is that performance varies between individuals: experts and novices approach problems differently, and personality traits can have a strong influence [46]. Classical cognitive biases such as the order effect can be significant [45]. Finally, the availability of more information does not necessarily lead to better decision-making [17]. For fast and frugal or other recent approaches [23, 25], human decision making does not rely so much on *risk* - when the decision rules and probabilities of outcomes are well modeled - than on *uncertainty* - where the indecisiveness is not just a consequence of unknowns quantities, but also of unknows on the suitability of the decision process itself -. Hence, making a decision heuristically, based on limited information, may yield better results than paying close attention to possibly irrelevant details. Burton [9] convincingly defends that, by design, algorithmic decision aids operate under models of *risk*, while humans need to consider the *uncertainties* of a situation. Consciously leveraging this difference may provide the means to make the best of human and algorithm complementarity.

3.2 Decision Support Systems

Algorithmic decision aids have existed for a long time, in slightly different contexts.

Semi-automation/Process Control: Our early focus was on measuring, and possibly reducing, automation bias, which we felt should occur in our context. A large portion of the literature on these biases focuses on tasks that involve less dedicated attention and analysis than business decisions. For instance, [42] finds attentional deficits at the onset of complacency biases. [5] identify this bias in process control tasks that involve verification rather than true decision making. Automation bias is clearly related to complacency bias. It can also result from attention deficits, which are even more prevalent in assisted driving tasks [21]. [2] finds a conformity bias: use by others increases trust in an algorithm. Finally, [24, 53] and [1] describe a major cause of biases: when the algorithm outperforms the human most of the time, motivation necessarily dwindles. Conversely, [41] provides some evidence that decision aids lose all usefulness when they provide less than 70% accuracy, which indicates that providing those in generic business processes requires some prior assessment of relevance.

Recommender Systems are algorithmic decision aids, but the tasks they support does not meet our focus: they don't help making a choice among predetermined outcomes, and decision quality is elusive: we often assimilate decision performance with user satisfaction [32]. Several types of cognitive biases can interfere, such as exposure bias [31]. Interestingly, recent literature in decision theory for recommender systems focuses on algorithm aversion, the opposite of automation biases: subjects avoid following recommendations, even when the algorithms perform better than humans [9]. The literature stresses the need to provide explanations [44, 52], especially for expert users [33]. We also notice that trust in the system degrades when bad recommendations occur [43], or when the task is highly subjective [13]. These findings should apply to our context of use.

Visual Analytics for decision making is an entire class of algorithmic decision aids. Visualization tools are geared towards exploratory analysis, which involves open decisions [20], thus is not in our focus. Still, work on identifying and reducing cognitive biases, such as the attraction effect [18] is relevant. More significant, the identification of the numerous biases [19] that may be found in visual decision aids provides a useful guiding framework.

3.3 Impact of Algorithmic Decision Aids on Work Practices, and Ethical Considerations

Medical decision support systems include decision aids and are extensively studied. Once again, they do not enter our scope, as the type of decision aids they provide are highly customized for specific purposes, and a medical decision can hardly qualify as a choice among predetermined possible outcomes. They support critical decisions, which explains why decision aids may be met with suspicion and some level of algorithm aversion [11]. Even in successful propositions [12], suspicion may not arise from the tool itself, but from the way it transforms work practices, perhaps for the better, but in directions which open avenues for high uncertainty [15]. At this point, addressing both algorithmic and cognitive biases in decision aids reaches beyond the scientific undertaking, into the realm of professional ethics. Determining the role of algorithmic decision aids requires a rigorous assessment of their power and their limitations in benefiting society.

From Scientific to Ethical Considerations. Health professions are not the only industry questioning the impact of decision aids on work practices. Morris [48] devotes a whole chapter on cognitive biases in decision-making for accounting, and how overcoming those biases is an ethical issue. Legal and administrative professions raise similar concerns [16], including how proper explanations improve the perception of legal decisions [7]. Decision automation also produces surprising adaptive behaviors to circumvent the loss of control associated with algorithm-driven activities. For instance, [38] shows that human players learn to control computer players in computer games. Kyung Lee [34] describes how Uber drivers use collaboration to understand and regain some level of control over the dispatch algorithms. One of the possible shortcomings of algorithm-driven decision making (and decision aids) is the potential to induce unwanted behaviors by reverse engineering the decision aids' logic: the decision maker becomes 'controlled' by the subjects impacted by those decisions.

To address these concerns, expert groups and regulatory bodies provide guidelines [3, 28] to design trustworthy decision support systems. *But in our context, we need more than design guidelines and regulations. We need metrics,* and possibly a partially automated method to ensure those metrics stay within safe boundaries in the variety of contexts were algorithmic decision aids will be generically embedded in business decision support systems. As a first step towards this ambitious goal, we propose some metrics applicable to business contexts, and we have conducted an empirical study on a simple task to assess their discriminatory power, in the hope of generalizing them to real-world tasks.

4 A Performance Model for Decision-Making

In machine learning, performance is most often synthesized by the F_β score, where the β term translates the cost differences between false positives and false negatives, and

F is the harmonic mean of the precision and recall of the classifier. Our target users, actuaries, financial analysts, budget planners and managers are more accustomed to a simple cost model, that includes cost of processing, and follows an equation similar to (for a binary decision):

$$P = (1 - E_n) G_n + (1 - E_p) G_p - C_p E_p - C_n E_n - C_t$$

Given a cost matrix:

C_p: *Cost of misclassification of a positive*
C_n: *Cost of misclassification of a negative*
G_p: *Positive identification gain*
G_n: Correct n*egative identification* gain
C_t: *Average cost of treatment* (typically human time and amortized time to develop the decision aid solution)
And some error terms:
E_n, E_p: *estimated error rate in the proposed configuration*

In a given situation, the equation should be weighted by the expected occurrence ratio of positives and negatives, or other priorities, such as keeping decisions homogenous rather than maximizing value. In our HCI context, the only parameters we may control are the error rates, and thus, we will assimilate performance with a strict reduction in the error rates, while neglecting, for now, C_t.

4.1 Decision Aid Effectiveness and Collaboration

Because we are interested in measuring the performance of decision aids, we define first a measure of human-algorithm collaboration. This is quantified as the ratio:

M_1 = performance with a decision aid/max (performance without a decision aid, performance of the classifier).

This ratio depends on a lot of factors:

- If a classifier clearly outperforms humans, there is little chance for this ratio to be >1, full decision automation is most likely the best solution.
- Conversely, a classifier will likely be useless when its accuracy is <70% [41].
- If the classifier and the humans tend to make the same type of mistakes, typically because they leverage the same information, then there is no reason for M_1 to be above 1.
- Finally, when the *internal decision model* (of the user) and *the computable decision model* (algorithm) leverage different sources of information, or prioritize the components of expected utility differently, we may find a measure above 1, demonstrating a collaboration effect.

4.2 Automation Bias and Resistance

Collaboration is easy to assess, explain, and it provides a nice metric to guide augmented Business Decision system design. It tells however little about how decision aids influence decision-making. We need to consider how a wrong recommendation influences the subject to let them lose their rationality, i.e. Automation bias, which can be one of two sub-categories:

- Authority bias: the subject follows (wrongly) the algorithm instead of their own reasoning because they perceive themselves as less accurate
- Complacency bias: the subject follows (wrongly) the algorithm out of a lack of motivation.

While we cannot distinguish the reason for the presence of *an automation bias*, we may still define it as *the probability that a subject who sees a wrong recommendation will make a non-rational decision, considering he would have made a rational decision had he not seen this recommendation.* We can define a dual measure of *resistance* as *the probability that the subject makes a rational decision when given a bad recommendation, knowing that if the recommendation had been correct, he would have made a rational choice.*

More rigorously, we can define a linear panel model [22]. Subjects are indexed by i, α_i corresponds to individual effects, while decision number are indexed by t. $Y'_{i,t} = 1_{\{response\ of (I,t)\ is\ rational\}}$. We compare the control group with the treatment group that received wrong recommendations: $X_{i,t} = (1, 1_{\{false\ recommendation\}})^T$. The linear panel model $Y_{i,t}$ is defined as:

$$Y_{i,t} = 1_{\{X_{i,t}^T \beta + \alpha_i + \epsilon_{i,t} > 0\}}$$
$$E[Y_{i,t}|X_{i,t}, \alpha_i] = X_{i,t}^T \beta + \alpha_i$$
$$\forall_i \in \{1, \ldots, n\}, t \in \{1, \ldots, m\}$$

With this panel model, automation bias is defined as:

$$B(\alpha_i) = P(\{Y_{i,t} = 0 | X_{i,t} = (1, 1)^T, \alpha_i\} | \{Y_{i,t} = 1 | X_{i,t} = (1, 0)^T, \alpha_i\})$$

While resistance is defined as:

$$C(\alpha_i) = P(\{Y_{i,t} = 1 | X_{i,t} = (1, 1)^T\} | \{Y_{i,t} = 1 | X_{i,t} = (1, 0)^T\})$$

Estimating those probabilities can be performed with pooled ordinary least squares (pooledOLS) when performing a between-groups study (individuals are randomly assigned to the control and treatment groups and trials are randomly distributed). Other biases and effects, such as decision fatigue, order effects, timing effects, expertise effect, can be measured with the same econometric tool, provided our experiments record the appropriate information. To the reader unaccustomed to econometric tools: in a trivial panel, B is simply the extra error rate introduced by false recommendations, while C is the error rate when bad recommendations are given over the error rate when no recommendation are provided.

The goal of our research is to embed this evaluation model in various business decision systems, to automatically assess the proper decision aids to provide users, on a case by case basis.

5 Study

Before we may consider embedding those metrics in an augmented BPM system, we need to assess their effectiveness and discriminatory power. To this effect, we have conducted an online study based on a real use case but gamified so as to attract a large and varied population of subjects. Our study relies on a simple decision task: some information describing a case, a choice to be made among predefined possible outcomes, a right choice that depends on some rules and heuristics presumed known to the user (with an acceptable degree of variability). We test a single decision aid, presented as a recommendation from a generic classifier, under a variety of presentation modes. Sometimes the recommender will be misleading. We want to measure the success rate of the subjects, the impact of "wrong" recommendations as well as other measures such as decision fatigue or time taken to reach a decision. The deviation from rationality is attributed to an automation bias which denotes that the subject choses to follow the recommender over their own reasoning or intuition. Once we have obtained measures for a control condition (without decision aids), we provide decision aids with various presentations and observe the performance variations.

5.1 Choice of a Decision Task to Evaluate

The task inspiring our use case is a fraud detection task: in large financial institutions, tens of thousands alerts on transactions are raised everyday as potential frauds. Scores of analysts review each of these alerts for further inspection, spending an average of 16 s on each alert. ML tools are currently being studied to help with this task, but actual deployment raises reliability and regulatory issues. Proper performance measures are needed to determine the optimal combination of algorithm and humans to handle this alert filtering. Resorting to a real-world task to define and assess our metrics is difficult: it requires extensive domain knowledge, and access to many expert users. Early pilots aimed at presenting a simplified version of the real task with a tutorial failed to provide the type of engagement we thought was needed: subjects would fall for a type of "impostor's" syndrome, and blindly follow recommendations rather than give a chance to their own intuition and their own *internal decision model*. Others have followed this path [54] and failed to demonstrate nuanced results regarding the possibility of actual complementarity of human and algorithm decision processes.

Instead, we propose a simple decision task, for which a large population can create their own *internal decision model* easily, and will therefore have some autonomy in deciding whether to trust their judgment or the algorithmic recommendation. We leverage the well-known Titanic dataset[1], a database of passengers on the Titanic ship that sunk in 1912. This dataset is widely used to teach classification algorithms, because it exhibits some obvious patterns: most women in 1st and 2nd class survived, while most men in 3rd and 2nd class died, and other attributes such as number of relatives on board have a significant but lesser influence on the fate of each passenger. Simple machine learning classifiers, as well as humans after a short study of the data, exhibit success rates of 70–80% in guessing correctly if a passenger survived or not.

---

[1] https://www.kaggle.com/c/titanic.

The decision task consists in, upon being presented with a passenger's information, choosing if it is more likely to have survived or died. The task is repeated 20 times. To create an incentive, the presentation is somewhat gamified: subjects are enticed to maximize their score of correct guesses. Unbeknown to the subjects, the passengers presented all follow the expected distribution of survivors: a logistics regression classifier has >70% chance of correct classification on those passengers. Hence, we are asking the subject to make a rational choice - maximizing their probability of scoring high -, not a chance guess. This means reaching a perfect score is possible and even likely. Obtaining less than 50% (less than random chance) is a sure sign the subject is not properly committed to the task.

5.2 Stimulus Presentation

The experiment starts with a few demographic questions: age range, level of studies and type of studies (humanities, business, engineering/science or other). Then the subject is presented with the goal, as well as some interactive visualizations (treemap) that let them create their *internal decision model*. We do not present explicit decision rules so as not to taint subjects (Fig. 1). Next, we introduce the task, indicating that the recommender (in the experimental condition) has about 76% success rate of guessing correctly. Then, we present the stimuli (Fig. 2). In accordance to the stated success rate of the recommender, 5 times in the run of 20 trials, the recommendation is wrong: it says "survived" when the subject has died or vice-versa.

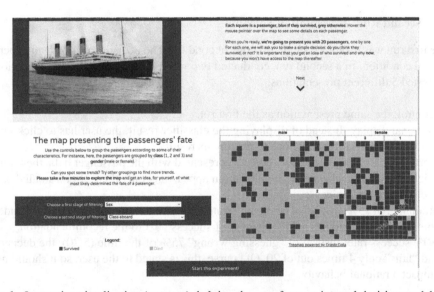

Fig. 1. Interactive visualization (treemap), helping the user form an internal decision model of who predominantly survived on the Titanic: Females from 1st and 2nd class, and who tended to die: males of 2nd and 3rd class.

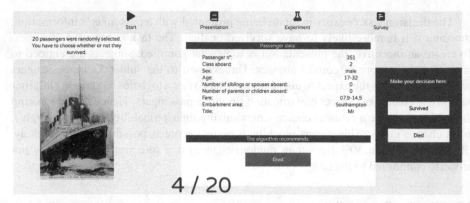

Fig. 2. Stimuli in the experimental condition: passenger data, followed by a recommendation (dies or survives), and, on the right, 2 buttons "survives" and "die". In the control condition, the recommendation panel is not shown.

Finally, after 20 trials, we ask a few experience questions: estimated success rate, did they choose intuitively or using self-made rules (or don't know), how many times they think the recommender provided the wrong answer, and a free comment box. Finally, we provide their score, and an invitation to an event that presented the early results. We set a cookie on their browser so they can't repeat the experiment for a few hours, so as not to taint our data collection with repeated trials by the same subject.

5.3   Second Run: Presentation Variants

The first run was meant to compare a control condition (no decision aid) with an experimental condition. In a second run, conducted two weeks later on a different population, we tested 5 different presentations:

- Control: the same presentation as the first run
- Optional display: Instead of displaying the classifier result, the user has to click on a button "show recommendation" to display its result.
- Forced acknowledgement: the subject is presented with the passenger data, then must click a button to make the recommendation appear, and only then, after a small delay, they enter their choice.
- Reminder of 75%: instead of being only stated at the beginning, the subject is reminded that the decision aid has a 75% chances of success next to the recommendation.
- 80% success rate: instead of "guessing wrong" 75% of the time (5/20), the decision aid "fails" only 4 times out of 20. Of course, this is stated to the user, so it should not impact a rational behavior.

Each subject was assigned to the same condition for all their trials (between-groups design). The goal of this run was to assess how different presentation strategies and recommender reliability affect the measures of performance, authority and resistance (defined below) in a significant way. This would be a strong indication that our metrics can be generalized to other context to drive the design of augmented business decision support systems.

5.4 Subjects Recruitment and Filtering

After a pre-run to calibrate expectations with ~20 subjects, we recruited subjects online. We did not want to use a survey service such as Amazon Mechanical Turk as we felt the subject's engagement would be distorted by a financial reward. Instead, we presented the experiment as a "fun and useful challenge". We announced the challenge on a variety of venues, starting in the company and student's forums and slowly extending our call to a wider audience, such as focused reddit and facebook groups, over a 2 months span.

75% of the incoming participants completed their trials run, which we take as indicative of the motivation we had managed to induce from our anonymous subjects (Fig. 3). A few participants (7) either failed to grasp the task or wanted to introduce noise and had less than 50% success (less than random chance), and we discarded them. In total, the first run had 231 participants and 155 usable trial runs, the second had 302 participants and 250 usable trial runs. The demographics reached is a mix of students and educated professionals, with more of an engineering/science background, roughly equally distributed in the 20–55 age range (Fig. 3).

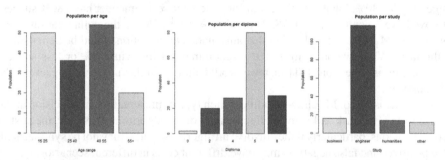

Fig. 3. Distribution of the subjects by age range, years of study after high school, and type of study (self-reported).

6 Results

6.1 Decision Aid Effectiveness

The first run shows a significant collaboration effect: subjects in the control condition obtain a score of 72.3%, while subject in the experimental condition (with decision aid) have a 76% success rate, giving $M_1 = 1.014$.

This collaboration effect is most useful to compare decision aids presentation synthetically. Our second run shows some modest but consistent variations:

While this improvement may appear modest, it is statistically significant, and it should be reminded that our experiment is tuned to obtain average scores in the realistic

Table 1. Decision aid effectiveness (first run result)

	Coefficient	95% confidence interval
Control condition (human alone)	0.7230	[0.6948, 0.7512]
With decision aid	0.7604	[0.7530, 0.7682]
"Algorithm alone"	0.75	–

Table 2. Measures of collaboration for various presentation modes of the recommender

	Coefficient	M_1
Control condition (human alone)	0.7230	1
With decision aid (new run)	0.7651	1.020
Optional display	0.7655	1.020
Forced acknowledgment	0.7660	1.021
Reminder of 75%	0.7619	1.016

range of 70%–80%. Finally, in the condition where the recommender has a 80% success rate, we have a coefficient of 0.7822 (p-value $< 10^{-4}$). Hence the collaboration effect disappears ($M_1 = 0.977$), indicating that automatic classification would be better suited to the task. While we have not tested a recommendaltion with 70% or less success rate, we can assume from [41] that we would find a similar negative impact on the collaboration.

These measures of M_1 allow deciding which type of presentation and decision aid to choose for a given task and a given effectiveness of the algorithm. However, the cost of wrong decisions, particularly if they involve an algorithmic bias, may not be symmetrical: false positives and false negatives may have different costs in different scenarios. Hence, the measure of biases is important to assess the full cost/benefit analysis of choosing appropriate decision aids.

6.2 Quantification of the Automation Bias

Coefficients β_1 and β_2 of the panel model are significantly nonzero at 5%. We can therefore reject the hypothesis that displaying a recommendation has no effect on the rationality of subjects. The model provides us with a metric that can be applied to various groups of the pool of subjects and compare their relative rationality ($B(\alpha_i)$, 0 = little influence) and resistance ($C(\alpha_i)$, 1 = maximal resistance). We can apply this model to study trends between different demographic classes recorded at the start of each run or presentation variants, between individuals, between trials (passengers) or any other available criteria. For instance, we display here the authority bias and resistance by type of studies (Table 3).

Table 3. Authority bias and resistance for different demographic groups.

Study type	Authority bias $B(\alpha_i)$	Resistance $C(\alpha_i)$	95% conf. $B(\alpha_i)$,	95% conf. $C(\alpha_i)$
Engineering/science	0.0666	0.8581	[0.0626, 0.0705]	[0.8152, 0.9011]
Business	0.0708	0.8423	[0.0663, 0.0753]	[0.7898, 0.8947]
Humanities	0.0684	0.8471	[0.0641, 0.0726]	[0.7970, 0.8971]
other	0.0737	0.8423	[0.0687, 0.0787]	[0.7900, 0.8946]

Age range	$B(\alpha_i)$	$C(\alpha_i)$	Level of study	$B(\alpha_i)$	$C(\alpha_i)$
15-25	0.0661	0.8606	2-	0.0688	0.8553
25-40	0.0687	0.8473	4	0.0681	0.8552
40-55	0.0663	0.8522	5	0.0657	0.8537
55+	0.0713	0.8548	8	0.0694	0.8545

While the bias and resistance differences are small, those measures can be useful to apply to varying levels of expertise on a real task. Data and detailed results are available in the supplementary material.

6.3 Comparison Between Presentation Variants

To choose the most effective presentation mode, depending if our goal is to maximize collaboration effectiveness, or to minimize authority bias while maintaining a high collaboration effectiveness, we compare the distributions of success under several conditions in Fig. 4.

In Fig. 4, we see success rate in the control condition as a horizontal line of blue marks, as a reference. Also for reference, the continuous horizontal line marks the "success rate" of the algorithm taken alone. The black marks indicate the success rate of the presentation mode. If the black marks are above both the blue marks (human alone) and the line ("computer alone"), then we can say the decision aid is effective in improving decision performance. This happens in all conditions but the last one, where the recommender has a much higher "success rate" of 80%. Based on this figure, the best performance is achieved with the "Forced acknowledgement" presentation mode (the subject must click to see the recommendation, then they can make their decision), although other presentations are quite close. This is the same information as Tables 1 and 2.

But more importantly, the red marks show the distribution of success with a wrong recommendation. We can see that in the "optional display" presentation mode, the authority bias is weaker. This suggests using the presentation mode "optional display" over "Forced acknowledgement" if one is particularly concerned about avoiding underlying algorithmic biases.

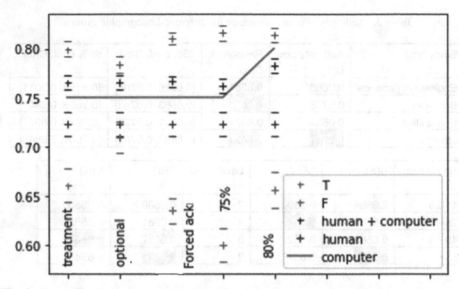

Fig. 4. Comparison of success rates with various stimuli presentations (black marks), success rates with wrong recommendation (red marks), success rate with good recommendations (green). Blue marks indicate the success without decision aid, and the line represent the "success rate" of the algorithm alone. (Color figure online)

6.4 Qualitative Feedback

Time spent on this experiment is not relevant enough to justify elaborate statistics: we needed a task that could be completed fast to reach a large population and match our target use case of alarm filtering. Aggregated data shows that, by and large, our assumptions hold. The average time to answer a trial is 10.3 s in the control condition vs. 9.5 s in the 1st experiment condition, with medians at 6.3 s and 5.4 s respectively, suggesting a small performance improvement with the decision aid. In the experiment condition, there is a slightly longer average time (9.6 s vs 9.1 s) when the recommendation is wrong than when it is correct, suggesting that subjects perceive the need to reflect when presented with a counter-intuitive proposition. Performance time by demographic category does not vary much, and finally, the time spent on the experiment influences very little the success rate (Fig. 5).

Subjects Feedback. Subjects showed a variety of reactions. Some explained their reasoning: "I only looked at sex and class, taking more things into account was too confusing", "The pattern is pretty obvious. First class was a high chance of survival. Female is a high chance of survival. Children did better than adults. I didn't trust that the algorithm would do better than saying survive for 1st class and female".

Others detailed their frustration at various constraints we had voluntarily set for the task: "I wish the algorithm had provided me with some explanation about its recommendations. Typically, when I disagreed with the recommendation, I would have loved to ask "why do you recommend this?"", "If the algorithm is only 80% accurate, why show us the algorithm answer before we make our decision?", "I would have needed a

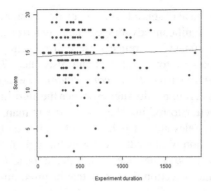

Fig. 5. 2D plot time spent x success rate.

few explanations on how the algorithm works before the experiment and while doing it some feedback on how it decided would have been helpful.", "I would have preferred to answer with probabilities rather than a binary choice.", "I would be interested to know the AI learning method".

Finally, many showed an understanding and appreciation for the study, noting that wrong recommendations could indeed affect their judgment: "Interesting experiment. Would love to see the end study!", "Funny (not topic, itself) and interesting", "AI = Random?", "I am very curious to understand the analyses process and the results. Would it be possible to receive the paper when published? Thanks". In debriefing interviews, subjects indicated that the test had made them aware of the complexity of the thought process at play when deciding to trust an algorithmic recommendation, which indeed, was the primary motivator of this study.

7 Discussion

7.1 Limitations

Our study results align with [24, 41, 52] and [1]. Taken together, they suggest that decision aids are useful only when the "algorithm alone" success is within a certain range, which we can roughly estimate as [70%, human success rate + constant]. Still, our measurements on this task may not be generalizable to other decision tasks. The causes of the uncertainty in a decision-making task may vary widely, the bias patterns may equally vary. Our contribution lies in the metrics of collaboration, automation bias and resistance, how to assess them and put them in production for our specific context, it is not a contribution to Decision Theory.

The task we have evaluated is not an expert task, it is more comparable to a routine managerial decision than to a complex decision such as medical diagnosis. Even though the metrics we have defined can be applied to those more complex contexts, experimental setup and access to many experts should make this very difficult, justifying more longitudinal approaches such as [12]. As mentioned in the introduction, our focus is in providing generic decision aids in the context of business decisions, and our task matches this context.

Finally, the effects we have observed, while statistically significant, may seem quite modest. We have shown a significant advantage of augmented decision-making in certain circumstances, and a significant difference in several presentation modes to contain, or, on the contrary, increase, automation bias and resistance. *The small amplitude of those effects is only a consequence of the narrow window in which augmented decision-making has its usefulness.* As our results suggest, when the algorithm clearly outperforms humans, it is probably better to rethink the role of the human. Conversely, when the algorithmic aid is of poor relevance, it is likely not useful, and, on the contrary, may lead to unwanted propagation of algorithmic biases through authority or complacency cognitive biases. This, by the way, has been confirmed a posteriori by the collaborative design sessions of the fraud detection workflow that inspired our study.

7.2 Towards a Methodology and Embedded Measures of Performance in Augmented Decision Making

Now that our model has shown its explanatory and discriminatory power, our next goal is to apply the model we have defined to real usage scenarios, first in the use case described before: fraud alert detection. Another important direction is to apply our methodology to other decision aids, such as nearest-neighbors' methods, that shows the data and outcomes of cases closely related to the present case.

In the longer run, we envision that decision aids will be generalized in business decision systems, provided they are instrumented with tooling that continuously assesses their relevance and performance so as to mitigate risks while improving the productivity and quality of decision-making.

8 Conclusion

We have presented a model, as a set of metrics to include in A/B testing of decision aids used in business decision tasks to assess their usefulness and control the biases a particular decision aid and its presentation may induce on the decision maker. Applied to a simple decision task, our metrics can be used to show the possibility of human-system collaboration (72% of success for humans alone, vs 76% for a human assisted by an algorithm that gives the correct answer 75% of the time). We have also defined measurements of automation biases and resistance to this bias. Applied to our decision task, we found a significant effect of wrong recommendations on the rationality of subjects (−5%), indicating that underlying algorithmic biases in the decision aid may be propagated in the decision process instead of compensated by the human.

Testing several presentation variants, we found that a technique that presenting the recommendation only on request (optional) was effective in increasing the resistance of the subjects, all the while preserving the performance of decision-making.

Our measurement system is meant to be embedded in A/B testing of generic decision support system used in many contexts of business decision management systems and business processes. *Augmented decision systems shift part of the responsibility of the decision maker to the system designer. Introducing systems that may induce authority, complacency or other cognitive biases creates liabilities for the system designers.*

Therefore, tools to objectivize the performance and impact of biases are needed to alleviate this liability, replacing impressions and subjective design guidelines with objective measures. We believe furthering this work is important to shape the future of augmented business decision-making.

Acknowledgments. We thank Grégoire Colombet and François Jaquin for introducing us to their client's decision problems that led to this research work. We also thank Pranivan Baudouin and Christopher Dolloff for their precious assistance along this project.

References

1. Alberdi, E., Strigini, L., Povyakalo, A.A., Ayton, P.: Why are people's decisions sometimes worse with computer support? In: Buth, B., Rabe, G., Seyfarth, T. (eds.) SAFECOMP 2009. LNCS, vol. 5775, pp. 18–31. Springer, Heidelberg (2009). https://doi.org/10.1007/978-3-642-04468-7_3
2. Alexander, V., Blinder, C., Zak, P.J.: Why trust an algorithm? Performance, cognition, and neurophysiology. Comput. Hum. Behav. **89**, 279–288 (2018). ISSN 0747-5632. https://doi.org/10.1016/j.chb.2018.07.026
3. Amershi, S., et al.: Guidelines for human-AI interaction. In: Proceedings of the 2019 CHI Conference on Human Factors in Computing Systems (CHI 2019), Paper 3, pp. 1–13. Association for Computing Machinery, New York (2019). https://doi.org/10.1145/3290605.3300233
4. Anderson, C.: The psychology of doing nothing: forms of decision avoidance result from reason and emotion. Psychol. Bull. **129**(1), 139–167 (2003). https://doi.org/10.1037/0033-2909.129.1.139. PMID 12555797. SSRN 895727
5. Elin Bahner, J., Hüper, A.-D., Manzey, D.: Misuse of automated decision aids: complacency, automation bias and the impact of training experience. Int. J. Hum.-Comput. Stud. **66**(9), 688–699 (2008). ISSN 1071-5819. https://doi.org/10.1016/j.ijhcs.2008.06.001
6. Bellamy, R.K., et al.: AI Fairness 360: an extensible toolkit for detecting, understanding, and mitigating unwanted algorithmic bias. arXiv preprint arXiv:1810.01943 (2018)
7. Binns, R., Van Kleek, M., Veale, M., Lyngs, U., Zhao, J., Shadbolt, N.: 'It's reducing a human being to a percentage': perceptions of justice in algorithmic decisions. In: Proceedings of the 2018 CHI Conference on Human Factors in Computing Systems (CHI 2018), Paper 377, pp. 1–14. Association for Computing Machinery, New York (2018). https://doi.org/10.1145/3173574.3173951
8. Bonaccio, S., Dalal, R.S.: Advice taking and decision-making: an integrative literature review, and implications for the organizational sciences. Organ. Behav. Hum. Decis. Process. **101**(2), 127–151 (2006). ISSN 0749-5978. https://doi.org/10.1016/j.obhdp.2006.07.001
9. Burton, J.W., Stein, M.-K., Jensen, T.B.: A systematic review of algorithm aversion in augmented decision making. J. Behav. Dec. Making **33**, 220–239 (2020). https://doi.org/10.1002/bdm.2155
10. Business Rules Journal: A brief history of the business rule approach, 3rd edn. Bus. Rules J. **9**(11) (2008). http://www.brcommunity.com/a2008/b448.html
11. Cabitza, F.: Biases affecting human decision making in AI-supported second opinion settings. In: Torra, V., Narukawa, Y., Pasi, G., Viviani, M. (eds.) MDAI 2019. LNCS (LNAI), vol. 11676, pp. 283–294. Springer, Cham (2019). https://doi.org/10.1007/978-3-030-26773-5_25

12. Cai, C.J., et al.: Human-centered tools for coping with imperfect algorithms during medical decision-making. In: Proceedings of the 2019 CHI Conference on Human Factors in Computing Systems (CHI 2019), Paper 4, pp. 1–14. Association for Computing Machinery, New York (2019). https://doi.org/10.1145/3290605.3300234
13. Castelo, N., Bos, M.W., Lehmann, D.R.: Task-dependent algorithm aversion. J. Mark. Res. **56**(5), 809–825 (2019)
14. Chalmers (ed.): The Extended Mind, Philosophy of Mind: Classical and Contemporary Readings. Oxford University Press (2002)
15. Char, D.S., Shah, N.H., Magnus, D.: Implementing machine learning in health care - addressing ethical challenges. N. Engl. J. Med. **378**(11), 981–983 (2018). https://doi.org/10.1056/NEJMp1714229
16. Coglianese, C., Lehr, D.: Regulating by Robot: Administrative Decision Making in the Machine-Learning Era (2017). Faculty Scholarship at Penn Law. 1734. https://scholarship.law.upenn.edu/faculty_scholarship/1734
17. Dijksterhuis, A., Bos, M.W., Nordgren, L.F., Van Baaren, R.B.: On making the right choice: the deliberation-without-attention effect. Science **311**(5763), 1005–1007 (2006)
18. Dimara, E., Bailly, G., Bezerianos, A., Franconeri, S.: Mitigating the attraction effect with visualizations. IEEE Trans. Vis. Comput. Graph. Inst. Electr. Electron. Eng. **25**(1), 850–860 (2019). TVCG 2019 (InfoVis 2018). https://doi.org/10.1109/TVCG.2018.2865233. (hal-01845004v2)
19. Dimara, E., Franconeri, S., Plaisant, C., Bezerianos, A., Dragicevic, P.: A task-based taxonomy of cognitive biases for information visualization. IEEE Trans. Vis. Comput. Graph. **26**(2), 1413–1432 (2020). https://doi.org/10.1109/TVCG.2018.2872577
20. Dimara, E., Bezerianos, A., Dragicevic, P.: Conceptual and methodological issues in evaluating multidimensional visualizations for decision support. IEEE Trans. Vis. Comput. Graph. (2018)
21. Endsley, M.R.: From here to autonomy: lessons learned from human-automation research. Hum. Factors **59**(1), 5–27 (2017). https://doi.org/10.1177/0018720816681350
22. Frees, E.: Longitudinal and Panel Data: Analysis and Applications in the Social Sciences. Cambridge University Press, New York (2004)
23. Gigerenzer, G., Gaissmaier, W.: Decision making: nonrational theories. In: Wright, J.D. (ed.) International Encyclopedia of the Social & Behavioral Sciences, 2nd edn., pp. 911–916. Elsevier (2015). ISBN 9780080970875. https://doi.org/10.1016/B978-0-08-097086-8.26017-0
24. Gombolay, M.C., Gutierrez, R.A., Clarke, S.G., Sturla, G.F., Shah, J.A.: Decision-making authority, team efficiency and human worker satisfaction in mixed human–robot teams. Auton. Robot. **39**(3), 293–312 (2015). https://doi.org/10.1007/s10514-015-9457-9
25. Hafenbrädl, S., Waeger, D., Marewski, J.N., Gigerenzer, G.: Applied decision making with fast-and-frugal heuristics. J. Appl. Res. Mem. Cogn. **5**(2), 215–231 (2016). ISSN 2211-3681. https://doi.org/10.1016/j.jarmac.2016.04.011
26. Hastie, R., Dawes, R.: Rational Choice in an Uncertain World, The Psychology of Judgment and Decision Making, 2nd edn. Sage Publications (2009)
27. Hirshleifer, D., Levi, Y., Lourie, B., Teoh, S.H.: Decision fatigue and heuristic analyst forecasts. J. Financ. Econ. **133**(1), 83–98 (2019)
28. HLEG-AI. Ethics guidelines for trustworthy AI. European Commision report, April 2019. https://ec.europa.eu/digital-single-market/en/news/ethics-guidelines-trustworthy-ai
29. Jeston, J., Nelis, J.: Business Process Management. Routledge, 21 January 2014. ISBN 9781136172984
30. Kahneman, D., Klein, G.: Conditions for intuitive expertise, a failure to disagree. Am. Psychol. **64**(6), 515–526 (2009). https://doi.org/10.1037/a0016755

31. Khenissi, S.: Modeling and counteracting exposure bias in recommender systems. Electronic theses and dissertations. Paper 3182 (2019). https://doi.org/10.18297/etd/3182
32. Knijnenburg, B.P., Willemsen, M.C., Gantner, Z., et al.: Explaining the user experience of recommender systems. User Model. User-Adap. Inter. **22**, 441–504 (2012). https://doi.org/10.1007/s11257-011-9118-4
33. Knijnenburg, B.P., Reijmer, N.J.M., Willemsen, M.C.: Each to his own: how different users call for different interaction methods in recommender systems. In: Proceedings of the Fifth ACM Conference on Recommender Systems (RecSys 2011), pp. 141–148. Association for Computing Machinery, New York (2011). https://doi.org/10.1145/2043932.2043960
34. Lee, M.K., Kusbit, D., Metsky, E., Dabbish, L.: Working with machines: the impact of algorithmic and data-driven management on human workers. In: Proceedings of the 33rd Annual ACM Conference on Human Factors in Computing Systems (CHI 2015), pp. 1603–1612. Association for Computing Machinery, New York (2015). https://doi.org/10.1145/2702123.2702548
35. Lemaire, A.: LOI n° 2016-1321 du 7 octobre 2016 pour une République numérique. https://en.wikipedia.org/wiki/Loi_pour_une_R%C3%A9publique_num%C3%A9rique
36. Logg, J.M., Minson, J.A., Moore, D.A.: Algorithm appreciation: people prefer algorithmic to human judgment. Organ. Behav. Hum. Decis. Process. **151**, 90–103 (2019). ISSN 0749-5978. https://doi.org/10.1016/j.obhdp.2018.12.005
37. Maggi, F.M., Di Francescomarino, C., Dumas, M., Ghidini, C.: Predictive monitoring of business processes. In: Jarke, M., et al. (eds.) CAiSE 2014. LNCS, vol. 8484, pp. 457–472. Springer, Cham (2014). https://doi.org/10.1007/978-3-319-07881-6_31
38. March, C.: The Behavioral Economics of Artificial Intelligence: Lessons from Experiments with Computer Players. CESifo Working Paper Series 7926, CESifo (2019). https://ideas.repec.org/p/ces/ceswps/_7926.html
39. Miller, T.: Explanation in artificial intelligence: insights from the social sciences. Artif. Intell. **267**, 1–38 (2019). https://doi.org/10.1016/j.artint.2018.07.007
40. Institut Montaigne: Algorithms: mind the bias! Report of the Institut Montaigne think-tank, March 2020. https://www.institutmontaigne.org/en/publications/algorithms-please-mind-bias
41. Onnasch, L.: Crossing the boundaries of automation—function allocation and reliability. Int. J. Hum.-Comput. Stud. **76**, 12–21 (2015). ISSN 1071-5819. https://doi.org/10.1016/j.ijhcs.2014.12.004
42. Parasuraman, R., Manzey, D.H.: Complacency and bias in human use of automation: an attentional integration. Hum. Factors **52**(3), 381–410 (2010). https://doi.org/10.1177/0018720810376055
43. Prahl, A., Van Swol, L.: Understanding algorithm aversion: when is advice from automation discounted? J. Forecast. **36**, 691–702 (2017). https://doi.org/10.1002/for.2464
44. Rader, E., Cotter, K., Cho, J.: Explanations as mechanisms for supporting algorithmic transparency. In: Proceedings of the 2018 CHI Conference on Human Factors in Computing Systems, Paper 103, pp. 1–13. Association for Computing Machinery, New York (2018). https://doi.org/10.1145/3173574.3173677
45. Romanov, D., Kazantsev, N., Edgeeva, E.: The presence of order-effect bias in Moscow administration. In: Di Ciccio, C., et al. (eds.) BPM 2019. LNBIP, vol. 361, pp. 337–341. Springer, Cham (2019). https://doi.org/10.1007/978-3-030-30429-4_26
46. Frederick, S.: Cognitive reflection and decision making. J. Econ. Perspect. **19**(4), 25–42 (2005). https://doi.org/10.1257/089533005775196732
47. Taddeo, M., Floridi, L.: How AI can be a force for good. Science **361**(6404), 751–752 (2018). https://doi.org/10.1126/science.aat5991

48. Morris, R., Mintz, S.: Cognitive processes and decision making in accounting, Chapter 2. In: Ethical Obligations and Decision-Making in Accounting: Text and Cases, 4th edn. McGraw Hill (2017). ISBN10: 1259543471

49. Tissandier, E., Baudel, T.: AIDA: Automatiser la prise de décisions métier en gardant l'humain dans la boucle. 31e conférence francophone sur l'Interaction Homme-Machine (IHM 2019), December 2019, Grenoble, France, pp. 2:1–2:6 (2019). ⟨hal-02407617⟩

50. Shneiderman, B.: Human-centered artificial intelligence: three fresh ideas. AIS Trans. Hum.-Comput. Interact. 12(3), 109–124 (2020). https://doi.org/10.17705/1thci.00131

51. Von Halle, B.: Business Rules Applied. Wiley (2001). ISBN 0-471-41293-7

52. Yeomans, M., Shah, A., Mullainathan, S., Kleinberg, J.: Making sense of recommendations. J. Behav. Dec. Making 32, 403–414 (2019). https://doi.org/10.1002/bdm.2118

53. Yetgin, E., Jensen, M., Shaft, T.: Complacency and intentionality in IT use and continuance. AIS Trans. Hum.-Comput. Interact. 7(1), 17–42 (2015)

54. Green, B., Chen, Y.: The principles and limits of algorithm-in-the-loop decision making. Proc. ACM Hum.-Comput. Interact. CSCW, Article 50, 3, 24 (2019). https://doi.org/10.1145/335 9152

Service-Oriented Justification
of Recommender System Suggestions

Noemi Mauro[✉], Zhongli Filippo Hu, and Liliana Ardissono

Computer Science Department, University of Torino, Torino, Italy
{noemi.mauro,zhonglifilippo.hu,liliana.ardissono}@unito.it

Abstract. In the selection of products or services, overviewing the list of options to identify the most promising ones is key to decision-making. However, current models for the justification of recommender systems results poorly support this task because, as they exclusively focus on item properties, they generate detailed justifications that are lengthy to skim. Moreover, they overlook the existence of a complex item fruition process which can impact customer satisfaction as well. For instance, consumer feedback shows that relevant factors in home booking include both the properties of apartments, and previous customers' perceptions of the interaction with the personnel who manages the homes. To address this issue, we propose a visual model that exploits an explicit representation of the service underlying item fruition to generate a high-level, holistic summary of previous consumers' opinions about the suggested items. From this overview, the user can identify the relevant items and retrieve detailed information about them, in a selective way, thus reducing information load. Our model is instantiated on the Airbnb *experiences* domain and uses the Service Blueprints to identify evaluation dimensions for the incremental presentation of data about items. A preliminary user study has shown that our model supports user awareness about items by enabling people to quickly filter out the unsuitable recommendations, so that they can analyze in detail the most relevant options.

Keywords: Summarization of recommendation lists · Service blueprints · Explainable AI · Sentiment analysis

1 Introduction

As reported in [6], product comparison is a crucial decision stage that buyers usually perform before they make a choice. Some recommender systems support this type of activity by generating post-hoc justifications of suggestions that highlight the main features of items which might interest the user [6,16–18]. However, these systems generate possibly lengthy, item-centric descriptions that only partially represent consumer experience, and might overload the user with too much data. For instance, in the e-commerce domain, it is not only a matter of liking the purchased item. The overall experience also includes the customer care,

© IFIP International Federation for Information Processing 2021
Published by Springer Nature Switzerland AG 2021
C. Ardito et al. (Eds.): INTERACT 2021, LNCS 12934, pp. 321–330, 2021.
https://doi.org/10.1007/978-3-030-85613-7_23

which might strongly impact the overall satisfaction about products. In service fruition, the user might have to interact with multiple actors, all of which might positively or negatively influence the final service evaluation.

We claim that, to enhance user awareness about suggestions, recommender systems should present both item-centric data, and perceptions about item fruition, in a compact format that helps the user identify the options to be evaluated in detail. For this purpose, we propose a service-oriented, visual model that supports the summarization of holistic information about items, taking the overall context in which they are experienced into account. The visualization is based on interactive bar graphs that describe customer experience quantitatively. Moreover, our model organizes the aspects emerging from online reviews around coarse-grained and fine-grained evaluation dimensions which support a selective and incremental inspection of consumer feedback. We use the Service Blueprints [3] to define the evaluation dimensions of customer experience for information summarization. Service Blueprints support the design and development of physical and online products and services, by focusing on the actions that the customer carries out, and on the tangibles (s)he encounters, during item fruition. They help organize the feedback about items around the user.

We apply our model to the presentation of Airbnb *experiences*, which consist of informal, leisure activities published by people in the Airbnb platform (https://www.airbnb.com). An experience could be a boat tour in a river, or a half day spent with somebody who teaches the preparation of a traditional dish. The *host* of the experience typically participates in it, and an experience can involve multiple *guests*. Thus the user interacts with other people during its enactment. Our service-oriented representation of items, centered around tangibles and human actors, is suitable to model all these stages of fruition. Moreover, it can be applied to other services involving multiple actors, such as home booking.

In the following, Sect. 2 outlines the related work. Section 3 presents the proposed summarization model, and Sect. 4 concludes the paper.

2   Background and Related Work

2.1   Service Blueprints

A Service Blueprint [3] is a visual description of the user experience with a service, such as a hotel, or an online retailer. It models the stages a person encounters when (s)he uses the service, from the start point (e.g., enter website or enter shop) to the end one (e.g., customer care), taking both onstage and backstage actions into account. Different from standard workflows, blueprints focus on customer actions. Therefore, they model the actors and the tangibles the user is expected to interact with. A typical Service Blueprint has five components. The *Physical evidence* includes the tangibles that the customer comes in contact with. For instance, in a hotel service, this component represents the hotel website, the parking, the desk, the elevators, the room, and so forth. The *Customer actions* include the actions that the guest performs when (s)he experiences the

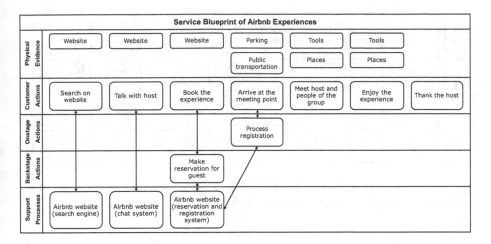

Fig. 1. Service blueprint of Airbnb experiences.

service; e.g., the reservation and the arrival at the hotel. The *Onstage/visible contact employee actions* are the actions that the contact employees perform while they interact with the customer; e.g., desk registration. The *Backstage/invisibile contact employee actions* are the actions carried out by the employees that are not visible to the customer but are useful to serve her/him. The *Support processes* include the activities carried out by non-contact employees, such as the reservation and registration systems used by the hotel.

2.2 Explaining and Justifying Recommendations

The research about recommender systems promotes their transparency to enhance user trust and acceptance of results [20,25]. In the systems based on a single item suggestion algorithm, results are typically explained in terms of inference traces [9,19,25]. For instance, some aspect-based recommender systems explain suggestions by highlighting the features of items which match, or mismatch, the target user's preferences [15]. Other ones support feature-based item comparison [5,14], or information exploration based on the visualization of the relevance of items to the keywords of search queries [4,24]. Graph-based recommenders use the connections between users and items as explanations [2,26]. A few systems fuse recommendation and explanation in the same process [7,12,15].

We aim at justifying recommendations, rather than explaining how the system generated them. The reason is that the traces of inference might be too complex for the user [19]. Moreover, if (s)he applies other evaluation criteria than those implemented in the recommender system, the explanations might be hardly convincing. However, different from previous justification approaches [6,16–18,20], which directly extract detailed features of items from reviews, we identify the aspects to be visualized by using the underlying service model, represented as a Service Blueprint, to steer the analysis of consumer feedback. This

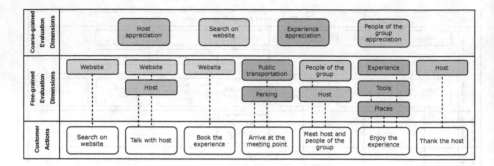

Fig. 2. Evaluation dimensions of Airbnb experiences. Colors represent the associations between fine-grained and coarse-grained dimensions. (Color figure online)

enables us to present items in a high-level, holistic perspective, which covers all the stages of interaction with services that are behind item fruition, and provides a synthesis of consumer opinions that facilitates the inspection of large sets of results. The usage of Service Blueprints also distinguishes our work from classical aspect-based justification and explanation [14,15,20], which focus on few peculiarities of items. By applying the blueprints, we extract the sentiment about a small set of evaluation dimensions that describe the overall experience with items.

3   Methodology

During April and May 2019, we scraped the Airbnb web site to collect data about the published experiences. We selected the content written in English. For each experience E, we extracted the reviews about it, and details such as name, host, price, planned activities, and URL of a picture of E. We collected data about 254,253 Airbnb users, 11,086 experiences and 336,288 reviews.

Reviews can cover different evaluation dimensions. For instance, the following example describes multiple aspects (tour, atmosphere) and provides feedback about the host: *"Very nice tour, very different than all the big commercial tours. The guide was really nice and created a friendly atmosphere from the start!"*.

3.1   Service-Based Representation of Airbnb Experiences

We introduce a service-oriented representation of items to capture the multiple perspectives about them emerging from online reviews. This representation is obtained in two steps. The first one is the **definition of the blueprint describing the service.** In this step, we represent the customer actions to be carried out during the fruition of the experiences. Moreover, we identify the actors and the tangibles which the guest is exposed to, as these elements contribute to her/his overall satisfaction. The second step is the **identification of evaluation dimensions** measuring consumers' perceptions about items, depending on those actors and tangibles.

We built the blueprint of Airbnb experiences, shown in Fig. 1, by studying both the service, and existing models available for the hotel booking domain [3]. The first tangible that the guest encounters is the Airbnb web site, through which (s)he can interact with the host of the experience and make the reservation. When the experience starts, the guest arrives at the meeting point and (s)he interacts with the host and with the other guests. Then, (s)he participates in the planned activities. Finally, (s)he closes the interaction with the other people.

While the Physical Evidence level of the blueprint describes the objects that the guest is expected to encounter, it does not represent human actors. However, the Customer Actions level provides both types of information. Thus, to obtain a holistic assessment of consumer perceptions, we map Customer Actions to evaluation dimensions associated with their involved tangibles and actors; see Fig. 2. To support both the summarization and a detailed organization of information, we define two levels of dimensions: a fine-grained one, related to the tangibles and actors involved in the Customer Actions, and a coarse-grained one, which describes the perceptions about the overall service at a high level. Fine-grained evaluation dimensions are grouped into coarse-grained ones, as shown by the colors in Fig. 2. For completeness, we introduced the *Experience* dimension, which is not strictly related to tangibles or human actors, because online reviews frequently mention intangible aspects such as ambience and time, which we want to represent to thoroughly model consumer feedback.

3.2   Analysis of Reviews

Given the Service Blueprint and the mappings to evaluation dimensions, we analyze the perceptions about an experience E in the following pipeline:

1. **Extraction of the aspects mentioned in the reviews of E.** Starting from the lemmatized text of each review R, we use the Spacy dependency parser [8] to build the syntax tree of the sentences of R. For each syntax tree, we apply an extension of the Double Propagation algorithm [22] to identify aspects and corresponding adjectives, as well as the adjectives referring to the host, who is frequently mentioned by name, or using pronouns, in nominal predicates. The output of this step is a list of $<aspect, adjective>$ pairs describing the mentioned aspects, combined with the adjectives used to qualify them. The second term is null when the adjective is missing.
2. **Computation of the sentiment about aspects.** We compute the polarity of each $<aspect, adjective>$ pair as the mean polarity value returned by the TextBlob [11] and Vader [10] opinion mining libraries. Then, we normalize this value in $[1, 5]$. We also count the occurrences of the pair in the reviews of E to measure how frequently people express the corresponding opinion.
3. **Classification of aspects w.r.t. service evaluation dimensions.** For this task, we combine entity recognition, which supports the identification of places and human actors, with the consultation of a dictionary for each fine-grained evaluation dimension. Each dictionary includes the lemmatized terms referring to the related tangibles or actors. The *Places* dictionary includes

Table 1. Aspects extracted from the reviews of an Airbnb experience. The rows are colored as the coarse-grained evaluation dimensions of Fig. 2.

Aspect	Adjective	Evaluation	Frequency	Fine-grained Evaluation Dimension
experience	great	4.43	39	Experience
tour	great	4.43	19	Experience
boat	big	3.00	17	Tools
time	great	4.43	15	Experience
host	great	4.43	14	Host
host	friendly	3.87	14	Host
experience	amazing	4.19	13	Experience
group	amazing	4.19	10	People of the group
snack	great	4.43	5	Tools

terms such as park, square, and river. The *People of the group* one includes words like people, group, and travelers. The *Experience* dictionary includes intangible concepts such as atmosphere, and time. Table 1 shows a subset of the aspects concerning an experience E. Each row shows an aspect and an adjective extracted from the reviews about E, the degree of appreciation (Evaluation) of the *<aspect, adjective>* pair in $[1, 5]$, and its frequency within these reviews. The last component of the row is the fine-grained evaluation dimension in which the aspect is classified.

To build the dictionaries, we first extracted the terms from a sample set of Airbnb reviews, by applying the techniques described in the step above. Then, three researchers from our University staff collaborated to map terms to the fine-grained evaluation dimensions of Fig. 2. When the researchers disagreed with each other, they discussed the outcome with the authors of the present paper. Notice that Airbnb experiences vary a lot, depending on the proposed activity. Therefore, a complete representation of terms within the dictionaries is practically impossible. Thus, when the aspect extraction returns a term that cannot be classified in any dictionary, we assume by default that it refers to the *Experience* dimension that has a broader scope than the other ones.

3.3 Visual Summary of User Feedback

We aim at enabling the user to overview a recommendation list, looking for the most promising items, and then focus on a few of them for a deeper analysis. This principle is inspired by Ben Shneiderman's zoom and pan information exploration model [1], which puts the user in control of the search process by supporting an incremental access to information. In our model, the classification of aspects in fine-grained and coarse-grained evaluation dimensions, and the computation of the associated sentiment, are the key elements to obtain this type of interaction because they support the presentation of a multi-faceted evaluation of consumer perceptions, at different levels of detail.

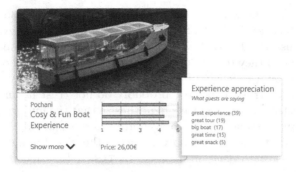

Fig. 3. Visualization of the Airbnb experience of Table 1. A visual legend, not shown, maps the colors of the bars to coarse-grained evaluation dimensions. (Color figure online)

Figure 3 shows the presentation of an Airbnb experience E. Below the picture of E, there are its host name, title, price, and a "Show more" link to retrieve its details. The bar graph summarizes consumer perceptions about E by showing the values of the coarse-grained evaluation dimensions emerging from its reviews. Each bar represents previous consumers' level of satisfaction about a dimension D, and it takes as value the weighted mean of the evaluations of the aspects classified in D. For each aspect, we use as weight its frequency in the reviews of E to tune its influence based on how many people share the opinion. The *Search on Web Site* bar is missing because the reviews do not refer to it.

By clicking on a bar, a box opens to present a few aspects extracted from the reviews of E that refer to the related coarse-grained dimension. For instance, see the "Experience appreciation" widget in Fig. 3. We aim at selecting diverse attributes to provide the user with rich qualitative data about previous guests' feedback. Thus, within the box of a coarse-grained dimension D, we show the most relevant aspects concerning each of its fine-grained dimensions, with their frequency. For instance, "great experience (39), ..., big boat (17), ..., great snack (5)". We use the frequency of aspects in the reviews of E as a measure of relevance because it reflects the conformity of consumer opinions.

3.4 Preliminary Test with Users in the Home Booking Domain

We tested with users a preliminary version of our model that is applied to the home booking domain and employs the Service Journey Maps [23] to represent items and to analyze online reviews. See [13] for details. This preliminary test makes sense because, similar to Airbnb experiences, the target of this system are young and middle-aged people who select items for leisure and work.

We recruited 11 participants (54.54% women; 45.46% men) representative of the target users. People joined the user study on a voluntary basis, without any compensation, and they gave their informed consent to participate in it.

Participants were between 19 and 57 years old (mean age = 36.36), and their educational level covered middle, high school and university. They declared that they regularly use the Internet. Based on the ResQue questionnaire [21], we asked participants if they tend to trust a person or thing, even though they have little knowledge about it: 9.09% of people declared that they very probably trust it, 18.18% probably trust it, 54.55% probably do not trust it, and 18.18% very probably do not trust it. We can thus hypothesize that the majority would desire to have a relevant amount of data to evaluate the recommended items.

We defined two tasks to test two versions of the visual model and we investigated their support to decision-making. In TASK1, for each presented home, we only showed the bar graph representing the coarse-grained evaluation dimensions we defined for home booking. In TASK2, for each presented home, we linked every bar of the graph to a set of aspects that justify its value. The user could view the aspects concerning a specific evaluation dimension by clicking on the associated bar. We asked participants to rate 5 homes for each task, or to opt out if they were not able to make a choice given the presented information.

In TASK1, 12.73% of the ratings were "I don't know"; in TASK2, participants rated all the homes. This means that, if the bar graph does not provide any qualitative data to justify the values of the evaluation dimensions, it poorly supports decision-making. Notice that, in the post-task questionnaire after completing TASK1, 54.54% of people declared that the given information was not enough to rate the homes. Differently, in TASK2, the number of people encountering decision-making problems was lower.

These findings suggest that a visual summary of previous experience with items, based on coarse-grained evaluation dimensions, helps the user efficiently filter out unsuitable options. However, users want to explore the details about the promising items before making any selection decisions, a typical attitude towards high-investment products and services. This finding highlights the importance of the method that is applied to select the aspects for summarization. As the Service Journey Maps do not explicitly represent onstage and backstage actions, tangibles and actors, they poorly support the classification of consumers' opinions in fine-grained evaluation dimensions. We thus concluded that we need the power of Service Blueprints, and a two-level representation of evaluation dimensions, to organize the aspects extracted from reviews in an efficacious way.

4   Conclusions and Future Work

We described a service-oriented visual model for the justification of item suggestions that enables the user to overview recommendation lists by means of a holistic analysis of consumer feedback, based on Service Blueprints. Different from previous work, our model summarizes previous consumers' perceptions about the whole item fruition process, rather than only focusing on item properties. In a preliminary user test, we collected positive feedback about the support of our model to user awareness and decision-making. These findings encourage to use the model to enhance information exploration support, and the presentation of recommender systems' results, with a user-centric perspective on items. A systematic user test of our model is part of our future work.

References

1. Ahlberg, C., Shneiderman, B.: Visual information seeking: tight coupling of dynamic query filters with starfield displays. In: Proceedings of the SIGCHI Conference on Human Factors in Computing Systems, CHI 1994, pp. 313–317. ACM, New York (1994). https://doi.org/10.1145/191666.191775
2. Amal, S., Tsai, C.H., Brusilovsky, P., Kuflik, T., Minkov, E.: Relational social recommendation: application to the academic domain. Expert Syst. Appl. **124**, 182–195 (2019). https://doi.org/10.1016/j.eswa.2019.01.061
3. Bitner, M.J., Ostrom, A.L., Morgan, F.N.: Service blueprinting: a practical technique for service innovation. Calif. Manage. Rev. **50**(3), 66–94 (2008). https://doi.org/10.2307/41166446
4. Chang, J.C., Hahn, N., Perer, A., Kittur, A.: SearchLens: composing and capturing complex user interests for exploratory search. In: Proceedings of the 24th International Conference on Intelligent User Interfaces, IUI 2019, pp. 498–509. ACM, New York (2019). https://doi.org/10.1145/3301275.3302321
5. Chen, L., Wang, F.: Explaining recommendations based on feature sentiments in product reviews. In: Proceedings of the 22nd International Conference on Intelligent User Interfaces, IUI 2017, pp. 17–28. Association for Computing Machinery, New York (2017). https://doi.org/10.1145/3025171.3025173
6. Chen, L., Wang, F., Qi, L., Liang, F.: Experiment on sentiment embedded comparison interface. Knowl.-Based Syst. **64**, 44–58 (2014). https://doi.org/10.1016/j.knosys.2014.03.020
7. Dong, R., Smyth, B.: User-based opinion-based recommendation. In: Proceedings 26th IJCAI, Melbourne, Australia, pp. 4821–4825 (2017)
8. Explosion AI: SpaCy - industrial Natural Language Processing in python (2017). https://spacy.io/
9. Herlocker, J.L., Konstan, J.A., Riedl, J.: Explaining collaborative filtering recommendations. In: Proceedings of the 2000 ACM Conference on Computer Supported Cooperative Work, CSCW 2000, pp. 241–250. Association for Computing Machinery, New York (2000). https://doi.org/10.1145/358916.358995
10. Hutto, C., Eric, G.: VADER: a parsimonious rule-based model for sentiment analysis of social media text. In: Proceedings of the 8th International AAAI Conference on Weblogs and Social Media, pp. 216–225. AAAI, New York (2014). https://www.aaai.org/ocs/index.php/ICWSM/ICWSM14/paper/viewPaper/8109
11. Loria, S.: TextBlob: Simplified text processing (2020). https://textblob.readthedocs.io/en/dev/index.html
12. Lu, Y., Dong, R., Smyth, B.: Why i like it: multi-task learning for recommendation and explanation. In: Proceedings of the 12th ACM Conference on Recommender Systems, RecSys 2018, pp. 4–12. Association for Computing Machinery, New York (2018). https://doi.org/10.1145/3240323.3240365
13. Mauro, N., Hu, Z.F., Ardissono, L., Izzi, G.: A service-oriented perspective on the summarization of recommendations. In: Adjunct Proceedings of the 29th ACM Conference on User Modeling, Adaptation and Personalization. ACM, Utrecht (2021)

14. Millecamp, M., Htun, N.N., Conati, C., Verbert, K.: What's in a user? Towards personalising transparency for music recommender interfaces. In: Proceedings of the 28th ACM Conference on User Modeling, Adaptation and Personalization, UMAP 2020, pp. 173–182. Association for Computing Machinery, New York (2020). https://doi.org/10.1145/3340631.3394844

15. Muhammad, K.I., Lawlor, A., Smyth, B.: A live-user study of opinionated explanations for recommender systems. In: Proceedings of the 21st International Conference on Intelligent User Interfaces, IUI 2016, pp. 256–260. Association for Computing Machinery, New York (2016). https://doi.org/10.1145/2856767.2856813

16. Musto, C., de Gemmis, M., Lops, P., Semeraro, G.: Generating post hoc review-based natural language justifications for recommender systems. User-Model. User-Adapt. Interact. **27** (2020). https://doi.org/10.1007/s11257-020-09270-8

17. Musto, C., Narducci, F., Lops, P., de Gemmis, M., Semeraro, G.: Linked open data-based explanations for transparent recommender systems. Int. J. Hum. Comput. Stud. **121**, 93–107 (2019). https://doi.org/10.1016/j.ijhcs.2018.03.003

18. Ni, J., Li, J., McAuley, J.: Justifying recommendations using distantly-labeled reviews and fine-grained aspects. In: Proceedings of the 2019 Conference on Empirical Methods in Natural Language Processing and the 9th International Joint Conference on Natural Language Processing (EMNLP-IJCNLP), pp. 188–197. Association for Computational Linguistics, Hong Kong, November 2019. https://doi.org/10.18653/v1/D19-1018

19. Nunes, I., Jannach, D.: A systematic review and taxonomy of explanations in decision support and recommender systems. User Model. User-Adapt. Interact. **27**(3–5), 393–444 (2017). https://doi.org/10.1007/s11257-017-9195-0

20. Pu, P., Chen, L.: Trust-inspiring explanation interfaces for recommender systems. Knowl.-Based Syst. **20**(6), 542–556 (2007). https://doi.org/10.1016/j.knosys.2007.04.004

21. Pu, P., Chen, L., Hu, R.: A user-centric evaluation framework for recommender systems. In: Proceedings of the Fifth ACM Conference on Recommender Systems, RecSys 2011, pp. 157–164. Association for Computing Machinery, New York (2011). https://doi.org/10.1145/2043932.2043962

22. Qiu, G., Liu, B., Bu, J., Chen, C.: Opinion word expansion and target extraction through double propagation. Comput. Linguist. **37**, 9–27 (03 (2011). https://doi.org/10.1162/coli_a_00034

23. Richardson, A.: Using customer journey maps to improve customer experience. Harv. Bus. Rev. (2015)

24. Di Sciascio, C., Sabol, V., Veas, E.E.: Rank as you go: user-driven exploration of search results. In: Proceedings of the 21st International Conference on Intelligent User Interfaces, IUI 2016, pp. 118–129. Association for Computing Machinery, New York (2016). https://doi.org/10.1145/2856767.2856797

25. Tintarev, N., Masthoff, J.: Explaining recommendations: design and evaluation. In: Ricci, F., Rokach, L., Shapira, B. (eds.) Recommender Systems Handbook, pp. 353–382. Springer, Boston (2015). https://doi.org/10.1007/978-1-4899-7637-6_10

26. Wang, H., et al.: RippleNet: propagating user preferences on the knowledge graph for recommender systems. In: Proceedings of the 27th ACM International Conference on Information and Knowledge Management, CIKM 2018, pp. 417–426. Association for Computing Machinery, New York (2018). https://doi.org/10.1145/3269206.3271739

Using the Design of Adversarial Chatbots as a Means to Expose Computer Science Students to the Importance of Ethics and Responsible Design of AI Technologies

Astrid Weiss[ID], Rafael Vrecar[(✉)][ID], Joanna Zamiechowska[ID], and Peter Purgathofer[ID]

Human Computer Interaction Group, Institute of Visual Computing and Human-Centered Technology, Technische Universität Wien, Karlsplatz 13, 1040 Vienna, Austria

`{astrid.weiss,rafael.vrecar,peter.purgathofer}@tuwien.ac.at,`
`e11936038@student.tuwien.ac.at`
`http://igw.tuwien.ac.at/hci/`

Abstract. This paper presents a reflection on a master class on "Responsible Design of AI" aimed at raising critical thinking among students about the pros and cons of AI technology in everyday life usage on the example of chatbots. In contrast to typical approaches teaching existing policies and design guidelines, we aimed to challenge students by setting up a project on the "most unethical chatbot imaginable". Our teaching concept therefore builds on students' self-identified issues and concerns and develops guidelines for ethical chatbot design according to students' interpretations of the capabilities and potential applications of these technologies. In our teaching we particularly focused on supporting mutual learning between teachers, students, and experts as foundational aspects. We conclude with reflections from the students regarding how this teaching approach can contribute to establish a critical and reflective mindset for future HCI researchers and developers.

Keywords: Education · Teaching · Responsible design · Responsible innovation · Artificial Intelligence · AI · Chatbots

1 Introduction

The topic of "Responsible Design of AI" is addressed from various disciplinary backgrounds. One can reasonably expect to find courses on this topic in a range of departments, including Computer Science (CS), Engineering, Psychology, Sociology, Philosophy, and many others. This interdisciplinary nature challenges teaching it within a Computer Science curriculum, as a given student body is unlikely to have expertise beyond their single, core area. Because of this, we considered

© IFIP International Federation for Information Processing 2021
Published by Springer Nature Switzerland AG 2021
C. Ardito et al. (Eds.): INTERACT 2021, LNCS 12934, pp. 331–339, 2021.
https://doi.org/10.1007/978-3-030-85613-7_24

"adversarial" chatbots as an opportunity to expose students to a broad range of new views and new ways of thinking about their work. In particular, chatbots can serve as a useful tool for training students with primary education in computer science to be aware of how related fields, such as sociology, psychology, philosophy and ethics deal with AI-based technology, and how these perspectives can be useful for practitioners in designing, implementing, and evaluating technologies. This broad perspective should help students to become critical and reflective future HCI scholars and technology designers/developers. In this paper, we explain why we consider chatbots as uniquely positioned and well-suited for introducing computer science students to more socially aware perspectives on AI and ethics and why we intentionally decided to challenge students' thoughts about chatbots through asking them to develop a most "unethical chatbot" during the course of the semester. We detail the different assignments we gave students to provoke their thinking and demonstrate the outcome of the course: a set of guidelines on "ethical chatbot development" students derived themselves from the course work. This description should serve fellow researchers as blueprint to develop HCI courses on related topics, such as accessibility and usability. We conclude with the students' personal reflections on the course.

2   "Responsible Design of AI" Exemplified by Chatbots

The scientific discipline of computer science is undergoing a transformation. Due to the increasing entanglement of technology with people and our society, the problems and research questions to be investigated are also changing. Subsequently, in computer science education we have to think of means how to equip students with relevant, critical, and reflective thinking to shape our technological future [2]. The HCI community is aware of the need to include the societal impacts and ethics into CS education. It was even placed into the ACM/IEEE CS Curriculum more than 20 years ago [9]. However, the implementation of such themes is challenging and often detached from other topics. Project-based teaching of Human-Robot Interaction has already proven to be a useful vehicle for exposing technologist students (e.g., in computer science or engineering) to social aspects of technology [10]. Similarly, a board game-based approach on responsible robotics aims to stimulate thinking beyond technology-centered concepts[1]. We aimed to create a similar learning experience under the constraints of virtual distance learning during the COVID-19 pandemic and therefore decided to work with chatbots as a boundary object to teach "Responsible Design of AI".

2.1   Pedagogical Goals

The primary superficial goal of the course is to critically examine potentially disruptive technologies, in this specific case, adversarial chatbots, in theory and practice. A main goal of the course is that students learn the skills necessary to

---

[1] https://responsiblerobotics.eu/wp-content/uploads/2019/12/Annex5.pdf.

extrapolate possible futures from this exploration and analysis, and to learn to see the difference between the hyperbole usually surrounding new technologies. A focus on the social implications of a technology, which most likely all of the students have experienced in some way in their own lives, requires a shift in how they approach, discuss, and work through the challenges and ideas in the project work. Instead of providing concrete truths about what a chatbot is and building small systems with extensive trial and error testing (which would be a more "traditional" CS approach), we wanted to show them techniques for engaging with the technology and its implications. Consequently, we put emphasis on oral discourse and peer-feedback.

The class format was a weekly 90-min slot in Zoom. It was a small seminar-like course with six participating students. The class followed a theme model where each class had a topic with associated readings or other inputs students should reflect upon. Additionally, a Slack channel was created for asynchronous discussions and inputs and Cryptpad was used to document every session. Each actual class can be broken down into three components: (1) input from the instructors, (2) discussion of the status of the student project, (3) reflection on prepared materials from the previous week. The following inputs and assignments were part of the course.

The first individual assignment was a *movie review*. Students were asked to watch a movie of their choice in which AI and robots play a major role. They were asked to pay close attention to human-robot interaction and how it is depicted in the film: What role does the technology have in society? What are its effects? How do people react (positively/negatively)? Further, they should comment on what they thought were the hard/easy social and technical problems involved with developing human-robot interaction of the sort shown in the movie, including potential ethical issues.

Next, a *reading reflection of two chapters of "Robot Futures"* [5] should serve as the scientific basis and discourse starting point on "Responsible Design of AI" for instructors and students. Students were asked to prepare short written reflections that not simply summarize what the chapters were about, but reflect their own understanding and thoughtful discussion of the material. Some of them focused on specific quotations made in the readings that they considered particularly relevant. Others described the most critical insights or posed the most important questions the readings raised.

Additionally, students were asked to *research on Turing Test* [7], *Chinese Room* [8], *and the Mirror Test* [3]. For this assignment, we asked them to pair up and research one of these topics. It turned out that the Turing Test was already well-known by the students as it is a prominent example when talking about Artificial Intelligence. However, the other two provided several new insights regarding aspects such as agency, human-likeness, and deception. They deemed to be a valuable starting point to discuss the similarities of human and machine intelligence, as well as crucial aspects in human-agent interaction, such as embodiment, personality simulation, and the Uncanny Valley phenomenon [4].

For one session we *invited a chatbot developer* to share her experience from a developer's perspective. Dr. Barbara Ondrisek, who calls herself "Bot Mother" and an enthusiastic software developer, presented several of the chatbot projects she was involved in and explained what makes a chatbot "successful" from a business perspective. Her talk also served as a starting point for the students how to set-up their own project work. For example, Dr. Ondrisek explained which ways of "exiting" the conversation have to be considered when letting a chatbot handle customer requests. Moreover, she also stated to always think about a suitable "personality"/"character" for the chatbot to create a positive user experience.

The final individual assignment of the course was to perform an *auto-ethnography of Woebot* (https://woebothealth.com). Woebot is a chatbot developed to serve as a digital therapist. Students were introduced to the concept of auto-ethnography [1] and provided with additional literature on the method. They were asked to install the Woebot chatbot on their phone, try it for several days, and share their experiences in class. For students who did not feel comfortable with the task, we offered a literature research on Woebot instead. Some students shared that they were experienced chatting with the bot as "uncomfortable and weird". This task led to critical discussions about the interaction of "AI and health care" in general and "persuasive technology" specifically. Additionally, some students used the opportunity to find ways to break the conversation flow with the bot and achieved surprising results, which also gave valuable insights for their own student projects.

2.2   Student Project

Students were assigned a project with the requirement that they should develop an adversarial chatbot, and over the course of the semester reflect what makes their chatbot unethical. Students were encouraged to develop their own ideas, but received input from the guest lecture on example chatbots and how they were implemented. Students were free to decide where to put the energy in their projects, for example, on using actual machine learning for their chatbot, visual design, or a specific story board. One project was completed by team of two students and four projects were done individually, all achieving valuable results and learning curves.

The primary goal of the project was for students to learn first-hand how many aspects of chatbots, besides "known machine learning aspects", are impacting ethics and responsible design. We believe that this was important for developing respect towards the efforts of responsible technology development and a trained, critical eye for appreciating its benefits and not just the "extra effort" it creates. Students were also encouraged to conduct a minimal user evaluation at the end of the course as part of their project, which helped in creating awareness of research ethics. The primary deliverable for the project was a working demonstration.

3   Outcome

The student activities resulted in two significant outcomes: (1) every student participated in conceptualizing and implementing a small chatbot, (2) students derived a set of guidelines which they deemed to be relevant when designing a chatbot with ethics in mind.

3.1   Student Projects

Inspirational Quotes Bot. Two students paired up to design a chatbot which would support conversations with occasional inspirational quotes found online. This chatbot incorporated machine learning algorithms for the generation of responses based on user input and its own database of sample conversations. The students added a list of inspirational quotes found online to the learning set. As users interacted with this chatbot, its responses were occasionally inappropriate. For example, some inspirational responses could be misinterpreted by a person suffering with anorexia as encouragement to continue losing weight. The two students were also challenged to apply ethical considerations to their user testing protocol. Without revealing the "unethical" aspect of the chatbot, users were encouraged to stop at any point, a wellness-check followup was conducted a week later.

Fitness Guru. The second project aimed towards building a "nasty" chatbot persona, modelled after a popular sports guru, that would give health advice and motivate people to exercise. The unethical twist was that it made toxic comments to users who entered an unhealthy BMI, instead of, for example, encouraging them to start a healthy diet. The bot was designed to have an offensive and arrogant "personality" with the intent on motivating the user through guilt and "tough love". This project demonstrates how the creator inserts their own values into the design, without considering the needs or cultural differences of the users.

Phishing Attack Bot. The third project developed around the idea of criminals intentionally using chatbots to gain a victim's trust during a phishing attack. The chosen setup was to open a malicious popup window which shows a quite intrusive warning that the anti-virus software has detected a virus on the victim's computer, and that the "smart" anti-virus customer support chatbot would help resolve the issue. However, this is just a way to gain the users' trust, and eventually to sell the user a "full package" anti-virus solution to solve their issue. While the harm here is intentional and a criminal will not follow these ethical guidelines, this project highlights the innate trust people put into technology without realizing how their data and privacy could be compromised.

Customer Service Agent. In this project the student decided to custom build a chatbot which would be deployed as a customer service agent on a commercial website to help a user resolve a problem, but would continuously encourage the user to leave a positive review about the product. This promotes the commercial interests of the company, over those of the user, in an annoying and unhelpful way. The intent of the chatbot is also deceitful and opaque, where the user believes its purpose is to solve a problem, the underlying motive is to increase the product rating. To eventually redirect the user to the review link, the chatbot conversation is programmed to follow several pre-defined paths.

Building Rapport. The final project implemented a social chatbot focused on gaining the trust of the user by convincing them that they are speaking with a real human. The chatbot attempts to emulate natural human conversation by strategically inserting humor, jokes, slang, and misspelling into the conversation flow. This can then be used towards various unethical ends, such as phishing, or spreading misinformation on social media. This is an ambitious task to achieve convincingly, and is a major focus of research and development in artificial intelligence. The student gained experience in working with Google DialogFlow and Google Assistant technologies to create a small working prototype. The experiences were mixed as it turned out that designing a chatbot despite using existing machine learning libraries is more complex than anticipated beforehand.

3.2   Guidelines on Ethical Chatbots

The last classroom activity was a retrospective look at the results from the projects, other assignments, and the discussions. In this session the students together with the instructors derived the following guidelines on ethical chatbot design:

– Be transparent: Openly show that your chatbot is a chatbot.
– Use a label or explain yourself: Be open about your intentions.
– Do not try emulating human behaviour: E.g., avoid human names, emotions.
– Avoid assigning gender to your chatbot.
– Provide a way to chat with a human and offer a way to end the conversation.
– Make an effort to detect urgency and relay the chat to a human.
– Be aware of vulnerable users/groups.
– Be aware of people with cognitive limitations/disabilities.
– Always question the values you encode into the chatbot when offering options, try to be comprehensive; offer a "none of the above" option.
– Aspire to be sensitive of context, e.g., culture; do not assume everyone celebrates on December 24.
– Inform users about how you handle their data and input, as is mandated by GDPR, and give people a chance to opt out.
– Assume the worst about your chatbot, and design for it.

Comparing these guidelines with the "Social and Ethical Considerations" of Conversational AI (CAs) [6] offers initial insights into potential successes of the course and future areas for improvement.

The authors of these Social and Ethical Considerations explain the importance of trust and transparency, and how it enables users to make informed choices in their interaction with a CA. They suggest making the CAs status as a non-human, and its motivations and capabilities explicit, which goes in line with the students' guidelines. In this paper, it is further explained that users assume a CA is neutral and unbiased, and that their data is secure, when this is often not the case. They describe the topic of user privacy as "paramount", and increasingly important to address on a societal and legislative level, due to the encroachment of these technologies into more aspects of our lives. Users are mostly unaware of the amount and scope of data that is collected on them, and how this data is used. In the case of CAs, the authors are in favor of legislative and legal compliance with respect to data privacy protection.

The authors are also aligned with the students' guideline of designing CAs to be androgynous. Not only does this avoid reinforcing gender stereotypes that are purposefully or unintentionally programmed into the CA, it also avoids influencing the user's interaction with the agent. Dehumanizing and not anthropomorphizing the chatbot also helps avoid a user subconsciously placing undue trust into it. Finally they discuss the dangers of unsupervised learning, where the CA could learn profanity, abusive language, or personal data from users, and then incorporate this into future conversations with different users. The importance of controlling the learning data and the chatbot responses was demonstrated in the "inspirational quote" chatbot.

The comparison of state-of-the-art "Social and Ethical Considerations" of Conversational AI (CAs) [6] with the guidelines derived by the students demonstrate that the course managed to convey the relevance that a developer or designer must always consider the unintended ethical consequences of their work in order to mitigate against possible harm. As we have seen from the student projects, even well-meaning chatbots can become problematic. As the projects progressed, the ethical considerations became increasingly nuanced and complex. Emerging themes of transparency, privacy, users' rights, protecting people, and the larger social impact of technology became central points of discussion. As such, the principles of digital humanism, and of putting the well-being of the person at the center of design considerations, underscore the guidelines constructed over the course.

4 Student Feedback

One of our pedagogical goals for the course was to show students reflective techniques for engaging with technology and its implications; through the provocative task of thinking about unethical chatbots for their student project we aimed to foster reflective stances. As a voluntarily final submission, we asked them to hand in a written reflection on their learning experience. Quotes such as the following suggest that we succeeded: *"I honestly can say that the lecture substantially changed my view on chatbots. First and foremost because I did not see how many negative implications can be caused by malfunctioning chatbots as people probably can be encouraged by the bot to do things to harm themselves or others"*.

Based largely on a constructivist learning theory, we believe that what you learn is to a great extent determined by the diverse and holistic ways you are enabled to think about a subject matter. Therefore, our meta-goal was that students learn skills that are necessary to extrapolate possible futures from the chatbot example. Again, a student feedback suggested that this was indeed the case: *"Furthermore, I underestimated the ethical implications that come with designing these. For me, chatbots before were just small gadgets which regularly totally mess up and annoy me when changing details on my, e.g., phone contract as they are often used to replace human assistance in my experiences [...] the lecture was insightful from many perspectives and also thinking about malicious use cases broadened my horizon in a way that we always have to think twice [...] when elaborating if our intended design can have negative implications [...]"* Another student stated that the course was "adventurous": *"We didn't have such strict tasks with rigid deadlines like in other courses but together we explored unethical chat bots, which I find really adventurous. [...] Frankly I never had in my technological education any focus on ethical aspect or social consequences of what I as an engineer create. Very big advantage of this course was opportunity to train creative thinking, as we weren't just ordered to perform very concrete strict tasks but had an opportunity to think about possible usage of our chat bot"*.

5   Conclusion

This paper illustrates why teaching "Responsible Design of AI" through the means of "adversarial" chatbots can be a useful mechanism for exposing CS students to a broader, socially-embedded view on technology. Students are exposed to readings and discussions that illustrate why it is important to be aware of social considerations, as such competence can influence algorithm and technology design and dictate how a technology is used, integrated, and ultimately, decide on whether it is successful or not. These are perspectives generally not covered in a technology-centered curriculum.

The brief overview of topics covered and the format of the course (including a student project) gives an indication how to engage students to reflect on the social implications of technology. Scaffolded by our input and the projects we gave them, students used the class as an opportunity to explore a range of social perspectives on technology. Furthermore, they designed chatbots and conducted evaluations, mostly using qualitative approaches. Overall, we believe that this paper illustrates the potential of adversarial chatbots as an accessible topic for providing CS students with education on how to be more socially reflective regarding their work.

Acknowledgements. We would like to thank all students who took part in the course described in this paper and who put so much effort into engaging with the material and developing exciting projects despite all COVID-19 limitations.

References

1. Ellis, C., Adams, T.E., Bochner, A.P.: Autoethnography: an overview. Hist. Soc. Res./Histor. Soz. **36**, 273–290 (2011)
2. Frauenberger, C., Purgathofer, P.: Ways of thinking in informatics. Commun. ACM **62**(7), 58–64 (2019). https://doi.org/10.1145/3329674
3. Haikonen, P.O.: Reflections of consciousness: the mirror test. In: AAAI Fall Symposium: AI and Consciousness, pp. 67–71 (2007)
4. Mori, M., MacDorman, K.F., Kageki, N.: The uncanny valley [from the field]. IEEE Robot. Autom. Mag. **19**(2), 98–100 (2012)
5. Nourbakhsh, I.R.: Robot Futures. Mit Press, Cambridge (2013)
6. Ruane, E., Birhane, A., Ventresque, A.: Conversational AI: social and ethical considerations. In: AICS, pp. 104–115 (2019)
7. Saygin, A.P., Cicekli, I., Akman, V.: Turing test: 50 years later. Mind. Mach. **10**(4), 463–518 (2000)
8. Searle, J.: Chinese Room Argument, the Encyclopedia of Cognitive Science (2006)
9. Tucker, A.B.: Computing curricula 1991. Commun. ACM **34**(6), 68–84 (1991). https://doi.org/10.1145/103701.103710
10. Young, J.E.: An HRI graduate course for exposing technologists to the importance of considering social aspects of technology. J. Hum. Robot. Interact. **6**(2), 27–47 (2017). https://doi.org/10.5898/JHRI.6.2.Young

Human-Centred Development of Sustainable Technology

DIY Homes: Placemaking in Rural Eco-Homes

Hongyi Tao⬛ and Dhaval Vyas⁽⊠⁾⬛

The University of Queensland, Brisbane, Australia
{h.tao,d.vyas}@uq.edu.com

Abstract. Eco-home makers are permaculturists, artists and environmentalists who actively engage with the environment and nature in order to build self-made, sustainable homes. Through the conceptual lens of "placemaking", we draw on an ethnographic study of eco-home makers and focus on unpacking important lessons for sustainable HCI research. Engaging with 15 eco-home makers in rural Australia and China, we aim to develop an in-depth understanding of how and why they design, build and retrofit their eco-homes. Our findings show that eco-home makers apply a material-first approach, align their designs with nature and are influenced by sociality and everydayness of making. We conclude by discussing how such insights can deepen our understanding of placemaking and DIY in HCI, and open up new avenues for future design and research of computing tools to empower residents as *place-makers,* enabling them to make their own living environments sustainable.

Keywords: DIY · Making · Placemaking · Sustainability · Eco-Home

1 Introduction

In recent years, HCI researchers have revised the traditional concept of "user" towards the "maker" [1] so to highlight people's abilities beyond using, such as upcycling, repurposing, retrofitting, fabricating, constructing and maintaining (e.g., [2–6]). In other words, instead of seeing people as passive recipients of products, designers should consider users as active makers of their own artifacts and built environments. Studies have been conducted to understand makers and makerspaces (e.g., [7–11]), and to design interactive technologies that better support DIY practices (e.g., [12–14]). More specifically, making in the domestic environment has been investigated to understand the interaction between residents and living environments [15, 16]. Subtle and incremental making and retrofitting the home fosters a reflective conversation [17] between makers and the place and cultivates the intimate relationship and complex entanglements [16].

Extensive studies have been conducted on urban DIY practices, but in rural context makers' perspectives, values, and approaches are rarely explored. Unlike urban DIY activities that rely on exiting industrial infrastructure, global supply chain, and emerging automatic tools, rural eco-home makers prefer manual tools, local materials, and low-tech primitive technology [18]. Eco-home makers are permaculturists, ecologists, architects, artists, and environmentalists who are interested in living in rural areas and

© IFIP International Federation for Information Processing 2021
Published by Springer Nature Switzerland AG 2021
C. Ardito et al. (Eds.): INTERACT 2021, LNCS 12934, pp. 343–364, 2021.
https://doi.org/10.1007/978-3-030-85613-7_25

eco-villages to have a self-reliant lifestyle. They completely immerse themselves in fabrication, growing food, making artifacts, and building eco-homes by themselves. Their perspectives, visions, and methods to work with nature could enhance our understanding of sustainability, however, such type of studies is relatively rare in the HCI community.

A growing focus within HCI is designing technologies to create a meaningful integration of people, place, and history for the common good of both humans and environment [19, 20]. HCI scholars borrowed placemaking from urban planning to improve residents' experience, cherish and value where they live [21], to study sustainability [22], and to inform the design of smart cities and urban informatics [19, 23]. However, approaches to placemaking are different in the rural context, where we may interact more directly with other beings, such as wildlife, raw materials, climate, and soil among other natural things. There is a research gap in ongoing rural eco-home making. Rather, the main questions of this research are: Q1) What are eco-home makers' motivations, perspectives, visions, and methods to engage in ongoing DIY home activities? Q2) How can technologies support everyday sustainable making?

In this paper, we focus on the interaction between makers and eco-homes and examine sustainable DIY home activities. We use Desjardins et al.'s [22] three themes of Sustainable Placemaking (longevity, unfinishedness, and multiplicity) as a conceptual lens to investigate how residents design, build and retrofit eco-homes and how they constantly reimage and reconfigure. DIY activities were chosen because they reveal makers' perceptions, visions and intentions, and the potential for design implications to empower individuals to shape their own living environments. We present the results of our ethnographic study with 15 eco-home makers in Australia and China. We identify three dimensions of DIY home practices from findings: Material-first approach maps the complex factors that shape how eco-home makers make decisions and interact with various materials; Working with nature charts the multiple strategies that eco-home makers use to understand the character and qualities of the place and interact with nature to minimize the impact of environment and maximize use of renewable resources during construction and occupation; and, Sociality and everydayness of making maps two-way dynamic interaction between residents and buildings (that individuals shape buildings, and buildings shape individuals) and how eco-home makers balance residents' needs and lifestyles that are more environmentally sustainable.

This paper makes two contributions to HCI research. First, it unpacks how eco-home makers design, build and retrofit their living spaces by discussing empirical evidence from the field and how this could deepen our understanding of placemaking in a rural eco-home context. In that process, it also draws parallels between urban placemaking work within HCI [19, 21–24]. Second, it provides insights into the co-design process that involves no-humans and discusses how HCI can support eco-home practices.

2 Related Work

2.1 Sustainable Placemaking

Place and placemaking could be useful concepts to understand the intentions and interactions of eco-home makers. Place is how individuals view and experience the world, and is dynamic, unfinished, and constantly changing [25]. Tuan [26] observes that a place is a time-based phenomenon created by the human experience, which contains memories, meaning and identity. Place is also a significant theme in HCI. Harrison and Dourish point out what distinguishes place from space is inhabitants' sense-making activities: human responses to their living environment, including understandings of behavioral appropriateness and cultural expectations, make place for a cultural and social phenomenon [27]. The theory of placemaking has also been taken up and investigated in the HCI community. This theory was originally developed in urban planning by Jane Jacobs [28] and William Whyte [29], who proposed a community-centered approach, and presented neighborhood designs that promoted public interaction. Their vision embraces collaboration, transformation, community-driven initiatives, and has a clear relation to the physical and historical context of a place [30]. Given the emerging agendas of ubiquitous computing and making movement, HCI researchers suggest that placemaking could be a viable strategy to design meaningful, future smart lives by making residents value and experience the place they live in [21, 31–33].

Placemaking is to intensify lived human experience and make residents cherish the place they live in [21]. Similar to the approach of user experience in HCI [34], by living in a place, inhabitants experience it naturally through perception, touch, meaning making and interpretation, and the spatial patterns of social interaction are formed over time. Then the place becomes distinctive to the individual and may get a unique name [35]. By integrating placemaking and smart environment, HCI researchers try to explore and design for a better life. For example, in the project Livehoods, Cranshaw et al. [36] present a clustering algorithm for mapping a city by analyzing patterns of residents' movements and behaviors. The project data portrayed a dynamic view of the social flows, and described how people go about placemaking across municipal neighborhood borders. Media facades [37], media architecture [32], and ongoing urban design [24] have also applied placemaking in HCI.

Focusing on sustainability and temporal dimension, Desjardins et al. [22] utilized sustainable placemaking to investigate how everyday place makers are engaged incrementally and over time in the making of a whole environment. They discussed three themes of sustainable placemaking: longevity, unfinishedness, and multiplicity, and proposed that a sustainable place should "invite people to continuously build, transform, and engage with that place and with each other in a long-term, creative, meaningful, and ongoing manner" [22]. The forming of a mature and long-lasting relationship between a place and people takes time, which is referred to as longevity. The making of place arises through the long-term periods of living within that place and it is this long temporal quality that allows design to facilitate and sustain the placemaking process. The quality of unfinishedness underlines the need for a balance between young and mature materials and that balance is necessary to reach an ongoing long-lasting process of creating a place – and thus achieve longevity. Through reflecting about their place, makers actively and creatively live and experience it, and are able to fluidly utilize multiple strategies to make their place. A holistic approach of placemaking is multiplicity. Place then becomes a result of the compound function of quality and people's engagement [22]. Their research work was the first step to frame sustainable placemaking in HCI community. Our study extends this work by contributing empirical insights from 15 eco-home makers, from the point of view of how they constantly reimage and reconfigure their personal living space.

We show that makers interact with materials, nature, and communities and highlight the ongoing, iterative, and unfinished design and making of the place.

2.2 DIY in HCI

DIY has been a major focus of the HCI community. Researchers identified DIY as a collaborative, creative hobbyist practice, which unifies playfulness, utility, and expressiveness [38]. Makers also attempt to transform consumer goods to better fit their own needs [16]. In the last decade, HCI researchers have been studying DIY makers and maker culture to create interactive technologies that better support DIY practices of maker communities (e.g., [11, 39–41]) as well as gaining insight into designing future collaborative technologies (e.g., [10, 42, 43]).

Ethos like sharing [44], care [4, 45] and open innovation [46] have been defined as the key aspects of DIY. These nuanced perspectives can be used in ethnographic studies [45] to understand and analyze the social setting and community-based DIY practices. For instance, Toombs et al. [45] focused on hackerspaces' maintenance labors and analyzed ethnographic encounters through the lens of care ethics to better understand social aspects. To Bellacasa [47] care is things we do to constantly maintain the world we live in, which encompasses our bodies, communities, and the physical environment where everyday making practices take place. More inclusively, HCI researchers proposed post-anthropocentric design [48] to care for nonhuman stakeholders [49–51] and the nature [52, 53]. DIY in this field attempts to involve human as catalysts for collaborative sustainable making.

More specifically, DIY activities in the domestic environment have been investigated to understand the interaction between makers and living environments. For example, Wolf and colleagues [15] introduced the concept of "home worlds" to understand DIY home repair and maintenance, and how homes are embedded in communities and everyday life. Desjardins and Wakkary [16] offered six qualities of the intimate relationship between makers and the lived-in prototype by presenting an autobiographical project of converting a camper van. Subtle and incremental making and retrofitting the home fosters a reflective conversation [17] between makers and the place and cultivates the intimate relationship and complex entanglements.

HCI researchers have also explored how computing tools could be designed to support everyday making, and interpreted the complex relations among technology, home and residents [54, 55]. Shewbridge et al. [56] designed technology probes to explore how normal people might use fabrication tools in their homes. DIY kits for smart homes have launched on the market with which users can create and modify their own smart homes by connecting various sensors, actuators, and social networks etc. [57]. Another related research area is end-user development (EUD). EUD for smart home provides a set of tools and interfaces that enable occupants shape their home environments [58]. A number of methods have been proposed: the adoption of a magnetic poetry metaphor for end-users to program their environment [59], tangible interfaces [60], end-user programming platforms [61–63].

3 Methodology

3.1 Research Settings

It is important to discuss the settings within which this research took place. An eco-home is when a maker has built or retrofitted all or some parts of his or her house to reduce environmental damage [18]. While there are various types of eco-buildings, we focused on self-built eco-home in rural settings. In our project, we wanted to engage with eco-home makers who either lived independently or in an eco-community. Our participants included makers who have no or little construction-related qualifications and experience, and those who are architects and DIY amateurs. The research involved visiting two eco-communities: one in Australian and another in China. 9 out of our 15 participants lived in eco-communities, while the other 6 participants lived on independent land that they owned. Table 1 shows a list of projects we considered as part of eco-home activity for this study.

Table 1. Project types

Project type	Description
Retrofitted house	Retrofitting an existing house towards sustainability
Tiny house	Caravan or shipping container house, or a house built on a trailer
Timber house	Timber as the main material to build frame, wall, and roof
Earth house	Earth as the main material to build foundation, floor, and wall – e.g., use of cob, earthbag, and clay brick
Off-grid system	Independent from public utilities. e.g., generation of electricity and conserving water on site
Edible garden	Growing food in the garden, composting kitchen waste, and recycling grey water for irrigation
Eco-community	A commune of eco-home makers, collaboratively building eco-homes and share common values

3.2 Methods and Participants

We conducted an ethnographic study in eco-homes and eco-communities. The criteria for participants recruitment were that they should have self-built (in parts) at least one home. A total of 15 participants (Table 2) from rural Australia (n = 8) and China (n = 7) were involved in this study to enable an international perspective, which also reflects the first authors' long-term work in DIY and sustainability. The first author had worked on eco-homes projects in both Australia and China and used this opportunity to conduct in-depth interviews with participants. The initial recruitment was done through the first author's personal network, followed by advertising it on permaculture-based Facebook groups. In Australia, the first author visited participants' places between February 2020

Table 2. Participant details (with pseudonym)

#	Name	Location	Age (DIY years)	Project types
1	Ben	Australia	58 (7 years)	Tiny house, edible garden
2	Nathan	Australia	46 (28 years)	Tiny house, off-grid systems, edible garden
3	Oliver	Australia	60 (40 years)	Tiny house, off-grid systems
4	Paul	Australia	50 (32 years)	Timber house, off-grid systems, edible garden
5	Lucas	China	45 (8 years)	Retrofitted house, edible garden, eco-community
6	Will	China	30 (11 years)	Retrofitted house, off-grid systems, eco-community
7	Iain	China	44 (11 years)	Timber house, eco-community
8	Eric	China	48 (4 years)	Retrofitted house, edible garden, eco-community
9	Victor	China	36 (5 years)	Retrofitted house, timber house
10	John	China	39 (11 years)	Retrofitted house
11	Martin	China	28 (7 years)	Earth house, off-grid systems
12	Thomas	Australia	68 (45 years)	Retrofitted house, off-grid systems, eco-community
13	David	Australia	75 (51 years)	Timber house, off-grid systems, eco-community
14	Bill	Australia	92 (50 years)	Timber house, off-grid systems, eco-community
15	Alan	Australia	82 (30 years)	Timber house, eco-community

to August 2020. In China, the first author visited these eco-home projects between years 2012 and 2017. Participants' ages ranged from 28 to 92.

The first author visited the participants and stayed on site for several days in order to get detailed insights around DIY of eco-homes. Semi-structured interview, field observations and sketches were employed during the data collection process. The first author also joined participants' daily activities, engaging in building, repairing, making, gardening and cooking. Through living with them, we aimed to study the natural circum-stances of everyday making activities, and daily interactions with eco-homes. In addition to participation and observation, we use sustainable placemaking [22] as a conceptual lens to design our contextual interviews, and aimed to learn participants' intentions, perceptions and visions of DIY home projects. Interviews focused on discussing specific DIY systems built by our participants and aimed to understand their rational in building those. Interviews also included participants' philosophical stand on environments and their role in it. Interviews were conducted in English and Mandarin Chinese. The interviews ranged in length from 40 min to up to 2 h.

All interviews were translated and transcribed. Furthermore, our research data included transcriptions of interviews, photos and field notes. We conducted thematic analysis [64] on our data. We used the professional online transcription software "Trint" to transcribe all the audio recordings, and coded our data using NVivo. We started by creating initial codes through open coding, and subsequently combined relevant codes into themes. Through iteratively reviewing and refining the coding, we summarized our analysis and developed three themes of DIY eco-home practices.

4   Findings

Our findings outline three sets of DIY home practices, and reveal how makers interact with materials, nature, and communities and highlight the ongoing, iterative, and unfinished design and making.

4.1   Material-First Approach

As the choice of materials influences the life-cycle cost, environmental impact, and comfort of eco-homes, eco-home makers prioritise the selection of materials and consider peculiarities of every material, and constantly experiment and iterate to make the best use of every piece.

Use of Economical Material
For economic factors, it was common to observe that eco-home makers tried to minimize the cost of materials. Their strategies include reducing the use of expensive materials, utilizing recycled and cheap local materials, and transforming waste and garbage into building materials. For example, the main materials of Martin's (P11) house are natural materials collected in his own farm. The wall, for example, is made from earth bags, and the roof is made from thatch. He also used construction waste removed from other houses to fill the foundation instead of gravel, and incorporated second-hand glass and beer bottles to make windows, and created mosaic with broken glass and tiles. He recounted how he chose and dealt with materials in his earthbag and cob houses.

> "Due to the financial constraint, the houses we built are relatively small, and more than 90% of the materials come from within 5 kilometers of our neighborhood. When I go to a place, I get used to looking at the rubbish on the ground and start thinking about what can this be used for. There is basically nothing that can be wasted. Rubbish can be turned into useful things through some techniques and methods". (Martin, P11)

After graduating from university, Martin (P11) had always wanted to return to his hometown in the province of Hubei, rather than staying in cities. He has been interested in permaculture since 2013 and started his first natural building project in 2015. So far, he has built 5 houses using natural and waste materials. Two of these are his own small houses, while he helped his friends and relatives build the other three houses. He believes that the process of turning soil, stones, straw and other free and waste materials into building houses is full of creative accomplishment. The local climate also played an important role in the selection of specific material. Martin commented that the thermal qualities of earthbags and cob would provide resistance against different weather conditions.

In order to find cheaper or free materials, eco-home makers usually pay more attention to the waste around them, and constantly think and experiment how to use these materials. As noted by Oliver (P3), who has been living in a caravan for 15 years, he has kept materials that he thought would be useful in the future, and then recycled them in different forms over a period of time. For instance, he has kept several canvases from different billboards for 20 years and repurpose them in different ways. He recently moved to a new place, re-glued them and made a new caravan annex roof. It is important to note here was that the quality and materiality of the canvas would enable Oliver to store it easily and re-use it to make walls, room dividers as well as to create ventilation during Australian summers. Similar behaviors are very common in DIY homes, where eco-home makers use free and cheap materials, experiment with them and re-purpose them for new situations.

Use of Natural and Local Material

As one of the main purposes of eco-homes is to reduce the impact on the environment, eco-home makers strongly consider whether the materials will cause any environmental hazards during construction and occupancy. Hence, they try to source mate-rial that is re-useable, recycled, locally available, and have suitable thermal functions. A good example would be Will's (P6) renovation of an old rammed earth house. Will is a 30-year-old artist. He left the city in 2009 to explore a self-sufficient life in the rural area and initiated an intentional community in 2015 to gather people with com-mon aspirations to practice a sustainable lifestyle. In the community, they experimented with many alternative construction methods, such as light steel, geodesic dome, earthship, timber structure, bamboo structure, and so on. This rammed earth house was an abandoned house he rented locally from 2018 and has been transformed into their residence together with other community members. The wooden structure and walls of the house had been damaged due to disrepair and the leaking roof. In the process of renovating, he tried to use local natural materials as much as possible, instead of using non-degradable materials and materials with long regeneration cycles. He followed the traditional method of using mixed soil, sand and lime to repair the wall without cement, and used tung oil for timber protection instead of industrial varnish. He also sorts and stores waste on-site for other purpose, such as building a small furnace to melt metal waste into ingots. When the accumulation reaches a certain amount, they can be melted and cast into tools again. As he commented:

> "Because we are concerned about the issue of environmental protection, and then we do this (self-sufficiency). The environment and people are one, and we respect the environment as the primary prerequisite for doing this, so basically we consider the use of natural materials as much as possible". (Will, P6)

Eco-home makers try to use local renewable recourses as much as possible, so that while acquiring resources, they can also maintain the local ecological balance. They

| (a) | (b) | (c) | (d) |

Fig. 1. Paul's (P4) garden and forest (a), the first house built in 1991 (b), the blacksmith workshop (c), the house they live in now (d)

reduce the impact of human activities on the environment by managing natural recourses like trees and plants. For example, the timber used in Paul's (P4) home was cut from his own farm (Fig. 1a). Most of the wood was first planted by his parents in the 1980s. He also plants new trees while cutting down. The continuous construction of his house began in 1991, starting with a small wooden house (Fig. 1b), then wood and black-smith workshops (Fig. 1c), and constantly built, fix, and change the houses due the birth of his children. So far, his houses are totally off-grid (Fig. 1d), living with his wife and three children. As he explained:

> "My philosophy is to reduce the damage I do. And it's making people feel safer and living in a way that makes people happier. Because I think people are happier when they feel independent. Um, and they're not limited by the money. Um, and the more resilient your own life is your community life will be as much resilient". (Paul, P4)

The examples of Will and Paul show that eco-home makers strive to use natural and locally sourced materials that will have less adverse impact on the environment while being able to manage their family lives.

Easy to Process and Maintain
In addition to supporting the basic structure, insulation and other functions, materials also need to be easy to process, operate and maintain manually. Since eco-home makers use hand tools and lack large construction machinery, they choose relatively light-weight materials that are easy to process by hand, such as wood, bamboo, straw, earth, and light steel. Take the case of Martin's (P11) houses, the reason why he chooses cob as the main construction method is because it is extremely fluid. Hand-formed from pliable mud, cob building requires little training, no machinery, and is accessible to everyone. Bill (P14), a 92-year-old male, gave the following comment:

> "I'm a lazy Australian. Australians find the easy way of doing things. My philosophy for building a house is that it should be easy. I did most of it myself. I had some help, but I did most of the construction myself. And, zero maintenance. No paint, so there's no paint in the place anyway. All timber is left natural. Yes, easy to construction, low cost, zero maintenance, they'd be the key points. A house set for me is easy to build". (Bill, P14)

Bill built his current house during his 60s. He had similar considerations when choosing the materials for his house. He used a pole structure to build his house, which allows the efficient use of small round timber. He did most of the construction by himself except the roof, which needed some additional help from his friends. He was able to build a house with a large open kitchen and two bedrooms, where additional guest can sleep.

4.2 Working with Nature

The design of eco-homes requires a good understanding of the character and qualities of the land, its topography, soil quality, climate, sun movements, wind patterns and existing biodiversity. Based on this knowledge, houses could minimize the impact on the environment and maximize use of renewable resources during construction and occupation. In this section, we discuss how eco-home makers utilize specific aspects associated with climate and landscape in order to live sustainably.

Climate

For eco-homes, acknowledging and understanding the local climate is often the starting point of designing a house. Climate will affect comfort and often long-term costs, more than any other factors. Houses in different climatic regions have very different requirements and designs: with those in cold temperate climates needing highly insulated walls and minimal heat leakage, whereas those in tropical or rainy climates might be quite structurally open to allow natural cross-ventilation to flow through and keep the house at a cooler temperature.

An eco-home ideally reflects its climatic location by managing, harnessing and maximizing the climatic features to enable a house to benefit from natural ventilation, solar gain and passive cooling. For example, David's (P13) eco-village was located in a sub-tropical region of Australia, where the climate offers 40 weeks of mild-warm to hot weather and 12 weeks of cool to cold weather. Passive solar design has been used in most of the houses in the village to keep cool in summer and warm in winter. In order to utilize passive solar gain (Fig. 2a), houses need to capture as much sun as possible. In the southern hemisphere, this is achieved by orientating houses to the north. By observing the sun's path throughout the year, eco-home makers could use the windows, wall and floors to collect, store and distribute heat from sunlight entering the building during the winter and exclude solar gain in summer. Like David (P13) explains:

"This house (Fig. 2b), is almost facing north. So, I built it this way to get the solar aspect. The roof goes up to let more of the sun in. Based on the design of the Queensland houses with the wide verandas, it stops the sun getting on your walls during the summertime and overheating the house". (David, P13)

In order to make full use of natural light, eco-home makers use various methods. New houses can use large windows to improve solar gain. For retrofitted projects, especially in colder area, the usual approach is to add a greenhouse because it is more difficult to change the size of the windows. For example, in Eric's (P8) home, he built a greenhouse to connect all the rooms in a courtyard type house. Before the renovation, the bedroom

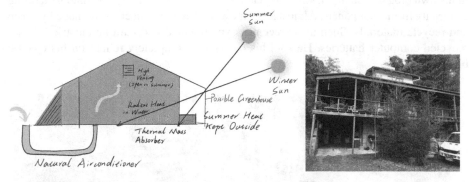

Fig. 2. Passive solar design (a), the passive solar design of David's house (b)

and living room were separate from the kitchen and bathroom. To go to the kitchen or bathroom, one had to pass through the open-air yard, which was not convenient in cold winter and rainy summer. Attaching a solar greenhouse not only increased the indoor space and makes it easier to move around in different rooms, the enclosed thermal mass walls can also store more heat in winter, thereby reducing the extra energy consumption of heating the rooms in winter. Eric and his family moved from the city to this rural old courtyard in 2014 because they wanted to shift to a lifestyle close to nature.

Conservation of Energy

Energy is an important part of a functioning home. It is required to heat water, heat or cool spaces of the house, cook, and provide electricity to power lights and run electrical appliances. Conventional houses often rely on fossil fuel energy sources, while eco-homes instead tend to harness less environmentally damaging renewable resources (sun, wind, water) through a variety of technologies. Most of the participants used micro-generation on-site technologies, small-scale equipment that either power a single house or an eco-community. Among our participants, the most popular technology used was photovoltaic panel, because of the simplicity in installation and use, they are often attached to old car batteries that is then used to power lights and laptops. Among other examples, Thomas (P12) made a biogas plant (Fig. 3b) for cooking, and built a standalone system by recycled solar panels (Fig. 3a), batteries and an inverter. As he noted:

"I got recycled solar panels to make a roof in my patio. It was given free to me as it came as a part of electronic waste. Generally, you can get them for nothing. And they put them in outer space. So that makes a very good roof, you know, very durable. Not all of them are fully functioning but some of them actually work. I have got batteries under my house, so I can save some power for later use". (Thomas, P12)

Thomas was an organic farmer and founded a community in 1975. He sold the farm due to the back injury, and now lives in a house with 800 square meters back-yard, which he called a small farm. He has been living a self-sufficient lifestyle for 45 years, growing his own food (Fig. 3d), keeping native bees, cooking from gas that is produced in his own biogas system, making biochar, collecting rainwater (Fig. 3c) and generating electricity from solar panels. Almost all of these alternative projects were made by waste and recycle materials. Such as he recently experimented and built an electric bike by recycled computer batteries. He sold his car and is completely reliant on his electric bike.

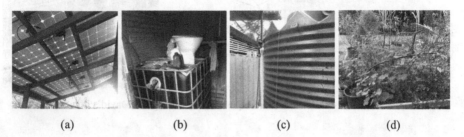

(a)   (b)   (c)   (d)

Fig. 3. Off-the-grid system in Martin's retrofitted house: (a) photovoltaic system, (b) biogas system, (c) rainwater collection, (d) edible garden

Wood energy is another solar energy and is accessible to everyone in the rural area. Using wood to cook and heat room is prevalent in eco-homes and is an easy way to achieve energy self-sufficiency. Different fireplaces and stoves were observed in this study. Eco-home makers attempt to experiment and develop appropriate methods to utilize wood and reduce the wood smoke. One approach is to increase burning efficiency. For example, rocket stoves [65] are very popular among participants' DIY projects. The goal of the rocket stove is to enable efficient wood burning in the room which reduces pollution and improves human comfort. Furthermore, the openness and flexibility of rocket stove enable eco-makers to DIY and fit their own needs.

4.3 Sociality and Everydayness of Making

To understand the effective functioning of eco-homes, one needs to attend to human behavior, practices, habits, and needs of people who inhabit those spaces. In this way, eco-homes are a balance between residents' needs and lifestyles that are more environmentally sustainable.

Sociality
Eco-homes are generally a part of larger eco-communities or eco-villages. Community members chose to work together in the pursuit of common ideas and intentions, and in this process, they help each other, share experience and provide technical support. Additionally, most eco-home methods and technologies are developed from grass-roots – via ongoing experiments involving a group of people and do not comply with contemporary building codes. It is often difficult to find professional builders to carry out the construction. Often, eco-homes are built by volunteers during the course of workshops. In this way, participating alongside other like-minded people not only saves labor costs, but also promotes the connection of individuals and the formation of communities. For example, Martin (P11) regularly holds natural building workshops and builds houses

with volunteers. He started his first workshop in 2015, and gradually more people followed him, wanting to learn how to build an eco-home by themselves. He argues that teaching others in workshop is the fastest way to learn, because in the process, he would find more information and reflect on previous projects. Moreover, he feels particularly meaningful and valuable to share his skills and ideas with others. He began to try to combine construction and healing in 2020, after his journey to other eco-villages in Thailand and India. He found that building together with other people not only promotes more sincere communication among individual, but also deepens the connection between human and the nature.

In addition to the construction of individual houses, eco-communities also organize workshops to build public landscapes and infrastructure, within which participants foster the sense of belonging and engaged relationships to the place. For example, John (P10) led a children's playground construction workshop in 2018. The playground is located in a small garden in an eco-village. In order to reduce the impact on the environment, they did not use any cement or concrete. Instead, they picked more than 1,000 small wooden stakes and smashed them into the soil by hand. A lid was made on the pit to create a primitive cave feeling. The entire construction process was completed by human labor without any machinery. As he noted:

> "We were divided into two groups, one for digging the pit and smashing stakes and one for making the lid. The two groups were separated by about 10 meters. In the end, we, about 20 people, lifted the lid together and move to the pit, and you can feel the power of the collective, and everyone worked together to accomplish this. There is individual work, and there are collective and community mutual support. We finally completed this together, which touched and shocked everyone". (John, P10)

Through building together, participants share not only physical labors but also emotional support. As we can see from cases, human well-being is also located at the central of eco-homes. Building collectively encourages makers to share their experience and stories. Then DIY eco-home becomes a convivial process and connection.

Ongoing Experiment

All the participants started DIY home from experiments. These grassroot innovations are rarely unproblematic. Eco-home makers make mistakes, learn from it and get bet-ter. Through such long-term interaction with materials, tools, nature and built environments, the relationship between inhabitants and the place which they live in is getting mature. As David (P13), who has been constantly being engaged in DIY home activities for 51 years, described his ongoing experiment:

> "I've never really finished a house yet, never will. But it's when I see something is functionally ready. I stop working on it for a small period of time. But then I start again whenever I learn something new".

Once eco-home makers start a DIY home practice, it tends to be a life-long experiment. For example, Oliver (P3), a 60-year-old maker, started an eco-community when he was young, and decided to live in a hunter-gatherer lifestyle, which he called an authentic life. 15 years ago, he began streamlining everything and started living in caravans. He had two caravans, which he later retrofitted: one for bedroom and office, one for kitchen and storage, and parked them both at his relative's place. In 2019, he moved to another place and sold one of his caravans. Now, he has divided his caravan into three parts, kitchen, bedroom and workshop. He cut the back off his caravan and put a door in, so that he could access the workshop from the rear. So that he had a large enough door to store large things. He built walls between the kitchen, the bedroom and the workshop, so that he does not smells or hear the fridge from his bedroom. He also recorded how much electricity and water he used every day to maintain his off-grid system. As He commented on his approach of this experiment:

> "I mean, I got I've got to a stage where if I want a solution and something, you know, you keep at it, and you'll find it. It's got to come out of somewhere. It's sort of like, you leave it to your subconscious to find it. And then all of a sudden you look at something down there, it is right in front of my face. I never even thought about doing it that way. Perfect. You know, that's the key, is to not try too hard to find the solution. Just let it come to you". (Oliver, P3)

Everyday Needs and Lifestyle

The most frequent word eco-home makers mentioned was the word "fit". The eco-home needs to fit into the environment, and fit around the needs of the people who live in it. What eco-home makers did firstly was to write down the basic needs of their house, so they knew what they were heading for. For instance, Bill (P14) noted that the first thing he needed is outdoor living space. Due to the climate in the east-coast of Australia (42 weeks of summer, 10 weeks of winter in a year) he wanted to spend most of his time in his verandah. He also needed a library for more than five hundred of his books, a proper kitchen space because he is enthusiastic cook, an aiding space and a living room with a big bay window. He wrote these requirements down and then did sketches of what he wanted. He wanted a house with the Japanese style, a living room with six sides, and "an engineer's cook kitchen" without drawers and cupboards (Fig. 4a), so it's easy to work in and doesn't have to go looking and rummaging around in a drawer. As he commented:

> "I love challenges. I love the whole concept of starting with nothing and building something which is actually felt like the house where you actually live in it when you're finished. And I think the whole thing about this was it starts off as a dream. And I knew I needed certain things in the house. The thing about the house is that it fits my needs. It's a comfortable house to live in". (Bill P14)

Bill lived on his own, but he did have children and grand-children who would visit him from time-to-time. His house is obviously built to cater to his own needs, but he also made sure that if he had his whole family coming over to visit, he would be able to entertainment in his house.

There are challenges for eco-home makers to balance environmental impact and comfort, such as dealing with human waste. Toilets enable us to explore the methods that makers use to live a comfortable and sustainable lifestyle. While various toilets are

(a)   (b)   (c)   (d)

Fig. 4. The "engineer's kitchen" (a), the circular bay window (b), the bookshelves (c) in the six sides living room, dry composting toilet (d) in Bill's house

available on market, eco-home makers prefer to design and build composting systems by themselves. For a small household, the dry composting toilet (Fig. 4d) is very common (P1, P3, P4, P5, P6, P11, P12, P13, P14, P15). By appropriate design, like a suitable location, long drop, balance moisture, and high chimney, it doesn't smell. Every year or two, when the wheelie bin under the toilet is full, people need to take out the bin and left for one more year to bury in the garden. For larger residential blocks, wet compost toilets are more efficient by introducing compost warm or biogas plants. In both cases, recycling humanure on-site makes everyday life a circular system and broaden possibilities of comfortable sustainability in eco-homes.

5 Discussion

In this paper, we have presented our findings from an ethnographic study of eco-home makers and aimed to highlight how they design, build and retrofit eco-homes and how they constantly reimage and reconfigure. These findings have outlined three overarching sets of practices: Material-first approach maps the complex factors that shape how eco-home makers make decisions and interact with various materials.

5.1 DIY Home as Placemaking

HCI researchers have borrowed and adapted the concept of place and placemaking to understand sustainability [22], offer strategies for Smart Cities [21], and understand domestic memories [66] in the urban context. However, the idea of placemaking is quite different in rural environment. In this paper, we grounded our work in rural DIY home activities and provided detailed description to our ethnographic encounters to investigate the goal of sustainability. In line with Desjardins et al.'s [22] framework of sustainable placemaking (longevity, unfinishedness and multiplicity), we observed how eco-home makers act as place makers and engage incrementally with the place they live in.

The forming of a mature and long-lasting relationship between a place and a maker takes time, which is referred to as longevity [22]. The design of 92-year-old David's house was a good example of longevity. The use of timber as the core material ensured David's long-term engagement with his house. The design of David's house has considered his everyday needs and routines through which he is able to function well. In a sense, the making of such a space arises through the long-term periods of living within that space and it is this temporal quality that allows new designs to emerge and sustain the placemaking process.

The quality of unfinishedness refers to a state that is constantly changing, and activities that are never finished [22]. In the eco-home context, the reason why the place is unfinished is because eco-home makers started DIY home from experiments and treated their homes as laboratories. Eco-home makers enjoyed the iterative process of learning, making mistakes and refining. Through such long-term interaction with materials, tools, nature and build environments, the intimate relationship between makers and the place is getting mature. From our fieldwork, we found that Oliver, for example, had been living in caravans for 15 years, and constantly retrofitted parts of the caravan when he moved to a new place. He started with two caravans, one for bedroom and office, one for kitchen and storage. When he moved to another place and started living in one caravan, he kept materials from the old caravan that he thought would be useful in the future, and then recycled them in different forms over a period of time. Through such ongoing adjustments, the place, the off-grid caravans, progressively fitted his needs and the environment he parked. Here, Oliver's living situation was always unfinished – as his life unfolded regularly, so did his living.

The multiplicity refers to the holistic approach that enables eco-home makers to reflect, experience and make the place [22]. All of our participants mentioned that permaculture [67] was the main method to guide their eco-home design. At the same time, they also had been learning and experimenting various techniques and methods based on their own interests and under-standings to make the place better. For example, Paul had three workshops for bicycle, woodwork, metal and mechanical work in his farm. He also grew food, raised native bees and produced wood for energy and making use. As we saw in our study, making an eco-home and living in a self-reliant lifestyle requires multiple competences. Moreover, multiple goals and strategies can co-exist to support sustainable placemaking.

However, apart from these three themes, we observed much more complex interactions between eco-home makers and their places. Eco-home makers have a deeper connection to the land and engage in a conversation with the natural world through placemaking. They hardly attempt to have an overall control of the construction and making processes, but engage in a shared autonomy with the place. Making and creating for eco-home makers also meant as reacting to nonstandard materials, complex nature, and diverse communities rather than just pleasure or executing a dream. Eco-homes became the stage that makers appreciate, where they collaborate with materials, nature, and communities and form an improvisation.

Unlike urban DIY activities that rely heavily on the use of existing industrial infrastructure and cutting-edge tools, rural eco-home makers preferred manual tools and appropriate technologies [68]. They value craftsmanship, self-sufficiency, respect unique qualities of every piece of material, and have more opportunities to access raw natural materials and heterogeneous nonstandard recycled materials. Thinking with hands [69] is the way they deal with these materials and shape their living environments. Even with specific goals, eco-home makers also reveal their personal perceptions, cultural expectations and unpredictable creativity. This kind of workflows not just give makers the sense of accomplishment but also constantly question and inspire them for further experiment and DIY to make the place better. Through these ongoing experiments and sense-making activities, an eco-home emerges as the unique spirit from inhabitants' attempts to constantly interact with materials and retrofit living environments.

For eco-home makers, human and non-humans are the stakeholders, adding natural entities, environmental surroundings and ecosystems in considerations. In order to build eco-homes to fit the environment, it usually takes a long time for makers to observe and understand the existing place, the landscape, sun movement, and various species. They believe that eco-homes should be able to minimize the adverse environment impact during construction and occupation compare to contemporary urban houses, in other words, they make the place better. Most of our participants had the options and ability to live in cities and enjoy a convenient life, but they choose to dive into ecology and care for the earth. DIY for them is not just a utility aspect but an expressiveness and sense-making feature of their lives. For example, Bill used tall frames and pole structure to build his house without any substantial excavation. He doesn't raise pets like dogs or cats so that wildlife like wallabies and kangaroos can hang around in his garden. Nathan and Paul plant native trees for birds every year in their farm and make beehives for native bees. They reject consumerism and industrial productivity that causes damage to the environment and pursue the self-reliance lifestyle as privileging diversity and nature. HCI researchers have shifted their empathy towards non-human elements to focus on post-anthropocentric design [50, 70]. However, this field still calls for a more inclusive and pro-found multidisciplinary base of methods and theories. Our ethnographic findings reveal human's perspectives, visions and abstract values as well as the diverse ways they work along with nature, which could inform future post-anthropocentric designs.

5.2   Co-design with Non-humans

In sustainable HCI, we are seeing an increasing interest in human-nature interaction [71, 72], and designing tools to sup-port interactions between non-humans and humans [52, 53, 73, 74]. Technology in this field is designed to connect human with nature and act as catalysts for collaborative sustainable making. From our ethnographic study, we saw a post-anthropocentric perspective. For example, eco-home makers not only built home for their own needs, but also emphasized the biodiversity they have achieved through the process. The design of eco-homes was always respectful towards other species, which showed that the process of building eco-homes as a co-design process that involved non-humans. How may HCI take up similar methods to support sustainable home making? One way is to develop tools to make such insights from non-humans more visible, by providing information about local species and ecosystem, soil and compost condition, sun movement, wind patterns, among others. From this standpoint, technology can play a role of a facilitator where eco-home makers could better understand the place they live in and get feedbacks for their DIY activities. Through making invisible visible, computing tools can help makers empathize the importance of non-human beings and foster a reflexive, speculative conversation with them. Design works such as Ode to Soil [75] and Collaborative Survival [50] provide starting points for explorations.

Where we saw the life-cycle cost, resource scarcity, fluidity and malleability as considerations of materials selection in DIY homes, we may care more about the value of craftsmanship, and the long-term relationship between makers and materials. HCI researchers aimed to decentralize human makers and regard materials as design collaborators [76] and have proposed digital craftsmanship. In this sense, materials call their own forms, making means in response to the living and changing qualities of materials. Our work reveals opportunities that computing technologies might create a dialogue between heterogeneous materials, manual tools and makers by asking open questions and not necessarily providing solutions. Keeping eco-homes open to change, mature and new materials can be integrated, and new forms can emerge beyond makers' imaginations.

The build process of eco-homes is similar to the "minimum viable prototype" [77], known in the software engineering field. They work on an assumption, build a prototype, and evaluate the idea. Keeping DIY practices at a smaller scale, not only provides flexibility for further optimization but also can be easily shared and adapted to by other makers. One possible way to foster these practices is Distributed System [78], making alternative experiments and sustainable practices replicable and connected [79]. Although social media platforms such as Facebook, YouTube, and Live Streaming can disseminate novel eco-home practices and help novices learn essential skills, many makers reject these applications for privacy, information overload, and political reasons. Additionally, some eco-communities and eco-villages are far from cities and lack infrastructures to connect the Internet. Decentralized technologies and distributed infrastructure could connect small elements and help them build an independent and resilient system. For example, decentralized applications like Secure Scuttlebutt [80] could be implemented without commercial network infrastructure, and as the alternative platform to share eco-home practices and knowledge.

6 Conclusion

Based on an ethnographic study of rural eco-home makers, we showed how they ap-ply a material-first approach, align their designs with nature and are influenced by sociality and everydayness of making. While we position our study alongside Desjardins et al.'s themes of sustainable placemaking [22] and other HCI studies on placemaking [21, 23, 27, 31] and DIY [1, 4, 9], this works has been able to deepens our under-standing of placemaking and DIY in HCI. Moreover, it sheds lights on how eco-home makers work with nature and constantly reimagine and renovate their home to fit the environmental and their own needs. With this paper, we foresee that our work will open up new avenues for future design and research of computing tools to empower residents as place-makers, where they can creatively co-design homes with non-humans, and make their own smart environments sustainable and resilient.

Acknowledgments. We thank all our participants for their valuable time. Dr. Dhaval Vyas is supported by the Australian Research Council's DECRA grant DE180100687.

References

1. Roedl, D., Bardzell, S., Bardzell, J.: Sustainable making? Balancing optimism and criticism in HCI discourse. ACM Trans. Comput. Interact. **22**, 1–27 (2015). https://doi.org/10.1145/2699742

2. Wakkary, R., Maestri, L.: The resourcefulness of everyday design. In: Proceedings of the 6th ACM SIGCHI Conference on Creativity & Cognition, pp. 163–172 (2007)
3. Buechley, L., Rosner, D.K., Paulos, E., Williams, A., Rosner, D.K., Williams, A.: DIY for CHI: methods, communities, and values of reuse and customization. In: CHI 2009 Extended Abstracts on Human Factors in Computing Systems, pp. 4823–4826. ACM Press, New York (2009)
4. Vyas, D.: Life improvements: DIY in low socio-economic status communities. In: Proceedings of the ACM Conference on Computer Supported Cooperative Work, CSCW, pp. 407–412. Association for Computing Machinery, New York (2020)
5. Fuchsberger, V., et al.: Fabrication & HCI: hobbyist making, industrial production, and beyond. In: Proceedings of the 2016 CHI Conference Extended Abstracts on Human Factors in Computing Systems, pp. 3550–3557. Association for Computing Machinery, New York (2016)
6. Smyth, M., et al.: Maker movements, do-it-yourself cultures and participatory design: implications for HCI research. In: Extended Abstracts of the 2018 CHI Conference on Human Factors in Computing Systems, pp. 1–7. Association for Computing Machinery, New York (2018)
7. Annett, M., Grossman, T., Wigdor, D., Fitzmaurice, G.: Exploring and understanding the role of workshop environments in personal fabrication processes. ACM Trans. Comput. Interact. **26**, 1–43 (2019). https://doi.org/10.1145/3301420
8. Deibert, R.: DIY Citizenship: Critical Making and Social Media. MIT Press, Cambridge (2014)
9. Bardzell, J., Bardzell, S., Lin, C., Lindtner, S., Toombs, A.: HCI's making agendas (2017)
10. Dew, K.N., Shorey, S., Rosner, D.: Making within limits: Towards salvage fabrication. In: Proceedings of the 2018 Workshop on Computing within Limits, pp. 1–11. Association for Computing Machinery, New York (2018)
11. Vyas, D., Vines, J.: Making at the margins: making in an under-resourced e-waste recycling center. Proc. ACM Hum.-Comput. Interact. **3**, 1–23 (2019). https://doi.org/10.1145/3359290
12. Berman, A., Thakare, K., Howell, J., Quek, F., Kim, J.: HowDIY: towards meta-design tools to support anyone to 3D print anywhere. In: 26th International Conference on Intelligent User Interfaces, pp. 491–503. ACM, New York (2021)
13. Peek, N., Jacobs, J., Ju, W., Gershenfeld, N., Igoe, T.: Making at a distance: teaching hands-on courses during the pandemic. In: Extended Abstracts of the 2021 CHI Conference on Human Factors in Computing Systems, pp. 1–5. ACM, New York (2021)
14. Radu, I., Joy, T., Schneider, B.: Virtual makerspaces: merging AR/VR/MR to enable remote collaborations in physical maker activities. In: Extended Abstracts of the 2021 CHI Conference on Human Factors in Computing Systems, pp. 1–5. ACM, New York (2021)
15. Wolf, C.T., Ringland, K.E., Hayes, G.R.: Home worlds: situating domestic computing in everyday life through a study of DIY home repair. Proc. ACM Hum.-Comput. Interact. **3**, 1–22 (2019). https://doi.org/10.1145/3359263
16. Desjardins, A., Wakkary, R.: Living in a prototype: a reconfigured space. Association for Computing Machinery (2016)
17. Schon, D.A.: The Reflective Practitioner: How Professionals Think in Action. Basic Books (1984)
18. Pickerill, J.: Eco-Homes: People, Place and Politics. Zed Books Ltd. (2016)
19. Foth, M.: Lessons from urban guerrilla placemaking for smart city commons. In: ACM International Conference Proceeding Series, pp. 32–35. Association for Computing Machinery (2017)
20. Wakkary, R., Tanenbaum, K.: A Sustainable identity: the creativity of an everyday designer. In: Proceedings of the 27th International Conference on Human Factors in Computing Systems - CHI 2009. ACM Press, New York (2009)

21. Freeman, G., Liu, S.Y., Bardzell, J., Lu, X., Bardzell, S., Cao, D.: Smart and fermented cities: an approach to placemaking in urban informatics. In: Conference on Human Factors in Computing Systems – Proceedings, p. 13. Association for Computing Machinery (2019)
22. Desjardins, A., Wang, X., Wakkary, R.: A sustainable place. In: Digital Technology and Sustainability, pp. 189–204. Routledge (2018)
23. Gonsalves, K., Foth, M., Caldwell, G., Jenek, W.: Radical placemaking: an immersive, experiential and activist approach for marginalised communities. Connect. Explor. Heritage Archit. Cities Art Media **20**(1) (2021)
24. Peacock, S., Anderson, R., Crivellaro, C.: Streets for people: engaging children in placemaking through a socio-technical process. In: Proceedings of the 2018 CHI Conference on Human Factors in Computing Systems,. pp. 1–14 (2018)
25. Malpas, J.: Thinking topographically: Place, space, and geography. Cannocchiale Riv. di Stud. Filos. **42**, 25–53 (2017)
26. Tuan, Y.-F.: Space and Place: The Perspective of Experience. U of Minnesota Press (1977)
27. Harrison, S., Dourish, P.: Re-place-ing space: the roles of place and space in collaborative systems. In: Proceedings of the 1996 ACM Conference on Computer Supported Cooperative Work, pp. 67–76. Association for Computing Machinery, New York (1996)
28. Jacobs, J.: The Death and Life of Great American Cities. Vintage (2016)
29. Whyte, W.H.: The Social Life of Small Urban Spaces (1980)
30. Schneekloth, L.H., Shibley, R.G.: Placemaking: The Art and Practice of Building Communities. Wiley, New York (1995)
31. Johnstone, S., Choi, J.H., Leong, J.: Designing for diversity: connecting people, places, and technologies in creative community hubs. In: Proceedings of the 28th Australian Conference on Computer-Human Interaction, pp. 135–139. Association for Computing Machinery, Launceston, Tasmania (2016)
32. Tomitsch, M., McArthur, I., Haeusler, M.H., Foth, M.: The role of digital screens in urban life: new opportunities for placemaking. In: Foth, M., Brynskov, M., Ojala, T. (eds.) Citizen's Right to the Digital City, pp. 37–54. Springer, Singapore (2015). https://doi.org/10.1007/978-981-287-919-6_3
33. Pang, C., Neustaedter, C., Moffatt, K., Hennessy, K., Pan, R.: The role of a location-based city exploration game in digital placemaking. Behav. Inf. Technol. **39**, 624–647 (2020)
34. McCarthy, J., Wright, P.: Technology as experience. Interactions **11**, 42–43 (2004)
35. Friedmann, J.: Place and place-making in cities: a global perspective. Plan. Theory Pract. **11**, 149–165 (2010)
36. Cranshaw, J., Schwartz, R., Hong, J., Sadeh, N.: The livehoods project: Utilizing social media to understand the dynamics of a city. In: Sixth International AAAI Conference on Weblogs and Social Media (2012)
37. Dalsgaard, P., Halskov, K.: Designing urban media façades: cases and challenges. In: Proceedings of the SIGCHI Conference on Human Factors in Computing Systems, pp. 2277–2286 (2010)
38. Tanenbaum, J.G., Williams, A.M., Desjardins, A., Tanenbaum, K.: Democratizing technology: pleasure, utility and expressiveness in DIY and maker practice. In: Proceedings of the SIGCHI Conference on Human Factors in Computing Systems, pp. 2603–2612 (2013)
39. Kuznetsov, S., Paulos, E.: Rise of the expert amateur: DIY projects, communities, and cultures. In: Proceedings of the 6th Nordic Conference on Human-Computer Interaction: Extending Boundaries, pp. 295–304 (2010)
40. Rosner, D., Bean, J.: Learning from IKEA hacking: i'm not one to decoupage a tabletop and call it a day. In: Proceedings of the SIGCHI Conference on Human Factors in Computing Systems, pp. 419–422 (2009)
41. Wakkary, R., Desjardins, A., Hauser, S., Maestri, L.: A sustainable design fiction: green practices. ACM Trans. Comput. Interact. **20**, 1–34 (2013). https://doi.org/10.1145/2494265

42. Andersen, K., Wakkary, R., Devendorf, L., McLean, A.: Digital crafts-machine-ship: creative collaborations with machines. Interactions. **27**, 30–35 (2019). https://doi.org/10.1145/337 3644

43. Woo, J., Lim, Y.: User experience in do-it-yourself-style smart homes. In: Proceedings of the 2015 ACM International Joint Conference on Pervasive and Ubiquitous Computing, pp. 779–790 (2015)

44. Cuartielles, D., Bean, J., Rosner, D.: Conversations on making. Interactions **22**, 22–24 (2015)

45. Toombs, A.L., Bardzell, S., Bardzell, J.: The proper care and feeding of hackerspaces: care ethics and cultures of making. In: Proceedings of the 33rd Annual ACM Conference on Human Factors in Computing Systems, pp. 629–638 (2015)

46. Lindtner, S., Hertz, G.D., Dourish, P.: Emerging sites of HCI innovation: hackerspaces, hardware startups & incubators. In: Proceedings of the SIGCHI Conference on Human Factors in Computing Systems, pp. 439–448 (2014)

47. de La Bellacasa, M.P.: Matters of care in technoscience: assembling neglected things. Soc. Stud. Sci. **41**, 85–106 (2011)

48. Loh, S., Foth, M., Caldwell, G.A., Garcia-Hansen, V., Thomson, M.: A more-than-human perspective on understanding the performance of the built environment. Archit. Sci. Rev. 1–12 (2020)

49. Clarke, R., Heitlinger, S., Light, A., Forlano, L., Foth, M., DiSalvo, C.: More-than-human participation: design for sustainable smart city futures. Interactions. **26**, 60–63 (2019)

50. Liu, J., Byrne, D., Devendorf, L.: Design for collaborative survival: An inquiry into human-fungi relationships. In: Proceedings of the 2018 CHI Conference on Human Factors in Computing Systems, pp. 1–13 (2018)

51. Liu, S.-Y., Bardzell, S., Bardzell, J.: Symbiotic encounters: HCI and sustainable agriculture (2019). https://doi-org.ezp01.library.qut.edu.au/10.1145/3290605.3300547

52. Liu, S.-Y.: Designing with, through, and for human-nature interaction (2019). https://doi.org/10.1145/3301019.3324874

53. Smith, N., Bardzell, S., Bardzell, J.: Designing for cohabitation: naturecultures, hybrids, and decentering the human in design. In: Proceedings of the 2017 CHI Conference on Human Factors in Computing Systems, pp. 1714–1725 (2017)

54. Kirk, D., Izadi, S., Hilliges, O., Banks, R., Taylor, S., Sellen, A.: At home with surface computing? In: Proceedings of the SIGCHI Conference on Human Factors in Computing Systems, pp. 159–168 (2012)

55. O'Brien, J., Rodden, T., Rouncefield, M., Hughes, J.: At home with the technology: an ethnographic study of a set-top-box trial. ACM Trans. Comput. Interact. **6**, 282–308 (1999)

56. Shewbridge, R., Hurst, A., Kane, S.K.: Everyday making: identifying future uses for 3D printing in the home. In: Proceedings of the 2014 Conference on Designing Interactive Systems, pp. 815–824 (2014)

57. Hwang, A., Hoey, J.: Smart home, the next generation: closing the gap between users and technology. In: 2012 AAAI Fall Symposium Series (2012)

58. Lieberman, H., Paternò, F., Klann, M., Wulf, V.: End-user development: an emerging paradigm. In: Lieberman, H., Paternò, F., Wulf, V. (eds.) End user development, vol. 9, pp. 1–8. Springer, Dordrecht (2006). https://doi.org/10.1007/1-4020-5386-X_1

59. Truong, K.N., Huang, E.M., Abowd, G.D.: CAMP: a magnetic poetry interface for end-user programming of capture applications for the home. In: Davies, N., Mynatt, E.D., Siio, I. (eds.) UbiComp 2004. LNCS, vol. 3205, pp. 143–160. Springer, Heidelberg (2004). https://doi.org/10.1007/978-3-540-30119-6_9

60. Horn, M.S., Jacob, R.J.K.: Designing tangible programming languages for classroom use. In: Proceedings of the 1st International Conference on Tangible and Embedded Interaction, pp. 159–162 (2007)

61. Dixon, C., et al.: An operating system for the home. In: Presented as part of the 9th {USENIX} Symposium on Networked Systems Design and Implementation ({NSDI} 12), pp. 337–352 (2012)

62. Hwang, A., Liu, M., Hoey, J., Mihailidis, A.: DIY smart home: narrowing the gap between users and technology (2013)

63. Zhang, T., Brügge, B.: Empowering the user to build smart home applications. In: ICOST 2004 International Conference on Smart Home and Health Telematics. Citeseer (2004)

64. Braun, V., Clarke, V.: Using thematic analysis in psychology. Qual. Res. Psychol. 3, 77–101 (2006)

65. Evans, I., Jackson, L.: Rocket Mass Heaters: Superefficient Woodstoves You Can Build. Cob Cottage Company (2006)

66. Sabie, D., Sabie, S., Ahmed, S.I.: Memory through design: supporting cultural identity for immigrants through a paper-based home drafting tool. In: Proceedings of the 2020 CHI Conference on Human Factors in Computing Systems, pp. 1–16 (2020)

67. Holmgren, D., Mollison, B.: Permaculture One. Int. Tree Crop Inst, USA (1978)

68. Schumacher, E.F.: Small is Beautiful: A Study of Economics as if People Mattered. Random House (2011)

69. Ruskin, J.: The Works of John Ruskin. G. Allen (1903)

70. Noz, F., An, J.: Cat cat revolution: an interspecies gaming experience. In: Proceedings of the SIGCHI Conference on Human Factors in Computing Systems, pp. 2661–2664 (2011)

71. Hirsch, T.: 13 beyond gardening: a new approach to HCI and urban agriculture. Eat Cook Grow Mix. Hum.-Comput. Interact. Hum.-Food Interact. 227 (2014)

72. Liu, S.-Y., Bardzell, S., Bardzell, J.: Out of control: reframing sustainable HCI using permaculture (2018). https://doi-org.ezp01.library.qut.edu.au/10.1145/3232617.3232625

73. Ballinger, M.L., Talbot, L.A., Verrinder, G.K.: More than a place to do woodwork: a case study of a community-based Men's Shed. J. Mens. health. 6, 20–27 (2009)

74. Mancini, C.: Towards an animal-centred ethics for animal-computer interaction. Int. J. Hum. Comput. Stud. 98, 221–233 (2017)

75. Liu, S.-Y.: Designing for multispecies collaboration and cohabitation. In: Conference Companion Publication of the 2019 on Computer Supported Cooperative Work and Social Computing, pp. 72–75 (2019)

76. Devendorf, L., De Kosnik, A., Mattingly, K., Ryokai, K.: Probing the potential of post-anthropocentric 3D printing. In: Proceedings of the 2016 ACM Conference on Designing Interactive Systems. pp. 170–181. Association for Computing Machinery, Inc., New York (2016)

77. Ries, E.: The lean startup: How today's entrepreneurs use continuous innovation to create radically successful businesses. Currency (2011)

78. Biggs, C.T.B., Ryan, C.J.R., Wiseman, J.R.: Distributed systems: a design model for sustainable and resilient infrastructure (2010)

79. Manzini, E., Coad, R.: Design, When Everybody Designs: An Introduction to Design for Social Innovation. Mit Press, Cambridge (2015)

80. Tarr, D., Lavoie, E., Meyer, A., Tschudin, C.: Secure scuttlebutt: an identity-centric protocol for subjective and decentralized applications. In: Proceedings of the 6th ACM Conference on Information-Centric Networking, pp. 1–11 (2019)

E-Scooter Sustainability – A Clash of Needs, Perspectives, and Experiences

Maria Kjærup$^{(\boxtimes)}$ ⓘ, Mikael B. Skov ⓘ, and Niels van Berkel ⓘ

Human-Centered Computing Group, Aalborg University, Selma Lagerløfs Vej 300,
9220 Aalborg East, Denmark
{mariak,dubois,nielsvanberkel}@cs.aau.dk

Abstract. Electric stand-up scooters (e-scooters) are introduced in several cities worldwide, providing new means for people to travel around the city. While praised for their flexibility, e-scooters are also met with negative sentiments due to fatal accidents and chaotic parking. In this paper, we seek to understand the mobility of shared e-scooters and point to gaps in the user interaction between the digital and physical world. We carried out three data collections, including interviews, *in situ* observation, analysis of news media coverage. Our findings illustrate integration with alternate modes of transportation in urban context, and how technologies facilitate or hinder (micro-) mobility. We found that users of e-scooters primarily view these devices as an alternative to walking rather than other transportation forms. Additionally, we found that users' and non-users' needs, perspectives and experiences of e-scooters clash, in particular with regard to perceptions of sustainability. Based on these findings, we present three relevant perspectives of sustainability, extending the ongoing debate of sustainable HCI research. We contribute with an empirically supported understanding of the perception of mobility and sustainability for e-scooters in a Scandinavian urban context.

Keywords: Transportation · Sustainability · E-scooters · Mobility

1 Introduction

Shared electric scooters are on the rise. Their introduction in many urban settings around the world enables new forms of mobility. Sometimes referred to as micro-mobility, this development is defined as *"the movement to unbundle the car with lightweight electric vehicles"* [3]. While such mobility may help to alleviate pollution problems, for example CO_2 emission or traffic congestion [20], several challenges emerge with the introduction of electric scooters and other lightweight motorized vehicles. These challenges include fitting with existing infrastructure, *e.g.* cluttering and obstructing side-walks and paths, or sharing of the roads with other traffic users [9,36]. Studies have shown that such challenges often lead to accidents with serious [4,14] or fatal [5,32] outcomes for riders and vulnerable

© IFIP International Federation for Information Processing 2021
Published by Springer Nature Switzerland AG 2021
C. Ardito et al. (Eds.): INTERACT 2021, LNCS 12934, pp. 365–383, 2021.
https://doi.org/10.1007/978-3-030-85613-7_26

road users (*e.g.* pedestrians). Additionally, the overall sustainability of the physical vehicle, from production to maintenance, has been questioned [29]. Despite such problems, shared electric scooters have become increasingly popular and are being introduced in new cities [6,46].

The emergence of shared electric scooters is highly relevant for mobile technology research as they provide new mobility forms through digital and ubiquitous technologies. E-scooters are a micro-mobility technology, which can be seen as a solution to address the last-mile problem of making connections to major transportation hubs [26,30,41], and thus serve to solve real and critical issues of transportation. The increased popularity of e-scooters presents a dualism, in which e-scooters can offer both a positive and negative effect on transportation sustainability. Prior work in Human-Computer Interaction (HCI) has commented positively on the hybrid nature of e-scooters for bringing fun user experiences, yet stresses the reliability and conflicts over public space [42]. While this highlights the value of ethnographic accounts of user experiences, we have limited empirical understandings of how people view and subsequently alter their transportation choices based on the sustainability of these shared e-scooters. In particular, we lack an understanding of how such shared e-scooter mobility compliments personal and walking transportation.

This paper investigates shared e-scooter schemes, so-called free-roaming rental e-scooters, in an urban context. We collect user and non-user perspectives through three distinct data collection techniques; interviews with riders, observations of riders in urban environments, and a preliminary analysis of social media comments. Our study provides insights into end-user motivation for (not) using e-scooters, highlighting implications for the acceptance of e-scooters as an alternative mode of transportation in society. This study builds on and contributes to the growing literature in HCI on sustainable mobility. In particular, addressing the tensions of HCI research's historical focus on technological novelty against the ethical imperative towards achieving sustainability goals [22,37]. We study the sustainability of e-scooters from three perspectives; green mobility, urban infrastructure and safety, and social and economic impact.

2   Related Work

Sustainability is an increasingly studied topic in the HCI research community. Through an analysis of published work on sustainable HCI, DiSalvo et al. identified different genres of study within this topic; persuasive technology, ambient awareness, sustainable interaction design, formative user studies, and pervasive and participatory sensing [22]. Our work falls within the genre of 'formative user studies', in which researchers aim to assess how users "*think about and approach sustainability*" [22]. While research on e-scooters is still relatively sparse, we next illustrate their role in a more extensive system of Mobility as a Service (MaaS) initiatives integrating micro-mobility, pointing towards the future of urban mobility. Additionally, we present the concept of hybridity as recently introduced in relation to research and design efforts.

2.1 Urban Sustainable Infrastructure and Micro-mobility

Contemporary use of the term sustainability touches on many perspectives. While traditionally used to denote initiatives that lower carbon emission, sustainable mobility now also refers to efforts such as reducing traffic congestion in cities, *e.g.* promoting ride pooling/-sharing, public transport and micro-mobility [43] and the planning of infrastructure to lower traffic injuries and increase safety for all road users [11]. Banister argues that local public transportation, cycling, and walking have become less attractive, giving way to car-dependence – fueled by the car's image of freedom and choice. However, when well planned, urban infrastructure will keep average trip lengths below the thresholds for walking and cycling and, in this manner, eliminate the need to have a car. This mental transformation of transportation needs depends on peoples understanding and acceptance of sustainable mobility [10]. Public Bike-Shares (PBS) have been around since the 1990s, and technological advances have since enhanced their efficiency and made them more accessible. PBS offer capacity to meet user needs for work, non-work, and leisure trips. In connection with public transportation, these bike-shares offer an improved first- or last-mile connectivity between home, public transport, and work places [15]. Bullock et al. found that while PBS offers an urban transport sustainable alternative, transportation modal shift from cars to bikes are infrequent. On the other hand, most shifts have been from walking, public transportation, or taxis. Bullock et al. argue that this shift resulted in journey timesavings, which is both a personal benefit of urban livability but also a considerable contribution to the urban economy [15]. PBS as a substitution for bus rides is further emphasized by Campbell and Brakewood, who argue that for mutually reinforcing sustainable transport networks it is vital to understand how public transit systems are interrelated with PBS [16]. Results from a PBS initiative in Beijing suggest that the placement of docks is critical for considering it a viable last-mile solution in connection with existing public transportation [30]. In an extensive literature review for KiM (Netherlands Institute for Transport Policy Analysis) from 2018, Durand et al. express the need for better insights on how free-floating e-scooter schemes impact travel behavior [23].

Smith and Schwieterman found that for short-distance travel (0.5–2 mi or 0.8–3.2 km) in parking-constrained areas, e-scooters would be cost-efficient and a reliable alternative to private cars. Furthermore, they found that dockless e-scooters (in comparison to docked bikes) could fill a void for intra-neighborhood trips where transit-coverage is limited [38]. Usage data from dockless bikes and dockless scooters in Austin in March 2019 – as collected during the technology and culture event SXSW – showed that while trips covered very short distances, the time spent covering the distance added up to an average speed of four miles per hours, considerably less than the topspeed and comparable to power-walking. This data suggests that people were not solely commuting but rather 'joyriding': *"More than a first- or last-mile solution, micromobility can actually be an extra-mile opportunity."* [4]. Reports from Portland [2] and NACTO [6] support these statements, highlighting that reasons for riding e-scooters include fun/entertainment or curiosity, and that shared e-scooter use is most common to usage with recreational bike-share use; social, shopping, and other.

2.2   Mobility as a Service and Ownership

The MaaS alliance describes Mobility as a Service as the *"integration of various forms of transport into a single mobility service accessible on demand."* [1]. Goodall et al. argue that transport operators must change their thinking in terms of business models, in favor of harnessing technological advances and enable a greater variety of choice of mobility modes, different uses of data, and a higher level of responsiveness [26]. Similarly, Spickermann et al. argue that the mobility sector, public authorities, and customers must break away from conventional thinking when it comes to the future of mobility and embrace integrated multi-stakeholder, multi-modal mobility scenarios [41]. Spickermann et al. argue that electric vehicles can be integrated into multi-modal concepts and help to promote the integration of transport modes in urban areas [41]. Empirical studies in HCI have investigated whether existing car-norms can be challenged by providing travelers with small electric vehicles [27] or creating awareness about the actual cost of car ownership and driving, that was transferable to other trips [40]. Hasselqvist et al. reported negative and positive experiences in the context of social structure, infrastructure, the individual, and near materiality. They further suggest sustainable HCI to focus on the *tension between the odd and the norm*. Spickermann et al. argue that a younger generation might be more likely than the older generation to relinquish the traditional ownership model [41]. Electric vehicles has also been suggested as a venue for design research to promote inclusion and thereby foster acceptance of new modes of transport and personal mobility. Don Norman express that design must strive to be inclusive of all ages, as a good example the Scooter for Life by PriestmanGoode is mentioned: *"Powerful lightweight motors and batteries promise to motorize many new things, including walkers, wheelchairs, bicycles, tricycles, baby carriages, and shopping carts. If these devices are stylish and useful, they will empower everyone, from the very young to the very old"* [33].

2.3   Hybrid Mobility

Recently, Fuchsberger introduced the notion of hybridity [24], in which the digital and physical are merged. Hybridity builds upon Weiser's vision of ubiquitous computing [47] and is used to evoke an image of merging: *"Everything computational may be considered hybrid, since it merges the digital with the physical"* [24]. Fuchsberger provides an example (among others) of hybridity; books have been adapted to viewing on smartphones and designers have tried to carry over this way of reading into physical books that can be held in one hand while flipping pages in a motion that resembles swiping a smartphone. Thus, understanding past developments may help overcome present issues. However, Fuchsberger warns that hybridity is not just mapping past development into current ways of living. Radical re-thinking is needed. Particular areas for HCI and design research are gaps where the physical and the digital world do not align with expectations *e.g.* concurrently keeping a physical calendar and a digital calendar and risk conflicting entries [24]. E-scooters can be viewed as a hybrid form of mobility, as digital (smartphone app functionality) and physical (e-scooter and road infrastructure) aspects are highly interdependent. Understanding the gaps in riding experiences can inform future directions for improving this mobility service and practice.

Tuncer and Brown illustrate through video-ethnography how e-scooter users perceive themselves as hybrid road users [42]. They observed riders instantaneously changing from riding in the bike lanes, to positioning themselves in the middle of the road 'like a car' and dismounting to jump red lights while positioning themselves as pedestrians in zebra crossings. Hildén et al. highlight the value of engaging with public transport users to identify their travel needs [28]. Prior work on sustainability also points to the importance of studying not solely the device or product, but instead focus on the perspectives of both user and non-users within the community [39]. These viewpoints motivate our work in the study of rider and non-rider perspectives and experiences concerning e-scooter sustainability.

3   Study

Our study focuses on riders' use and perception of shared e-scooter mobility services, as well as the co-existence of riders with other road users while moving around the city. We applied a mixed-methods approach consisting of three separate data collections: individual interviews with e-scooter riders, observations and first-hand experiences by riding along with other riders, and finally an analysis of social media comments (analyzing experiences from both riders and non-riders). In total, we conducted eight one-on-one interviews, seven *in situ* (group) observations of a total of sixteen people, and analyzed 300 comments from a Facebook group of a prominent Danish national newspaper (Politiken) on news about e-scooters in Denmark.

3.1   Individual Interviews

Eight people (four women, four men) participated in the individual interviews, ranging in age between 25–58 years (M = 33.1 see Table 1). We recruited participants through postings on personal as well as specific group pages on Facebook and through our own networks. Our participants had a diverse range of experience using rental e-scooters, with four of them having taken more than ten rides. As illustrated in Table 1, our eight participants had used e-scooters from different cities in primarily Denmark (Copenhagen, Aalborg, Aarhus) and secondarily New Zealand (Auckland, Christchurch). Participants had used various digital electric scooter services or platforms (*e.g.*, VOI, Lime).

Interviews were conducted as semi-structured interviews using an interview guide either in person or through a video conference call. The interview guide contained questions about experiences with riding e-scooters and adherence to regulations, general views on urban mobility, the role of electric motorized vehicles and technologies, and the digital facilitation of mobility. Examples of questions include: *"In which instances would you prefer the e-scooter over other forms of transportation?"* or *"How well do you know the regulations for riding e-scooters in your local area?"*

The interviews lasted between 25 to 70 min, with six of the eight interviews lasting more than 45 min. All interviews were audio-recorded for subsequent analysis.

Table 1. Demographics of the eight participants in our individual interviews.

ID	Gender (age)	Trips	Purpose (city)	Usual means of transport
P1	F (25)	>10	Sightseeing (Auckland, Christchurch)	Public, bike
P2	M (28)	3	Appointment (Copenhagen)	Public, bike
P3	M (25)	>10	Sightseeing & commuting (Auckland, Christchurch, Aalborg)	Public, bike
P4	M (30)	6	Job errands (Copenhagen)	Public, car
P5	F (32)	>10	Commuting (Aarhus)	Public, car, privately owned e-scooter
P6	M (38)	>10	Commuting (Copenhagen)	Public, car, e-skate board
P7	F (58)	1	Commuting (Copenhagen)	Bike, car
P8	F (29)	1	Appointment (Copenhagen)	Public, Bike, motorcycle

3.2   In Situ Observations and Interviews

We further conducted seven *in situ* observations and interviews with a total of sixteen people while riding e-scooters in Copenhagen, Denmark (Table 2). Our motivation for this data collection was to obtain first-hand experiences of riding these scooters and to observe e-scooter users while riding. We chose Copenhagen as city for this part of the study as its size fits e-scooters because many significant attractions are reachable using scooters, but also due to the fact that Copenhagen has a long tradition for bike riding and bike lanes, and thus provides a potential infrastructure for scooter riders (in line with argumentation from *e.g.* [8]). We chose to conduct these *in situ* interviews while riding with other riders as a kind of research in the wild as inspired by Rogers and Marshall [35] for conducting research in the everyday and in naturalistic environments.

We conducted our observations and interviews over two consecutive days. Observations were carried out in two distinct ways; 1) As a pedestrian, observing central points in the city center of Copenhagen at predetermined time frames – *e.g.* an hour outside the central train station during the morning commute, and 2) observation while riding an e-scooter, following the flow of traffic and clusters of e-scooters (as it appeared in the apps). We took observation notes to be written up later (interpretive description) inspired by the anthropological

Table 2. Demographic details of the participants in the *in situ* study.

ID	Demographics	Nationality	Trips	Purpose
W1	F (24) + M (34)	France	1	Tourist commuting
W2	F (52) + M (56)	England	3	Tourist commuting
W3	F (15 + 16)	Denmark	2	Joyriding
W4	F (14 + 13)	Denmark	2	Riding to train station
W5	F (10) + parent	Denmark	1	Joyriding
W6	M (15 + 15 +16)	Denmark	>10	Joyriding
W7	M (41 + 43) + F (38)	Germany	1	Tourist commuting

tradition of field notes [18]. To immerse in the environment, we carried out most of the observations as participant observation while riding an e-scooter around the city. Using the e-scooter as a *personality prosthesis* helped in approaching people on or by e-scooters [17] and most of the in-situ interviews resulted from this observation mode. We approached riders in traffic, taking into account the traffic flow and complying with local traffic regulations. We provide an illustrative example. When approaching W1 waiting at a red light, the observer made introductions, initiated interviews, and proceeded to follow them when the light turned green in order not to disturb the flow of traffic. The seven *in situ* interviews were carried out using the same semi-structured interview guide as used in the aforementioned individual in-person interviews. We proactively supplemented the guide with questions related to the current environment and situation of the riders. The duration of these interviews was considerably shorter due to the context of our observations.

3.3 Social Media Comments

Lastly, we analyzed social media comments on e-scooter newspaper articles to obtain experiences and opinions from both users and especially non-users. Introducing new modes of transportation to an urban context already surging with mobility offers is noticed by all road users, and therefore we wanted to obtain a first-person perspective on both user and non-user experiences. Inspired by prior work by Vistisen et al. [44], we collected and analyzed feedback and interactions from the comment section of an internationally recognized Danish news media called Politiken. During spring 2019, Politiken requested stories and experiences from citizens' everyday interactions and encounters with e-scooters. Two follow-up articles based on the responses to these requests and the corresponding social media comments were used for this part of our study.

3.4 Data Analysis

Interviews were transcribed for analysis and subjected to thematic analysis inspired by Braun and Clarke [13]. One author was responsible for data collec-

tion. All observation and *in situ* notes and transcripts were read by this author
for recall purposes, then coded, and subsequently arranged into themes using
affinity diagramming. Identified themes were scrutinized and iterated on in collaboration by all authors. Our analysis of the collected social media comments is
based on a total of 300 comments. Comments were individually assigned an ID
reference and manually sorted in an analysis framework consisting of two axes
with two sets of dichotomous stances. This allowed us to assess the comments
qualitatively based on of what was posted: 1) user (e-scooters) and non-user,
2) positive statements and negative statements. Each comment was plotted into
one of four quadrants of our analysis framework, while keeping in mind that
the individual comment was often to be read as part of a larger discussion. We
proceeded to identify clusters of comments. Comments that solely contributed
with unsolicited ridicule or spite (commonly known as trolling) were excluded
from the analysis, as well as comments that merely pointed critique towards the
news media and its journalism rather than the topic of interest.

4   Results

We next present our findings under the themes identified during analysis. These
themes include the diverse range of mobility needs expressed by e-scooter users,
the environmental perceptions and motivations towards the e-scooters as a *green*
mobility solution, the hybrid mobility experience of these devices, and finally
the non-user perceptions as observed through social media comments found on a
news article. P1-P8 refers to individual interview participants, whereas W1-W7
refers to *in situ* interview participants (riders in the wild).

4.1   Mobility Needs

Our first finding concerns the mobility need of the participants and generally we
found that the participants would use these scooters for shorter rides, but also
for more causal rides and activities. Most of our interview and *in situ* participants viewed the scooters as *walking on wheels* rather than substituting other
transportation modes (*e.g.*, bike, car). As the pricing scheme of these services
is generally counted by the minute, rides often preferred to use the scooters for
shorter distances (less than 5 km, approximately 3 mi) – comparable to walking
distance. Most participants found it less physically straining to move around by
e-scooter as compared to walking or biking. We further found that our participants would use rental e-scooters for one of three purposes; convenience and
ad-hoc trips, everyday commuting, and tourist or sightseeing purposes.

Six of our eight interview participants found the e-scooters more conveniently
available than other transportation modes (e.g. buses or metro), which supports
the comparison to walking (P1-P4, P6, P7). They all emphasized the ease that
comes with the free-floating, dock-less scheme of retrieving and parking the e-
scooters as compared to locating a transportation hub – *e.g.* train station, bus
stop, bike rack that has a fixed placement. Although, as participant P3 pointed

out, this required a critical mass of available e-scooters for the convenience to be noticeable. P2 particularly enjoyed how the free-floating scheme of the e-scooters offered a door-to-door solution rather than going by bus. P6 owned multiple transportation means, even an e-skateboard, but every now and then made use of the shared e-scooters.

"It's simply faster. A walk of 30–40 min I can ride in 10 min, especially for routes that cuts through bus corridors. if you have to change buses, even once, it gets annoying." (P6)

Participant P4 only used the e-scooters for running errands on the job, due to them being ready-at-hand and in close proximity. While P8 thought of e-scooter riding as a fun experience, she also found it too expensive compared to her usual means of transportation and would prefer to walk every now and then.

Some participants (3/8) primarily used the e-scooters for commuting (P5, P6, P8). Note that participant P5 was the only one included in this study that owned an e-scooter instead of renting; she primarily used an e-scooter as a last-mile solution. She argued that parking in the inner city is costly, and free spots are hard-to-find. Therefore, she often parked her car outside the city and used the e-scooter to cover the distance from the parking lot to her destination.

Finally, several of our participants would use the scooters for causal activities like being a tourist for sightseeing activities, as they were seen as useful for tourist transportation due to the need to get around to planned destinations and take ad-hoc detours to visit places on a whim. Several of our participants (P1, P3, P7, W1, W2, W7) used e-scooters to get around while abroad to avoid the strain of walking everywhere:

"We had walked ourselves half to death. I think one day we walked a half-marathon [distance]... We just wanted to experience all the things." (P3)

4.2 Environmental Motivations and Perceptions

Our participants, both those interviewed individually and *in situ*, generally held the perception that the e-scooters had a positive environmental impact. Two teenagers (W3) even noted the positive environmental impact as a factor for choosing e-scooters: *"It's environmentally friendly because of the electricity."* P7 would like to see urban centers completely emission-free, and in this regard welcomed the small electric vehicles (e-scooters and e-bikes) although she preferred the use of regular bikes.

Interestingly, more of the participants seemed to perceive the e-scooters as environmental neutral or positive due to the fact that they would compare the scooters to petrol-fueled cars. In this sense, they indirectly argued that alternative transportation to the scooters would be by driving a car or taking a taxi. However, as noted above, often scooters were used when walking and walking would be the natural alternative. As articulated by P3: *"... I like the idea of riding or driving on electricity compared to petrol ... not that it is the most important thing in the world, but it is sort of a feel good thing ...*". Some of the participants even followed Youtubers on the green transition or pro-environmental behavior. E.g. P6 occasionally watched a show called Fully Charged on using electricity for various types of transportation means like scooters or cars. Also, P6 considered buying an electric car and believes that more restrictions will be implemented in major cities in the years to come. A few of them even stressed that cities in Denmark, e.g. Copenhagen, ought to brand themselves for being sustainable or green due to the fact that a lot of electricity is produced from wind turbines in Denmark.

Our analysis of social media comments showed a big contrast in the perception of the environmental impact of e-scooters. Almost as many social media comments welcomed e-scooters as a green, environmentally sound mobility choice as the number of comments which rejected this perception.

Positive statements regard the emission of riding e-scooters: "*E-scooters don't emit CO_2.*" In particular when compared to the emission of other forms of public transportation; "*All in all a very green way of transporting yourself. It is greener than taking the bus.*" Whereas negative comments state that e-scooters are "*CO_2 sinners on a large scale!*" One comment linked to a report on the negative climate impact, while other comments presented concerns regarding the lifecycle assessment of the production and discarding of e-scooters and their batteries. Another comment emphasized that charging electric vehicles is dependent on sourcing electricity from other resources than fossil fuels.

4.3   Digital and Physical: Hybrid Mobility Experiences

Rental e-scooters are physical vehicles that require a digital counterpart to be used (*e.g.*, unlocking/locking in the mobile application). As such, e-scooters merge physical and digital aspects of mobility. We observed several digital factors that influenced the use of these devices. Understanding the concept on the first encounter was expressed by all interviewees as an initial challenge, albeit quickly overcome. However, all applications require a data connection, which was perceived as a challenge when *e.g.* traveling abroad without a suitable data plan. Two participants (P1, P3) explained how they would ad-hoc create temporary hotspots for locking/unlocking the e-scooter or even have to drag the e-scooter to a Wi-Fi hotspot to commence a ride.

Digital regulations affected the user's driving behavior in the physical world. For example, some rental companies have mapped out zones that can only be viewed digitally, and while you can physically park your e-scooter in a red zone, it is not possible to end your ride in such a location. Adversely, in response to the many complaints of haphazard parking of e-scooters, green zones have been implemented to nudge riders into parking in more appropriate areas by offering a payback of an amount of the cost for the trip.

While only two participants mentioned having noticed (and understood) the red zones on the map, P3 consciously used the app to earn free riding credits. Riding without credits was discouraging to the point where he would instead use another mode of transportation. Additionally, W6 stated that they were *"trying to find a way around"* paying for the rides, as one of them demonstrated how they successfully hacked the e-scooters to double the hard-set speed limit.

4.4 Non-user Perceptions

Social media comments presented a mixed perception in terms of e-scooter mobility. Interestingly, several of the non-users perceived e-scooters as a substitution for *e.g.* a private car or public transportation, rather than walking (as opposed to the riders that we interviewed): *"Every time someone travels by e-scooter instead of a car or a bus they will contribute to reduce congestion and that is something I would like to applaud.".* A few of the comments perceived e-scooters as a lazy substitution for walking and urged people to make better lifestyle choices regarding their transportation habits.

Challenges arise when reckless e-scooter riders are driving among pedestrians and other vulnerable road users. Lack of consideration demonstrated by some riders are expressed in several social media comments, *e.g. "They drive way too fast for anyone to react or sidestep."* Challenges additionally arise in connection with inconsiderate parking, cluttering up streets and sidewalks. One social media comment expressed the view of e-scooters as a toy rather than a vehicle: *"Scooters, skateboards and the likes are playthings and has no place on public roads, paths or sidewalks."* In response, comments from the social media analysis stressed that the physical infrastructure is seen as a necessary part of better regulation of e-scooter riding and micro-mobility in general.

Some comments emphasized the number of accidents involving e-scooters since their widespread introduction. One comment included a link to a report supposedly supporting their statement *"e-scooters have significantly more accidents per driven kilometer than other related vehicles."* Another comment stated that emergency rooms report a dramatic increase in head trauma injuries for e-scooter riding. In response to this, a person commented that they did not see accidents as a result of introducing the e-scooters but urged to direct the attention to the people riding them to regulate themselves rather than more external regulation: *"You wouldn't ban cars just because some are drunk driving."*

5   Discussion

Given their increasing popularity and impactful presence on existing infrastructure, the topic of e-scooters fits well within the ongoing efforts of sustainable HCI research. In particular, the clashes between users and non-users of e-scooters proves that the e-scooter is not introduced into a transportation vacuum. Instead, it stirs a critical question at the center of discussions: The role of HCI in technology innovation. Disalvo et al. and Silberman et al. emphasize the tensions between a historical focus on technological novelty and the ethical imperative of HCI towards sustainability goals [22,37]. In this discussion, we present different sustainability perspectives for e-scooters and integrate knowledge within and beyond the HCI literature to accommodate the need for studies to inform the design and operation of systems people use in their everyday practices [37]. Further, we demonstrate that e-scooter mobility is not solely a derived demand but also a valued activity [10].

5.1   Green Mobility/Environmental Focus

The perspective of e-scooters as a sustainable mobility mode, as based solely on their limited emission, has been widely critiqued. While Hollingsworth et al. agree that e-scooters as a substitute for private car usage results in a universal net reduction in environmental impacts [29], there are many other factors to take into account. The results of a Monte Carlo analysis, in which the total life cycle of e-scooters is assessed, point towards initiatives for e-scooter collection and charging approaches, *e.g.* fuel-efficient vehicles for collection, only collecting and charging in case of low battery, and reducing driver distance for collection. Importantly, they found that these results were susceptible to e-scooter lifetime, concluding that the positive environmental impacts will not be substantial unless the individual scooter lifetime exceeds two years [29]. Similar conclusions for PBS are found in a study by Luo et al., who conclude that if replacing car trips, both docked and dockless PBS can be seen as sustainable modes of transport when well designed and operated. They add that in particular environmental positive impacts are gained when PBS is used as a first/last-mile solution in combination with public transportation. Adversely, PBS is not necessarily the more sustainable choice compared to the bus, electric bikes, personal bikes, and walking [31].

In line with findings from Smith and Schwieterman [38], our findings show that the use of a shared e-scooter was primarily viewed as an alternative to walking over other modes of transportation. Additionally, shared e-scooters were preferred for relatively spontaneous mobility needs where routes can be navigated ad-hoc, *e.g.* more direct routes than offered by public transportation. Survey data from several U.S. cities suggest that people using docked bikes are more likely than people using e-scooters to commute for work or connect to other modes of transit [6].

Our findings show that both users and non-users generally perceive e-scooters as a sustainable mode of transportation in relation to *e.g.* a private car, due to running on electricity. However, e-scooters are not necessarily viewed as a sustainable *green* mobility offer when looking at a lifecycle assessment of production, upkeep, and discarding, as well as the source of the vehicle's energy. Our results indicate that the general public typically does not consider all these aspects when forming their opinion on green transportation alternatives. This observation holds for both users and non-users alike. How to effectively communicate the impact of e-scooters on the environment, balancing both the benefits and drawbacks of their production and expected (long-term) use, is an open research question with a potentially extensive impact. For example, work within HCI is being carried out to meet demands for charging small electric vehicle fleets, as their large quantity could pose a threat to power grid consumption and demand in the future [34]. Our results provide insight into the conflicting needs of end-users of such transportation technology, with a desire for e-scooters that are both widely and instantly available at an attractive price point.

5.2 Urban Infrastructure and Safety

Our findings mention infrastructure as a determining factor of the riding experience, *e.g.* dedicated bike lanes vs. cobblestone surface. Among others, Tuncer and Brown argue for HCI research to open the delicate debate on the amount of space currently dedicated to cars and how this prioritization misaligns with expectations of urban transport sustainability goals [42]. Banister also addresses the role of policy measures to widen the notion of the street, not only as a road, but also a space for people, green modes, and public transportation [10]. Redesigning infrastructure has also been attributed to increased safety for the individual, as presented in the 'vision zero' policy regarding transport safety, and sets itself apart by stating that designers of road safety policies and infrastructure initiatives are held responsible instead of the individual drivers in cases of serious or fatal accidents [11]. In 2019, the Norwegian capital Oslo proved successful in implementing Vision Zero with zero bicyclist or pedestrian deaths [19]. However, HCI research has questioned the implementation of a universal road safety culture and urges researchers to be attentive to local history, understandings, and practices of road safety [45]. The impact of these policies on sustainable HCI research and practice is currently poorly understood, providing opportunities for future study and engagement with policymakers. Furthermore, recent work highlights how the assessment of recent governmental policies provides HCI researchers with an additional tool to identify topics of societal relevance for future work [12]. To the best of our knowledge, this perspective has not yet been explored within the context of e-scooters.

Our findings showed that the dockless, free-floating scheme was crucial to considering the e-scooter over *e.g.* the docked (e-)bikes or public transportation, as they were viewed as a convenient door-to-door transport solution. Along with the aspect that it was considered as a more fun way to travel. However, the application of free-floating e-scooters requires reaching a mass that accounts for the density of a city and distribution of scooters to be available – as similarly argued by Campbell and Brakewood in relation to PBS [16]. Adversely, inconsiderate behavior and reckless riding was seen as detrimental to the acceptance of e-scooters. Research has pointed to e-scooter riders being more likely to ignore traffic regulations than other road users [9]. Unsurprisingly, our findings suggest that not following traffic regulations could result in insecurity in traffic for other road users, in the worst case leading to collisions and accidents.

Banister argues that public acceptability is an essential and often neglected part of sustainable mobility policies [10]. Our findings point towards different stakeholders, both public and private, that are expected to regulate better driving experience for riders to co-exist with other road users. Examples include the municipality for infrastructure and local regulations, rental companies for responsibilities towards respecting local regulations, and riders themselves to ride with more respect for other road users. Multi-modal mobility requires all stakeholders to engage in its success [10,23,26,43]. Rental companies have committed in different ways to communicate good riding practices to their users through *e.g.* campaigns rewarding users for demonstrating good practices along with investing in projects for appropriate infrastructure.

5.3   Social and Economic Sustainability

Ridesharing schemes have received negative attention for being mostly beneficial to middle and high-income households. In particular, low-income and transportation-scarce households, where vehicle ownership may not be an option, have been found to be disadvantaged in terms of accessibility to these services [21]. Our participants generally found e-scooters expensive to rent. Additionally, the use of e-scooters requires a certain level of (digital) literacy skills. HCI research has suggested that these factors, in other shared mobility schemes, point towards an unfair disadvantage for socio-economically disadvantaged groups [21]. Organized campaigns of vandalism have appeared, *e.g.* 'Uber Plätten!' (translation: 'Puncture Uber'), which incite and guide activist action against Uber vehicles, primarily bikes and e-scooters in Berlin against a perceived negative contribution to social mobility [7]. HCI research has focused on how the introduction of on-demand MaaS initiatives have created a mobile workforce. While this reliance on 'gig-economy' might increase worker flexibility and create new job opportunities, we also need to be aware of how this affects work conditions [25]. Future HCI research could investigate the social and economic sustainability of e-scooter pricing and availability.

Our findings indicate the sharing of e-scooters as a resource for tourists. This specific user group expressed a preference for e-scooters based on their ease of accessibility. At the same time, some noted that access to data networks and potential roaming costs could hinder their actual use.

Hasselqvist et al. found that one of the most echoed concerns of choosing small electric vehicles over cars was how other people characterized it as odd or extreme. Participants found that it can be unpleasant to break with social norms and expectations, and carefully chose how they explicated motivations of swapping their car with electric vehicles to non-participants [27]. Similarly, the clash of user and non-user perspectives demonstrated in our findings suggest that e-scooters are not yet fully socially accepted as a mobility mode. We argue that ethnographic studies of mobility can offer a lot in the discussion on how different modes of transportation may continue to co-exist in an urban context.

5.4   Utilizing Hybridity to Regulate Riding

The inherent hybridity of e-scooters as a mobility service is an interesting case on how digital and physical elements are combined to form the rider experience. We present our considerations on utilizing vehicle design and interaction in designing for e-scooters, based on our study's findings and prior work.

Our findings suggest practices of exploiting the hybrid aspects of e-scooters, both in detrimental approaches like 'hacking the system' *e.g.* tinkering with hard-set speed limits and positive approaches of 'gaming the system', *e.g.* earning credits in intended and legal ways. Facilitating ways of earning credits may contribute to viewing rental e-scooters as an attractive option. Tuncer and Brown additionally observed how e-scooter users 'hacked the city' by *e.g.* rental users utilizing e-scooters as a first- or last-mile transportation, to establish routes ad-hoc to more direct train lines that were previously too far away from their starting point [42]. We see potential to support this type of transportation navigation with real-time data, taking into account saturation across a range of transportation modes and suggest alternative routes that feature intra-modal travel plans. As addressed by our participants, ideally a payment plan that rewards users for *e.g.* frequent use outside of peak hours or for making sustainable transportation choices could be coupled with this dynamic application of route planning. Recent mobility research has suggested embracing the thought of mobility as a service to implement payment plans that resemble other services like streaming [43].

The mobile applications used to rent the e-scooters already provide various 'nudging' mechanisms, *e.g.* financial incentives when parking in appropriate locations. We see this as an open space for HCI researchers who wish to explore how the riding behavior of e-scooter users can be improved. Our findings showed that only a few participants were aware of how rental companies intervene or nudge users to regulate their e-scooter use, *e.g.* through no-parking zones or by directing riders to suitable parking zones by offering ride credits. Data-capabilities of these hybrid vehicles and companion apps may be utilized to determine where zones may be conveniently located – meanwhile increasing the risk that the free-roaming nature of e-scooters is reduced. Additionally, to accommodate the data connection issues, public Wi-Fi hotspots could be created that would encourage parking next to one, and to make it easier to ride for tourists or people with restricted access to data.

Our findings emphasize the need for a reasonable mass of e-scooters to increase the reliability of this transportation mode to be available when needed, as riders dynamically and rapidly re-position e-scooters around the city. Tuncer and Brown also point to rental e-scooters having issues with the reliability of position and availability [42]. In response to availability and reliability, a reservation feature might be considered. Reserving a particular scooter in advance will ensure that it will be available even if you have to walk to get to it. Further research following these lines of thought may uncover interesting potential solutions to make shared e-scooters more attractive. Additionally, in an effort to challenge the idea of ownership, application supported initiatives could facilitate sharing instead of renting schemes [42].

Limitations. Our *in situ* approach to both participant recruitment and observation enabled us to participate in and experience the physical elements of e-scooters on the streets. A challenge we have encountered in this regard has been recruitment, as the real world is characterized as being multi-located, hybrid, and mobile. We have attempted to accommodate the recruitment challenge by triangulating data collection approaches. Additionally, as we have studied e-scooters in the context of a Scandinavian country already well-known for its biking culture, results will not be readily transferable to other countries.

6   Conclusion

This study investigated dockless, free-roaming shared e-scooter schemes in an urban context by inquiring about the mobility needs of their users, as well as the issues they present for users and non-users alike. We explored this research question through three distinct data collections; individual interviews, in-situ observation, and an analysis of comments on social media. We present implications for the acceptance of e-scooters as a new mode of transportation, that is introduced into an existing multitude of alternate transportation modes. Our work extends the existing debate on policies of urban infrastructure, in particular within sustainable HCI research – highlighting the urgent ethical imperative of innovation and designing new technologies. We discuss three sustainability perspectives to take into account when imagining how e-scooters may make beneficial integration with a multi-modal urban mobility system; Green Mobility/environmental focus, urban infrastructure and safety, and social and economic sustainability. Additionally, we argue that the e-scooter is well suited for this integration as we view it as a hybrid vehicle, incorporating both digital and physical components. These hybrid qualities motivate design possibilities with respect to sustainability goals for an urban society.

Acknowledgements. The authors would like to extend their gratitude to all participants in this study.

References

1. What is MaaS. MaaS Alliance. https://maas-alliance.eu/homepage/what-is-maas/
2. 2018 e-scooter pilot: User survey results. Portland Bureau of Transportation (2018). https://www.portlandoregon.gov/transportation/article/700916
3. The car will be unbundled. Micromobility Industries (2019). https://micromobility.io/our-vision
4. Driving is work but riding is fun. The Microbility Newsletter (May 2019). https://micromobility.substack.com/p/driving-is-work-but-riding-is-fun
5. Electric scooters: Europe battles with regulations as vehicles take off. BBC (Aug 2019). https://www.bbc.com/news/world-europe-49248614
6. Shared micromobility in the u.s.: 2018. NACTO (2019). https://nacto.org/shared-micromobility-2018/
7. Uber plätten: News & einsendungen. Uber Platt Machen (2020). https://uberplaetten.blackblogs.org/news/
8. Abend, L.: Cyclists and e-scooters are clashing in the battle for europe's streets. TIME (Aug 2019). https://time.com/5659653/e-scooters-cycles-europe/
9. Bai, L., Liu, P., Guo, Y., Yu, H.: Comparative analysis of risky behaviors of electric bicycles at signalized intersections. Traffic Inj. Prev. **16**(4), 424–428 (2015). https://doi.org/10.1080/15389588.2014.952724. pMID: 25133656

10. Banister, D.: The sustainable mobility paradigm. Transp. Policy **15**(2), 73–80 (2008). https://doi.org/10.1016/j.tranpol.2007.10.005. new Developments in Urban Transportation Planning
11. Åke Belin, M., Tillgren, P., Vedung, E.: Vision zero - a road safety policy innovation. Int. J. Inj. Control Saf. Promot. **19**(2), 171–179 (2012). https://doi.org/10.1080/17457300.2011.635213
12. van Berkel, N., Papachristos, E., Giachanou, A., Hosio, S., Skov, M.B.: A systematic assessment of national artificial intelligence policies: perspectives from the nordics and beyond. In: Proceedings of the 11th Nordic Conference on Human-Computer Interaction: Shaping Experiences, Shaping Society. NordiCHI 2020 (2020). https://doi.org/10.1145/3419249.3420106
13. Braun, V., Clarke, V.: What can "thematic analysis" offer health and wellbeing researchers? Int. J. Qual. Stud. Health Well-being **9**(1), 26152 (2014). https://doi.org/10.3402/qhw.v9.26152
14. Brownson, A.B., Fagan, P.V., Dickson, S., Civil, I.D.: Electric scooter injuries at Auckland City Hospital. N Z Med. J. **132**(1505), 62–72 (2019)
15. Bullock, C., Brereton, F., Bailey, S.: The economic contribution of public bike-share to the sustainability and efficient functioning of cities. Sustain. Urban Areas **28**, 76–87 (2017). https://doi.org/10.1016/j.scs.2016.08.024
16. Campbell, K.B., Brakewood, C.: Sharing riders: how bikesharing impacts bus ridership in New York city. Transp. Res. Part A Policy Pract. **100**, 264–282 (2017). https://doi.org/10.1016/j.tra.2017.04.017
17. Chamberlain, A., Crabtree, A. (eds.): Into the Wild: Beyond the Design Research Lab. SAPERE, vol. 48. Springer, Cham (2020). https://doi.org/10.1007/978-3-030-18020-1
18. Clifford, J.: Notes on (field) notes. Fieldnotes Mak. Anthropol. **1990**, 47–70 (1990)
19. Coulon, J.: Oslo just proved vision zero is possible. Bicycling (Jan 2020)
20. Dargay, J., Gately, D., Sommer, M.: Vehicle ownership and income growth, worldwide: 1960–2030. Energy J. **28**(4), 143–170 (2007)
21. Dillahunt, T.R., Kameswaran, V., Li, L., Rosenblat, T.: Uncovering the values and constraints of real-time ridesharing for low-resource populations. In: Proceedings of the 2017 CHI Conference on Human Factors in Computing Systems, pp. 2757–2769. CHI 2017, Association for Computing Machinery, New York, NY, USA (2017). https://doi.org/10.1145/3025453.3025470
22. DiSalvo, C., Sengers, P., Brynjarsdóttir, H.: Mapping the landscape of sustainable HCI. In: Proceedings of the SIGCHI Conference on Human Factors in Computing Systems, pp. 1975–1984. CHI 2010, Association for Computing Machinery, New York, NY, USA (2010). https://doi.org/10.1145/1753326.1753625
23. Durand, A., Harms, L., Hoogendoorn-Lanser, S., Zijlstra, T.: Mobility-as-a-Service and changes in travel preferences and travel behaviour: a literature review. Netherlands Institute for Transport. Policy Analysis (2018)
24. Fuchsberger, V.: The future's hybrid nature. Interactions **26**(4), 26–31 (2019). https://doi.org/10.1145/3328481
25. Glöss, M., McGregor, M., Brown, B.: Designing for labour: uber and the on demand mobile workforce. In: Proceedings of the 2016 CHI Conference on Human Factors in Computing Systems, pp. 1632–1643. CHI 2016, Association for Computing Machinery, New York, NY, USA (2016). https://doi.org/10.1145/2858036.2858476
26. Goodall, W., Fishman, T.D., Bornstein, J., Bontrhon, B.: The rise of mobility as a service-reshaping how urbanites get around. deloitte review (2017)

27. Hasselqvist, H., Hesselgren, M., Bogdan, C.: Challenging the car norm: opportunities for ICT to support sustainable transportation practices. In: Proceedings of the 2016 CHI Conference on Human Factors in Computing Systems, pp. 1300–1311. CHI 2016, Association for Computing Machinery, New York, NY, USA (2016). https://doi.org/10.1145/2858036.2858468

28. Hildén, E., Ojala, J., Väänänen, K.: A co-design study of digital service ideas in the bus context. In: Bernhaupt, R., Dalvi, G., Joshi, A., Balkrishan, D.K., O'Neill, J., Winckler, M. (eds.) INTERACT 2017. LNCS, vol. 10513, pp. 295–312. Springer, Cham (2017). https://doi.org/10.1007/978-3-319-67744-6_20

29. Hollingsworth, J., Copeland, B., Johnson, J.X.: Are e-scooters polluters? The environmental impacts of shared dockless electric scooters. Environ. Res. Lett. 14(8), 084031 (2019). https://doi.org/10.1088/1748-9326/ab2da8

30. Liu, Z., Jia, X., Cheng, W.: Solving the last mile problem: ensure the success of public bicycle system in Beijing. Procedia Soc. Behav. Sci. 43, 73–78 (2012). https://doi.org/10.1016/j.sbspro.2012.04.079. 8th International Conference on Traffic and Transportation Studies (ICTTS 2012)

31. Luo, H., Kou, Z., Zhao, F., Cai, H.: Comparative life cycle assessment of station-based and dock-less bike sharing systems. Resour. Conserv. Recycl. 146, 180–189 (2019). https://doi.org/10.1016/j.resconrec.2019.03.003

32. Nellamattathil, M., Amber, I.: An evaluation of scooter injury and injury patterns following widespread adoption of e-scooters in a major metropolitan area. Clin. Imaging 60(2), 200–203 (2020). https://doi.org/10.1016/j.clinimag.2019.12.012

33. Norman, D.: "i wrote the book on user-friendly design. what i see today horrifies me". Fast Company (2019)

34. Quintal, F., Scuri, S., Barreto, M., Pereira, L., Vasconcelos, D., Pestana, D.: Mytukxi: low cost smart charging for small scale EVs. In: Extended Abstracts of the 2019 CHI Conference on Human Factors in Computing Systems, pp. 1–6. CHI EA 2019, Association for Computing Machinery, New York, NY, USA (2019). https://doi.org/10.1145/3290607.3312874

35. Rogers, Y., Marshall, P.: Research in the wild. Synth. Lect. Hum.-Cent. Inform. 10(3), i–97 (2017)

36. Shaheen, S., Cohen, A.: Shared micromoblity policy toolkit: docked and dockless bike and scooter sharing (2019). https://doi.org/10.7922/G2TH8JW7

37. Silberman, M.S., et al.: Next steps for sustainable HCI. Interactions 21(5), 66–69 (2014). https://doi.org/10.1145/2651820

38. Smith, C.S., Schwieterman, J.P.: E-scooter scenarios: evaluating the potential mobility benefits of shared dockless scooters in chicago (2018)

39. Soro, A., Brereton, M., Taylor, J.L., Lee Hong, A., Roe, P.: A cross-cultural noticeboard for a remote community: design, deployment, and evaluation. In: Bernhaupt, R., Dalvi, G., Joshi, A., Balkrishan, D.K., O'Neill, J., Winckler, M. (eds.) INTERACT 2017. LNCS, vol. 10513, pp. 399–419. Springer, Cham (2017). https://doi.org/10.1007/978-3-319-67744-6_26

40. Southern, C., Cheng, Y., Zhang, C., Abowd, G.D.: Understanding the cost of driving trips. In: Proceedings of the 2017 CHI Conference on Human Factors in Computing Systems, pp. 430–434. CHI 2017, Association for Computing Machinery, New York, NY, USA (2017). https://doi.org/10.1145/3025453.3025686

41. Spickermann, A., Grienitz, V., von der Gracht, H.A.: Heading towards a multimodal city of the future?: Multi-stakeholder scenarios for urban mobility. Technol. Forecast. Soc. Change 89, 201–221 (2014). https://doi.org/10.1016/j.techfore.2013.08.036

42. Tuncer, S., Brown, B.: E-scooters on the ground: lessons for redesigning urban micro-mobility. In: Proceedings of the 2020 CHI Conference on Human Factors in Computing Systems, pp. 1–14. CHI 2020, Association for Computing Machinery, New York, NY, USA (2020). https://doi.org/10.1145/3313831.3376499

43. Utriainen, R., Pöllänen, M.: Review on mobility as a service in scientific publications. Res. Transp. Bus. Manag. **27**, 15–23 (2018). https://doi.org/10.1016/j.rtbm. 2018.10.005. special Issue on Mobility as a Service

44. Vistisen, P., Poulsen, S.B.: Return of the vision video: can corporate vision videos serve as setting for participation? Nordes **7**(1), 1–8 (2017)

45. Wang, M., Lundgren Lyckvi, S., Chen, F.: Why and how traffic safety cultures matter when designing advisory traffic information systems. In: Proceedings of the 2016 CHI Conference on Human Factors in Computing Systems. p. 2808–2818. CHI 2016, Association for Computing Machinery, New York, NY, USA (2016). https://doi.org/10.1145/2858036.2858467

46. Wanger, I.: Worldwide number of battery electric vehicles in use from 2012 to 2019. Statista (2019). https://www.statista.com/statistics/270603/worldwide-number-of-hybrid-and-electric-vehicles-since-2009/

47. Weiser, M.: The computer for the 21st century. Sci. Am. **265**(3), 94–105 (1991)

Objective Evaluation of Subjective Metrics for Interactive Decision-Making Tasks by Non-experts

Yann Laurillau[1]([✉]), Joëlle Coutaz[1], Van Bao Nguyen[1], Gaëlle Calvary[1], and Daniel Llerena[2]

[1] LIG, Univ. Grenoble-Alpes, CNRS, Grenoble INP, 38000 Grenoble, France
{yann.laurillau,joelle.coutaz,van-bao.nguyen,
gaelle.calvary}@univ-grenoble-alpes.fr
[2] GAEL, Univ. Grenoble-Alpes, CNRS, Grenoble INP, 38000 Grenoble, France
daniel.llerena@univ-grenoble-alpes.fr

Abstract. This work addresses the evaluation of interaction techniques for decision-making tasks performed by non-experts in the context of multi-objective optimization problems. Such tasks require making trade-offs between antagonistic criteria, according to individual subjective preferences. Evaluating such techniques is made difficult by the subjective nature of such tasks, as well as by a lack of rigorous methods for assessment. Our primary contributions to this problem are two-fold: (1) a set of subjective metrics including decision accuracy, choice satisfaction, and incentives to explore; (2) the use of a pragmatic approach to map these subjective metrics onto objective quantitative measures. To illustrate how this subjective-objective mapping can be performed in a pragmatic manner, we have conducted an experiment involving 177 participants to objectively measure and compare two multi-slider interaction techniques for decision-making tasks performed by non-experts in the context of domestic energy management. The results of this evaluation constitute a secondary contribution.

Keywords: Multi-criteria decision-making · Evaluation · Decision-making task · Pareto front · Optimization problem · Tightly coupled sliders · Energy management

1   Introduction

In Psychology, decision-making is a cognitive process that results in the selection of an alternative from multiple possibilities. To help this process, the field of Multi-Criteria-Decision Making (MCDM) has developed mathematical models, methods and algorithms that generate solutions for problems that involve multiple, possibly conflicting,

Electronic supplementary material   The online version of this chapter (https://doi.org/10.1007/978-3-030-85613-7_27) contains supplementary material, which is available to authorized users.

criteria [29]. For such problems, there is no unique solution but a set of alternatives from which decision makers must choose the solution that best fits their objectives or preferences. To make informed decisions, decision makers should be supported by appropriate tools such as visualization techniques.

Most work on visualization for decision-making has focused on Multi-Attribute Decision Analysis, a subclass of MCDM for which the solution space is discrete, finite, and predetermined (such as finding a hotel room for a vacation). Dimara et al. refer to a *"multi-attribute choice task (MACT) as a task that consists of choosing the best alternative among a fixed set of alternatives where alternatives are defined across several attributes"* [9]. In this article, we are concerned with Multi-Objective Optimization problems, another subclass of MCDM problems, for which the set of alternatives is continuous, possibly infinite, not known explicitly in advance, and where the criteria are strongly interdependent. To complement Dimara et al., we define a *"multi-objective choice task (MOCT) as a task that consists of choosing the best alternative from a continuous set of alternatives where criteria are strongly interdependent"*.

For Multi-Objective Optimization problems, it is impossible to find a solution that simultaneously gives the optimal value for all the criteria. Rather, there exist many solutions, called Pareto-optimal [1], that satisfy the problem mathematically. Because all Pareto-optimal solutions are equally good from the mathematical point of view, decision makers have to select the preferred "best" solution. This requires making trade-offs between the criteria, where making trade-offs means giving up on at least one criterion to allow the improvement of others.

As a typical example of this class of problems, consider Alice who would like to be warm with good air quality at the lowest possible cost. Suppose that her home is equipped with an e-coach energy management system capable of generating Pareto-optimal solutions for her problem [3]. The Pareto front, which corresponds to the set of optimal solutions, delimits the frontier between the set of feasible but non-optimal solutions from the set of unfeasible solutions. To be optimal, Alice must select her preferred solution from the Pareto front by deciding how much she is ready to give up on thermal comfort and air quality to reduce financial cost or vice versa. To make this final decision, Alice must draw on her subjective preferences.

In this article, we are concerned with the problem of objectively evaluating and comparing interaction techniques designed for tasks that are inherently subjective. There is a growing research interest in addressing this issue in the field of interactive visualization [2, 4, 5]. In this area, evaluation generally consists of assessing the usability of the technique as in [30], or evaluating the capacity of the technique to support data exploration for analytical tasks such as retrieving a particular value [10]. Based on qualitative studies, Boukhelifa et al. [6] show how experts resolve conflicts between competing objectives but do not address the comparative evaluation of multiple techniques. In [9], Dimara et al. investigate metrics, such as decision accuracy, to objectively compare interactive visualizations for MACTs. In this article, we address this issue for MOCTs – which, by definition, are more complex than MACTs, when performed by non-experts – who, like Alice, are not trained in this type of tasks.

Our primary contributions to the objective evaluation of interaction techniques for MOCTs are two-fold: (1) a set of subjective metrics including decision accuracy, choice satisfaction, and incentives to explore, that can be objectively and quantitatively measured; (2) the use of a pragmatic approach to map these subjective metrics onto objective quantitative measures. To illustrate how this subjective-objective mapping can be performed in a pragmatic manner, we have conducted an experiment involving 177 participants to objectively measure and compare Sliders4DM and P4DM, our own re-implementations of two existing multi-slider interaction techniques for exploring Pareto fronts, respectively, TOP-Slider [19] aimed at non-experts performing multi-objective choice tasks, and 'Pareto sliders' developed for expert surgeons [24].

In the following, we provide an overview of related work and justify our choice for multi-slider interaction techniques as representative case studies for MOCTs. We then propose a set of objective and subjective metrics for assessing these techniques and show how a pragmatic approach can be used to measure the proposed subjective metrics, both quantitatively and objectively, from logged data. The experiment conducted to show the feasibility of our approach and the results are then presented in detail. We finally discuss our findings and conclude with implications for future research.

2 Related Work

In this section, we provide an overview of previous work on visualization techniques for optimization problems, along with the requirements for supporting non-experts. We then cover related work on the evaluation of tools for MOCTs.

2.1 Visualization Techniques for Optimization Problems

Visualization techniques for optimization problems have been proposed for experts in specific areas such as engineering design, business intelligence, and surgery. A number of methods including HSDC [1], 3D-RadVis [14], and ParetoBrowser [27] have been developed to visualize Pareto fronts for complex optimization problems. In particular, 3D-RadVis maps large dimensional objective spaces to 3D representations while preserving the shape of the Pareto front. However, 3D representations require specific training for interpretation. To alleviate this problem, ParetoBrowser combines 2D and 3D graphs with parallel coordinates representations. However, ParetoBrowser is intended for domain experts.

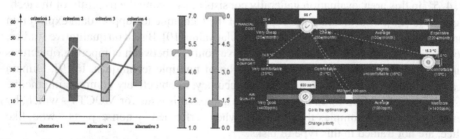

Fig. 1. Alternatives represented as value paths (extract from [21]) (left); The Pareto Slider for surgery (PSS) (extract from [24]) for two criteria (middle); TOP-Slider with three criteria (right): financial cost, thermal comfort, and air quality (extract from [19]).

For an untrained user such as Alice who has little or no knowledge in thermal models, we hypothesize the following requirements. Visualization techniques targeted at non-experts performing multi-objective choice tasks should: (R1) Hide the complexity of the optimization problem while facilitating the understanding of the mutual influence between the criteria; (R2) Favor the exploration of the Pareto front to find the preferred "best" solution in an informed manner; (R3) Notify users when moving away from the optimal solution space; (R4) Make the Pareto front observable in order to limit the attraction effect bias and to incite users to select optimal solutions [10].

Sliders are commonly used interactive tools for exploring data spaces and selecting values. Thus, we hypothesize that multi-slider based techniques can provide an appropriate foundation for supporting non-experts performing multi-objective choice tasks. As illustrated by Value Paths [21], Pareto Slider [24], and TOP-Slider [19] discussed below, multiple sliders can be combined to implicitly represent Pareto fronts in a 2D-space (cf. R4), and thereby, hiding the complexity of the underlying optimization problem (cf. R1) while favoring the exploration of the solution space (cf. R2).

Value Paths visualize Pareto optimal solutions as a set of parallel vertical bars in a 2D-coordinate space (See Fig. 1-left). Each criterion is represented by a bar whose size and location on the y-axis express the range (provided that it is known) of the criterion in the Pareto optimal set. Alternatives are represented by polygonal lines called value paths. Similarly to the parallel coordinates technique, the number of criteria can be increased to a certain degree, but having too many alternatives makes interpretation and comparison difficult [21].

Many multi-slider interactive techniques have been developed for multi-attribute choice tasks [23, 25, 26, 31], but very few have targeted multi-objective choice tasks. Pareto Slider designed for Surgeons (PSS in short) [24] and TOP-Slider [19] are notable exceptions. Both of them are composed of parallel sliders, using one slider per criterion. The Pareto front is represented implicitly as ranges of optimal values distributed across the sliders. Whereas Value Paths represent Pareto optimal ranges only, PSS shows both the optimal and unfeasible ranges using color-coding (see Fig. 1-middle). TOP-Slider goes one step further by representing the optimal, unfeasible, as well as feasible but non-optimal Pareto ranges using white, red and grey color-coding respectively (see Fig. 1-right as an illustration). Color-coding is one way to indicate users when moving away from the Pareto front (cf. R3).

Both PSS and TOP-Slider express the interdependence between criteria in a tightly-coupled manner (cf. R1). However, these techniques differ in the way they provide feedback when a cursor is moved. In PSS, moving the cursor of one slider to modify the value of its corresponding criterion, moves the cursor of the other sliders automatically so that the new position of the cursors corresponds to a Pareto optimal solution. The strategy used for choosing the new Pareto optimal solution among the possible ones is computed algorithmically, not decided by users. By contrast, with TOP-Slider, moving one cursor does not move the other cursors. Instead, as shown in Fig. 1-right, two pairs of lines pop up to show the impact of the current position of the cursor on the Pareto ranges of the other criteria. As a consequence and contrary to PSS, TOP-Slider allows users to choose their preferred optimal solution as well as to explore trade-offs that are not necessarily Pareto optimal (cf. R2).

2.2   Evaluation of Tools for Multi-objective Choice Tasks

In their analysis of evaluation methods of tools for multi-attribute choice tasks (MACT) [9], Dimara et al. observe that *"there is a lack of methodological guidance in the information visualization literature on how to do so"*. The problem is two-fold: (1) Objective metrics are not enough to capture the quality of a decision, given that *"finding a good trade-off"* is subjective. Subjective metrics such as self-reported satisfaction are useful, but unreliable as they may be subject to cognitive biases [10]. (2) There is a lack of clear references for identifying an appropriate baseline for comparative assessment.

As a first step towards a more rigorous approach to the evaluation of tools for multi-attribute choice tasks, Dimara et al. [4] propose a combination of objective and subjective metrics for comparing parallel coordinates, scatterplot, and tabular visualizations, three commonly used elementary visualization techniques: accuracy and time-on-task as objective metrics; technique preference, satisfaction, confidence, easiness, and attachment as subjective metrics. Dimara et al. report that, for decision-making, the three techniques are comparable across the metrics with *"a slight speed advantage for the tabular visualization"*. Therefore *"time-on-task can be a useful differentiating factor"*. Another interesting conclusion is that *"testing real decision tasks can provide more insights"*.

Although table-based visualization techniques seem more effective for decision-making than scatter plots and parallel coordinates [15], they are not applicable to optimization problems where the set of alternatives is continuous and possibly unknown in advance. As we are concerned with multi-objective choice tasks, we have elected the slider, another commonly used elementary interactive tool that supports choosing a value in a range of continuous numeric values. Although Dimara et al.'s work is an important contribution to the problem of evaluating tools for decision making by non-experts, sliders have not been covered by their study.

Sharing similarities with Multi-Objective Optimization problems, geospatial multi-criteria decision-making (GIS-MCDM) problems deal with an infinite and continuous set of alternatives (e.g. geographical distance). Milutinovic et al. [22] developed GISwaps, a novel method based on the concept of Even Swaps, *"a trade-off-based method for multiple criteria decision-making under certainty"*. This method consists of adjusting alternatives depending on a reference criterion, and a response criterion depending on a set of *"virtual alternatives"*: the key idea is to make the reference criterion "irrelevant" thanks to a compensation value applied to the response criterion. Based on this method, they conducted a quantitative comparative study to objectively evaluate the impact of interactive visualization on trade-off-based geospatial decision-making. To do so, they compute *"the average trade-off value for each virtual alternative in each swap turn (ranking results)"* and *"variation in compensation values in trade-offs"*. The key result shows that interactive visualization leads to more consistent trade-offs.

Boukhelifa et al. [6] have conducted an observational study in order to understand how experts, in a collaborative setup, develop strategies to deal with "multiple competing objectives" for exploring complex solutions spaces in the context of Multi-objective Optimization. In this study, the underlying optimization model is a multi-dimensional Pareto front. One key observed strategy for trade-off is prioritization: experts often start with the most important criterion according to their expertise, then refine their exploration based on a secondary criterion.

PSS targets surgeons for planning medical radiofrequency ablation, and has been evaluated with only 2 surgeons. As discussed above, PSS enforces the choice for an optimal solution as the result of the value change of one criterion. The experiment does not address the adequacy of this strategy. To the best of our knowledge, TOP-Slider is the only example of a multi-slider interaction technique targeted at non-experts for multi-objective choice tasks. TOP-Slider, however, has only been evaluated qualitatively with 16 participants [19].

3 Mapping Subjective Metrics with Objective Measures Using Pragmatism: Comparing TOP-Slider (S4DM) with PSS (P4DM) as a Case Study

In this section, we address the following research question: how to objectively and experimentally evaluate and compare interaction techniques designed for MOCTs? More specifically, in addition to the usual objective metrics such as time-on-task, what objective measures should be used in practice to evaluate metrics that are inherently subjective? In the following, we first present our approach to address these questions using a pragmatic approach. We then detail each step of this approach.

3.1 A 3-step Pragmatic Approach

As discussed in [9], decision-accuracy and decision-satisfaction are inherent to decision-making tasks. However, defining a measure for these metrics is challenging because of the subjective nature of decision tasks and because of the difficulty to find "good" solutions without objective methods such as Pareto-based models. To address this difficulty, we have adopted a pragmatic approach, drawing on the experimental context to map aggregated logged data as objective measures for subjective metrics.

Pragmatism is *"thinking about solving problems in a practical and sensible way rather than by having fixed ideas and theories"* (Cambdridge Dictionnary). In research, a pragmatic approach focuses on finding useful/practical solutions in a realistic context through experiential inquiry [13], *"rather than becoming mired in discussions regarding generalizability"* [16]. For this study, we propose a 3-step pragmatic approach that consists for the experimenters (1) to elicit the characteristics shared by the target users, (2) to consider the key differentiating features of the interaction techniques under evaluation, and (3) to draw on the context of use.

As a concrete example of interaction techniques and realistic context of use, we considered TOP-Sliders [19] and PSS respectively [24], in the context of residential homes equipped with a smart energy management system. Typically, users are not experts in thermal modeling, but they are familiar with thermal comfort, air quality and financial cost. Using either one of these techniques, inhabitants would express their preferences as a trade-off between comfort, air quality and financial cost. As users modify their preferences, the system would update the Pareto-based optimal solution space from which users could iteratively pick the most appropriate solution for them.

The choice for TOP-Sliders and PSS is motivated by the following: (1) They both address MOCTs using sliders as the elementary interactive technique; and (2) both of them use color-coding but differ in the way the interdependence of the criteria is reflected as well as how they suggest or enforce the choice for optimal solutions. For the sake of conformity and comparison with the qualitative study performed in [19] for TOP-Sliders, we have elicited the same three criteria for expressing users' preferences: financial cost, thermal comfort, and air quality.

The choice for energy management as context of use is motivated by the following: (1) energy is a major world societal grand challenge for the upcoming decades (e.g., United Nation's sustainable development goals [28]); and (2) energy management is a typical example addressed by research on optimization models such as finding trade-offs between energy consumption and thermal comfort (e.g., [32]).

3.2 Step 1: Profiling with a Preliminary Study

As a first step, we propose to *identify a primary criterion that reflects the participants' profile*. This contrasts with Dimara et al. who, to measure decision-accuracy [9], relied on self-reported preferences, which are not necessarily reliable [10].

We conducted a preliminary users study [19] to evaluate TOP-Sliders qualitatively involving a limited number of participants in order (1) to improve the design of TOP-Sliders until the requirements were met satisfactorily, (2) to identify the strategies that users developed to find their preferred solution. Participants ranged between 17 and 71, of which 6 were over 40, with an average of ~ 38. The participants included 1 computer scientist, 9 students, and 6 family members (of which 4 retired healthy persons). 7 participants had concerns for energy consumption and financial cost and 3 of the retired participants used a technical solution to manage their own consumption at home (e.g., programming heating periods). In particular, the semi-structured interviews uncovered that all the students asserted that financial cost was more important than thermal comfort. Therefore, in the context of energy saving by participants with low income, we hypothesized that financial cost is the primary criterion.

In the following, we will refer to Sliders4DM as the reimplementation and improvement of TOP-Slider [19] and to P4DM as our own implementation of PSS [24].

3.3 Step2: Metrics for Comparison

We considered a combination of objective and subjective metrics to compare Sliders4DM with P4DM: time-on-task and interaction-workload as objective metrics; decision-accuracy, decision-satisfaction, and incentive-to-explore as subjective metrics. Time-on-task is frequently used in HCI in comparative studies. Interaction-workload is relevant, as decision-making tasks are cognitively demanding. Incentive-to-explore makes it possible to assess Requirement R2 (cf. Sect. 2).

C1 – Decision-Accuracy as a Subjective Metrics. As in [9], decision-accuracy is our first class metrics. In the experiment presented here, we considered students with limited financial resource. Thus, as observed in step 1, the choice made by the participants for financial cost can serve as an objective measure for decision-accuracy. This is motivated by the following: (1) the solution space is already Pareto optimal. As a result, the difficulty to find optimality is alleviated and (2) the participants share the same profile.

C2 – Decision-Satisfaction as a Subjective Metrics. Instead of post-questionnaire for subjective choice assessment [9], we propose the final position of the sliders as an objective measure. This is motivated by the following: (1) in the instructions, the participants were asked to click the '*Validate*' button when they "were satisfied" with their choice; (2) according to Cialdini's influence principles [8], a person always tries to seek for consistency while taking decisions, especially when a decision is recorded – which was the case, as the participants were made aware that their choice was logged. In addition, referring to step 1, all interviewees involved in the preliminary users study, but one, indicated that they were satisfied with their choice.

C3 – Incentive-to-Explore as a Subjective Metrics. For this criterion, we used the order in which the participants used the sliders. In particular, we focused on the order of the first three sliders used to analyze the exploration and possibly detect corrective actions. Data exploration is a basic analytic task, a necessary component for multi-attribute choice tasks [8]. Furthermore, according to Dimara et al. [8], "analytic tasks are informative when evaluating visualization tools for decision support, because good decisions require a good understanding of the relevant data". Consequently, we consider that a "good understanding" implies understanding the impact of each criterion through the manipulation of each slider.

C4 – Time-on-Task as an Objective Metrics. As in [9], we considered the time to achieve the task as well at the fine grain action level using the time spent to drag cursors or to reach and click buttons. This duration includes the durations of idle moments (e.g., no interaction) and the total activity duration that is the sum of the duration of the atomic actions such as moving a cursor.

C5 – Interaction-Workload as an Objective Metrics. For the purpose of comparing P4DM with Sliders4DM at the interaction level, we have considered the number of atomic actions (e.g., dragging a cursor or a restrictor knob, clicking a button), the number of mouse movements to drag a cursor or a restrictor knob, as well as trajectory lengths (in pixels) of the cursors when moved with the mouse. The goal is to ensure that usability does not impact the decision-making task.

3.4 Step 3: Comparing Sliders4DM with P4DM

Figure 2 shows Sliders4DM and P4DM. For both of them, we have reused the color-coding scheme and layout of TOP-Sliders [19]. Similarly, Sliders4DM and P4DM share the same Pareto front modeled by Eq. (1) where each criterion is represented by a normalized value between 0 and 1. This model was developed with experts in energy consumption to satisfy the "real decision task" condition put forward by Dimara et al. [9]. The goal is to focus on the intrinsic differences between the two interaction designs.

$$4\left((x-1)^2 + \frac{1}{5}\right)(y-1) - \frac{8}{15}x^2 - 2z + \frac{3}{10} = 0 \text{ with } (x, y, z) \in [0, 1] \quad (1)$$

In the following, we detail the main characteristics of Sliders4DM and P4DM as well as their key differences. From this link [20] the interested reader can play with the two techniques.

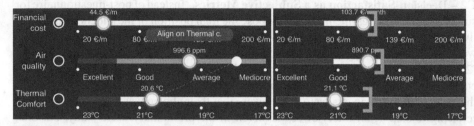

Fig. 2. (left) Screenshot of Sliders4DM, the adapted version of TOP-Slider used for the comparative experiment. Here, financial cost has been selected as the primary criterion. The user is now moving the cursor for Thermal comfort. As a result, a dashed-white line pops up and links this cursor to a small white circle that suggests an optimal solution for the third criterion. As the cursor is moved, the white-filled circle moves accordingly in a tightly-coupled manner. (right) Screenshot of P4DM, our own implementation of PSS.

Sliders4DM: TOP-Slider Adapted. As shown in Fig. 2-left, Sliders4DM integrates the suggestions from [19], such as introducing radio buttons as an explicit means to support the priority-based strategy developed by the participants during the qualitative experiment. This is backed up by Milutinovic et al.'s observational study [22] (see Sect. 2.2). In addition, we have improved the interactive behavior of TOP-Slider as the result of a number of expert evaluations conducted with colleagues.

The notable differences between Sliders4DM and TOP-Slider are the following:

Primary Criterion. When a primary criterion is selected using one of the radio buttons, two pairs of dashed-white lines pop up to show the interdependence with the other two criteria. This is a change from TOP-Slider where the interdependence lines were visible only during the displacement of a cursor. Like for TOP-Slider, the Pareto ranges are updated in a tightly-coupled manner with cursor displacement, but only for the cursor of a primary criterion.

Secondary Criterion. Differing from TOP-Slider, when moving the cursor of a secondary criterion, the two pairs of dashed lines are now re-placed with a single dashed-white line resulting in a simplification of the visual cues. This line links the cursor of the secondary criterion to a white-filled circle that moves within the slider bar of the third criterion synchronously with the displacement of this cursor. The circle suggests an optimal choice for the third criterion, given the current choice for the primary criterion and the position of the secondary criterion.

Tight-Coupling Visualization. As with TOP-Slider, the Pareto ranges are updated in a tightly-coupled manner with cursor displacement. Differing from TOP-Slider with the introduction of these radio buttons, the Pareto ranges of the sliders are updated only for the cursor of a primary criterion and are kept unchanged for the other criteria. By doing so, we improve screen visual stability.

'Align on ...' Button. A contextual *'Align on ...'*, green button replaces the contextual pop-menu of TOP-Slider that was used rarely in the qualitative experiment [15]. Clicking the green button would then move the linked cursor to the current position of the white circle. The green button, which appears only when the cursor of a secondary criterion is moved, has been introduced to facilitate the alignment of the cursors on the Pareto front while leaving the user free to explore non-optimal solutions.

P4DM: Pareto Slider for Surgery Adapted. Like PSS, one distinctive feature of P4DM is the presence of a square bracket shape cursor, named "restrictor knob" whose position on a slider delimits the optimal from the undesired values for the corresponding criterion (cf. Fig. 2-right). By moving the restrictor of a slider, users can exclude values for the corresponding criterion. In addition, a cursor cannot be moved outside its white range: moving the round cursor of one slider moves the cursor of the other sliders automatically so that the new position of the cursors corresponds to a Pareto optimal solution.

In PSS, the strategy used for choosing the new Pareto optimal solution is decided by the designer of the algorithm, not by the user. In our re-implementation, we have reproduced the strategy described in [24]: a point on the Pareto front is selected so that the movement of the two untouched cursors is kept minimal.

4 Experimental User Study

This section presents the details of the experimental study conducted with 177 students to compare Sliders4DM with P4DM. In this experiment, objective quantitative data was logged automatically then processed to measure the objective and subjective metrics presented in Sect. 3.

4.1 Apparatus

Using standard web browsers, both Sliders4DM and P4DM were available as web applications developed with JavaScript (client and server), SVG (visual rendering), node.js (storage of interaction traces, and participant authentication). Both user interfaces were designed with a minimal 900 × 560 pixels footprint. Therefore, the participants were asked to use a standard desktop computer with mouse for input, and connected to the Internet with regular communication speed (i.e. no tablet or smartphone device). Logs show an average resolution width of 1419 px ($\sigma = 168$ px).

The code of the two interaction techniques was instrumented to collect mouse events where a log entry includes: a timestamp, an event type (motion, press, release) and the widget concerned (slider cursor, priority button, alignment button, restrictor knob), the slider index, and the cursor position (value normalized between 0 and 1). The log files, one per participant, were stored on a server in JSON format. Logged data was analyzed with Python scripts using the SciPy library.

4.2 Participants

The experiment was the third and last session of a larger experiment that involved 201 students over a two-month period. The subjects were told that they could earn up to 20€ for participating in the first two sessions and that they could earn a 5€ bonus if they achieved the task of the third session, the scope of this article. Students were told that payment would occur at the end of the third session. In addition, they did not know how much they had already earned in participating in the first two sessions before the end of the third session. Therefore, the participants share the same profile, that is, students with limited financial resources: only 24 over 201 students chose not to participate in our experiment. It is thus reasonable to consider that (1) money was the motivation for the remaining 177 students; and (2) that financial cost is effectively the primary criterion for this experiment.

Table 1. Groups of participants: mean age and studies.

Group	# Part.	Mean age	Studies			
			Eco.	Lit.	Law	Sci.
S4DM	91 (50 m/42 f.)	21.3 ($\sigma = 2.1$)	45 (49.4%)	16 (17.6%)	16 (17.6%)	14 (15.4%)
P4DM	86 (49 m/36 f.)	21.4 ($\sigma = 1.6$)	36 (41.9%)	20 (23.2%)	17 (19.8%)	13 (15.1%)

Table 1 shows the distribution of the participants: 99 males and 78 females (average age: 21.35) studying economy and/or management (81), literature (36), law and/or politics (33), and sciences (27). We used a between-subjects approach with the interaction technique as the independent variable [12]. As in experimental economics [7, 17], we adopt a between-subjects (or between-groups) experimental design, so that each person is exposed to a single interaction technique. The main reasons for this choice are the following: first, this experimental design minimizes learning and transfer across experimental conditions. In a within-subjects design, the subjects are more knowledgeable about the domain after the first user interface's use, and that knowledge will likely help subjects to become more efficient on the second tested user interface. In our case, the learning effect is precisely in the course of our study. Secondly, between-subjects studies have shorter sessions than within-subject ones, which allows it to be less tiring or boring, and also more appropriate for remote non-moderated testing. Between-subjects experimental design requires care in the constitution of the two subject groups. The groups must meet homogeneity conditions to ensure that the assignment of subjects does not affect the results of the study. For this reason, in our experiment, subjects were randomly distributed into two groups, one for each interaction technique. We chose to recruit students as subjects because Step 1 indicated their sensitivity to financial cost for decision making. In addition, socio-economic diversity is less pronounced for this class of subjects making it easier to satisfy the requirements for similarity in characteristics between the two groups. In the following, we denote S4DM the group of participants that used Sliders4DM, and P4DM the group of participants that used P4DM.

4.3 Decision Task

Participants were asked to perform the following decision task: *"As a student with limited financial resources, you are asked to select the values for financial cost, air quality and thermal comfort that best suit you for your home. When you have found a combination that satisfies your objectives, please click the 'Validate' button"*.

As shown in Fig. 2, financial cost ranged between 20 €/month and 200 €/month, air quality between excellent (400 ppm) and mediocre (1400 ppm), and thermal comfort between 17 °C and 23 °C. The maximum and minimal values for air quality and thermal comfort were chosen in accordance with the outdoor conditions at the time of the experiment (i.e., early April in France).

4.4 Procedure

The first step of our experiment consisted of providing the participants with the necessary information displayed on their screen, including a detailed description of the interaction technique to be used (either S4DM or P4DM), color-coding schemes, tight-coupling of the sliders, and the task to achieve. For both P4DM and Sliders4DM, the sliders were displayed in the same order as follows: financial cost (top), air quality (middle), thermal comfort (bottom).

The participants were informed that: (1) the goal was to set the cursors on a position suitable for them; (2) the initial position of the sliders cursors corresponded to an arbitrary choice (i.e. minimal cost, bad air quality, and cold temperature); (3) there was no time limit to achieve the decision task but one trial only was taken into account; (4) they had to click the 'Validate' button when satisfied with their choice; (5) validating was mandatory to record their choice and to earn the financial bonus; (6) all their actions were recorded automatically; and (7) the session would start in two days and would be available online for only 24 h.

In the second step of the experiment, participants had to authenticate themselves using an identification number and a password in order to be able to interact with one of the two interaction techniques.

5 Results

This section reports and analyzes the data logs from the experiment. Interval estimation is used to interpret the inferential statistics [11]: we adopted the approach recommended in [11] based on the overlapping of the confidence intervals (disjoint, less than 25%, more than 25%) to assess practical evidence (respectively: strong, some, none). In the following, the graphs that report a mean value also display a 95% BCa bootstrap confidence interval (CI) [18], graphically and numerically (within square brackets). As well, as recommended by [11], effect size for mean difference (diff. = P4DM-S4DM) is reported as a 95% BCa confidence interval. In addition, we used the following color-coding scheme: dark grey for S4DM, and light grey for P4DM.

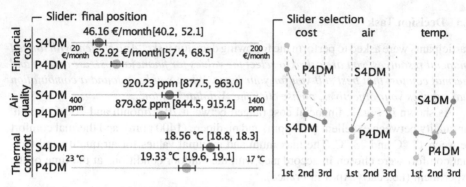

Fig. 3. Final cursor position for each slider denoting the choice of the decision task (left); The first three sliders used by the P4DM and S4DM groups (right).

Multi-objective Choice Task. The results are shown in Fig. 3-left. Each of the three horizontal panels corresponds to a criterion: financial cost, air quality, and thermal comfort. An horizontal panel reports the mean final position of the cursor for both interaction techniques, representing the result of the decision task.

For financial cost, there is strong evidence that the P4DM group is willing to spend more money (62.92 €/month) than the S4DM group (46.16 €/month), by 36% (diff. = 16.76 €/month, CI = [9, 24.4]). For thermal comfort, there is strong evidence that the P4DM group chose a more comfortable level for thermal comfort (19.33 °C) than the S4DM group (18.56 °C), by 8.4% (diff. = 0.77 °C, CI = [0.38, 1.13]). For air quality, with strong evidence, both groups chose a similar level of air quality between good (733 ppm) and average (1066 ppm), respectively ~ 920 ppm for the S4DM group, and ~879 ppm for the P4DM group (diff. = −40.41 ppm, CI = [−97.81, 13.59]).

In short, we observe a strong correlation between financial cost and thermal comfort: a lower financial cost for the S4DM group, and a higher level of thermal comfort for the P4DM group.

Table 2. Statistics for the first three sliders used (including standardized residuals); residuals (dof = 2) are in bold if the value is greater than 1.96 (or less than −1.96).

Group	First use		Second use		Third use	
	S4DM	P4DM	S4DM	P4DM	S4DM	P4DM
Financial cost	52 (**−2.50**)	65 (**2.50**)	28 (**−2.10**)	40 (**2.10**)	24 (−1.26)	29 (1.26)
Air quality	20 (0.59)	16 (−0.59)	45 (**2.51**)	27 (-2.51)	27 (−1.11)	31 (1.11)
Thermal Com	18 (**2.79**)	5 (**−2.79**)	16 (−0.53)	18 (0.53)	35 (**2.41**)	18 (**−2.41**)
χ^2 (p-value)	9.15 (0.01)		6.64 (0.036)		5.82 (0.054)	

The First Three Sliders Used. The results are reported in Table 2 as well as in Fig. 3-right. Table 2 shows the numerical values used to generate the three graphs of Fig. 3-right, one per slider, respectively from left to right: financial cost, air quality, and thermal comfort. Each graph represents the number of participants (vertical axis) using the related slider for their first three uses (horizontal axis).

In order to identify differences between the two groups, we applied a multivariate statistical test using 3×2 contingency tables based on the χ^2 probability law (dof = 2). The bottom row of Table 2 reports the computed χ^2 value and p-value of the statistical test. For each count, Table 2 also reports the standardized residuals (dof = 2). For the first use, with strong evidence, both groups use the slider related to financial cost. In addition, we observe that: (1) a higher number of users (u.) of P4DM (65 u.) used the financial cost slider first compared to S4DM (52 u.); (2) a very few number of P4DM users (5 u.) used the thermal comfort slider.

For the second use, with strong evidence, a majority of the S4DM group (45 u.) used the air quality slider while the majority of the P4DM group (40 u.) still used the financial cost slider.

For the third use, there is a small difference between the two groups (p ~ 0.05). Analyzing the use of the thermal comfort slider in details by computing a 2×2 contingency table where the data related to financial cost and air quality criteria are aggregated (35 vs. 51 for S4DM, 18 vs. 60 for P4DM), we observe with strong evidence ($\chi^2 = 5.0285$, dof = 1, p-value = 0.025) that, as a third use, the S4DM group has used the thermal comfort slider more than the P4DM participants.

In summary, the "first three sliders used" patterns are the following:

- For S4DM: financial cost/air quality/thermal comfort.
- For P4DM: financial cost/financial cost/(air quality or financial cost).

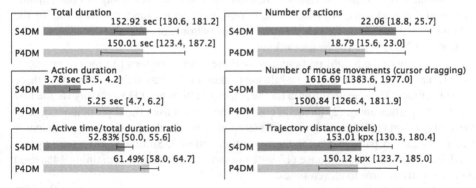

Fig. 4. Durations of the decision task and of actions (left); Interaction statistics (right).

Completion Time and Duration. The results are presented in Fig. 4-left. With strong evidence, both groups achieved the decision task by the same amount of time (Fig. 4, left-top panel): 2 min and 32.92 s for the SADM group, and 2 min and 30.01 s for the P4DM group (diff. = −2.91 s, CI = [−40.0, 38.2]).

At a finer grain though, with strong evidence (Fig. 4, left-middle panel), the S4DM group achieved atomic actions faster (3.78 s) than the P4DM group (5.25 s, diff. = 1.473 s, CI = [0.77, 2.35]). This result is based on measuring the time spent to achieve actions including the time used to drag cursors between two positions and the time to click a 'Priority' or 'Align on ...' button.

We calculated the active time ratio as the total of each action duration divided by the total duration of the task. With strong evidence (Fig. 4, left-bottom panel), the P4DM group (61.49%) spent more time to interact than the S4DM group (52.83%), by 8.7% (CI = [4.3,12.9]).

Interaction-Workload. As shown in Fig. 4 (right-top panel), the S4DM group achieved the decision task within a mean number of ~22 actions while the P4DM group used a mean number of 18.78 actions, without significant difference (diff. = −3.26 actions, CI = [−8.23, 2.12]). Using raw mouse events, we considered the number of mouse movements for dragging cursors or restrictor knobs during the decision task (Fig. 4, right-middle panel). The S4DM group moved the mouse ~1616 times while the P4DM group moved the mouse ~ 1500 times, without significant difference (diff. = −116 times, CI = [−512, 275]).

We measured the length in pixels (1 Kpx = 1000 pixels) of the trajectory followed by the mouse cursor. For this purpose, we considered a mean display width (1419 pixels) computed from the logs (see Sect. 4.1, Apparatus). For S4DM, a trajectory included the mouse movements to reach and click buttons (radio buttons to select a criteria priority and the alignment buttons). For both groups (Fig. 4, right-bottom), the distance is about 150 Kpx, without significant difference (diff. = −2.89 Kpx, CI = [−43.7, 35.7).

Use of Buttons and Restrictor Knobs. We computed how many times the S4DM buttons and the P4DM restrictor knobs were used, as well as the percentage of participants that used these widgets. We observe that some participants have not used one of the following widgets: 44% for the 'Priority' radio buttons, 68.13% for the 'Align on...' button, and 27,91% for the restrictor knobs.

A majority of the S4DM participants used the priority buttons (3 times in average), once (20.88%), or twice (13.19%) while the remaining 23% used the buttons from three to twelve times. The selected criteria for the priority buttons are: (1) air quality for the first use (37/51 participants); (2) financial cost for the second use (18/32 participants), over thermal comfort (10/32 participants); (3) air quality for the third use (12/21 participants) and between 4–5 participants for the two other criteria). Similarly, most participants used the 'Align on...' button once (10.99%) or twice (6.59%). The remaining 14% used this button from three to eleven times.

As for P4DM, the restrictor knobs were used from once to seven times by 47.67% of the participants. The remaining 24.42% used them from eight to thirty-eight times.

6 Discussion

Based on the quantitative details presented above, we now analyze and interpret the results according to the 5 metrics specified in Sect. 3.1. We then summarize and generalize the main findings and point out the limits of this work.

6.1 Analysis

Decision-Accuracy. Using financial cost as an objective measure for decision-accuracy, we observe a significant difference between the two interaction techniques: Sliders4DM leads to a more optimal decision than P4DM as the S4DM group save 16.76 €/month. The P4DM group chose a more expensive option by ~36%. For Sliders4DM, these results are consistent with the preferences provided by the students involved in the qualitative experiment for TOP-Slider (i.e. low financial cost priming over thermal comfort). Moreover, air quality might be more important over thermal comfort as participants selected air quality twice as the primary criterion. This might explain why they chose a better level of air quality over thermal comfort.

Decision-Satisfaction. In terms of satisfaction, we may consider that Sliders4DM helps users to reach a suitable compromise faster than P4DM. As reported in Sect. 5 for the "three first sliders used", the P4DM group changed the value of the financial cost twice while the S4DM group did so only once. Furthermore, 2/3 of the P4DM group needed to manipulate the restrictor knob. We interpret this as an initial unsatisfactory choice for financial cost.

More specifically, Sliders4DM may help users to reach a satisfactory choice in an efficient manner as (1) each slider is used once at the beginning (cf. the 'financial cost-air quality-thermal comfort' pattern reported in Sect. 5) and (2) only 1/3 of the S4DM participants used the '*Align on…*' button, meaning that often the cursors were already set at a suitable position.

Incentive-to-Explore. In terms of exploration, the "three first sliders used" patterns show differences between the two interaction techniques. Correlated to our previous observation, whereas the P4DM group achieved a corrective pattern 'financial cost-financial cost-air quality', the S4DM group used each slider once in a 'financial cost-air quality-thermal comfort' sequence. Moreover, 2/3 of the S4DM group adopted the 'air quality-financial cost-air quality' pattern for the priority criteria. We suspect that the tight coupling between cursor positions enforced by P4DM results in corrective patterns.

Time-on-Task. Although both groups spent a similar amount of time to achieve the decision task (~150 s), we observe differences at the action level: with Sliders4DM, participants' actions are clearly shorter than with P4DM (~30% less). This is correlated with a significant smaller ratio *(total active time)/(total duration)* for Sliders4DM. We hypothesize that Sliders4DM allows users to find a suitable compromise more quickly.

Interaction-Workload. We expected that interaction workload would be higher for Sliders4DM given that Sliders4DM includes three radio buttons and one contextual

'*Align on...*' button displayed next to the sliders. In fact, both interaction techniques show very similar results. The presence of the radio buttons and the '*Align on...*' button did not increase trajectory lengths significantly. The total number of mouse movements to drag a slider cursor or to drag a restrictor knob is also similar for the two techniques. Consequently, both interaction techniques seem to impose a similar interaction workload.

6.2 Summary of the Findings

Our comparative study indicates that Sliders4DM is more effective than P4DM in terms of decision-accuracy, decision-satisfaction, and incentive-to-explore. This may be due to the difference in the way the interdependence between the criteria is expressed in the two techniques. P4DM automatically positions cursors at optimal solutions, necessarily guiding users to safe choices at the risk of imposing non-preferred best solutions[1], and thereby restricting "what if" thinking. Sliders4DM encourages users to explore by decoupling cursor placements. In this way, users are free to position cursors in any range, whether it be optimal, non-optimal or even unfeasible. This freedom is necessary to accommodate situations in which users may not be looking for optimality, but for a satisfactory solution.

However, if cursor placements rely on human decision, then two conditions must be satisfied: (1) The implementation must provide *tightly-coupled visual feedback for cursor displacements* to express the interdependence between the criteria; and (2) The system must warn users when moving away from the Pareto front, for example, using color coding. These features can be complemented with *a system-suggested optimal solution* that users may choose to accept, for example, through a contextual speed-up button.

The experiment has provided significant results with the aggregated logged data used to objectively measure key subjective metrics: decision-accuracy, decision-satisfaction, and incentive-to-explore. In particular, for decision-accuracy, we were able to observe a clear difference between the two techniques using a metrics based on financial cost and a metric based on the final position of the cursors. In addition, the "three first sliders used" pattern allowed us to assess decision-satisfaction as well as incentive-to-explore. For the latter, the observation of the use of the '*Priority*' radio buttons was considered in conjunction with the "three first sliders used" pattern to assess decision-satisfaction. This allowed us to observe clear differences between the two groups.

Compared to Dimara et al.'s methodology [9], our approach goes one step further as we were able to objectively measure decision-accuracy and decision-satisfaction without asking participants to self-report their confidence about the decision made. Besides, Dimaral et al. concede that self-reported confidence "can be subject to biases" [10]. Instead, we have adopted a pragmatic approach, drawing on the experimental context to map aggregated logged data as objective measures for subjective criteria, that is: (1) a controlled profile for participants (students with limited financial resources), (2) a clear primary criterion (financial resources), and (3) a limited number of interdependent

---

[1] Although they have not explicitly investigated this lack of freedom, Schuman et al. observed that the two surgeons recruited for their experiment preferred manual selection to using PSS [24].

criteria (financial cost, air quality, thermal comfort). Our approach, nevertheless, requires a preliminary user study to identify the primary criterion to be used for the participants' profile. For this, we relied on a preliminary study for documenting that financial cost is primary for students whereas thermal comfort is primary for elderly people.

The design choices made for a particular user interface dedicated to decision-making may introduce biases that influence the decision process (this has been demonstrated in the context of information visualization [10]). First, in order to minimize this side effect, we choose to reimplement TOP-Slider and PSS to share the same visual and feedback design, while respecting their interactional differences. Consequently, even if the final design might introduce biases, the results of our study show significant differences between the two interaction techniques. Second, to avoid framing, we chose to set the cursors on an ultimate but impossible best solution (best comfort at lowest cost).

6.3 Limitations and Caveats

All the participants involved in the comparative experiment were students. This may have affected the results. In addition, the mapping we used between the objective logged data and the subjective metrics may have also influenced the results. In particular, we have assumed that financial cost was a primary criterion and thus used the choices made by the participants for financial cost to measure decision-accuracy. While this assumption is confirmed with strong evidence, it may not be valid when applied to participants with very different cultural backgrounds. Despite these limitations, although a pragmatic approach does not seek for generalizability, our approach opens perspectives to investigate these metrics further as well as to consider new subjective metrics to cover heterogeneous profiles and/or multiple primary criteria. At the methodological levels, it also requires to investigate how to design preliminary studies to build relevant profiles in relation to criteria.

7   Conclusion and Take-Away Message

In this research, we have explored the problem of evaluating interaction techniques for multi-objective decision-making. These techniques are difficult to rigorously evaluate due to the subjective nature of decision-making as well as a lack of methodological guidance. Qualitative methods such as self-reporting, are commonly used for evaluating subjective metrics. However, self-reporting is known to be sensitive to cognitive bias. We believe that objective measures can bring additional rigor to the evaluation process.

In this article, we have shown how objective quantitative measures, aggregated from logged data, can be used to evaluate subjective metrics including decision accuracy, choice satisfaction, and incentive to explore. We have shown how these metrics can serve for conducting objective comparative experiments of interaction techniques for multi-objective decision-making tasks with a significant number of participants. We have selected two existing multi-slider interaction techniques as a case study and involved 177 participants.

We have proposed the following pragmatic considerations for defining the mapping of subjective metrics from objective aggregated data: (1) the characteristics shared by the target users, such as the "primary criterion for choice", (2) the key differentiating features of the interaction techniques under evaluation such as "suggestion vs enforcement of optimal solution", (3) the context of use such as energy management. We hope our approach will inspire researchers to extend these heuristics as methodological guidelines and principles for objectively evaluating and comparing interaction techniques designed for tasks that are inherently subjective.

Acknowledgements. This work has been partially sponsored by the French ANR, project INVOLVED reference ANR-14-CE22–0020, as well as by PIA project reference ANR-11-EQPX-0002, Amiqual4Home, and by Eco-SESA, a "Cross Disciplinary Program" project of the IDEX of Université Grenoble-Alpes, France, ANR project ANR-15-IDEX-02. We also thank Marie Cronfalt-Godet for her help for the organization of the experimental study.

References

1. Agrawal, G., Bloebaum, C., Lewis, K., Chugh, K., Huang, C.-H., Parashar, S.: Intuitive visualization of pareto frontier for multiobjective optimization in n-dimensional perfor-mance space. In: 10th AIAA/ISSMO Multidisciplinary Analysis and Optimization Confe-rence, 2004-4434. American Institute of Aeronautics and Astronautics (2004)
2. Akram Hassan, K., Liu, Y., Besançon, L., Johansson, J., Rönnberg, N.: A study on visual representations for active plant wall data analysis. Data **4**(2), 74 (2019)
3. Alzhouri Alyafi, A., et al.: From usable to incentive-building energy management systems. Model. Using Context **2**(1) (2018). http://openscience.fr/Issue-1-372
4. Bajracharya, S., et al.: Interactive visualization for group decision analysis. Int. J. Inf. Technol. Decis. Mak. **17**(6), 1839–1864 (2018)
5. Booshehrian, M., Möller, T., Peterman, M., Munzner, T.: Vismon: facilitating analysis of trade-offs, uncertainty, and sensitivity in fisheries management decision making. Comput. Graph. Forum **31**(3pt3), 1235–1244 (2012)
6. Boukhelifa, N., Bezerianos, A., Trelea, C., Perrot, N., Lutton, E.: An exploratory study on visual exploration of model simulations by multiple types of experts. In: Proceedings of the 2019 CHI Conference on Human Factors in Computing Systems (CHI 2019), pp. 1–14. ACM Press, Glasgow (2019)
7. Charness, G., Gneezy, U., Kuhn, M.: Experimental methods: between-subject and within-subject design. J. Econ. Behav. Organ. **81**(1), 1–8 (2012)
8. Cialdini. R.: Influence. William Morrow and Company, New York (1984)
9. Dimara, E., Bezerianos, A., Dragicevic, P.: Conceptual and methodological issues in evaluat-ing multidimensional visualizations for decision support. IEEE Trans. Vis. Comput. Graph. **24**(1), 749–759 (2018)
10. Dimara, E., Franconeri, S., Plaisant, C., Bezerianos, A., Dragicevic, P.: A task-based taxonomy of cognitive biases for information visualization. IEEE Trans. Vis. Comput. Graph. **26**(2), 1413–1432 (2018)
11. Dragicevic, P.: Fair statistical communication in HCI. In: Robertson, J., Kaptein, M. (eds.) Modern Statistical Methods for HCI. HIS, pp. 291–330. Springer, Cham (2016). https://doi.org/10.1007/978-3-319-26633-6_13
12. Fréchette, G.R., Schotter, A.: Handbook of Experimental Economic Methodology. Oxford Univ. Press, Oxford (2015)
13. Goldkuhl, G.: Pragmatism vs interpretivism in qualitative information systems research. Eur. J. Inf. Syst. **21**(2), 135–146 (2012)

14. Ibrahim, A., Rahnamayan, S., Martin, M.V., Deb, K.: 3D-RadVis: visualization of Pareto front in many-objective optimization. In: IEEE Congress on Evolutionary Computation (CEC 2016), pp 736–745. IEEE (2016)
15. Inselberg, A., Dimsdale, B.: Parallel coordinates for visualizing multi-dimensional geometry. In: Kunii, T.L. (ed.) Computer Graphics 1987, pp. 25–44. Springer, Tokyo (1987). https://doi.org/10.1007/978-4-431-68057-4_3
16. Kelly, L.M., Cordeiro, M.: Three principles of pragmatism for research on organizational processes. Methodol. Innov. **13**(2), 2059799120937242 (2020)
17. Keren, G.B., Raaijmakers, J.G.W.: On between-subjects versus within-subjects comparisons in testing utility theory. Organ. Behav. Hum. Decis. Process **41**(2), 233–241 (1988)
18. Kirby, K.N., Gerlanc, D.: BootES: An R package for bootstrap confidence intervals on effect sizes. Behav. Res. Methods **45**(4), 905–927 (2013)
19. Laurillau, Y., et al.: The TOP-slider for multi-criteria decision making by non-specialists. In: Proceedings of the 10th Nordic Conference on Human-Computer Interaction (NordiCHI 2018), pp. 642–653. ACM, New York (2018)
20. Laurillau, Y., Nguyen, V.-B., Coutaz, J., Calvary, G.: Slider4DM and P4DM widgets. http://iihm.imag.fr/laurillau/S4DM/. Accessed 01 June 2021
21. Miettinen, K.: Survey of methods to visualize alternatives in multiple criteria decision making problems. OR Spect. **36**(1), 3–37 (2012). https://doi.org/10.1007/s00291-012-0297-0
22. Milutinović, G., Ahonen-Jonnarth, U., Seipel, S., Brandt, S.A.: The impact of interactive visualization on trade-off-based geospatial decision-making. Int. J. Geogr. Inf. Sci. **33**(10), 2094–2123 (2019)
23. Pajer, S., Streit, M., Torsney-Weir, T., Spechtenhauser, F., Möller, T., Piringer, H.: WeightLifter: visual weight space exploration for multi-criteria decision making. IEEE Trans. Vis. Comput. Graph. **23**(1), 611–620 (2017)
24. Schumann, C., et al.: Interactive multi-criteria planning for radiofrequency ablation. Int. J. Comput. Assist. Radiol. Surg. **10**(6), 879–889 (2015)
25. Sifer, M.: Filter co-ordinations for exploring multi-dimensional data. J. Vis. Lang. Comput. **17**(2), 107–125 (2006)
26. Tweedie, L., Spence, R., Dawkes, H., Su, H.: Externalising abstract mathematical models. In: Proceedings of the SIGCHI Conference on Human Factors in Computing Systems (CHI 1996), p. 406–412. ACM, New York (1996)
27. Vallerio, M., Hufkens, J., Van Impe, J., Logist, F.: An interactive decision-support system for multi-objective optimization of nonlinear dynamic processes with uncertainty. Expert Syst. Appl. **42**(21), 7710–7731 (2015)
28. United Nations. www.un.org/sustainabledevelopment/energy/. accessed 11 May 2021
29. Velasquez, M., Hester, P.T.: An analysis of multi-criteria decision making methods. Int. J. Oper. Res. **10**(2), 56–66 (2013)
30. Weng, D., Zhu, H., Bao, J., Zheng, Y., Zu, Y.: HomeFinder revisited: finding ideal homes with reachability-centric multi-criteria decision making. In: Proceedings of the 2018 CHI Conference on Human Factors in Computing Systems (CHI 2018), pp. 1–12. ACM Press, Montreal (2018)
31. Wittenburg, K., Lanning, T., Heinrichs, M., Stanton, M.: Parallel bargrams for consumer-based information exploration and choice. In: Proceedings of the 14th Annual ACM Symposium on User Interface Software and Technology (UIST 2001), pp. 51–60. ACM, New York (2001)
32. Wu, B., Cai, W., Chen, H.: A model-based multi-objective optimization of energy consumption and thermal comfort for active chilled beam systems. Applied Energy **287**, 116531 (2021)

Human-Robot Interaction

Design Guidelines for Collaborative Industrial Robot User Interfaces

Helena Anna Frijns$^{(\boxtimes)}$ and Christina Schmidbauer

Institute of Management Science, TU Wien, Vienna, Austria
{helena.frijns,christina.schmidbauer}@tuwien.ac.at

Abstract. Collaborative industrial robot (cobot) systems are deployed to automate tasks or as a tool for Human-Robot Interaction (HRI) scenarios, especially for manufacturing applications. A large number of manufacturers of this technology have entered the cobot market in recent years. Manufacturers intend to offer easy control possibilities to make cobots suitable for different user groups, but there are few evaluation tools for assessing user interface (UI) design specifically for cobots. Therefore, we propose a set of design guidelines for cobots based on existing literature on heuristics and cobot UI design. The guidelines were further developed on the basis of modified heuristic evaluations by researchers with robotics expertise, as well as interviews with cobot UI/User Experience (UX) design experts. The resulting design guidelines are intended for identification of usability problems during heuristic evaluation of the UI design of cobot systems.

Keywords: Human-robot interaction · Human-robot collaboration · Collaborative robots · Design guidelines · Heuristic evaluation · User interface design

1 Introduction

This paper is concerned with the design of robots and associated UIs that are part of collaborative industrial robot systems (cobots). Cobots are systems that are intended for collaborative operation, i.e. the concurrent execution of tasks by human(s) and robot(s) in the collaborative workspace (as defined in [14]). Such a system is not collaborative by itself; rather, the collaborative nature arises from the way the application and interaction are designed. A cobot system usually includes a robotic arm and a graphical user interface (GUI) with which, for instance, a factory worker can program the robot to do a specific task in a manufacturing context. The last decade has seen increased interest in the introduction of cobots to the shop floor [7]. Various manufacturers of automation solutions (e.g., ABB, COMAU, FANUC, KUKA, Stäubli, Yaskawa/Motoman, Doosan) have extended their product portfolio with cobots, and new suppliers such as Universal Robots, Techman Robot, and Franka Emika have entered

© IFIP International Federation for Information Processing 2021
Published by Springer Nature Switzerland AG 2021
C. Ardito et al. (Eds.): INTERACT 2021, LNCS 12934, pp. 407–427, 2021.
https://doi.org/10.1007/978-3-030-85613-7_28

the market. Examples of cobots are Universal Robots' UR5 [35], Kuka's LBR iiwa [17], and Franka Emika's Panda [10] (Fig. 1).

The design of current cobot UIs that are on the market can be improved. Researchers have evaluated several cobot systems and found them to have low usability scores[1]. High ease of use is especially important, as the promise of cobot systems is that these will enable reprogramming by factory workers with limited programming expertise [23]. The importance of making industrial robot systems easier to use is further exemplified by several recent research projects that aim to make cobot UIs easier to use or introduce different concepts for the design of programming environments on cobot UIs [12,15,27,32]. Companies are entering the market offering alternative UIs for existing cobot hardware with the proposition that these are easier to use [6], which indicates that improvement of the usability of cobots is seen as a market opportunity. Other researchers have pointed to the importance of designing cobots to be easy to use and intuitive to interact with [23,36] and that are positively evaluated by operators, in order to make the shift from traditional manufacturing robotics to user-friendly cobot systems [20]. Therefore, we claim that establishing factors that are important for cobot design and providing cobot UI designers with a tool for usability inspection is a relevant endeavor.

In this paper, we propose design guidelines for heuristic evaluation of cobot UIs. We argue that cobot UIs require a separate, more specific set of guidelines as the context these systems operate in is distinct from other HRI (Human-Robot Interaction) or HCI (Human-Computer Interaction) applications for which heuristics have been developed previously. One of the main tasks is the programming of the cobot's task, which is a rather specific HRI application for which factors such as reuse of previous work are important. This sets it apart from applications such as teleoperation in field robotics. Moreover, cobots have a specific use, as these systems are integrated in a work context in which they are subject to interaction with operators repeatedly over long periods of time, which increases the importance of human factors and accessibility [36]. Cobots also represent a challenge in terms of the variety of users, who differ insofar as their roles, preferences, and abilities to modify the cobot control program are concerned (levels of interaction [31]). The UI should support all these users in programming, maintaining, and monitoring the cobot.

We propose a set of 24 design guidelines that can be used during the development, design, and implementation phases of cobot systems to identify UI design problems by means of heuristic evaluation. The contribution of this paper is the identification and refinement of cobot design guidelines based on literature and expert evaluation, thereby providing a resource for design and evaluation of cobot UIs (a form of intermediate-level knowledge for HRI design [18]). In Sect. 2, a short literature review is provided. The procedure and database search to establish the initial guidelines are described in Sect. 3. The guidelines were further

---

[1] Several usability evaluations yielded SUS scores between 50–70 for different cobot systems [8,31], which has been argued to indicate that a product is marginal in terms of usability and should be improved [3].

developed by means of an evaluation study as reported in Sect. 4, and interviews with UI/UX design experts as described in Sect. 5. Finally, Sect. 6 contains the proposed guidelines.

Fig. 1. Franka Emika Panda cobot

2 Related Work

2.1 Interaction with Cobot Systems

With regard to design, several factors must be considered by a manufacturer to enter the market and be competitive. Besides the main factors functionality and safety, other factors such as risk and ergonomics assessment, risk reduction in the workspace, and specifications of use limits and transitions to other operations are required for the design of cobot applications [14]. The interaction is characterized by the levels of interaction based on safety implications of cobots. Cobots are partly completed machinery; these systems have to be designed in compliance with regulations (e.g. [33]) and include safety mechanisms [19]. Cobots have particular challenges, as they are intended to be operated in close proximity by end users with differing levels of programming experience, in the context of different types of tasks. For instance, users can take on the role of programmer, operator/supervisor, or maintainer [7,20]. Programming and maintenance activities are usually of limited duration or even restricted to single events, while supervision requires more continuous levels of interaction and attention [20].

Another consideration is that of UI design. The cobot user interface is that part of the system that enables the user to interact with the cobot. The interaction takes place by means of system inputs and outputs, and can be realized using multiple different interaction modalities (multimodal interaction). The design of the interface determines how commands can be given to the machine or application and how information is represented to the user. Several different interaction modalities exist (e.g. visual, acoustic, haptic) and are realized in different ways (keyboard, mouse, buttons, sounds, signal lamps, projectors) (see [7,31] for an overview). A common piece of hardware that is part of the UI is the teach pendant, which is a hand-held device that is usually equipped with physical buttons and a GUI. This is often the main interface for programming and maintenance activities [20]. Examples of GUIs are Franka Emika's web-based Desk interface [10] and the GUI of UR5, which runs on a teach pendant [35]. Teach pendants and other associated screens enable the user to program and control the cobot and to observe status information. Programming environments often contain representations of the robotic arm and its configuration, and location and trajectories of the end effector.

In order to introduce cobots in industrial environments, research has been conducted into enabling human awareness and so-called *intuitive* programming of cobots [7]. The term *intuitive* is often used to characterize UIs and refers to an effective interaction between a user and a technical system without conscious use of previous knowledge [25]. Moreover, it refers to the use of design strategies that appeal to prior knowledge in a way that makes it easier to (learn to) use an interface and reduces user effort. Another relevant term is *usability*, which has been defined as the *"extent to which a system, product or service can be used by specified users to achieve specified goals with effectiveness, efficiency and satisfaction in a specified context of use"* [13]. It has been argued that making technologies more intuitive and easier to learn may promote access to jobs that typically require higher skills [23]. Developments towards making cobot programming more intuitive include integration of teach pendants and other input devices, programming by demonstration, multimodal HRI, and virtual and augmented reality (VR, AR) [16]. A drawback of using communication modes such as speech and gesture is that they add additional uncertainty; GUIs may be better suited for use in industry. Ways of programming a cobot through a GUI include making use of cobot teach pendants, Icon-based programming, CAD-based programming, and task-based programming. Another way to control the cobot is by means of haptics and force [7]. Krot and Kutia distinguish between online, offline, and hybrid programming approaches [16]. For more information on cobot programming we refer to [7,16].

2.2   Evaluating Cobots: Metrics, Measures, Methodologies

Several researchers have performed usability evaluations of cobot systems. Ferraguti et al. [8] propose a methodology for executing a comparative analysis of cobots, which they apply to the cobots KUKA LWR 4+, UR5, and Franka Emika Panda. They propose that technical data as provided by the manufacturer, experimental verification, usability evaluation and required physical and mental effort to program the robot should be taken into account for such a comparative analysis. For the usability score, they used the SUS (System Usability Scale) and the Questionnaire for the Evaluation of Physical Assistive Devices (QUEAD). Schmidbauer et al. [31] evaluated three cobots UIs (Franka Emika, UR, Fanuc) using the SUS. Weintrop et al. [37] evaluated the time on task, task success, ease of use, learnability and satisfaction of the CoBlox environment they developed using Blockly, ABB's FlexPendant, and Universal Robots' Polyscope. For an overview of metrics, we refer to Marvel et al.'s metrology framework for

Human-Robot Collaboration in manufacturing [20]. We conclude that for the evaluation of the usability of cobot systems, often qualitative and quantitative measures are combined. Examples of quantitative metrics for assessing interfaces are learning time, expert use time, and error cost, while qualitative metrics include the NASA-Task Load Index (NASA-TLX) and the SUS scale [20].

2.3   Design Guidelines and Heuristic Evaluation

Heuristics are principles that can be used to identify usability problems with a particular UI. Examples of heuristics are: *"Does the interface provide feedback?"* [5] and *"Provide indicators of robot health/state"* [1]. Heuristic evaluation refers to a type of evaluation that is usually conducted by UI/UX experts, during which they use heuristics or design guidelines to identify usability problems. Quiñones and Rusu [29] describe the method of heuristic evaluation. First, each evaluator individually compiles a list of problems with the help of a set of heuristics. The evaluators combine the problems to form a list of unique problems, which are then rated for severity, criticality, and frequency by each individual evaluator. Advantages are (1) the low cost of heuristic evaluation, (2) that no extensive planning is required, (3) the broad applicability of the method, especially early in the software development process, and (4) that the method can help find many usability problems without involving end users. On the downside, heuristic evaluation requires experienced evaluators with task-specific knowledge. Additionally, the method helps identifying problems but does not offer pre-packaged solutions to these problems [29]. Heuristics and design guidelines can be considered as intermediate-level knowledge for HRI design [18].

Different sets of design guidelines and heuristics exist, many of which are targeted at the design of computer software, such as the usability heuristics proposed by Nielsen [26]. For robotics, alternative sets have been proposed for applications such as field robotics [24], robot teleoperation [1], assistive robotics [34], and HRI in general [5] (these have also been applied in video-based heuristic evaluation [38]). Robots are embodied and HRI often requires different interfaces to support multiple user roles, which sets HRI apart from HCI applications [24]. While these arguments apply to cobots as well, cobots present a different application area compared to field robotics, teleoperation, and assistive robotics. When interacting with a cobot, the human and the robot are co-located, which distinguishes this type of interaction from scenarios such as teleoperation, as operators have access to more contextual information [20] and users can, for instance, switch between physical interaction and interaction through a GUI. Cobots can be interacted with and observed via different means (e.g. programmed on a computer or using a teach pendant, or hand-guided). Cobot status can be observed on the teach pendant or by looking at the cobot itself (e.g. checking indicator LEDs). Interaction modalities such as AR, VR, and a variety of handheld devices are subjects of ongoing investigation [36]. This makes it important to guarantee consistency with respect to the way information is presented to the user across different modalities, as well as to support the user in managing their attention. Teach pendants of cobots can be rather heavy, but existing sets of heuristics (e.g. [5,26]) do not refer to physical ergonomics, which is a relevant factor for usability of cobot systems. This means that existing design guidelines for HCI or HRI in general are not sufficient, nor are sets that have been developed for other applications such as teleoperation. In the next section, the development of a set of guidelines for heuristic evaluation of cobot systems is described.

3   Development of the Cobot UI Design Guidelines

With regards to the realization of a new set of heuristics, Quiñones and Rusu [29] recommend establishing which features of the target domain are application-specific, identifying existing heuristics that can be reused, specification of heuristics according to a template, and validation of the heuristics. Common methods include collecting design recommendations from industry, from the public domain [2], and from academia [1]. The collected guidelines can then be clustered using asynchronous affinity diagramming [2] or other methods, and sorted using methods such as open or closed card sorting [1]. Methods to evaluate heuristics include performing modified heuristic evaluations, user studies based on heuristic evaluation [2,5,34], and expert reviews [2]. Other practices include the use of templates for problem reporting [5], customizing heuristics to the application domain [5], and using an iterative process [2,5,29]. We make use of these methods and recommendations to establish heuristics for cobots, as described below.

3.1   Procedure for Establishing Cobot UI Guidelines

The methodology for establishing the cobot UI guidelines was as follows (see Fig. 2). Prior to establishing the design guidelines, an informal heuristic evaluation was conducted using existing sets of heuristics, namely [1,26], to determine if these were sufficient or if some issues were not appropriately covered by those heuristics. In order to establish which design guidelines had previously been proposed in the academic literature, papers were collected that propose guidelines for HRI design by searching academic research databases (ACM digital library, IEEE Xplore®, and SpringerLink, Sect. 3.2). Design recommendations that were listed in those papers were collected and categorized during an affinity diagramming session. This resulted in clusters of guidelines that were summarized into individual heuristics. Additional heuristics and clusters were proposed on the basis of literature on cobot systems in manufacturing (beyond literature focusing on design guidelines, e.g. [7]). The preliminary heuristics were used in an evaluation of two cobot systems, after which they were revised to make them more clear, actionable, and applicable. During the first empirical evaluations (Sect. 4), study participants (early-career researchers with HRI expertise) were asked to apply the guidelines in the context of a modified heuristic evaluation of a cobot system, and rate the guidelines for clarity. Based on participant feedback, the guidelines were revised. Experts in cobot UI/UX design (such as UX designers at companies developing cobot systems) were invited to participate in interviews to collect feedback on the guidelines (Sect. 5), which led to a final revision of the guidelines. For the final version of the guidelines, see Tables 1 and 2.

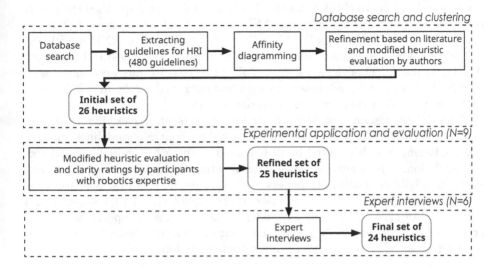

Fig. 2. Overview of the research process, in which different sources of information were used to propose design guidelines for heuristic evaluation.

3.2 Literature Review with Database Search

We performed a database search with the aim of finding design guidelines, recommendations, and heuristics that have previously been proposed in the academic literature, especially for HRI and cobots. The inclusion criteria were that the publication had to be in English, that it contained specific recommendations and heuristics, and that its topic should concern design guidelines, heuristics, or interaction design for an interactive technology or robotics. The research question was: *What are specific design guidelines, recommendations, and heuristics that have been proposed in the academic literature, especially for HRI?*

The databases ACM digital library, IEEE Xplore®, and SpringerLink were searched for combinations of keywords. The timeframe was restricted to 1999–2019. Databases were searched for combinations of one of the terms "Human Robot Interaction", "cobot", "collaborative robot", "robot", **plus** one of the following terms: "heuristics", "design guidelines", "design recommendations", "usability guidelines", "design principles". If possible, it was specified that these terms needed to appear in the abstract of the paper. After searching for combinations of keywords, duplicates were removed. Then, the paper's title, keywords, and abstract were reviewed and the paper was excluded if it did not meet the inclusion criteria. For the ACM database search (conducted 25-11-2019, 28-11-2019), 354 results were checked, resulting in 32 papers. For the IEEE Xplore® database search (on 19-11-2019), checking 2808 results led to selection of 53 papers. The Springer database search (on 3-12-2019 and 4-12-2019) yielded too many search results to check manually. For this database, we specified the search terms as a combination: ((Human AND Robot AND interaction) OR robot OR (collaborative AND robot)) AND (heuristics OR (design AND guidelines) OR (design AND recommendations) OR (design AND principles) OR (usability AND guidelines)). This yielded a total of 35,851 results. Results were sorted with SpringerLink's "sort by relevance" feature and restricted to the first 500 items. Of these items, 51 papers met the inclusion criteria.

The database search yielded 131 unique papers after checking titles and abstracts for relevance. Each paper was checked for concrete guidelines and recommendations, which resulted in 42 papers containing 561 guidelines and recommendations. The main application domains that these papers were concerned with, were HRI in general (11 papers, e.g. [38]), rescue robotics, field robotics, safety-critical systems and tactical systems (11 papers, e.g. [1,24]), assistive and service robotics (10 papers, e.g. [34]), telepresence systems (3 papers), and industrial robotics (2 papers, [9,21]). After removing duplicate guidelines, this resulted in 480 guidelines, heuristics, and other recommendations.

3.3   Clustering of Guidelines Based on Affinity Diagramming

All 480 design recommendations were clustered into groups of similar topics by means of affinity diagramming (similar to [2]). This resulted in 38 clusters, each of which contained between 2 and 27 recommendations. Additional design issues specific to cobots were identified, mostly based on [7,16], such as the use of multiple modalities and providing information on ways a user can teach the cobot. Finally, some clusters were merged, changed, or deleted (e.g. the cluster "cultural expectations" was deleted, as the recommendations collected in that section mostly applied to conversational agents). We summarized each cluster into a single design guideline, resulting in a total of 35 guidelines.

3.4   Revision Based on Modified Heuristic Evaluation

The first version of the guidelines was applied by the authors of this paper in an evaluation session that was structured as a modified heuristic evaluation modeled after [2]. The interface of Franka Emika Panda and UR5 were evaluated. The Panda cobot was controlled from the Desk environment, version 2.1.1 ced048bda3. The UR5/CB3 (version 3.9) cobot was equipped with software 3.9.1 64192 (April 1 2019), installed on a teach pendant (12 in. touchscreen) with the PolyScope GUI. A Robotiq gripper [30] plus custom 3D printed safety encasing was attached to the UR5 robot, and functionality of the gripper was embedded in the GUI with URCaps. During the evaluation, examples of applications and violations of the guidelines were collected. If no applications or violations of the guidelines were found, deleting the guideline was considered, as this was an indication that the guideline would be difficult to evaluate by means of heuristic evaluation. If there was overlap between applications and violations listed for different guidelines, we considered merging them. This resulted in 26 guidelines. Items regarding technical capabilities, human-oriented perception, and safety were removed, as these are basic requirements of robotic systems. Assessing safety or privacy is outside the scope of UI/UX design or heuristic evaluation, as safety of the cobot system must comply with (legal) standards [14].

4 Evaluation Study Based on Modified Heuristic Evaluation

After the database search and subsequent refinement of the proposed guidelines, an evaluation study was conducted (N = 9) that was based on modified heuristic evaluation of two cobot systems by participants with robotics and/or cobot systems expertise. The goal of this evaluation study was to find out if the formulations of the guidelines were clear and if they could be applied to existing cobot systems. We used feedback by participants, clarity scores given by participants to guidelines, and survey responses to revise the guidelines established in Sect. 3.

4.1 Procedure of the Evaluation Study

The evaluation study was structured as a modified heuristic evaluation. The evaluated cobots were described in Sect. 3.4. The study took place at the teaching and learning factory at TU Wien [28]. Participants were asked to sign an informed consent form and complete a personal information survey. They were explained what heuristic evaluation is, what it is used for, and they were given some examples of applications and violations of a heuristic in the context of HCI and HRI. Next, they received a safety briefing for the cobot they were going to work with. Participants were asked to read the guidelines and the survey form was explained to them (see next section). They were asked to identify applications and violations of each design guideline, to rate each guideline for clarity and to make notes if they had any other feedback. Participants were informed that their performance on the task would not be scrutinized and that constructive criticism was welcomed, as this would help to improve the guidelines. Then, they worked with the cobot by themselves and completed the survey form. Participants took about one hour to complete the evaluation study.

Participant Task in the Evaluation Study. Each participant interacted with a cobot for an hour. They were supplied with a programming task, but were allowed to deviate from it. The task contained instructions to program a movement trajectory with several intermediate points for the cobot and to open and close the gripper. The task for UR5 was as follows: *1) Use the Move tab to program a trajectory. Program at least 3 points. 2) Change the second point of the* *trajectory you programmed. 3) Open the gripper. 4) Add another Move trajectory: Use the Freedrive button to move the robot and store some points for a trajectory. 5) Close the gripper.* The task for Panda was similar. We asked participants to complete a survey form while programming the task on which they 1) gave a rating for clarity of each guideline, 2) wrote examples of applications and violations of guidelines they encountered in the UI (for example, one participant noted *"It is not clear what is the exact location of the end effector"* as a violation regarding accessibility of information), and 3) gave feedback on guidelines. We asked for examples to check whether people could apply the guidelines.

Survey Forms. The personal information sheet included questions regarding participants' professional occupation, specialization, name of employer, and asked participants to estimate their experience working with cobots in hours and robotics expertise in years. The survey form contained every guideline in the set. The first question for every guideline was *"The formulation of this guideline is very clear/clear/neutral/confusing/very confusing"*. Participants were asked to circle the answer they felt was appropriate. There were open fields where participants could list applications and violations of each guideline. They were informed that they did not need to list any examples if they did not find any, but that they could also list multiple examples. The final question on the survey form asked participants for feedback on the guidelines. Half of the participants received a survey form on which the guidelines were sorted alphabetically and the other half in reverse alphabetical order.

4.2 Participants

A total of 9 participants (5 male, 4 female) took part in the first evaluation sessions. Participants were recruited internally, thus 8 of 9 participants reported being employed by TU Wien. The participants were mostly early-career researchers (average age $M = 29.3$, $SD = 2.2$ years), with specializations in the areas of (industrial) robotics, mechanical engineering, assistive systems, HRI, and social robotics. Regarding their robotics expertise, one participant reported that their robotics experience was limited, 3 reported between 18–24 months of experience, 3 reported 4–5 years experience, and 2 reported 10 years experience. All participants had experience directly working with cobots (e.g. programming cobots).

4.3 Evaluation Results

The explanation phase of the experiment, including reading the guidelines, took 20 min on average and the average working time was 63.3 min. Of the participants, 4 evaluated the UR5 UI and 5 the Franka Emika Panda UI. See Fig. 3a for an overview of the clarity scores for each of the guidelines. Then, the listed applications and violations were analyzed. Items were excluded if they were not

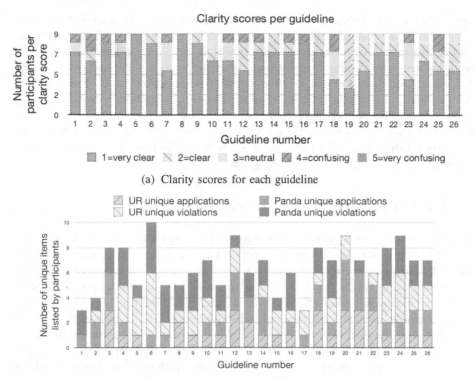

(a) Clarity scores for each guideline

(b) This figure shows the number of unique applications and violations of each guideline were listed for both the Panda cobot and the UR cobot.

Fig. 3. Results of the evaluation study.

specific enough, did not apply to the guideline, or were simply stated as a confirmation of the guideline. For instance, one participant listed *"Panda is very intuitive"* as a response to *Support user learning*, which was removed on the grounds of not being specific enough. Another wrote *"indicating system state"* in response to *System state awareness*, which was removed as it does not specify how the guideline is applied or violated in the UI. See Fig. 3b for an overview of the unique number of applications and violations for each guideline (if multiple participants listed the same application/violation, these would be counted as one unique application/violation). As multiple examples were listed for each guideline, we conclude that the guidelines could be applied to the cobot systems and that guidelines could be interpreted by the evaluation participants.

4.4 Revision of the Guidelines

Guidelines were revised on the basis of the participants' feedback and if a guideline's clarity score was higher than 1.5 (guidelines with a score of 1 were very clear, guidelines with a score of 5 very unclear). During the revision process, the applications and violations listed by the participants on the survey form were compared to the meaning the researchers intended to capture with the guideline. Guidelines were revised by changing terms that were not understood, changing complex words to simpler formulations, removing word repetitions, and ensuring guidelines contained between 5–12 words as recommended in [2]. For example, item 12 had a clarity score of 1.67, thus *12. Errors: Accommodate troubleshooting when errors occur* was changed to *12. Errors: Give clear explanations and steps to recover when errors occur*. Terminology was made consistent (e.g. referring to the person interacting with the system as "user"). Guidelines were grouped into categories and initial category headings were added.

5   UI/UX Design Expert Interviews

In order to get a practitioner perspective on the guidelines and on the practice of developing cobot UIs in industry, cobot UI/UX design experts were invited to participate in interview sessions. The main aims of the interviews were to evaluate if participants could recognize and relate to the guidelines, as well as to gather feedback to the guidelines and check whether they needed revision. In other words, both the relevance of individual guidelines to participants' work practices and the formulation of the guidelines were evaluated. Six online interviews were conducted, which resulted in 41–74 min of recorded material per interview (average 52 min). The interviews were transcribed and coded using a thematic analysis approach [4]. On the basis of interviewees' feedback, minor changes were made to the guidelines.

5.1   Participants

We contacted 9 companies and company branches via email and contact forms. Additionally, 16 individuals were contacted who had cobot UI/UX design experience and/or had a leading design or innovation role at companies that developed cobots, who were found via company LinkedIn pages, referrals by university colleagues, and referrals by interview participants. We found 6 suitable participants who agreed to an interview, four of whom worked at two different companies producing cobot systems in the role of (senior or junior) UX designer or engineer. One participant worked at a university as a researcher and had prior experience in software development for cobot systems. The final participant worked at an industrial automation company and was responsible for usability testing of industrial robotic systems. Five were based in Europe and one in China.

5.2   Procedure and Interview Protocol

Prior to the interview, participants received the guidelines for reference, information regarding storage of data in accordance with GDPR, and an informed consent form. At the start of the interview, the interviewer (the first author of this paper) thanked the interviewee for participating, introduced the goal of the research study, and gave the participant an overview of the topics that would be discussed. Participants were informed that constructive criticism was welcome, that they could withdraw at any time, and that they could notify the researcher if they did not want to answer a particular question. The participant was informed that the recording was started and was first asked to answer introductory questions regarding their job description, the main (design) activities and evaluation methods they used in their job, and their familiarity with cobots. Subsequently, participants were asked for feedback regarding the individual guidelines, their response to the whole set, and the categorization. Finally, participants were asked what challenges they encountered in the cobot UI design process. Participants were not informed regarding previous steps of the development of the guidelines.

5.3   Interview Themes

A thematic analysis approach [4] was used to analyze the interviews using the software MAXQDA [22]. First, transcripts were read by both authors of this paper. One of the interview transcripts was analyzed and coded separately by both researchers (generating initial codes), who then agreed on a coding scheme, which was used to (re)code all six transcripts. The coding scheme included responses to guidelines and other categories such as design methods used. Both researchers were involved in coding the transcripts and subsequent analysis. Based on the analysis of the interviews, recurring themes were identified regarding goals, methods, and design constraints. Job-related goals mentioned by interviewees were focusing on and solving problems for the end user (explicitly mentioned by 3 different participants), improving ease of use and the user experience (2x), improving efficiency (2x), changing the minds of engineers on the team, improving system understanding, conducting research, and solving problems in the company product (1x). Methods that were mentioned most were getting feedback from team members or customers (5x), interviews with end users/customers, persona development or definition of target end users (4x), getting familiar with or explicitly evaluating competitor products (3x), comparing interfaces using metrics (such as time to complete certain tasks), identifying dependencies and requirements, drawing, and prototyping (2x).

Design Constraints. Interviewees indicated that the implementation of the guidelines not only depended on the design of the cobot, but also on the application that the cobot was used for, regulations, safety measures, company culture, and differences between users. Different users need different information (mentioned 3x), have different backgrounds and levels of expertise (3x), and have different expectations. Human factors is influenced by the application and the way the work environment is organized, by regulation, and different users have different abilities (e.g. some users are color blind). Cultural effects and country-specific regulations will also influence how the guidelines can be implemented. One person mentioned that autonomy given to workers by the companies varies greatly from one country to another. While we would propose that information that is necessary to (better) achieve the user's task should not be hidden by the system manufacturer, we note that company culture, the culture of the region, and commercial interests will influence how guideline number 3 (in Table 1), accessibility of information, is implemented in practice.

Diversity of End Users as an Effect on Guideline Implementation.
Interviewees emphasized that there are many different end users for whom they are designing interfaces. People who interact with cobots have different roles in the company (such as operator or programmer). The type of interface that is desirable depends on the previous knowledge and expertise of the end user, but also on what kind of application the user wants to implement on the cobot. A software developer with several years of coding experience, but no previous interaction experience with any robot needs different user guidance than a shop floor worker who has several years of experience in working with machines and industrial robots but has never programmed or controlled them by themselves. Novices were often contrasted to expert users during the interviews. In addition, different stakeholders of the cobot development process were mentioned, such as company salespeople, system integrators, customers, end users, engineers, and programmers. We connect the fact that different users have different needs to the frequent use of methods such as developing personas. While many of the interviewees emphasized that their focus is on the end user, they also noted that it can be difficult to get access to end users. One participant mentioned that in specific industries, exchange of information is not desired by companies, although this information is much needed to improve cobot UI/UX design.

Response to Design Guidelines and Revisions. Some participants responded to almost every guideline, either by stating a confirmation, supplying a practical example, asking for clarification, or voicing disagreement. Guidelines *13. Human factors* and *17. Adaptable system architecture* were responded to by most participants (5 out of 6). Participants also remarked on the whole set, its potential uses, and on the categorization of the guidelines. One participant noted that *"it is something I can relate to, even though I never had this struc-tured list before (...) it's (...) putting a word on most items I do here at work"*. Two participants explicitly stated they thought the guidelines were quite complete. A few extra topics were suggested, such as safety (which we had previously decided to exclude) or learning about safety (which is implicitly included in item 9). Possible alternative uses of the guidelines were mentioned, such as using the guidelines as a checklist, using them for discussion with top management to indicate which items need to be worked on, or applying the guidelines to other machine interfaces in a manufacturing context. Two participants remarked that similar UI/UX guidelines exist, which is understandable as the guidelines are based on literature search. Participants made comments that many of the issues touched on by the guidelines were large research projects in themselves. One participant also emphasized that cobots are part of larger systems, and that programming cobots is just one piece of the puzzle when it comes to solving automation problems.

Interviewee feedback indicated that the guidelines did not need substantial revision. Details in the wording were adjusted, for instance *"operator attention"* was adapted to *"user attention"* as this guideline did not apply only to operators on the shop floor. Several guidelines were adapted to reflect remarks by participants. For instance, the item *accessibility of information* was adapted, as participants pointed out that some information is not understandable to end users (such as raw data), and information requirements and accessibility also depend on the user, culture of the region and company, and user access. Guidelines 3, 8, 9, 11, 13, 15, 17, and 18 were adapted slightly, 20 was adapted substantially for clarification and merged with a different guideline, and several initial category headings were revised based on participant feedback (the numbering refers to the guidelines as presented in Table 1 and 2).

6   Proposed Set of Guidelines

The proposed set of cobot UI design guidelines consists of 24 items, see Table 1 and 2. An explanation and an example are included for each of the guidelines. The guidelines cover the main topics of situation awareness, system understanding, task efficiency, human factors, configurability, and interaction design of the UI, with a focus on the usability and user experience of the cobot system. The guidelines should be considered from the perspective that the user group is diverse and that different users will have different needs, for instance in terms of the information they need to achieve their task, that they might need different levels of support and complexity, and have different abilities, all of which have consequences for the required interface design. Regarding intuitive use (guideline 22), mental models (guideline 7), and user learning (guideline 9), we remark that the differences in users' backgrounds will also have an influence on how these guidelines are operationalized; for different people, different things are familiar, and (thus) different UI features will be easy to use or easy to learn.

6.1   Comparison with Existing Heuristics and Usability Guidelines

After the final revision based on the expert interviews, we compared our proposed guidelines with heuristics for robot teleoperation [1], assistive robotics [34], and HRI [5]. Guidelines 2, 5, 7, 9, 11, 12, 15–18, and 20, as proposed in the current paper are not included in the set for assistive robotics [34]. While the compact form of the HRI heuristics [5] is useful for heuristic evaluation, not all issues indicated by the guidelines proposed in the present paper are covered (guidelines 5, 9–13, 16, 18, 24, and to some extent 23 are not covered by [5]). The set that was the most similar to the guidelines proposed in the current paper was the one for teleoperation [1]. We note that while there is some overlap of many guidelines on a surface level regarding the topics, the formulation and

Table 1. Guidelines for heuristic evaluation of cobot UIs, continued in Table 2.

Situation awareness
1. System state awareness: Inform the user on the cobot's state. The interface should support the user in maintaining appropriate awareness of the system's state. *Example: The cobot informs the user via lights on the robotic arm about the current state, for instance a green light means a program is running.*
2. Situation awareness: Inform the user regarding the cobot's environment and configuration. Help the user in understanding the configuration of the cobot in its environment, as well as other sensor inputs. *Example: The GUI shows a 3D model of the robot, which indicates the cobot's configuration and end effector position.*
3. Accessibility of information: Allow users to access information required for the task. Make sure the information the user needs for the task is available and accessible, considering possible restrictions. *Example: When editing a trajectories, a user can access information about the exact end effector location on the GUI.*

System understanding
4. Feedback: The UI is responsive to user actions. Respond to user actions so the user can follow task progress and understand the effects of their actions. *Example: The UI is responsive when buttons are clicked, when the user navigates to a different menu, or when values are updated.*
5. Affordances: Signify how the user can interact with the cobot. The interface should indicate which actions are currently possible and which ones are not. *Example: An icon of a trash bin next to a stored point indicates the point can be deleted by clicking on the icon.*
6. Errors: Give clear explanations and steps to recover when errors occur. Tolerate minor user errors, prevent critical system errors, support undo and redo. *Example: When a trajectory cannot be executed, a popup appears with an explanation why the error occurred and steps to recover from the error.*
7. Mental model: Support the user in understanding the way the system works. Support the user in understanding the connection between user actions and system response, for instance by providing feedback and using appropriate terminology. *Example: The user can play a programmed trajectory as an animation on the GUI before execution by the cobot.*
8. Help and documentation: Provide contextual help and documentation. Give users clear explanations of functionality and errors. *Example: When the help icon is clicked, the help menu displays help items that relate to the functions that are currently on the display.*
9. Support user learning: Help the user solve their (automation) problem. Support trial-and-error behavior and provide templates, contextual instructions or other clues that indicate how the cobot can be interacted with. *Example: Templates for robot tasks are provided, so the user has an idea what a program should look like.*

Task efficiency
10. Efficiency: Avoid unnecessary work on the users side. Minimize the number of steps required to achieve goals and provide shortcuts. *Example: The user does not have to set the speed and acceleration for each point in a trajectory, but can specify these values for the whole trajectory.*
11. Task progress: Communicate to the user which task is being executed. The GUI should make it easy for the user to follow task execution by indicating previous, current and next steps. *Example: When the robot is executing a series of actions, the current action that is being executed is highlighted on the GUI.*
12. Reuse: Enable reuse of previous work. Support users in reusing their work or the work of others. *Example: Previous programs can be copied and edited.*

Table 2. Guidelines for heuristic evaluation of cobot user interfaces

Human factors
13. Human factors: Design cobot and UI with ergonomics and accessibility in mind. Ensure the cobot UI is comfortable to work with for the necessary duration. *Example: The teach pendant is light to carry or can be placed on a table, so it will be comfortable to work with it for a few hours.*
14. Avoid cognitive overload: Reduce mental strain. Support recognition instead of requiring users to recall information, and limit the number of options that are presented. *Example: A function name such as "Wait" is easy to remember and indicates its function.*
15. User attention: Support the user in directing their attention. Make menu items that need attention visually salient. Do not attract attention unnecessarily. *Example: When the user is in the submenu for editing a trajectory, the menu items for editing points are the largest items.*

Configurability
16. Level of automation: Let the user determine the level of human input. The user can decide to integrate human input or to make the program fully automatic. *Example: There is a function for integrating human input, which requires the operator to press a button before the robot continues its task.*
17. Adaptable system architecture: Enable easy software integration after hardware exchange. The system architecture should allow for adapting the system to different types of tasks and application scenarios. *Example: It is easy to exchange the gripper and add sensors to the system.*
18. Adaptable tasks: Support easy editing of robot programs. Robot programs, trajectories, configurations should be editable by the user. *Example: Points in a previously stored trajectory can be deleted or changed.*

Interaction design of the UI
19. Consistent behavior: Make sure cobot and UI behave in a consistent way. Cobot behaviors, movement, and responses are predictable. *Example: The cobot always executes the same motion trajectory the same way.*
20. Multimodal UI: Consider the relation between different interaction modalities. Manage user attention across modalities and ensure the way information is presented via different modalities is consistent. *Example: The system provides feedback with LED lights on the cobot, which matches specific events on the UI.*
21. Graphic design: Design GUI items with usability, accessibility, and aesthetics in mind. Make sure information is presented in a clear and structured way, and use color, contrast and salience appropriately. *Example: Fonts are legible and the interface has appropriate contrast.*
22. Clarity of interface: Ensure the UI is easy and intuitive to use. Avoid a complex UI design; make use of simple graphics and icons. *Example: When selecting an action for the cobot, a sub menu for editing this action opens automatically.*
23. High vs. low complexity: Display programming functions at different levels of detail. Allow users to switch between simple and more complex ways of programming the cobot. *Example: There is the possibility to change between a simple version of the UI and a more complex version that provides more options.*
24. Customizability: Support user preferences. Enable users to change the interface according to their wishes and needs. *Example: It is possible to adapt different features based on user preference, such as the size of windows on the UI.*

meaning of the guidelines is different. Several guidelines we propose for cobots are not included in the teleoperation guidelines, namely guidelines 12 (reuse of previous work), 13 (human factors/ergonomics), and 19 (consistent behavior), due to the differences between the domains of robot teleoperation and cobots for manufacturing. Several guidelines had overlaps, but with different practical implications. For example, guideline 20 (Multimodal UI) is in a sense similar to the item *"Complement video stream with feedback information from other sensors"* [1, pp. 257–258], but the presented information is very different (video stream from remote teleoperated robot versus a programming environment on a GUI in a manufacturing context). Some items relevant for teleoperation are not relevant in the context of cobot systems (e.g. *"Ability to self-inspect the robot's body for damages or entangled obstacles"* [1]).

6.2   Validity and Generalizability of Guidelines

In this section, potential threats to validity are considered. In the evaluation study (Sect. 4), participants worked in a factory-like setting with equipment and robots [28]. This gives the experiment some level of ecological validity (findings generalize to the real world [11]). The first evaluation study indicates that guidelines can be applied to cobot systems. The external validity of the study is threatened to some level as the participants did not have specific expertise in applying design guidelines. Ideally, participants would have known how to work safely with cobots, would have previously worked with heuristics, and would have design-related expertise, besides having time to participate. As the most important aspect was being able to safely program the cobot, we chose robotics expertise as most relevant criterion. We chose to conduct the interviews with participants who had expertise in cobot UI/UX design to balance this initial focus with people with design-related expertise. Participants in the expert interviews had experience with other cobots besides those used in our experimental evaluation. This provides indications that the findings generalize to other cobots (external validity). Feedback by participants given in the studies may be biased by their desire to cooperate, which may have led to feedback that was skewed on the positive side. We aimed to lessen this effect by specifically asking for (constructive) criticism and by using the clarity scores in the evaluation study as an indication of those items that were most unclear and that thus needed revision. The sample size was small for the both the evaluation study and the interviews. In both studies, the main aim was to obtain detailed feedback to be able to improve the proposed guidelines, which was achieved. Next, quantitative evaluation can be used to validate the guidelines. Such an evaluation study could also evaluate the use of heuristics that comprise a shortened, summarized version of the presented guidelines, which could lead to possible additional refinement.

7   Conclusion

In this paper, a set of 24 design guidelines for the heuristic evaluation of cobot UIs is proposed. Three different sources of information were used, namely a database search, modified heuristic evaluations with participants with robotics expertise (N = 9), and interviews with cobot UI/UX design experts (N = 6). On the basis of a comparison with existing design guidelines for HRI, we note that the proposed guidelines are specific to cobot UI design in a manufacturing context and that they are distinct from existing guidelines in the literature.

Visions of future manufacturing in which human workers can reprogram cobots in collaborative interaction settings [31] can only be realised if cobot technologies are sufficiently usable. The design guidelines that were proposed in this paper indicate which design features are important in such interaction scenarios. However, more research into cobot design and design proposals to improve current cobot UIs are necessary.

Acknowledgements. Supported by Doctoral College TrustRobots, TU Wien. The first author of this publication was responsible for the research project and writing of the publication, and was supported by the second author. We thank Hans Küffner-McCauley, Tanja Zigaert, Michael Hornáček, all paper reviewers, evaluation study participants, and interviewees.

References

1. Adamides, G., Christou, G., Katsanos, C., Xenos, M., Hadzilacos, T.: Usability guidelines for the design of robot teleoperation: a taxonomy. IEEE Trans. Human-Mach. Syst. **45**(2), 256–262 (2015). https://doi.org/10.1109/THMS.2014.2371048
2. Amershi, S., et al.: Guidelines for human-AI interaction. In: Proceedings of the 2019 CHI Conference on Human Factors in Computing Systems - CHI '19, pp. 1–13. ACM Press (2019). https://doi.org/10.1145/3290605.3300233
3. Bangor, A., Kortum, P.T., Miller, J.T.: An empirical evaluation of the system usability scale. Int. J. Hum.-Comput. Interact. **24**(6), 574–594 (2008). https://doi.org/10.1080/10447310802205776
4. Bladford, A.: Semi-structured qualitative studies. In: The Encyclopedia of Human-Computer Interaction. The Interaction Design Foundation, 2 edn. (2013). https://www.interaction-design.org/literature/book/the-encyclopedia-of-human-computer-interaction-2nd-ed/semi-structured-qualitative-studies
5. Clarkson, E., Arkin, R.C.: Applying heuristic evaluation to human-robot interaction systems, American Association for Artificial Intelligence (2007)
6. drag&bot: Industrieroboter wie ein smartphone bedienen (2020). https://www.dragandbot.com/de/. Accessed 10 Sept 2020
7. El Zaatari, S., Marei, M., Li, W., Usman, Z.: Cobot programming for collaborative industrial tasks: an overview. Robot. Auton. Syst. **116**, 162–180 (2019). https://doi.org/10.1016/j.robot.2019.03.003
8. Ferraguti, F., Pertosa, A., Secchi, C., Fantuzzi, C., Bonfè, M.: A methodology for comparative analysis of collaborative robots for Industry 4.0. In: 2019 Design, Automation Test in Europe Conference Exhibition (DATE), pp. 1070–1075 (2019). https://doi.org/10.23919/DATE.2019.8714830
9. Fletcher, S.R., Johnson, T.L., Larreina, J.: Putting people and robots together in manufacturing: are we ready? In: Aldinhas Ferreira, M.I., Silva Sequeira, J., Virk, G.S., Tokhi, M.O., Kadar, E.E. (eds.) Robotics and Well-Being. ISCASE, vol. 95, pp. 135–147. Springer, Cham (2019). https://doi.org/10.1007/978-3-030-12524-0_12

10. Franka Emika GmbH: Franka Emika Panda (2020). https://www.franka.de/technology
11. Hoffman, G., Zhao, X.: A primer for conducting experiments in human-robot interaction. ACM Trans. Hum.-Robot Interact. **10**(1), 1–31 (2020). https://doi.org/10.1145/3412374
12. Ionescu, T.B., Schlund, S.: A participatory programming model for democratizing cobot technology in public and industrial fablabs. Procedia CIRP **81**, 93–98 (2019). https://doi.org/10.1016/j.procir.2019.03.017
13. ISO: ISO 9241–210 Ergonomics of human-system interaction - Part 210: Human-centred design for interactive systems (2010). https://www.sis.se/api/document/preview/912053/
14. ISO: ISO/TS 15066:2016(en) Robots and robotic devices - Collaborative robots (2016)
15. Komenda, T.: SAMY - semi-automatische modifikation (2020). https://www.fraunhofer.at/de/forschung/forschungsfelder/SAMY.html. Accessed 10 Sept 2020
16. Krot, K., Kutia, V.: Intuitive methods of industrial robot programming in advanced manufacturing systems. In: Burduk, A., Chlebus, E., Nowakowski, T., Tubis, A. (eds.) ISPEM 2018. AISC, vol. 835, pp. 205–214. Springer, Cham (2019). https://doi.org/10.1007/978-3-319-97490-3_20
17. KUKA AG: LBR iiwa (2020). https://www.kuka.com/en-de/products/robot-systems/industrial-robots/lbr-iiwa
18. Lupetti, M.L., Zaga, C., Cila, N.: Designerly ways of knowing in HRI: broadening the scope of design-oriented HRI through the concept of intermediate-level knowledge. In: Proceedings of the 2021 ACM/IEEE International Conference on Human-Robot Interaction. pp. 389–398. ACM, Boulder (2021). https://doi.org/10.1145/3434073.3444668. https://dl.acm.org/doi/10.1145/3434073.3444668
19. Malik, A.A., Bilberg, A.: Developing a reference model for human–robot interaction. Int. J. Interact. Design Manuf. (IJIDeM) **13**(4), 1541–1547 (2019). https://doi.org/10.1007/s12008-019-00591-6
20. Marvel, J.A., Bagchi, S., Zimmerman, M., Antonishek, B.: Towards effective interface designs for collaborative HRI in manufacturing: metrics and measures. ACM Trans. Hum.-Robot Interact. **9**(4), 1–55 (2020). https://doi.org/10.1145/3385009
21. Maurice, P., Allienne, L., Malaise, A., Ivaldi, S.: Ethical and Social Considerations for the Introduction of Human-Centered Technologies at Work. In: 2018 IEEE Workshop on Advanced Robotics and its Social Impacts (ARSO). pp. 131–138. IEEE, Genova (2018). https://doi.org/10.1109/ARSO.2018.8625830
22. MAXQDA, VERBI GmbH: MAXQDA—All-In-One Qualitative & Mixed Methods Data Analysis Tool (2020). https://www.maxqda.com/
23. Michaelis, J.E., Siebert-Evenstone, A., Shaffer, D.W., Mutlu, B.: Collaborative or simply uncaged? understanding human-cobot interactions in automation. In: Proceedings of the 2020 CHI Conference on Human Factors in Computing Systems, pp. 1–12. ACM (2020). https://doi.org/10.1145/3313831.3376547
24. Murphy, R.R., Tadokoro, S.: User interfaces for human-robot interaction in field robotics. In: Tadokoro, S. (ed.) Disaster Robotics. STAR, vol. 128, pp. 507–528. Springer, Cham (2019). https://doi.org/10.1007/978-3-030-05321-5_11
25. Naumann, A.: Intuitive use of user interfaces: defining a vague concept. In: Harris, D. (ed.) EPCE 2007. LNCS (LNAI), vol. 4562, pp. 128–136. Springer, Heidelberg (2007). https://doi.org/10.1007/978-3-540-73331-7_14
26. Nielsen, J.: Enhancing the explanatory power of usability heuristics. In: CHI '94: Proceedings of the SIGCHI Conference on Human Factors in Computing Systems, pp. 152–158 (1994). https://doi.org/10.1145/191666.191729

27. Paxton, C., Hundt, A., Jonathan, F., Guerin, K., Hager, G.D.: CoSTAR: instructing collaborative robots with behavior trees and vision. In: 2017 IEEE International Conference on Robotics and Automation (ICRA), pp. 564–571 (2017). https://doi.org/10.1109/ICRA.2017.7989070

28. Pilotfabrik TU Wien: Pilot Factory TU Vienna - Industry 4.0 (2021). https://www.pilotfabrik.at/?lang=en

29. Quiñones, D., Rusu, C.: How to develop usability heuristics: a systematic literature review. Comput. Stand. Interfaces 53, 89–122 (2017). https://doi.org/10.1016/j.csi.2017.03.009

30. Robotiq: Products: Grippers, Camera and Force Torque Sensors (2021). https://robotiq.com/products

31. Schmidbauer, C., Komenda, T., Schlund, S.: Teaching cobots in learning factories - user and usability-driven implications. Procedia Manuf. 45, 398–404 (2020). https://doi.org/10.1016/j.promfg.2020.04.043

32. Steinmetz, F., Wollschläger, A., Weitschat, R.: RAZER-a HRI for visual task-level programming and intuitive skill parameterization. IEEE Robot. Autom. Lett. 3(3), 1362–1369 (2018). https://doi.org/10.1109/LRA.2018.2798300

33. The European Parliament and the Council of the European Union: Directive 2006/42/EC of the European Parliament and of the Council of 17 May 2006 on machinery, and amending Directive 95/16/EC (recast). Official Journal of the European Union (2006). https://eur-lex.europa.eu/LexUriServ/LexUriServ.do?uri=OJ:L:2006:157:0024:0086:EN:PDF

34. Tsui, K.M., Abu-Zahra, K., Casipe, R., M'Sadoques, J., Drury, J.L.: Developing heuristics for assistive robotics. In: 2010 5th ACM/IEEE International Conference on Human-Robot Interaction (HRI), pp. 193–194 (2010). https://doi.org/10.1109/HRI.2010.5453198

35. Universal Robots: UR5 collaborative robot arm—flexible and lightweight robot arm (2019). https://www.universal-robots.com/products/ur5-robot/

36. Villani, V., Pini, F., Leali, F., Secchi, C.: Survey on human-robot collaboration in industrial settings: safety, intuitive interfaces and applications. Mechatronics 55, 248–266 (2018). https://doi.org/10.1016/j.mechatronics.2018.02.009

37. Weintrop, D., Afzal, A., Salac, J., Francis, P., Li, B., Shepherd, D.C., Franklin, D.: Evaluating CoBlox: a comparative study of robotics programming environments for adult novices. In: Proceedings of the 2018 CHI Conference on Human Factors in Computing Systems, pp. 1–12. ACM, Montreal (2018). https://doi.org/10.1145/3173574.3173940

38. Weiss, A., Wurhofer, D., Bernhaupt, R., Altmaninger, M., Tscheligi, M.: A methodological adaptation for heuristic evaluation of HRI. In: 19th International Symposium in Robot and Human Interactive Communication, pp. 1–6. IEEE (2010). https://doi.org/10.1109/ROMAN.2010.5598735

Intention Recognition in Human Robot Interaction Based on Eye Tracking

Carlos Gomez Cubero and Matthias Rehm[✉]

Technical Faculty of IT and Design, Aalborg University, Aalborg, Denmark
{cgcu,matthias}@create.aau.dk

Abstract. In human robot interaction any input that might help the robot to understand the human behaviour is valuable, and the eyes and their movement undoubtedly hold valuable information. In this paper we propose a novel algorithm for intention recognition using eye tracking in human robot collaboration. We first explore how the Cascade Effect hypothesis and a LSTM-based machine learning model perform to classify intent from gaze. Second, an algorithm is proposed, which can be used in a real time interaction to infer intention from the human user with a small uncertainty. A data collection with 30 participants was conducted in virtual reality to train and test the algorithm. The algorithm allows to detect the user intention up to two seconds before any user action with a success rate of up to 75%. These results open the possibility to study human robot interaction, where the robot can take the initiative based on the intention recognition.

Keywords: Human-robot interaction · Intention recognition · Eye tracking

1 Introduction

When robots start collaborating in close proximity with humans it becomes necessary for the robot to be able to predict human behavior for allowing safe interactions. On a low level this would mean predicting trajectories for human movement to prevent path overlaps and collisions with the human worker and thus ensure safety when working in the same space [12]. On a higher level this means recognizing the intent of the user in relation to the current task in order to predict the user's next action in the shared work space, e.g. predicting the need for a specific tool and being ready to give it to the user when s/he needs it. Intention recognition for such pick and place or give and take actions is both relevant for social scenarios [20] and industrial settings [2]. The reason for this is that the collaboration between robot and human will be more natural, fluent and effective, when the robot is able to predict, which object the human user will require in the next step [11].

© IFIP International Federation for Information Processing 2021
Published by Springer Nature Switzerland AG 2021
C. Ardito et al. (Eds.): INTERACT 2021, LNCS 12934, pp. 428–437, 2021.
https://doi.org/10.1007/978-3-030-85613-7_29

Three sources have been identified by Liu and colleagues [11] for inferring intentions in interactions: motion intention, object arrangement (environmental layout), and daily activities (task semantics). On the other hand, studies of human intention recognition show that especially eye gaze and head orientation are instrumental for intention recognition [6]. In this paper, we thus investigate a fourth source for inferring intentions, by utilizing eye tracking data for training a deep learning model for intention recognition in human robot collaboration.

2   State of the Art

While frequently used in collaborative robotics, intention is not clearly defined. From a cognitive point of view, intention is a high level concept that allows real-time synchronization of tasks and actions to achieve the intention. Vernon and colleagues for instance describe shared intention for cognitive robotics [21]. Schlenoff and colleagues [16,17] present an approach based on ontologies where intentions can best be described as the overall task a user wants to perform and the state of the work space is used to infer the corresponding intention based on the model. On the other side we can find low level concepts of intention that are often concerned with user movements, such as utilizing the force applied to joints of a robot arm to predict where the user wants the arm to go to [23] or where the user wants to go [22], predicting upper limb motion using FMG [1], hand motor intention with EMG [8], or computer vision to infer if an approaching user intents to interact with a robot [13]. Others focus on the manipulated objects in collaborative tasks and bind intentions to the manipulations possible with the given objects in object intention networks [7]. A similar approach is described in [10] that also integrate NLP and derived semantics in the object-guided intention recognition.

As we have seen above, different sensors have been used for predicting human intention such as EMG [8], FMG [1], EEG [5], or Computer Vision [13]. In this paper, we are investigating eye tracking as a source for intention recognition. Bader and colleagues [3] have used fixations and saccades as features for gaze-based intention classification and provide a first theoretical account of the causal relations between gaze behavior and interaction context. Singh and colleagues [19] show the advantage of gaze as a predictive cue to intention recognition. In their case, the goal is to predict a player's intention in a board game and they can show that the integration of gaze analysis in the prediction model allows to recognize the players intention ca. 90 s before the necessary actions take place. In contrast to a board game, collaboration in robotic scenarios is usually more fast paced but it nevertheless indicates that gaze might be a useful method for intention recognition in close proximity interactions. The Cascade Effect hypothesis was introduced by Shimojo and colleagues [18]; it states that in a selection task it is more likely that an object is selected the more attention it accumulates before the selection. It was also shown that this effect can be used to influence the selection by presenting a certain item for a longer period. Bird and colleagues [4] revised this experiment by changing the position where the items

Fig. 1. Screenshots of the Virtual Reality scenario for the data collection. It contains a Sawyer robot and a table with three objects. The participant selects an item using the VR controller. Left image: an eagle eye view of the interaction, the camera icon represent the position of the headset, the yellow line shows the ray cast from the headset to the position of gaze on the table. Right image: the participant's point of view. (Color figure online)

were presented obtaining similar results. The Cascade Effect thus relies on only one variable – the amount of attention – but does not take other features into account as saccades or fixations that occur when using the gaze in a cognitive process. The gaze can be treated as a time series which makes it feasible to apply machine learning for predicting user intention based on the gaze behavior.

In the following we describe the data collection and training of a LSTM model for intention prediction from eyetracking data.

3 Data Collection

The data collection was designed in Virtual Reality (VR), consisting of a simple human-robot collaborative task. The task is to select an item between three possibilities on a table while a Sawyer robot is at the other side. The participant is asked to take their time and select the object that they like the most, without choosing an item at random. The robot then takes the selected item and places it in a box after which three new items appear. The participant has to perform this task several times for four different stages. In stage one, the participant has to select one of three identical bricks, in stage two, the bricks have different colors, in stage three, the bricks have different shapes, and in stage four, the participant has to decide between different objects (see Fig. 1). The number of rounds in the first and second stages is smaller, as the task is more simple, in order to spend more time in the last two stages and keep the attention of the participants.

The hardware used for the data collection was a HTC Vive Headset together with a Pupil Labs VR/AR add-on eye tracker system. The computer used was a VR ready computer tower capable of running the VR experiment with around 140 frames per second. The participants were 30 students and staff from the university, 22 male and 8 female, age between 22 and 32 years and with different study backgrounds, non of them related to Robotics.

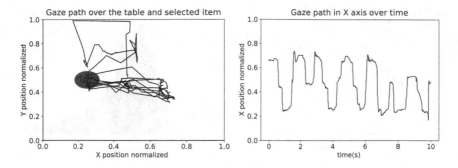

Fig. 2. Graphic representation of a series. Left image: in black a representation of the path travelled by the position of gaze over the table during an entire action, the red circle represents the position of the item selected. Right image: the plot of the X position (long side of the table) of the position of gaze of the same series over the time. (Color figure online)

The collected data consists of the values of the position of gaze (POG) over the table, being the X axis the long side of the table and Y axis the short side, and the item selected in the end. The data was recorded with the eye tracking system at maximum frame rate, this is 140 Hz but it fluctuates, therefore the data-set was re-sampled 100 Hz as a common sampling rate using the nearest neighbour method. The data is then normalized to values between 0 and 1 according to the size of the table. In Fig. 2 a series from the data is shown, plotting the path of the POG on the table and the position on the X axis over the time.

The duration of the selection process for the different stages varies between three and ten seconds. Figure 3 presents the histogram of duration. We collected 885 series, 162 for stage one, 189 for stage two, 272 for stage three and 261 for stage 4. The number of items selected for each of the three possibilities is evenly distributed in the dataset.

Russo and Leclerc [14] define three stages in a decision process based on gaze:

1. Orientation: occurs when the task starts and the participant orients the gaze towards the region that contains the items.
2. Evaluation: occurs when the participant gaze is scanning the items and its attention is engaged in the task. The POG jumps from one item to another in a move called saccade and between saccades the POG is hold for some instants which are called fixation [15]. During this stage the participant is performing a cognitive process that will result in a final selection.
3. Verification: is the last stage, the participant has already made a decision and now is about to signal the decision. During this stage the POG is steady on the item while the participant is moving the hand, in this case, to reach the item.

Figure 3 shows the percentage of series in which the attention is fixed in the item selected along the time. It is expected that during the verification most

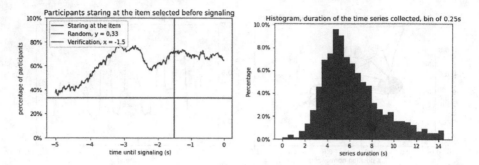

Fig. 3. Left image: for the series longer than 5 s, the percentage of participants staring at the item signaled withing the last 5 s. Used to estimate the start of the verification stage (green line). Right image: histogram of the duration of the series collected. (Color figure online)

of the participants will fix the attention on the item as they try to reach for it. We can approximate from Fig. 3 that the verification stage in this specific task takes around 1,5 s since there is a steady percentage of participants staring at the selected item. Identifying the verification stage is key to understand the amount of time that passes since the participant makes the decision until it is signaled to the system. In Sect. 5.3 we observe an increase in the accuracy of the trained models by removing the verification stage in the dataset.

4　Cascade Effect

According to the Cascade Effect hypothesis it is expected that the item selected on average would have more time of attention than the others. To calculate the accuracy of the Cascade Effect the table was divided in three equally sized zones in the horizontal plane, with an item placed in the middle of each zone. The attention for each item is calculated by accumulating the time the POG dwells in each zone. This parameter is stored for each zone and then compared with each other to infer the selection. Figure 4 also shows the accuracy of using this method over time, with around 75% at the time when the item is signaled and around 65% three seconds before.

5　Machine Learning

We use Long Short-Term Memory Neural Networks (LSTM) [9] as the machine learning approach. LSTMs are a type of Recurrent Neural Networks (RNN), a deep learning architecture designed to handle time series. LSTMs are widely used for both classification and regression of time series. The data used is the raw POG, which present a time series suitable for processing with a LSTM, unlike other previous work presented in the state of the art, which usually uses static analysis of fixation and saccades.

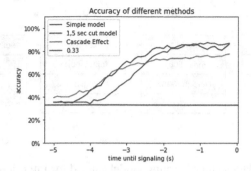

Fig. 4. Accuracy of the different methods to infer intention over the time. In blue the LSTM model trained with the dataset unedited, in orange the LSTM model trained without the verification stage (last 1.5 s), in green the inference based on cascade effect, in red the random inference (accuracy = 0.33). (Color figure online)

Using a LSTM-based machine learning model it is expected to achieve a classification of the series if there are features that differentiate them. As seen before, the amount of attention is already a feature, the model could easily learn it. But the great advantage of using machine learning is that other features can be extracted during training that otherwise would go unnoticed. The process to obtain a good model is described in the following paragraphs. In case of a different scenario this process can be repeated to find a model that suits better.

5.1 Accommodating the Data

The data collected was duplicated in two datasets, one of which was truncated the last 1,5 s minding the verification stage. For both datasets the series shorter than three seconds and longer than 14 s were discarded. Then the series were truncated to the last 5 s, in order to train a model with a size large enough to analyze up to 5 s at the same time, series shorter than that were padded with zeros at the beginning. This leave us with a data set of 755 series split in 60% for training, 20% for validation and 20% for testing.

5.2 Model Topology and Training Method

The topology of the model consists of two LSTM layers where the node size of the first layer is twice as big as the second layer, and followed by a fully connected neural network of output three for classification. The LSTM layers perform the feature extraction and the fully connected layer the classification based on the features. A training battery was conducted with different node sizes in order to find out, which what number fits the data better. To prevent overfitting and increase the accuracy of the model dropout layers were placed in between, with a dropout rate of 0,2. The loss function used was the Categorical Cross-Entropy, which is used for multi-class classification.

Topology of the model

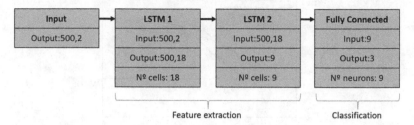

Fig. 5. Topology of the machine learning model trained for intention recognition. Consist on a sequence of two LSTM layers and a Fully Connected Neural Network. Shape and size of each layer is given with each layer.

The model with the best fit is presented in Fig. 5, a sequential model with a first LSTM layer with node size of 18, a second LSTM layer with size 9 and a fully connected layer with output 3.

5.3 Testing the Model

As a first test, the model input consists of series from the test dataset, obtaining a single output that corresponds to the most likely item to be selected. Both models output an accuracy around 80% in this test. To test the model's performance during and interaction (and not only at the end), the series are tested for each sample that has been logged. This is done by starting with a series full of zeros and entering the samples by the tail one by one, then the series are given to the model with each new sample. This simulates a real time operation of the model and gives a set of results dependent on the time.

The results for this test are shown in Fig. 4. Both models have an identical accuracy at the end but the model trained without the last 1,5 s has a better accuracy. This can be explained as a consequence of training with the verification stage, because as the attention is fixed on the object it is easier for the model to classify it at the last moment without taking the rest of the series into account, thus causing overfitting. We can conclude that the model trained without verification stage performs better, classifying around 80% of the series two seconds before signaling and 70% of the series three seconds before signaling.

6 Proposed Algorithm Combining both Methods

The LSTM approach has an acceptable accuracy to infer the intention of the participant with around 80%. It can be used in scenarios where the signaling time is fixed. But it fails to work in a more relaxed interaction where the signal time is not known, as it outputs a great amount of false positives the rest of the time and therefore would not be reliable to use in most of the cases. To overcome this problem an algorithm is proposed that combines both methods.

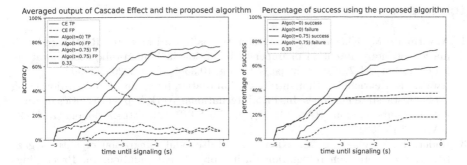

Fig. 6. Left image: comparison of the output from using Cascade Effect method (CE) and the proposed algorithm (Algo) using threshold t = 0 s and t = 0,75 s. The graph shows the True Positives (TP) with solid line, and False Positives (FP) with dotted line. Right image: the success or failure when taking the very first output of the algorithm to infer the result. The solid line represents the success, the dotted line the failures.

It consists in comparing the output of the LSTM model with the cascade effect plus a threshold. If the classification of the LSTM model matches with the item that accumulates more attention and this accumulated attention is higher than the threshold, then the prediction is valid.

This drastically decreases the number of false positives but also the accuracy. Applying a threshold of 0 s the accuracy of the prediction at the end of the actions is close to 70% while the false positives move from 10% to 5%. If the threshold is adjusted to 0.75 s the prediction decreases but the false positives also decrease to a steady 5%. These results are presented and compared to the cascade effect in Fig. 6. Filtering out the false positives leads to an increase in the number of successful inferences when taking the first output of the algorithm. This can be seen in Fig. 6, where the algorithm with higher threshold has an overall lower accuracy but a better percentage of success.

7   Conclusion

We can conclude that the cascade effect and the LSTM model on their own have a good performance to infer intention when the interaction has been concluded, but lack robustness for a real time interaction, due to its uncertainty the rest of the time. To decrease this uncertainty, the algorithm proposed here is based on both methods and can be used during the interaction. Tweaking the parameters allows adjusting the number of false positives and increasing reliability.

This makes it possible to study the effect of a proactive robot that could infer user intention based on the user's gaze behavior while the interaction is taking place. In such a scenario, the robot can take the initiative and reach for the item before the user has made his/her final decision. It remains to be shown if such a proactive behavior is increasing the task efficiency and trust in the robot or has a detrimental effect, e.g. due to a feeling of loss of control.

References

1. Anvaripour, M., Khoshnam, M., Menon, C., Saif, M.: FMG- and RNN-based estimation of motor intention of upper-limb motion in human-robot collaboration. Front. Robot. AI **7**, (2020). https://doi.org/10.3389/frobt.2020.573096
2. Awais, M., Henrich, D.: Human-robot collaboration by intention recognition using probabilistic state machines. In: 19th International Workshop on Robotics in Alpe-Adria-Danube Region (RAAD 2010), pp. 75–80 (2010). https://doi.org/10.1109/RAAD.2010.5524605
3. Bader, T., Vogelgesang, M., Klaus, E.: Multimodal integration of natural gaze behavior for intention recognition during object manipulation. In: Proceedings of the 2009 International Conference on Multimodal Interfaces., pp. 199–206. Association for Computing Machinery, New York (2009). https://doi.org/10.1145/1647314.1647350
4. Bird, G.D., Lauwereyns, J., Crawford, M.T.: The role of eye movements in decision making and the prospect of exposure effects. Vision. Res. **60**, 16–21 (2012)
5. Buerkle, A., Eaton, W., Lohse, N., Bamber, T., Ferreira, P.: EEG based arm movement intention recognition towards enhanced safety in symbiotic human-robot collaboration. Robot. Comput.-Integr. Manuf. **70**, 102137 (2021)
6. Duarte, N.F., Raković, M., Tasevski, J., Coco, M.I., Billard, A., Santos-Victor, J.: Action anticipation: reading the intentions of humans and robots. IEEE Robot. Autom. Lett. **3**(4), 4132–4139 (2018). https://doi.org/10.1109/LRA.2018.2861569
7. Duncan, K., Sarkar, S., Alqasemi, R., Dubey, R.: Scene-dependent intention recognition for task communication with reduced human-robot interaction. In: Agapito, L., Bronstein, M.M., Rother, C. (eds.) ECCV 2014. LNCS, vol. 8927, pp. 730–745. Springer, Cham (2015). https://doi.org/10.1007/978-3-319-16199-0_51
8. Feleke, A.G., Bi, L., Fei, W.: EMG-based 3D hand motor intention prediction for information transfer from human to robot. Sensors **21**(4), 1316 (2021). https://doi.org/10.3390/s21041316
9. Hochreiter, S., Schmidhuber, J.: Long short-term memory. Neural Comput. **9**, 1735–80 (1997). https://doi.org/10.1162/neco.1997.9.8.1735
10. Li, J., Lu, L., Zhao, L., Wang, C., Li, J.: An integrated approach for robotic sit-to-stand assistance: control framework design and human intention recognition. Control Eng. Pract. **107**, 104680 (2021). https://doi.org/10.1016/j.conengprac.2020.104680
11. Liu, T., Lyu, E., Wang, J., Meng, M.Q.H.: Unified intention inference and learning for human-robot cooperative assembly. IEEE Trans. Autom. Sci. Eng. 1–11 (2021). https://doi.org/10.1109/TASE.2021.3077255
12. Luo, R., Mai, L.: Human intention inference and on-line human hand motion prediction for human-robot collaboration. In: 2019 IEEE/RSJ International Conference on Intelligent Robots and Systems (IROS), pp. 5958–5964 (2019). https://doi.org/10.1109/IROS40897.2019.8968192
13. Pattar, S.P., Coronado, E., Ardila, L.R., Venture, G.: Intention and engagement recognition for personalized human-robot interaction, an integrated and deep learning approach. In: 2019 IEEE 4th International Conference on Advanced Robotics and Mechatronics (ICARM), pp. 93–98 (2019). https://doi.org/10.1109/ICARM.2019.8834226
14. Russo, J.E., Leclerc, F.: An eye-fixation analysis of choice processes for consumer nondurables. J. Consum. Res. **21**(2), 274–290 (1994)

15. Salvucci, D., Goldberg, J.: Identifying fixations and saccades in eye-tracking protocols, pp. 71–78 (2000). https://doi.org/10.1145/355017.355028
16. Schlenoff, C., Kootbally, Z., Pietromartire, A., Franaszek, M., Foufou, S.: Intention recognition in manufacturing applications. Robot. Comput.-Integr. Manuf. **33**, 29–41 (2015). Special issue on knowledge driven robotics and manufacturing
17. Schlenoff, C., Pietromartire, A., Kootbally, Z., Balakirsky, S., Foufou, S.: Ontology-based state representations for intention recognition in human-robot collaborative environments. Robot. Auton. Syst. **61**(11), 1224–1234 (2013). Ubiquitous robotics
18. Shimojo, S., Simion, C., Shimojo, E., Scheier, C.: Gaze bias both reflects and influences preference. Nature Neurosci. **6**(12), 1317–1322 (2003)
19. Singh, R., Miller, T., Newn, J., Velloso, E., Vetere, F., Sonenberg, L.: Combining gaze and AI planning for online human intention recognition. Artif. Intell. **284**, 103275 (2020)
20. Trick, S., Koert, D., Peters, J., Rothkopf, C.A.: Multimodal uncertainty reduction for intention recognition in human-robot interaction. In: 2019 IEEE/RSJ International Conference on Intelligent Robots and Systems (IROS)., pp. 7009–7016 (2019). https://doi.org/10.1109/IROS40897.2019.8968171
21. Vernon, D., Thill, S., Ziemke, T.: The role of intention in cognitive robotics. In: Esposito, A., Jain, L.C. (eds.) Toward Robotic Socially Believable Behaving Systems - Volume I. ISRL, vol. 105, pp. 15–27. Springer, Cham (2016). https://doi.org/10.1007/978-3-319-31056-5_3
22. Wang, Y., Wang, S.: A new directional-intent recognition method for walking training using an omnidirectional robot. J. Intell. Robot Syst. **87**, 231–246 (2017). https://doi.org/10.1007/s10846-017-0503-z
23. Ye, L., Xiong, G., Zeng, C., Zhang, H.: Trajectory tracking control of 7-DOF redundant robot based on estimation of intention in physical human-robot interaction. Sci. Progr. **103**(3) (2020)

Interaction Initiation with a Museum Guide Robot—From the Lab into the Field

Laura-Dora Daczo, Lucie Kalova, Kresta Louise F. Bonita,
Marc Domenech Lopez, and Matthias Rehm[✉]

Department of Architecture, Design, and Media Technology, Aalborg University,
9000 Aalborg, Denmark
matthias@create.aau.dk

Abstract. The use of social robots is making its way into public spaces such as schools and museums. In this paper we investigate initiation of interaction between a museum guide robot and visitors. First, we conducted a lab experiment, based on a previous Japanese study, which confirmed that participants prefer the robot with appropriate greeting behavior to the robot without. Thus, we concluded that the results obtained in the original study can be applied in the Danish cultural context. Based on these finding, we conducted a field study in a Danish museum to evaluate whether the same principles apply in the wild and to investigate spatial behavior between robot and visitors in real world settings.

Keywords: Human robot interaction · Field study · Cross cultural comparison

1 Introduction

Social robots are envisioned to provide services in public spaces such as schools and museums, which means that people will be interacting with robots more often. This has brought researchers to study the different aspects of the robot's behaviour and to find out how humans react to it. For instance, Shiomi et al. [14] studied the interaction between a humanoid robot and visitors in a science museum, and Yousuf et al. [20] studied the best way to start interaction through greeting with a humanoid robot.

In all these studies, mobile robots provide services like education, information, entertainment and assistance to people [11]. However, most studies were not conducted in the wild, even though studying social robots in the real world plays an important role in improving their acceptance. We decided to replicate the study by Yousuf et al. [20], to find out if their findings also apply to the Danish culture. We then verified this in the context of a museum through a field study.

Published by Springer Nature Switzerland AG 2021
C. Ardito et al. (Eds.): INTERACT 2021, LNCS 12934, pp. 438–447, 2021.
https://doi.org/10.1007/978-3-030-85613-7_30

2   Related Work

Human-Robot Interaction. Within the field of HRI, multiple studies focus on how humans approach robots [1,3], and how robots should behave after the initiation phases of the interaction [15,19]. However, we found only two studies focusing on how a robot should initiate interaction through greetings. Heenan et al. [5] implemented some of Kendon's [7] greeting behaviours from human human interaction into a 58 cm tall humanoid robot. Based on informal observations of how people reacted to their prototype they found the robot's greeting capability effective, however there's is no indication about how they measured effectiveness. Yousuf et al. [20] used a 108 cm tall, humanoid robot with hands and wheels, to study how robots that perform greeting impact people's perception. They compared the robot that greeted people before providing information, with one that did not. The sighting phase consisted of participants looking at the robot. During the distance salutation, the robot positioned itself to form a transactional segment, while in the approach phase the robot decreased the original distance from the participants to a distance of 1 to 1.3 m. Finally, the close salutation consisted of a verbal greeting, "Welcome", without additional gestures. The experimental area was 3.5 m^2, so the starting distance was within the social distance. The robots were assessed through a questionnaire that used Likert-scale on greeting capability and general impression, participants preferring the robot that performed the interaction initiating behaviors.

Interaction with Museum Guide Robots. Other studies focus on exploring how humanoid robots can serve as guides [8,15,19–21]. Shiomi et al. [15] studied a guide robot that served as an advertiser in a shopping mall, while the other studies investigated the interaction in the context of museums. Apart from Yousuf et al. focusing on greetings, the other studies investigated the coordination of verbal and non-verbal interactions as well as spatial formations. Two of these studies modelled the interaction based on observations and video analysis of human guides [19,21]. From their ethnographic studies, they found that humans automatically form F-formations, and if a visitor's facial or body orientation was not facing the guide or the exhibit, the human guide stopped and restarted sentences in order to re-capture the visitor's attention. Further, they also found that guides frequently turned their heads to look at both the visitors and the exhibit while explaining, and pointed towards the exhibit that was being explained. These non-verbal cues were most often performed at sentence endings. If these patterns were adopted by robots, participants found them more favorable compared to cases were they were missing.

In the Wild. Except for Yamazaki et al. [19] and Shiomi et al. [15], all experiments mentioned here were conducted in labs. Considering the lack of studies in which museum guide robots were tested in the wild, we explored challenges that can appear in real world settings when interacting with a robot. In in-the-wild studies, people use systems without being explicitly instructed about tasks, so the ecological validity is higher than in case of lab studies. This on the other hand leads to the researchers not being able to control the outcome [9,16]. According to Marshall et al. [9], these studies are most beneficial early in the development process to gain insights into design challenges. However, Siek et al. [16] mentions that the used prototypes should be at a level where they are robust enough to be used *in situ*. Not being highly familiar with the environment and the participants can often lead to unexpected situations that are very specific to the study and that the researchers cannot prepare for based on other studies and literature. This can lead to situations in which actions are taken based on the environment and not on the needs of the researchers [4]. This can eventually lead to further findings about aspects that need to be improved to achieve a prototype that is robust enough to function in the wild [2,17]. While doing experiments in the wild Williamson and Williamson and Mueller et al. [10,18] found that it can take a long time to find people who are willing to interact with their artifacts placed at public places, as, unlike lab experiments, these sessions are not scheduled. Therefore, it is important to plan ahead when conducting these studies, keeping in mind when there would be people willing to interact with a given artifact [16]. Furthermore, permission to conduct or, on occasion, document these studies should also be obtained [9]. While not everything can be planned, the prototype should be usable and the researchers should be prepared to encounter unexpected situations.

3   Lab Experiment

This experiment was a replication of the study by Yousuf et al. [20], conducted a) to verify their results; b) to explore if there are any culture-related effects; and c.) to explore whether using a different robot (we use a Pepper robot from SoftBank Robotics) influences the results. The experiment was conducted in a lab, where we marked an area of 3.5 m^2, within which the participants had to stay, just as in the original experiment. We placed a drawing at eye level in one corner of the area, while the robot's starting position was in the opposite corner.

16 Danish two person groups participated (8 female, 24 male), both graduate and undergraduate students recruited at Aalborg University Create campus. One of the participants had previous experience with humanoid robots. The experiment was counterbalanced and consisted of two separate conditions, condition A (experimental condition) and condition B (control condition), with within-subject and post-test only design. Participants filled out a set of two questionnaires. The original questionnaire consisted of three questions on a 7-point Likert scale: (1) Do you think the robot was able to greet you properly?; (2) Do you think that the robot attended to you adequately?; (3) What is your overall evaluation of the robot? Additionally, participants filled out a *Godspeed Questionnaire Series* (GQS) for additional data, after each condition. The experiment took approximately 8–10 min to complete including filling in the questionnaires.

In the experimental condition (A), the guide robot approached the person looking at it and said: "Welcome, may I explain the exhibit to you?". If the participant replied "Yes", the robot moved towards the exhibit and started the explanation. In the case that neither of the participants was looking at the robot in the beginning of the experiment and they were both looking at the exhibit instead, or anywhere else in the room, the guide robot approached closer, eventually moving into the participants' field of view to get their attention. With at least one of the participants gazing at the robot, the experiment continued in the same way as in the case mentioned before. In the control condition (B) the robot moved directly to the painting and started the explanation immediately without any greeting.

3.1   Results

Original questionnaire. In a Wilcoxon signed ranked test, we discovered that the participants found the robot's greeting capability significantly higher in condition A (Mdn = 5) compared to condition B (Mdn = 2.5) $T = 16.5, p < 0.01, r = 0.55$. In question 2, the Wilcoxon signed ranked test revealed that the participants found robot's attendance in condition A (Mdn = 5) significantly more adequate compared to the condition B (Mdn = 4), $T = 18, p < 0.01, r = -0.45$. Finally, the participants evaluated the robot significantly higher in condition A (Mdn=5) compared to condition B (Mdn = 4), $T = 24, p = 0.01, r = 0.45$.

Godspeed Questionnaire. On average, the participants rated the robot in condition A higher in all of the categories. Each of these categories were then individually compared using a Wilcoxon signed rank test. The results revealed that the anthropomorphism of the robot in condition A (Mdn = 3) was significantly higher, than the anthropomorphism of the robot in condition B (Mdn = 3) $T = 268, p < 0.01, r = -0.69$. The animacy lead to similar results, condition A (Mdn = 3) being significantly more animous than B (Mdn = 3) $T = 1953, p < 0.01, r = -0.81$. We also found that the likeability (Mdn = 4) in condition A was significantly higher than of condition B (Mdn = 4), $T = 739, p < 0.01, r = -0.52$. The perceived intelligence (Mdn = 4) was also significantly higher than in condition B (Mdn = 3), $T = 2654, p < 0.01, r = -0.45$. Finally, there was no significant difference in perceived safety (Mdn = 3, Mdn = 3), $p = 0.23, r = -0.15$.

3.2   Discussion

In the original study, participants rated the robot significantly higher in all three questions in condition A. We obtained the same results, which also seem to be supported by the answers to the GQS, where we got significantly higher results in four out of the five categories. Looking at the categories of the GQS individually, we can see that the Likeability results are aligned with the findings from the follow-up comments. Further, people attributed higher intelligence to the robot that was greeting and asking for permission to explain the exhibit, despite the fact that in both conditions the robot was exhibiting a pre-programmed behaviour and was unable to interact freely with the participants.

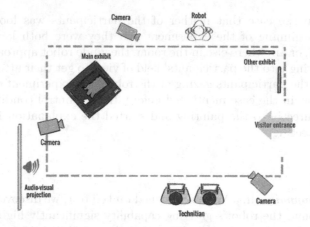

Fig. 1. The setup for the field study inside the museum.

Based on these findings we can conclude that starting the interaction by greeting is appreciated in Denmark. Having similar results to original study it is difficult to conclude how the differences in the robots influenced greetings. Overall, achieving significant preference for the experimental condition in both our and the original study suggests that these results are strong enough to conduct an experiment in the wild with a robot that starts interacting with people by greeting them.

4   Field Study

Following the success of the lab study, we decided to test the robot in a real museum. The purpose of the study was to evaluate the performance of our robot as a guide and to see how visitors in the context of a real museum interact with it. For data collection, we used the qualitative method of video analysis to observe the interaction, and interview to gather user responses from participants.

The second experiment was conducted at a local museum, the Utzon Center in Aalborg, Denmark. In the museum, we occupied an area where a wooden model of the Romsdal museum was used as the main exhibit for this field study experiment (see Fig. 1). We set up three video cameras at different angles to document the whole experiment.

Seeing that Williamson and Williamson [18] and Mueller et al. [10] warned about how difficult it can be to find participants in public places, we wanted to make sure we could recruit enough people willing to participate in the experiment. Thus, we chose the weekend day after a new exhibit was opened, when the Utzon Center usually has the most visitors. There was a total of 26 participants, 15 female and 11 male. Three people participated alone, while there were eight groups of two, one group of three and one group of four participants in the experiment. Two of the participants had previous experience with robots in the

Fig. 2. Left: L-shaped F-formation; Center: Horseshoe arrangement; Right: Horseshoe arrangement with Pepper.

Fig. 3. Left: Circular F-formation with Pepper; Center: Participants leaning in to hear the robot better; Right: Participants smiling when interacting with the robot.

form of robot vacuum cleaners. All participants were Western European, two of them native English speakers from the UK and 24 Danish with various levels of knowledge of the English language.

Three researchers were present during each test i.e. one facilitator and two technicians. The facilitator lead and explained each test while the two technicians operated the robot manually to avoid any unpredictable problems that might arise when using the fully automatic behaviour. Each test started with the facilitator verbally explaining the procedure and showing the participants to the designated experiment area. Then, the robot would approach the group, greet them and ask if it could explain the Romsdal Folk model. Shortly after, the robot would ask participants to follow it towards the model to explain the specific exhibit. The entire test took 2 to 5 minutes to complete for each group, followed by a 3 minutes follow-up group interview.

4.1 Findings

Observation. The videos were analyzed using Interaction Analysis, following a subset of the categories defined by [6]. These were turn-taking, spatial organization and trouble and repair. In the turn-taking theme, we observed 12 instances of groups of participants waiting with speaking or walking after robot has done so first. We also noticed that 5 participants were replying to the robot even when it was not needed for the interaction and were polite, saying things like "Yes, please" even though politeness does not matter when interacting with a robot.

With spatial organization we focused on the F-formation, looking into which one participants tend to use and when. We uncovered that every time a participant was interacting with Pepper alone they were in a vis-a-vis F-formation in the beginning, usually after they greeted each other and before Pepper lead them to the exhibit. After that, they regrouped into an L-shaped F-formation when the robot was explaining the exhibit (Fig. 2 left). In groups with several participants (2 to 4) there was more diversity in where people stood during the experiment. Most popular was the side-by-side F-formation, where 4 groups of 2 people chose to stand next to each other, opposite to Pepper, both in the greeting and the explanation phase. Furthermore, we observed 4 horseshoe arrangement cases, 2 of which consisted of people in this formation facing Pepper (Fig. 2 center) and 2 groups that included Pepper in this arrangement (Fig. 2 right). In two cases groups of 2 people formed a circular F-formation together with Pepper, once during the explanation phase and once during greeting (Fig. 3 left).

Analysing the videos through the trouble and repair theme brought to our attention that when the robot suddenly stopped moving during 3 trials, the participants became uncomfortable and confused and waited for the robot to start moving again. We also confirmed that the background noise, which was present during the testing, was intrusive and made it harder for the participants to hear and understand the robot, as two participants leaned in when it was talking to hear better (Fig. 3 center) and two people mentioned it was difficult to understand the robot. In general, we observed that participants in 5 groups were smiling and in 4 laughing when interacting with the robot, especially when they were in a group (Fig. 3 right).

Follow-Up Interviews. We analysed the follow-up interviews by six topics.

Main Impressions of the Experience. Participants' main impressions from the experiment were mostly positive, 6 people thinking it was fun, 2 that it was fine, 1 saying that it was a special experience and 1 calling it a positive experience. On the other hand, it was also apparent that none of the participants have ever interacted with a humanoid robot before, as 4 of them mentioned it was strange, 4 said it was a new experience and 2 participants felt it was surreal.

Participants' Feelings and Preoccupations During the Experiment. During the experiment, 6 participants felt confused, because they were not sure what they should say or where the robot would lead them. Nevertheless, 4 participants felt curious and 1 was fascinated by the robot's movement and gestures.

Participants' Overall Impressions of the Robot. The participants described the robot with positive attributes. 3 of them regarded it polite, 2 found it friendly and 2 others found it useful. There were 2 participants who described the robot as cute.

The Robot's Voice. However, most participants had problems with the robot's voice, 10 of them mentioning that it was difficult to understand what it was saying, 3 participants explaining that the problem was the loud background voice coming from the neighbouring exhibit. Furthermore, 3 people thought the robot had a monotonous voice, while 3 others said it was mechanical and 2 regarded its voice high-pitched.

Further Problems. Other problems people had with robot were its speed, 4 participants saying that it moved too slowly, while 2 complained about the lack of open interaction and 1 about the lack of eye contact.

4.2 Discussion

We observed that people anthropomorphized the robot by treating it as they would be treating a human guide, being polite and answering its greetings. During the interviews they also referred to it with terms that are commonly used to describe people. On the other hand, they were fully aware that it was impossible to have the same kind of interaction with the robot as they have with each other e.g. impossible to have an open conversation. These findings are aligned with Reeves' media equation [12] and have also been confirmed by other studies [13].

Conducting the study in the wild resulted in the benefit of uncovering environmental influences on the efficiency of the robot. During the lab test people understood what the robot explained but in the museum the presence of another synthetic voice made it difficult to follow what the robot was saying. While people were able to understand each other, the similarity of the robot's voice to the sound coming from other exhibits made it difficult to understand. Besides human voices being easier to understand, people also mentioned preferring a human voice. However, even though this would be both preferred and easier to understand it would not only break the design by not conforming to expectations but also limit the verbal interaction to predefined speech. Additionally, changes in pitch, intonation and timbre could be made.

In terms of formations, there was no overall preference for a specific type of F-formation. As Kendon found in human interactions, the formations created with the robot were also dependent on the number of participants and the interaction phase. This suggests that during HRI both the number of participants and the specifics of the interaction should be considered before aiming to establish a formation. Due to the fact that participants sometimes excluded the exhibited model from their formations, focusing only on the robot, the robot should actively aim to draw attention to the exhibit. Yamazaki et al. [19], observed that gesturing towards the exhibit was often used during explanations. In our study we observed that this and the exhibit made the participants look at it, therefore these behaviours should be employed more frequently.

In general it can be noticed that the aspects that participants complained about were different from how humans interact with each other e.g. lack of possibility for free interaction or synthetic voices. These aspects should be improved to achieve an interaction that is more natural for the participants.

5   Conclusion

In this paper we have proposed a museum guide robot able to initiate interaction with museum visitors, using human human interaction as reference. We have conducted an experiment based on Yousuf et al.'s paper [20] and confirmed that their findings are correct and also apply to Denmark. Seeing that there was a lack of studies investigating HRI in the wild, our second step was to conduct a field study in a real museum setting. We can conclude that greetings are a good way of initiating interaction between a museum visitor and a museum guide robot in Denmark. Additionally, our observations suggested that aspects of interaction that were different from human human interaction, such as the speed of the robot and its voice, were not appreciated. Therefore, these aspects should be further investigated. Another area that could be investigated in the future is whether these findings apply in other contexts, such as a library or a shopping mall.

References

1. Aaltonen, I., Arvola, A., Heikkilä, P., Lammi, H.: Hello pepper, may i tickle you? Children's and adults' responses to an entertainment robot at a shopping mall. In: Proceedings of the Companion of the 2017 ACM/IEEE International Conference on Human-Robot Interaction, pp. 53–54. Association for Computing Machinery, New York (2017). https://doi.org/10.1145/3029798.3038362
2. Behrens, M., Valkanova, N., gen. Schieck, A.F., Brumby, D.P.: Smart citizen sentiment dashboard: a case study into media architectural interfaces. In: Proceedings of The International Symposium on Pervasive Displays, pp. 19–24. Association for Computing Machinery, New York (2014). https://doi.org/10.1145/2611009.2611036
3. Bergstrom, N., Kanda, T., Miyashita, T., Ishiguro, H., Hagita, N.: Modeling of natural human-robot encounters. In: 2008 IEEE/RSJ International Conference on Intelligent Robots and Systems, pp. 2623–2629(2008). https://doi.org/10.1109/IROS.2008.4650896
4. Boyd, L.E., Rector, K., Profita, H., Stangl, A.J., Zolyomi, A., Kane, S.K., Hayes, G.R.: Understanding the role fluidity of stakeholders during assistive technology research "in the wild,". In: Proceedings of the 2017 CHI Conference on Human Factors in Computing Systems, pp. 6147–6158. Association for Computing Machinery (2017). https://doi.org/10.1145/3025453.3025493
5. Heenan, B., Greenberg, S., Aghel-Manesh, S., Sharlin, E.: In: Designing social greetings in human robot interaction. In: Proceedings of the 2014 Conference on Designing Interactive Systems, pp. 855–864. Association for Computing Machinery, New York (2014). https://doi.org/10.1145/2598510.2598513
6. Jordan, B., Henderson, A.: Interaction analysis: foundations and practice. J. Learn. Sci. 4(1), 39–103 (1995). https://doi.org/10.1207/s15327809jls0401_2
7. Kendon, A.: Conducting Interaction: Patterns of Behavior in Focused Encounters. Cambridge University Press, New York (1990)
8. Kobayashi, Y., Shibata, T., Hoshi, Y., Kuno, Y., Okada, M., Yamazaki, K.: Choosing answerers by observing gaze responses for museum guide robots. In: 2010 5th ACM/IEEE International Conference on Human-Robot Interaction (HRI), pp. 109–110 (2010). https://doi.org/10.1109/HRI.2010.5453240
9. Marshall, P., Rogers, Y., Pantidi, N.: Using f-formations to analyse spatial patterns of interaction in physical environments. In: Proceedings of the ACM 2011 Conference on Computer Supported Cooperative Work pp. 445–454. Association for Computing Machinery, New York (2011). https://doi.org/10.1145/1958824.1958893

10. Müller, J., Walter, R., Bailly, G., Nischt, M., Alt, F.: Looking glass: a field study on noticing interactivity of a shop window. In: Proceedings of the SIGCHI Conference on Human Factors in Computing Systems, pp. 297–306. Association for Computing Machinery, New York (2012). https://doi.org/10.1145/2207676.2207718

11. Pateraki, M., Trahanias, P.: Deployment of robotic guides in museum contexts. In: Mixed Reality and Gamification for Cultural Heritage, pp. 449–472. Springer, Cham (2017). https://doi.org/10.1007/978-3-319-49607-8_18

12. Reeves, B., Nass, C.: The Media Equation: How People Treat Computers, Television, and New Media Like Real People and Places. CSLI Publications (1996)

13. Rehm, M.: She is just stupid: analyzing user-agent interactions in emotional game situations. Interact. Comput. **20**(3), 311–325 (2008). https://doi.org/10.1016/j.intcom.2008.02.005. Special issue: on the abuse and misuse of social agents

14. Shiomi, M., Kanda, T., Ishiguro, H., Hagita, N.: Interactive humanoid robots for a science museum. In: Proceedings of the 1st ACM SIGCHI/SIGART Conference on Human-Robot Interaction, pp. 305–312. Association for Computing Machinery (2006). https://doi.org/10.1145/1121241.1121293

15. Shiomi, M., Kanda, T., Ishiguro, H., Hagita, N.: A larger audience, please! encouraging people to listen to a guide robot. In: Proceedings of the 5th ACM/IEEE International Conference on Human-Robot Interaction, pp. 31–38. IEEE Press (2010)

16. Siek, K.A., Hayes, G.R., Newman, M.W., Tang, J.C.: Field deployments: knowing from using in context. In: Olson, J.S., Kellogg, W.A. (eds.) Ways of Knowing in HCI, pp. 119–142. Springer, New York (2014). https://doi.org/10.1007/978-1-4939-0378-8_6

17. Vaizman, Y., Ellis, K., Lanckriet, G., Weibel, N.: Extrasensory app: data collection in-the-wild with rich user interface to self-report behavior. In: Proceedings of the 2018 CHI Conference on Human Factors in Computing Systems, pp. 1–12. Association for Computing Machinery, New York (2018). https://doi.org/10.1145/3173574.3174128

18. Williamson, J.R., Williamson, J.: Understanding public evaluation: quantifying experimenter intervention. In: Proceedings of the 2017 CHI Conference on Human Factors in Computing Systems, pp. 3414–3425. Association for Computing Machinery, New York (2017). https://doi.org/10.1145/3025453.3025598

19. Yamazaki, A., Yamazaki, K., Burdelski, M., Kuno, Y., Fukushima, M.: Coordination of verbal and non-verbal actions in human-robot interaction at museums and exhibitions. J. Pragmatics **42**, 2398–2414 (2010). https://doi.org/10.1016/j.pragma.2009.12.023

20. Yousuf, M.A., Kobayashi, Y., Kuno, Y., Yamazaki, A., Yamazaki, K.: How to move towards visitors: a model for museum guide robots to initiate conversation. In: 2013 IEEE RO-MAN, pp. 587–592 (2013). https://doi.org/10.1109/ROMAN.2013.6628543

21. Yousuf, M.A., Kobayashi, Y., Kuno, Y., Yamazaki, A., Yamazaki, K.: Development of a mobile museum guide robot that can configure spatial formation with visitors. In: Huang, D.-S., Jiang, C., Bevilacqua, V., Figueroa, J.C. (eds.) ICIC 2012. LNCS, vol. 7389, pp. 423–432. Springer, Heidelberg (2012). https://doi.org/10.1007/978-3-642-31588-6_55

Recognition of a Robot's Affective Expressions Under Conditions with Limited Visibility

Moojan Ghafurian[1]([⊠]), Sami Alperen Akgun[2], Mark Crowley[1],
and Kerstin Dautenhahn[1,2]

[1] Department of Electrical and Computer Engineering, University of Waterloo,
Waterloo, ON, Canada
{moojan,mcrowley,kerstin.dautenhahn}@uwaterloo.ca
[2] Department of Systems Design Engineering, University of Waterloo,
Waterloo, ON, Canada
saakgun@uwaterloo.ca

Abstract. The capability of showing affective expressions is important for the design of social robots in many contexts, where the robot is designed to communicate with humans. It is reasonable to expect that, similar to all other interaction modalities, communicating with affective expressions is not without limitations. In this paper, we present two online video studies (72 and 50 participants) and investigate if/to what extent the recognition of affective displays of a zoomorphic robot is affected under situations with different levels of visibility. Recognition of five affective expressions under five visibility effects were studied. The intensity of the effects was more pronounced in the second experiment. While visual constraints affected recognition of expressions, our results showed that affective displays of the robot conveyed through its head and body motions can be robust and recognition rates can still be high even under severe visibility constraints. This study supported the effectiveness of using affective displays as a complementary communication modality in human-robot interaction in situations with visibility constraints, e.g. in the case of older users with visual impairments, or in outdoor scenarios such as search-and-rescue.

Keywords: Affective displays · Impaired visibility · Social robots · Zoomorphic robots · Miro

1 Introduction

Emotional expressions have been designed on many different robots [8,13,43, 50] and using different modalities, such as, facial expressions [8,43], light [10], sound [40], body gesture [18], motion [45], and other more abstract methods [31]. Each of these methods (or a combination of them) can be used to improve

© IFIP International Federation for Information Processing 2021
Published by Springer Nature Switzerland AG 2021
C. Ardito et al. (Eds.): INTERACT 2021, LNCS 12934, pp. 448–469, 2021.
https://doi.org/10.1007/978-3-030-85613-7_31

emotional displays of a robot and increase its social capabilities. This capability is especially beneficial in many context where humans interact directly with robots, such as in health and safety applications.

It is important to ensure that emotions expressed by a social robot can be perceived reliably by humans who are interacting with the robot or working alongside it (e.g., in healthcare or search and rescue applications of robots). Otherwise, robots that lack clearly identifiable expressions of emotions may be socially unacceptable to their users [5], and might be unable to sustain successful social interactions.

Sometimes end users are less familiar with robotics technologies, such as children and older adults, or medical staff. For such cases, expressions of emotions that can be perceived reliably becomes more crucial since those users often assume that the emotions expressed by the robot are real and genuine [26,42]. In addition, many real-life applications of emotionally expressive robots include scenarios with limited visibility that might affect perception of emotions [22], possibly related to the different visual capabilities of different user groups (e.g., children [4] or older adults [15]). Also, depending on the specific application area, the environment in which the robot operates might introduce conditions that can result in limited visibility such as in search and rescue [54], firefighting [29], or service robotics [19].

Misinterpreting a robot's emotional displays can have a significant impact on the quality of the interaction itself, as well as the acceptability and usability of the robot across a variety of different application areas and user groups [5,33]. Therefore, here, we investigate how situations limited by visibility constraints affect recognition of a robot's affective expressions. We investigated the robustness of recognition of affective expressions of a robot expressed through its head and body gestures. Our choice of robotic platform is the Miro robot, a zoomorphic robot designed not to look like any specific animal, but which can express emotions via many modalities, such as body language [11,35]. This zoomorphic robot was selected since (1) animal-like robots are widely used in many applications in health (e.g., therapeutic situations and with older adults) and safety (e.g., search and rescue scenarios), and (2) a recent study designed and evaluated different affective displays for the Miro robot, all of which involved head and body gestures which are of interest in the present study [18].

In the following, we will first detail our research questions followed by a discussion of background and related work. Two experiments and their results are presented afterwards. We conclude with a discussion of the results and identifying limitations of this work.

Research Questions and Expectations: We investigate the robustness of human observers' recognition of affective expressions of a zoomorphic robot (including emotions and moods) conveyed through its body language, under different visibility conditions. Our specific research questions are as follows.

RQ1. To what extent is the recognition of a robot's affective expressions robust with regards to the visibility of the robot?

RQ2. How does the degree of visibility (moderate versus severe) impact the recognition of a robot's affective expressions?

Concerning RQ1, since to our knowledge this is the first study of its kind on this particular topic, RQ1 was exploratory in nature. However, we expected that some affective expressions might be easier to recognize than the others under the same visibility constraints. Regarding RQ2, we found it reasonable to expect that severe constraints on visibility will have a larger impact than moderate constraints. And again, we expected that some affective expressions might be more affected than others.[1]

2 Background and Related Work

In many application areas, social robots may operate in an environment that introduces constraints. For example a noisy environment can make sound less effective, or an environment with limited visibility can affect visibility of the robot's expressions, such as its facial expressions. These situations are very common in robots that assist in search and rescue (in which emotions have been recently proposed as a new modality [1]) or fire fighting missions. In these missions many conditions such as rain [27,49], smoke [6], limited available light [6], or even temperature [21] can affect visibility of robots. Further, some users, such as older adults may be affected by a condition that can influence their vision, such as blurred vision. For robots to be successful in these situations, it is important to ensure that both robots and users can continue to communicate successfully despite these constraints.

From the perspective of robots, many studies have investigated improving performance of a robot in situations with limited visibility, for example in smoky environments [44,48], dark areas [12], underwater [23], or to detect humans at different distances [38]. To this end, different machine learning methods, computer vision techniques, as well as sensors have been proposed for the robots to enhance their navigation and detection of humans in situations with similar visibility constraints [12,37,38,44,48]. For instance, Naḍ et al. suggested using smart gloves to overcome limited visibility problem in water for gesture recognition [37].

However, visibility of emotional expressions of robots by humans is also important for the success of interactions between humans and robots, a research area that has so far attracted little attention, but will ultimately determine to what extent emotional expressions can be used successfully in real life situations. In general, visibility of robots has been studied in many situations where humans need to locate a robot [30]. For example, with the goal of designing a socially assistive service robot, McGinn et al. used lights to improve visibility of the robot and suggested that while it is commonly believed that a social robot with

---

[1] Note, we had originally envisaged to conduct both studies as in-person experiments, but due to COVID-19 this was not possible and we had to move the study online.

a head/face is most effective for interactions, having a head can limit the observation angle and result in a poor visibility of the robots' expressive states [34]. This can be particularly true if the robot's expressiveness is restricted to facial expressions. However, an approach that uses both head and body gestures to convey expressions could be beneficial in overcoming this challenge. However, even when the observation angle is not an issue, there are still other visual constraints as mentioned above that can affect the visibility of a robot's expressions. Therefore in this article we ask how such situations affect recognition of a robot's affective expressions.

3   Experiment 1

In this experiment we evaluate the recognition of five affective expressions of the Miro robot under five different situations that *moderately* affect visibility through a crowdsourcing video study, which is a common approach in many of the related studies in human-robot interaction (e.g., [8,17,31]).

3.1   Methodology

Affective Expression Selection. As discussed earlier, we study the affective expressions of the zoomorphic Miro robot. For this particular robot, prior work designed and evaluated eleven affective expressions (including emotions and moods) [18], inspired by various sources of information, including ethology, cartoon animations, etc. These affective expressions were conveyed through the robot's eyes, ears, tail, and body movements. The Miro robot has the potential to be used as a companion robot for older adults for applications such as pet therapy, and the emotional expressions (used in this study) have the potential to be implemented on the other zoomorphic robots. Further, in other applications, such as in search and rescue, body and head motions could be effective for communicating emotions, because these motions can, to some extent, be applied to appearance constrained robots used, e.g., in search and rescue [7].

Out of the proposed 11 affective expressions of Miro, we selected expressions that (1) were highly recognized by the majority of the participants who evaluated these expressions in a previous study [18], and (2) were found to be important in situations where the robot's visibility can be affected, such as in search and rescue situations [1]. This resulted in the selection of five affective expressions: happy, sad, tired, excited, and surprised.

Video Effect Selection. After careful consideration of different situations that can affect the visibility of a robot, five visual effects were selected: dark, rain, smoke, blurred vision (called blur in this paper), and the robot located at a far distance (called zoom hereafter). Here are some real-life situations with limited visibility that can be represented by the selected video effects:

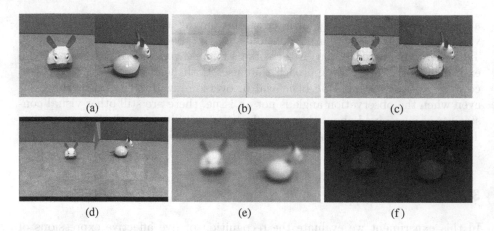

Fig. 1. Snapshots taken from the start of the tired expression for (a) actual videos used in training, (b) smoke effect, (c) rain effect, (d) zoom effect, (e) blur effect, and (f) dark effects

- **Dark:** Other than many common situations where the robot may operate in a dark room or a room with dimmed lights, during almost all types of search and rescue operations, the rescue might be conducted under diminishing light conditions. During wilderness search and rescue [20], maritime/sea search and rescue [36], or mountain rescue [27], the reason for darkness might just be related to the operation time (i.e., the missions need to start or continue at night). On the other hand, for other search and rescue situations such as urban search and rescue [2] or cave rescue [24], areas of interest can be dark regardless of the operation time, since these types of rescues involve confined spaces. This can be the case for firefighters, too, since they sometimes have to operate in dark areas [6]. Therefore, this effect can represent many situations in which the robot is used to increase safety.
- **Smoke:** This effect, similar to dark, mostly represents situations in which the robot is used to increase safety. In general, smoke is the main factor that firefighters need to deal with [6]. Further, the areas involved in search and rescue situations might be affected by the smoke caused by either fire at the scene [9] or by dust of collapsed structures [32]. This effect also represents situations where the rescue workers need to deal with dense fog in open areas like mountain rescue [46].
- **Rain:** Similar to dark and smoke effects, heavy rain (and, with a similar effect, snow) can introduce many different challenges in search and rescue situations (for example in mountain search and rescue situations [27,49]). Limited visibility due to rain is present in many maritime search and rescue operations since most of the time rescue workers need to operate either in or near to water [36].
- **Blur:** This effect can represent situations happening both in robots designed in the context of healthcare and those designed for safety. For example,

blurred vision (or a similar condition) can affect many older adults, as well as other individuals, and constrain the visibility of the robots. Furthermore, a blurred vision may happen in firefighting scenarios, or search and rescue scenarios due to high humidity/temperature [21] or low-lighting conditions [41].

- **Zoom:** As many of the social robots may be used in large areas, for example in a care home or in a search and rescue scene, it is expected that the robot will not always remain close to its users. For example, a companion robot in a care home may be farther from some residents/caregivers and closer to the others. Also, while rescue robotics involves situations that requires co-located interactions between humans and robots [14], the distance between the human and robot teammates varies significantly depending on the search area (e.g., they may need to operate at very distant locations during wilderness search and rescue [25] or forest fire missions [28]).

All the videos were adjusted to have the same length. The videos were modified in a way that each effect was identical for all the affective expressions. Figure 1 shows a snapshot of these effects.[2]

Design and Procedure. Upon signing the consent form, the participants followed four steps of the study as below.

Step 1 - Training: The participants first saw a video of all five expressions of the robot, in which the affective expressions were clearly stated overlaying text on the video. The purpose of this step was to teach participants about the affective expressions of Miro, and to ensure that they would know each expression and its label under clear visibility conditions. The participants were told that this was a training part and we wanted them to learn the meaning of each expressions. They were able to replay this video as many times as they wished.

After watching the training video (as many times as needed), we tested the success of the training, i.e., participants' ability to recognize the expressions, to ensure that they paid sufficient attention to the video learned the five expressions. The expressions were shown to them one by one, and they were asked to indicate what each expression was. If they passed a test for each expression, that expression was removed from the testing set. Otherwise, it remained in the test set and we showed them that expression again at a later time and in a random order. This continued until the participants were either able to complete training successfully, or if they exceeded "15" test videos (i.e., watching each video three times on average). In the latter case, participants were allowed to continue with the study but their data was removed since it indicated that for those participants training was unsuccessful.

This step was essential, because (1) while these affective expressions were previously designed and their recognition was evaluated correctly in the majority of

---

[2] A combination of widely available video editing software (i.e., iMovie, Wondershare Filmora, and HitFilm Express) was used to create the video effects. The choice of software depended on the effect. Please contact the authors if you are interested to see the videos.

instances, it is not reasonable to assume that all participants would recognize the affective expressions 100% correctly, and (2) without training, and thus ensuring that all participants will recognize the affective expressions correctly when visual constraints are not present, it is not possible to know whether any recognition errors observed in our study may be due to individual participant's difficulties in evaluating those affective expressions (which is not the focus of this study) or is due to visual constraints (which is the focus of this study). Furthermore, in many contexts, such as search and rescue, it is expected that those interacting with the robots will get prior information and training regarding the interpretation of the robots' affective expressions, if they are used as a communication modality.

Step 2 - Evaluating Video Effects: After the training phase, participants read instructions about the next phase, and they were informed that the videos are intentionally not as visible as those that they saw in the training phase, in order to avoid the remote participants to worry that reduced visibility of the videos might be due to internet issues, etc.

In this step, the participants evaluated 10 videos with different effects. They were allowed to only select one option as their response. The first 5 videos were selected in a way that both the order of expressions (EM_1 to EM_5) and effects (EF_1 to EF_5) were random. Afterwards, they saw another combination as below:

- The order of effects were similar to what they originally saw
- The order of affective expressions were the same as before, except for one shift, moving the first expression to the last.

In other words, participants first saw $[EM_1, EF_1]$ to $[EM_5, EF_5]$, where EM_n and EF_n were randomly selected from the set of five expressions (i.e., happy, sad, surprise, excited, and tired) and effects (i.e., rain, smoke, blur, dark, and zoom). After completing these five combinations, the participants then saw $[EM_2, EF_1]$, $[EM_3, EF_2]$, $[EM_4, EF_3]$, $[EM_5, EF_4]$, $[EM_1, EF_5]$ (a total of 5 videos). This way, (a) all participants saw 10 videos, (b) evaluated each effect and each expression twice, and (c) the combinations (i.e., order of effects, affective expressions, and the combination of effect+expression) were counterbalanced. As it is suggested by previous work (e.g., see [16]) and to avoid fatigue, we did not expose each participant to all 25 videos.

Step 3 - Test: After evaluating the 10 videos, we tested participants to see how well they recalled the original expressions, to ensure that the errors in the recognition of the affective expressions were actually due to the video effects, as opposed to the participants forgetting the expressions. In this step, participants saw the original 5 videos that they saw in the training phase, and were asked to select the correct expression.

Step 4 - Questionnaire: A Questionnaire was designed to obtain information on participants' demographics, as well as their perception of the effects and their familiarity with pets and emotions (which are shown to affect recognition of a zoomorphic robot's expressions [18]). The questionnaire asked about participants' (1) age, (2) gender, and (3) ethnicity. We also included questions asking participants (4) if they had pets, (5) if they had a friend with a pet, (6) if they wear glasses or contact lenses, and if yes, if they were wearing them at the time of the study, (7) whether they liked pets, (8) whether they were scared of pets, (9) how good they thought they are in recognizing pets' emotions, and (10) if they had difficulty understanding pets emotions. Finally, participants were asked to report how difficult it was for them to understand Miro's expressions under each of the five effects (questions 11–15).

Questions 7 through 15 were responded to on a continuous scale. Questions 9 and 10 were designed to complement each other, as an attention check. One additional attention check question was added, which asked participants if they thought that cats and dogs were popular pets in North America (we assumed that the correct answer to this question would be YES and removed the data from those whose answers were anywhere from the centre of the continuous scale to "Completely Disagree").

Step 5 - Human Emotion Understanding: As a previous study suggested that understanding human emotions can be correlated with understanding Miro's affective expressions [18], in this step we asked participants to evaluate 14 images of human emotions (i.e., angry, fearful, disgusted, happy, neutral, sad, and surprised; two images of each). All images were taken from the FacesDB dataset.[3] Gender, age, and skin color were counterbalanced in the two images representing the same emotion, as well as among all the 14 images. In order to avoid fatigue we decided on 14 images. This step was added as a previous study showed that the recognition of affective expressions of the selected robot can be significantly affected by the ability to recognize human emotions [18].

All the steps were performed on the same day and one right after the other.

Participants: A total of 116 participants who had an approval rate of over 97% based on at least 100 HITs completed the study on Amazon Mechanical Turk. Data from 37 participants were removed as they failed the attention checks. This left 79 participants (44 male, 34 female, 1 unknown; age range [19,58], average: 35.2 yrs). The study received full Ethics clearance from the University of Waterloo's Research Ethics Committees.

4   Results - Experiment 1

The results for recognition of each affective expression under each effect is shown in Table 1 and Fig. 2 summarizes the results. The correct expression was selected significantly more than the others for all expressions and effects. The accuracy was very similar for all the effects and were either 86% or 87%. We also studied the accuracy in recognition of each affective expression. While all accuracies were high (82% to 92%), the lowest accuracy belonged to surprised (82%), and the

---

[3] http://app.visgraf.impa.br/database/faces/.

Table 1. Results for the recognition of each affective expression for each visibility effect. The last column shows the overall accuracy for each effect. The last row shows the overall accuracy for each affective expression. Through binomial tests, we show if each choice was selected significantly more than the others: ***: $p < .001$, **: $p < .01$. The differences in number of results for affective expressions are due to (1) the random assignment of sets of effects+emotions, and (2) removal of data from those who failed the study.

		Happy	Sad	Surprised	Tired	Excited	Accuracy
Rain	Happy	22***	0	0	1	3	86%
	Sad	0	29***	0	3	0	
	Surprised	4	0	26***	2	3	
	Tired	0	5	0	28***	0	
	Excited	1	0	0	0	31***	
Blur	Happy	35***	0	0	1	3	87%
	Sad	0	27***	0	1	0	
	Surprised	1	2	22***	0	4	
	Tired	0	5	0	35***	0	
	Excited	3	0	0	1	18***	
Dark	Happy	28***	1	0	0	1	86%
	Sad	0	39***	0	4	0	
	Surprised	0	2	30***	1	1	
	Tired	0	3	0	18***	0	
	Excited	3	1	5	0	20**	
Smoke	Happy	28***	0	3	0	2	87%
	Sad	0	25***	0	1	0	
	Surprised	1	1	24***	2	3	
	Tired	0	4	0	26***	0	
	Excited	2	0	2	0	34***	
Zoom	Happy	26***	0	1	0	3	87%
	Sad	0	26***	0	3	0	
	Surprised	0	1	27***	1	0	
	Tired	0	5	0	27***	1	
	Excited	4	0	1	0	32***	
Accuracy		88%	92%	82%	85%	85%	

highest to sad (92%). It is in fact reasonable for surprise to have a lower accuracy when visibility is affected, since the associated behavior is not as continuous as in the other expressions and the behavior change is fast and sudden.

To study how other factors affected recognition of expressions, we fit a linear model predicting the number of correctly recognized expressions of Miro based on (a) participants' understanding of human emotions measured through the

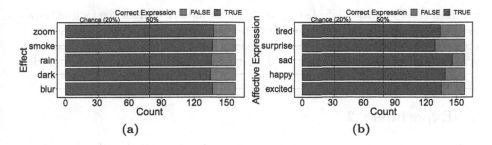

Fig. 2. Overall results for (a) recognition of each effect, and (b) recognition of each affective expression

Table 2. Linear model predicting the number of correct responses to the affective expressions.

Covariate	Estimate	SE	t	Pr (>|t|)
Intercept	7.078	1.328	5.331	<.0001
humanUnderstanding	−0.075	0.101	−0.750	0.455
petEmotionDifficulty	−0.001	0.001	−2.077	<.05
test	1.057	0.150	7.046	<.0001
training	−0.276	0.069	−4.028	0.0001

images, (b) their reported difficulty in understanding pets' emotions, (c) their accuracy in the post-test results, and (d) how long training took for them. Results are shown in Table 2.

A higher reported difficulty in understanding pets' emotions significantly and negatively affected recognition of Miro's expressions ($se = 0.001, t = −2.077, p < .05$). Participants' performance in the post-test was also a significant predictor for recognition of expressions: as expected, those who performed better in their test results had a better recognition of Miro's affective expressions under different visibility constraints ($se = 0.150, t = 7.046, p < .0001$). Performance in training was also a significant predictor of the correct responses ($se = 0.069, t = −4.028, p < 0.0001$), the faster the participants finished the training (i.e., less errors they had), the better they performed in recognizing Miro's expressions in the videos with effects. This can be because (a) Miro's expressions were more intuitive for those who learned them quicker and finished faster, thus they recognized them better also in other conditions, or (b) those who finished the training faster paid more attention to the study in general and Miro's expressions shown in videos in particular. We did not observe any effect of participants' age or gender on recognition of the affective expressions.

Finally, as the difficulty level of the effects can affect recognition of affective expressions, we asked participants to report how difficult it was to recognize each affective expression under each of the five effect conditions. Figure 3 shows the results. Recognition was reported to be relatively easy for all the effects. After controlling for the other effects (i.e., using linear models and for the factors shown in Table 2), only for the rain effect the reported difficulty level was a predictor of the accuracy of recognition of the expressions ($se = 0.000, t = -3.308, p = .001$). We did not observe any effect of the reported difficulties on the recognition accuracies for the other visibility effects.

5   Experiment 2

In this experiment we investigated how the recognition of the affective expressions changes in extreme situations, when visibility of the expressions are *severely* affected.

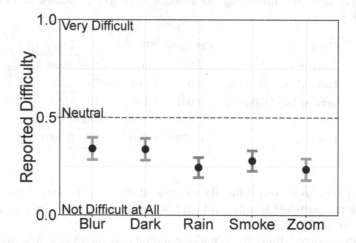

Fig. 3. Reported difficulty of each effect on the recognition of the robot's affective expressions

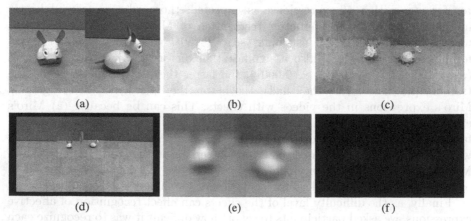

Fig. 4. Snapshots taken from the start of the tired expression for (a) actual videos used in training, (b) smoke effect, (c) rain effect, (d) zoom effect, (e) blur effect, and (f) dark effect

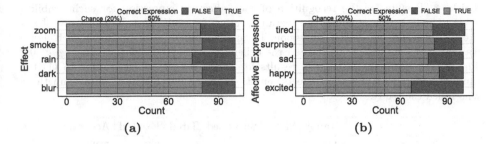

Fig. 5. Overall results for (a) recognition of each effect, and (b) recognition of each affective expression

5.1 Methodology

The procedure and all the steps of this experiment were similar to Experiment 1. Participants followed the exact same five steps, except that new videos with more extreme effects were used and, as our intention was to use severe constraints on visibility in this experiment, as compared to moderate effects in Experiment 1, participants were given specific instructions to adjust their screens' brightness prior to evaluation of Miro's expressions in the videos.

Video Effects. Considering that participants will use different computers, screens, settings, etc., and to ensure that the videos are suitably manipulated and reflect extreme situations, we did two pilot tests. The first test was conducted by asking five people in the authors' research group (who were not involved in this study) to evaluate different effects. Three extreme versions of the effects (changing in intensity) were created and the pilot group were asked to select the video which they thought was most extreme, but they could still see Miro. According to this feedback, five videos were selected and used in the second pilot study. The second pilot study was conducted on Amazon Mechanical Turk, where we asked seven participants to complete the experiment with the new videos. We then referred to the difficulty levels that the participants reported for each effect. As the difficulty levels were initially not as high as expected, the videos were further manipulated and the effects were intensified. Figure 4 shows snapshots of the final videos that were used in this experiment.[4]

Participants: 92 participants were recruited on Amazon Mechanical Turk. The same qualification criteria as used in Experiment 1 were applied (i.e., participation was limited to North America, and those with an acceptance rate of over 97% based on at least 100 HITs). Data from 42 participants was removed as they failed the attention checks (attention checks were identical to those in Experiment 1). This left 50 participants (35 male, 15 female; age range [21, 61],

---

[4] Please contact the authors if you are interested to see the videos.

Table 3. Results for the recognition of each affective expression for each visibility effect. The last column shows the overall accuracy for each effect. The last row shows the overall accuracy for each expression. Through binomial tests, we show if each choice was selected significantly more than the others: ***: $p < .001$, **: $p < .01$, *: $p < .05$. The differences in the number of results for affective expressions are due to (1) the random assignment of sets of effects+emotions, and (2) removal of data from those who failed the study.

		Happy	Sad	Surprised	Tired	Excited	Accuracy
Rain	Happy	**16****	1	0	2	3	**72%**
	Sad	1	**21*****	0	4	0	
	Surprised	1	0	**18*****	1	0	
	Tired	0	3	1	**15****	1	
	Excited	7	0	0	0	4	
Blur	Happy	**14****	0	1	1	3	**80%**
	Sad	1	**17****	0	3	1	
	Surprised	1	1	**13*****	0	0	
	Tired	0	1	0	**15*****	1	
	Excited	5	1	0	0	**21****	
Dark	Happy	**21*****	0	1	0	0	**84%**
	Sad	0	**15****	0	2	0	
	Surprised	2	0	**16*****	0	1	
	Tired	2	1	0	**19*****	0	
	Excited	2	1	3	0	9	
Smoke	Happy	**18*****	0	1	0	1	**80%**
	Sad	1	**10**	0	5	0	
	Surprised	1	0	**21*****	0	2	
	Tired	0	3	1	**16****	0	
	Excited	3	0	2	0	**15****	
Zoom	Happy	**16*****	0	0	0	1	**77%**
	Sad	1	**15****	0	2	0	
	Surprised	1	3	**14****	1	1	
	Tired	1	1	0	**16*****	1	
	Excited	8	0	0	0	**18***	
Accuracy		85%	79%	81%	83%	68%	

average: 34.7 yrs). The study received full Ethics clearance from the University of Waterloo's Research Ethics Committees.

6   Results - Experiment 2

Results for the new, more extreme effects are shown in Fig. 5 and Table 3. While the accuracies were still high, in three situations (i.e., Rain-Excited, Dark-Excited, and Smoke-Sad) the correct expression was no longer selected significantly more than the other options, and in the Rain-Excited situation it was not even selected significantly more than random. The accuracies in recognition of the expressions dropped from the previous experiment, with excited having the largest drop and the least accuracy among the other expressions.

A linear model with the same dependent variables as the previous experiment (i.e., human emotion understanding results, reported difficulty in understanding pet emotions, training results, and test results) was fit to predict the number of correct expressions recognized by the participants. Two effects were consistent with the previous experiment: a higher test performance resulted in a better recognition of Miro's expressions ($se = 0.266, t = 3.079, p < .01$) and the longer it took the participants to learn the expressions in the training phase, the lower their recognition rates were ($se = -0.014, t = -3.539, p < .001$). The results are shown in Table 4.

Finally, Fig. 6 shows the results for the reported difficulties of the effects. The effects were perceived to be more difficult than those in Experiment 1. However, after controlling for the other effects (i.e., using linear models and for those factors shown in Table 4), reported difficulty levels were not significant predictors for the accuracy of recognition of expressions.

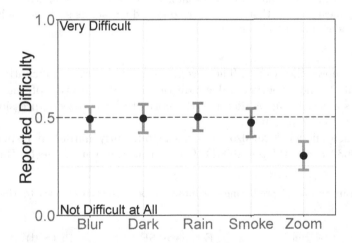

Fig. 6. Reported difficulty of each effect on the recognition of the robot's affective expressions

7   Results - Combined

To study the effect of the intensity of the video effects (moderate vs. severe) on the recognition of the robot's affective expressions, and to check that the difficulty levels changed indeed to more severe conditions in Experiment 2, we pooled the data. Note that while intensity of the effects was not intended to be a condition, the two studies were conducted very close and within 1 month of each other, and anything except for the intensity of videos were identical in both. Therefore, pooling the data and doing a between-participants condition would be valid in this situation.

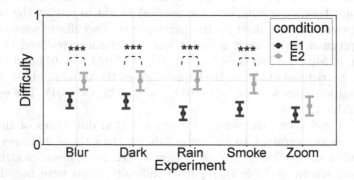

Fig. 7. Comparison between the reported difficulty levels in Experiment 1 and Experiment 2. 95% confidence intervals are visualized. ***: $p < .001$. Significance was calculated using linear models that took other confounding factors such as results related to human understanding into account.

Table 5 shows the results. The recognition rates were significantly lower in Experiment 2, and experimental condition (i.e., the severity of the visibility effects) was a significant predictor of the correctly recognized expressions ($se = -0.937, t = -3.477, p < .001$).

The video effects were also rated as significantly harder in Experiment 2 ($se = 19.8632, t = 8.314, p < .0001$). Comparing the pair of effects, Rain, Blur,

Table 4. Linear model predicting the number of correct responses to the affective expressions.

Covariate	Estimate	SE	t	Pr (>|t|)
(Intercept)	5.916	2.147	2.755	<.01
humanUnderstanding	0.153	0.170	0.903	0.371
petEmotionDifficulty	0.000	0.001	0.262	0.794
test	0.819	0.266	3.079	<.01
training	−0.414	0.117	−3.539	<.001

Table 5. Linear model predicting the number of correct responses to the robot's affective expressions under different visibility conditions. Condition shows whether data belonged to Experiment 1 (E1) or Experiment 2 (E2).

Covariate	Estimate	SE	t	Pr ($>|t|$)
Intercept	6.801	1.171	5.806	<.0001
humanUnderstanding	0.033	0.0885	0.375	0.708
conditionE2	−0.937	0.270	−3.477	<.001
petEmotionDifficulty	−0.001	0.001	−1.023	0.308
training	−0.323	0.061	−5.246	<.0001
test	0.952	0.136	6.982	<.0001

Dark, and Smoke were all rated to be significantly more difficult in Experiment 2 as compared with Experiment 1. However, while the robot's size (shown in the video) was halved from Experiment 1 to Experiment 2, the difference between the difficulty ratings was not significant for zoom (See Fig. 7).

8   Discussion

This study investigated the feasibility of using a zoomorphic robot's affective expressions as a communication method in situations where users' vision or visibility of the robot are affected. Two experiments investigated recognition of five affective expressions (happy, excited, sad, tired, and surprised) under five situations with visual constraints (blurred vision, rain, far distance, smoke, and dark). The intensity of effects differed across the two experiments and were significantly intensified in the videos shown in Experiment 2. The two experiments helped us understand how visibility constraints affect recognition of emotions, while we controlled for the other confounding factors that may affect recognition in general.

Although, as expected, the accuracies dropped when the effects were intensified, the results suggested that the recognition of the affective expressions, as conveyed through head and body gestures of a zoomorphic robot, can be relatively robust to visual constraints, once the observer has received training in recognizing those expressions when they are clearly visible. This could be a great advantage in many application areas of HRI, as other communication methods may not be as effective under similar visual constraints. For example, text displayed on a screen mounted on the robot might not be readable if visibility is impaired, especially in conditions with severe effects (e.g., those in Experiment 2). Communication through voice can be affected by hearing impairments (e.g., in social robots used for older adults or situations with a high background noise that occur in search and rescue situations). If we had only relied on facial expression, e.g., by using a robot with a large repertoire of facial expressions (as are used in many humanoid robots), recognition accuracies might have been much lower since in many of the visibility conditions the face of the robot was not even visible.

Thus, our results highlight that affective expressions of a social robot, which are conveyed through its head and body gestures, can be an effective modality to improve interactions with a social robot in many application areas affected by low visibility (as well as other situations such as when hearing is impaired).

Among the five expressions, recognition of excited was affected the most when the effects were intensified, and it was mostly confused with happy: an expression that involved similar body movements, but executed with a lower speed. While future work is needed to understand why this happened, one explanation could be that intensity of the effects can obscure more frames of the video, thus reducing the number of frames in which the participants can see the robot and its movements (similar to motion illusions that happen in real scenarios [52]), and therefore, the sense of speed might have been affected as a result of those obscured frames. This could suggest that affective expressions differing only in speed can be mostly affected by visual constraints, and the one with faster motions is likely to be confused with an expression that has similar movements but at a lower speed.

Interestingly, for the more severe effects (Experiment 2), we did not find the reported difficulty to be a predictor of accuracy in recognition of the expressions. This might suggest that the participants might have thought that their selections were correct, and therefore reported the difficulty to be less than it actually was. As another possible explanation, as difficulty was rated only for the specific observed effects (and not as a direct comparison with other difficulty levels), people possibly judged the difficulties based on their perception of how accurate their responses were, and how well they learned/recognized Miro's expressions in general. In this case, those who did poorly in training and testing would then have reported the difficulties to be higher. Our data supports this possibility, as we found correlations between the reported difficulties of different effects and participants' performance in test and training.

Note, while we mainly focused on the situations where social robots are used for search and rescue or for the care of older adults, these results may be applicable to a wider range of applications where emotions can strengthen communication with social robots, such as in education, healthcare, and entertainment.

9   Limitations and Future Work

Our study had several limitations. First, being an online, remote study, despite our efforts (i.e., adding instructions on adjusting brightness, using Google Chrome only, using a laptop's screen and not a phone or a connected large screen, etc.), we could not guarantee that all the participants indeed saw the videos similarly. However, with the size of the data, we can expect that variations have been similar across different effects and expressions. Another limitation is that the participants did not see the actual robots as the study was online. However, this is a common approach in studies in human-computer/robot interaction, which is shown to be comparable to the direct recruitment methods [3] and can reduce biases such as experimenter bias [39]. This approach has become even more common as a result of COVID-19, and it helped us with further controlling the effects. For example, it would be extremely difficult to simulate smoke and rain effects and ensure that the effects are similar for all the participants in a laboratory and in person setting. Also, it has been suggested in previous studies that there might be a high agreement between video studies and live studies (e.g., see [53]), in particular in cases where there is no direct interaction (e.g. more "observation" than "contingent engagement") involved, and in these situations video studies could be beneficial [47]. However, in another study, the results of an online experiment could not be replicated through an in person experiment [51]. While in that case the task was playing a game with a robot and did require interactions, future work is needed to study how visibility of the affective expressions change when the participants interact with the physical robot in similar but real-world conditions. Also, while we did our best to ensure that the effects in the second study were representative of extreme situations, it is possible that more extreme situations happen depending on the application areas. Finally, this study investigated five affective expressions in five different situations with visual constraints. Future work is needed to investigate recognition of other expressions and in other situations with limited visibility. Future work could also consider comparative studies with differently embodied robots with different affective expressions. A particular challenge here could be to create affective expressions for already existing robot designs (e.g., those used in service or search and rescue). Lastly, the affective expressions used in our study were conveyed through the robot's eyes, ears, tail, and body movements. Future work is needed to understand whether emotions and affective expressions that are shown using other methods (e.g., light) can be as recognizable, or if these results are only valid for affective expressions that are conveyed through motion.

10   Conclusion

In many contexts, affective expressions can complement human-robot interaction, improve quality and efficiency of interactions, and increase users' enjoyment. But similar to other modalities of interaction, there might be limitations in conveying affective expressions. This study evaluated recognition of a zoomorphic robots' affective expressions in different conditions with limited visibility and showed that expressions of a robot reflected through its head and body gestures can be an effective modality of communication for social robots in situations where vision is impaired.

Acknowledgment. This research was undertaken, in part, thanks to funding from the Canada 150 Research Chairs Program and funding from the Network for Aging Research at the University of Waterloo. We would like to thank the members of the Social and Intelligent Robotics Research Laboratory (SIRRL) at the University of Waterloo for their comments on the video effects.

References

1. Akgun, S.A., Ghafurian, M., Crowley, M., Dautenhahn, K.: Using emotions to complement multi-modal human-robot interaction in urban search and rescue scenarios. In: Proceedings of the 2020 International Conference on Multimodal Interaction, pp. 575–584 (2020)
2. Baker, M., Casey, R., Keyes, B., Yanco, H.A.: Improved interfaces for human-robot interaction in urban search and rescue. In: 2004 IEEE International Conference on Systems, Man and Cybernetics (IEEE Cat. No. 04CH37583), vol. 3, pp. 2960–2965. IEEE (2004)
3. Bartneck, C., Duenser, A., Moltchanova, E., Zawieska, K.: Comparing the similarity of responses received from studies in amazon mechanical Turk to studies conducted online and with direct recruitment. PLOS ONE 10(4), 1–23 (2015)
4. Beck, A., et al.: Interpretation of emotional body language displayed by a humanoid robot: a case study with children. Int. J. Soc. Robot. 5(3), 325–334 (2013)
5. Beer, J.M., Prakash, A., Mitzner, T.L., Rogers, W.A.: Understanding robot acceptance. Technical report, Georgia Institute of Technology (2011)
6. Bennett, M.V., Matthews, I.: Life-saving uncooled IR camera for use in firefighting applications. In: Infrared Technology and Applications XXII, vol. 2744, pp. 549–554. International Society for Optics and Photonics (1996)
7. Bethel, C.L., Murphy, R.R.: Non-facial and non-verbal affective expression for appearance-constrained robots used in victim management. Paladyn J. Behav. Robot. 1(4), 219–230 (2010)
8. Breazeal, C.: Emotion and sociable humanoid robots. Int. J. Hum. Comput. Stud. 59(1–2), 119–155 (2003)
9. Chen, A.Y., Peña-Mora, F., Plans, A.P., Mehta, S.J., Aziz, Z.: Supporting urban search and rescue with digital assessments of structures and requests of response resources. Adv. Eng. Inform. 26(4), 833–845 (2012)
10. Collins, E.C., Prescott, T.J., Mitchinson, B.: Saying it with light: a pilot study of affective communication using the MIRO robot. In: Wilson, S.P., Verschure, P.F.M.J., Mura, A., Prescott, T.J. (eds.) LIVINGMACHINES 2015. LNCS (LNAI), vol. 9222, pp. 243–255. Springer, Cham (2015). https://doi.org/10.1007/978-3-319-22979-9_25
11. Collins, E.C., Prescott, T.J., Mitchinson, B., Conran, S.: Miro: a versatile biomimetic edutainment robot. In: Proceedings of the 12th International Conference on Advances in Computer Entertainment Technology, pp. 1–4 (2015)
12. Dang, Q.K., Suh, Y.S.: Human-following robot using infrared camera. In: 2011 11th International Conference on Control, Automation and Systems, pp. 1054–1058. IEEE (2011)
13. Cañamero, L.D.: Playing the emotion game with Feelix: what can a LEGO robot tell us about emotion? In: Dautenhahn, K., Bond, A., Cañamero, L., Edmonds, B. (eds.) Socially Intelligent Agents. MASA, vol. 3, pp. 69–76. Springer, Boston (2002). https://doi.org/10.1007/0-306-47373-9_8
14. Delmerico, J., et al.: The current state and future outlook of rescue robotics. J. Field Robot. 36(7), 1171–1191 (2019)
15. D'Onofrio, G., et al.: Assistive robots for socialization in elderly people: results pertaining to the needs of the users. Aging Clin. Exp. Res. 31(9), 1313–1329 (2019)
16. Fleischer, A., Mead, A.D., Huang, J.: Inattentive responding in MTurk and other online samples. Ind. Organ. Psychol. 8(2), 196 (2015)

17. Gácsi, M., Kis, A., Faragó, T., Janiak, M., Muszyński, R., Miklósi, Á.: Humans attribute emotions to a robot that shows simple behavioural patterns borrowed from dog behaviour. Comput. Hum. Behav. **59**, 411–419 (2016)
18. Ghafurian, M., Lakatos, G., Tao, Z., Dautenhahn, K.: Design and evaluation of affective expressions of a zoomorphic robot. In: Wagner, A.R., et al. (eds.) ICSR 2020. LNCS (LNAI), vol. 12483, pp. 1–12. Springer, Cham (2020). https://doi.org/10.1007/978-3-030-62056-1_1
19. Giambattista, A., Teixeira, L., Ayanoğlu, H., Saraiva, M., Duarte, E.: Expression of emotions by a service robot: a pilot study. In: Marcus, A. (ed.) DUXU 2016. LNCS, vol. 9748, pp. 328–336. Springer, Cham (2016). https://doi.org/10.1007/978-3-319-40406-6_31
20. Goodrich, M.A., et al.: Supporting wilderness search and rescue using a camera-equipped mini UAV. J. Field Robot. **25**(1–2), 89–110 (2008)
21. Greatbatch, I., Gosling, R.J., Allen, S.: Quantifying search dog effectiveness in a terrestrial search and rescue environment. Wilderness Environ. Med. **26**(3), 327–334 (2015)
22. Hortensius, R., Hekele, F., Cross, E.S.: The perception of emotion in artificial agents. IEEE Trans. Cogn. Dev. Syst. **10**(4), 852–864 (2018)
23. Islam, M.J., Ho, M., Sattar, J.: Understanding human motion and gestures for underwater human-robot collaboration. J. Field Robot. **36**(5), 851–873 (2019)
24. Jackovics, P.: Standard of operation for cave rescue in Hungary. Int. Fire Fighter **2016**(9), 84–86 (2016)
25. Jones, B., Tang, A., Neustaedter, C.: Remote communication in wilderness search and rescue: implications for the design of emergency distributed-collaboration tools for network-sparse environments. Proc. ACM Hum.-Comput. Interact. 4(GROUP) (2020). https://doi.org/10.1145/3375190
26. Kahn, P.H., Jr., et al.: "Robovie, you'll have to go into the closet now": children's social and moral relationships with a humanoid robot. Dev. Psychol. **48**(2), 303 (2012)
27. Karaca, Y., et al.: The potential use of unmanned aircraft systems (drones) in mountain search and rescue operations. Am. J. Emerg. Med. **36**(4), 583–588 (2018)
28. Karma, S., et al.: Use of unmanned vehicles in search and rescue operations in forest fires: advantages and limitations observed in a field trial. Int. J. Disaster Risk Reduction **13**, 307–312 (2015)
29. Kim, J.H., Starr, J.W., Lattimer, B.Y.: Firefighting robot stereo infrared vision and radar sensor fusion for imaging through smoke. Fire Technol. **51**(4), 823–845 (2015)
30. Kitade, T., Satake, S., Kanda, T., Imai, M.: Understanding suitable locations for waiting. In: 2013 8th ACM/IEEE International Conference on Human-Robot Interaction (HRI), pp. 57–64. IEEE (2013)
31. Korcsok, B., et al.: Biologically inspired emotional expressions for artificial agents. Front. Psychol. **9**, 1191 (2018)
32. Larochelle, B., Kruijff, G.J.M., Smets, N., Mioch, T., Groenewegen, P.: Establishing human situation awareness using a multi-modal operator control unit in an urban search & rescue human-robot team. IEEE (2011)
33. Li, J., et al.: Usability of a robot's realistic facial expressions and peripherals in autistic children's therapy. arXiv preprint arXiv:2007.12236 (2020)
34. McGinn, C., et al.: Meet Stevie: a socially assistive robot developed through application of a 'design-thinking' approach. J. Intell. Robot. Syst. **98**(1), 39–58 (2020)

35. Mitchinson, B., Prescott, T.J.: MIRO: a robot "Mammal" with a biomimetic brain-based control system. In: Lepora, N.F.F., Mura, A., Mangan, M., Verschure, P.F.M.J.F.M.J., Desmulliez, M., Prescott, T.J.J. (eds.) Living Machines 2016. LNCS (LNAI), vol. 9793, pp. 179–191. Springer, Cham (2016). https://doi.org/10.1007/978-3-319-42417-0_17

36. Mu, L., Zhao, E.: The optimization of maritime search and rescue simulation system based on CPS. In: Hu, S., Yu, B. (eds.) Big Data Analytics for Cyber-Physical Systems, pp. 231–245. Springer, Cham (2020). https://doi.org/10.1007/978-3-030-43494-6_11

37. Nađ, Đ., et al.: Towards advancing diver-robot interaction capabilities. IFAC-PapersOnLine **52**(21), 199–204 (2019)

38. Pan, Y., Gao, F., Qi, C., Chai, X.: Human-tracking strategies for a six-legged rescue robot based on distance and view. Chin. J. Mech. Eng. **29**(2), 219–230 (2016)

39. Paolacci, G., Chandler, J., Ipeirotis, P.G.: Running experiments on Amazon mechanical Turk. Judgm. Decis. Mak. **5**(5), 411–419 (2010)

40. Ritschel, H., Aslan, I., Mertes, S., Seiderer, A., André, E.: Personalized synthesis of intentional and emotional non-verbal sounds for social robots. In: 2019 8th International Conference on Affective Computing and Intelligent Interaction (ACII), pp. 1–7 (2019)

41. Rivera, A., Villalobos, A., Monje, J., Mariñas, J., Oppus, C.: Post-disaster rescue facility: human detection and geolocation using aerial drones. In: 2016 IEEE Region 10 Conference (TENCON), pp. 384–386. IEEE (2016)

42. Sabelli, A.M., Kanda, T., Hagita, N.: A conversational robot in an elderly care center: an ethnographic study. In: 2011 6th ACM/IEEE International Conference on Human-Robot Interaction (HRI), pp. 37–44. IEEE (2011)

43. Saldien, J., Goris, K., Vanderborght, B., Vanderfaeillie, J., Lefeber, D.: Expressing emotions with the social robot probo. Int. J. Soc. Robot. **2**(4), 377–389 (2010)

44. Sales, J., Marin, R., Cervera, E., Rodríguez, S., Pérez, J.: Multi-sensor person following in low-visibility scenarios. Sensors **10**(12), 10953–10966 (2010)

45. Sharma, M., Hildebrandt, D., Newman, G., Young, J.E., Eskicioglu, R.: Communicating affect via flight path exploring use of the laban effort system for designing affective locomotion paths. In: 2013 8th ACM/IEEE International Conference on Human-Robot Interaction (HRI), pp. 293–300. IEEE (2013)

46. Silvagni, M., Tonoli, A., Zenerino, E., Chiaberge, M.: Multipurpose UAV for search and rescue operations in mountain avalanche events. Geomat. Nat. Haz. Risk **8**(1), 18–33 (2017)

47. Soegaard, M., Dam, R.F.: The Encyclopedia of Human-computer Interaction (2012)

48. Starr, J.W., Lattimer, B.: Evaluation of navigation sensors in fire smoke environments. Fire Technol. **50**(6), 1459–1481 (2014)

49. Stott, S.: Critical Hours: Search and Rescue in the White Mountains. University Press of New England (2018)

50. Velásquez, J.D.: An emotion-based approach to robotics. In: Proceedings of the International Conference on Intelligent Robots and Systems, vol. 1, pp. 235–240. IEEE (1999)

51. Wallkotter, S., Stower, R., Kappas, A., Castellano, G.: A robot by any other frame: framing and behaviour influence mind perception in virtual but not real-world environments. In: ACM/IEEE International Conference on Human-Robot Interaction, pp. 609–618 (2020). https://doi.org/10.1145/3319502.3374800

52. Weiss, Y., Simoncelli, E.P., Adelson, E.H.: Motion illusions as optimal percepts. Nat. Neurosci. **5**(6), 598–604 (2002)

53. Woods, S.N., Walters, M.L., Koay, K.L., Dautenhahn, K.: Methodological issues in HRI: a comparison of live and video-based methods in robot to human approach direction trials. In: ROMAN 2006 The 15th IEEE International Symposium on Robot and Human Interactive Communication, pp. 51–58. IEEE (2006)
54. Zhao, J., Gao, J., Zhao, F., Liu, Y.: A search-and-rescue robot system for remotely sensing the underground coal mine environment. Sensors **17**(10), 2426 (2017)

ToolBot: Robotically Reproducing Handicraft

Kim Wölfel[1]([⊠]) [iD], Jörg Müller[2] [iD], and Dominik Henrich[1] [iD]

[1] Chair for Robotics and Embedded Systems, University of Bayreuth,
95447 Bayreuth, Germany
{kim.woelfel,dominik.henrich}@uni-bayreuth.de
[2] Chair of Serious Games, University of Bayreuth, 95447 Bayreuth, Germany
joerg.mueller@uni-bayreuth.de

Abstract. We present ToolBot, a robotic system for creating handicraft with hand-held tools. Through using our process users are able to work with their favorite tools when producing handicraft. We observe the production process using motion capture. We provide a trajectory editor, which allows non-robotics-experts to semi-automatically edit the tool motion. Finally, ToolBot executes the movements using a lightweight robot arm. This is non-trivial for three reasons. First, the original tool trajectory might be non-replicable due the robots limited workspace, collisions, or singularities. Second, the robots maximum velocities and accelerations can be exceeded. Third, the user might want to let the robot use a different tool or replicate downscaled tool motion. We resolve these issues, such that the hand-held tool can be mounted on a robot arm, which can then mass-produce the handicraft. We evaluate the usability of ToolBot through a user study.

Keywords: Fabrication · Human-robot interaction · Robot programming by demonstration

1 Introduction

Artisanal handicraft is arguably the first personal fabrication technology. Carrying a long tradition, an enormous variety of hand-held tools and techniques exist for creating objects. A large fraction of the world's population possess considerable skill in operating these tools. Handicraft with hand-held tools allows for expressivity and detail. The main limitation of handicraft is that it does not scale for mass production. Produced objects are unique, and the effort of production grows linearly with the number of objects produced.

Industrial technologies allow a production of objects on a large scale. A huge variety of production technologies, including milling, injection molding, forming

Electronic supplementary material The online version of this chapter (https://doi.org/10.1007/978-3-030-85613-7_32) contains supplementary material, which is available to authorized users.

C. Ardito et al. (Eds.): INTERACT 2021, LNCS 12934, pp. 470–489, 2021.
https://doi.org/10.1007/978-3-030-85613-7_32

etc. have been developed. This greatly reduced the cost of producing additional objects, once an object is designed and a production line is set up.

Recently, personal fabrication machines, such as 3D printers, have been available at low cost. Additive, subtractive, and formative manufacturing allows individuals to produce, and mass-produce, self made objects. There has been extensive research in how to enable individuals to easily produce objects using these technologies. New approaches add considerable power and flexibility to the design process compared to handicraft. However, due to the different manufacturing process used, objects fabricated with mass-fabrication technologies do have very different appearances and detail from handicraft. Each fabrication technology comes with its unique fabrication artifacts and constraints.

Fig. 1. Using ToolBot, users can produce handicraft with their personal hand-held tools. Tool motion is recorded using a Motion Capture System (I). Using our trajectory editor, non-robotics experts can then fix errors semi-automatically and adjust the tool movement to robot capabilites or other aspects and validate the execution with a simulation (II). The real-world robot can then reproduce the handicraft arbitrarily often, possibly at home or in a central factory (III).

We propose to solve this problem with the seemingly simple idea of replicating the production process using the hand-held tool and robotic technology (see Fig. 1). Users handcraft their objects working with their own favorite tools. The tool movement is captured using motion capture technology. We provide a trajectory editor that allows non-robotics experts to semi-automatically fix errors and adjust the tool trajectory to robot capabilities. The tool is then installed on a robotic arm, which recreates the production process with a new object. In this way, the desired number of copies of the hand-crafted object can be created at low cost.

This approach poses three major technical challenges. First, the tool trajectory might be non-replicable for the robot, due to its limited workspace, collisions, or singularities. In this paper, we present several solutions for these problems consisting of a mix of automatic and manual modifications of the recorded trajectory. Second, our data shows that hand-held tools often reach velocities and accelerations which are beyond robot capabilities. We present an approach that deals with this problem by using a special interpolation technique. Third, the user might want to let the robot use a different tool or replicate downscaled tool motion. Our approach enables the use of different or scaled tools for modelling and replicating a motion.

One particular strength of our approach is that it works for almost any hand-held tool. This includes classical tools such as knifes and brushes, but also extends to modern tools such as Dremel and 3Doodler.

2 Handicraft and Mass Fabrication

Two major differences between handicraft and mass fabrication are that, first, they use very different tools and fabrication techniques, and second, that Handicraft is unique, while mass fabricated items are usually perceived as not being unique. Regarding the first point, each fabrication technology comes with its own unique fabrication artifacts and constraints. Injection moulding, for example, creates visible grates where the mould sides connect, where the material enters the mould, and at the ejector pins. Furthermore, products containing "overhangs" need to be produced from multiple parts. Materials that can be injection moulded are also very limited.

Hand-carved items, on the other hand, have very visible traces of the carving tool. The traces are often irregular, and of the pattern that is created by guiding the tool with a human hand. The entire workpiece often contains irregularities which create the distinct "Handicraft" appearance. Materials are limited to those soft enough to be carved with human strength, such as wood. Many people prefer the appearance of Handicraft objects (e.g., hand carved) to those created by mass-production (e.g., injection moulded).

Regarding the second point, hand crafted items are often perceived as unique, while mass-produced items are usually not. The impact of the reproducability of art on its perception has been discussed by Walter Benjamin [3]. He argues that some art has been reproducible since ancient times, e.g., terracotta and bronze. Modern technologies like printing and photography extended the range of art that could be reproduced, thereby changing the nature of art and becoming a new art themselves. Benjamin coins the term of the "Aura" of a unique art-piece, describing the effects of its unique existence at one location. The "Aura" encompasses chemical and physical changes over time, as well as the history of owners and events happening to the art piece. Only in this case it makes sense to speak of the "original" and of authenticity. We think that it is important to realize that ToolBot is only one new reproduction technology in a long history of these. One difference is that ToolBot replicates the production process itself, not merely the end product. This means for example, that the influence of the raw material is preserved in the final product. The economic impact of such a technology on artisans is also not forseeable. On one hand, the ability to create handicraft without additional human labor might increase competition for them. On the other hand, the ability to mass-produce their work could allow artisans to reach more customers and compete with industrial companies. In this paper, we concentrate on the technical aspects of this reproduction process. While we want to mention the possible implications of our work to media and art, we prefer to leave these aspects to future work in the fields that possess more expertise in these areas, such as media studies.

3   Related Work

3.1   Personal Fabrication

Personal fabrication has been described as "the ability to design and produce your own products, in your own home, with a machine that combines consumer electronics with industrial tools" [10]. In recent years, a wealth of knowledge and new ideas has been generated on the topic of personal fabrication. A comprehensive summary is provided by [2]. The majority of research deals with additive (e.g., 3D printing), followed by subtractive (e.g., milling, laser cutting) and formative fabrication technologies, i.e. by applying mechanical forces, restricting forms, heat, or steam to form a material into a desired shape [11]. Many researchers investigate how to design models for 3D printing or milling machines in an easier way, such as [20].

3.2   Assisted Handicraft

Several smart handheld tools have been developed, which are actuated jointly by the users' hands and computer-controlled actuation, e.g. [13] or [21]. An excellent overview of this topic is provided by [24]. Furthermore, systems allow users to create 3D models both by forming clay and by editing the model digitally, such as ReForm [19], or by wax coiling using a hand-held actuated extruder (*D-Coil* [15]). The *Makers' Marks* System [17] allows the fabrication of functional objects via annotation stickers and *Drill Sergeant* [18] applies the concept of software tutorials onto physical craft processes through augmented tools.

3.3   3D Photocopying

Several mechanisms have been proposed for "photocopying" existing objects. Scotty [12] is a "3D teleporter" that destructively scans an object, while reproducing it at a different location, as well as ensuring that only one copy exists. The work in [4] also maintains the physical deformation behavior of objects while photocopying. Even commercial 3D photocopying machines have been available for this purpose [22].

3.4   Painting Robots

When it comes to replicating paintings or decorating eggs some systems, like the WaterColorBot, AxiDraw or the EggBot, have been presented which are able to generate astonishing results. Most of these systems take an actual image as an input and then reproduce it on a sheet of paper or a 3D surface if it is possible to fixate it in the system. These approaches differ from our framework, because the input is limited to a 2D graphic. While this is satisfactory for painting an image using water color or projecting it on a 3D surface, task like modelling clay with an appropriate tool is hard or impossible to realize.

3.5   Robot Programming by Demonstration

Robot programming by demonstration [1] enables users to teach robots by performing motions without having to write code. Many approaches perform the teaching phase by tracking the human wrist [16] or guiding the robot arm by hand (*kinesthetic programming*) [14,23]. The later approaches work well in pick-and-place scenarios, but may limit the users in cases where more dynamic motions are needed. We found only two papers mentioning direct tracking of the users' tool [6,8].

The contribution presented in [8] is a novel tracking system with a custom active marker and a stereo camera. The marker can be attached to a tool and the recorded motion can then be executed by a robot arm. However, the proposed tracking system is considerably less accurate than state-of-the-art motion capture systems. The application proposed is that of tracking a large spray paint gun. Motions are slow due to the large mass of the gun, and the required accuracy is relatively low. The user is required to record the motion at the actual robot location within the workspace of the robot. Therefore, the authors of [8] are able to directly map their recordings to robot motion without modification.

In [6] an approach is presented which records not only the position-controlled human motion but also takes care of the occuring forces. This is done by utilizing a reciprocating electric carving tool. These tools are normally used to facilitate carving actions by lowering the force needed to penetrate the material. These forces can also be extracted and therefore used for later applications. The worker is tracked while performing a carving task a few times and the recorded motion is then used to train a neural network. The neural network is able to generate robot trajectories containing the performed carving motion for work pieces with varying grain direction, length or depth. Therefore, their system is able to perform learned carving *skills* through a multi-shot learning pipe-line.

Our contribution includes features of these two approaches to allow the replication of a complete manipulation (like [8]) together with a high accuracy (<1 mm) and the possibility to perform the motion by oneself [6]. Additionally, we enable the user to edit the recorded data manually in a post processing step.

4   Methods

In this section we briefly describe important definitions from the area of robotics which are necessary to understand the rest of the paper. Desired poses of the robot arm (joint configurations) can be set in *joint space*, i.e. angles for each joint J_i of the robot arm (see Fig. 2 right), or in *Cartesian space*, i.e. in the form of a transformation matrix in an *NSA* coordinate system (see Fig. 2 left) for the tool center point (TCP) located at the end of the robot arm with a potential offset (ignoring multiple solutions in the case of redundant robot arms). Here, $\vec{n} \in \mathbb{R}^3$ is the direction perpendicular to the finger movement of an attached gripper, $\vec{s} \in \mathbb{R}^3$ is the slide direction of its fingers and $\vec{a} \in \mathbb{R}^3$ is the approach direction of the gripper. The transformation between the two spaces is achieved by *forward kinematics* (FK), from joint to cartesian space, and *inverse kinematics* (IK),

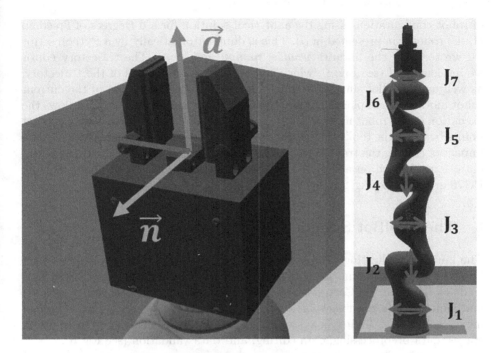

Fig. 2. NSA coordinate system of the gripper (left) and robot arm (right) with joints $J_i, i \in \{1, 7\}$ and orientations.

from cartesian to joint space. When moving the robot arm through given joint configurations, an adequate interpolation strategy is required.

While we want to imitate human motions, time-optimal trajectories between these configurations are important, so as to be able to replicate movement in a realistic way. During the execution, the necessary robot configurations are then computed using these trajectories.

5 Implementation

Our ToolBot system consists of five main steps: recording a tool's motion, transforming the tracking data into configurations in the robot workspace, editing the transformed trajectory by hand, validating the configurations using a robot simulation and executing the final motion on a real robot arm.

For recording the tool's motion, we built a motion capture setup comprising twelve OptiTrack Flex 3 cameras mounted on a cube-like rack (see Fig. 3). This setup is located on the table the user is working at and can easily be adapted, if different camera poses are needed. We record and export the tracking data with the *Motive* software. The tracked data is modified and transformed into a series of robot configurations using the analytical solution for a 6 Degrees of Freedom (DoF) robot arm presented in [7]. This is done automatically by a Python script we wrote using the libraries *pandas*, *numpy* and *scipy*. The trajectory editor we implemented (see Fig. 4), which can be used to edit parts of the trajectory, as well as the robot simulator, which allows a virtual validation of the current robot motion, are implemented in C++. The robot simulator not only allows the execution of the robot motion in a virtual environment, but also renders contact points between the tool's tip and the workpiece (see Fig. 5), which highlights the impact of editing the trajectory. The last step, the execution of the transformed data, is performed on a KUKA LWR IV robot arm with 7 DoF and a Schunk PG70 gripper (see Fig. 2 right).

6   The ToolBot System

The limits of replicating hand-held tool movement by using a robot arm are set by the robot's maximum joint angles, velocities, accelerations, and jerks. This leads to limits in the Cartesian space (e.g. collisions or unreachable positions) and joint space (e.g. unreachable configurations). We adapt the recorded human movement to these limits via a data processing pipeline consisting of three major stages: data preprocessing, data editing, and data validation (see Fig. 6).

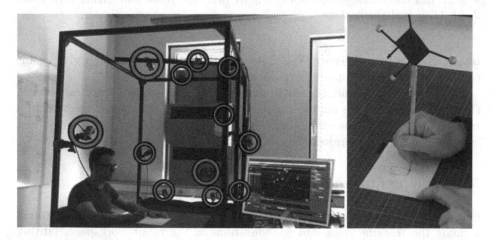

Fig. 3. Left: Optitrack Setup: Twelve Optitrack Flex 3 cameras (red circles) located around the executed motion and the visualization of the data using the Motive software (green rectangle) Right: Pencil with attached marker. (Color figure online)

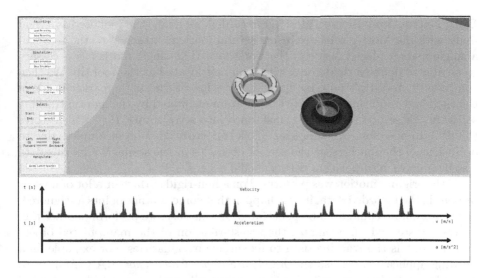

Fig. 4. The ToolBot Editor. Enables users to transform and delete selected vertices of a recorded motion (blue) in the rendering window (right) via mouse input or through GUI widgets (left). It also renders the velocity and acceleration data of the TCP in the lower left area. (Color figure online)

6.1 Data Preprocessing

The main challenge during this stage is to modify the data exported from the motion capture software, such that irregularities and data loss are fixed as effectively as possible.

Fig. 5. Two example painting motions replicated in the robot simulation. Contact points are connected using blue lines. (Color figure online)

Data Extraction. Before a motion is recorded, we define the tool used as a rigid body with the Motive software, using several markers attached to the tool and a single marker placed inside of the workspace. The single marker is necessary to be able to define a rigid body, with a marker located at the tool tip. We then compute the tool-tip's pose by using the position of the single marker inside of the rigid body and the rigid body's orientation estimated by the motion tracking software. These poses are then transformed into a trajectory T_{init}, which stores the tool-tip pose for each time-step. This trajectory may be incomplete due to occlusions of the markers by the user or obstacles in the scene. We fix this data loss by a linear interpolation between valid entries.

If the original motion was performed on a non-rigid surface or a lot of noise is present in the recorded data, it may happen that some contact points are ignored, or the workpiece could even be penetrated. In this case, we perform another pre-processing step which estimates the transformation of the manipulated object and transforms the tracking data to fix surface irregularities. For example, in a drawing application we use the *Random Sample Consensus* (RANSAC) [9] to fit a plane into the drawing pane and project all tracking points lying behind this plane on its surface. At this point, a trajectory T_{prep} is available that stores the tool-tip position along with the corresponding tool orientation for the entire tracked motion.

Data Transformation. The main challenge of this stage is to find an appropriate transformation of the tool tip trajectory T_{prep} into the robot workspace and an adequate fallback method to adjust the gripper's transformation, if there are still unreachable configurations after the transformation of T_{prep}.

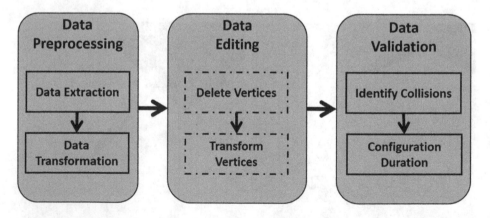

Fig. 6. ToolBot data processing pipeline. Boxes with round corners represent main stages, boxes with sharp corners represent mandatory steps (straight lines) and optional steps (dashed lines).

We transform T_{prep} from the coordinate system in which it was recorded, into the robot's workspace as follows: Let $\vec{z}_{\text{wp}} \in \mathbb{R}^3$ be the normalized axis of the workpiece, pointing away from the underlying surface. We compute a homogenous transformation matrix $M_{\text{robot}} \in \mathbb{R}^{4 \times 4}$, which represents a rotation from $\vec{z}_{\text{wp}}$ onto the z-Axis of the robot base $\vec{z}_{\text{robot}} \in \mathbb{R}^3$ and a translation of the motion into the center of the robot's workspace. Therefore, the resulting trajectory T_{trafo} is computed for n tracking points as follows:

$$T_{\text{trafo},i} = M_{\text{robot}} \cdot T_{\text{prep},i}, \forall i \in \{0, \ldots, n-1\}. \tag{1}$$

All entries of T_{trafo} are then converted into a trajectory of NSA transformations T_{TCP} for the robot arm. This is done by projecting the tool-tip along the z-axis of its orientation for an appropriate length l_m. The TCP orientation is computed by transforming the rigid body's orientation. For example, in the case of a pen, the tip position $\vec{x}_t \in \mathbb{R}^3$ and orientation $\vec{q}_m$ are extracted from the tracking data. The rotation $\vec{q}_m$ is then used to rotate a unit vector $\vec{x}_z$ pointing into the z-direction with the length l_m to compute the TCP position via:

$$\vec{x}_{\text{TCP}} = \vec{x}_t + l_m \cdot \vec{q}_m \vec{x}_z. \tag{2}$$

These transformations are then converted into joint configurations using an IK algorithm. In our case, we set the robot's joint J_3 (see Fig. 2, right) to zero, and use an analytical IK solution to overcome problems like singularities associated with numerical solutions for 7 DoF robot arms. This results in a list of valid joint configurations for the motion, as long as these exist.

Instead of immediately marking an execution as not executable if an unreachable transformation is found, we give the user the opportunity to adapt the trajectory by hand in the Data Editing stage. At this point we mark the configuration as not reachable with the user's configuration and attach a default rotation for the gripper. In the future, we plan to investigate more elaborate fallback methods using motion planning approaches.

6.2   Data Editing

In case users are not satisfied with the result of their work, they would normally have to repeat the work from scratch, which can be time consuming and tends to annoy the artist. To overcome this problem, we implemented a trajectory editor, which enables the user to manipulate the recorded trajectory. Similar to proportional editing of vertices in the 3D modelling software "Blender", users can manipulate single or sets of vertices by translating them along fixed directions (see Fig. 7(III) and (IV)) or deleting them (see Fig. 7(I) and (II)). At the moment the translation is done by mapping the users mouse input to a 3D motion. Depending on the currently locked 3D axis the vertices are then translated and highlighted as soon as invalid robot configurations are reached.

To avoid discontinuities in the trajectory, translating vertices does not only affect the selected vertices but also some of the adjacent vertices. Starting from the selected vertex, adjacent vertices are also manipulated, if the distance to their preceding vertex does exceed a pre-defined distance d_{limit}. This guarantees, that the robot stays inside of its velocity limits while executing the trajectory. To preserve the smoothness of the trajectory while translating vertices, adjacent vertices are only manipulated by a fraction the distance or orientation displacement per time step. In our editor this is done using a weight function $\omega(d) \in [0, 1[$ computing the displacements depending on the distance $d \in \mathbb{R}$ to the selected vertex. While $\omega(d)$ should be symmetric around 0 and smooth, we use a wide normal distribution which results in a smooth transition between the vertices (see Fig. 7).

To improve the usage of our editor for experts as well as non-experts, we also implemented three features which prevent the user from generating potentially invalid configurations. The first feature is, that the robot is rendered in a transparent way while a vertex is selected. This is useful to check for potential collisions between the gripper and the environment. The second feature is

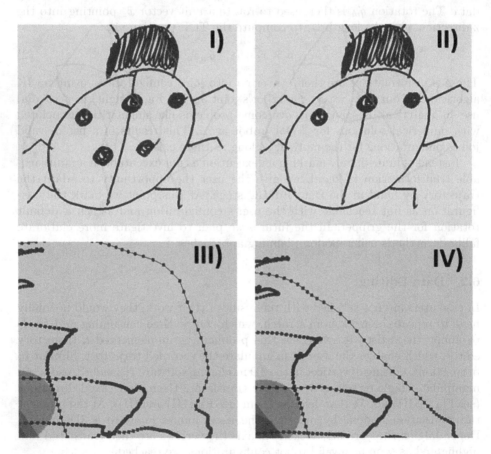

Fig. 7. Applications of our trajectory editor: easily deleting parts from an original recording (I) while preserving the rest of it (II). Transforming vertices of the original trajectory (III) to correct unwanted movements (IV).

highlighting non-reachable configurations in red. As long as these configurations are present in the trajectory, an execution is not possible. The last feature are the velocity and acceleration profiles rendered at the bottom of the editor. They show the velocities and accelerations necessary to move between vertices and can therefore be used to estimate to which extent a vertex can be manipulated. Those may be not of interest for every user of the system, but is helpful to estimate, if dynamic limitations are reached soon. These features lead to a trajectory which can be executed by the robot arm and satisfies the user's requirements.

6.3   Data Validation

The main challenge at this stage consists of two tasks. The first is to identify and handle collisions between the robot and its environment by adjusting T_{TCP} based on the type of collision. The second challenge is to find durations between two configurations that lead to the fastest possible replication.

Collision Detection. Before the trajectory can be executed by a robot arm, the list of configurations is validated as follows: We first simulate the motion in our robot simulation framework, as described in the Implementation section, to automatically identify the location of collisions between the robot gripper and the table which may occur as a result of the difference in size between the gripper and a human hand. This has to be done, because such collisions corrupt the replicated motion and can lead to severe damage to the workpiece, tool, or robot. If such a collision is identified, the affected vertex of our trajectory is highlighted in red and the trajectory is marked as not valid. To be able to execute the manipulation by the robot the user has to fix these vertices by manipulating the trajectory with our trajectory editor (see Fig. 4).

Configuration Duration. The last pipeline step is to speed up the robot's execution. We use linear functions with parabolic blends presented in [7] to interpolate between our configurations Θ_i and speed up the execution by varying the durations d_i which specify the time the robot should take to move from one configuration to another. As long as d_i is high enough, the necessary linear path segment between each two parabolic path segments can be generated. Because of this, we start with an initial duration of d_{init} which is valid in most cases. We then iterate over all configurations and check, whether or not they are valid. While a configuration is valid, we adapt its duration by decreasing d_i by a constant d_Δ. If a configuration is not valid, we adapt its duration by increasing d_i by d_Δ until a valid result is reached. This is repeated until all configuration durations are set to a valid value, depending on d_Δ resulting in the fastest possible execution.

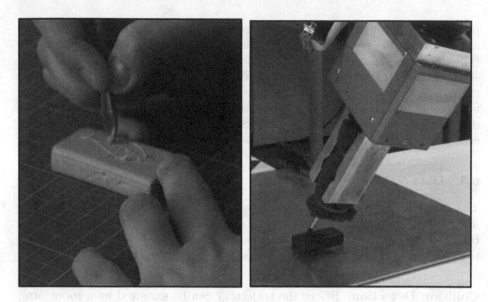

Fig. 8. Recording a motion with a Fimo modelling tool, length $l = 12.7$ cm, (left) and its replication using a screwdriver, $l = 25.4$ cm, (right).

7   Scaling Tool or Workpiece

Besides the need to know the contact point computed in the data preparation stage, in later process steps, this also allows the replication of the same contact point trajectory using a different tool as long as the tool's geometry is known. We had already tested this feature several times with different tools (see Fig. 8) and by scaling the tool. Until now, scaling the tool had to be done for each replication, because the gripper is usually larger than the tool used while recording the motion. By doing this, the user is even able to use an abstract tool for recording the motion, which is replaced by the desired tool in the real-world execution.

An advantage of using the transformation in the data transformation stage is that the recorded motions can be imitated not only for workpieces of the same size, but also for scaled work pieces. This enables users for example to model details on enlarged workpieces which are then executed on smaller workpieces by the robot.

8   User Study

In order to evaluate the usability and user experience with using Toolbot, we conducted a user study. We observed users while using the Toolbot system and conducted a semi-structured interview with them. As questionnaires, we used the System Usability Scale (SUS) and the User Experience Questionnaire (UEQ). Additionally, we asked whether they experienced the manipulated trajectory and the object produced by the robot arm as their own work.

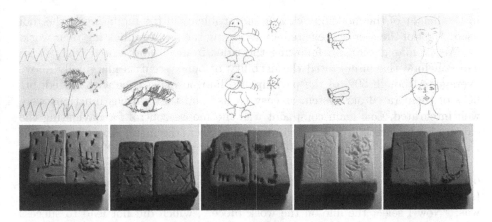

Fig. 9. Examples from the user study. The top row shows five drawing examples (top: participant, bottom: robot arm). The bottom row shows five modelling examples (left: participant, right: robot arm). Some artifacts, like the missing part of the duck, originated from calibration problems, others, like the additional lines in the most left and most right image, from the trajectory editing during the study.

Overall 15 users (5 female, 10 male) with a mean age of 27 participated at our study. Before they began they had to rate their experience regarding the three topics programming, robotics and 3D editors on a scale of 1 to 7, and name any 3D editors they had already used. Their mean experience in programming was 4.1, the mean experience in robotics was 2.9 and the mean experience in using 3D editors was 3. 50% of the users had been working with a 3D editor before.

8.1 Procedure

Users created two pieces with an optically tracked tool. They drew on a postcard and carved an image into modelling paste (see Fig. 9, row 1 and 2). The system transformed the recorded data as described in the data preprocessing Sect. 6. Users then edited their trajectories in our Toolbot editor. During the editor use, we used a think aloud protocol. After deleting and transforming data points, the users did run the robot motion in the simulation and saved their results. The users then watched the real robot arm executing their edited motion. For each motion the user was able to attach the tool used to the gripper and examine the robot motion. After the users have saw the motion, they filled the SUS, UEQ and the custom questionnaire. Finally, we performed a semi-structured interview.

8.2 Results

The results produced by the robot arm are shown in Fig. 9. Overall the robot was able to replicate the recorded and edited motions in most cases. Some problems were caused by calibration problems, e.g. the correct positioning and differences in the height of the modelling clay or the problems in the mounting of the tool used. Most of the users felt excited about seeing the robot replicating their work.

We evaluated the SUS following the rules from [5] and scored 68.4, so we can conclude that users rated the usability of our system as marginally above average. Although 50% of the participants had no experience with 3D editors 66% of them rated our system as easy to use and that various functions were well integrated. One main complaint was the mouse control for navigating the camera in the virtual world, which resulted in user statements like: "The view is zooming too fast.", "The other 3D editors i am using have a different control." and "I would like to have pre defined camera views". This inspired us to add a dropdown menu which enables the user to switch to pre defined camera views (see Fig. 10) and updated the camera control. Another comment of some users was: "Now i select the line on the work piece.", which did not lead to success

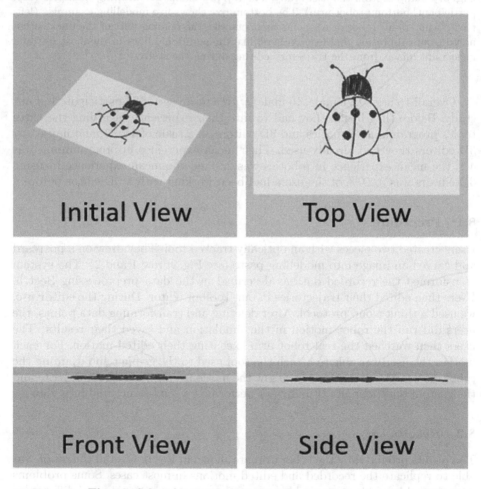

Fig. 10. Selectable camera views in our ToolBot editor.

because it was only possible to select the TCP trajectory above the line. We fixed this problem by transforming the TCP trajectory into a tooltip trajectory and highlighted contact points in solid blue, free space points in transparent red and selected points in solid orange (see Fig. 11). It was also mentioned by the users that operating the system was easier in the second task.

We evaluated the UEQ with the tool presented on the UEQ website[1]. Results for the UEQ are shown in Fig. 12. The values show that users generally enjoyed the experience of using the system. Lower scores for efficiency and dependability show that, due to the prototype nature of Toolbot, users were not yet able to solve all tasks without effort.

In the custom questionnaire and semi-structured interview, 73% of the users stated that they did not feel restricted by the system when creating their handicraft. Some participants stated that there were some restrictions by holding the tool in a steep enough angle such that the gripper would not collide with the table. We observed that, while working with the hand-held tools, contacts between the users hand and the table were common. Additionally, users often changed the grip of the tool to reach different poses. Because such contacts with the surface should be avoided for robots, and the robot cannot change the grip, this poses challenges for the robot motion. Our current solution is to extend the length of the tool for the robot. An alternative solution would be to place the workpiece on an elevated platform, so it can be reached from flatter angles by the robot. After seeing the robot result, 80% of the users identified with the edited tool motion, because they manipulated them by themselves. Even 66% of the users still identified the result produced by the robot as their own work.

Fig. 11. Revised trajectory visualization (contact points in solid blue, free space points in transparent red) for a drawing and modelling trajectory. (Color figure online)

---

[1] https://www.ueq-online.org/.

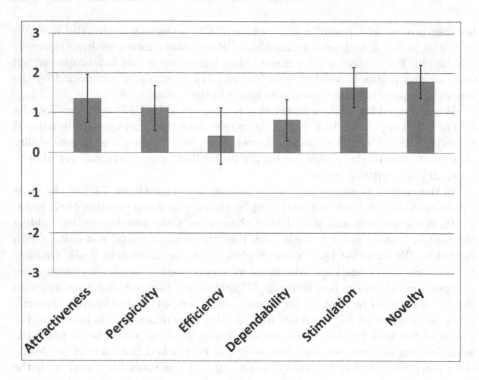

Fig. 12. Evaluation of the performed UEQ between −3 (bad) and 3 (good).

The remaining users disagreed because of imperfections resulting from calibration errors, positioning of the work pieces and the insufficient accuracy of the robot arm used. A majority of the participants (80%) would give away the result as a present or sell it. Conclusively, the majority (73%) of the participants would use such a system in the future. The remaining users disagreed, because of the calibration errors and restrictions while recording the motion. These findings show that more work is to be done to further increase the accuracy of the robot replication. A major area of future work would be to detect variations in the size of the work piece, and develop accurate calibration methods of the work piece relative to the robot arm.

9   Discussion

In this section limitations of the presented system are discussed. At this point, tool motions can be recorded, are automatically transformed into robot configurations, and can be manipulated per configuration. Forces occuring at the workpiece or tool are not considered yet, but plannend to be integrated in future work. As stated in Sect. 6, unreachable configurations are reset to a default orientation at the moment as a fallback. We are planning to improve this fallback in the future by using further visual feedback or estimating more appropriate fallback orientations. Since the robotarm geometry differs from that of a human arm, adding a platform on which the workpiece is manipulated would be helpful in future work as well.

10 Conclusion

We have presented a novel approach to robotically creating handicraft with hand-held tools. ToolBot is directed towards non-robotics-experts and allows them to mass-produce their handicraft without writing code. We have presented a novel approach for transforming tool motions executed by humans to robot arms. Our approach allows the scaling of the tool used, automatically identifies collisions between the robot arm and the scene, and offers solutions that allow an execution of the recorded motion, even if this would not have been possible with the initial motion data. To ensure the validity of the final robot configurations, our framework contains a robot simulation which is able to perform the motion using a simulated robot controller. To enable the user to delete or adjust mistakes we implemented a trajectory editor for translating and deleting samples of the recorded trajectory.

The system is clearly still in prototype stage. To develop it towards a product, particularly the accurate calibration of the work piece relative to the robot needs to be improved. However, the result of the user study we conducted shows, that we can already conclude that the robotic replication of hand-held tool movements is a promising idea that warrants further investigation in the future. We hope that robotic fabrication with traditional tools might inspire and augment research in fabrication in Human-Computer Interaction, Robotics, and related disciplines.

Acknowledgements. This work has partly been supported by Deutsche Forschungsgemeinschaft (DFG) under grant agreement He2696-18.

References

1. Argall, B.D., Chernova, S., Veloso, M., Browning, B.: A survey of robot learning from demonstration. Robot. Auton. Syst. **57**(5), 469–483 (2009)
2. Baudisch, P., Mueller, S.: Personal fabrication: state of the art and future research. In: Proceedings of the 2016 CHI Conference Extended Abstracts on Human Factors in Computing Systems, pp. 936–939. ACM (2016)
3. Benjamin, W.: The Work of Art in the Age of Its Technological Reproducibility, and Other Writings on Media. Harvard University Press (2008)
4. Bickel, B., et al.: Design and fabrication of materials with desired deformation behavior. ACM Trans. Graph. (TOG) **29**, 63 (2010)
5. Brooke, J., et al.: SUS-a quick and dirty usability scale. Usabil. Eval. Ind. **189**, 4–7 (1996)
6. Brugnaro, G., Hanna, S.: Adaptive robotic training methods for subtractive manufacturing. In: Proceedings of the 37th Annual Conference of the Association for Computer Aided Design in Architecture (ACADIA), pp. 164–169. Acadia Publishing Company (2017)

7. Craig, J.J.: Introduction to Robotics: Mechanics and Control, vol. 3. Pearson/Prentice Hall, Upper Saddle River (2005)
8. Ferreira, M., Costa, P., Rocha, L., Moreira, A.P.: Stereo-based real-time 6-DoF work tool tracking for robot programing by demonstration. Int. J. Adv. Manuf. Technol. **85**(1–4), 57–69 (2016)
9. Fischler, M.A., Bolles, R.C.: Random sample consensus: a paradigm for model fitting with applications to image analysis and automated cartography. In: Readings in Computer Vision, pp. 726–740. Elsevier (1987)
10. Gershenfeld, N.: Fab: the Coming Revolution on Your Desktop-from Personal Computers to Personal Fabrication. Basic Books, New York (2008)
11. Kolarevic, B.: Digital fabrication: manufacturing architecture in the information age (2001)
12. Mueller, S., Fritzsche, M., Kossmann, J., Schneider, M., Striebel, J., Baudisch, P.: Scotty: relocating physical objects across distances using destructive scanning, encryption, and 3D printing. In: Proceedings of the Ninth International Conference on Tangible, Embedded, and Embodied Interaction, pp. 233–240. ACM (2015)
13. Mueller, S., Lopes, P., Baudisch, P.: Interactive construction: interactive fabrication of functional mechanical devices. In: Proceedings of the 25th Annual ACM Symposium on User Interface Software and Technology, pp. 599–606. ACM (2012)
14. Orendt, E.M., Fichtner, M., Henrich, D.: Robot programming by non-experts: intuitiveness and robustness of one-shot robot programming. In: 2016 25th IEEE International Symposium on Robot and Human Interactive Communication (ROMAN), pp. 192–199. IEEE (2016)
15. Peng, H., Zoran, A., Guimbretière, F.V.: D-coil: a hands-on approach to digital 3d models design. In: Proceedings of the 33rd Annual ACM Conference on Human Factors in Computing Systems, pp. 1807–1815. ACM (2015)
16. Rueckert, E., Lioutikov, R., Calandra, R., Schmidt, M., Beckerle, P., Peters, J.: Low-cost sensor glove with force feedback for learning from demonstrations using probabilistic trajectory representations. arXiv preprint arXiv:1510.03253 (2015)
17. Savage, V., Follmer, S., Li, J., Hartmann, B.: Makers' marks: physical markup for designing and fabricating functional objects. In: Proceedings of the 28th Annual ACM Symposium on User Interface Software & Technology, pp. 103–108. ACM (2015)
18. Schoop, E., Nguyen, M., Lim, D., Savage, V., Follmer, S., Hartmann, B.: Drill sergeant: supporting physical construction projects through an ecosystem of augmented tools. In: Proceedings of the 2016 CHI Conference Extended Abstracts on Human Factors in Computing Systems, pp. 1607–1614. ACM (2016)
19. Weichel, C., Hardy, J., Alexander, J., Gellersen, H.: ReForm: integrating physical and digital design through bidirectional fabrication. In: Proceedings of the 28th Annual ACM Symposium on User Interface Software & Technology, pp. 93–102. ACM (2015)
20. Weichel, C., Lau, M., Kim, D., Villar, N., Gellersen, H.W.: MixFab: a mixed-reality environment for personal fabrication. In: Proceedings of the SIGCHI Conference on Human Factors in Computing Systems, CHI 2014, pp. 3855–3864. ACM, New York (2014). https://doi.org/10.1145/2556288.2557090 http://doi.acm.org/10.1145/2556288.2557090
21. Willis, K.D., Xu, C., Wu, K.J., Levin, G., Gross, M.D.: Interactive fabrication: new interfaces for digital fabrication. In: Proceedings of the Fifth International Conference on Tangible, Embedded, and Embodied Interaction. pp. 69–72. ACM (2011)

22. ZEUS: The world's first all-in-one 3D printer/copy machine (2018). http://www.zeus.aiorobotics.com

23. Zoliner, R., Pardowitz, M., Knoop, S., Dillmann, R.: Towards cognitive robots: building hierarchical task representations of manipulations from human demonstration. In: Proceedings of the 2005 IEEE International Conference on Robotics and Automation, ICRA 2005, pp. 1535–1540. IEEE (2005)

24. Zoran, A., Shilkrot, R., Goyal, P., Maes, P., Paradiso, J.A.: The wise chisel: the rise of the smart handheld tool. IEEE Pervasive Comput. **13**(3), 48–57 (2014)

Information Visualization

An Immersive Approach Based on Two Levels of Interaction for Exploring Multiple Coordinated 3D Views

Carlos Quijano-Chavez(ID), Luciana Nedel(ID), and Carla M. D. S. Freitas(✉)(ID)

Institute of Informatics, Federal University Rio Grande do Sul,
Porto Alegre, RS, Brazil
{carlos.chavez,nedel,carla}@inf.ufrgs.br

Abstract. Multiple coordinated views have often been used for visual analytics purposes over the last years. In this context, if the exploration of 2D visualizations is not an obstacle, adding an extra dimension can be an issue. The interaction with multiple 3D visualizations in 2D conventional displays lacks usability and does not guarantee the usefulness the extra dimension would provide. Immersive visualization techniques can potentially fulfill these gaps by providing 3D visualizations and novel 3D interactions simultaneously. In this paper, we propose a new approach for interacting with composite and multiple coordinated visualizations in immersive virtual environments. We use a 3D-WIMP-like concept, i.e., virtual cubes (*Spaces*), for encapsulating views, which the user can freely control in the virtual environment. Moreover, operations like "cloning" and "coordinated interactions" features provide a way for performing composed tasks. We compared our approach with a desktop version to evaluate its performance when dealing with composed tasks. A user study with 19 participants was conducted, and the results show that the immersive approach has advantages over the corresponding desktop version regarding interaction with multiple coordinated 3D views.

Keywords: Multiple coordinated views · Virtual reality · Immersive analytics

1 Introduction

Multiple Coordinated Views (MCV) are among the most commonly used ways of composing visualization techniques to show different perspectives of the same or potentially correlated data to facilitate insight into a complex dataset [16]. Such an approach is especially suited for visual analytics applications [40]. Depending on the data, using multiple 2D views in conventional 2D displays demands large displays, while for 3D visualizations, such setup may not guarantee a useful tool. Earlier studies showed that the interaction with multiple 3D visualizations in 2D displays does not meet usability criteria [33]. This lack of usability could be

© IFIP International Federation for Information Processing 2021
Published by Springer Nature Switzerland AG 2021
C. Ardito et al. (Eds.): INTERACT 2021, LNCS 12934, pp. 493–513, 2021.
https://doi.org/10.1007/978-3-030-85613-7_33

overcome if the exploration happens in immersive environments, where the user has an extra degree of freedom for interacting with 3D visualizations [14]. Additionally, human spatial awareness and organizational capabilities can help the analytical process performed interactively with the visualizations [19]. Immersive analytics approaches have been developed to take advantage of these characteristics.

Immersive Analytics (IA) is defined as an interdisciplinary field where any technology that remove barriers between users and their data can be used for building tools to support data exploration, communication, reasoning and decision making [29]. Technologies like Augmented Reality (AR) let the user navigate the physical environment to interact with different devices such as multiple displays [31]. The use of multiple devices helps collaborative tasks involving multiple views [37], while Virtual Reality (VR) techniques allow the user to be completely unaware of the surroundings providing a feeling of reality to the end-user [6]. A recent survey on immersive analytics [12] found more than one hundred papers related to VR, and only 15 employing AR technologies from 1991 to 2019, which shows a general preference for VR technology. One of the authors' conclusions is that the IA community should focus on real-life scenarios that require novel strategies for interacting with multiple views.

Developing techniques for using multiple views in VR is a challenge because they require more complex control of interaction techniques [19]. Furthermore, there is a need for interaction methods capable of achieving the functionalities of the predominant WIMP (windows, icons, menus, pointer) used for visual analysis tasks [23]. Some experiments performed with FiberClay [15] for exploring trajectories allowed the authors to report suggestions for improving the user experience in VR environments with multiple views, such as: avoid 2D graphical user interface components, limit the number of interaction modes, facilitate the navigation and preferential use of one primary view.

Although multiple views have been used for years [32], it is worth mentioning that the potential cognitive overload introduced by interaction makes designers ask themselves when and to what extent it should be used. Baldonado et al. [41] identified a list of issues of a multiple views system, where the first four concern to cognitive aspects, and the last three, to system requirements: (1) the time and effort required to *learn* the system, (2) the *load* on the user's working memory, (3) the effort required for *comparison*, (4) the effort required for *context switching*, (5) the *computational requirements* for rendering the additional display elements, (6) the *display space* requirements for the additional views, and (7) the *design, implementation, and maintenance* resources required by the system. Moreover, multiple views share a relationship that is used for coordination. Scherr [36] analyzed coordination techniques, the most common one being *brushing* where, given a selection of elements in one view, the same or related elements are highlighted in the other linked views. There is also *navigational slaving* that describes the relation between views and data, based on a 2x3 taxonomy: selecting items – selecting items, navigating views – navigating views, and selecting items – navigating views.

In this paper, we present an approach for interacting with multiple coordinated views that display 3D visualizations. Our technique uses a virtual cube as a 3D-WIMP version – we call it *Space*, inspired by Mahmood et al.'s work [28] –, for encapsulating each view, and two modes of interaction with the views: the *macro* mode for interacting with the Spaces, and the *micro* mode for interacting with the data displayed in the Space (see Fig. 1). In addition to standard interaction techniques, we provide "cloning" and "coordinated interactions" features.

Overview. Given that similar 3D-WIMPs could be displayed on 2D displays, we designed a similar desktop version to compare it with our VR Spaces approach and decided to focus our study on the following research question: *Do our Spaces approach improve the manipulation of multiple coordinated 3D views when they are explored in an immersive virtual environment? How does the approach differ from a 3D conventional desktop version?* We formulated hypotheses inspired by the problems described in the MCV studies reported in the literature. Then, we conducted a user study with 19 participants. The results contribute to future studies to develop new ways to interact with multiple views. Additionally, the 3D-WIMPs approach opens possibilities for investigating whether free control views are better than common metaphors (e.g., small multiples) in virtual reality.

Contributions. We propose a new approach for interacting with MCVs using a head-mounted display (HMD) to give users full control of the three-dimensional visualizations. Then, we report the lessons learned from the comparative study with 19 participants to create a basis for future works using multiple coordinated views in immersive 3D environments.

The remainder of the paper is structured as follows. In Sect. 2, we briefly review previous works on multiple coordinated views. The concept of *Spaces*, the interaction techniques proposed and additional technical details are introduced in Sect. 3. Sections 4 and 5 present the users' experiment design and the results, respectively, while Sect. 6 discusses our findings. Finally, Sect. 7 presents our conclusions and future work.

2   Related Work

Multiple coordinated views approaches implement the concept of "composite visualization views (CVVs)", which was recently formalized by Javed and Elmqvist [16]. Their proposal followed the concepts inherited from Card et al.'s pipeline [5]: *visual composition*, i.e., the placement or arrangement of multiple visual objects; *visual structure*, i.e., the graphical result of a visualization technique; and *view*, the physical display where a visual structure is rendered. A "composite visualization" is the visual composition of two or more visual structures in the same view. They identified different forms of composing visualizations and came up with *CVVs design patterns* as follows: *juxtaposition*, that corresponds to placing visualizations side-by-side; *superimposition*, which corresponds to overlaying two visualizations in a single view; *overloading*, which uses the space of one visualization for another; *nesting*, which is having the contents of one visualization inside another visualization, and *integrating*, which places visualizations in the same view with visual links.

Several immersive analytics studies have used diverse strategies to provide multiple views [19] regarding different CVVs design patterns, coordination techniques and settings. In this section, we briefly review the studies mostly related to ours, highlighting the limitations and challenges addressed by them.

2.1 Multiple Views on Large Displays

Several authors have explored multiple views in wall-sized displays, usually adopting a *juxtaposition* pattern. Febretti et al. [11] presented OmegaLib, a software framework for supporting the development of immersive applications using Hybrid Reality Environments (HREs), which integrates high-resolution wall-sized displays with immersive technologies. This framework allows the linking of 2D and 3D views, and is designed for a group to discuss the visualizations showed in the wall displays, while another group using laptops is in charge of the control management of the multiple views. With OmegaLib, they try to overcome known problems of these alternative approaches: the static spatial allocation of 3D and 2D used in most systems and the lack of unified interaction between the 2D and 3D visualizations.

Similarly, Langner et al. [21] presented a study based on an MCV system using interaction on a wall-sized display for analyzing the behavior of multiple users exploring more than 45 coordinated views. Their study implemented a general layout with multiple numbers and different sizes of views, and users could swap the views' positions (*juxtaposition*). The authors highlight that view management was not the focus of their study. To support interaction from varying positions, they combined direct touch and distant interaction using mobile devices. To interact with views, the users had to select the region's border showing the desired visualization. It is worth noting the importance of interactions for free navigation and the use of the border to change the mode for manipulating the data shown in the view.

A hybrid application developed by Su et al. [39] allowed the user to visualize 2D and 3D information using a Large High-Resolution Display (LHRD) and VR technology, respectively. The study qualitatively compared 2D/3D coordination data displayed in 2D displays, 2D/3D data without coordination, and 2D/3D coordinated data displayed in the 2D display and in the VR environment. The visualizations used in the study were: a geolocation map, chord and horizon time plots in 2D views, and a 3D scene of a city. The 2D visualization shows the location and link data over time for the highlighted assets and links in the 3D visualization. The location trail is *superimposed* to the 2D and 3D maps, while the chord and time plots show coordinated actions. The results favored to 2D/3D coordinated environment in understanding and interactivity, but 2D/2D was the global favorite due to the facility of staying in one context only. The participants showed signals of discomfort because removing the headset was too disruptive for the data analysis workflow. Nonetheless, the users agreed there are benefits in using hybrid environments.

2.2 Multiple Views in AR and VR Environments

An alternative way to avoid the problem of changing the environment is to adopt augmented reality (AR) solutions. Mahmood et al. [28] proposed a 3D version of a conventional MCV designing a Multiple Coordinated Spaces workspace. AR techniques were used to integrate a physical environment and to combine 2D views and virtual 3D spaces, such as 2D displays with virtual 3D visualizations. This workspace is built by obtaining positions of 2D surfaces, and then plotting 3D spaces. The workspace area is adjusted and subdivided into multiple spaces with similar sizes. The visualization methods used were based on 2D WIMP, displaying 3D parallel coordinates that linked real or virtual views (*overloading*) and topographic maps with *superimposed* scatterplots. Three-dimensional visualizations contained maps and 3D scatterplots included in 3D spaces. The interaction techniques implemented were data/view selection, scaling, and translating (allowing *juxtaposing* views), show/hide visualizations, and creation of history, which saves a configuration of the workspace, all with the help of hand gestures and voice commands provided by the Microsoft HoloLens. This work focused mainly on Coordinated Spaces for supporting immersive analytics in a physical environment and motivated our approach.

The number of works using MCVs in VR environments has been increasing over time. ImAxes [8] is an interactive tool that allows users to manipulate multiple charts' axes like physical objects in a VR environment to design visualizations. The user can manipulate one axis for observing a 1D histogram. Two or three axes placed perpendicularly create 2D and 3D scatterplots, while parallel coordinates are created distributing the axes in parallel in the VR environment. ImAxes was used by experts for economic analysis in a subsequent study by Batch et al. [2]. Since ImAxes is based on placing axes in the VR environment, users can *juxtapose* them. In addition, the proximity between visualizations can create linked 2D and 3D scatterplots (*integration* pattern).

Other studies using the *juxtaposition* pattern are presented by Johnson et al. [18]. In Bento Box, a VR technique for exploring multiple 3D visualizations juxtaposed in a grid, like small multiples. Their tool was evaluated within a CAVE, and results showed that the users found it good for data analysis because it facilitates collaborative discussion. More recently, Jiazhou Liu et al. [26] also used 3D visualizations in small multiples in an immersive environment.

Coordination techniques were studied by Prouzeau et al. [30]. The authors proposed a design space for routing visual links between multiple 2D views in immersive environments, which we classify as the *integration* pattern. Their realtime algorithm allows them to draw links to connect multiple visualizations considering their coordination and the users' views. These visualizations were evaluated without interactive techniques showing the challenges of strategies for MCVs applied in VR.

Two recent works describe approaches that allow users to interact with multiple views in a way close to ours. Satriadi et al. [34] describe the exploration of multiple 2D maps in a VR environment. Each map view could be created, scaled, and arranged by the users. Their study focused on the exploration of user-generated patterns with the maps views. Based on a *juxtaposition and over-load* patterns, their work shows an interesting way to arrange 2D maps to better understand how users arrange the views. More recently, Lee et al. [22] developed FIESTA, a system for collaborative data analysis in immersive environments using VR. FIESTA uses static visualizations floating in a virtual room (*juxtaposition*). Its interactions are based on direct contact with UI elements and distant contact using a laser pointer.

Finally, we should mention the toolkits and frameworks that have been developed for supporting data visualization in VR and AR environments. DXR [38], IATK [7], VRIA [4] are examples of such tools. DXR and IATK are based on the *juxtaposition* pattern [16], while VRIA supports also the *overlaying* pattern.

In summary, an increasing number of works report experiments with multiple views and highlight the limitations of the methods provided to control composite visualizations with coordinated interactions using 2D/3D views. For example, the studies surveyed herein commonly used the juxtaposition pattern followed by superimposition, which is typical of geographical maps. The absence of methods and practical guidelines to use composite views in IA induced the development of different strategies, which showed disadvantages, especially in VR environments [13]. Our work presents an approach to allow users to compose visualizations moving MCVs for improving the scene layout, facilitating data exploration.

3   The *Spaces* Approach

The change from standard 2D to 3D WIMP induces differences in perception and interactivity [29]. Following the design space of composite visualization [16], where multiple "visual structures" are combined in the same "view", we designed our approach based on similar concepts. The "visual structure" is mapped to a virtual cube where it is rendered. The virtual cube is called *Space* inspired by Mahmood et al. [28]. An overview of the approach is shown in Fig. 1 and its details are presented below.

3.1   *Spaces*

A *Space* is a container for one visualization only and can be manipulated similarly to an object but without physics, weight, or texture associated. The objective of a *Space* is to facilitate the interaction across multiple visualizations. We chose a cuboid shape to represent a *Space* to have a reference point for the coordinate system, and added a title identifying the dataset being visualized in the *Space*. It can be cloned, and then the title is customized with the version number to distinguish it from the original *Space* (see Fig. 2-left). To interact with a *Space*, the interacting agent must be in *macro* mode, while to interact with the data displayed inside a Space, it must be in *micro* mode (see Subsect. 3.2).

In a VR environment, the interacting agent used is the virtual hand, which is considered the most natural interaction paradigm [3] for 3D interaction with

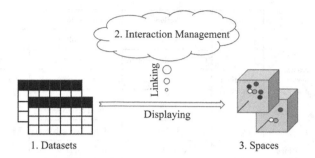

Fig. 1. Overview of the *Spaces* approach: reading from the datasets (1); a visualization instance is added to the interaction manager (2) for coordination techniques (Brushing and Navigational Slaving); data is rendered in the virtual environment, in the *Spaces* graphical representation (3).

Fig. 2. The proposed macro/micro modes of interaction allow the user to interact with the Spaces and the data. The Spaces can be grabbed and overlaid to facilitate comparison of the data represented inside each one (left). The two virtual hands arc independent from each other: the user can grab a Space with one hand and explore its information with the other one (center). Our approach allows the exploration of Multiple Coordinated Spaces (right).

near objects. The user can change between macro and micro modes of interaction through the proximity sensor of the index finger. For evaluation purposes, we developed a similar 3D desktop version. In that version, the mouse cursor is the interacting agent, and the mode change is based on events. We present the distribution of the events for both the VR and desktop versions in Fig. 3.

3.2 Interaction Techniques

The standard WIMP functions are moving, close, and minimizing or maximizing. We developed similar functions for both the VR and desktop versions of our approach for manipulating the *Spaces*, except for minimizing and maximizing. These functions are presented in Fig. 3.

As mentioned before, the interaction techniques are divided into *macro* and *micro* modes.

Macro Mode Interaction. For *selecting* a *Space*, the *virtual hand* must be inside it. The *Space* chosen will slightly change color, avoiding perception

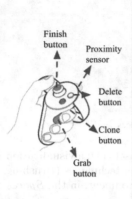

Target	Action	Virtual Reality	Desktop
Container (macro)	Select	Hand collision	Pointer collision
	Grab/Translate/Rotate	Select + Grab button	Select + Right click
	Clone	Select + Clone button	Select + Space bar
	Scale	Grab container with both controllers	Select + Mouse wheel
	Delete	Select + Delete button	Select + Delete button
Data (micro)	View detail	Index finger collision	Cursor pointer
	Highlight	View detail + Grab button	View detail + left click
Navigation	Virtual movement	Head movement	FPS control (A/W/S/D buttons)
System	Finish task	Finish button	Enter button

Fig. 3. Distribution of actions for each interactive command used in the Virtual Reality and Desktop versions. We propose two easily interchangeable modes of interaction, the *micro* mode to manipulate data displayed in the *Space*, and the *macro* mode to interact with the *Spaces*. A **controller module** manages how the user interacts with the *Spaces* and data, while an **interaction module** connects data to *Spaces*. All features needed for coordinating interactions are provided by this module.

changes in the visualization technique. In order to **grab** a *Space*, the user must keep the Grab button pressed, allowing to grab one Space per hand. We selected the Grab button because it resembles the behavior of holding an object. Once grabbed, the user can **move** and **rotate** the *Space* freely according to their movement. To **scale** a *Space*, the user must grab it with both hands, and by separating or joining them, the scale will increase or decrease the size of the *Space*, accordingly. To **clone** a *Space*, it is necessary to select it and press the Clone button: a copy of the *Space* will be created, including the same visual features. To **remove** a *Space*, one must select the *Space* and then press the Delete button: a confirmation window will open on the user's hand to verify whether or not the *Space* should be deleted.

Micro Mode Interaction. Two commands are available in the *micro* mode. The **view** interaction is based on touching a data item with the virtual hand: it shows details about the data on the *Space* at hand. The second command is **highlight**, which allows changing the color of a data item for contrasting with others. The way to highlight or remove the highlight is to point at the data item and press the Grab button.

Multiple Coordinated *Spaces.* are based on the **coordinate interactions**. Each time a *Space* is rotated, the linked spaces will rotate too (**navigation slaving**). When the data is highlighted or not, the linked data will undergo the same change, thus providing the **linking-and-brushing** functionality.

3.3   Implementation Details

We developed our proof-of-concept prototype using the Unity game engine, C#, and the SteamVR plug-in to build a tool compatible with the HTC Vive and Oculus Rift head-mounted displays. As we can see in Fig. 1, datasets are read, and the visualizations are created in *Spaces*. A reference to the dataset and *Space* is instantiated in the **interaction module**, which is responsible for the interaction management thus linking both data and *Space* to support coordination. Also, each *Space* can be linked to other *Spaces* for *navigational slaving* and *brushing-and-linking* interactions. Each *Space* keeps track of the virtual hands that are inside it managed by the **controller module**, allowing the communication between them for *scaling* interaction. Axes of the coordinate system of each *Space* are drawn, which is useful when the user superimposes *Spaces* for comparison purposes, for instance.

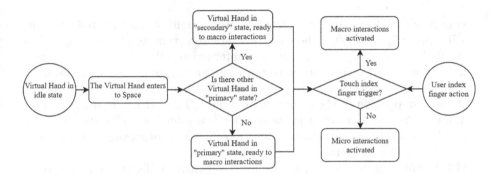

Fig. 4. Overview of the interaction flow and change of interaction modes.

The **controller module** manages the *macro/micro* modes of interaction (Fig. 4). We use three states for managing the modes. The *idle* state is the default state, which indicates that the virtual hands are not inside any *Space*. The **primary use** state indicates that a virtual hand is ready to interact or is interacting with a *Space*, and the **secondary use** state is used for controlling interactions that need two virtual hands. Also, to differentiate the *macro/micro* modes for the virtual hands, the controller device is showed in the VR environment every time the *macro* mode is active. The method chosen for the mode change is the index finger's proximity sensor.

4   Evaluation

The evaluation of our approach of multiple coordinate three-dimensional views in VR using the *Spaces* approach was performed through an experiment with users. We implemented a VR-based and a similar 3D desktop version with the same interactions to standardize the experiment variables. The *First Person* navigation technique was implemented for the desktop because it is more immersive than a third-person point of view (POV) [9] approach. Our user study compares the users' behavior while handling 3D visualizations in Desktop and Virtual Reality.

4.1   Hypotheses

To evaluate if our approach improves the MCV issues (mentioned in Sect. 1) [41], we focused on the comparative performance between the desktop (3D) and the virtual reality (VR) versions. We excluded the learning issue because it is challenging to have non-expert users available. Furthermore, issues related to infrastructure and implementation capacity were also not addressed because we assume that new technologies such as HMDs give support for those. The hypotheses that guided our user study are:

– **H1:** It will be faster to complete tasks using multiple coordinated views in VR than in 3D. Although there are several interaction techniques mapped to the desktop version, which can lead to interaction difficulties, the familiarity with mouse + keyboard can overcome those and allow a fair comparison.
– **H2:** The user will keep more information in VR than in 3D. We aim to analyze the first impression of the environment's data. The VR environment can be more fun for the user, and they would pay less attention to the data than in the desktop with physical space limitation. However, proprioception can help users in the VR version.
– **H3:** It will be easier to compare views in VR than in 3D. We aim to analyze the use of multiple visualizations, including cloning them.
– **H4:** The context switching will be hardest in VR than in 3D. The composed tasks let the user change visualization with different data interpretation. We displayed bar chart filters in one scene and increased the scatterplot chart filters in another.
– **H5:** Interacting with multiple coordinate views will be more comfortable in VR than in 3D.
– **H6:** Interacting with multiple coordinated views using the Spaces approach will be more efficient in VR than in 3D.
– **H7:** Multiple coordinated views using the Spaces approach will be easier to use in VR than in 3D.

4.2   Use Case

The use case we designed for testing our hypotheses is the exploration of a music dataset because music is a well-known topic that does not demand introduction effort.

The dataset used is the same previously used by Liang et al. [25], and it contains the following data for each music album: year, artist, genre, and also feature data from sound signals. For the experiment, the dataset was processed to avoid missing data. Finally, a total of 338 tracks were chosen.

The visualizations implemented are 3D scatterplots of music tracks, artists, and genres, obtained from a multidimensional projection technique, and bar charts showing the number of tracks per year, artist, and genre. The primary view is a scatterplot showing music tracks, and the other visualizations operate as music filters by brushing. Each visualization result is displayed in a *Space*.

The coordination between *Spaces* allows obtaining data corresponding to the intersection of filters applied to different visualizations and data corresponding to the union when more than one filter is applied to a single visualization. The *Spaces* of the genre and artist scatterplots are linked to the *Space* of the music scatterplot letting the *navigational slaving* interaction.

The 3D scatterplots are the result of the dimensionality reduction technique t-SNE [27] configured as follows: 100,000 iterations and perplexity equal to 40. We selected these parameters because they provided the best possible clusterization of genres. Then, to obtain the artist and genre scatterplots, we calculate the centroid using an average of their tracks' positions. Additionally, the centroids were multiplied by a weight (20) because more than one centroid was overlapping.

The implemented *brushing* interaction is based on highlighting data. Initially, the data is displayed with a shade that is sufficient for viewing details about the data item. A limitation of our brushing technique is that the information on the number of tracks is not refreshed (nor the height of the bar plots). The year, genre, and artist visualizations filter directly to the music scatterplot. Additionally, the user can clone any visualization for saving filtered data.

4.3 Tasks

For our user study, we designed composed tasks involving the manipulation of multiple views. The contexts used are artist, genre, and music tracks. Our test tries to emulate real system solutions. To finish each task, the user had to state the answer. A confirmation dialog similar to deleting cloned *Spaces* was used to confirm the end of each task.

T1. Select the Artist with More Music Tracks of Genre Punk Between 2005 and 2010. A comparison of dense selected data from different filters is required. Cloning and comparing *Spaces* is the expected goal. Given multiple comparisons, this task exclusively tests H3 and helps to measure time for H1.

T2. Select the Closest Artist to the Music Most Different from the Majority of Genre Folk Between 2005 and 2010. This task aims at two objectives, the selection of the most atypical filtered data and the selection of the nearest data to a different context. We look for the overlapping *Spaces* – this task measures time to evaluate H1 and the accuracy to evaluate H4.

T3. Given to the User 2 Min of Free Exploration, Answer Ten Questions. About genres, years, and artists with more and fewer music tracks (we asked 6 medium level questions), the more similar artists (2 difficult level questions) and music genres from the year 1991 and 1995 (2 very difficult level questions). With this task, we want to measure the memorization rate related to H2.

The hypotheses H5, H7 are evaluated through questionnaires, while H6 is assessed through the correct responses in tasks T1 and T2.

4.4   Training and Pilot Test

A brief description of the environment (VR and desktop), data, and visualizations were presented at the beginning of the experiment. The instructions of use for each environment were explained before it started. The first training took approximately 15 min (10 min to VR and 5 min to 3D Desktop) and included *macro* and *micro* interactions.

In a pilot test, we noted that the users could not perform the tasks taking advantage of the functionalities of cloning, overlaying, and walking navigation, and consequently, the tasks would demand too much time. In order to reduce the testing time, we extended the training, inviting them to walk over the virtual area to improve confidence. Also, short recommendations were given to deal with tasks that involved overlapping and cloning.

4.5   Experiment

The experiment was carried out in a 4×4 m room; the users were aware of the space where they could walk. A similar virtual room was set up to improve immersion. Additionally, an existing TV in the room was also modeled in the VR environment for displaying the tasks (see Fig. 5).

The user study followed a within-subjects design, combining VR and 3D desktop environments, 6/4 *Spaces*, where genre and artist scatterplots were added in the second case, and three tasks (independent variables). A Latin-square design counterbalanced the order of the environments and the number of *Spaces*. Each participant performed four sessions, where they started using 4 and 6 *Spaces* (or vice-versa) in the VR environment and later continued in a similar order on the desktop version (or vice-versa). Each of these scenarios started with a short training (learned from pre-testing) followed by the experimental session. We collected the time to complete each trial and correct answers as dependent variables.

The average training time was 30 min (20 min for VR and 10 min for 3D Desktop). After completing a task, the users were consulted through a Web version of the Subjective Mental Effort Questionnaire (SMEQ) [35], and one-select Emocards [10] used to validate H7 and H5, respectively. Finally, completing the number of *Spaces* series (6 or 4), a UMUX-lite form was asked to analyze H7.

The target population consisted of 19 participants (16 males and 3 females), where 18 were computer science students and 1 was a student on ecology. Their

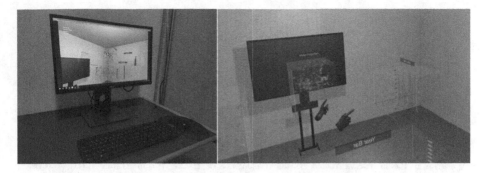

Fig. 5. The virtual room had a TV that showed the tasks. The participants started the exploration in the middle of the room, and the visualizations were displayed around them. Users interacted with the visualizations using keyboard + mouse (left), while in the VR environment they used controllers as virtual hands (right).

average age was 23 years. The majority of the participants had none or minimal experience with VR headsets; only three reported high experience.

5   Results

To validate the usability of the environments, we compared the perceived difficulty of the tasks T1 and T2 with the SMEQ "How difficult or easy was to conclude the Task overall?". Results (Fig. 6) showed a normal distribution by Shapiro-Wilk, and the statistical analysis by ANOVA indicates that VR was easier than 3D Desktop ($p = .0163$).

Additionally, the System Usability Score (SUS) was calculated from UMUX-lite [24]. ANOVA analysis was used for finding the effects of the number of *Spaces* using the SUS score (normal distribution validated by Shapiro-Wilk), resulting in significant differences. Post-hoc analysis by Tukey's HSD suggests that using 4 Spaces in VR is significantly more usable than in a 3D Desktop with 4 Spaces ($p = .0121$) and 6 Spaces in VR shows a higher usability score than in 3D Desktop with 4 Spaces ($p = .0184$). H7 is validated in both analyzes (results can be visualized in Fig. 7-left).

Analyzing the duration of tasks for validating H1, the time showed a normal distribution validated by Shapiro-Wilk. We found through ANOVA that there was no significant difference for T1 ($p = .7380$) and T2 ($p = .2830$) in the duration of tasks.

We selected the correct answers to calculate the efficiency for validating H3, H4 and verify H6. From 152 answers, we obtained only 8 wrong answers in T1, and 17 errors in T2. The time of correct answers did not show significant differences for T1 ($p = .9170$) and T2 ($p = .9070$). The efficiency distribution can be observed in Fig. 8.

SMEQ

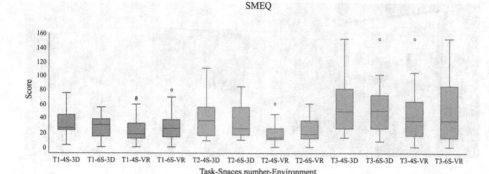

Fig. 6. Box-and-whiskers plot of SMEQ scores for each trial. For T1, the VR version with 4-Spaces was the easiest (Mean = 26.57, SD = 21.16), the 3D Desktop version with 4-Spaces was the most difficult (Mean = 34.21, SD = 20.24). Also, T2 in the VR version with 4S was the less difficult (Mean = 18.26, SD = 16.40) and the 3D Desktop version with 4-Spaces, the most difficult (Mean = 39.94, SD = 29.89). T3 had similar result, the VR version was hardly less difficult (Mean = 47.50, SD = 41.24) than 3D Desktop (Mean = 55.28, SD = 36.55).

Friedman test was performed to compare the number of correct answers for T3 (Shapiro-Wilk showed no normal distribution). Results demonstrate that there are no significant differences ($p = .7960$), not validating H2 (see Fig. 8-right).

The comfortability of each environment was evaluated based on emotional categories using emocards (Fig. 7-right). We calculated Cohen's kappa of 114 responses (6 answers by user), evaluating the two environments per categorical answers ("pleasant", "unpleasant" and "neutral"). The results are summarized in Table 1. Cohen's kappa was 0.26 and conducted a reliability "fair" [20]. We concluded that the VR version was "average pleasant" (Mdn = 3) over the "calm pleasant" for 3D Desktop (Mdn = 4) with fair reliability validating H5.

The SUS ranged from 28.32 to 87.90 for 3D Desktop (M = 66.80, SD = 13.07) and from 44.57 to 87.90 for the VR version (Mean = 77.64, SD = 10.44). According to surveys that compare SUS scores for different systems, our VR version is ranked as "Good" [1].

In summary, only H5 had significant differences and was validated, showing that our approach is more comfortable than the 3D version. The other hypotheses could not be proved nor rejected due to lack of statistical significance.

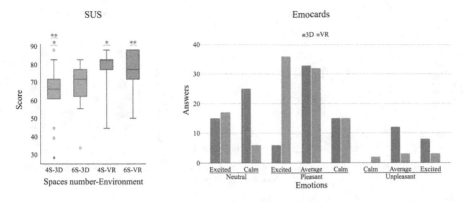

Fig. 7. Box-and-whiskers plot (left) of SUS score for each condition. * and ** indicate significant differences. Histogram of emocards (right) selected by users per environment (VR and 3D).

Table 1. Results of 114 emotional answers per environment.

		3D Desktop			
		Pleasant	Neutral	Unpleasant	Total
VR	Pleasant	46	24	13	83
	Neutral	6	15	2	23
	Unpleasant	2	1	5	8
	Total	54	40	20	114

6 Discussion and Limitations

While visual analytics systems often use multiple coordinated views to explore and analyze complex datasets in 2D desktop environments, literature shows that fully-immersive analytics applications lack well-established techniques to use similar approaches.

We analyzed the difficulties of multiple coordinated views and proposed and evaluated an approach to provide multiple three-dimensional views in immersive Virtual Reality. Our method allows the user to use virtual hands to grab the visualizations displayed in three-dimensional versions of WIMPs (the *Spaces*) for free interaction in *macro* mode and interacting with the data items in *micro* mode. This way, the approach divides the interaction between *Spaces* and data, respectively. Moreover, the use of two modes for each *virtual hand* increases the number of grouped interactions that can be implemented (*macro, micro, macro - macro, micro - micro, macro - micro*). Another significant aspect is that our approach does not depend on the user's dominant hand.

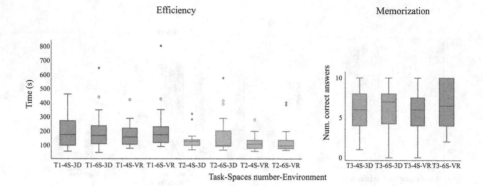

Fig. 8. Box-and-whiskers plot of time (seconds) for correct answers for T1 and T2 (left). Similar distributions were obtained for T1 in the 3D Desktop version (Mean = 187.54, SD = 104.33) and VR (Mean = 202.68, SD = 136.39), and T2 in the 3D Desktop version (Mean = 135.57, SD = 74.58) and VR (Mean = 123.44, SD = 86.31). Box-and-whiskers plot of trials per number of correct answers (right). No significant differences were found.

6.1   Findings

The evaluation of our approach was based on comparing it with a 3D desktop version for testing 7 hypotheses. We designed and conducted an experiment where 19 subjects explored a music dataset, employing 4 and 6 coordinated views in both environments.

Before the actual experiment, a pilot test with five users made us recognize that although the case study was easy, the manipulation of multiple views required users with experience in data exploration. Interactions, as navigation and visualization grabbing, cloning, and overlaying, were not known, so they did not learn the most optimal manner to perform the tasks, and the tests demanded excessive time. The training was then improved, reducing the experiment time and the difficulties of the tasks.

However, the pilot test also showed that the usability of grabbing and manipulating visualizations had good results in comfort, in favor of our VR version. The three-dimensional visualization could be placed in different locations for better exploration. In addition, the training in physical walking for navigation caused the users to trust our system. This is reflected in the comfort results and comments. Furthermore, the navigation for the 3D desktop version was intuitive because most users knew the FPS format, but the translation and rotation interactions were hated due to the depth.

Concerning the hypotheses, although the quantitative results indicated no significant differences between the VR and 3D desktop, some interesting findings came from the questionnaires.

As for hypothesis **H1**, "It will be faster to complete tasks using multiple coordinated views in VR than in 3D." (tasks T1 and T2), one might assume that the familiarity with mouse + keyboard could lead the desktop version to be faster than VR but that was not confirmed. This might suggest that our approach did not introduce difficulties even for users with no experience in VR, presenting competitive execution times.

Regarding hypothesis **H2**, "The user will keep more information in VR than in 3D", it was evaluated based on the correct answers for task T3. Results were also non-significant, most likely due to a learning effect. We noticed that the participants acquired memorization strategies after completing task T3 and applied them to the other tasks. The shuffled questions ordering did not avoid the learning effect as we assumed it would.

The time spent and correct answers for tasks T1 and T2 allowed us to evaluate hypothesis **H3**, "It will be easier to compare views in VR than in 3D" and **H6**, "Interacting with multiple coordinated views using the *Spaces* approach will be more efficient in VR than in 3D". Both hypotheses were not statistically confirmed. However, participants commented that they had better confidence using the VR version, probably by novel technology. Also, most of them liked being able to organize the visualizations in the 3D virtual environment.

Regarding **H4**, "The context switching will be hardest in VR than in 3D", was also assessed by task T2, which was far more complex than the others. Since there were no significant differences in time or number of correct answers between the VR and 3D versions, this hypothesis was also not confirmed. Such a result might suggest that our approach did not increase the cognitive effort demanded to complete the task compared to a well-known setting such as the desktop.

Finally, the hypotheses **H5**, "Interacting with multiple coordinate views will be more comfortable in VR than in 3D", and **H7**, "Multiple coordinated views using the *Spaces* approach will be easier to use in VR than in 3D", were evaluated through questionnaires. The results showed that the comfort of handling multiple *Spaces* is higher in our fully-immersive environment than in the 3D desktop version, which probably might have influenced the same good result regarding usability.

Summary. Motivated by the challenges related to multiple views [17,19,41] and the increasing use of immersive analytics applications [29], we proposed an approach that allows composite visualization patterns in VR and comfortable and easy ways of interacting with multiple 3D visualizations in such environments. Our results show that the Desktop version is not significantly better than the VR version in terms of time and accuracy despite using the standard FPS approach with keyboard and mouse. Multiple 3D views are not typically used in desktop versions, and this could be the reason for the non-significant results. Subjective results show that our VR approach is significantly better than the Desktop version. We infer that the participants are not able to explore multiple 3D visualizations with common desktop interaction devices.

6.2 Limitations

When designing our approach regarding the composite visualization patterns, we chose to support the juxtaposition and superimposition patterns. However, our application's architecture separates interaction with the *Spaces* (macro mode) from interaction with the data (micro mode), allowing a *Space* to be used with any data visualization. Therefore, overloading (by proximity) and integration (showing linking) are feasible patterns to evaluate in future works.

Another limitations are related to our experimental application. Multiple views are used to solve complex tasks, which is not feasible with non-expert participants. Having only non-expert users as subjects may be the most probable cause of not finding significant differences.

The brushing technique also introduced a limitation because the information on the number of music tracks is never updated. If we had that feature, we could have proposed other comparison tasks. Finally, the interaction techniques are based on direct contact between the users' hands and the virtual cube representing the *Spaces*. So, far interaction strategies using ray casting are missing.

7   Conclusions and Future Work

In this work, we have presented an Immersive Analytics approach to interact with multiple coordinated three-dimensional views in Virtual Reality. The main idea is that the user can grab the visualizations inside a virtual cube container (a *Space*) ,allowing composite patterns.The proposed technique combines different components to provide users with a comfortable interaction. We have demonstrated the usability of our approach in a user study with non-expert participants comparing with a similar 3D desktop version. It suggests that our approach can be used in real-life scenarios.

From the lessons learned with this experiment, in an on-going work we are considering to offer to the users the possibility of interacting with near objects using the virtual hand and also with far objects, through ray casting.

As future work, we would like to conduct an extensive experimental study involving a more complex use case involving different visualization techniques and employing the overloading and integration CVVs patterns, with the support of expert participants. Considering that expert users in visualization are not necessarily familiar with immersive VR and the use of the proprioception in virtual environments, we will also extend the training to motivate them to better explore the real environment and their body movements. In this way, we believe we will be able to better investigate the hypotheses that could not be demonstrated statistically here, and reason on the results achieved.

Acknowledgements. We are deeply grateful to the subjects of our study, conducted before the COVID-19 pandemics. We also thank the insightful comments from the reviewers that helped us to improve our paper. Special thanks to Arnaud Prouzeau, whose comments led to a much better final version of this paper. This work was financed by the Brazilian funding agencies CNPq and CAPES - Finance Code 001.

References

1. Bangor, A., Kortum, P., Miller, J.: Determining what individual SUS scores mean: Adding an adjective rating scale. J. Usab. Stud. 4(3), 114–123 (2009). https://dl.acm.org/doi/10.5555/2835587.2835589
2. Batch, A., et al.: There is no spoon: evaluating performance, space use, and presence with expert domain users in immersive analytics. IEEE Trans. Visual Comput. Graph. 26(1), 536–546 (2019). https://doi.org/10.1109/TVCG.2019.2934803
3. Bowman, D., Kruijff, E., LaViola, J., Poupyrev, I.: 3D User Interfaces: Theory and Practice, CourseSmart eTextbook. Pearson Education (2004). https://books.google.com.br/books?id=JYzmCkf7yNcC
4. Butcher, P.W.S., John, N.W., Ritsos, P.D.: Vria - a framework for immersive analytics on the web. In: Extended Abstracts of the 2019 CHI Conference on Human Factors in Computing Systems, CHI EA '19, pp. 1–6. Association for Computing Machinery, New York (2019). https://doi.org/10.1145/3290607.3312798
5. Card, S.K., Mackinlay, J.D., Shneiderman, B. (eds.): Readings in Information Visualization: Using Vision to Think. Morgan Kaufmann Publishers Inc., San Francisco (1999). https://dl.acm.org/doi/10.5555/300679
6. Chandler, T., et al.: Immersive analytics. In: 2015 Big Data Visual Analytics (BDVA), pp. 1–8 (2015). https://doi.org/10.1109/BDVA.2015.7314296
7. Cordeil, M., et al.: IATK: an immersive analytics toolkit. In: 2019 IEEE Conference on Virtual Reality and 3D User Interfaces (VR), pp. 200–209 (2019). https://doi.org/10.1109/VR.2019.8797978
8. Cordeil, M., Cunningham, A., Dwyer, T., Thomas, B.H., Marriott, K.: ImAxes: immersive axes as embodied affordances for interactive multivariate data visualisation. In: Proceedings of the 30th Annual ACM Symposium on User Interface Software and Technology, UIST '17, pp. 71–83. Association for Computing Machinery, New York (2017). https://doi.org/10.1145/3126594.3126613
9. Denisova, A., Cairns, P.: First person vs. third person perspective in digital games: do player preferences affect immersion? In: Proceedings of the 33rd Annual ACM Conference on Human Factors in Computing Systems, CHI '15, pp. 145–148. Association for Computing Machinery, New York (2015). https://doi.org/10.1145/2702123.2702256
10. Desmet, P., Overbeeke, K., Tax, S.: Designing products with added emotional value: development and application of an approach for research through design. Des. J. 4(1), 32–47 (2001). https://doi.org/10.2752/146069201789378496
11. Febretti, A., Nishimoto, A., Mateevitsi, V., Renambot, L., Johnson, A., Leigh, J.: Omegalib: a multi-view application framework for hybrid reality display environments. In: 2014 IEEE Virtual Reality (VR), pp. 9–14 (2014). https://doi.org/10.1109/VR.2014.6802043
12. Fonnet, A., Prié, Y.: Survey of immersive analytics. IEEE Trans. Visual. Comput. Graph. 27(3), 2101–2122 (2021). https://doi.org/10.1109/TVCG.2019.2929033
13. Gračanin, D.: Immersion versus embodiment: embodied cognition for immersive analytics in mixed reality environments. In: Schmorrow, D.D., Fidopiastis, C.M. (eds.) AC 2018. LNCS (LNAI), vol. 10915, pp. 355–368. Springer, Cham (2018). https://doi.org/10.1007/978-3-319-91470-1_29
14. Greffard, N., Picarougne, F., Kuntz, P.: Beyond the classical monoscopic 3D in graph analytics: An experimental study of the impact of stereoscopy. In: 2014 IEEE VIS International Workshop on 3DVis (3DVis), pp. 19–24 (2014). https://doi.org/10.1109/3DVis.2014.7160095

15. Hurter, C., Riche, N.H., Drucker, S.M., Cordeil, M., Alligier, R., Vuillemot, R.: FiberClay: sculpting three dimensional trajectories to reveal structural insights. IEEE Trans. Visual. Comput. Graph. **25**(1), 704–714 (2019). https://doi.org/10.1109/TVCG.2018.2865191

16. Javed, W., Elmqvist, N.: Exploring the design space of composite visualization. In: 2012 IEEE Pacific Visualization Symposium, pp. 1–8 (2012). https://doi.org/10.1109/PacificVis.2012.6183556

17. Javed, W., Elmqvist, N.: Exploring the design space of composite visualization. In: 2012 IEEE Pacific Visualization Symposium, pp. 1–8. IEEE (2012)

18. Johnson, S., et al.: Bento box: an interactive and zoomable small multiples technique for visualizing 4D simulation ensembles in virtual reality. Front. Robot. AI **6**, 61 (2019). https://doi.org/10.3389/frobt.2019.00061

19. Knudsen, S., Carpendale, S.: Multiple views in immersive analytics. In: IEEE VIS 2017 Workshop on Immersive Analytics (2017). https://tinyurl.com/immersiveviews

20. Landis, J.R., Koch, G.G.: The measurement of observer agreement for categorical data. Biometrics **33**(1), 159–174 (1977). http://www.jstor.org/stable/2529310

21. Langner, R., Kister, U., Dachselt, R.: Multiple coordinated views at large displays for multiple users: empirical findings on user behavior, movements, and distances. IEEE Trans. Visual. Comput. Graph. **25**(1), 608–618 (2019). https://doi.org/10.1109/TVCG.2018.2865235

22. Lee, B., Hu, X., Cordeil, M., Prouzeau, A., Jenny, B., Dwyer, T.: Shared surfaces and spaces: collaborative data visualisation in a co-located immersive environment. IEEE Trans. Visual. Comput. Graph. **27**(2), 1171–1181 (2021). https://doi.org/10.1109/tvcg.2020.3030450

23. Lee, B., Isenberg, P., Riche, N.H., Carpendale, S.: Beyond mouse and keyboard: expanding design considerations for information visualization interactions. IEEE Trans. Visual. Comput. Graph. **18**(12), 2689–2698 (2012). https://doi.org/10.1109/TVCG.2012.204

24. Lewis, J.R., Utesch, B.S., Maher, D.E.: UMUX-LITE: when there's no time for the SUS. In: Proceedings of the SIGCHI Conference on Human Factors in Computing Systems, CHI '13, pp. 2099–2102, Association for Computing Machinery, New York (2013). https://doi.org/10.1145/2470654.2481287

25. Liang, D., Gu, H., O'Connor, B.: Music genre classification with the million song dataset. Machine Learning Department, CMU (2011). https://www.ee.columbia.edu/~dliang/files/FINAL.pdf

26. Liu, J., Prouzeau, A., Ens, B., Dwyer, T.: Design and evaluation of interactive small multiples data visualisation in immersive spaces. In: 2020 IEEE Conference on Virtual Reality and 3D User Interfaces (VR), pp. 588–597 (2020). https://doi.org/10.1109/VR46266.2020.00081

27. van der Maaten, L., Hinton, G.: Visualizing data using t-SNE. J. Mach. Learn. Res. **9**(86), 2579–2605 (2008). https://jmlr.org/papers/v9/vandermaaten08a.html

28. Mahmood, T., Butler, E., Davis, N., Huang, J., Lu, A.: Building multiple coordinated spaces for effective immersive analytics through distributed cognition. In: 2018 International Symposium on Big Data Visual and Immersive Analytics (BDVA), pp. 1–11 (2018). https://doi.org/10.1109/BDVA.2018.8533893

29. Marriott, K., et al.: Immersive analytics: time to reconsider the value of 3D for information visualisation. In: Immersive Analytics. LNCS, vol. 11190, pp. 25–55. Springer, Cham (2018). https://doi.org/10.1007/978-3-030-01388-2_2

30. Prouzeau, A., Lhuillier, A., Ens, B., Weiskopf, D., Dwyer, T.: Visual link routing in immersive visualisations. In: Proceedings of the 2019 ACM International Conference on Interactive Surfaces and Spaces, ISS '19, pp. 241–253. Association for Computing Machinery, New York (2019). https://doi.org/10.1145/3343055.3359709

31. Ran, X., Slocum, C., Gorlatova, M., Chen, J.: ShareAR: communication-efficient multi-user mobile augmented reality. In: Proceedings of the 18th ACM Workshop on Hot Topics in Networks, HotNets 2019, pp. 109–116. Association for Computing Machinery, New York (2019). https://doi.org/10.1145/3365609.3365867

32. Roberts, J.C.: State of the art: coordinated multiple views in exploratory visualization. In: Fifth International Conference on Coordinated and Multiple Views in Exploratory Visualization (CMV 2007), pp. 61–71 (2007). https://doi.org/10.1109/CMV.2007.20

33. Russo Dos Santos, C., Gros, P.: Multiple views in 3D metaphoric information visualization. In: Proceedings Sixth International Conference on Information Visualisation, pp. 468–473 (2002). https://doi.org/10.1109/IV.2002.1028815

34. Satriadi, K.A., Ens, B., Cordeil, M., Czauderna, T., Jenny, B.: Maps around me: 3D multiview layouts in immersive spaces. In: Proceedings of the ACM on Human-Computer Interaction, vol. 4, no. ISS (2020). https://doi.org/10.1145/3427329

35. Sauro, J., Dumas, J.S.: Comparison of three one-question, post-task usability questionnaires. In: Proceedings of the SIGCHI Conference on Human Factors in Computing Systems, CHI '09, pp. 1599–1608. Association for Computing Machinery, New York (2009). https://doi.org/10.1145/1518701.1518946

36. Scherr, M.: Multiple and coordinated views in information visualization. Trends Inf. Visual. **38**, 33 (2008). https://www.mmi.ifi.lmu.de/lehre/ws0809/hs/docs/scherr.pdf

37. Sereno, M., Wang, X., Besancon, L., Mcguffin, M.J., Isenberg, T.: Collaborative work in augmented reality: a survey. IEEE Trans. Visual. Comput. Graph. 1 (2020). https://doi.org/10.1109/TVCG.2020.3032761

38. Sicat, R., et al.: DXR: a toolkit for building immersive data visualizations. IEEE Trans. Visual. Comput. Graph. **25**(1), 715–725 (2019). https://doi.org/10.1109/TVCG.2018.2865152

39. Su, S., Perry, V., Dasari, V.: Comparative study for multiple coordinated views across immersive and non-immersive visualization systems. In: Chen, J.Y.C., Fragomeni, G. (eds.) HCII 2019. LNCS, vol. 11574, pp. 321–332. Springer, Cham (2019). https://doi.org/10.1007/978-3-030-21607-8_25

40. Thomas, J.J., Cook, K.A.: Illuminating the path: the research and development agenda for visual analytics (2005). https://www.hsdl.org/?abstract&did=485291

41. Wang Baldonado, M.Q., Woodruff, A., Kuchinsky, A.: Guidelines for using multiple views in information visualization. In: Proceedings of the Working Conference on Advanced Visual Interfaces, AVI '00, pp. 110–119. Association for Computing Machinery, New York (2000). https://doi.org/10.1145/345513.345271

Directing and Combining Multiple Queries for Exploratory Search by Visual Interactive Intent Modeling

Jonathan Strahl[1] , Jaakko Peltonen[2]([⊠]) , and Patrik Floréen[1,3]

[1] Department of Computer Science, Aalto University, Espoo, Finland
jonathan.strahl@aalto.fi
[2] Faculty of Information Technology and Communication Sciences, Tampere University, Tampere, Finland
jaakko.peltonen@tuni.fi
[3] Department of Computer Science, University of Helsinki, Helsinki, Finland
patrik.floreen@helsinki.fi

Abstract. In interactive information-seeking, a user often performs many interrelated queries and interactions covering multiple aspects of a broad topic of interest. Especially in difficult information-seeking tasks the user may need to find what is in common among such multiple aspects. Therefore, the user may need to compare and combine results across queries. While methods to combine queries or rankings have been proposed, little attention has been paid to interactive support for combining multiple queries in exploratory search. We introduce an interactive information retrieval system for exploratory search with multiple simultaneous search queries that can be combined. The user is able to direct search in the multiple queries, and combine queries by two operations: intersection and difference, which reveal what is relevant to the user intent of two queries, and what is relevant to one but not the other. Search is directed by relevance feedback on visualized user intent models of each query. Operations on queries act directly on the intent models inferring a combined user intent model. Each combination yields a new result (ranking) and acts as a new search that can be interactively directed and further combined. User experiments on difficult information-seeking tasks show that our novel system with query operations yields more relevant top-ranked documents in a shorter time than a baseline multiple-query system.

Keywords: Interactive information retrieval · Information visualization · Exploratory search · Intent modeling · Query combination

---

Work supported by Academy of Finland (FCAI flagship and grants 313748 & 327352), Business Finland (grants 2115754 & 211548), and Aalto Science-IT.

C. Ardito et al. (Eds.): INTERACT 2021, LNCS 12934, pp. 514–535, 2021.
https://doi.org/10.1007/978-3-030-85613-7_34

1 Introduction and Related Work

Information seeking is an everyday task in domains ranging from internet pages to specialized corpora such as scientific publications, healthcare information and legal documents. Simple lookup search is not sufficient for all information seeking: studies estimated up to 50% of searching is informational and the search behavior is exploratory, spreading over multiple queries [9,16]. For example, academic search is exploratory, uncertain, multifaceted and successive [33]: an average scientific search session requires 15 queries [14]. Exploratory search is related to the concept of recommender systems: both help the user find new items of interest. Exploratory search benefits from active engagement with the user, through novel user interfaces and relevance feedback [21]. Exploratory search is hard as it can be difficult for the user to formulate appropriate queries for their information need [40], especially in standard search systems that only support typed queries and show results as document lists; if a query does not yield good results it can take much cognitive effort to explore query reformulations [32].

Methods have been proposed supporting exploratory search [11,12,25,37, 42]. Early work on adaptive search [5] and adaptive visualization [1] noted search results improved when the system adapted to the user. Correspondingly, in context-aware search [41] explicit or inferred context can be used to adapt results. In search the user's information need is also called "intent", and search systems must model it from limited data [29]. A dashboard visualizing document similarity was proposed [20], allowing relevance feedback to documents or terms but without visualizing term relationships, similar to a baseline system in [29].

Searching by building Boolean queries has been supported by interactive visualization of Boolean expressions [31], but without recommendation and needing manual construction. Further, the Cluster Map [15,39] can create a graph of document subgroups sharing particular ontology terms such as keywords. The user can select such keywords; documents having them are then shown in clusters. The user can combine keywords with logical "AND" to find documents with intersecting keywords. However, there is no modeling of user intent, users must go through a complete keyword list to select relevant ones, and documents must explicitly contain selected keywords or their combinations to be shown which may rule out relevant documents; in contrast, we will propose a system that models user intent, infers and presents recommended relevant keywords, and infers a probabilistic document ranking more tolerant to variability of keyword use.

A system for exploratory search building a probabilistic "interactive intent model" of the user's search intent was shown in [29], and extended to allow negative feedback in [27]. We will propose a system which supports exploratory search with multiple simultaneously shown queries which we call "search streams", each with recommendation of content based on probabilistic models of user intent, and allows combing streams by operations between the models themselves.

In the "interactive intent modeling" approach [27,29,30], a radial keyword visualization communicates the beliefs of the intent model with the user:

predicted relevant keywords are shown according to the underlying user intent model and organized as directions in an information space. Radial visualization has proven beneficial also in other work [24] not featuring user modeling or keyword recommendation, but in the interactive intent modeling approach the visualization directly shares the beliefs of the model with the user [29], so the user can learn about the search space and provide relevance feedback to direct the search. We propose a system where radial visualization is used over multiple search streams.

In exploratory search, web search logs revealed users open several tabs [17,18] and work on them concurrently [7]. In academic search tasks users use multitasking with parallel and recurrent reformulation [29]. Such results motivate making multiple searches available in the same view. Andolina et al. [3] showed benefits of letting the user work on multiple exploratory searches with intent modeling in parallel, where each user search query and related visualization is denoted as a "stream". They showed side-by-side streams and allowed keyword dragging from one stream to another. This requires each keyword to be transferred separately and assigned a suitable relevance weight, and the result does not yield an intersection of the information needs; our proposed approach is much simpler for the user, combining two entire streams in two mouse clicks.

A challenge for exploratory search and information retrieval are difficult queries [10,22], where few or none of the top ranked documents are relevant. A recent work [27] showed interactive intent modeling [29] could resolve many difficult queries, but in some queries positive relevance feedback did not sufficiently improve relevance of top documents; adding negative relevance feedback improved such search results. Our new system further improves performance on difficult queries; an example is seeking documents that should contain multiple subtopics, e.g. "machine learning" and "mobile phones" in each document.

Combining evidence from multiple queries [2,6,13] and combining data sources for a query [35] are shown to improve results, motivating a system to aid in combining queries. However, interactive systems for combining evidence are missing. Some work on exploratory search uses interactive visualizations [3,20,23,27,29,30], but without combinations of search streams, which we emphasize in this work.

We address a crucial need of users working with multiple exploratory search streams: a user may want to find what is in common between two searches, and what is the difference between them. In the previous example, given two queries "machine learning" and "mobile phones" a user may want to find documents relevant to both queries (both "machine learning" and "mobile phones"), or documents relevant to one but not the other (relevant to "machine learning" but not to "mobile phones"). Simple set-theoretic operations on queries or on document sets would not suffice for these needs; for example, a query with the concatenated query terms can return documents with keywords in only one set, but we need documents having keywords in both sets. To solve the problem, we introduce two operations between pairs of streams: **intersection** and **difference**. Intersection lets the user see what relevant content is in common between two search streams, and difference finds content relevant to one stream but not the other. They are inspired by set-theoretic analogues but are novel **operations on search intent models themselves**. The intent-model based operations result in novel probabilistic relevance-scoring methods. Both operations support exploration: they produce a new stream the user can interact with.

In this work we create the first exploratory visual system supporting operations on intent models. We provide a mathematically well-grounded solution for such operations. We support the user to visually explore the result, and direct the search, through a new visualized intent model. Our main contributions are:

1. **We address challenging exploratory search** where simple lookup search or naive Boolean operations on document lists/keyword filters are not enough. The user seeks documents relevant to an underlying information need rather than initial keywords; the user must find documents beyond initial ones and novel keywords leading to them. Our interactive intent modeling uses parallel search streams, probabilistic user intent modeling, operations on intent models, and interactive visualization for relevance feedback; through the models even relevant papers not having any original keywords can be found.
2. **Multiple streams.** Previous work [27,29,30] only considers individual streams. We extend the single-stream system in [27], allowing positive and negative feedback, to multiple streams shown side-by-side in one display. Each stream has its own intent model and result list; the user can interact with all streams.
3. **Novel operations.** We add novel interaction between these streams: operations that combine streams as intersections and differences. These operations go beyond simple set-theoretic Booleans of document list and keyword filters [31]: they operate on probabilistic intent models.
4. **Novel ranking.** We show that simple mathematics do not suffice for operations on intent models, and develop a new nontrivial solution yielding novel ranking criteria. We prove it works where a simple concatenation would not; and it produces a new intent model that can be further directed by the user.
5. **Exploration of potentially relevant keywords.** This is the first work with multiple streams including both relevant keywords and predicted future relevant keywords. Previous work on multiple streams [3] did not allow visual exploration of potentially relevant keywords.
6. We introduce a **visual interface** for exploring and combining multiple queries. Prior work only supports a single query [27,29,30], lacks operations between queries [3], or only facilitated query construction [31].

We demonstrate our system on exploratory search of scientific articles, although it is applicable to other domains. We compare to Peltonen et al. [27].

2   Directing and Combining Queries

We propose an exploratory search system that allows multiple streams side by side and enables operations between streams. Each stream is based on the UI and

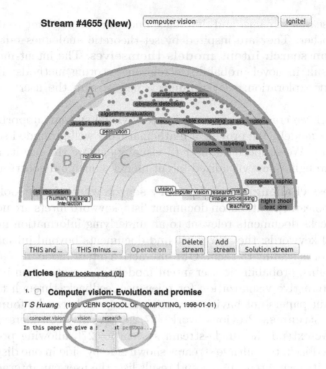

Fig. 1. A single search stream: query box at the top, visualization as a half-circle radar of keywords below, operation buttons below the visualization and article list at the bottom. The ten most relevant keywords are displayed in area C, predicted future relevant keywords in area B, and unwanted keywords in area A when negative feedback is given. Relevance +1 or −1 can be given to keywords in the article list using a pop-up button D. See https://github.com/strahl2e/OpsOnExploratorySearchIntentModels for high-resolution Figs. 1–2.

model of [27], represented both by a ranked document list and by a visualization of the estimated search intent as relevant keywords organized in a radar-like interactive visualization, see Fig. 1; for an example with multiple streams side by side, see Fig. 2. We now present a walk-through of the interface.

The system in [29,30], further developed in [27], had a query box, a radar interface showing keyword relevance and the resulting list of documents retrieved; we made minor modifications to this design in order to more conveniently display multiple search streams side-by-side and added buttons for implementing our operations, see Fig. 1. On the radar, the ten keywords estimated to be most relevant are displayed in the inner area (C), with the most relevant closest to the center. The ten most unwanted keywords, i.e., those predicted to be most unwanted based on negative feedback, are in the outer area (A). The intermediate area (B) contains predicted future relevant keywords; the user can hover the mouse over the "bubbles" to enlarge them and show the text following the principle of "overview first, zoom and filter, then details on demand" [34]. Similar keywords are placed at a similar angle on the radar.

The user initializes a search by entering a query and clicking "Ignite" (Fig. 1). This displays the intent visualization and article results for the query.

Fig. 2. Result (left stream) of an intersection operation between "computer vision" (right) and "remote sensing" (middle).

Feedback on a Single Search. As in [27], a user can drag a keyword on the radar to give feedback: placing it in the center gives maximum relevance 1, in area C relevance drops linearly to 0 moving outwards, in area B it is 0 and in area A it drops linearly from 0 to −1 moving outwards, yielding negative feedback. Feedback +1 or −1 can also be given to a keyword in the document list by hovering over it and pressing a + or − pop-up button (D). Feedback can be given to multiple keywords; the search can then be updated by clicking the center of the radar. The search can be refined by repeating this process.

Multiple Query Streams. On pressing the "Add stream" button a new stream appears at the left end of the view. The user can inspect and give feedback to all streams in the view, scrolling left/right if needed. The user can make an intersection or difference operation on any two streams; this results in a new stream to the left of the view. Feedback can be given to the new streams and further intersection and difference operations can be applied to them. Users can also delete streams with the "Delete stream" button.

Stream Operations. An **intersection** operation between streams A and B is done by pressing the "THIS and ..." button on A and the "Operate on" button on B. This creates a new stream that shows a combination of keywords in A and B and ranks documents based on relevance to both searches, see Fig. 2. A **difference** operation between A and B is done by clicking "THIS minus ..." on A and the "Operate on" on B. This creates a new stream that shows keywords relevant to A but not B, and ranks documents relevant to A but not B.

3   Exploratory Search with Interactive Intent Modeling

An interactive intent model is a probabilistic representation of what content is relevant to the user, parameterized by keywords and their relevance. We describe the model of [27] and our modifications at different phases of exploratory search.

3.1   Initializing the Search Stream

Typing a query initializes the search. We use query likelihood with Jelinek-Mercer (JM) smoothing [43] to rank documents; initial query terms have weight 1. The top N (we use $N = 100$) ranked documents are retrieved. Keyword propagation is then applied: for each unique keyword from the top N documents that keyword is added to keyword sets of other documents containing it in the text. Instead of keeping the ranking from Lucene as in [27], we rerank the documents based on the propagated keywords, with a modified smoothing, see Sect. 3.4.

3.2   User Feedback

The user can give feedback to keywords to update the search. The intent model, with the accumulated user feedback, estimates relevance for all keywords; the relevance estimates are used to retrieve documents and draw the visualization.

A user feedback is a scalar $r_k \in [-1, 1]$ for a keyword $k \in \{1, 2, ..., M\}$, where M is the number of unique keywords. Each keyword has a TFIDF feature vector $\mathbf{x}_k \in \mathcal{R}^N$ over N documents. Multi-step transition smoothing [27] spreads influence of keywords to related documents: one step is $\mathbf{P} : [\mathbf{P}]_{ij} = \frac{[\mathbf{X}^\top \mathbf{X}]_{ij}}{\sum_{k=1}^{N} [\mathbf{X}^\top \mathbf{X}]_{ik}}$ and the Markov-transition matrix is $\mathbf{P}_{multi} = 0.5\mathbf{I} + 0.25\mathbf{P} + 0.1875\mathbf{P}^2 + 0.00625\mathbf{P}^3$, and the new keyword feature space becomes $\mathbf{X}_{new} = \mathbf{X}\mathbf{P}_{multi}$.

To address the problem of little user feedback, [27] uses exploration-exploitation: predicting relevance scores with upper confidence bounds (UCBs). We addressed a weakness in the LinRel [4] UCB model they used; linear regression can overemphasize uncertain keywords yielding UCB scores above the maximal relevance of 1. It could confuse users if such keywords were shown as top ones instead of those that received even maximal feedback. We instead use Gaussian process (GP) regression [36] so that $\hat{r}^{UCB}(\mathbf{x}) = E_f[f(\mathbf{x})] + \alpha Var_f[f(\mathbf{x})]$, where the expectation and variance are over the GP prior $f \sim GP(0, C(\mathbf{X}_{new}))$ with a radial basis kernel function C, and α controlling the amount of exploration; relevance spreads mostly to similar keywords and uncertain keywords are closer to 0.

3.3   Intent Visualization

The intent visualization represents user intent as keywords on a radial display [26,27]; users can explore the search space and give feedback. The visualization is computed from relevance UCBs (Sect. 3.2) to aid exploration (showing potentially relevant keywords) and exploitation (showing estimated relevant keywords).

For each keyword its relevance UCB is used as its radius. Their angles are organized by similarity: two keywords are considered similar *if their relevance predictions behave similarly with respect to relevance feedback*. A pseudo-feedback (value 1) is added in turn to each of the current inner top ten keywords, to infer new UCBs for all other keywords. The ten pseudo feedbacks thus yield for each keyword ten UCBs, which we collect into a vector representing how relevance of that keyword is affected by user feedback. Two keywords are considered similar if their length-normalized UCB vectors are similar. The neighborhood retrieval visualizer method [38] is used to map the keywords to one-dimensional angles so that similar keywords get neighboring angles on the radial display.

Intent models, UCBs, and optimized angular organization differentiate our display from previous radial search visualizations [24], and the handling of multiple streams and streams representing results of operations with intent models differentiates our display from previous interactive intent visualizations [27,29,30].

3.4   Document Retrieval

Query Expansion. With a UCB score for each keyword, the ten keywords with highest UCB scores are added to the existing query weighted by their UCB scores, and are the new inner keywords for the visualization in Sect. 3.3.

Retrieval. Using the reformulated query, the JM unigram language model is used to retrieve a new set of N top-ranking documents from the full collection.

As in [27], a query may include both wanted (positive-weighted) keywords and unwanted (negative-weighted) keywords. Consider a query $\mathcal{Q} = (\mathcal{K}, \mathcal{R})$ with keywords $\mathcal{K} = \{k_1, \ldots, k_R\}$ and their predicted UCB relevance weights $\mathcal{R} = \{r_1, \ldots, r_R\}$. Let us split the keywords into the set of positive keywords $\mathcal{K}^+ = \{k_1, \ldots, k_{R+}\}$ with weights $\mathcal{R}^+ = \{r_1, \ldots, r_{R+}\}$ and the set of negative keywords $\mathcal{K}^- = \{v_1, \ldots, v_{R-}\}$, whose weights $\mathcal{R}^- = \{w_1, \ldots, w_{R-}\}$ are absolute values of their original negative weights, for convenience of notation. The query likelihood ranking of a document d is based on the likelihood ratio

$$\frac{p(\mathcal{K}^+, \mathcal{R}^+ \mid d)}{p(\mathcal{K}^-, \mathcal{R}^- \mid d)} = \frac{p((k_1, r_1), \ldots, (k_{R+}, r_{R+}) \mid d)}{p((v_1, w_1), \ldots, (v_{R-}, w_{R-}) \mid d)} = \frac{\prod_{i=1}^{R^+} p(k_i \mid d)^{r_i}}{\prod_{i=1}^{R^-} p(v_i \mid d)^{w_i}}, \quad (1)$$

where $p(k_i|d)$ is the probability of generating keyword k_i from document d, $p(v_i|d)$ is the probability of generating unwanted keyword v_i, and the second equality follows because of the independence assumption.

The above principle is used for an original stream; streams created by stream operations require more advanced ranking of documents, described in Sect. 4.

Document Reranking. Documents are retrieved from the full collection with a unigram query-likelihood model scoring each document based on the title, keywords and abstract [27]; we rerank documents based on the propagated keywords only. The propagated keywords may be sparse, hence even with JM smoothing the ranking might not tell apart relevant documents; to mitigate the sparsity, we also reward documents for keywords that tend to co-occur with desired keywords. To do so, we introduce Markov transition smoothing, as described in Sect. 3.2, as an extra component of JM smoothing. The score for keyword k_i of query Q for the jth document from the N retrieved is $p(k_i|d_j) = (1 - \lambda - \beta)\tilde{p}(k_i|d_j) + \lambda p(k_i|C) + \beta[\mathbf{X}_{new}]_{ij}$, where d_j is the jth document, k_i is a query keyword at position i in the set of keywords, $\tilde{p}(k_i|d_j)$ is the keyword frequency in the document divided by document size, $p(k_i|C)$ is the collection probability for keyword k_i that we compute from the N retrieved top-ranking documents, $\lambda \in [0,1]$ and $\beta \in [0,1]$ are strengths of the collection smoothing and Markov-transition smoothing respectively: $\lambda + \beta \leq 1$. We do not renormalize $\mathbf{X}_{new}$ per document, which adds a small ranking preference towards documents well-connected in the transition graph.

4   Operations on Exploratory Search Queries

We motivate need for new operation mathematics, show a naive solution fails (Sect. 4.1) and explain **intersection** and **difference** operations (Sects. 4.2 and 4.3).

Simple Set-Theoretic Operations do not Suffice for Exploratory Search. If two search streams were simply finite unordered document sets $\mathcal{D}^A$ and $\mathcal{D}^B$, set-theoretic intersection $\mathcal{D}^A \cap \mathcal{D}^B$ would find all documents in common between the sets, and set-theoretic difference $\mathcal{D}^A \backslash \mathcal{D}^B = \mathcal{D}^A \cap (\mathcal{D}^B)^c$ would exclude all documents in B. However, in search streams this does not suffice:

- Ranks of documents are crucial: a search stream scores and ranks every document, hence the unordered sets $\mathcal{D}^A$ and $\mathcal{D}^B$ both contain the whole corpus (only with different rankings) and rank-unaware set-theoretic operations would do nothing (intersection) or yield an empty set (difference).
- For computational scalability, search systems do not score and rank every document in a corpus, but exclude low-relevance documents early on. Naive intersection of top documents does not suffice: for complicated scientific concepts, it is likely that top documents of any search stream are about that concept only (probabilistic query-based ranking criteria favor such results) so two streams are likely to have no top documents in common.
- Working with documents alone is not enough: in interactive search, each stream must represent a model of the user's search intent, here relevances of keywords, and incorporate user feedback. So operations must also produce a model of intent and its uncertainty to allow further exploration and feedback.

Naive Boolean searches for specific keywords also do not suffice in exploratory search: a hard Boolean requirement, such as "must include machine learning AND mobile phone", would not work to find documents about the underlying concept rather than the specific keywords. Our novelty is enabling operations for this exploratory task, as combinations of intent models and corresponding probabilistic rankings rather than hard Boolean constraints, and integrating them in an interactive system where visualizations suggest related concepts.

4.1   Intersection Operation

The intersection operation aims to find documents relevant to two search streams. Next, we show that a naive query likelihood scoring, resulting from a naive Boolean AND operation of two search queries, is not sufficient to find documents relevant to both searches; then we introduce our model and its scoring.

Naive Scoring Fails for Ranking Intersecting Results. Given two queries we wish to rank highly documents that are relevant to both queries. If one simply concatenates the keywords of both queries and ranks them with a query likelihood model, the highest ranking documents may only contain positive keywords from one query. We formalize this problem as follows.

Lemma 1. *When documents are ranked by a query likelihood language model with a bag-of-words document representation, a Boolean AND operation between two queries Q^A and Q^B can yield higher scores for documents without intersecting terms than for documents with intersecting terms.*

Proof. The contents of a query are its keywords and their relevances $(\mathcal{K}, \mathcal{R}) = \{(k_i, r_i)\}_{i=1}^{R}$. For simplicity, we assume each query contains only positive keywords so that $(\mathcal{K}^+, \mathcal{R}^+) = (\mathcal{K}, \mathcal{R})$. In a query likelihood model, the query is treated as an observed random event and documents are ranked by the probability to generate the event; two queries $Q^A = (\mathcal{K}^A, \mathcal{R}^A) = \{(k_i^A, r_i^A)\}_{i=1}^{R^A}$ and $Q^B = (\mathcal{K}^B, \mathcal{R}^B) = \{(k_i^B, r_i^B)\}_{i=1}^{R^B}$ are treated as two events, and a Boolean AND means both events have happened; the query likelihood for a document is then the probability to generate both events simultaneously from the document.

Let document d contain a set of keywords $\mathcal{T}_d$. For simplicity, assume the probability $p(k|d)$ to generate a keyword k has a uniformly high value ϕ for all $k \in \mathcal{T}_d$ and a uniformly low value γ for other keywords, as would happen with document smoothing. The likelihood ratio (1) has a constant denominator for a query Q with positive keywords; the numerator becomes the query likelihood

$$\prod_{i=1}^{R} p(k_i|d)^{r_i} = \phi^{\left(\sum_{i:k_i \in Q \cap \mathcal{T}_d} r_i\right)} \cdot \gamma^{\left(\sum_{i:k_i \in Q \setminus \mathcal{T}_d} r_i\right)}.$$

The query likelihood is the probability that the content of query Q is generated by document d from its language model. The probability to generate two queries $(\mathcal{K}^A, \mathcal{R}^A)$ and $(\mathcal{K}^B, \mathcal{R}^B)$ is the product of their independent probabilities; in the resulting query likelihood, exponents of ϕ and γ can be divided into six terms:

$$\left(\prod_{i=1}^{R^A} p(k_i^A|d)^{r_i^A}\right)\left(\prod_{i=1}^{R^B} p(k_i^B|d)^{r_i^B}\right) = \phi^{r^{A,d}+r^{B,d}+r^{A,B,d}} \cdot \gamma^{r^A+r^B+r^{A,B}},$$

where $r^{A,d} = \sum_{i:k_i \in (\mathcal{K}^A \setminus \mathcal{K}^B) \cap \mathcal{T}_d} r_i^A$, $r^{B,d} = \sum_{i:k_i \in (\mathcal{K}^B \setminus \mathcal{K}^A) \cap \mathcal{T}_d} r_i^B$, $r^{A,B,d} = \sum_{i:k_i \in (\mathcal{K}^A \cap \mathcal{K}^B) \cap \mathcal{T}_d} (r_i^A + r_i^B)$, $r^A = \sum_{i:k_i \in (\mathcal{K}^A \setminus \mathcal{K}^B) \setminus \mathcal{T}_d} r_i^A$, $r^B = \sum_{i:k_i \in (\mathcal{K}^B \setminus \mathcal{K}^A) \setminus \mathcal{T}_d} r_i^B$, $r^{A,B} = \sum_{i:k_i \in (\mathcal{K}^A \cap \mathcal{K}^B) \setminus \mathcal{T}_d} (r_i^A + r_i^B)$. Clearly, only the total of the terms in each exponent matters: a document can get a high query likelihood even if it has keywords from one query only, for example several keywords in $(\mathcal{K}^A \setminus \mathcal{K}^B) \cap \mathcal{T}_d$ which yields a high $r^{A,d}$ value, even if the two other terms in the exponent of ϕ are zero. Thus naive query likelihood does not suffice to rank documents by how well they generate terms from two or more sets of terms.

4.2 Ranking for Intersecting Documents

To find documents relevant to two search intent models, and avoid the problem illustrated in Lemma 1, we introduce a novel query likelihood that ranks documents based on the joint probability of generating a keyword from one search stream and a different keyword from another search stream. We consider two queries, each of which may contain both positive and negative keywords, $\mathcal{Q}^A = (\mathcal{K}^{A,+}, \mathcal{R}^{A,+}, \mathcal{K}^{A,-}, \mathcal{R}^{A,-})$ and $\mathcal{Q}^B = (\mathcal{K}^{B,+}, \mathcal{R}^{B,+}, \mathcal{K}^{B,-}, \mathcal{R}^{B,-})$. Our probabilistic ranking for an intersection can be interpreted as a special query likelihood model for the positive keywords: the probability to generate two different keywords such that one is relevant to query A and the other to query B. This is computed based on several probabilities: the probability $p(k, k' \mid d)$ to generate a pair of keywords k and k' from a document d, the probability $p(k \in A)$ that the first keyword is relevant to stream A, the probability $p(k' \in B)$ that the second keyword is relevant to stream B, and the probability $p(k \neq k')$ that the two keywords are different.

We also want to penalize documents for being able to generate negative (unwanted) keywords of the two queries, i.e., keywords in either $(\mathcal{K}^{A,-}, \mathcal{R}^{A,-})$ or $(\mathcal{K}^{B,-}, \mathcal{R}^{B,-})$. This yields a document score interQL which is a likelihood ratio:

$$
\begin{aligned}
interQL(\mathcal{K} \mid d) &= \frac{p(k \text{ rel. to } A, \text{ distinct } k' \text{ rel. to } B|d)}{p(v \text{ or } v' \text{ an unwanted keyword } |d)} \\
&= \frac{\sum_{k,k' \in \mathcal{K}^+} p(k,k' \mid d)p(k \text{ rel. to } A)p(k' \text{ rel. to } B)p(k \neq k')}{\sum_{v,v' \in \mathcal{K}^-} p(v,v' \mid d)p(v \text{ or } v' \text{ unwanted in } A \text{ or } B)} \\
&= \frac{\sum_{k,k' \in \mathcal{K}^+} p(k \mid d)p(k' \mid d)r_k^A r_{k'}^B \delta_{k \neq k'}}{2(\sum_{v \in \mathcal{K}^-} p(v \mid d)w_v) - (\sum_{v \in \mathcal{K}^-} p(v \mid d)w_v)^2}, \quad (2)
\end{aligned}
$$

where $\mathcal{K}^+ = \mathcal{K}^{A,+} \cup \mathcal{K}^{B,+}$ and $\mathcal{K}^- = \mathcal{K}^{A,-} \cup \mathcal{K}^{B,-}$ are the unions of the positive and negative keyword sets of the two queries, and $\delta_{k \neq k'} = 1$ if $k \neq k'$ and 0 otherwise. We use the relevance values as probabilities that the keywords are relevant: $p(k \text{ rel. to } A) = r_k^A \in [0,1]$ and similarly for $r_{k'}^B$. In the denominator, either keyword can independently be unwanted, in either query or in both, thus in the result we denote $w_v = p(v \text{ unwanted in } A \text{ or } B) = w_v^A + w_v^B - w_v^A w_v^B$, which reduces to $w_v = \max(w_v^A, w_v^B)$ if the unwanted sets are nonoverlapping.

This probabilistic score solves the issue presented in Lemma 1, as shown next.

Lemma 2. *In an intersection of queries A and B having positive keywords, interQL (2) ranks documents such that documents having intersecting content rank higher than documents without such content.*

Proof. Consider two queries A and B. Assume for simplicity each query contains only positive keywords. Let document d contain a set of keywords $\mathcal{T}_d$. Assume the probability $p(k|d)$ to generate a keyword k has a uniform high value ϕ for all $k \in \mathcal{T}_d$ and a uniform low value γ for other keywords. Then only the numerator of (2) is relevant and becomes

$$\sum_{k,k' \in \mathcal{K}^{A,+} \cup \mathcal{K}^{B,+}} p(k \mid d)p(k' \mid d)r_k^A r_{k'}^B \delta_{k \neq k'}$$

$$= \sum_{k \in \mathcal{K}^{A,+} \cap \mathcal{T}_d, k' \in \mathcal{K}^{B,+} \cap \mathcal{T}_d} \phi^2 r_k^A r_{k'}^B \delta_{k \neq k'} + \sum_{k \in \mathcal{K}^{A,+} \setminus \mathcal{T}_d, k' \in \mathcal{K}^{B,+} \cap \mathcal{T}_d} \gamma \phi r_k^A r_{k'}^B$$

$$+ \sum_{k \in \mathcal{K}^{A,+} \cap \mathcal{T}_d, k' \in \mathcal{K}^{B,+} \setminus \mathcal{T}_d} \phi \gamma r_k^A r_{k'}^B + \sum_{k \in \mathcal{K}^{A,+} \setminus \mathcal{T}_d, k' \in \mathcal{K}^{B,+} \setminus \mathcal{T}_d} \gamma^2 r_k^A r_{k'}^B \delta_{k \neq k'},$$

where the latter three sums are small as γ is low compared to ϕ; thus the rank of the document is mainly determined by the first sum. That sum is over pairs (k, k') with $k \neq k'$, such that $k \in \mathcal{K}^{A,+} \cap \mathcal{T}_d$ and $k' \in \mathcal{K}^{B,+} \cap \mathcal{T}_d$, so document d must contain at least one term from $\mathcal{K}^{A,+}$ and a different term from $\mathcal{K}^{B,+}$ to get a nonzero value of this sum. It is then easy to see that such a document scores higher, and thus outranks, another document having zero terms in the first sum, as long as the probability ϕ is sufficiently higher than γ.

Lemma 2 shows our formulation solves the limitation of traditional query likelihood in Lemma 1. While other formulations with such benefit are possible, to our knowledge ours is the first solution and yields good results in experiments.

Ideally we would rank all documents with our probabilistic intersection ranking, but in very large corpuses computational efficiency is key. We thus propose to first use a special unigram query-likelihood based ranking, detailed below, to retrieve a subset of documents, and then rerank them by InterQL. The advantage is that this first-stage retrieval is directly implementable in efficient packages like Apache Lucene, and still yields good enough documents.

First-Stage Retrieval for Intersection by Unigram Query Likelihood.

We use a special unigram query likelihood retrieval to filter out low-scoring documents as nonrelevant; then rerank the higher-scoring documents with interQL.

Unigram Query Likelihood Retrieval: Keyword Weight Balancing. We build a unigram query (with JM smoothing in Apache Lucene) from the two original queries for an intersection of streams A and B, with their weighted keywords $(\mathcal{K}^A, \mathcal{R}^A)$ and $(\mathcal{K}^B, \mathcal{R}^B)$, by concatenating the relevance-weighted keywords and balancing the weights so that the resulting L highest ranking documents are maximally relevant to both queries ($L = 100$ in experiments). We found that if we simply use given weights for keywords and multiply the query likelihood ratios for A and B of Eq. (1), top ranked documents are often only related to one of the searches, so we apply a search strategy to balance the weight for each search. The unigram query likelihood ratio of (1) is then

$$\left(\prod_{i=1}^{R^Q} p(k_i|d)\right) \left(\frac{\prod_{i=1}^{R^{A+}} p(k_i|d)^{r_i}}{\prod_{i=1}^{R^{A-}} p(v_i|d)^{w_i}}\right)^{\beta} \left(\frac{\prod_{i=1}^{R^{B+}} p(k_i|d)^{r_i}}{\prod_{i=1}^{R^{B-}} p(v_i|d)^{w_i}}\right)^{2-\beta},$$

where the first product is over the R^Q keywords in the concatenated query, other products are over the predicted relevant keywords of A and B, and $\beta \in [0,2]$ is a balancing factor. An efficient strategy to find a good value of β is to choose a set of values and run them in parallel, then pick the one that maximizes the number of documents having a non-empty positive-set intersection $(\mathcal{K}^{A+} \cap \mathcal{K}^{B+}) \cap \mathcal{T}_d$.

Before the balancing is applied, we: 1) normalize weights in A and B to have the same sum (average of their original sums); 2) multiply weights of keywords in $\mathcal{K}^A \cap \mathcal{K}^B$ by 1/2 to avoid one shared keyword dominating the score of a document. This is to ensure enough good documents are near the top.

Selecting Keywords from Intersecting Searches. *Inner Keywords.* For the ten inner keywords on the visualization of a new intersection search we use the top keywords from each search (top five in the experiments) in the operation. If the two keyword sets have no keywords in common we concatenate the two sets. If the same keyword is in common to both streams, it is added only once, we then add a new keyword from the stream that had higher UCB for the keyword in common, ensuring we get ten unique high-ranking keywords from both streams.

Ranking. In an intersection of searches A and B we use 20 keywords to rank documents according to (2), 10 each from A and B, selected similarly as above.

Removal of "Covered" Unigram Keywords. Keywords with more than one term (e.g. "machine learning") are decomposed into unigrams during efficient retrieval. These introduced unigrams can dominate the intersection ranking due to being more common, but worsen the results due to being generic single words. To solve this, if a unigram and a larger n-gram containing ("covering") it appear in a document, for document ranking we omit the covered unigram.

Feedback on an Intersection. An intersection stream has two underlying intent models. Each inner keyword on the visualization belongs to one of the models; feedback on it goes to that model. Keywords in the intermediate area of the visualization use average UCB values from both models making it unclear which model should get the feedback. For such a keyword, we aim to assign feedback to the intent that the keyword is more related to. We assign the feedback to the model with the smallest uncertainty for the keyword: keywords with small uncertainty in our intent model either already have feedback or are similar to ones with feedback, and are thus likely to be related to the intent of that model.

4.3 Difference Operation

A difference operation returns documents relevant to one stream A and not relevant to the other stream B. Its components are constructed as follows.

Query-Text. As it represents desired content, we set it to the query-text of A.

Feedback Sets. Differing amounts of feedback in A and B should not make a difference operation overly favor either stream in document ranking or keyword scoring. To ensure an equal role for both streams we take the top-five relevant keywords from A, and give positive implicit feedback to the new stream, and we take the top-five relevant keywords from B, and give negative implicit feedback.

Intent model. With the query and feedback we infer the intent model and learn relevance estimates of all keywords (Sect. 3.2), with TFIDF vectors for keywords computed using the set of $2N$ documents from both original searches.

Given the intent model, we run visualization and retrieval (Sects. 3.3 and 3.4).

5 User Experiments

User experiments investigate the effect of the intersection and difference operations. We compare two versions of the same system, one with our two operations (ours) and the other with them disabled (baseline). The single-stream behavior of both systems corresponds to the state-of-the-art system in [27], modified as detailed at the end of Sect. 3.4. Comparison between the system with negative feedback [27] and without it [29] is in [27], and between [29] and a common typed query system is in [29]; thus we focus on the effects of our two operations.

Hypothesis*: With the intersection and difference operations in our system, the user reaches (1) more relevant results (2) more easily and faster.*

5.1 Task Design

The baseline exploratory search system gives support beyond standard queries or keyword-only search [29]. As it is a well-performing system, we do not claim multiple searches and operations between them yield strong benefit in all exploratory tasks—if the user aims to narrow down on one topic, exploration with one stream may suffice; even in some initially difficult queries negative feedback to the stream may yield good results [27]. We thus focus on those difficult queries where such easy fixes do not work, as discussed in Sect. 1. Recent studies of user-perceived causes of difficult queries revealed multiple subtopics as a main cause [22]. Our intersection operation is designed to rank documents relevant to multiple streams, essentially multiple subtopics, so we focus on difficult queries with multiple subtopics. We explored a number of tasks with multiple subtopics, where the user's goal is to find what is in common between the subtopics. Many could be resolved with single-stream relevance feedback, with enough effort. For the user study we chose three exploratory search tasks that were challenging for the single stream system: 1. "machine learning" and "signal processing", 2. "machine learning" and "mobile phones" and 3. "sparse regression" and "expectation maximization". In each task, the user's goal is to make the top ten ranked documents relevant to the topic of the task, which is a combination of subtopics.

5.2 Experiment Setup

As our experiment is on scientific papers we used computer science university students as a realistic user group. The 17 participants (14 male, 3 female) were PhD (13), MSc (2), and BSc (1) students and 1 postdoc, all experienced search engine users. They were given the three information seeking tasks (Sect. 5.1) to be performed on both systems. We also asked about familiarity about the topics in our tasks. Each user had a HP EliteBook laptop, 24" monitor, mouse, and keyboard. They were shown a ten-minute instructional video on the system, and had five minutes practice on each system before starting the tasks.

We used a balanced within-subjects study design: each user completed all three tasks on both systems. Tasks and systems were ordered with a counterbalanced design to reduce learning bias: for each task essentially equally many users completed it first on our system vs. first on the baseline, and for each task essentially equally many users completed it as the first/second/third task. Users could stop when satisfied; after ten minutes they were requested to finalize and submit their remaining feedback and then stop, ensuring overall experiment time was not excessive. They clicked a button below the stream they considered to have the most relevant top ten documents to denote it as the solution stream. After completing the tasks, users filled in a user satisfaction questionnaire with 25 questions based on two established frameworks: ResQue [28] and SUS [8].

Data. Both systems used the same data: about 50 million articles from Web of Science, ACM, IEEE, and Springer.

System Setup. For the intent model we used an RBF kernel for GP-UCB, where we tuned the width parameter using distances to three nearest neighbors on data samples, and chose a small exploration parameter $\alpha = 0.1$ tuned by testing searches. For the language model (Sect. 3.4), following [43], we set the multi-step Markov transition smoothing parameter and the collection probability smoothing parameter to small values $\beta = 0.05$ and $\lambda = 0.05$.

5.3 Evaluation of Results

Retrieval Performance. We collected all the top ten documents from the solution stream of each user for each task on each system, leaving 17 (users) $\times$ 3 (tasks) $\times$ 2 (systems) = 102 result sets of ten documents. For each task, we extracted the list of unique documents from the result sets. Three evaluators (the authors) then gave each unique document a relevance score of 0=certainly not relevant, 1=likely not relevant, 2=likely relevant, 3=certainly relevant without knowledge

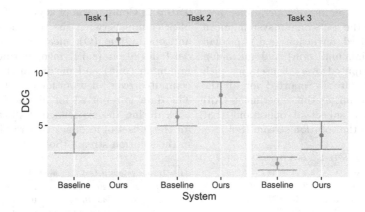

Fig. 3. Discounted cumulative gain (DCG) for tasks 1–3 for the baseline (red) and our system (cyan). Bars are 95% confidence intervals. DCG ranges from 0 (no relevant documents) to 13.6 (all documents certainly relevant).

of which result set(s) the document belonged to. Each evaluator scored independently (average inter-rater correlations in tasks 1–3: 0.75; 0.87; 0.67); the evaluators then discussed discrepancies and came to consensus for each document score. We used discounted cumulative gain (DCG) [19] on the relevance scores of the top ten documents to reward the system for ranking relevant documents higher. Figure 3 shows the mean DCG score for the top ten documents for each task and system, including the 95% confidence interval, over the 17 users. Our system yields clearly better results than the baseline. The improvement is statistically significant: repeated measures 2-way ANOVA with users as subjects, performing each task on each system, showed a statistical significance for the system effect (p-value < 0.01). We also verified by another repeated measures 2-way ANOVA that the presentation order of the tasks and systems to the users did not have a statistically significant effect. Thus it is clear from the results that operations gave an overall advantage, especially for task 1.

Task Speed. We recorded task durations, and computed the average time for each task on each system. With one-way repeated measures ANOVA tasks 2 and 3 showed no statistically significant difference, but task 1 had a statistically significant difference (p-value $< 10^{-5}$): average task time was 563 s on the baseline and 258 s on our system, thus operations made the search faster.

User interaction. Tables 1 and 2 contain statistics of the counts of all stream operations and feedbacks executed by each user. Users took advantage of the operations: all users used operations in all tasks. On average users made several intersection operations for each task, but the difference operation was used only occasionally. Moreover, with the operations users had less need of keyword feedback: they needed clearly less feedback on our system to arrive at their solutions.

Our system yielded results quickly with few operations and little feedback. As shown in Table 1, for task 1 most users needed only one intersection, and as shown

Table 1. Counts of operations performed by the users on our system: mean (μ), standard deviation (s.d.), median (med), minimum (min) and maximum (max) computed over all users for each task. The data is reported for all the operations during the experiment (All) and for the subset of operations that resulted in the solution stream (Sol.).

Action	Data	Task	μ (s.d.)	Med	Min	Max
Intersection	All	1	2.2 (1.9)	1	1	6
	Sol.	1	0.9 (0.2)	1	0	1
	All	2	5.8 (2.2)	7	2	9
	Sol.	2	1 (0.4)	1	0	2
	All	3	5.6 (2.3)	6	1	10
	Sol.	3	1.2 (1.0)	1	0	4
Difference	All	1	0 (0)	0	0	0
	Sol.	1	0 (0)	0	0	0
	All	2	0.3 (0.7)	0	0	3
	Sol.	2	0.1 (0.2)	0	0	1
	All	3	0.6 (1.5)	0	0	5
	Sol.	3	0.2 (0.4)	0	0	1

Table 2. Comparison of keyword feedback counts between the baseline (B) and our system (O): mean (μ), standard deviation (s.d.), median (med), minimum (min) and maximum (max) computed over all users for each task. The data is reported for all the feedback during the experiment (All) and for the subset of feedback that resulted in the solution stream (Sol.).

Task	Data	System	μ (s.d.)	Med	Min	Max
1	All	B	20.2 (12.8)	17	3	53
		O	4.5 (6.3)	0	0	18
	Sol.	B	13.6 (14.0)	12	0	47
		O	3.1 (6.2)	0	0	18
2	All	B	29.1 (16.8)	24	5	65
		O	18.2 (11.7)	14	2	39
	Sol.	B	18.1 (21.6)	8	0	65
		O	11.1 (13.0)	6	0	39
3	All	B	23.1 (17.5)	20	2	77
		O	19.1 (17.7)	13	2	68
	Sol.	B	10.9 (9.6)	8	0	34
		O	13.7 (17.6)	8	0	68

in Table 2 often without further tuning, to easily get good results outperforming the baseline in speed and result quality. On the baseline, users did not achieve corresponding result quality even with multiple feedback. Tasks 2 and 3 show similar behavior. The only case where users of our system used more feedback than on the baseline was for their solution stream (Sol.) of task 3, but even there the total amount of feedback (All) was smaller on our system than on the baseline. Thus, having operations yields good results with less effort and faster.

Intersections were used both for exploration and for constructing the solution: in all tasks, the total count of intersections (All) in Table 1 is greater than the count for solution streams (Sol.). The difference operation was much less used, but was used in up to three operations per user in task 2 and five in task 3 and contributing to solution streams in those tasks. From interaction data on our system, we found users preferred to make operations first and fine-tune later: a 74% majority of feedback was given to streams produced by an operation.

Serendipity. Unlike manual query construction, intent modeling predicts likely relevant keywords that the user did not directly type, and likely relevant documents having those keywords. This enables finding serendipitous documents: non-trivial relevant documents that are not found by naive filtering for query keywords. Our system allows combining intent models, maintaining the advantage of serendipity in the results. We evaluate serendipity in top ten results for each task and system by counting the total number of serendipitous documents found by the users, i.e., relevant documents that did not contain the query terms of the original queries and would not be found by a logical AND of two queries.

Table 3. User feedback. Average scores and p-values between the baseline (B) and our system (O), for each question and group of questions (bold font). Responses on a Likert scale: strongly disagree = -2, disagree = -1, neither agree or disagree = 0, agree = 1, strongly agree = 2. We reversed scores for questions where disagree was better (marked with *), so higher numbers are always better. See full table at https://github.com/strahl2e/OpsOnExploratorySearchIntentModels.

Question	B	O	p-value
I. Quality of Recommended Items	0.2	0.9	$2 \cdot 10^{-6}$
1. The keywords displayed to me matched the search objective	0.5	1.2	$6 \cdot 10^{-4}$
2. The articles displayed to me matched the search objective	0.2	1.2	$2 \cdot 10^{-5}$
3. The system produced good results	-0.2	1.1	$3 \cdot 10^{-6}$
4. The system helps me discover new articles	0.7	1.3	0.03
5. The articles displayed to me are similar to each other*	0.0	-0.2	0.33
II. Interaction Adequacy	-0.4	0.8	$2 \cdot 10^{-5}$
6. The search streams provides an adequate way for me to conduct my search	-0.7	1.0	$3 \cdot 10^{-5}$
7. The keyword feedback provides an adequate way for me to refine my search	0.0	0.6	0.04
IV. Perceived Ease of Use	-0.4	0.8	$8 \cdot 10^{-6}$
10. I easily found the articles that were relevant to my search	-0.5	0.8	$3 \cdot 10^{-6}$
11. It is easy to learn to tell the system what to search for	-0.4	1.1	$3 \cdot 10^{-5}$
12. I feel in control of telling the system what I want	-0.4	0.8	$1 \cdot 10^{-3}$
13. I understood why the articles were recommended to me	-0.1	0.7	$4 \cdot 10^{-3}$
V. Attitude	-0.3	1.0	$1 \cdot 10^{-5}$
14. Overall, I am satisfied with the system	-0.3	1.0	$1 \cdot 10^{-5}$
VI. Behavioral Intentions	0.3	0.7	$5 \cdot 10^{-4}$
15. If a system such as this exists, I would use it to find scientific articles	-0.2	1.1	$3 \cdot 10^{-6}$
16. I think I would use this system frequently if given the opportunity	-0.4	0.6	$2 \cdot 10^{-4}$
21. I thought there was too much inconsistency in the system*	-0.1	0.5	0.01
24. I felt very confident using the system	-0.1	0.4	$7 \cdot 10^{-3}$

Both systems find serendipitous documents; our system finds 55, 72, and 22 serendipitous documents in tasks 1, 2, and 3 respectively, overall better than the baseline, which found 56, 58, and 14.

User satisfaction. In our feedback questionnaire, users were most satisfied with our system. We ran a 1-way repeated measures ANOVA for each question. Table 3 shows the 15 questions with statistically significant difference between systems (p-value < 0.05) out of the 25 questions in total. All significant differences favor our system. Users had better results, keywords, and articles, could conduct and refine the search better, found articles more easily, learned more easily to use the system effectively and felt more in control, were more satisfied, and would use the system and use it more frequently. Thus users had a clearly better experience on our system for these tasks.

The questions in Table 3 were divided into six groups: Quality of Recommended Items (questions 1–5), Interaction Adequacy (6–7), Interface Adequacy (8–9), Perceived Ease of Use (10–13), Attitude (14) and Behavioral Intentions (15–25). Group-wise difference between systems was tested by 2-way repeated measures ANOVA per group, with users as subjects and question and system as factors. The Interface Adequacy group of questions showed no statistically significant difference (thus omitted from Table 3) showing that the addition of the operations did not hurt ability to operate the interface. All other groups had a significant difference, and all significant differences again favor our system.

6   Conclusions and Discussion

We address multiple parallel searches and highlight the complexity of combining user models for exploratory search. As shown in Sect. 4, simple set-theoretic operations on documents or queries do not suffice. We described a novel system with an interactive visual interface, supporting intersection and difference of search streams. The system allows relevance feedback to the keywords in an interactive visual interface, and involves novel document scoring and keyword exploration models. Our experimental results validate our hypothesis that stream operations improve user performance and satisfaction on difficult queries with multiple subtopics: results were clearly better for all three tasks, average time of task one was clearly lower, and users stated in the questionnaire they found relevant documents more easily. Future work could include experiments on further domains and extension to collaborative search.

References

1. Ahn, J., Brusilovsky, P.: Adaptive visualization for exploratory information retrieval. Inf. Process. Manag. **49**(5), 1139–1164 (2013). https://doi.org/10.1016/j.ipm.2013.01.007
2. Anava, Y., Shtok, A., Kurland, O., Rabinovich, E.: A probabilistic fusion framework. In: Proceedings of the 25th ACM International Conference on Information and Knowledge Management (CIKM'16), pp. 1463–1472. ACM (2016)
3. Andolina, S., et al.: IntentStreams: smart parallel search streams for branching exploratory search. In: Proceedings of the 20th International Conference on Intelligent User Interfaces (IUI'15), pp. 300–305. ACM (2015)
4. Auer, P.: Using confidence bounds for exploitation-exploration trade-offs. J. Mach. Learn. Res. **3**(Nov), 397–422 (2002)
5. Backhausen, D.T.J.: Adaptive IR for exploratory search support. In: Proceedings of the 35th International ACM SIGIR Conference on Research and Development in Information Retrieval (SIGIR'12), p. 992. ACM (2012). https://doi.org/10.1145/2348283.2348416

6. Belkin, N.J., Kantor, P., Fox, E.A., Shaw, J.A.: Combining the evidence of multiple query representations for information retrieval. Inf. Process. Manag. **31**(3), 431–448 (1995). https://doi.org/10.1016/0306-4573(94)00057-A

7. Bilenko, M., White, R.W.: Mining the search trails of surfing crowds: identifying relevant websites from user activity. In: Proceedings of the 17th International Conference on World Wide Web (WWW'08), pp. 51–60. ACM (2008)

8. Brooke, J.: SUS: A 'quick and dirty' usability scale. In: Jordan, P. W., Thomas, B., McClelland, I. L., Weerdmeester B. (eds.) Usability Evaluation In Industry, pp. 189–194. Taylor & Francis (1996)

9. Byström, K., Kumpulainen, S.: Vertical and horizontal relationships amongst task-based information needs. Inf. Process. Manag. **57**(2), 102065 (2020). https://doi.org/10.1016/j.ipm.2019.102065

10. Carmel, D., Yom-Tov, E., Darlow, A., Pelleg, D.: What makes a query difficult? In: Proceedings of the 29th Annual International ACM SIGIR Conference on Research and Development in Information Retrieval (SIGIR'06), pp. 390–397. ACM (2006)

11. Chang, J.C., Hahn, N., Kittur, A.: Mesh: Scaffolding comparison tables for online decision making. In: Proceedings of the 33rd Annual ACM Symposium on User Interface Software and Technology (UIST'20), pp. 391–405. ACM (2020). https://doi.org/10.1145/3379337.3415865

12. Chang, J.C., Hahn, N., Perer, A., Kittur, A.: SearchLens: composing and capturing complex user interests for exploratory search. In: Proceedings of the 24th International Conference on Intelligent User Interfaces (IUI'19), pp. 498–509. ACM (2019). https://doi.org/10.1145/3301275.3302321

13. Croft, W.B.: Combining approaches to information retrieval. In: Croft, W.B. (ed.) Advances in Information Retrieval: Recent Research from the Center for Intelligent Information Retrieval, vol. 7, pp. 1–36. Springer, New York (2000). https://doi.org/10.1007/0-306-47019-5_1

14. Du, J.T., Evans, N.: Academic users' information searching on research topics: characteristics of research tasks and search strategies. J. Acad. Librariansh. **37**(4), 299–306 (2011). https://doi.org/10.1016/j.acalib.2011.04.003

15. Fluit, C., Sabou, M., van Harmelen, F.: Ontology-based information visualization: toward semantic web applications. In: Geroimenko, V., Chen, C. (eds.) Visualizing the Semantic Web: XML-based Internet and Information Visualization, pp. 45–58. Springer, Heidelberg (2002). https://doi.org/10.1007/1-84628-290-X_3

16. Hearst, M.A.: Search User Interfaces, 1st edn. Cambridge University Press, Cambridge (2009)

17. Huang, J., Lin, T., White, R.W.: No search result left behind: branching behavior with browser tabs. In: Proceedings of the Fifth ACM International Conference on Web Search and Data Mining (WSDM'12), pp. 203–212. ACM (2012)

18. Huang, J., White, R.W.: Parallel browsing behavior on the web. In: Proceedings of the 21st ACM Conference on Hypertext and Hypermedia (HT'10), pp. 13–18. ACM (2010)

19. Järvelin, K., Kekäläinen, J.: Cumulated gain-based evaluation of IR techniques. ACM Trans. Inf. Syst. (TOIS) **20**(4), 422–446 (2002)

20. Krishnamurthy, Y., Pham, K., Santos, A., Freire, J.: Interactive exploration for domain discovery on the web. In: Proceedings of the ACM KDD Workshop on Interactive Data Exploration and Analytics (IDEA'16), pp. 64–71 (2016)

21. Marchionini, G.: Exploratory search: from finding to understanding. Commun. ACM **49**(4), 41–46 (2006)

22. Mizzaro, S., Mothe, J.: Why do you think this query is difficult?: A user study on human query prediction. In: Proceedings of the 39th International ACM SIGIR Conference on Research and Development in Information Retrieval (SIGIR'16), pp. 1073–1076. ACM (2016)

23. Moraes, F., Santos, R.L., Ziviani, N.: On effective dynamic search in specialized domains. In: Proceedings of the ACM SIGIR International Conference on Theory of Information Retrieval (ICTIR'17), pp. 177–184. ACM (2017)

24. Nitsche, M., Nürnberger, A.: QUEST: querying complex information by direct manipulation. In: Yamamoto, S. (ed.) HIMI 2013. LNCS, vol. 8016, pp. 240–249. Springer, Heidelberg (2013). https://doi.org/10.1007/978-3-642-39209-2_28

25. Oppenlaender, J., Kuosmanen, E., Goncalves, J., Hosio, S.: Search support for exploratory writing. In: Lamas, D., Loizides, F., Nacke, L., Petrie, H., Winckler, M., Zaphiris, P. (eds.) INTERACT 2019. LNCS, vol. 11748, pp. 314–336. Springer, Cham (2019). https://doi.org/10.1007/978-3-030-29387-1_18

26. Peltonen, J., Belorustceva, K., Ruotsalo, T.: Topic-relevance map: visualization for improving search result comprehension. In: Proceedings of the 22nd International Conference on Intelligent User Interfaces (IUI'17), pp. 611–622. ACM (2017). https://doi.org/10.1145/3025171.3025223

27. Peltonen, J., Strahl, J., Floréen, P.: Negative relevance feedback for exploratory search with visual interactive intent modeling. In: Proceedings of the 22nd International Conference on Intelligent User Interfaces (IUI'17), pp. 149–159. ACM (2017). https://doi.org/10.1145/3025171.3025222

28. Pu, P., Chen, L., Hu, R.: A user-centric evaluation framework for recommender systems. In: Proceedings of the Fifth ACM Conference on Recommender Systems (RecSys'11), pp. 157–164. ACM (2011)

29. Ruotsalo, T., et al.: Directing exploratory search with interactive intent modeling. In: Proceedings of the 22nd ACM International Conference on Information and Knowledge Management (CIKM'13), pp. 1759–1764. ACM (2013)

30. Ruotsalo, T., et al.: Interactive intent modeling for exploratory search. ACM Trans. Inf. Syst. (TOIS) **36**(4), 44 (2018)

31. Russell-Rose, T., Chamberlain, J., Shokraneh, F.: A visual approach to query formulation for systematic search. In: Proceedings of the Conference on Human Information Interaction and Retrieval (CHIIR'19), pp. 379–383. ACM (2019)

32. di Sciascio, C., Sabol, V., Veas, E.E.: Rank as you go: user-driven exploration of search results. In: Proceedings of the 21st International Conference on Intelligent User Interfaces (IUI'16), pp. 118–129. ACM (2016). https://doi.org/10.1145/2856767.2856797

33. di Sciascio, C., Veas, E., Barria-Pineda, J., Culley, C.: Understanding the effects of control and transparency in searching as learning. In: Proceedings of the 25th International Conference on Intelligent User Interfaces (IUI'20), pp. 498–509. ACM (2020). https://doi.org/10.1145/3377325.3377524

34. Shneiderman, B.: The eyes have it: a task by data type taxonomy for information visualizations. In: Proceedings 1996 IEEE Symposium on Visual Languages, pp. 336–343 (1996)

35. Shokouhi, M., Si, L.: Federated search. Found. Trends Inf. Retr. **5**(1), 1–102 (2011). https://doi.org/10.1561/1500000010

36. Srinivas, N., Krause, A., Kakade, S., Seeger, M.: Gaussian process optimization in the bandit setting: no regret and experimental design. In: Proceedings of the 27th International Conference on Machine Learning (ICML'10), pp. 1015–1022. Omnipress (2010)

37. Umemoto, K., Yamamoto, T., Tanaka, K.: Search support tools. In: Fu, W.T., van Oostendorp, H. (eds.) Understanding and Improving Information Search. HIS, pp. 139–160. Springer, Cham (2020). https://doi.org/10.1007/978-3-030-38825-6_8
38. Venna, J., Peltonen, J., Nybo, K., Aidos, H., Kaski, S.: Information retrieval perspective to nonlinear dimensionality reduction for data visualization. J. Mach. Learn. Res. **11**(Feb), 451–490 (2010)
39. Verbert, K., Parra, D., Brusilovsky, P.: Agents vs. users: visual recommendation of research talks with multiple dimension of relevance. ACM Trans. Interact. Intell. Syst. (TiiS) **6**(2), 1–42 (2016). https://doi.org/10.1145/2946794
40. White, R.W., Roth, R.A.: Exploratory search: beyond the query-response paradigm. In: Synthesis Lectures on Information Concepts, Retrieval, and Services, Morgan & Claypool Publishers (2009)
41. Xiang, B., Jiang, D., Pei, J., Sun, X., Chen, E., Li, H.: Context-aware ranking in web search. In: Proceedings of the 33rd International ACM SIGIR Conference on Research and Development in Information Retrieval, SIGIR '10, pp. 451–458. Association for Computing Machinery, New York (2010). https://doi.org/10.1145/1835449.1835525
42. Yogev, S.: Exploratory search interfaces: blending relevance, diversity, relationships and categories. In: Proceedings of the Companion Publication of the 19th International Conference on Intelligent User Interfaces (IUI Companion '14), pp. 61–64. ACM (2014). https://doi.org/10.1145/2559184.2559187
43. Zhai, C., Lafferty, J.: A study of smoothing methods for language models applied to ad hoc information retrieval. In: Proceedings of the 24th Annual International ACM SIGIR Conference on Research and Development in Information Retrieval (SIGIR'01), pp. 334–342. ACM (2001)

Situated Visualization of Historical Timeline Data on Mobile Devices: Design Study for a Museum Application

Kerstin Blumenstein(✉), Victor Oliveira, Magdalena Boucher, Stefanie Größbacher, Markus Seidl, and Wolfgang Aigner

St. Pölten University of Applied Sciences, St. Pölten, Austria
{kerstin.blumenstein,victor.oliveira,magdalena.boucher,
stefanie.groessbacher,markus.seidl,wolfgang.aigner}@fhstp.ac.at

Abstract. Many museums offer mobile apps to extend the brief descriptions of physical exhibits. However, these apps often reproduce on-site content, are not location-aware, or demand several user interactions to view the content. Therefore, we propose using visitors' mobile devices to extend static information with time-oriented, situated information visualization. We present a design study using visualizations to guide visitors through an exhibition. In total, we performed two comparative studies: 1) with clickable mockups of three visualization concepts (Timeline, Bookshelf, and Timeflower), and based on these results, 2) with three functional prototypes of timeline visualization concepts (Stack-based, Section-based, and All-in-one) both in a lab and museum setting. Our main finding is, that museum visitors prefer familiar and linear visualization techniques. We reflect on our results and the process and define guidelines for future studies on visualization for casual users in museums.

Keywords: Information visualization · Mobile · Situated visualization · Casual user · Museum · Design study

1 Introduction

Although some research has already been done to augment exhibits in the museum (e.g., [30,40,41,46]), many exhibits are still passive and silent, i.e., the objects themselves do not provide any additional information or recommendations. This is why the artifacts are often augmented through short textual descriptions or explanations from a guide. However, commonly there is more data available than what can be written on a small plate or told in a short time (e.g., knowledge of curators or information in databases and documents). Using mobile devices to convey this extra information has been proven effective in several research projects [10,43].

Electronic supplementary material The online version of this chapter (https://doi.org/10.1007/978-3-030-85613-7_35) contains supplementary material, which is available to authorized users.

Fig. 1. Museum setting showing the visitor using the mobile application with visualization (a), the physical object in the museum (b), and Bluetooth beacons at exhibits telling the app where the user is located (c).

Many museums enable their visitors to download additional information to their smartphones (e.g., Mumok [42], Deutsches Museum [22]). However, this content is often identical to that presented within the exhibition. Besides, while most museum apps do offer maps and lists to assist users in navigation [23], the apps are not location-aware, and visitors still have to select the objects of interest themselves.

Providing a friendly and efficient user interface is crucial when conveying the vast amount of information behind an exhibition, so an app can also reach less experienced visitors and, thus, more users in general [44]. We believe this can be achieved through Information Visualization (InfoVis) methods. While there is much research on human-computer interaction in museums [31], the use of interactive data visualization in museums is still a growing area of research (e.g., [13,59]). Our research aims to bring the perspective of InfoVis to the visitors' mobile devices.

We conducted a design study to identify a suitable visualization for a location-aware mobile application that guides visitors through a museum exhibition (see Fig. 1). Our overall goal was to develop a visualization that is integrated into a mobile application for a museum exhibition. Therefore, we first explored three different visualization concepts and evaluated them in a lab test. In the second stage, we built upon the results of the first stage, developed variations of the preferred visualization concept, and evaluated them in both a lab and the actual museum setting. The main contributions of this work are:

- the design of situated, mobile visualization concepts, their prototypical implementation using web technologies and application in a real museum setting (Sect. 4.1 and 5.1),
- the results of two consecutive comparative studies (Sect. 4 and 5), as well as
- a set of lessons learned and implications about visualization & interaction and the insights derived from the study process (Sect. 6).

In the following, we will describe the background of our study and the design process (Sect. 2). We present relevant related work focusing on mobile devices in museums as well as on timeline visualization and InfoVis on mobile devices and in museums. Section 4 and 5 document the two performed iterations to evaluate visualization concepts. In Sect. 6, we reflect on the results and the design process.

2   Background and Design Process

The exhibition "Des Kaisers neuer Heiliger" (The Emperors New Saint) at the Klosterneuburg Monastery, Austria, told the stories of Emperor Maximilian I (Habsburg) and Margrave Leopold III (Babenberg) at a time of media in transition [56]. The exhibition was a mixture of the two extreme museum types (highly interactive science museums vs. do-not-touch art museums and galleries) described in [31]. Our study was performed in the context of this exhibition.

2.1   Method

We followed a design process with two iterations. First, we developed three basic visualization concepts and implemented them as clickable mockups for evaluation (Iteration 1). Based on the chosen timeline concept, we noticed there were multiple options for visualizing the data. Therefore, we conceived three concepts, which were developed as fully functional prototypes and assessed (Iteration 2). Figure 2 illustrates the timeline of the iterative development phases.

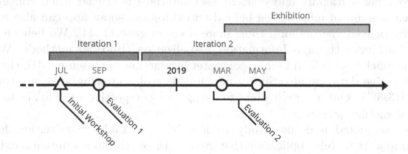

Fig. 2. Timeline of the development phases from July 2018 to November 2019.

The concepts were developed by experts in mobile development, HCI, and InfoVis. The same concepts were refined based on feedback provided by three other experts not only in InfoVis and HCI but also on the development of digital artifacts to enhance museum visits. As part of our co-design process, we also performed an initial workshop with the five exhibition curators with a background in history and as cultural mediators as domain experts. In this workshop, we got to know the exhibition concept, discussed existing data, and defined the requirements. Furthermore, we brainstormed about how the visualization could look like. One of the ideas was a timeline that looked like a newspaper, which after the contribution from different experts became the timeline concepts designed for Iteration 1. We got back with the ideas to the curators in one of our monthly workshops with them in the course of preparing the entire interactive exhibition. Thus, we regularly discussed the progress of the visualization design and specified the underlying data.

2.2   Problem Analysis

Based on the results of the initial workshop with the exhibition curators, we defined data and requirements for the visualization.

Data Overview. The data contained a title, time (year(s)), a detailed description in text form, images, and additional interactive components (e.g., AR or a single choice game). The temporal dimension was not visible in the exhibition except on the exhibit labels which showed title, short description, and year. Thus, including time in the visualization interested the curators and us.

In total, 27 exhibits were planned for the exhibition. Because of the storytelling aspects, the curators decided not to integrate all exhibits into the application. This is why the exhibits within the app were reduced to 13. These exhibits were divided into six content-related sections.

Requirements for Visualization. Together with the curators, we defined requirements for our visualization concepts:

RQ1. The visualization should function as a guide through the exhibition. Thus, the order of the individual exhibits within the museum has to be shown.
RQ2. Depending on the visitor's location, exhibits should appear dynamically. The focus should be on the closest exhibit.
RQ3. To visualize the time dependency within the exhibition, exhibits appear chronologically within each section.
RQ4. Complementary information is shown for the selected exhibit, thus providing the visitors with additional information.

3   Related Work

Based on the data and requirements, we focus on time-oriented data visualization for a location-aware mobile application in a museum. Therefore, in this section, we cover related work in four areas. First, we summarize the use of mobile devices in museums. Additionally, we take a closer look at timeline visualization, InfoVis on mobile devices, and InfoVis in museums.

3.1   Mobile Devices in Museums

In the 1950s, Acoustiguide [1] introduced the first audio guides with mobile devices in museums. Around 40 years later, the first museum applications using PDAs and Pocket PCs were documented. E.g., HyperAudio [45] is an early mobile guide based on a PDA with additional infrared sensors developed in the late 1990s. HyperAudio displayed hypermedia pages with an audio channel depending on location in the museum. Several other visitor guides followed (e.g., [18,43]). Economou and Meintani [23] evaluated museum applications for mobile phones. Most of them function as guided tours and representations of exhibitions, which is why maps or lists are often integrated to allow visitors to navigate according to the spatial layout or the chronological or alphabetical order of exhibits. In addition to functioning as guides, mobile phones are used to augment exhibits or exhibition spaces. Luna et al. [37] analyzed Augmented Reality (AR)-integrating heritage applications in Europe. Most of the 35 studied apps (23) used AR to reconstruct spaces and buildings. Interestingly, fewer apps (10) extended exhibits. Mobile devices have also been integrated into multi-device ecologies (MDEs). Such MDEs are often studied in the context of games [33] and as a combination of guides and games [25]. Ghiani et al. [25] extended large screens by combining a mobile guide with games. An underlying architecture for such MDEs integrating the visitor's mobile device has been proposed by Blumenstein et al. [8]. The authors distinguish between active (interactive, e.g., which connect to a multi-touch table) and passive (traditional) exhibits.

3.2   InfoVis on Mobile Devices and in Museums

Timeline Visualization. Using time-based approaches [2] to visualize data dates back to the 18th century. Already in 1765, John Priestley used timelines to visualize the lifespans of famous people [49] for his 'Chart of Biography'. Khulusi et al. [34] created an interactive version of Priestley's chart with data of musicians. Such timelines were also used to visualize personal histories based on medical records [47] and interactions of movie characters [39]. Newer research explores timelines in combination with storytelling [14].

InfoVis on Mobile Devices. In 2006, Chittaro [19] published an article about visualizing information on mobile devices. The main conclusion was that "visualization applications developed for desktop computers do not scale well to mobile devices". The arguments mainly followed the lines of the smaller size, lower resolution, different aspect ratio, and less powerful hardware. Over the years, the performance of smartphones has been enhanced considerably. However, a survey article by Isenberg & Isenberg [32] seven years later showed that smartphones had only been used in 6% of the 100 analyzed research projects, although the user base of smartphones had been continuously growing during these years. In recent years, visualization on mobile devices has attracted more and more attention in research [9,15,20,35] and practice [51,53].

Several research works focused on tablets as target devices. Baur et al. [5] presented TouchWave (touchable stacked graphs). Sadana and Stasko [52] implemented multiple coordinated views for tablets. Later research on tablets explores details-on-demand techniques for interactive visual exploration [57] or proposes consistent interaction across different types of visualization [55]. Compared to research on tablet devices, research on smartphones is underrepresented [9]. Besides, Hoffswell et al. [29] proposed design guidelines for responsive visualization addressing news visualization.

InfoVis in Museums. Previously, visualization research used to heavily focused on expert users (e.g., [48]). When designing InfoVis for museum visitors, however, users of the visualization are not domain experts [7]. Research by Börner et al. [11] revealed a rather low level of data visualization literacy among science museum visitors. A promising fact, however, is that participants showed interest in the presented visualization. In 2012, the utilization of casual InfoVis in museums was described "as a rudiment of utopia in the cultural organization" [36]. However, some applications show that data visualization fits very well into the museum space. Hinrichs et al. [28] demonstrated the potential and challenges of such applications with InfoVis on a large touch display. Other examples of visualization in museums included tools with which visitors were able to explore scientific data [38] or a visualization that showed the area around Hamburg through space and time from the Middle Ages to the present [3]. The target device of those applications was a horizontal touch display (tabletop).

Rogers et al. [50] performed a comparison of in-situ and remote exploration of museum collections with three visualizations (Choropleth map, bar graph, and list of artifacts) on tablets. Results showed that a keyword search was mostly likely to be used rather than visualization filters. One reason for this might be that the app was not implemented as *situated visualization*, which is why it did not react to the visitors' location, and visitors had to figure out which exhibit was next to them. *Situated visualization* is defined as data representation, which depends on the situation of the user or the object closest to the user [64].

Currently, there is hardly any focus on InfoVis on mobile devices (especially smartphones) in museums. Nevertheless, museums have utilized mobile applications as an additional way of extending visits. Therefore, introducing InfoVis to this area seems like a more promising approach for enhancing the design possibilities for navigation through exhibits.

4   Iteration 1: Visualization Concepts

We combined basic InfoVis premises (e.g., overview first and then details on demand [54]) and mobile guidelines (e.g., screen size limitation, vertical scrolling, occlusion and fat finger problem [19,63]) to propose different visualization options. For presenting time-oriented information, we selected three of five representation aspects as described in [14] (linear, grid, and radial). We designed a conventional linear timeline (*Timeline*) and a radial approach that is optimized to take advantage of mobile screen size (*Timeflower*). Since our data are also historical, which is often connected to documents and books, we also created a grid visualization based on a bookshelf as a metaphor (*Bookshelf*).

4.1   Visualization Concepts

In *Timeline*, data are represented as a linear vertical timeline (Fig. 3 (a)). A box represents each exhibit containing its title (Fig. 3 (a) 1) and is anchored to a year on the timeline (Fig. 3 (a) 2). If a museum visitor has not yet passed an exhibit, it is displayed as inactive (Fig. 3 (a) 5). Addressing RQ2, an exhibit is activated on the timeline whenever visitors walk by. Besides, it automatically moves to the center of the screen. The year of the closest exhibit is marked with

Fig. 3. Three design concepts for visualizing historical data on a mobile device: Timeline (a), Bookshelf (b), and Timeflower (c).

a border (Fig. 3 (a) 6). If the visitor selects an exhibit by tapping on the box, a larger box appears containing additional text (Fig. 3 (a) 4, RQ4). A section-introduction element introduces each section (Fig. 3 (a) 3), which, in contrast to regular exhibits, features a different icon and starts a new timeline instead of displaying a year.

The *Bookshelf* visualization shows the data in a bookshelf-like grid layout in which each tier represents one section of the exhibit (Fig. 3 (b)). Bookshelves were used as a metaphor in visualization before (e.g., [4,58]). In contrast, we intended to visualize a real bookshelf. Each book corresponds to one exhibition object and shows a keyword on its back (Fig. 3 (b) 1). Labels on the underlying tiers show the year of the exhibits (Fig. 3 (b) 2). Book holders represent section introductions (Fig. 3 (b) 3). While the tiers (sections) are aligned vertically, the horizontal alignment of the books shows the chronological order of the exhibits (RQ1, RQ3). If the years of multiple exhibits are the same, the books are stacked on top of each other (Fig. 3 (b) 7). Once again, the books are marked as inactive until the visitor has passed the corresponding exhibit. The book which represents the closest exhibit is shown with a border (Fig. 3 (b) 6). Its tier scrolls to the middle of the screen upon activation (RQ2). Tapping on the book reveals detailed information as an overlay (Fig. 3 (b) 4, RQ4).

Timeflower was inspired by People Garden [65] which is a graphical representation of users based on their past interactions. The entire content of the exhibition is represented by a flower-like structure (Fig. 3 (c)) in which each exhibit is a petal (Fig. 3 (c) 1). Stamens mark section introductions (Fig. 3 (c) 3). By swiping across the screen, the flower can be rotated. While the flower takes up the lower half of the screen, an information box is displayed on the upper half (Fig. 3 (c) 4, RQ3). This box contains the title and a teaser text of the exhibit petal that is currently facing upwards. Between the box and the petal, the year of the corresponding exhibit is shown (Fig. 3 (c) 2). When visitors pass an exhibit, the flower automatically rotates so that the corresponding petal is in the middle of the screen, and its information is displayed. An additional border marks the petal that represents the closest exhibit (Fig. 3 (c) 6, RQ2).

Our three concepts address the defined requirements. The order of the exhibits in all three concepts represents the path through the museum (RQ1). This order also represents a chronological order within each section (RQ3). As *Timeline* and *Timeflower* have a sequential scale, we do not visualize the period in between the exhibits. *Bookshelf*, on the other hand, visualizes such data as a chronological scale. To address RQ3, we activate exhibits that are close to the visitors, center, and highlight them in all three concepts. Besides, we show additional information for selected exhibits (RQ4). However, our three designs have different strengths and weaknesses. *Timeline* has the look and feel of a news app, which is well known. The vertical scrolling is familiar to the user [16]. Yet, it is a classic approach that might offer the least fun experience. *Bookshelf* provides a good overview and looks well structured. Its weakness is the covering of parts when showing detailed information. The strength of *Timeflower* is the excellent mixture between overview and detail, but it is less known for presenting data and uses vertical text orientation, which could influence readability.

4.2   Evaluation

As the three designs are quite different in their approaches, we conducted a comparative evaluation of clickable mockups to see which concept was the easiest to understand and use. To focus on the different design concepts, we added neither the location-aware aspect nor coloring in this first evaluation step. The evaluation was counter-balanced with a within-subject design. We selected four tasks to find out 1) how participants interpret our designs, 2) whether it is possible for them to navigate within the prototype, 3) find additional information, and 4) get back to the overview page. During these tasks, participants were asked to think aloud. Afterward, they answered three post-task questions about 1) the comprehensibility of the navigation, 2) the comprehensibility of changing between exhibition objects, and 3) the ease of use of the visualization. Once all three concepts had been tested, participants were requested to fill in a post-study questionnaire to directly compare the concepts. All questions were presented as a seven-point Likert scale varying from negative to positive scores.

Subjects. Twenty-four persons (P) participated in the assessment (13 female and 11 male), with an age range of 19 to 77 years ($M = 41.6$, $SD = 14.9$). Seventeen participants used Android as the operating system, while the others used iOS. Only one user reported not having experience using smartphones. As Iteration 1 was conducted in a university, participants recruited were students and administrative staff who had not previously been involved in the project.

Data Analysis. Data were analyzed with R. When distributions were not Gaussian (according to the Shapiro-Wilks test), the effect of the three designs on the participants' scores was evaluated using the non-parametric Friedman test with posthoc Wilcoxon analyses (paired samples).

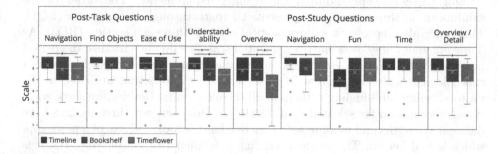

Fig. 4. Iteration 1. Scores from post-task and post-study questionnaires across designs. The y-axis maps the Likert scale from 1 (negative) to 7 (positive).

4.3   Results

When performing the assigned tasks, the design did not affect user performance. Participants reached correct results in 79% ($SD = 23.2$) of cases with the *Timeline* design, in 78% ($SD = 21.2$) of cases with *Bookshelf*, and in 74% ($SD = 23.0$) of cases with *Timeflower*. However, results regarding informal feedback are in contrast to these findings. Figure 4 summarize the results for the post-task and post-study questionnaires.

Post-task Questions. The design had an effect on the comprehensibility of the navigation ($\chi^2(2) = 9.30$, $p < .01$). Posthoc tests showed that *Timeline* provided an easier navigation than *Timeflower* ($p < .01$). In addition, there was an effect of the design on the ease of use of the visualization ($\chi^2(2) = 6.03$, $p < .05$) where *Timeline* also supported a better usage than *Timeflower* ($p < .05$). However, designs did not differ in the ratings for comprehensibility when changing between exhibition objects.

Post-study Questions. The design also had an effect on the understandability rating of the visualization ($\chi^2(2) = 9.95$, $p < .01$). The *Timeline* design was assessed as more understandable than both *Bookshelf* ($p < .05$) and *Timeflower* ($p < .01$). In addition, the design affected the quality of the overview offered by the visualization ($\chi^2(2) = 11.05$, $p < .01$). This time, *Timeflower* was judged to be less suitable for overview compared to both *Timeline* ($p < .01$) and *Bookshelf* ($p < .05$). Both results seem to be related to the responsiveness of *Timeflower*. The design also had an effect on how easy it was to navigate through the visualization ($\chi^2(2) = 11.39$, $p < .01$). Again, *Timeline* was rated as supporting navigation better than *Timeflower* ($p < .01$). In addition, regarding the combination between overview and detailed information, there was also a difference between designs ($\chi^2(2) = 6.11, p < .05$). *Timeline* offered a better balance between overview and detailed information than *Timeflower* ($p < .05$).

Informal Feedback. Qualitative results showed that the idea behind *Timeline* was received well. Comments like "one can scroll, and there are exhibits" (P2), "I would expect it when I download a museum app" (P7), and "exhibition topic with historical order of objects" (P9) documented this fact. For *Bookshelf*, we recognized two different opinions within the comments of the participants: "overloaded, do not know where to look" (P10) vs. "well structured and numbered" (P18). *Timeflower* was hardly recognized as a flower. Participants recognized, e.g., a crown, a sun, or arrows. The most critical issue design-wise referred to the sectioning; in each respective design, 14 (for *Timeline* and *Bookshelf*) and 18 (for *Timeflower*) participants could not imagine what the subdivision meant.

5   Iteration 2: Linear Timelines

Based on the results of the first evaluation, in which the *Timeline* concept received the better overall rating, we developed the linear concept further. Since we had to visualize time and duration for six different sections, we noticed different options concerning scale and layout [14]. First, we reproduced the same timeline concept, which focused on the exhibits' order. Therefore, such a visualization displayed the different sections consecutively (*Stack-based*, Fig. 5 (a)). In general, stacking items is common for mobile screens. However, it means having stacked timelines as well, which corresponds to a faceted layout [14]. To avoid a very long list of six chronological timelines, a sequential scale was chosen, which means that distances between exhibits do not correspond to chronological distances [14]. In our second approach, we used pagination (*Section-based*, Fig. 5 (b)) to overcome the stacking (faceted layout). Thus, we could use a chronological scale to visualize the exhibits. Alternatively, we also implemented a unified option prioritizing time over exhibits' order by including all exhibits in one timeline (*All-in-one*, Fig. 5 (c)) with a chronological scale.

5.1   Visualization Concepts

In all three visualizations, exhibits are represented as cards with a title and the exhibits time frame either on the card (Fig. 5 (b, c) 1) or on the timeline next to it (Fig. 5 (a) 1). The card representing the exhibit closest to the visitors is highlighted (Fig. 5 (a, b, c) 5, RQ2), and a location button can be used to scroll to the corresponding card (Fig. 5 (a, b, c) 7). Inactive cards represent exhibits visitors have yet to unlock by walking by them and are indicated by higher transparency (Fig. 5 (a, b, c) 4). Once an exhibit is unlocked, the visualization scrolls to the corresponding object card (RQ2). In case this exhibit is in a different section, both the section color and the background image change accordingly. In

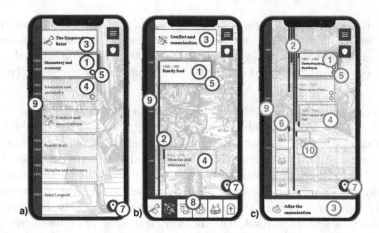

Fig. 5. Timeline visualizations showing different areas of the exhibition: (a) Stack-based, (b) Section-based, and (c) All-in-one visualization.

all three visualization prototypes, clicking on a card opens the exhibit's detail page showing detailed descriptions in the form of text, images, and/or additional interactive components (RQ4). In both *Stack-based* and *Section-based* visualization, the current exhibit's section is displayed on section introduction cards showing its title and icon (Fig. 5 (a, b) 3). In the *All-in-one* visualization this information is shown as a footer instead (Fig. 5 (c) 3).

In the *Stack-based* visualization (Fig. 5 (a)), a timeline is divided into sections. Whenever visitors walk into a new section, the timeline's color as well as the background color and image change. Within these colored sections, the objects are listed chronologically, but the time axis jumps between years according to the sequence of the displayed objects (Fig. 5 (a) 9).

The *Section-based* visualization shows each section as a page. For navigation through these pages, we positioned a navigation bar at the bottom (Fig. 5 (b) 8). The time frame of the time axis (Fig. 5 (a) 9) remains the same through all sections. The coloring of this axis is based on the section's color. Objects within the sections are listed chronologically. Timelines [60] on the left side of the object's cards indicate the temporal assignment as their height is determined by the start and end years the exhibit is assigned to (Fig. 5 (b) 2).

The *All-in-one* visualization shows one time axis (Fig. 5 (a) 9), integrating all exhibits. Within each section, exhibits still appear based on the order in the exhibition. To differentiate between the exhibition's sections, each card is connected to a timeline showing the temporal assignment (Fig. 5 (c) 2). The timelines are colored according to the section they belong to. Whenever a visitor is located in a section, the background color, and the image change accordingly. In addition, all cards which belong to this section are shown in full size (Fig. 5 (c) 1). The other cards are reduced to a small card showing the dedicated section icon (Fig. 5 (c) 10) such as a fisheye [24]. In case exhibits are allocated to the same year or time frame, their cards are shown as aggregated (Fig. 5 (c) 6).

Our three visualizations are well-suited for getting to know the time the exhibits are related to (RQ3). Nevertheless, these visualizations have different strengths and weaknesses. The *Stack-based* visualization is a simple and straight-forward concept, backed by Iteration 1. However, the focus is on the exhibits' order within the exhibition rather than on time (RQ1). The *Section-based* visualization tries to solve this by displaying each section on demand. In this way, it is possible to compare the time between objects of different sections, as the time axis stays in the same position. On the other hand, it might present too much white space, as exhibits in each section are spread over different years of the same time axis. The focus of the *All-in-one* visualization is on the chronological order (RQ3) rather than on the exhibit's order within the exhibition (RQ1). Its strengths are the overview of all exhibition objects and the ease of comparing the time of exhibits. However, such a concept might be overwhelming for first-time users.

5.2 Evaluation

To evaluate which visualization is the easiest to understand and provides the best experience, we once again prepared a counter-balanced evaluation of the visualizations (within-subjects), this time in a lab and a museum setting (between-subjects). We implemented the three visualizations with web technologies (HTML, CSS, Javascript, and D3 [12]). As we used Bluetooth tags to trigger the location of the exhibits, we wrapped the web content in a native application for iOS and Android. All subjects were provided with prepared iPhone devices (iPhone 7 and 8) to ensure that different devices did not influence results. The three tasks were the same for all visualization: 1) Describe the visualization. 2) Which year(s) is/are assigned to the last object you activated? 3) Show us two objects which are linked in the same year(s). After each visualization, participants answered three questions about 1) ease of use, 2) understandability of the temporal assignment, and 3) ease of comparing the time between exhibits. When all three visualizations were tested and rated, users completed an additional questionnaire where the visualizations were directly compared. For both the post-task and the post-study questions, we used a 7-point Likert scale varying from negative to positive scores.

For both the lab and the museum setting, we used the same process. Each visualization was tested in two sections (two exhibits in the first section, one exhibit in the second section). For the lab setting, we prepared a path comparable to the museum setting with five sections. Additionally, the test in the museum setting was carried out at a time when there were hardly any visitors in the museum so that we could reduce distractions.

Subjects. Overall, thirty-six persons participated in the assessment. The evaluation was conducted in two different locations: first, with 24 participants (14 female and 10 male, age range 20 to 56 years ($M = 32.8$, $SD = 11.2$)) in a lab setting. The second location was in the field, testing 12 users (6 female and 6 male, 11 and 12 years old ($M = 11.8$, $SD = 0.6$)) in the actual exhibition.

As the laboratory setting of Iteration 2 was conducted in a university, participants recruited were students and administrative staff who had not previously been involved in the project. The museum setting was conducted with a school class visiting the museum.

In the pre-questionnaire, 25 (museum: 9) participants reported their daily usage time on their smartphone to be 61 min and more, 6 (museum: 2) participants reported 30 to 45 min daily usage time, 3 participants in the lab setting use it 45 to 60 min, while 15 to 30 min (museum) and 10 to 15 min (lab) have each been reported once. Participants were also asked to rate their data visualization experience on a 7 point Likert scale (low to high), resulting in a mean of 4.0 ($SD = 1.4$) for participants in the lab setting and 2.3 ($SD = 1.7$) in the museum setting.

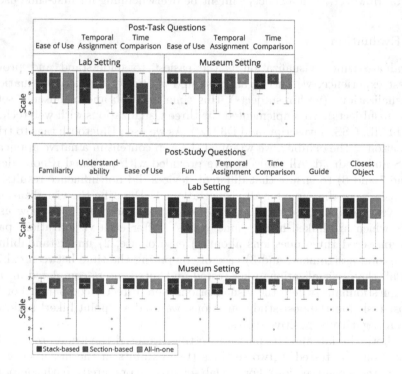

Fig. 6. Iteration 2. Scores from post-task and post-study questionnaires across visualization. The y-axis maps the Likert scale from 1 (negative) to 7 (positive).

Data Analysis. The same methods from Iteration 1 were applied. There were no significant differences between the assessed treatments. Following an exploratory analysis [61], Pearson tests were also performed for testing correlation between the users' scores and their demographics: gender (male, female), age group (child & adolescent (under 18, n = 12), young adult (18 to 30, n = 13), middle and old aged (above 30, n = 11)), smartphone usage, data visualization experience, setting group (lab vs. museum), and condition type (order of design during the test). After detecting significant correlations, a factorial analysis was adopted with a factorial ANOVA test and Tukey test for posthoc analysis.

5.3   Results

Performing the tasks, participants reached correct results in 68% of cases with *Stack-based* (SD = 32.0) and *Section-based* design (SD = 33.1), and in 78% (SD = 33.7) of cases with *All-in-one* design. These findings reflect the overall results regarding user experience. Figure 6 shows the aggregated results for the post-task and post-study questionnaires.

Post-task Questions. ANOVA test reported a significant effect of setting group (lab vs. museum) on ease of use ($F(1,102)$ = 4.44, p = .04). Ease of use was rated significantly better (p = .04) by the museum group than the lab group. Additionally, there was a significant effect of setting group on comparing the time ($F(1,102)$ = 16.11, $p < .001$), which was better rated ($p < .001$) by the museum group than the lab group.

Age group had an effect on comparing the time ($F(2,99)$ = 8.76, $p = < .001$). Young adults and middle & old aged rated this task significantly lower ($p < .01$ & $p < .001$) than children & adolescents.

There was also an effect of data visualization experience on comparing the time ($F(6,87)$ = 2.62, p = .02). Participants with medium experience (M = 4.48, SD = 2.01) rated significantly lower (p = .02) than participants with the lowest experience (M = 6.33, SD = 1.28) in general.

Post-study Questions.   Correlation   tests   revealed   positive   correlations between setting groups and each of the post-task questions. For familiarity, ANOVA revealed a significant difference between designs ($F(2,102)$ = 3.29, p = .04). Participants had more fun with the *Section-based* visualization than with the *All-in-one* visualization ($p < .001$). There was also a significant difference between setting groups ($F(1,102)$ = 11.73, $p < .001$). The museum group rated significantly better than the lab group ($p < .001$) in general. We found the same significant differences for understandabilty ($F(1,102)$ = 9.83, $p < .01$), fun ($F(1,102)$ = 19.25, $p < .001$), temporal assignment ($F(1,102)$ = 4.64, p = .03), comparing the time ($F(1,102)$ = 18.75, $p < .001$), suitability as guide ($F(1,102)$ = 20.97, $p < .001$), noticing the closest object ($F(1,102)$ = 5.76, p = .02), and ease of use ($F(1,102)$ = 11.22, p = .001). The designs also had an effect on ease of use ($F(2,102)$ = 3.34, p = .04). Again, the *Section-based* visualization was easier to use than the *All-in-one* visualization (p = .04).

Both designs ($F(2,99)$ = 3.28, p = .04) and age groups ($F(2,99)$ = 3.28, p = .04) had an effect on familiarity. On the one hand, there was a marginally significant difference (p = .05) showing that the *Section-based* visualization is more familiar than the *All-in-one* visualization. On the other hand, young adults and middle & old aged rated familiarity significantly lower ($p = .04$ & $p < .01$) than children & adolescents. In terms of understandability, we found a significant difference based on age groups ($F(2,99) = 5.28, p < .01$). Again, the posthoc test showed that young adults and middle & old aged gave significantly less points ($p = .02$ & $p = .01$) than children & adolescents. Additionally, there was an effect on interaction between designs and age groups ($F(4,99) = 3.04, p = .02$). For middle & old aged the *Section-based* design is more understandable than the *Stack-based* design ($p = .04$). Design exhibit a significant effect ($F(2,102) = 3.38, p = .04$) on ease of use. The *Section-based* design was easier to use than the *All-in-one* design ($p = .03$). Additionally, ease of use ($F(2,99) = 5.99, p < .01$) as well as fun ($F(2,99) = 9.80, p < .001$), comparing the time ($F(2,99) = 9.64, p < .001$), and suitability as a guide ($F(2,99) = 10.38, p < .001$) showed effects with age groups. Young adults and middle & old aged rated significantly lower than children & adolescents. For temporal assignment, we also found significant differences between age groups ($F(2,99) = 4.05, p = .02$). This time, only middle & old aged rated significantly lower ($p = .16$) than children & adolescents.

ANOVA showed a significant difference between designs ($F(2,102) = 3.93, p = .04$). Also, in combination with data visualization experience, participants reported that the *Section-based* visualization is easier to use than the *All-in-one* visualization ($p = .03$). Data visualization experience had an effect on comparing times ($F(6,87) = 2.26, p < .05$) and on suitability as a guide ($F(6,87) = 2.64, p = .02$). Participants with the lowest experience ($M = 6.61, SD = 1.04$) gave significantly ($p = .03$) more points than participants with experience three ($M = 5.10, SD = 1.84$).

Informal Feedback. Qualitative results show that the general "timeline" concept is received well. However, both qualitative and quantitative results show that user opinions on the different designs diverge considerably. The *Stack-based* design is properly recognized as "multiple stacked timelines". Participants describe it as "clear" or "looking ordered". At the same time, others called it "not clear", "overwhelming", or found the time "complete messy". The *Section-based* design is described as a "vertical timeline with multiple parallel timelines" which "feels like a conventional app layout". Comments regarding this visualization were that it is "irritating" or "cool, but hard to understand". One participant reported that they "need longer to do something, but with the sections, it is straightforward". Another participant states that "the comparison is not possible". However, she had given the correct answer for the comparison task. The *All-in-one* design is described as "multiple timelines side by side with colors and icons". Judging from the comments, it seems to cause the most diverging opinions. On the one hand, *All-in-one* is praised for providing "a good overview", for being "easy to understand", "well organized", and for having "a clean layout". On the other hand, participants' comments included remarks such as "loose orientation", "totally overwhelming", "looks more confusing", "overloaded", or "very complicated". Overall, participants liked the section coloring, which supported guidance within the exhibition.

6   Reflections and Lessons Learned

In this section, we reflect on visualization & interaction and the process of our design study and derive implications. Based on our reflections, we derived the following guidelines for future studies on InfoVis for casual users in museums:

- Choose familiar and linear visualization techniques.
- The prototype should consider the interaction needed.
- Choose participants with different profiles.
- Combine quantitative scores with qualitative feedback.
- Perform tests in the museum is always essential, leave highly controlled comparison tests for the lab.

Choose Familiar and Linear Visualization Techniques. Our results show that the general public may lean towards more familiar and linear visualization techniques. Börner et al. [11] already stated the importance of familiarity for visitors with low data literacy. In Iteration 1, participants were able to perform the tasks well with all three designs, although the user experience with the designs was different. Based on the users' ratings, there was no difference between designs regarding their ability to display content about exhibits (Find Objects). However, participants rated *Timeflower* as the least preferred approach regarding navigation and ease of use. *Timeflower* was functional and attended the system requirement of focusing mainly on the current exhibit, which was shown by the scores it got for the overview. Nevertheless, it was also a somewhat unfamiliar technique and metaphor. Whenever users were unable to identify which object *Timeflower* represented, they were not able to see its affordance, which negatively influenced usability. The *Bookshelf* and *Timeline* designs, on the other hand, were more apparent and more familiar to the users, yielding close scores in many aspects such as navigation and overview. However, participants rated *Bookshelf* as significantly less understandable than *Timeline*. Even when the meaning of the metaphor of *Bookshelf* was clear, *Timeline* shows objects straightforwardly and functionally. *Timeline* also reflects the same visual metaphor found in news feeds and social media (e.g., card-based layout). This is why we chose *Timeline* as the basis for Iteration 2. With three versions of a linear timeline in Iteration 2, users were again able to perform the tasks well with all three designs with no significant differences in performance and user experience.

Clickable Mockups Are Not Always the Optimal Choice. In Iteration 1, we produced medium-fidelity clickable mockups as we wanted to make use of the real physical device [27]. Nevertheless, we noticed that there might be an effect of the static mockup setup, particularly on the *Timeflower* assessment. The design of *Timeflower* included a wheel interaction not present on the other designs. Missing interaction elements (e.g., a smooth spinning of *Timeflower*) may influence the perception of the visualization representation, especially when comparing familiar (*Timeline* or *Bookshelf*) with non-familiar techniques (*Timeflower*).

Therefore, we conclude that click dummies are not always optimal for comparing different visualization techniques. In future projects, interaction should be the primary key when deciding on prototype fidelity. If the interaction varies between designs, all interactions must be implemented as they should work in the final version (i.e., with higher fidelity). Otherwise, it is possible to use lower-fidelity prototypes and simulate interactions (e.g., with a wizard-of-oz technique [62]).

Age vs. Design Alternatives. Different age groups responded differently to the assessed prototypes. The *Stack-based* and *Section-based* visualization yielded close scores, but the *Section-based* design was shown to be easier to use for older users (middle & old aged). Finally, we consistently observed the prevalence of older visitors despite our museum partner reporting its target group as people from a wide age range. In such a scenario, considering only the differences between age groups, the final design should follow a *Section-based* implementation. However, both *Stack-* and *Section-based* visualizations were shown to be suitable.

Combine Quantitative Scores with Qualitative Feedback. In our studies, we wanted to perform a comparative evaluation but still consider the user's experience. That is why we selected a combination of a task-based method and structured Likert-scale questions, which could work even in the real museum setting and have been used before (e.g. [33]). Thus, we could adequately observe when the performance of the users differed from their perceived performance. With a mixed-method, we could search for statistical effects between the designs. Also, asking participants about the motivation for their ratings provided us additional qualitative information, which could be combined with the ratings. Quantitative data could also support the interpretation of qualitative data [21].

Choose Participants with Different Profiles. Correlation tests in Iteration 2 revealed participants who reported having more experience with data visualization consistently rated their experience lower than those with less data visualization experience. Therefore, more experienced participants might be more analytical than less experienced users. Regarding the age of our participants, we could not determine a correlation between smartphone usage and age. However, our youngest age group (children & adolescents) consistently rated their experience higher than the older participants. The younger ones are surrounded by technology [17] and use them frequently [6]. Hence, they might have shown a higher motivation to use their smartphone within the museum and a different perspective when rating the designs. Visually impaired people are an underrepresented target group in visualization research [26]. Although accessibility was not in the focus of our study, we have provided each element with the required ARIA[1] labels enabling users to read all visualization elements via screen reader. We observed a blind person using the *Section-based* visualization (final version). We observed that accessing an exhibit in the middle of the timeline was a main issue, as users had to go through all previous exhibits in the timeline to reach the desired item every time the screen was reloaded. To solve this problem, we

---

[1] ARIA stands for Accessible Rich Internet Applications.

had to add anchor points to jump to exhibits directly. As casual users differ in visualization literacy (cf. [48]), motivations in using technology, and limitations, there is a need for future studies to select participants with different profiles, especially when targeting casual users.

Weighing Up Lab Against Museum Setting. In Iteration 2, we tested our location-aware visualization in two different settings. The Lab provided a controlled setting aiming at high internal validity. Besides, we wanted to address the lack of knowledge about the context of usage [9] through additional testing in the museum. In our study, the two questions focusing on the location-aware aspect (noticing the closest object & suitability as a guide) were rated significantly higher by the museum group, which might indicate a clear benefit in using the real exhibition setting. However, the museum group was the same as the youngest age group. Therefore, we cannot differentiate between the effects of age group and test setting. Performing a comparative study in a running exhibition environment meant much effort. That is why we used a school class. On the other hand, in such classes, the population was far too homogeneous, with participants presenting similar profiles.

7   Conclusion

In the context of an exhibition in an Austrian museum, we contribute a design study on visualizing historical data through a mobile museum application. In total, we performed two comparative studies: 1) with clickable mockups of three basic visualization concepts, and based on these results, 2) with three functional prototypes of timeline visualization concepts both in a lab and museum setting. As a final step, we defined guidelines for the design and development of future studies on visualization for casual users in museums based on the lessons learned. The guidelines should support the design of interactive visualizations for cultural heritage applications, covering aspects from the visualization and interaction implementation, as well as the general design process.

Acknowledgments. This work was supported by the Austrian Federal Ministry of Science, Research and Economy under the FFG COIN program (MEETeUX project, #856308), the Federal Government of Lower Austria via the project Dataskop (K3-F-2/015-2019), and Internet Foundation Austria (IPA) with a Ph.D. scholarship (#1587). Besides, we want to thank C. Stoiber for giving critical feedback on our manuscript. A heartfelt thank you to the team of the library of Klosterneuburg Monastery for letting us contribute our ideas to the exhibition.

References

1. Acoustiguide: Acoustiguide Audio Tour: Company Profile (2014). https://web.archive.org/web/20140426142620/. http://www.acoustiguide.com/company-profile. Accessed 11 Aug 2019

2. Aigner, W., Miksch, S., Schumann, H., Tominski, C.: Visualization of Time-Oriented Data. Springer, London (2011). https://doi.org/10.1007/978-0-85729-079-3
3. ART + COM Studios: The Formation of Hamburg (2012). https://artcom.de/en/project/the-formation-of-hamburg/. Accessed 30 July 2019
4. Aslan, I., Murer, M., Primessnig, F., Moser, C., Tscheligi, M.: The digital bookshelf: decorating with collections of digital books. In: Proceedings of the ACM Conference on Pervasive and Ubiquitous Computing Adjunct Publication Adjunct, pp. 777–784. ACM Press (2013)
5. Baur, D., Lee, B., Carpendale, S.: TouchWave: kinetic multi-touch manipulation for hierarchical stacked graphs. In: Proceedings of the ACM International Conference on Interactive Surfaces and Spaces, pp. 255–264. ACM Press (2012)
6. Bitkom Research: Kinder und Jugendliche in der digitalen Welt (2019). https://www.bitkom.org/sites/default/files/2019-05/bitkom_pk-charts_kinder_und_jugendliche_2019.pdf
7. Block, F., Horn, M.S., Phillips, B.C., Diamond, J., Evans, E.M., Shen, C.: The DeepTree exhibit: visualizing the tree of life to facilitate informal learning. IEEE Trans. Vis. Comput. Graph. 18(12), 2789–2798 (2012)
8. Blumenstein, K., Kaltenbrunner, M., Seidl, M., Breban, L., Thür, N., Aigner, W.: Bringing your own device into multi-device ecologies: a technical concept. In: Proceedings of the ACM International Conference on Interactive Surfaces and Spaces, pp. 306–311. ACM Press (2017)
9. Blumenstein, K., Niederer, C., Wagner, M., Schmiedl, G., Rind, A., Aigner, W.: Evaluating information visualization on mobile devices: gaps and challenges in the empirical evaluation design space. In: Proceedings of the Workshop on Beyond Time and Errors on Novel Evaluation Methods for Visualization, pp. 125–132. ACM Press (2016)
10. Boiano, S., Bowen, J.P., Gaia, G.: Usability, design and content issues of mobile apps for cultural heritage promotion: the malta culture guide experience. In: Proceedings of the EVA London Conference on Electronic Workshops in Computing, pp. 66–73. British Computer Society (2012). arXiv:1207.3422
11. Börner, K., Maltese, A., Balliet, R.N., Heimlich, J.: Investigating aspects of data visualization literacy using 20 information visualizations and 273 science museum visitors. Inf. Vis. 15(3), 198–213 (2016)
12. Bostock, M., Ogievetsky, V., Heer, J.: D^3 data-driven documents. IEEE Trans. Vis. Comput. Graph. 17(12), 2301–2309 (2011)
13. Boucher, M., Blumenstein, K., Oliveira, V.A.D.J., Seidl, M.: BYOD - bringing your own device into single-surface interaction models. In: Proceedings of the International Conference on Tangible, Embedded, and Embodied Interaction, Salzburg, Austria. ACM Press (2021)
14. Brehmer, M., Lee, B., Bach, B., Riche, N.H., Munzner, T.: Timelines revisited: a design space and considerations for expressive storytelling. IEEE Trans. Vis. Comput. Graph. 23(9), 2151–2164 (2017)
15. Brehmer, M., Lee, B., Isenberg, P., Choe, E.K.: Visualizing ranges over time on mobile phones: a task-based crowdsourced evaluation. IEEE Trans. Vis. Comput. Graph. 25(1), 619–629 (2019)
16. Buchanan, G., Farrant, S., Jones, M., Thimbleby, H., Marsden, G., Pazzani, M.: Improving mobile internet usability. In: Proceedings of the International Conference on World Wide Web, pp. 673–680. ACM Press (2001)
17. Burns, T., Gottschalk, F.: What do we know about children and technology? (2019). https://www.oecd.org/education/ceri/Booklet-21st-century-children.pdf

18. Cardoso, P.J.S., et al.: Cultural heritage visits supported on visitors' preferences and mobile devices. Universal Access in the Information Society (2019)
19. Chittaro, L.: Visualizing information on mobile devices. Computer **39**(3), 40–45 (2006)
20. Choe, E.K., Dachselt, R., Isenberg, P., Lee, B.: Mobile data visualization (Dagstuhl Seminar 19292). Dagstuhl Rep. **9**(7), 78–93 (2019)
21. Creswell, J.W., Creswell, J.D.: Research Design: Qualitative, Quantitative, and Mixed Methods Approaches, 5th edn. SAGE, Los Angeles (2018)
22. Deutsches Museum: Deutsches Museum: App (2018). https://www.deutsches-museum.de/en/whats-on/app/. Accessed 30 Mar 2020
23. Economou, M., Meintani, E.: Promising beginning? Evaluating museum mobile phone apps. In: Rethinking Technology in Museums 2011: Emerging experiences. University of Limerick, Ireland (2011)
24. Furnas, G.W.: Generalized fisheye views. In: Proceedings of the CHI Conference on Human Factors in Computing Systems, pp. 16–23. ACM Press (1986)
25. Ghiani, G., Paternò, F., Santoro, C., Spano, L.D.: A location-aware guide based on active RFIDs in multi-device environments. In: Lopez, J.V., Montero, S.F., Molina, M.J., Vanderdonckt, J. (eds.) Computer-Aided Design of User Interfaces VI, pp. 59–70. Springer, London (2009). https://doi.org/10.1007/978-1-84882-206-1_6
26. Grinstein, G.: How data visualization and regulation meet on the modern web. In: IEEEVIS 2016 Panel (2016)
27. Hartson, R., Pyla, P.S.: The UX Book: Agile UX Design for a Quality User Experience. Morgan Kaufmann (2018)
28. Hinrichs, U., Schmidt, H., Carpendale, S.: EMDialog: bringing information visualization into the museum. IEEE Trans. Vis. Comput. Graph. **14**(6), 1181–1188 (2008)
29. Hoffswell, J., Li, W., Liu, Z.: Techniques for flexible responsive visualization design. In: Proceedings of the CHI Conference on Human Factors in Computing Systems, pp. 1–13. ACM Press (2020)
30. Hornecker, E.: Interactions around a contextually embedded system. In: Proceedings of the International Conference on Tangible, Embedded, and Embodied Interaction, pp. 169–176. ACM Press (2010)
31. Hornecker, E., Ciolfi, L.: Human-computer interactions in museums. Synth. Lect. Hum.-Centered Inform. **12**(2), i–153 (2019)
32. Isenberg, P., Isenberg, T.: Visualization on interactive surfaces: a research overview. I-COM **12**(3), 10–17 (2013)
33. Jimenez, P., Lyons, L.: An exploratory study of input modalities for mobile devices used with museum exhibits. In: Proceedings of the CHI Conference on Human Factors in Computing Systems, pp. 895–904. ACM Press (2011)
34. Khulusi, R., Kusnick, J., Focht, J., Jänicke, S.: An interactive chart of biography. In: Proceedings of the IEEE Pacific Visualization Symposium, pp. 257–266 (2019)
35. Lee, B., Brehmer, M., Isenberg, P., Choe, E.K., Langner, R., Dachselt, R.: Data visualization on mobile devices. In: Proceedings of the CHI Conference on Human Factors in Computing Systems - Extended Abstracts, p. W07. ACM Press (2018)
36. Li, Y.C., Liew, A.W.C., Su, W.P.: The digital museum: challenges and solution. In: Proceedings of the International Conference on Information Science and Digital Content Technology, vol. 3, pp. 646–649. IEEE (2012)
37. Luna, U., Rivero, P., Vicent, N.: Augmented reality in heritage apps: current trends in Europe. Appl. Sci. **9**(13), 2756 (2019)

38. Ma, J., Liao, I., Ma, K.L., Frazier, J.: Living liquid: design and evaluation of an exploratory visualization tool for museum visitors. IEEE Trans. Vis. Comput. Graph. **18**(12), 2799–2808 (2012)

39. Munroe, R.: Movie Narrative Charts (2009). https://xkcd.com/657/. Accessed 2 Mar 2020

40. Nofal, E., Panagiotidou, G., Reffat, R.M., Hameeuw, H., Boschloos, V., Moere, A.V.: Situated tangible gamification of heritage for supporting collaborative learning of young museum visitors. J. Comput. Cult. Heritage **13**(1), 1–24 (2020). https://dl.acm.org/doi/10.1145/3350427

41. Not, E., Cavada, D., Maule, S., Pisetti, A., Venturini, A.: Digital augmentation of historical objects through tangible interaction. J. Comput. Cult. Heritage **12**(3), 1–19 (2019). https://dl.acm.org/doi/10.1145/3297764

42. NOUS Knowledge Management: mumok guide (2017). https://apps.apple.com/us/app/mumok-guide/id982518019. Accessed 22 June 2019

43. Othman, M.K., Young, N.E., Aman, S.: Viewing Islamic art museum exhibits on the smartphone: re-examining visitors' experiences. J. Cogn. Sci. Hum. Dev. **1**(1), 102–118 (2015)

44. Palumbo, F., Dominici, G., Basile, G.: Designing a mobile app for museums according to the drivers of visitor satisfaction. In: Recent Advances in Business Management and Marketing - Proceedings of MATREFC. Social Science Research Network (2013)

45. Petrelli, D., Not, E.: User-centred design of flexible hypermedia for a mobile guide: reflections on the HyperAudio experience. User Model. User-Adap. Inter. **15**, 303 (2005)

46. Petridis, P., Pletinckx, D., Mania, K., White, M.: The EPOCH multimodal interface for interacting with digital heritage artefacts. In: Zha, H., Pan, Z., Thwaites, H., Addison, A.C., Forte, M. (eds.) VSMM 2006. LNCS, vol. 4270, pp. 408–417. Springer, Heidelberg (2006). https://doi.org/10.1007/11890881_45

47. Plaisant, C., Milash, B., Rose, A., Widoff, S., Shneiderman, B.: LifeLines: visualizing personal histories. In: Proceedings of the CHI Conference on Human Factors in Computing Systems, pp. 221–227. ACM Press (1996)

48. Pousman, Z., Stasko, J.T., Mateas, M.: Casual information visualization: depictions of data in everyday life. IEEE Trans. Vis. Comput. Graph. **13**(6), 1145–1152 (2007)

49. Priesley, J.: A Chart of Biography (1765). https://jrnold.github.io/priestley/articles/priestley.html. J. Johnson, St. Paul's Church Yard

50. Rogers, K., Hinrichs, U., Quigley, A.: It doesn't compare to being there: in-situ vs. remote exploration of museum collections. In: The Search Is Over! Exploring Cultural Collections with Visualization (2014)

51. Ros, I.: Bocoup: MobileVis (2016). http://mobilev.is/. Accessed 23 Aug 2019

52. Sadana, R., Stasko, J.: Designing multiple coordinated visualizations for tablets. EG Comput. Graph. Forum **35**(3), 261–270 (2016)

53. Sadowski, S.: Mobile Infovis and Dataviz Pattern (2018). https://mobileinfovis.com/. Accessed 23 Aug 2019

54. Shneiderman, B.: The eyes have it: a task by data type taxonomy for information visualizations. In: Proceedings of the IEEE Symposium on Visual Languages, pp. 336–343. IEEE (1996)

55. Srinivasan, A., Lee, B., Riche, N.H., Drucker, S.M., Hinckley, K.: InChorus: designing consistent multimodal interactions for data visualization on tablet devices. In: Proceedings of the CHI Conference on Human Factors in Computing Systems, pp. 1–13 (2020)

56. Stift Klosterneuburg: Jahresprogramm Stift Klosterneuburg 2019 (2018). https://www.stift-klosterneuburg.at/wp-content/uploads/2018/11/Stift_Klosterneuburg_Jahresprogramm_2019.pdf
57. Subramonyam, H., Adar, E.: SmartCues: a multitouch query approach for details-on-demand through dynamically computed overlays. IEEE Trans. Vis. Comput. Graph. **25**(1), 597–607 (2019)
58. Thudt, A., Hinrichs, U., Carpendale, S.: The bohemian bookshelf: supporting serendipitous book discoveries through information visualization. In: Proceedings of the CHI Conference on Human Factors in Computing Systems, pp. 1461–1470. ACM Press (2012)
59. Trajkova, M., Alhakamy, A., Cafaro, F., Mallappa, R., Kankara, S.R.: Move your body: engaging museum visitors with human-data interaction. In: Proceedings of the CHI Conference on Human Factors in Computing Systems, pp. 59:1–13. ACM Press (2020). https://doi.org/10.1145/3313831.3376186
60. Tufte, E.R.: The Visual Display of Quantitative Information, 2nd 5th Print edn. Graphics Press, Cheshire (2007)
61. Tukey, J.W.: Exploratory Data Analysis, 1st edn. Pearson, Reading (1977)
62. White, K.F., Lutters, W.G.: Behind the curtain: lessons learned from a Wizard of Oz field experiment. ACM SIGGROUP Bull. **24**(3), 129–135 (2003)
63. Wigdor, D., Forlines, C., Baudisch, P., Barnwell, J., Shen, C.: Lucid touch. In: Proceedings of the ACM Symposium on User Interface Software and Technology, pp. 269–278. ACM Press (2007)
64. Willett, W., Jansen, Y., Dragicevic, P.: Embedded data representations. IEEE Trans. Vis. Comput. Graph. **23**(1), 461–470 (2017)
65. Xiong, R., Donath, J.: PeopleGarden: creating data portraits for users. In: Proceedings of the ACM Symposium on User Interface Software and Technology, pp. 37–44. ACM Press (1999)

Strategies for Detecting Difference in Map Line-Up Tasks

Johanna Doppler Haider[1], Margit Pohl[1(✉)], Roger Beecham[2],
and Jason Dykes[3]

[1] University of Technology, Vienna, Austria
{johanna.haider,margit}@igw.tuwien.ac.at
[2] University of Leeds, Leeds, UK
r.j.beecham@leeds.ac.uk
[3] City University London, London, UK
j.d.dykes@city.ac.uk

Abstract. The line-up task hides a plot of real data amongst a line-up of decoys built around some plausible null hypothesis. It has been proposed as a mechanism for lending greater reliability and confidence to statistical inferences made from data graphics. The proposition is a seductive one, but whether or not line-ups guarantee consistent interpretation of statistical structure is an open question, especially when applied to representations of geo-spatial data. We build on empirical work around the extent to which statistical structure can be reliably judged in map line-ups, paying particular attention to the strategies employed when making line-up judgements. We conducted in-depth experiments with 19 graduate students equipped with a moderate background in geovisualization. The experiments consisted of a series of map line-up tasks with two map designs: choropleth maps and a centroid-dot alternative. We chose challenging tasks in the hope of exposing participants' sensemaking activities. Through structured qualitative analysis of think-aloud protocols, we identify six sensemaking strategies and evaluate their effects in making judgements from map line-ups. We find five sensemaking strategies applicable to most visualization types, but one that seems particular to map line-up designs. We could not identify one single successful strategy, but users adopt a mix of different strategies, depending on the circumstances. We also found that choropleth maps were easier to use than centroid-dot maps.

Keywords: Graphical inference · Cognitive strategies · Spatial autocorrelation · Geovisualization · Visual perception · Sensemaking · Thinking-aloud

1 Introduction

If statistical graphics are to be used in data analysis and reporting, there needs to be reassurance that the statistical effect implied by a graphic can be reliably perceived. The possibility of a mismatch between statistical effect and its

© IFIP International Federation for Information Processing 2021
Published by Springer Nature Switzerland AG 2021
C. Ardito et al. (Eds.): INTERACT 2021, LNCS 12934, pp. 558–578, 2021.
https://doi.org/10.1007/978-3-030-85613-7_36

visual perception is especially relevant to geovisualization. Whilst maps convey information around the location and extent of phenomena that may be difficult to imagine using non-visual techniques, they may also lead to artefacts that are incidental to the statistical structure under investigation and that may even induce interpretation of false structure.

The graphical line-up test [24] is a practical means of effecting more reliable interpretation. Graphical line-ups, as depicted in Fig. 1, can be considered as visual equivalents of test statistics. Line-up tests were developed in analogy to line-ups in the criminal justice system. The accused (the real data set) is hidden among several innocents (decoys). The innocents are data sets that conform to the null hypothesis. The null hypothesis assumes that there are no significant differences among the data sets. Significant differences between data sets can be tested statistically but also visually by human observers. If an impartial observer, an individual who has not previously seen the plot, is able to correctly identify the real from the decoys, then this lends confidence to the claim that a statistical effect exists – or rather, following null hypothesis significance testing, that the observed data are not consistent with the specified null hypothesis.

Graphical line-up tests are straight-forward to implement and conceptually appealing. They offer much potential to geo-spatial analysis [1]. However, they do not fully negate concerns around reliability of perception. Recent empirical studies have demonstrated that perception of statistical effects varies systematically with the intensity of effect [20], with visualization design [7] and in the case of geovisualization, with the geometric properties of the regions being studied [1]. Whilst there is evidence to suggest that these variations in perception are sufficiently systematic to be modelled (e.g. [7]), the evidence is less compelling for representations of geo-spatial data in choropleth maps (e.g. [1]).

Beecham et al. [1] speculated around the various explanations for why this is the case – why it is that, after modelling for variation due to intensity of statistical effect and geometric irregularity, there is much variation in perception of statistical structure encoded in maps. Elsewhere, Hofmann [8] and later VanderPlas & Hofmann [23] investigated whether or not ability to make correct

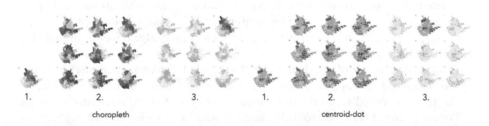

Fig. 1. A line-up is a visual equivalent to a test statistic. 1. Analyst observes neighbourhood-level pattern of crime rates. 2. Informal observer asked to pick the real data from a group of decoys constructed under CSR. 3. If the real is correctly selected from the decoys, we reject the null that crime distributes independently of location.

judgements in (non geo-spatial) line-up tests varies as a function of individuals' perceptual capability and reasoning or some other demographic characteristics. Whilst both studies found variation in individual ability to interpret line-up tests, this variation was not consistent with demographics or visual abilities.

This study attempts to address the problem from a different perspective. Through structured qualitative analysis of think-aloud protocols, we attempt to expose the *sensemaking processes* through which judgements are made during line-ups displaying geo-spatial data. Specifically, we wanted to find out whether participants adopt different sensemaking strategies to solve the tasks. If this is the case, some variation might be explained by the use of different strategies. Using the materials made available by Beecham et al. [1], we developed a series of map line-up tasks with line-ups consisting of nine data graphics: one plot of *real* data hidden amongst a set of eight decoy plots. We conducted a randomised controlled study (N = 19) where the following conditions were varied:

- Geovisualization design: choropleth map | centroid-dot map
- Geometric irregularity: artificial grid | real geography, regularly shaped | real geography, irregularly shaped
- Graphic size: small | large
- Statistical intensity: low | high

We analysed how ability to perform line-up tasks – that is, to correctly identify the real from the decoys – varies by these different conditions. We also paid attention to participants' perceived confidence in making line-up judgements under different conditions and their preferences amongst the different conditions. We conducted a qualitative study, therefore the sample size is fairly small due to the extensive analysis process of the thinking aloud protocols.

The three main contributions of our investigation are:

- An exposition of the cognitive strategies users adopt when performing map line-up tasks. We identify six cognitive strategies; most are strategies generalisable across visualization types, but one is specific to geo-spatial data.
- Findings around the factors influencing performance of map line-up tasks. These factors may result from differences in the stimulus (map size, low/high statistical intensity) or from the strategies the participants adopted (cognitive strategies, time spent on task). The most important factor influencing performance is time spent on task.
- Insight into the role of geovisualization design in influencing task performance. We compared choropleth maps and centroid-dot maps to find out which of the two supported more reliable judgements of statistical structure in maps. We conjectured that centroid-dot maps would be associated with higher success rates, especially in the more irregular geographies, as they overcome the problems associated with different sizes and shapes of spatial units, visual artefacts that are inherent to chropleth maps. Our investigation indicates that this assumption is inaccurate. Participants performance is better when using choropleth maps.

2   Related Work

The process of making inferences from graphics can be regarded as one of sense-making. Individuals tend to apply a range of different strategies or heuristics, often in combination. Newell and Simon [17] describe how heuristics can be used to cut down the large problem space to manageable dimensions. They especially describe two heuristics – hill-climbing and means-end analysis. Gigerenzer [5] argues that reasoning processes in everyday situations are often based on a specific heuristic – gut feeling. Based on empirical research he shows that this heuristic can at times be very efficient. Fast inferences made from visualization can also be described as resulting from this heuristic. Lemaire and Fabre [15] discuss cognitive strategies from a conceptual point of view. They distinguish between general and domain specific strategies and argue that many reasoning processes are a combination of the two. In Information Visualization and Visual Analytics such issues have been discussed within the framework of sensemaking theories. In this context, Klein's approach has been especially influential [9–11]. Klein distinguishes between five different processes that enable people to gain insight: making connections, finding coincidences, emerging curiosities, spotting contradictions, and being in a state of creative desperation [9]. Sedig et al. [22] point out that complex cognitive activities can be described at different levels of abstraction. Lee et al. [14]. analysed sensemaking processes and developed a model that is rather similar to Klein's approach.

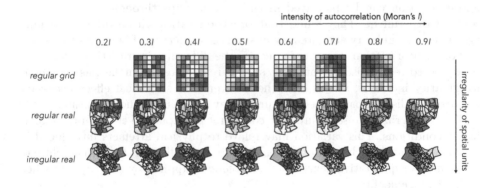

Fig. 2. We base our geographic stimuli – spatial regions – on conditions used by Beecham et al. [1]. We chose to test performance with two background levels of auto-correlation (*Moran's I*): low (0.3) and high (0.8).

Doppler Haider et al. [3] developed a model of sensemaking strategies, which is partly based on Klein's research [9]. They identify the following general sensemaking strategies: comparing (finding connections), laddering, storytelling, summarising, eliminating, verifying. They also found task specific sensemaking strategies which will not be discussed here. Pohl and Doppler Haider [19] provide a general overview of the literature on heuristics and sensemaking strategies. Our research is especially influenced by the last two papers. In the study presented in this paper we focus on sensemaking strategies used when comparing levels of autocorrelation in maps. We especially want to compare the strategies found for geo-spatial vizualisations with the strategies found for other visualization types and analyse whether there are strategies specific for detecting autocorrelation. In addition, we also want to analyse whether there are strategies that are more successful than others.

3   Study

3.1   Analytic Background and Study Aim

When presenting data in maps, analysts are often concerned with the role of space, or spatial association, in phenomena: to what extent are high crime rates concentrated in certain neighbourhoods of a city and low crime rates concentrated in others? *Spatial autocorrelation* is a concept used widely for describing this tendency [18] and *Moran's I* a formal statistic for quantifying the amount or *intensity* of autocorrelation that exists. A test statistic for spatial autocorrelation is typically derived by comparing an observed intensity of *Moran's I* against a distribution that would be expected under *complete spatial randomness* (CSR) or some sensible prior knowledge [1].

Beecham et al. [1] measured the precision with which differences in spatial autocorrelation can be perceived in choropleth maps through a large crowd-sourced experiment. They found that precision varies within different stimuli (geometric irregularity and intensity of statistical effect, cf. Fig. 2). As the intensity of autocorrelation structure increases, the difference in statistical effect necessary to correctly discriminate that structure decreases. Further, as geometric irregularity increases, so too does the difference in statistical effect necessary to correctly discriminate that structure. They also found much variation in the ability to discriminate structure that could not be explained through the experiment conditions. This variation may relate to physical artefacts introduced in choropleth maps which was not systematically controlled for. Or it may relate to differences in qualitative heuristics – *strategies* – applied by participants when making judgements.

3.2   Study Conditions

This research aims to expose and characterise the *strategies* used when making judgements in *map* line-up tests and the study conditions tested were generated using resources published through Beecham et al. [1]. A summary of the conditions tested is displayed in Table 1. We vary geometric irregularity in the same way as Beecham et al.: we use the same geographic regions, cf. Figure 3, but add a further set of three regions with approximately the same levels of geometric irregularity and twice the number of spatial units (from ≈50 to ≈100 units).

One hypothesis for the large variation in perception identified in Beecham et al. [1] relates to geovisualization design. In a choropleth map, the entirety of each spatial units is given a single colour, which can result in salience bias in favour of larger regions and other artefacts that are incidental to statistical effect. We therefore also test a centroid-dot alternative. Introducing the centroid-dot maps brings some additional challenges: with a white background, dark dots gain greater saliency, whilst the contrary is true of a black background. A light grey background appeared to minimise these artefacts. Additionally, we design line-up tests with two intensities of baseline statistical effect: *Moran's I* of 0.3 (low) and 0.8 (high).

Table 1. Study conditions.

3	Geometric irregularity (grid, regular, irregular)	×
2	Map size (small ≈50 units, large ≈100 units)	×
2	Statistical effect (low 0.3, high 0.8 – Moran's I)	×
2	Geovis types (choropleth, centroid-dot)	×
19	Participants	=
456	Tests overall	
24	Unique test conditions	

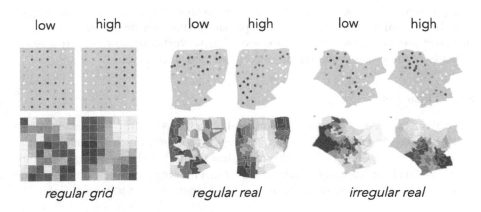

low   high   low   high   low   high

regular grid   *regular real*   *irregular real*

Fig. 3. The difficulty of line-up tests is assumed to increase with increasing irregularity of spatial units, i.e., grids and regular geometries are easier to assess than more complex, irregular geometries. The lower autocorrelation condition is assumed to be easier than the high condition for each geometry.

Since we wish to expose the various strategies employed when making line-up judgements we wished to generate line-up tasks that were relatively challenging. We therefore selected "difference" values for decoy plots based on the thresholds published in [1]. These thresholds loosely represent the minimum difference necessary to correctly judge between two choropleth maps 75% of the time – a quantity referred to as *just noticeable difference* (JND) – and take into account the modelled influence of geometric irregularity and intensity of statistical effect. By choosing difference values in this way, we hope to control for the influence of geometry and intensity of statistical effect – that is we *expect* no difference in performance due to these factors.

3.3   Design and Tasks

We used a within-subject ($N = 19$), counter-balanced design, where every participant performed 24 line-up tasks in random order. Each line-up was composed of nine images: eight *decoy plots* and one correct *target*, randomly positioned in a 3×3 array. The *target* was made different from the decoys by increasing its autocorrelation value in line with the thresholds published in Beecham et al. [1] – one JND higher than the decoys given the geometric irregularity (grid | regular | irregular) and baseline intensity of *Moran's I* (low | high). All eight decoys contain approximately the same autocorrelation level. Note that each decoy is unique – even if it contains the same spatial autocorrelation value. The decoys were generated using a permutation approach published in [1].

For each map line-up we asked the following three questions: 1) Which is the plot with the highest spatial autocorrelation? 2) How confident are you in your choice? 3) Are there possible alternatives? We specifically decided to develop challenging tasks that forced participants to reflect explicitly about the problem and possible solutions. In this way, we were better able to study the strategies used by the participants than with simple tasks that can be solved at a glance. In easier scenarios, participants are less able to verbalise how they reached a solution because the reasoning process is fast and unconscious.

3.4   Data Set

We arrived at threshold values for our conditions based on the experience of two pre-tests. Important considerations here were the time taken to complete the experiment (we wished to keep this to within 60 min) and generating stimuli of sufficient levels of difficulty to trigger slow sensemaking processes, and therefore expose *strategies*, rather than testing for pre-attentive perceptive abilities.

Difference in the Decoys of the Line-Ups. Beecham et al.'s [1] JND thresholds were generated under a very different setting to ours. Rather than a full map line-up, participants had to compare two images at a time in an established staircase procedure where the difficulty level changed due to participant performance. The aim was to encourage learning and improve performance to the extent that the JND level represents the minimum perceptible difference between the two stimuli. Since only two stimuli are used, the intuitive explanation of JND – the difference necessary to correctly discriminate 75% of the time – cannot be easily transferred to our study since the 75% figure must also include some chance-guessing.

We started by constructing line-up tests using the minimum JND threshold values published by Beecham et al. [1] and completed two pre-tests with two and three participants in each. We hypothesise that a 50:50 success rate would suggest tests that are sufficiently challenging to expose user strategies, provide sufficient number of correct and incorrect tests in order to analyse the circumstances under which correct and erroneous judgements are made, as well as maintain the motivation of the participants.

In a second round we increased the difference to the median JND thresholds used by Beecham et al. [1] and found that the target was too easy to identify with the effect that almost all answers were correct. Based on this observation we chose the value midway between minimum and mean JND's per geometry $(mean(JND) - (mean(JND) - min(JND))/2)$ and Moran's I which yielded the anticipated 50:50 performance (compare results).

3.5 Participants and Procedure

We conducted a study with 19 computer science students with a Bachelor's degree or higher, from which eleven were male and eight female. Participants were between 23 and 31 years old with fair knowledge of geovisualization (average 3.15 on a 5-point Likert scale). We asked *"How familiar are you with map visualizations?"* with ranges from extremely, moderately, somewhat, slightly to not at all familiar. One participant reported a mild red-green colour perception deficiency, who afterwards stated that she did not feel challenged with the task. We chose a colour-blind safe colour palette from colorbrewer2.org for the visualisations. Participants were trained on both map types with different data than in the experiment.

Participants trained for 10–15 min prior to the experiment. They were furnished with an explanation of spatial autocorrelation and six examples, one per map type and geography (2×3). In the trial we first collected demographic information, followed by the line-up tasks and finally preferences on the map types. We asked participants to complete line-up tasks as depicted in Fig. 1 with the exception that we specifically asked participants to identify the plot with the *greater* level of spatial autocorrelation. Participants were given feedback on these answers, but in the experiment proper, no feedback on participant performance was given. Additionally, we deliberately provided no context around the phenomena and spatial processes under investigation. Special attention was paid to instances where participants provided explanations behind judgements that included storytelling. Experiment sessions lasted between 50 and 60 min.

4 Results

4.1 Participant Performance

Overall around 50% of line-ups were correctly answered: 213 correctly and 219 incorrectly identified the target from the decoys. For each test condition we consider the number of participants that performed the line-up correctly. Figure 4 displays this information as well as a frequency plot of participants' self-reported confidence in their answers for that condition on a 5-point Likert scale ($1 =$ not at all confident; $5 =$ very confident).

The test condition with the highest success rate was the small centroid-dot map with a regular geometry and low level of baseline autocorrelation. Comparing success levels between geovisualization type, we found, counter to expectation, that the choropleth maps were associated with higher success rates than were centroid-dot maps (Cohen's d. effect size 0.64). An even larger effect was observed between the high and low baseline autocorrelation cases ($d.1.64$), with the low autocorrelation conditions associated with higher success rates than the lower cases. There is no obvious difference in success rates between map size (small and large) ($d = .02$).

On average, participants needed 42 min to complete the line-ups. There is a small correlation between used time and performance ($\rho\ (T, P) = .27$). The greater the time spent studying the line-ups, the better the performance. We have eight participants with a good success rate of more than 50%. The remaining 10 answered less than half of the test cases correctly. The individual performances differ significantly. The best performance is 18 out of 24 line-up tasks correctly answered (75%), the worst performance is 5 out 24 (20,8%). We can neither observe a clear increase nor decrease in performance over time: whilst participant performance did not improve over time, neither did it deteriorate towards the end of the experiment, although verbal protocols include statements regarding fatigue in the last third of the experiment (compare Fig. 5).

4.2 Participant Preference

Participants expressed a strong preference for choropleth maps over the centroid-dot maps. This was true of all geometries (grid 29:9, regular 32:6, irregular 32:6). Only a small number of participants preferred the centroid-dot maps and in a small number of specific cases: in the grid geometry five participants expressed a preference for the centroid-dot maps.

Overall the centroid-dots irritated the participants due to overlaps and differently sized areas between the dots. Nevertheless, when reporting this frustration, participants reflected on the importance of inter-zone distances. In one dot case a participant pitied a "lonesome" dot, as it "stands all alone by itself", reporting that it would especially catch their attention. Our design seemingly did not overcome the saliency problem with large areas and may have exacerbated it.

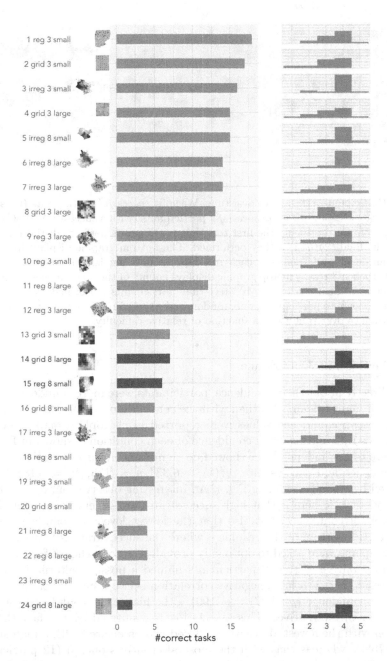

Fig. 4. Success and confidence per condition shows that participants were overconfident in the incorrect cases. Red lines show conditions that get discussed in the strategies examples. The map line-up stimuli with strategies used to form a judgement are shown in Fig. 6. (Color figure online)

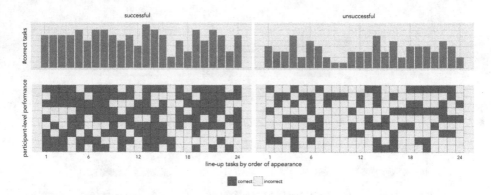

Fig. 5. Participant performance over time. We split *successful* participants (those with a success rate of >50%) from *unsuccessful* participants (with a success rate <50%). The left-most column represents the first test that participants performed; the right-most column the final (24th) test they performed. The bottom graphic displays individual, participant-level performance – each row represents a participant and each column identifies their n^{th} test. The top graphic displays counts of these columns – the number of correct identifications for the nth test that participants performed. Note that the conditions shown to participants were randomised – therefore we do not expect patterns of performance over time to be a function of relative difficulty.

4.3   Participant Confidence

Asked directly about their confidence, participants were more confident with the choropleth maps (mean 3.49) than with the centroid-dot maps (mean 3.33). The top four mean confidence values were reported in choropleth map conditions. The success rate and reported confidence of each condition is shown in Fig. 4. A chi-square test of independence showed no significant linear association between the confidence and success rate, $\chi^2(1) = 6.334, p = .175, (V = .118)$. This is confirmed by visually scanning Fig. 4. An interesting observation, hidden by the summary statistic here is that high success rates are generally associated with high levels of confidence, but also that the lowest levels of confidence do not appear at the bottom of the graphic – where the success rate is lowest.

Participants were asked to optionally provide a 'second choice' for the target. On average only 6 of the 19 participants named a possible alternative for the line-up test. There is a small negative correlation between number of alternatives and mean confidence ($\rho\,(A, C) = -.190$) – the higher the confidence the fewer the number of alternatives. This association is confirmed by the fact that the condition with the fewest alternatives offered was associated with a high success rate (>75%), whereas that with the most alternatives offered (12 participants in total volunteered an alternative target) had a success rate of only 50%.

Table 2. The sensemaking codes show a high inter-coder agreement (Cohen's Kappa $\kappa = .976$, N= 19).

Code	Frequency	Agreement rate
Cluster	499	99.6%
Transition	355	98.7%
Outlier	354	99.1%
Colour	162	97.6%
Figure	70	85.1%
Gut feeling	58	93.9%

4.4 Strategies

After transcription of the think-aloud protocols one researcher suggested possible codes for sensemaking strategies, which were consequently discussed with a second researcher. For the interpretation of the thinking aloud data we used qualitative content analysis [16,21]. This is an empirical methodology for the systematic investigation of textual data that preserves some of the advantages of quantitative content analysis but still yields rich qualitative information about textual communication. Qualitative content analysis can either adopt a bottom-up or a top-down approach. The top-down approach requires investigators to develop a frame of categories before the study, the bottom-up approach consists of a repeated processing of the material with the goal to structure the material in a way to derive the categories from the material itself. We adopted a bottom-up approach but were inspired by categories identified in previous research. The final six codes were used by both researchers and their high inter-coder agreement (Cohen's Kappa $\kappa = .976$, compare Table 2) shows that the codes are efficient and easily distinguishable. The strategies will be described in detail in the following.

To assess the performance of strategies proved to be difficult but we found a dependency of performance and strategy change. Better performing participants switched less frequently, i.e., applied fewer strategies than participants with a success rate of less than 50%. They employed clusters followed by outliers and transitions as most successful strategies, as did the participant with the overall best performance. The worse performing group could not employ the transition strategy as successfully, and was rather successful with analysing clusters and outliers. A clear pattern, however, does not emerge.

The individual performances differ to a high degree, from the best performance with 18 out of 24 line-up correct cases (75%) to the worst performance of 5 out of 24 (20,8%). The best participant took more time (55 min) than the average (42 min) for the tasks and looked at every map in close detail. She reported that the centroid-dot condition was harder as was the higher autocorrelated condition than the lower, a truly good assessment as 5 out of the 6 wrong answers showed low autocorrelations. The best participant used 81 strategies (the average ≈83). Most often *Clusters* was used and secondly, *Outliers*. The participant with the least correct answers reported a red-green colour-vision impairment but afterwards reported that she had no problems discerning the colours. She noted that lighter colours seemed to stick out less than the dark ones. Although she completed the line-ups in average time, far more strategies (118) than the average (≈83) were used. We observed quick switching between strategies and insecurity about whether a strategy was useful for the task. Interestingly, three out of the five correct line-ups were the supposedly more difficult ones, the low autocorrelated centroid-dot regular real and the high autocorrelated irregular real small and large choropleth map. Most often *Clusters* were used to come to a decision and secondly, *Outliers*, which were the only successfully used strategies that led to correct answers.

Searching for Clusters. The grouping of units into clusters of the same colour has a big influence on the decision about autocorrelation. *Examples: "There is one big cluster in the middle", "Here we have two clusters on the sides", "I take the one with the fewer clusters", "I will choose the one with the big centered cluster above this one which also looks nice, with the left to right separation".*

Identifying clusters was the most dominantly used strategy, including mentioning the number of clusters, the size of clusters and the position of the cluster. If the form of a cluster was explicitly mentioned the statements were coded as both, cluster and figure strategy. We can summarise the following observations.

– Bigger and fewer clusters were favoured. The size and consequently the number of cluster had an effect on the decision making. If there are fewer clusters in the decoys it can happen that they look more homogeneous than the higher autocorrelated plot with, e.g., two clusters having a smooth transition, and, therefore, a higher Moran's I value. This happened for example in the small, regular, choropleth map line-up (compare *Cluster* line-up in Fig. 6 plot nr.6: one yellow and one red cluster).
– Centred clusters were favoured. The position of the cluster influenced the decision in some cases and centred clusters had a greater effect than those on the side. The cluster in the middle got over-emphasised, e.g., in the case of small, grid, high autocorrelated centroid-dot maps (compare *Position* line-up in Fig. 6 plot nr.5).

These strategies seem intuitive and can lead to good decisions, however, they are not reliable for autocorrelation judgements. The clusters in the high autocorrelated regular small choropleth map condition, for example, were often wrongly interpreted and decoy plots seemed to fit better to these strategies than the correct real (compare low success rate in Fig. 7 and *Cluster* example in Fig. 6).

Analysing Transitions. This strategy summarises all statements on transitions, where participants looked for smoother changes within each plot. *Examples: "There is a nice transition to the center", "This evolves beautifully from light to dark".*

Transition was remarkably well reported in the condition of high autocorrelated regular large choropleth line-up, which led to a good success rate compared to the centroid-dot (compare Fig. 7) and fairly confident decisions (compare *11 reg 8 large* in Fig. 4).

Elimination Due to Single Outliers. Participants used single outliers in a plot as a reason to exclude the plot from the possible range of answers. Hence, this elimination strategy was sometimes heavily applied when no positive example stood out. The maximum of 8 times per line-up, however, was rarely employed, but instead, a switch to a different strategy happened with the reduced set of plots. *Examples: "I will exclude this because of these high contrasts here", "Here are also these high contrasts", "There is a very light one right next to a very dark one".*

Emphasis on Colour. Dark hues had a greater impact than light ones. Darker colour hues were more often explored than the yellow, light hues when looking for clusters and transitions in both the choropleth map and the centroid-dot map. Some participants reported on looking at orange *"mid-level"* colours, others again tried to look at both and change their focus when they were stuck in an impasse, but those were the exception. *Examples: "I mostly look at dark areas", "Maybe I should look more on light colours.. I will try that now.".*

Regarding outliers light and dark hues were equally distracting, e.g., *"One light in the middle of this dark area"*, as well as *"..but then there is this one dark dot here".*

Recognising Shapes (Storytelling). Storytelling as a possibility of designing visualizations has been discussed in the visualization community [12,13]. It has been argued that the development of a storyline supports users to form connections between disparate facts to make them memorable. Similar issues have been discussed in cognitive psychology for some time (see e.g. [26]). In cognitive psychology, the emphasis is on the activities of the study participants and how they make sense of the material that is being presented to them. Participants try to construct coherent models based on this material. We called a strategy storytelling when participants identified meaningful shapes in the maps that helped them to solve the tasks. Figure-like cluster arrangements have a big impact. *Examples: "Here are dark clouds", "A blob or an island", "..like a mountain range", "This looks somewhat like Vienna".*

If a random plot resembles some kind of figure, a recognisable pattern with some kind of meaning, it has a strong effect on the user's decision, although it is unrelated to the task of judging autocorrelation, e.g., *"This looks somehow like a man with a stick"* (compare decoy nr.8 of the *Figure* line-up in Fig. 6). This can, of course, also help if the figure is seen in the correct real, as it was the case in the low autocorrelated large choropleth grid condition where the highest autocorrelated plot was described as the shape of a *pincer* (compare real of condition *8 grid 3 large* in Fig. 4). Confidence, however, was not high in this case (compare confidence in Fig. 4).

Trusting a "Gut Feeling". This strategy summarised statements about first impressions and *gut feelings*, where no rationale could be verbalised. It is hard to discern aesthetics and other statements from this category, but we wanted to grasp how often participants were stuck in an impasse and had to give up like this, or just liked to trust their guts. We think it is due to the difficulty of the line-up tasks that this strategy was not employed very often. *Examples: "I don't know, it is just a feeling", "This was my first impression".*

Although participants mostly could not make a decision at first glance, they often had first choices as a starting point. However, this depends very much on the participant and the verbal reporting (participants usually do not verbalise in the same amount of detail). For example, participant 17 mentioned a first idea in 16× of the 24 line-ups, where she then stuck with this choice only in five of the cases. The explanation then was, e.g., *"Here I will stick to my gut feeling".* More cautious people, on the other hand, stated their gut feeling only when they were more or less sure about it, e.g., participant 19 verbalised 8× a first idea and then stuck with it in seven of the cases.

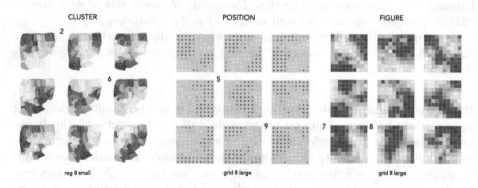

Fig. 6. Participants favoured plot 6 over 2 in the left choropleth line-up because of the smaller number of clusters; In the centroid-dot map (center) most participants chose plot 5 because of the centered cluster instead of the smoother, higher autocorrelated plot 9 leading to the worst success rate. Most participants chose plot 8 in the right choropleth line-up because of a perceived figure although plot 7 shows a higher autocorrelation value.

5 Discussion

5.1 Strategies

We conducted an investigation to study the processes underlying the perception and interpretation of autocorrelation in maps and how persons with knowledge

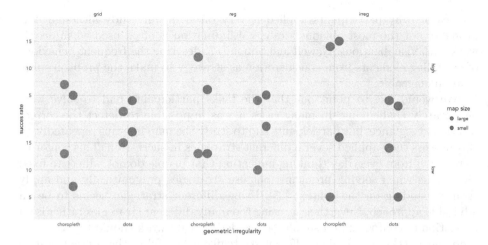

Fig. 7. Each dot represents a unique line-up – a line-up representing each experiment condition. The vertical position of dots varies according to the *success rate* for that line-up – the number of participants that correctly identified the real from the decoys.

in computer science and visualization try to solve such tasks. One of the main goals was to identify the most important cognitive strategies people use in such a context. We identified six such strategies: searching for clusters/identifying connections, analysing transitions, identifying outliers, emphasising colour, seeing meaningful figures (storytelling) and gut feeling.

The most popular trategies are *searching for clusters, analysing transitions, identifying outliers* and *emphasising colour*. The other two strategies are less important. Contrary to our expectation, we could not find any relationship between the strategy used and the performance of the participants. We specifically assumed that the strategy analysing transition would be more successful than the others because it is tightly related to the task of finding autocorrelation. This was not the case. We also had assumed that participants would use this strategy most often because it seems to be most appropriate for the task of finding autocorrelation but they relied most often on the strategy of finding clusters.

Some of the strategies can be applied to other tasks and are not specific to the spatial and spatial-autocorrelation or map-lineup context: finding clusters, identifying outliers (elimination), storytelling and gut feeling [3,6]. Especially finding clusters seems to be a very general strategy. It has some similarities with finding connections in Klein's model [9] where it is an important element. Klein argues that finding connections often occurs in the context of problem solving activities. In our experiment participants described clusters as elements having some connection with each other. From this they concluded that autocorrelation exists. Doppler Haider et al. [3] also found that finding connections is a strategy that is often adopted. Finding connections seems to be a kind of default strategy people adopt when they are not sure how to solve a problem. This might be the reason why participants applied it very often in our study although it is probably not the most obvious strategy. Elimination is often used when people work with visualizations. Newell and Simon [17] describe the frequent behaviour of excluding elements from consideration as strategy to make the problem space more manageable.

We would like to point out that the tasks participants had to solve were deliberately challenging. In many cases it was impossible to detect the correct solution at a glance, but participants had to study the map line-ups repeatedly. In this process they applied several different strategies in succession. This conforms to research from everyday thinking indicating that people do not adhere to fixed algorithms when solving problems, but use strategies pragmatically and apply them depending on the context [25]. Using different strategies seems to be an advisable approach. Nevertheless, using too many different strategies rather is an indication of confusion and should be avoided. Future work should try to clarify the issue whether combining different strategies is helpful in the context of map line-ups or not. Our experiment indicates that challenging tasks in map line-ups are difficult to solve. Drawing statistical inferences under such conditions is not a straight-forward task.

5.2   Performance and Confidence

The quantitative analysis also provides interesting results. The performance of the participants was influenced by level of autocorrelation (high vs. low autocorrelation), but not by map size. This is surprising as we have deliberately designed our line-ups to control for this effect using empirically-informed prior knowledge [1]. We assume that the 0.3 and 0.8 cases are equally difficult. That we find a lower success rate associated with 0.8 may suggest that Beecham et al.'s [1] modelling might have overrepresented the effect of statistical intensity, that the staircase procedure used in Beecham et al. [1] disproportionately improves ability to detect differences in the high autocorrelation cases and/or that line-up designs 'work harder' where the level of statistical effect is low.

There is one approach that is helpful to solve map line-up tasks. This is analysing the material in detail and spending more time on the tasks. This is probably an indication of increased motivation. This also shows that challenging map line-up tasks require the users to study the material repeatedly for a considerable amount of time.

There was no relationship between confidence about the correctness of the results and the performance of the participants. The participants apparently had difficulties to assess the correctness of their solutions, especially when the tasks were very difficult. This probably indicates that the participants need more training in detecting autocorrelation.

5.3   Map Design and Spatial Autocorrelation

We also compared choropleth and centroid-dot maps. We had assumed that centroid-dot maps would be associated with higher success rates, especially in the more irregular geographies, as they negate certain artefacts inherent to choropleth maps. Contrary to our expectation, participants performed significantly better with choropleth maps. This might be due to the fact that people are better acquainted with choropleth maps and feel more comfortable with them. Subjective ratings of the participants indicate that they prefer choropleth maps to dot maps. This could be addressed by adapting the centroid-dot design, e.g., varying size of dots, prominence of region borders or different colour palettes.

From our investigation, we can derive a few tentative ideas about factors influencing perception of autorcorrelation in maps. There are some factors that might distract viewers from detecting the real data. We saw that bigger and fewer clusters as well as clusters in the center were favoured. This indicates that other autocorrelations might be overlooked. Shapes conveying some imaginary meaning resulting in storytelling may also distract users.

The different autocorrelation levels (low and high) were received with mixed feelings. On the one hand participants liked the higher autocorrelation plots, calling them *"more pleasing"* just to realise that it made the task not easier because *"all look very good now"* (highest autocorrelated plot was not such an obvious visual outlier). In the high autocorrelated conditions participants would quickly find one or more possible candidates and while looking at each plot participants would add more and more to this subset ending up with a long list of possible answers.

We observed higher discomfort when confronted with the lower autocorrelated line-ups. Participants did not like them at first sight because they found them chaotic and could not make out any clusters or good transitions, i.e., the two most frequently applied strategies could not be applied.

5.4 Methodological Challenges

Thinking-aloud is a good method to analyse thought processes while a task is solved or a specific tool is used. It can show up what participants have in mind while they are working [2,4]. This information cannot be complete because humans are not thinking about everything they do and look at, and only verbalise certain information at a time, hence, this method has its limits.

The analysis of our verbal protocols indicate differently employed reading directions of line-ups. The starting position was deliberated by some participants - if the top most left plot or the centre position was more investigated than other. One participant was concerned, e.g., that she was always coming back to the centre. The participant stated *'I don't really know why I decided for plot 5, maybe because it's in the middle'*. From the protocols we could observe starting from the top left to the right line-by-line, chaotically jumping between plots as well as pairwise comparison between likely candidates for the answer. For a complete analysis, however, eye-tracking is necessary to see in which order the plots get fixated and commented on. This would provide more detail on the specifics of the strategies used to solve line-ups and help establish whether there are differences in performance. It would also provide detail on whether the position of the target plot makes a difference when judging spatial autocorrelation in map line-up tasks.

6 Limitations and Future Work

This work aimed to identify sensemaking strategies used in solving line-up tasks in a qualitative manner. We could identify sensemaking strategies that were used in the line-up tasks, but the relationship between usage of strategies and performance is still not entirely clear. More work is necessary to clarify this issue.

We observed that participants adopted several different strategies for the same task, but we do not know whether or not such combinations are beneficial. Analysing the order of strategies seems like an important next step - left to right, or top to bottom or scan then check - are very different. We might find that performance is better if the outlier is checked first as a baseline. Capturing eye movements may provide detailed information that could inform this work.

Similarly to Beecham et al. [1] we found great variability among participants concerning performance and strategies used. The reason for this is not clear. It would also be interesting to investigate whether people use different strategies for different levels of difficulty of the tasks or different levels of autocorrelation. We also noticed that the confidence about the solution deviated from the performance. Participants were sometimes very confident about incorrect solutions.

The sample we investigated was fairly small and consisted of computer science students. When conducting qualitative research, it is not possible to analyse larger samples because qualitative methods are very time-consuming. As far as the composition of the sample is concerned, we think that computer science students are representative of the kind of persons who might work with interactive choropleth maps and who might be interested in this topic. Nevertheless, the results may not apply to a wider population.

7 Conclusion

We conducted a study of graphical line-up tests to investigate how statistical inferences are drawn from data graphics. In this context, we are especially interested in the users' sensemaking strategies. We conducted an in-depth experiment with 19 graduate students with choropleth and centroid-dot maps. We could identify six strategies users adopt to solve challenging line-up tasks. Some of the strategies are comparable to strategies used when interacting with other visualizations (clustering/finding connections, elimination, storytelling). There is one strategy that is specific for the interpretation of map line-up tasks (transition).

Our research indicates that a successful detection of autocorrelation depends on a combination of various different strategies. Further research should clarify on which conditions specific strategies can successfully be applied. It is, for example, possible that strategies like storytelling are less successful and might be distracting. We found that using too many different strategies is an indication of confusion and should be avoided. Spending more time on the task, in contrast to that, is a condition for a successful solution of the tasks. Detecting autocorrelation sometimes apparently requires extensive exploration. We also compared choropleth maps and centroid-dot maps. In general, choropleth maps out performed centroid-dot maps. We were also able to identify some adverse conditions that may distract users (large clusters in the centre, dark clusters). We think that the results of such research can help us begin to understand the reliability of map lineup tests, how people conduct them and how we may train map readers to interpret autocorrelation and perform these tests more reliably.

Acknowledgments. The research reported in this paper has received funding from the European Union 7th Framework Programme FP7/2007-2013, through the VALCRI project under grant agreement no. FP7-IP-608142, awarded to B.L. William Wong, Middlesex University London, and Partners.

References

1. Beecham, R., Dykes, J., Meulemans, W., Slingsby, A., Turkay, C., Wood, J.: Map LineUps: effects of spatial structure on graphical inference. IEEE Trans. Vis. Comput. Graph. **23**(1), 391–400 (2017)
2. Boren, T., Ramey, J.: Thinking aloud: reconciling theory and practice. IEEE Trans. Prof. Commun. **43**(3), 261–278 (2000)
3. Doppler Haider, J., Seidler, P., Pohl, M., Kodagoda, N., Adderley, R., Wong, B.L.W.: How analysts think: sense-making strategies in the analysis of temporal evolution and criminal network structures and activities. In: Proceedings of the Human Factors and Ergonomics Society 61st Annual Meeting 2017, Austin (2017)
4. Ericsson, K.A., Simon, H.A.: Protocol Analysis. MIT Press, Cambridge (1993)
5. Gigerenzer, G.: Gut Feelings: The Intelligence of the Unconscious. Penguin (2007)
6. Haider, J., et al.: Exploring the challenges of implementing guidelines for the design of visual analytics systems. In: Proceedings of the Human Factors and Ergonomics Society Annual Meeting, vol. 59, no. 1, pp. 259–263 (2015)
7. Harrison, L., Yang, F., Franconeri, S., Chang, R.: Ranking visualizations of correlation using Weber's Law. In: IEEE Conference on Information Visualization (InfoVis), vol. 20, pp. 1943–1952 (2014)
8. Hofmann, H., Follett, L., Majumder, M., Cook, D.: Graphical tests for power comparison of competing designs. IEEE Trans. Vis. Comput. Graph. **18**(12), 2441–2448 (2012)
9. Klein, G.: Seeing What Others Don't: The Remarkable Ways We Gain Insights. PublicAffairs, a Member of the Perseus Book Group, New York (2013)
10. Klein, G., Moon, B., Hoffman, R.R.: Making sense of sensemaking 1: alternative perspectives. IEEE Intell. Syst. **21**(4), 70–73 (2006)
11. Klein, G., Moon, B., Hoffman, R.R.: Making sense of sensemaking 2: a macrocognitive model. IEEE Intell. Syst. **21**(5), 88–92 (2006)
12. Kosara, R., Mackinlay, J.: Storytelling: the next step for visualization. Computer **46**(5), 44–50 (2013)
13. Lee, B., Riche, N.H., Isenberg, P., Carpendale, S.: More than telling a story: transforming data into visually shared stories. IEEE Comput. Graph. Appl. **35**(5), 84–90 (2015)

14. Lee, S., Kim, S., Hung, Y., Lam, H., Kang, Y., Yi, J.S.: How do people make sense of unfamiliar visualizations?: a grounded model of novice's information visualization sensemaking. IEEE Trans. Vis. Comput. Graph. **22**(1), 499–508 (2016)
15. Lemaire, P., Fabre, L.: Strategic aspects of human cognition: implications for understanding human reasoning. In: Methods of Though: Individual Differences in Reasoning Strategies, pp. 11–56 (2005)
16. Mayring, P.: Qualitative Inhaltsanalyse: Grundlagen und Techniken Beltz Verlag Weinheim (2003)
17. Newell, A., Simon, H.A.: Human Problem Solving, vol. 104. Prentice-Hall, Englewood Cliffs (1972)
18. O'Sullivan, D., Unwin, D.: Geographic Information Analysis, 2nd edn. Wiley, Hoboken (2010)
19. Pohl, M., Doppler Haider, J.: Sense-making strategies for the interpretation of visualizations-bridging the gap between theory and empirical research. Multimodal Technol. Interact. **1**(3) (2017)
20. Rensink, R., Baldridge, G.: The perception of correlation in scatterplots. Comput. Graph. Forum **29**, 1203–1210 (2010)
21. Schreier, M.: Qualitative Content Analysis in Practice. Sage Publications (2012)
22. Sedig, K., Parsons, P., Liang, H.N., Morey, J.: Supporting sensemaking of complex objects with visualizations: visibility and complementarity of interactions. In: Informatics. vol. 3, p. 20. Multidisciplinary Digital Publishing Institute (2016)
23. VanderPlas, S., Hofmann, H.: Spatial reasoning and data displays. IEEE Trans. Vis. Comput. Graph. **22**(1), 459–468 (2016)
24. Wickham, H., Cook, D., Hofmann, H., Buja, A.: Graphical inference for Infovis. IEEE Trans. Vis. Comput. Graph. **16**(6), 973–979 (2010)
25. Woll, S.: Everyday Thinking: Memory, Reasoning, and Judgment in the Real World. L. Erlbaum Associates, Mahwah (2001)
26. Zwaan, R.A., Magliano, J.P., Graesser, A.C.: Dimensions of situation model construction in narrative comprehension. J. Exp. Psychol. Learn. Mem. Cogn. **21**(2), 386 (1995)

TEVisE: An Interactive Visual Analytics Tool to Explore Evolution of Keywords' Relations in Tweet Data

Shah Rukh Humayoun[1(✉)], Ibrahim Mansour[2], and Ragaad AlTarawneh[3]

[1] San Francisco State University, San Francisco, CA, USA
humayoun@sfsu.edu
[2] University of Kaiserslautern, Kaiserslautern, Germany
[3] Intel Labs, Intel Corporation, Santa Clara, CA, USA
ragaad.altarawneh@intel.com

Abstract. Recently, a new window to explore tweet data has been opened in TExVis tool through visualizing the relations between the frequent keywords. However, timeline exploration of tweet data, not present in TExVis, could play a critical factor in understanding the changes in people's feedback and reaction over time. Targeting this, we present our visual analytics tool, called TEVisE. It uses an enhanced adjacency matrix diagram to overcome the cluttering problem in TExVis and visualizes the evolution of frequent keywords and the relations between these keywords over time. We conducted two user studies to find answers of our two formulated research questions. In the first user study, we focused on evaluating the used visualization layouts in both tools from the perspectives of common usability metrics and cognitive load theory. We found better accuracy in our TEVisE tool for tasks related to reading exploring relations between frequent keywords. In the second study, we collected users' feedback towards exploring the *summary* view and the new *timeline evolution* view inside TEVisE. In the second study, we collected users' feedback towards exploring the *summary* view and the new *timeline evolution* view inside TEVisE. We found that participants preferred both view, one to get overall glance while the other to get the trends changes over time.

Keywords: Information visualization · Visual analytics · Social media exploration · Twitter · Tweet data · Adjacency matrix diagram · Chord diagram · User study

1 Introduction

Twitter has become a powerful tool for people to express their feedback, feelings, and reactions precisely towards recent topics. This create opportunities to researchers developing visual analytics (VA) tools to help users exploring and understanding underlying tweet data from different perspectives. For example, Nokia Internet Pulse [10] visualizes the evolution of Twitter discussions with a time series of stacked tag clouds, SparkClouds

© IFIP International Federation for Information Processing 2021
Published by Springer Nature Switzerland AG 2021
C. Ardito et al. (Eds.): INTERACT 2021, LNCS 12934, pp. 579–599, 2021.
https://doi.org/10.1007/978-3-030-85613-7_37

[18] integrates spark lines into the cloud tags to convey the trends between multiple tag clouds, and ScatterBlogs [34] visualizes geo-located Twitter messages.

We previously developed a tool, called TExVis [9], that enables exploration of data based on the relations between the frequent keywords. For this, TExVis used an enhanced Chord diagram to show the frequent keywords (e.g., hashtags, nouns, or verbs) and the relations between these keywords based on some criteria (e.g., the common tweets). In the TExVis user study [9], we showed that visualizing the relations between the frequent keywords based on some criteria helps users to explore and understand people' feedback and feelings towards an event. However, we found two main limitations of TExVis. First, it struggles from the visual cluttering issue in the relation area of the proposed extended Chord diagram due to the high number of relation chords between the frequent keywords (nodes), as mentioned by the participants in the TExVis user study. Second, TExVis shows the behavior of overall tweet data without considering the timeline evolution of underlying tweets. Such option can play an important role to enhance our understanding of how people's feedback and reaction are changed over time towards a particular event or product.

Targeting these limitations, we developed a visual analytics tool called **TEVisE** (**T**weets **T**imeline **E**volution **V**isual **E**xplorer). To avoid the visual cluttering, we decided to use an enhanced version of interactive adjacency matrix diagram to show the high-frequency keywords (e.g., hashtags, nouns, verbs) and the relations between these keywords based on certain criterion (e.g., the co-occurrence of keywords in same tweets). However, some researchers have suggested in the past that radial (circular) layouts produce compact visualizations and use the space efficiently than rectangular or square layouts [14, 15]. Keeping this in view, our *first research question* was which visualization layout, between the Chord diagram used in TExVis (i.e., a radial layout) and the adjacency matrix diagram used in TEVisE (i.e., a square layout), works better for the tasks related to reading and exploring the relations between the frequent keywords in tweet data.

To find out the answer of our first research question, we conducted a controlled user study with 12 participants in a lab environment. Our contributions in this regard are:

- A comparison of the visualization layouts in both tools to check the common usability aspects (i.e., *accuracy, efficiency,* and *user satisfaction*) with regard to exploring underlying tweet data. We were especially interested to see how the tasks related to the exploration of the relations between the frequent keywords effect the mentioned usability metrics.
- Assessing the cognitive load of the used visualization layouts in both tools to see their effect on users' limited working load memory capacity, which is utilized during information processing [26].

Targeting the second limitation in TExVis, we made enhancements in our TEVisE tool to show the *timeline evolution* of the frequent keywords and the relations between these keywords. With this new timeline evolution facility in TEVisE, our *second research question* was to analyze how users utilize the *timeline evolution* view for exploring an event compared to the overall *summary* view. To find the answer of this research question, we conducted a second user study with 10 new participants. Our contribution in this regard is:

- Getting the participants' subjective feedback to compare between the overall *summary* view and the *timeline evolution* view in order to see the usefulness of timeline view in exploring the underlying event.

The remainder of the paper is structured as follow. In Sect. 2, we provide the related work. In Sect. 3, we present our TEVisE tool with the enhanced adjacency matrix diagram and the timeline evolution view. In Sect. 4, we provide details of our first user study design and present the results. In Sect. 5, we describe our second user study design and present the results. In Sect. 6, we discuss the findings of both studies. Finally, we conclude the paper in Sect. 6 and shed light on future directions.

2   Related Work

As social media platforms (e.g., Twitter, Facebook) provide large amount of text data (e.g., tweets, comments, opinions, etc.), researchers developed powerful visualization and visual analytics tools to help users exploring and analyzing this huge amount of text data from different perspectives. Nokia Internet Pulse, developed by Kaye et al. [10], was one of the earliest visualization tools targeting tweet data. It visualizes the keywords frequency using a time-series of stacked clouds corresponding to a topic.

We see a deep interest in visualizing the sentiment analysis of tweets. One of the earliest works in this direction was done by Claster et at. [2], in which they visualized the sentimental polarity of over 80 millions tweets showing the effects on tourism in Thailand due to the unrest in early months of 2010. While Zhao et al. [40] examined Weibo, a Chines version of Twitter, provided timeline sentimental analysis of Weibo-based tweets in their MoodLens tool using four categories, i.e., *angry, disgusting, joyful,* and *sad*. Other examples are: Liu et at. [21] worked on the sentiment classification in tweet events. Nguyen et al. [29] used the case study of UK royal birth in 2013 and showed the sentimental polarity of tweets using a UK heat-map and a tile-map representation. Torkildson et al. [36] showed the sentiment frequency results of collected tweets, related to 2010 Gulf Oil Spill, through stacked-area chart. Wang et al. [37] developed Senti-Compass to help users exploring and comparing the sentiments of time-varying tweet data and combined the 2D psychology model of motion with a time-tunnel representation. Kempter et al. [11] proposed multi-category emotion sentiment and visualized the summary of public emotion in Olympics 2012 related tweets. Lu et al. [22] used the map view and timeline chart view to show sentiments in tweet data of disaster scenarios. Munezero et al. [28] proposed the *enduring sentiments* concept that is based on psychological descriptions of sentiments, which is built over time while enduring emotional depositions. Mohammad et al. [27] combined the stance and sentiment analysis in tweets towards a target and showed the result using different visualizations (e.g., treemap, bar charts, etc.). Hoeber et al. [7] targeted sport event tweet data to visualize distribution of top terms, hashtags, user mentions, and authors in each of three sentiment polarity class using timeline charts geo-map. Dai and Prout [3] used a continuous word representation algorithm (Word2Vec) to train vector model on sentiment and collected Super Bowl 50 related tweets to demonstrate their classification method. Recently, Kucher et al. [16] developed StanceVis Prime tool for the analysis of sentiment and stance in temporal test data in social media data source.

There are also examples of tools that focus on analyzing and exploring tweet data based on the geo-spatial information. Few examples are: MacEachren et al. [23] developed SensePlace2 tool where they focused on using the geospatial information in tweets, obtained either through extracting information from the tweets or through user profiling location. Thom et al. used ScatterBlogs to visualize geo-located Twitter messages [34] and to study crisis intelligence [35]. Kraft et al. [12] focused on extracting the structural representations of events in tweet data. While Godwin et al. [6] developed TypoTweets Map tool for associating tweets to their spatial locations.

Exploring topics and analyzing their evolution over time has also been investigated by researchers. Few examples are in this directions are: Wanner et al. [38] developed Topic Tracker tool that uses shape-based time-series visualization to show trends and sentiment tracking of user defined topics. SparkClouds tool, developed by Lee et al. [18], integrates spark lines into the cloud tags to convey the trends between multiple tag clouds. Dork et al. [5] visualized tweet data in three modes: topics over time through Topics Streams layout, people and their activity through spiral layout, and popularity of event photos through Image Cloud. TopicFlow tool, developed by Malik et al. [24], visualizes the evolution of tweets for statistical topic modeling. Sopan et al. [32] did an analysis of academic conferences hashtags over time to analyze popular trends. Stojanovski et al. [31] visualized the topic distribution in the underlying tweet data in their TweetViz tool where users can also search for any hashtag or keywords. Recently, Li et at. [20] focused on the topic popularity in tweets over space and time.

Other researchers examined tweet data from different perspectives, e.g.: Krstajić et al. [13] focused on how real-time tweets can be used to early detecting any unexpected events. Kumamoto et al. [17] analyzed the impression building of a user through the posted tweets on the user's timeline. Humayoun et al. [9] developed TExVis tool to show the relations between the frequent keywords. Martins et al. [25] developed StanceXplore tool for the interactive exploration of stance in social media.

Except TExVis [9], other tools lack investigating the impact of relations between the frequent keywords inside tweet data. We tackle the limitations of TExVis tool from two directions: providing an enhanced adjacency matrix diagram to minimize the visual cluttering issue, and providing the timeline evolution of these relations through a series of proposed adjacency matrix diagrams.

3   TEVisE: Tweets Timeline Evolution Visual Explorer

TEVisE visualizes tweet data using an enhanced interactive adjacency matrix diagram (see Fig. 1) to show the frequent keywords (e.g., hashtags, nouns, verbs) and the relations between these keywords based on a certain criterion (e.g., the *co-occurrence* of two keywords in same tweets). TEVisE was developed as a web-based tool using web technologies (e.g., HTML5, CSS, and JavaScript) and libraries such as *JQuery, d3.js* and *node.js* server.

As a proof of concept in this paper, we use the same dataset that was used by TExVis [9], which is consisted of 41,199 tweets (with 56,701 distinct keywords) and was extracted from Twitter using the "brexit" keyword. We assigned random ID numbers to individual tweets in order to anonymize the real users' IDs. The tweets (only in English and excluding the retweets) were fetches from Twitter using the *Tweetinvi* and *Twitter REST* APIs using a requesting loop for the time period between July 01 to July 10, 2016. The tweets were then tokenized based on hashtags, nouns and verbs using the *Apache OpenNLP* natural language processing library. Frequently used non-noun or non-verb hashtag were also separated as a token to use for frequent keywords. In order to classify tweets based on the contained sentimental polarities [30], we used the Aylien.TextApi library for each retrieved tweet. The library returns the polarity value (e.g.,*positive, negative,* or *neutral*) alongside the confidence value (between 0% to 100%) of the stated polarity value. We used MongoDB as a database system to store the retrieved tweets and the above-mentioned data after pre-processing on stored tweets.

3.1 The Enhanced Adjacency Matrix Diagram

Some participants of TExVis user study [9] mentioned the visual cluttering problem in the relation area of the used Chord diagram (i.e., radial layout). Therefore, we decided to use a square layout (i.e., an adjacency matrix diagram) in TEVisE rather than a radial layout in order to avoid the visual cluttering issue. We argue that the implicit fashion of showing the relations using the intersections between the rows and columns in an adjacency matrix diagram reduces visual cluttering in the relation area. Due to this, we also argue that it enhances the readability of relations and supports users to preserves the mental map of the underlying data. Also, it is easy to compare a series of adjacency matrix diagrams in the case of timeline evolution.

We designed an enhanced interactive version of adjacency matrix diagram to show the high-frequency keywords, the relations between these keywords, and the sentimental polarity of the associated tweets to each keyword. Figure 1 shows the proposed enhanced adjacency matrix diagram using the "brexit" dataset having the most frequent twenty keywords. Initially, TEVisE shows only one adjacency matrix diagram, called the *summary* view, as in Fig. 1, representing the overall summary result of all tweets collected against a specific keyword. This view can be changed into the *timeline evolution* view (see Fig. 2(a)) to show the change over time, see the forthcoming section.

The nodes in our adjacency matrix diagram represent the high-frequency keywords (i.e., most popular *hashtags, nouns,* or *verbs*), which were extracted as tokens from the underlying tweet dataset. Initially, the nodes are arranged in the descending order based on keyword frequency, from top to bottom or left to right. A bar is attached to each node representing the corresponding keyword's frequency. The inside colors of these attached bars represent the division of sentimental polarity of associated tweets (i.e., green for *positive*, blue for *neutral*, and red for *negative*), where each color's length represents the frequency of associated tweets to a certain sentimental polarity. Mouse hovering over a particular node (keyword) or the attached bar shows further details through a tool tip (e.g., number of associated tweets, average confidence level, etc.).

The matrix cells are used to show the relations between the frequent keywords, based on a certain criterion (e.g., in *co-occurrence* a relation occurs if both keywords are in

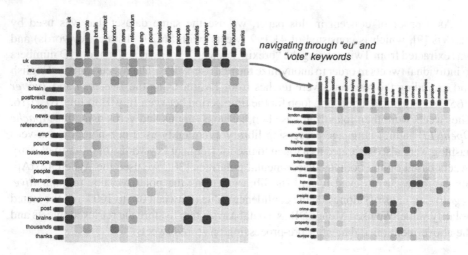

Fig. 1. The initial enhanced adjacency matrix diagram for "brexit" dataset *(left)* and the new diagram after navigating through "eu" and "vote" keywords *(right)*.

the same tweet or the *word-similarity* relation of two keywords with a value of (0, 1] using the WordNet.Net library, etc.). The opacity of a matrix cell's grey color represents the value of the relation, e.g., Fig. 1 (left) shows that people are talking more about "uk" and "startups" in same tweets, as these keywords show a high relation value in the co-occurrence relation. We decided to use only grey color scaling rather than color coding for the relation cells' values, so users would not confuse it with the attached bars' sentiment color coding. Mouse hovering over a particular matrix cell highlights this cell and the corresponding keywords in red color and brings a tooltip to show further details, e.g., the total number of associated tweets to this relation.

Navigation in the proposed enhanced adjacency matrix diagram is provided on-demand, which enables inspecting and exploring tweets that contain the selected keyword(s). This is achieved by clicking on a particular keyword or a matrix cell, which results in showing a menu with the option of navigation. In both cases, selecting navigation option results a new matrix diagram as a next level-of-details and deals with only those tweets that contain the selected keyword(s), see Fig. 1. Selecting this option from a keyword brings the new matrix diagram with a one-level-down details, while selecting it from a matrix cell brings the new matrix diagram with a two-levels-down details. For example, navigating "eu" and then "vote" in two steps in Fig. 1 brings a new matrix diagram related to only those tweets that have "brexit", "eu", and "vote" keywords together in them. This can be achieved directly in one step by navigating from the relation cell between the "eu" and "vote" keywords.

3.2   The Timeline Evolution of Tweets

Timeline analysis of tweets can play a critical role in enhancing our understanding of how people's feedback and reaction are changed over time towards a particular event or product. TEVisE uses a series of adjacency matrix diagrams (see Fig. 2) to provide the timeline evolution of tweets, where each matrix diagram represents tweet data of a certain time period. In the *timeline evolution* view, the number of resulting matrix diagrams is based on the user's selection of time period over the total time period of underlying tweet data (e.g., based on hours, days, weeks, or months). These matrix diagrams are arranged from left to right and right to left at alternatively rows (starting from the top row) to provide a smooth viewing from one timeline to another one. TEVisE provides three categories to represent the timeline evolution of tweets:

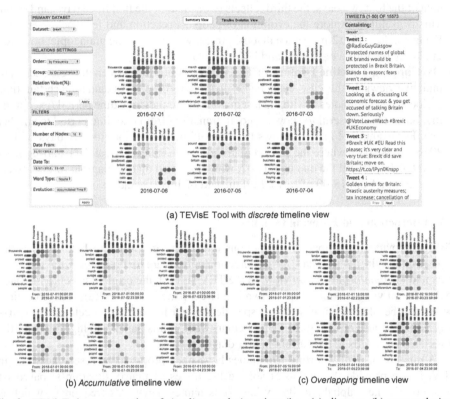

(a) TEVisE Tool with *discrete* timeline view

(b) *Accumulative* timeline view   (c) *Overlapping* timeline view

Fig. 2. TEVisE three categories of *timeline evolution* view (i.e., (a) *discrete*, (b) *accumulative*, and (c) *overlapping*) using the tweets from the first six days of "brexit" dataset.

- **Discrete Timeline Evolution:** In this case, each matrix diagram reflects tweet data of a certain time period in a way that the underlying data of this diagram is mutually exclusive with the data before that time period and after that time period. Figure 2(a) shows the "brexit" dataset in this view over the first six days of July 2016. In this case, each matrix diagram represents tweet data of only a particular day of the selected six days. Such discrete timeline visualizations are useful to explore the changes of people's reaction and feedback from one time period to another one. For example in Fig. 2(a), we see initially that on July 01 and 02 people talked more about those topics and keywords that are related to initial protests (e.g., "protest", "march", "london", "thousand"); however, on July 04 and 05 people were more concerned about Europe future as they talked more about "eu", "uk", "vote", and "postbrexit". We also see the same trend in the relation cells between these keywords.

- **Accumulative Timeline Evolution:** In this case, each timeline division accumulates tweet data from the beginning to the current time period. Therefore, each matrix diagram reflects tweet data from the beginning to the current time period. For example, Fig. 2(b) shows the "brexit" dataset over the first six days of July 2016, where the first matrix diagram reflects tweet data only of the first day, the second reflects tweet data of the first two days, the third reflects tweet data of the first three days, and so on. This is useful to explore the evolution of people's reaction and feedback over time. For example in Fig. 2(b), we see that the protest was initially the main topic; however, gradually the future of Europe and UK took place over it.

- **Overlapping Timeline Evolution:** This is a hybrid form between discrete and accumulative views. In this case, each matrix diagram reflects tweet data for a certain time period and accumulates it with the last quarter of the previous time period (except the first one). This is useful to show a smooth transition from one time period to another one. For example, Fig. 2(c) shows the "brexit" dataset of the first six days of July 2016 in this style, where the second matrix diagram reflects tweet data starting from 18:00 of July 01 till the end of July 02, while the third matrix diagram reflects tweet data starting from 18:00 of July 02 till the end of July 03, and so on.

3.3   Interaction and Filtering Options

TEVisE provides a number of interactions and filtering options to help users better explore underlying tweet data. These interaction options are for both views, the *summary* view and the *timeline evolution* view. In the TEVisE tool, the original tweets associated to the current visualization(s) are shown in a tweet panel (see Fig. 2(a)). These original tweets can be filtered out based on a specific keyword or a relation cell in the matrix diagram(s). Mouse hovering over a particular tweet in this panel also highlights all the associated keywords in the current matrix diagram(s).

A number of matrix sorting techniques have been proposed by researchers [1]. In TEVisE, we provide the option of sorting the nodes of matrix diagram(s) based on three criteria, i.e.: alphabetically by keywords names, keywords frequency (which is the default option) with descending or ascending order, or relation value. In the case of relation-based sorting, a keyword (node) gets the position (descending or ascending) based on the total of all corresponding relation values. In the *timeline evolution* view, mouse hovering over a keyword highlights this keyword and if presents then in all other matrix diagrams as well, while mouse hovering over a particular cell highlights this cell and the associated keywords and if presents then in all other matrix diagrams as well. Furthermore, individual zoom and panning facility is provided for all matrix diagrams.

In addition, users can filter the current matrix diagram(s) in both views through a number of filtering options using the filter-panel (see Fig. 2(a)) in the tool, e.g.: selecting the relation type (e.g., *co-occurrence* or *word-similarity*), selecting relation percentage range (between any value from 0% to 100%), navigating the matrix diagram(s) based on a given keyword, selecting the number of nodes, selecting tweet data based on time by giving a starting and ending time value, and selecting what specific type of keywords should be shown (e.g., hashtags, nouns, verbs, or all). During the exploration and analysis of tweet data, users can switch between the summary view and the timeline evolution view while using all the interaction and filtering options, either provided directly on the matrix diagram or through the filtering panel.

4   User Study 1: TEVisE vs. TExVis

TExVis used radial layout (Chord diagram) [9], as it has also been claimed by researchers [14, 15] in the past that radial layouts encourage eye movement to proceed along the curved line of the circular diagrams, which helps viewers to better understand and explore the underlying data. However, we used the adjacency matrix diagram in TEVisE to avoid the visual cluttering in the relation area, which was mentioned by TExVis user study participants. In order to find the answer of our first research question, i.e., which layout amongst the used ones in both tools works better for the tasks related to reading and exploring the relations between the frequent keywords in tweet data, we conducted our first user study with 12 participants in a lab environment.

4.1   Study Goals

The goal of our first user study was to compare between the used visualization layouts in both tools from the perspective of common usability aspects, i.e., *effectiveness aka accuracy*, *efficiency*, and *user acceptance*. We were interested on how these usability aspects are effected due to the tasks related to reading and exploring the relations between frequent keywords using the visualizations in both tools.

Furthermore, we decided to investigate the cognitive load and the mental efforts that users needed while working with the underlying visualization layouts in both tools. Cognitive load theory was initially postulated by John Sweller [33] to measure the load of lessons and assessing learning. Current findings in the theory supports a three-factor approach, i.e., *intrinsic load:* the load associated with the material or subject matter, *extraneous load:* the load type predicated on the design, instructional and task complexity, and *germane load:* the load type measuring the elements contributing to learning [4]. In general, cognitive load theory is based on a limited working memory capacity, which is utilized during information processing [26]. Evaluating the used visualization layouts in both tools from the perspective of these three cognitive load factors would help us understanding the effect of the used visualization layouts on users' limited working memory capacity with respect to exploring tweet data.

4.2   Participants and Material

We were able to requite 12 participants (4 females and 8 males with average age of 27.3) on volunteer basis. The participants were either master-level students (i.e., 9) or recently graduated (i.e., 3). Amongst the participants, 10 were from computer science background while the remaining 2 were from electrical engineering background. All the participants reported not having any prior experience working with any of the underlying visualization layouts. Furthermore, none of them reported any color deficiency or any kind of color blindness.

The study was conducted as a *between-subject* study, where the participants were allocated randomly to either TEVisE or TExVis. Before starting an experiment, participants gave their informed consent and filled the pre-questionnaires form for collecting demographic information (i.e., age, gender, educational background, experience with underlying visualization, color deficiency or blindness). Then the participants were introduced to the experiment set-up with a 10-min tutorial of the underlying tool and the used visualization. The same examiner was presented during all experiments. The study took place in a quite office environment using a 15.6-in. display laptop, where both web-based tools were installed locally to avoid any network latency. We used the "brexit" dataset as it was supported by both tools. We used only the *summary* view of TEVisE in this study, as TExVis does not support timeline evolution view.

Figure 3 shows two examples of the visualization layouts in both tools for this study. In the case of TExVis [9] (the Chord diagrams in Fig. 3), nodes (arcs) represent the high-frequency keywords where a node's width represents the frequency, while the chords between nodes represent relations between the keywords based on some criteria (e.g., occurring in the same tweet). The width of a chord represents the relation value. Arcs outside of nodes are used to show the sentimental polarity of the associated tweets.

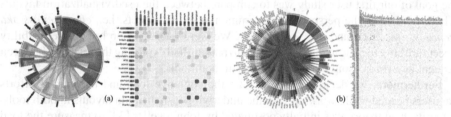

Fig. 3. The Chord diagram of TExVis [9] and the enhanced adjacency matrix diagram of TEVisE with 20 high-frequency keywords (a) and 100 high-frequency keywords (b). The participants in the study were allowed to configure the node size (frequent keywords) between 5 to 100.

4.3 Tasks, Hypotheses, and Metrics

We distilled 12 tasks in a way that encourages insight and sense-making and structured these 12 tasks into four categories (i.e., *overview, adjust, detect pattern,* and *match mental model*), according to the insight-gaining process by Yi et al. [39]. After the completion of each task category, participants were asked to fill out an adaptation version of the cognitive load questionnaire (with an eleven-point scale from 0 to 10) by Leppink et al. [19] to assess the cognitive load of the last tasks' category. There were 8 questions in this questionnaire classified into *intrinsic, extraneous,* and *germane* load sections. At the end, participants filled out a subjective closed-ended questionnaire with 10 questions using a 5-points Likert-scale, and an open-ended questionnaire.

We treated the used visualization as an independent variable, while the common usability aspects, i.e., effectiveness, efficiency, and user satisfaction, were taken as a dependent variables. Based on this, we formulated four hypotheses. Due to the visual cluttering issue in the relation area of the Chord diagram in TExVis:

- **H1:** We were expecting that TEVisE participants would achieve a higher accuracy value: *Accuracy(TEVisE) > Accuracy(TExVis)*
- **H2:** We were expecting that TEVisE participants would need less time to complete tasks compared to TExVis participants: *Time(TEVisE) < Time(TExVis)*
- **H3:** We were expecting that TEVisE would get higher user acceptance score in the subjective feedback than TExVis:
  User Acceptance(TEVisE) > User Acceptance(TExVis)
- **H4:** We were expecting that TEVisE would get lower rating of extraneous load (EL) and higher rating of germane load (GL):
  EL(TEVisE) < EL(TExVis) & GL(TEVisE) > GL(TExVis)

There were four tasks in the *overview* category with the nature of gaining insight about the underlying visualization, e.g., detecting nodes with specific qualities or detecting nodes having specific relation values; three tasks in the *adjust* category with the nature of filtering data and adjusting the underlying visualization, e.g., filtering the visualization per specific period of time or finding out nodes with a certain type of relation; three tasks in the *detect pattern* category with the nature of discovering detailed information from the underlying visualization, e.g., extracting some information from the visualization based on a certain keyword or identifying some relations with a certain values; and two comparative complex tasks in the *match mental model* category with the aim of ensuring how much the user has grasped the whole idea of underlying data as well as the underlying visualization, e.g., identifying and exploring keywords with higher positive or negative associated polarities.

4.4 Usability Results

Figure 4 shows the average accuracy per task for both tools. In the *overview* category, TEVisE achieved 93.75% overall average accuracy compared to 59.5% for TExVis. In the *adjust* category, TEVisE achieved 100% overall average accuracy compared to 63% for TExVis. In the *detect pattern* category, TEVisE achieved 83.33% overall average accuracy compared to 100% for TExVis. While in the *match mental model* category, both tools achieved 100% overall average accuracy. Overall, participants of TEVisE achieved 93.75% overall average accuracy in all twelve tasks compared to 77.25% for TExVis. When we check the results of both tools through applying the independent sample t-test statistically for hypothesis H1; we get $t = 2.02123, p\text{-}value = 0.027794$ at $p < 0.05$. These results support the acceptance of our hypothesis H1.

We found out that TEVisE participants performed much better in those tasks that were related to identifying the relations between the keywords, which indicates the effectiveness of TEVisE in examining and exploring the relation area. Also, the cluttering appeared in the relation area of the Chord diagram played critical role for the low accuracy of TExVis participants in those tasks. On the other side, we found that TExVis participants performed better in those two tasks where they were asked to give answer

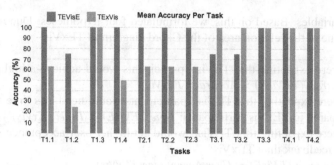

Fig. 4. Average accuracy results per task for TEVisE and TExVis

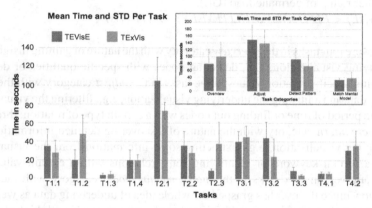

Fig. 5. Average efficiency results per task of TEVisE and TExVis participants. The top right-side box shows the average efficiency results per task-category.

related to a particular node. This can indicate that TExVis participants were more comfortable answering the tasks related to individual nodes, while TEVisE participants were more comfort for answering the tasks related to the relations among nodes.

Figure 5 shows the time required per task by participants of both tools and the overall time in each task-category. Participants using both tools achieved very comparative response with an overall average of 29.33 s for TEVisE compared to 29.58 s for TExVis. We found that participants had higher standard deviation values in the first two categories, which indicates that they reached to a common learning ground of the tool throughout the experiment duration. When we check the results of both tools through applying the independent sample t-test statistically for hypothesis H2; we get $t = -0.02522, p\text{-}value = 0.490053$ at $p < 0.05$. In this case, we failed to reject the null hypothesis. We think that participants spent more time in understanding the implicit relations in the TEVisE matrix diagram of. At the same time, we think due to the cluttering issue in the TExVis Chord diagram, participants' latency also got affected.

In the closed-ended questionnaire, TEVisE received higher average score on five questions, TExVis received higher average score on two questions, while both tools received same average score in the three questions. Overall, TEVisE received an average score of 4.2 compared to 3.9 for TExVis. When we check the results of both tools through applying the independent sample t-test statistically for hypothesis H3; we get $t = 1.19839$, $p\text{-value} = 0.123153$ at $p < 0.05$. In this case as well, we failed to reject the null hypothesis. However, we found a major difference in the question 4, which was about the ease of discovering the relations between the keywords, where TEVisE received 4.5 score compared to 3.0 for TExVis. This again indicates the cluttering issue in the relation area of TExVis Chord diagram.

In the open-ended feedback, TExVis participants mentioned explicitly that they found it difficult to follow the relation-paths between the nodes due to the visual cluttering issue, even though filtering options were provided in the used Chord diagram. On the other side, TEVisE participants mentioned that the node-relation discovery in the used adjacency matrix diagram was useful in related tasks.

4.5 Cognitive Load Results

Based on the cognitive load theory's differentiation between the three loads, a minimum rating of extraneous load and a maximum rating of germane load is preferred in the results [19]. Intrinsic load is a load imposed by the inherent difficulty of the subject matter and cannot be influenced by the design of the visualization. Figure 6 shows the average factor scores for the three load types in all four categories of tasks.

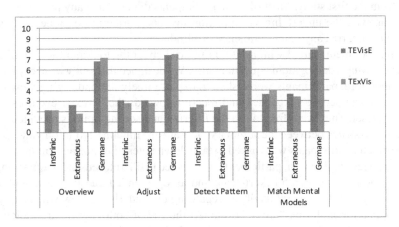

Fig. 6. Average factor scores for the three load types in the four categories of tasks.

As intrinsic load is independent of the resulting visualization; therefore, we were expecting the same kind of results in both tools. This is confirmed as the results show a quite similar score of intrinsic load in all categories of tasks between both tools. The extraneous load is based on the design, instructional and task complexity. In this case, the overall average score for TEVisE is 2.9 compared to 2.6 for TExVis ($t = 0.65311$, $p\text{-value} = 0.268945$ at $p < 0.05$). The difference between both tools is notably caused by the overview task category with an average extraneous load of 2.6 for TEVisE compared to 1.8 for TExVis. This could give an indication that the Chord diagram is more effective initially to provide the insight of underlying visualization at the beginning. The germane load is used to measure the elements contributing to learning. In this case, we do not find much difference between both groups, as TEVisE average rating is 7.5 compared to 7.6 for TExVis ($t = -0.26726$, p-value $= 0.399109$ at $p < 0.05$). In this case, we also failed to reject the null hypothesis.

5   Study 2: TEVisE Exploratory Study Between the Summary View and the Timeline Evolution View

We conducted a second user study to find the answer of our *second research question*, i.e., to analyze how users utilize the new *timeline* evolution view for exploring tweet data for an event compared to the *summary* view. The study was conducted as a *within-subjects* style, where half of the randomly selected participants first used the summary view and then the timeline evolution view and the other half did it in the reverse order. Initially, we recruited 12 participants on volunteer basis; however, 2 participants were not able to work on both tools due to some technical issues; therefore, we excluded these 2 participants feedback form the study. The remaining 10 participants (3 females, aged 24–37, M = 28.4) were master-level students, where 9 of them were from computer science background and one was from business analytics background. We recruited those participants who did not participate in the first study in order to avoid any learning effects from the first study. Most of these participants did not have any prior experience of working with the underlying visualization layouts. Furthermore, none of these 10 participants reported any color deficiency or blindness.

Each experiment started with a 10-min tutorial about the tool and the visualization layout, following a demographic questionnaire. We designed this study in an exploratory format; therefore, participants were asked to explore freely the underlying view for 10 min and analyze people's feedback and reaction towards the "brexit" event using the "brexit" dataset. They were free to use the filtering and sorting options provided by the tool, except to switch between the summary view and the timeline evolution view. During the experiment, participants were asked to take down notes of important findings. At the end of each view exploration, participants were asked to fill a closed-ended questionnaire with five questions using a 5 Likert-scale and an open-ended questionnaire with three questions to give their general feedback regarding the underlying view when analyzing the tweet data for exploring "brexit" event. At the end of both views' exploration, participants were also asked to provide their overall feedback about the both views. Each experiment lasted no more than one hour, including a 10-min break between the two views' exploration. The study was conducted in a quite office environment using a 32-in. monitor, where the TEVisE tool was installed locally to avoid any network latency.

5.1   Results

In the first four questions of closed-ended questionnaire (i.e., *intuitiveness of the underlying visualization, easiness of finding the important information, support of underlying view to analyze the tweet data, and recommending the underlying view to use in future*), participants showed comparative more positive feedback towards the timeline evolution view compared to the summary view (i.e., 4 vs 3.7, 4.2 vs 4.3, 4.2 vs 3.9, and 4.3 vs 4.2

respectively for timeline evolution vs summary view). In the case of summary view, the fifth question was *"whether there is no need of timeline exploration view"* then all the participants, irrespective of whether they had already worked on the timeline evolution view or not, either strongly disagreed or disagreed (1.8 average score) with this statement. While in the timeline evolution view, the fifth question was *"importance of the timeline evolution exploration"*. In this case, most of the participants strongly agreed with the statement (4.8 average score). In spite of the same underlying visualization in both views, participants were better able to explore the underlying event and this can be the reason for getting a comparative positive feedback towards the timeline evolution view. The importance of timeline evolution view for better exploration is also shown from the feedback of question 5 in both cases.

In the open-ended questionnaire, we asked the participants to give their feedback about the important visual cues that they used in the underlying view when analyzing the "brexit" event. In the case of summary view, most of the participants told that they used all the important visual cues of the proposed matrix adjacency diagram like the frequency bars, the sentimental polarities, and the co-occurrence relation matric cells. However, few participants said that they focused more towards a particular visual cues among them. While in the case of timeline evolution view, most of the participants (i.e., 7) also mentioned explicitly the timeline in addition to the above-mentioned visual clues. They greatly appreciated the timeline evolution exploration of tweet data. Three examples are: *"Got a sense of time and how events were happening"*, *"How easy it is to look at different combination of the data, and how the relationships change as you include some history"*, and *"I liked how easy it is to see trends change over a few days. The timeline view allowed me to see how the first couple of days were focused more on the protests, and how people started talking more about voting over time"*.

At the end of both views' exploration, we asked the participants to give their general feedback towards the both views. Many participants recommended that they would prefer to use both, e.g., one participant said: *"Both are necessary and complement each other"*. Participants mentioned that the summary view is good to get an overall glance of underlying tweet data, e.g., one participant said: *"Summary is useful to see the overall picture about an event. It can give us insights into the most talked topics and the relations between them"*. However, most of the participants mentioned that the timeline evolution view is important to see the changing of people's reaction and feedback over time, e.g.: *"The timeline mode can reveal more information about a particular day which can help users to dive deep into the data to explore the information"* or *"Timeline works better to see the changing trend"*. When asked which view is their first preference between both, 7 participants chose the timeline evolution view while 3 participants chose the summary view. These results indicate that both views help the user in exploring the event, the summary view for giving the accumulative glance of the event while the timeline evolution view for seeing the trends changes over time.

6   Discussion

We carried out two user studies to find the answers of our two research questions. Finding of our first user study can be summarized as the following:

- **Effectiveness aka accuracy:** In our first user study, TEVisE participants gained comparative higher accuracy compared to TExVis participants (i.e., overall average of 93.75% accuracy compared to 77.25% respectively), which indicates the effectiveness of the used enhanced adjacency matrix diagram in TEVisE. Mainly, TExVis achieved low accuracy in those tasks that were somehow related to the relations between the keywords, probably due to the visual cluttering issue in the relation area of the used Chord diagram. When we look into the results, we can infer that the used Chord diagram was useful when extracting information visualized on the curved line of the layout (e.g., information regarding nodes in it), as the radial layout encourages eye movement to proceed along the curved line of the underlying layout. However, the high density of relations between the nodes lowered down the accuracy due to the visual cluttering in the relation area of Chord diagram.
  Proper utilization of filtering and interaction options in the relation area of radial layouts can be useful for getting more accurate results. In TExVis, mouse hovering over a particular node results in fading of all other nodes' relations and changing the colors of this node's relations according to the opposite associated nodes. However, this did not help much TExVis participants in the related tasks, as keeping track of all or targeted relations was difficult due to visual cluttering. Therefore, we suggest investigating more about the kind of filtering and interaction options before applying them in the relation area of radial layouts. On the other side, the implicit fashion of using the transactions between the rows and columns in the used adjacency matrix diagram reduces the visual cluttering in the relation area, thus helped the TEVisE participants in executing the related tasks more accurately. Overall, we can infer that if tasks are more oriented towards extracting information regarding nodes, then radial layouts could be better choice for getting higher accuracy, while square layouts showing the relations implicitly (like our enhanced adjacency matrix diagram) could be better choice for tasks related to the relations between nodes.
- **Efficiency aka Latency:** In the case of time to complete the tasks, we received very mixed results, as in few tasks TEVisE participants performed better while in other tasks TExVis participants performed better. We also did not find any relation with efficiency to the accuracy. For example, in the tasks where TEVisE participants achieved higher accuracy, sometimes they took more time while in other cases they took less time than TExVis participants. In two tasks where TExVis participants achieved higher accuracy, we also see the same pattern. Overall both tools achieved the same latency average.
- **User acceptance:** The closed-ended feedback score endorses the accuracy finding, as TExVis received lower score in the relation related statement. This finding is further supported by the open-ended feedback, as some TExVis participants explicitly highlighted the difficulty of following paths to discover information about a relation due to the visual cluttering. As mentioned earlier that although the filtering options were provided in the used Chord diagram; however, it seems that TExVis participants became confused from the initial cluttering in the relation area of the diagram. On the other hand, TEVisE participants found the used matrix adjacency visualization useful in relation discovery and exploration. Few suggestions were provided by the participants for improving the interaction in our enhanced adjacency matrix diagram,

e.g., highlighting the whole column and row when selecting a specific relation cell rather than just highlighting the corresponding keywords.

- **Cognitive Load:** Based on our results, TExVis showed a relatively better cognitive load indication rather than TEVisE. Although, a comparative low extraneous load rating and a slightly high germane load rating indicates the higher complexity of the adjacency matrix diagram compared to the Chord diagram; however, participants required nearly the same overall average time to finish the target tasks in both visualizations. We think that another reason of having low extraneous load score and high germane load score for TExVis might be due to the radial layout, as it encourages the eye movement to proceed along the curved lines rather than a zig-zag fashion in a square or rectangular figure [15]. Overall, participants of both visualizations mentioned an average of low mental effort for the *overview* and *adjust* sections, and very low mental effort for the *detect pattern* and *match mental model* sections.

With regard to answering our first research question, it is clear from the results that the adjacency matrix diagram used in TEVisE is more suitable for the tasks related to reading and exploring the relations between the keywords in tweet data, as it received higher accuracy score with nearly the same level of efficiency. Also, it provided a comparative overall higher user acceptance score with a clear difference in the question related to the relation area. On the other side, the Chord diagram used in TExVis showed a low extraneous load rating and a slightly high germane load rating, which indicates a comparative lower effect on users' limited working load memory when using this layout. However, the difference is not significantly different from TEVisE ratings. Therefore, we think it is comparable to use a square visualization layout, such as in TEVisE, in many real scenarios (e.g., analyzing tweets regarding an event for journalism, exploring tweets towards a new launched product to understand people's feedback, etc.), in order to get more accurate answers of relations-related questions. On the other side, we also suggest using the radial visualization layout, such as in TExVis, if emphasize is driven more towards tasks related to exploration of nodes. However, in such cases we suggest investigating more about the effectiveness of used filtering and interaction options before applying them in the relation area for getting higher accuracy.

There are some limitations in our study. Although, the used tweet data was real for the "brexit" event; however, the study was carried out with students only. Using a real interested user group for such event (e.g., journalists) would provide more insight of our first research question. Furthermore, we were able to compare only the summary view of TEVisE, as TExVis does not support timeline evolution view. Comparing the two visualizations from the timeline evolution perspective may reveal new findings both from usability and cognitive load perspectives, which is missing in our study. Also, the study was done with a limited pool of users; therefore, further studies are required in order to generalize the results between both visualization layout types.

In the case of second user study, the participants' feedback show the importance of timeline evolution view when exploring and analyzing people's feedback and reaction changing over time due to the continuous developments concerning the event. We also asked whether they would like to use both views or only one of the views, then 8 participants preferred to use both views while just two participants preferred to use the timeline evolution view only. This shows that both, the summary view as well as the timeline evolution view are necessary as one gives the overall glance of underlying tweet data while the other is useful to explore and analyze people's feedback and reaction over time for an in-depth analysis.

7 Conclusion and Future Work

In this paper, we presented our TEVisE tool to overcome the two main limitations of a previously developed tool TExVis, which struggles from the visual cluttering issue in the relation area and lacks in providing the timeline exploration of underlying tweet data. Visualizing the timeline of frequent keywords and their relations based on a certain criteria opens the doors to provide in-depth exploration of how people's reaction and feedback are changed over time towards some topics. Furthermore, such facility can be useful for many user groups and application domains, e.g., journalists can analyze tweets to explore and understand people's feedback and reaction over time towards an event, companies can analyze customers' reaction towards their new launched products, etc. We conducted two user studies to find the answers of two formulated research questions. We found out that using our enhanced adjacency matrix diagram in TEVisE increases the accuracy for the tasks related to reading and exploring relations between the frequent keywords. However, we found out that the Chord diagram used in the TExVis tool is slightly more preferable in terms of the cognitive load metrics. We discussed our general findings of both user studies in the previous section.

In the future, we intend to assess both views within our TEVisE tool (i.e., the summary view and the timeline evolution view) from the cognitive load perspective in order to see their impact on users' memory. We also want to analyze those factors that can improve the cognitive load in the case of cross-link multi-view visualizations such as the case of timeline evolution view. Furthermore, we plan to include additional functionalities in the tool, e.g.: the geo-spatial information in order to see people's feedback and reaction based on their locations (as few of the participants mentioned about it in their feedback), support of other social media platform (e.g., Facebook), and visual comparison of tweet data of two or more identical events/products in order to compare people's feedback and reaction towards these events/products.

References

1. Behrisch, M., Schreck, T., Pfister, H.: GUIRO: user-guided matrix reordering. IEEE Trans. Visual Comput. Graph. **26**(1), 184–194 (2020)
2. Claster, W.B, Cooper, M, Sallis, P.: Thailand – tourism and conflict: modeling sentiment from twitter tweets using naïve bayes and unsupervised artificial neural nets. In: Proceedings of the International Conference on Computational Intelligence, Modelling and Simulation (CIMSim), pp. 89–94 (2010)
3. Dai, X., Prout, R.: Unlocking super bowl insights: weighted word embeddings for twitter sentiment classification. In: Proceedings of the the 3rd Multidisciplinary International Social Networks Conference on Social Informatics 2016, Data Science 2016 (MISNC, SI, DS 2016), Article 12, pp. 1–6. Association for Computing Machinery, New York (2016)

4. DeLeeuw, K.E., Mayer, R.E.: A comparison of three measures of cognitive load: evidence for separable measures of intrinsic, extraneous, and germane load. J. Educ. Psychol. **100**(1), 223 (2008)

5. Dörk, M., Gruen, D., Williamson, C., Carpendale, S.: A visual backchannel for large-scale events. IEEE Trans. Vis. Comput. Graph. **16**(6), 1129–1138 (2010)

6. Godwin, A., Wang, Y., Stasko, J.T.: TypoTweet maps: characterizing urban areas through typographic social media visualization. In: Short Papers of the Eurographics Conference on Visualization (EuroVis 2017), Barcelona, 12–16 June 2017 (2017)

7. Hoeber, O., Hoeber, L., Meseery, M.E., Odoh, K., Gopi, R.: Visual twitter analytics (vista): temporally changing sentiment and the discovery of emergent themes within sport event tweets. Online Inf. Rev. **40**(1), 25–41 (2016)

8. Huang, W., Hong, S.-H., Eades, P.: Predicting graph reading performance: a cognitive approach. In: Proceedings of the 2006 Asia-Pacific Symposium on Information Visualisation - Volume 60, APVis 2006, pp. 207–216. Australian Computer Society, Inc., Darlinghurst (2006)

9. Humayoun, S.R., Ardalan, S., AlTarawneh, R., Ebert, A.: TExVis: an interactive visual tool to explore Twitter data. In: 19th EG/VGTC Conference on Visualization (EuroVis 2017), Eurographics and EEE VGTC, Barcelona, 12–16 June 2017 (2017)

10. Kaye, J.J., Lillie, A., Jagdish, D., Walkup, J., Parada, R., Mori, K.: Nokia internet pulse: a long term deployment and iteration of a twitter visualization. In: CHI 2012 Extended Abstracts on Human Factors in Computing Systems (CHI EA 2012), pp. 829–844. Association for Computing Machinery, New York (2012)

11. Kempter, R., Sintsova, V., Musat, C., Pu, P.: EmotionWatch: visualizing fine-grained emotions in event-related tweets. In: Proceedings of the International AAAI Conference on Weblogs and Social Media (ICWSM), pp. 236–245 (2014)

12. Kraft, T., Wang, D.X., Delawder, J., Dou, W., Yu, L., Ribarsky, W.: Less after-the-fact: investigative visual analysis of events from streaming Twitter. In: Proceedings of the IEEE Symposium on Large-Scale Data Analysis and Visualization (LDAV), pp. 95–103 (2013)

13. Krstajić, M., Rohrdantz, C., Hund, M., Weiler, A.: Getting there first: real-time detection of real-world incidents on Twitter. In: Proceedings of the IEEE Workshop on Interactive Visual Text Analytics (TextVis), October 2012

14. Krzywinski, M.I., et al.: Circos: an information aesthetic for comparative genomics. Genome Res. **19**(9), 1639–1645 (2009)

15. Krzywinski, M. I.: Benefits of a circular layout. Circos. http://circos.ca/intro/circular_app roach/. Accessed 20 May 2021

16. Kucher, K., Paradis, C., Kerren, A.: Visual analysis of sentiment and stance in social media texts. In: Proceedings of the Eurographics/IEEE VGTC Conference on Visualization: Posters (EuroVis 2018), pp. 49–51, Eurographics Association, Goslar (2018)

17. Kumamoto, T., Wada, H., Suzuki, T.: Visualizing temporal changes in impressions from tweets. In: Proceedings of the 16th International Conference on Information Integration and Web-based Applications & Services (iiWAS 2014), pp. 116–125. Association for Computing Machinery, New York (2014)

18. Lee, B., Riche, N.H., Karlson, A.K., Carpendale, S.: SparkClouds: visualizing trends in tag clouds. IEEE Trans. Vis. Comput. Graph. **16**(6), 1182–1189 (2010)

19. Leppink, J., Paas, F., Van der Vleuten, C.P.M., Van Gog, T., Van Merriënboer, J.J.G.: Development of an instrument for measuring different types of cognitive load. Behav. Res. Methods **45**(4), 1058–1072 (2013). https://doi.org/10.3758/s13428-013-0334-1

20. Li, J., Chen, S., Andrienko, G., Andrienko, N.: Visual exploration of spatial and temporal variations of tweet topic popularity. In: Proceedings of the EuroVis Workshop on Visual Analytics (EuroVA), pp. 7–11 (2018)

21. Liu, S., et al.: Co-training and visualizing sentiment evolvement for tweet events. In: Proceedings of the 22nd International Conference on World Wide Web (WWW 2013 Companion), pp. 105–106. Association for Computing Machinery, New York (2013)
22. Lu, Y., Hu, X., Wang, F., Kumar, S., Liu, H., Maciejewski, R.: Visualizing social media sentiment in disaster scenarios. In: Proceedings of the International Conference on World Wide Web (WWW), pp. 1211–1215 (2015)
23. MacEachren, A.M., et al.: SensePlace2: GeoTwitter analytics support for situational awareness. In: Proceedings of the IEEE Conference on Visual Analytics Science and Technology (VAST), pp. 181–190 (2011)
24. Malik, M, et al.: TopicFlow: visualizing topic alignment of Twitter data over time. In: Proceedings of the 2013 IEEE/ACM International Conference on Advances in Social Networks Analysis and Mining (ASONAM 2013), pp. 720–726. Association for Computing Machinery, New York (2013)
25. Martins, R., Simaki, V., Kucher, K., Paradis, C., Kerren, A.: Stancexplore: visualization for the interactive exploration of stance in social media. In: 2nd Workshop on Visualization for the Digital Humanities VIS4DH 17, 02 October 2017 (2017)
26. van Merriënboer, J.J.G., Sweller, J.: Cognitive load theory and complex learning: recent developments and future directions. Educ. Psychol. Rev. **17**, 147–177 (2005)
27. Mohammad, S.M., Sobhani, P., Kiritchenko, S.: Stance and Sentiment in tweets. Sepc. Sect. ACM Trans. Internet Technol. Argument. Soc. Media **17**(3), 1–23 (2017)
28. Munezero, M., Montero, C.S., Mozgovoy, M., Sutinen, E.: EmoTwitter – a fine-grained visualization system for identifying enduring sentiments in tweets. In: Gelbukh, A. (ed.) CICLing 2015. LNCS, vol. 9042, pp. 78–91. Springer, Cham (2015). https://doi.org/10.1007/978-3-319-18117-2_6
29. Nguyen, V.D., Varghese, B., Barker, A.: The royal birth of 2013: analysing and visualising public sentiment in the UK using Twitter. In: Proceedings of the IEEE International Conference on Big Data, pp. 46–54 (2013)
30. Pang, B., Lee, L., Vaithyanathan, S.: Thumbs up? Sentiment classification using machine learning techniques. In: Proceedings of the ACL-02 Conference on Empirical Methods in Natural Language Processing - Volume 10 (EMNLP 2002), pp. 79–86, Association for Computational Linguistics, USA (2002)
31. Sijtsma, B., Qvarfordt, P., Chen, F.: Tweetviz: visualizing tweets for business intelligence. In: Proceedings of the International ACM SIGIR Conference on Research and Development in Information Retrieval (SIGIR), pp. 1153–1156 (2016)
32. Sopan, A., Rey, P.J., Butler, B., Shneiderman, B.: Monitoring academic conferences: real-time visualization and retrospective analysis of backchannel conversations. In: 2012 International Conference on Social Informatics, Lausanne, pp. 62–69 (2012)
33. Sweller, J.: Cognitive load during problem solving: effects on learning. Cogn. Sci. **12**(2), 257–285 (1988)
34. Thom, D., Bosch, H., Koch, S., Worner, M., Ertl, T.: Spatiotemporal anomaly detection through visual analysis of geolocated Twitter messages. In: Proceedings of the 2012 IEEE Pacific Visualization Symposium (PACIFICVIS 2012), pp. 41–48. IEEE Computer Society, USA (2012)
35. Thom, D., et al.: Can Twitter really save your life? A case study of visual social media analytics for situation awareness. In: 2015 IEEE Pacific Visualization Symposium (PacificVis 2015), Hangzhou, pp. 183–190 (2015)
36. Torkildson, M.K., Starbird, K., Aragon, C.: Analysis and visualization of sentiment and emotion on crisis tweets. In: Luo, Y. (ed.) CDVE 2014. LNCS, vol. 8683, pp. 64–67. Springer, Cham (2014). https://doi.org/10.1007/978-3-319-10831-5_9

37. Wang, F.Y., Sallaberry, A., Klein, K., Takatsuka, M., Roche, M.: SentiCompass: interactive visualization for exploring and comparing the sentiments of time-varying Twitter data. In: Proceedings of the IEEE Pacific Visualization Symposium (PacificVis 2015), pp. 129–133 (2015)
38. Wanner, F., Weiler, A., Schreck, T.: Topic tracker: shape-based visualization for trend and sentiment tracking in Twitter. In: Proceedings of the IEEE Workshop on Interactive Visual Text Analytics (2012)
39. Yi, J.S., Kang, Y., Stasko, J.T., Jacko, J.A.: Understanding and characterizing insights: how do people gain insights using information visualization? In: Proceedings of the 2008 Workshop on BEyond Time and Errors: Novel evaLuation Methods for Information Visualization (BELIV 2008). Association for Computing Machinery, New York (2008)
40. Zhao, J., Dong, L., Wu, J., Xu, K.: MoodLens: an emoticon-based sentiment analysis system for Chinese tweets. In: Proceedings of the 18th ACM SIGKDD International Conference on Knowledge Discovery and Data Mining (KDD 2012), pp. 1528–1531. Association for Computing Machinery, New York (2012)

Visualization of User's Behavior in Indoor Virtual Environments Through Interactive Heatmaps

Luca Chittaro and Marta Serafini[✉] [iD]

HCI Lab, Department of Mathematics, Computer Science and Physics, University of Udine,
via delle Scienze 206, 33100 Udine, Italy
serafini.marta@spes.uniud.it

Abstract. Three-dimensional virtual environments (VEs), such as those used in video games and virtual reality experiences, pose new challenges to the study of user's behavior. This paper proposes a system based on the combination of two heatmaps for the analysis of user's movement in the VE and of the areas looked at by him/her. It also describes a pilot study aimed at assessing the efficacy of the system. Results of the study indicate that the system can effectively support analysts in identifying user's look-at behaviors as well as navigation strategies, patterns, and coverage of specific areas during movement.

Keywords: Virtual environment · Information visualization · Heatmap · User behavior · Visual analytics

1 Introduction

Three-dimensional virtual environments (VEs), such as those used in video games and virtual reality experiences, pose new challenges to the study of user's behavior. Recent years saw a growth in interest in tools that support the analysis of user behavior in VEs by visualizing data collected during usage [1, 6, 8–10, 12–15, 18, 19, 21–23, 25, 26]. For example, visualizations can highlight the most frequented areas of the VE and the paths followed by users, helping analysts understand users' navigation behavior and how different design choices can affect it. In the literature, research on tools for the analysis of user's behavior in VEs has typically focused on two-dimensional representations such as maps [1–3, 6, 10–12, 14, 18, 19, 24–26], while solutions that visualize behavioral data directly in the three-dimensional VE are still rare, motivating further research.

This paper focuses on an innovative combination of existing ideas to propose a system that, given a VE that represents an indoor, real or imaginary, environment (indoor VE), provides a visualization of user's movement together with a visualization of how much different parts of the VE have been looked at by the user. We also evaluate the effectiveness of the proposed system by conducting a pilot study with a group of experts in the field of virtual reality and games.

© IFIP International Federation for Information Processing 2021
Published by Springer Nature Switzerland AG 2021
C. Ardito et al. (Eds.): INTERACT 2021, LNCS 12934, pp. 600–609, 2021.
https://doi.org/10.1007/978-3-030-85613-7_38

The paper is organized as follows: we first discuss the related work in Sect. 2, then Sect. 3 illustrates the proposed system, while Sect. 4 presents the pilot study and its results. Finally, Sect. 5 discusses results and outlines future work.

2   Related Work

In the literature, tools for visual analysis of user's movement typically employ two alternative types of techniques. The first type visualizes the path followed by each user on a 2D map of the VE [2, 3, 6, 12, 14, 18, 19, 26] to support detailed analysis. The second type is the 2D heatmap, which highlights the most frequented areas of the VE [4, 6, 24]. Most studies of spatiotemporal user's behavior have focused on 2D top-down representations of user's movement, but some of them have started to allow the analyst to examine the visualization from different viewpoints [8, 9, 13, 15, 16, 21, 23]. Bidimensional heatmaps are widely used in the literature also to visualize the frequency of specific events (e.g., user's death, gunshot) [10, 12, 26].

However, when the analyst needs to study where users looked at in the VE, this kind of heatmaps is not sufficient because the information on the third dimension is lost. For this reason, heatmaps superimposed on the entire VE, called 3D heatmaps, have been proposed as an alternative to the traditional 2D heatmap. For example, Stellmach et al. [22] proposed two different techniques for visualizing looked-at objects of the VE with an eye tracker. The first technique (object-based attentional map) considers the entire surface of each object in the VE and assigns to it a color that indicates how much the user looked at the object. Since this technique considers the object as a whole, it provides an overview of the looked-at objects but does not give detailed information on which areas of the object have been looked at. The second technique (surface-based attentional map, also called triangle-based attentional map) visualizes observational data directly on the surface of each object in the VE using vertex-based mapping (i.e., it first colors the vertices based on looked-at data and then the triangles of the 3D model are colored by interpolation). This heatmap should allow the analyst to see which areas of the object have been looked at but is affected by two issues. First, the accuracy of the visualization depends on the resolution of the triangulation (i.e., objects with a small number of vertices will not produce accurate attentional maps). Second, when triangles are colored, if the object is relatively small, the coloring may extend to parts of the object that were not visible from the user's viewpoint. It must also be noted that an object is considered to be looked-at when the eye-tracker detects a fixation on that object, and both visualizations ignore the other objects in close proximity, possibly leading to a lack of coloring of nearby objects in the user's field of view. Maurus et al. [17] proposed a 3D heatmap that considers occlusions of the user's view by objects and as Stellmach et al., uses an eye tracker to collect user's precise gaze data. Unlike [22], they perform the computation of the looked-at areas at the pixel level instead of the vertex level. Pfeiffer et al. [20] presented a 3D heatmap based on special textures, called attention textures, applied to the surfaces of objects and created by mixing the colors of the heatmap with those of the original object so that its original texture remains distinguishable. Kraus et al. [16] proposed a visualization technique of looked-at areas that wraps all the surfaces to be monitored in the VE with a uniform grid. Each vertex of the grid increases a counter every time a user looks at it. In this way, the visualization allows to clearly distinguish among looked-at, not looked-at and occluded areas by coloring the grid in green, red, and blue respectively according to a threshold value.

To summarize, current techniques show that heatmaps are able to properly represent both user's movement and looked-at areas, but their combinations are still rare in 3D VEs. An exception is the recent work by Kepplinger et al. [15] who proposed a combination of visualizations that shows in the 3D VE the user's path and the objects (s)he looked at. The former is represented by connected segments while the latter is represented by a gradient heatmap on the contours of the looked-at objects of interest.

In this work, we aim at integrating a 3D heatmap of looked-at areas with a heatmap of movement, making them viewable from any angle inside the VE. The combination of these two visualizations can help the analyst to better understand user behavior, e.g. by highlighting what is the object the user looked at from each of his/her positions.

3   The Proposed System

The system we propose aims at helping in the analysis of single user's behavior in indoor VEs by visualizing usage data directly within the VE and supporting exploration of the visualization from arbitrary view angles. As shown in Fig. 1, the system integrates two heatmaps into an interactive interface, using two different gradients. To visualize user's movement, we adopted the 2D heatmap proposed by Kraus et al. [16], with a black-to-yellow gradient. To visualize looked-at areas, we combined instead the surface-based attentional map [22] and the 3D heatmap by Maurus et al. [17], with a black-to-red gradient. The resulting heatmap operates on pixels instead of vertices of 3D objects, thus becoming independent from the number of vertices used to model the object. Moreover, it is able to exclude occluded objects [17], with the possible exception of some parts of the objects that are not visible from the user's viewpoint, as in surface-based attentional maps [22].

To determine looked-at objects and areas in the VE, the system uses a raycast that points to the center of the scene viewed by the user and colors a circular area around that point on the surface of the object. Furthermore, unlike Stellmach et al., it does not consider as looked-at only the object in the center of the field of view, but spreads the attention to the objects in its close proximity under a distance threshold, obtaining a more accurate result. Furthermore, the system works without the need for an eye tracker, supporting collection of data from large numbers of online users who do not have special hardware.

The interactive interface of the system adds the possibility for the analyst to select objects of interest: they will be circled in the VE to highlight their location and facilitate visual retrieval. The analyst can turn on or off each visualization as well as object-circling. In addition, (s)he can apply a temporal filter to visualize only data in a time interval. For example, in Fig. 2 time is restricted to the first 30 s of data, allowing the analyst to discover the following behaviors. From the movement visualization, the analyst can conclude that the user walked only along the upper corridor and moved continuously instead of using teleportation. From the visualization of looked-at objects, the analyst can conclude that the user: (i) passed close to the "Luggage" object but did not look at it because (s)he was looking towards the middle row of seats, and (ii) saw the "Ball" object even though it was on the corridor (s)he did not travel.

Both visualizations use gradients that scale on brightness because color maps such as the classic rainbow map: (i) are not perceptually ordered, (ii) are not suitable for presenting small details because the human visual system cannot perceive small hue changes which can thus obscure information, and (iii) can introduce artifacts into the visualization. The last problem arises from the fact that sharp transition between the different hues of the rainbow color map can be perceived by the analyst as a sharp difference in the visualized data, leading to misinterpretations [5].

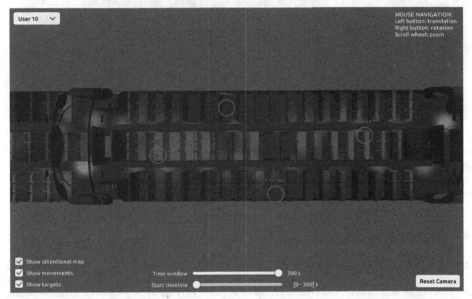

Fig. 1. Top-down view with both visualizations activated. The black-to-yellow gradient on the floor allows to quickly notice that this user's navigation strategy is based on teleportation. Visualization of looked-at areas uses instead a black-to-red gradient: black coloring of the "Pillow" and "Fire truck" objects indicates they have not been looked at by the user. For the interpretation of color in this figure, the reader is referred to the web version of this article.

Our proposed system shows user's behavior directly in the VE, representing user's movement and the observed areas with a 2D and 3D heatmap, respectively. In this way, unlike Keppliger et al. [15], it is possible to recognize the navigation strategy used (e.g., to distinguish continuous motion from teleportation), as well as identify which parts of the objects' surfaces were looked at, by highlighting them directly on the 3D objects, and examining the objects from different angles. For example, in Fig. 2., the arbitrary viewpoint allows one to see that even though the user did not look at the top row of seats, (s)he still looked at the sides of seats facing the corridor, including their armrest.

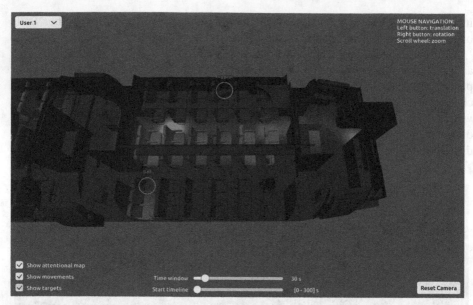

Fig. 2. The system with arbitrary view angle active, both visualizations active, and a time interval set to 30 s since the beginning of the session. The black-to-yellow gradient on the floor highlights that the user moved continuously instead of using teleportation. The black-to-red gradient highlights that the user looked at the "Ball" object but not at the "Luggage" object. For the interpretation of color in this figure, the reader is referred to the web version of this article.

4   Pilot Study

4.1   Objectives, Dataset and Participants

A pilot study was conducted with a group of experts in VEs to evaluate the effectiveness of the interactive visualization system. We used a dataset of real users' behavioral data that was collected in an experiment whose purpose was to test users' ability to remember the position of target objects placed on some seats of an indoor VE that could be navigated with a continuous or teleportation strategy. The indoor VE was a reproduction of the cabin of a Boeing 777 twin-aisle aircraft, and users carried out a visual inspection that flight attendants have to perform with no passengers on board. We chose this dataset because it is representative of the typical datasets concerning users moving in a VE and at the same time puts central aspects of our system under test. Indeed, it allows to evaluate the effectiveness of: (i) the visualization of movement, which should allow analysts to recognize the general and detailed patterns of movement followed by each user, and (ii) the visualization of looked-at areas, which should allow analysts to recognize which target objects were looked at or not by each user.

The pilot study involved four experts in the field of VEs. They were members of the HCI Laboratory at the University of Udine, and none of them was involved in the design of the system or had previously used it. They were asked to carry out four different analysis tasks on the data of each of 10 users taken from the dataset. We chose the 10 specific cases from a total of 127 in a way that covered different possibilities such as:

users who relied on teleportation vs. users who did not, users who visited the entire VE vs. users who left some areas unexplored, users who looked at all target objects vs. users who looked only at some target objects.

4.2 Procedure

Since the study was carried out during the Covid-19 lockdown, it was conducted remotely. Each expert was sent a link to download the system and a document that described the visualizations and the interface. They used the system on their own computer and completed a questionnaire on Google Forms. This actually contributed to make the context more naturalistic, since analysts are going to use this kind of tools on their computers, in the places where they work.

The effectiveness of the system in supporting the experts was measured by asking them to perform four different analysis tasks on each of the 10 users, resulting in 40 analyses performed by each expert. The questionnaire was organized in 10 identical sections, one for each of the 10 cases. Each section was organized into 4 subsections, one for each task. The aim of task T1 was to recognize the general user's navigation pattern, and experts were asked to identify whether the user moved in the VE using a continuous movement strategy or teleportation. In T2, the goal was to detect whether the user followed a specific path: experts were asked to report whether or not the user had followed a path that was suggested to him/her, i.e. traveling from the starting point (identical for all users) to the opposite side of the VE through only one aisle, and then returning to the starting point through only the other aisle. T3 focused on the ability to detect whether the user had explored a specific wide area of the VE, and experts were asked to report whether or not the user had completed at least one full tour of the VE. Experts were informed that a tour of the VE was to be considered complete if the user had visited the entire VE without leaving areas unexplored, thus fully using both corridors in the VE. T4 focused on the ability to identify which objects were looked at and which were not by the user: for each of the 8 target objects in the VE, experts were asked to indicate whether or not it had been looked at by the user.

4.3 Results

The results obtained with the proposed visualization system were compared with those that would be obtained if the contribution of the visualization was not better than chance. For each of the four tasks, the proportion of correctly identified user behaviors was thus subjected to the appropriate non-parametric test (binomial test), after checking its assumptions were met, following Cohen [7]. Since the outcome of each answer obtained from experts was dichotomous, the expected proportion of correct answers if the effects of the visualization were not different from chance is 50%. For each task, the obtained proportions were instead ideal (100%) or close to ideal (95%), and the binomial test indicated that they were significantly higher than those expected. The obtained results for each task are illustrated respectively by Tables 1, 2, 3 and 4, for each expert as well as for all experts combined. For all 10 users, all experts correctly recognized the type of navigation (T1) and identified whether users had followed the suggested path (T2). Experts were able to recognize if users had covered a specific area (T3) for a number of users that was 9 or 10 (M = 9.5, SD = 0.58). Finally, in T4 they were able to correctly identify which target objects were looked at or not for a number of objects that ranged from 72 to 80 (M = 76.0, SD = 4.08).

Table 1. Results for task T1

Expert	Right answer	Wrong answer	Significance test
E1	10	0	p < 0.01
E2	10	0	p < 0.01
E3	10	0	p < 0.01
E4	10	0	p < 0.01
All	40	0	p < 0.001

Table 2. Results for task T2

Expert	Right answer	Wrong answer	Significance test
E1	10	0	p < 0.01
E2	10	0	p < 0.01
E3	10	0	p < 0.01
E4	10	0	p < 0.01
All	40	0	p < 0.001

Table 3. Results for task T3

Expert	Right answer	Wrong answer	Significance test
E1	10	0	p < 0.01
E2	10	0	p < 0.01
E3	9	1	p < 0.05
E4	9	1	p < 0.05
All	38	2	p < 0.001

Table 4. Results for task T4

Expert	Right answer	Wrong answer	Significance test
E1	72	8	$p < 0.001$
E2	80	0	$p < 0.001$
E3	73	7	$p < 0.001$
E4	79	1	$p < 0.001$
All	304	16	$p < 0.001$

5 Discussion and Conclusions

This paper proposed a visualization system to support the analysis of user's behavior in indoor VEs. The results obtained in the pilot study provide an indication that the system can effectively support analysts in detecting navigation strategies, patterns, and coverage of specific areas in terms of movement as well as look-at behaviors. By discussing with experts about the errors made with the movement visualization (a total of 2 errors, both in task T3), it came out that one expert had considered a tour complete also when the user reached the opposite side of the VE and then returned to the starting point, even if the user did not walk through all the in-between areas. The discussion with experts also allowed us to identify the four reasons behind the relatively few errors made in identifying which target objects were looked at or not by users. First, in 4 of the 16 errors, the expert concluded that the target object was looked at by the user even if the visualization had correctly painted the object in black, e.g., the target "Fire Truck" in Fig. 1. This happened because the expert reasoned that, since nearby objects had been looked at (e.g., some seats near "Fire Truck" in Fig. 1), then the user might have looked at the target too. Second, 2 errors were due to a slip by the expert in selecting the answer in the questionnaire. Third, for 2 errors, the reason was particularly interesting because it highlighted a difficulty in interpretation that may arise in a specific case, i.e. when the visualization paints a small object in dark red because it has been briefly looked at by the user, but the small object is placed on a large object which has mostly not been looked at and is thus painted in black. This highlights the need for further refinement of 3D heatmaps of the areas looked at by the user. For example, it should be evaluated whether changing the size of the colored area for each looked-at point on objects could make it easier to clearly recognize that the target object has been seen in the above described case. The remaining 8 errors revealed that some experts concluded that the user had not looked at the target object even if it was painted in dark red. This coloring reflected the fact the user had looked at the target briefly compared to the total duration of the session. However, the expert reasoned that, since the object was painted in very dark red, it was unlikely that the user had looked at it.

Our research will now continue along two main lines, also considering the above mentioned issues. First, we will introduce new features into the system to increase the level of support offered by the interface to the analyst. For example, the system could semi-automatically propose an identification of the objects that were looked at based on thresholds defined by the analyst. This would also help preventing the last source of error described above. Second, we will assess the effectiveness of the system in supporting the detection of VE design problems, e.g. finding the VE areas where the user got stuck, due to the used navigation techniques or the architectural modeling of the VE. In addition, we will compare our system with visualization tools that use 2D representations, such as those presented in Sect. 2, to highlight the strengths and weaknesses of both solutions. A larger sample of participants will also be considered.

References

1. Ahmad, S., Bryant, A., Kleinman, E., Teng, Z., Nguyen, T. H. D., Seif El-Nasr, M.: Modeling individual and team behavior through spatio-temporal analysis. In: Proceedings of the Annual Symposium on Computer-Human Interaction in Play, pp. 601–612 (2019). https://doi.org/10.1145/3311350.3347188

2. Almeida, S., Mealha, O., Veloso, A.: Video game scenery analysis with eye tracking. Entertain. Comput. **14**, 1–13 (2016). https://doi.org/10.1016/j.entcom.2015.12.001

3. Aung, M., et al.: The trails of just cause 2: spatio-temporal player profiling in open-world games. In: Proceedings of the 14th International Conference on the Foundations of Digital Games, pp. 1–11 (2019). https://doi.org/10.1145/3337722.3337765

4. Barros, V.P., Notargiacomo, P.: Big data analytics in cloud gaming: Players' patterns recognition using artificial neural networks. In: 2016 IEEE International Conference on Big Data (Big Data), pp. 1680–1689 (2016). https://doi.org/10.1109/BigData.2016.7840782

5. Borland, D., Taylor, R.M., II.: Rainbow color map (still) considered harmful. IEEE Comput. Archit. Lett. **27**(02), 14–17 (2007)

6. Chittaro, L., Ranon, R., Ieronutti, L.: Vu-flow: A visualization tool for analyzing navigation in virtual environments. IEEE Trans. Visual Comput. Gr. **12**(6), 1475–1485 (2006). https://doi.org/10.1109/TVCG.2006.109

7. Cohen, B.H.: Explaining Psychological Statistics, 4th edn. John Wiley & Sons, Hoboken (2013)

8. Dixit, P.N., Youngblood, G.M.: Understanding information observation in interactive 3d environments. In: Proceedings of the 2008 ACM SIGGRAPH symposium on Video games, pp. 163–170 (2008). https://doi.org/10.1145/1401843.1401874

9. Dixit, P.N., Youngblood, G.M.: Understanding playtest data through visual data mining in interactive 3d environments. In: 12th International Conference on Computer Games: AI, Animation, Mobile, Interactive Multimedia and Serious Games (CGAMES), pp. 34–42 (2008)

10. Drachen, A., Canossa, A.: Analyzing spatial user behavior in computer games using geographic information systems. In: Proceedings of the 13th International MindTrek Conference: Everyday Life in the Ubiquitous Era, pp. 182–189 (2009). https://doi.org/10.1145/1621841.1621875

11. Drachen, A., Canossa, A.: Towards gameplay analysis via gameplay metrics. In: Proceedings of the 13th International MindTrek Conference: Everyday life in the Ubiquitous Era, pp. 202–209 (2009). https://doi.org/10.1145/1621841.1621878

12. Drachen, A., Canossa, A.: Evaluating motion: spatial user behaviour in virtual environments. Int. J. Arts Technol. **4**(3), 294–314 (2011). https://doi.org/10.1504/IJART.2011.041483

13. Drenikow, B., Mirza-Babaei, P.: Vixen: interactive visualization of gameplay experiences. In: Proceedings of the 12th International Conference on the Foundations of Digital Games, pp. 1–10 (2017). https://doi.org/10.1145/3102071.3102089

14. Hoobler, N., Humphreys, G., Agrawala, M.: Visualizing competitive behaviors in multi-user virtual environments. In: IEEE Visualization 2004, pp. 163–170. IEEE (2004). https://doi.org/10.1109/VISUAL.2004.120
15. Kepplinger, D., Wallner, G., Kriglstein, S., Lankes, M.: See, Feel, Move: player behaviour analysis through combined visualization of gaze, emotions, and movement. In: Proceedings of the 2020 CHI Conference on Human Factors in Computing Systems, pp. 1–14 (2020). https://doi.org/10.1145/3313831.3376401
16. Kraus, M., Kilian, T., Fuchs, J.: Real-time gaze mapping in virtual environments. In: EUROVIS 2019: 21st EG/VGTC Conference on Visualization (2019). https://doi.org/10.2312/eurp.20191135
17. Maurus, M., Hammer, J.H., Beyerer, J.: Realistic heatmap visualization for inter- active analysis of 3d gaze data. In: Proceedings of the Symposium on Eye Tracking Research and Applications, pp. 295–298 (2014). https://doi.org/10.1145/2578153.2578204
18. Moura, D., El-Nasr, M.S., Shaw, C.D.: Visualizing and understanding players' behavior in video games: discovering patterns and supporting aggregation and comparison. In: ACM SIGGRAPH 2011 game papers, pp. 1–6 (2011). https://doi.org/10.1145/2037692.2037695
19. Mueller, S., et al.: HeapCraft: interactive data exploration and visualization tools for understanding and influencing player behavior in Minecraft. In: Proceedings of the 8th ACM SIGGRAPH Conference on Motion in Games, pp. 237–241 (2015). https://doi.org/10.1145/2822013.2822033
20. Pfeiffer, T., Memili, C.: Model-based real-time visualization of realistic three-dimensional heat maps for mobile eye tracking and eye tracking in virtual reality. In: Proceedings of the Ninth Biennial ACM Symposium on Eye Tracking Research & Applications, pp. 95–102 (2016). https://doi.org/10.1145/2857491.2857541
21. Schertler, R., Kriglstein, S., Wallner, G.: User guided movement analysis in games using semantic trajectories. In: Proceedings of the Annual Symposium on Computer-Human Interaction in Play, pp. 613–623 (2019). https://doi.org/10.1145/3311350.3347156
22. Stellmach, S., Nacke, L., Dachselt, R.: 3D attentional maps: aggregated gaze visualizations in three-dimensional virtual environments. In: Proceedings of the International Conference on Advanced Visual Interfaces, pp. 345–348 (2010). https://doi.org/10.1145/1842993.1843058
23. Stellmach, S., Nacke, L., Dachselt, R.: Advanced gaze visualizations for three-dimensional virtual environments. In: Proceedings of the 2010 Symposium on Eye-tracking Research & Applications, pp. 109–112 (2010). https://doi.org/10.1145/1743666.1743693
24. Tremblay, J., Torres, P., Rikovitch, N., Verbrugge, C.: An exploration tool for predicting stealthy behaviour. In: Proceedings of the AAAI Conference on Artificial Intelligence and Interactive Digital Entertainment, vol. 9 (2013)
25. Wallner, G., Kriglstein, S.: Multivariate visualization of game metrics: an evaluation of hexbin maps. In: Proceedings of the Annual Symposium on Computer-Human Interaction in Play, pp. 572–584 (2020). https://doi.org/10.1145/3410404.3414233
26. Wallner, G., Kriglstein, S.: Plato: a visual analytics system for gameplay data. Comput. Graph. **38**, 341–356 (2014). https://doi.org/10.1016/j.cag.2013.11.010

VizInteract: Rapid Data Exploration Through Multi-touch Interaction with Multi-dimensional Visualizations

Supratim Chakraborty[(✉)] and Wolfgang Stuerzlinger[(✉)]

School of Interactive Arts and Technology, Simon Fraser University, Vancouver, Canada
w.s@sfu.ca

Abstract. Creating and editing multi-dimensional data visualizations with current tools typically involves complex interactions. We present VizInteract, an interactive data visualization tool for touch-enabled displays. VizInteract supports efficient multi-touch data exploration through rapid construction of and interaction with multi-dimensional data visualizations. Building on primitive visualization idioms like histograms, VizInteract addresses the need for easy data exploration by facilitating the construction of multi-dimensional visualizations, such as scatter plots, parallel coordinate plots, radar charts, and scatter plot matrices, through simple multi-touch actions. Touch-based brushing-and-linking as well as attribute-based filter bubbles support "diving into the data" during analysis. We present the results of two explorative studies, one on a tablet and another on a large touchscreen and analyze the usage patterns that emerge while participants conducted visual analytics data exploration tasks in both conditions.

Keywords: Visualization · Visual analytics · Multi-touch · Large touchscreen

1 Introduction

With the increasing availability of data and need for analysis, data visualization is becoming ubiquitous [8]. Thus, sensemaking, as a skill, is becoming essential to address complex data-related questions across all domains. From novice to expert users, there is a need for tools that facilitate easy data exploration, a critical component of sensemaking [28]. Visual Analytics (VA) focuses on analytical reasoning facilitated by interactive visual interfaces [13]. Desktop VA tools like Tableau or Cognos offer powerful user interfaces for data exploration and analysis, but have a steep learning curve [24]. Most current VA tools are based on traditional WIMP metaphors. Although the operations that users can perform on such tools are overall standardized [3], post-WIMP [34] implementations of data exploration tools have demonstrated significant improvements in maintaining a user's understanding of data [31, 45]. To facilitate data exploration on the

Electronic supplementary material The online version of this chapter (https://doi.org/10.1007/978-3-030-85613-7_39) contains supplementary material, which is available to authorized users.

C. Ardito et al. (Eds.): INTERACT 2021, LNCS 12934, pp. 610–632, 2021.
https://doi.org/10.1007/978-3-030-85613-7_39

growing set of touch-enabled devices, we use multi-touch interaction to enable easier and faster construction of and interaction with multi-dimensional data visualizations. To cater to both novices and experts, we leverage the power of commonly used and easy-to-learn multi-touch interaction techniques in VizInteract to allow users to quickly compose primitive visualizations into multivariate data visualizations.

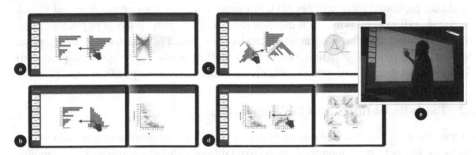

Fig. 1. VizInteract affords rapid and easy creation of multi-dimensional visualizations through a multi-touch interface on a tablet. a) Dragging two vertically oriented data dimensions into proximity creates a parallel coordinate plot, b) two orthogonally oriented dimensions combine into a scatter plot, c) multiple dimensions at other angles form a radar chart, and d) multiple scatter plots combine to a scatter plot matrix. e) Participant using VizInteract on a large touchscreen.

The interface leverages the proximity of individual dimensions and their orientation to produce new visualizations. For an example, two orthogonal histograms brought close together generate a scatter plot. VizInteract currently supports five types of visualizations: histograms (corresponding to a single data dimension), scatter plots (SCPs), parallel coordinate plots (PCPs), radar charts, and scatter plot matrices (SPLOMs). As such, visualizations can be easily and rapidly created and modified in VizInteract, and the system thus facilitates analytical reasoning on the underlying data (Fig. 1).

We conducted two exploratory user studies to investigate how users interact with our tool. Our goals were to: a) observe user strategies and their progress with simple touch-based interaction on a tablet during VA tasks and b) investigate data exploration behaviors while users interact with VizInteract on a large touch display.

2   Related Work

2.1 Ad-Hoc Visualization Construction

Even though Excel [60] offers quick ways to create charts with its PivotChart feature and Tableau [61] supports quick chart creation through query operations, none of these tools support multi-touch for rapid chart construction. In contrast, tools like Voyager [54], reduce the manual interaction required to create visualizations. Such systems instead recommend visualizations to display significant relationships. APT [38] ranked visualizations with an effectiveness criterion. VizDeck [43] showed a gallery of recommendations based on the statistical effectiveness of chart types.

Faceted metadata [56] dynamically reduced the data dynamically through filters and then identified relationships between attributes. OnSet [46] explored set relationships for elements through logical operations on grid cells, where each cell represents the same item in two different sets. GraphTrail [20] enabled exploration through nodes and edge-based aggregation of data. The idea of filters can also be extended to multiple views. Snap-Together [42] introduced coordinate selection and filters across multiple views and DynDash presented filter bubbles [41]. For more complex data processing and visualization workflows, toolkits, such as d3.js [58] or VTK [63], provide application programming interfaces that programmers can use to connect to data sources and generate custom visualizations. The limitation of these toolkits is that they require programming skills and that the authoring of visualizations requires detailed specifications.

2.2 Touch-Based Interaction for Visualizations

Interacting with visualizations using gesture or touch-based interfaces has been widely explored. Isenberg et al. identified interactive tabletops and touch surfaces as a medium for effective data visualization [30]. Lee et al. recognized the importance of using post-WIMP metaphors and using naturalistic interactions for sensemaking in VA [34]. The combination of pen and touch for object selection [25] has also been used in data visualization [10, 16, 35, 52]. Further, interactive whiteboards and/or pens can facilitate fluid and easy data exploration. SketchVis [10] used sketching to transform data and perform filter operations. VizDom [17] also used pen and touch to support conducting interactive visual data analysis on a whiteboard. SketchInsight [35] proposed drawing simple charts on a whiteboard to explore data. VisWall [1] explored construction of multivariate visualizations using attributes of previously created visualizations on a large display. It combined collaborative touch-based interactions and visualization recommendations. TouchViz [19] compared traditional WIMP-based interface with their gesture-based interface for VA on a tablet. It focused on gesture-based data querying operations. VizInteract builds on these ideas by supporting touch-based visualization construction without the need for auxiliary input devices and providing data filtering and querying operations. Kinetica [45] used physics-based affordances for multivariate data exploration and filtering. Each query required the user to trace a significant portion of the canvas. VizInteract uses simpler drag-and-drop interactions to manipulate filters. Multi-touch interaction have also been used for dynamic scatter plots [48]. TouchWave [6] offered multi-touch gestures for interacting with stacked graphs. All these tools offer only touch-based interactive data exploration with a *single* type of chart. In contrast, VizInteract's canvas allows the user to construct and interact with multiple types of multi-dimensional charts.

2.3 Interaction with Multi-dimensional Data Visualizations

Tukey et al. [51] introduced scatter plot matrices (SPLOMs) for exploring multivariate data, which display scatter plots for each pair-wise combination of dimensions. Another popular visualization for multivariate data is parallel coordinate plots, PCPs. Inselberg et al. [29] introduced PCPs for effective data exploration in a 2D space, and found PCPs to have low representational complexity. Wong et al. surveyed much multivariate data visualization research [53]. They identified visualizations that explore interactivity in multi-dimensional data visualization, including Starfields [2] and parallel sets [32]. Common data analysis operations like brushing-and-linking in multivariate visualizations have also been explored in the past [39]. DataMeadow [21] used a canvas of starplots, each with an interactive filter slider to adjust the distribution of a selected dimension in a query. All these interactive multi-dimensional visualizations were designed primarily for desktop-based user interfaces and have minimal multi-touch affordances. VizInteract expands on these works by introducing multi-touch interactions to explore multivariate data. In VizInteract, any number of dimensions can be selectively dragged and placed on the canvas and combined to produce new visualizations.

With Flexible Linked Axes [11] users can draw lines between axes on the canvas to explore multi-dimensional data. Depending on the lines drawn and their configuration, the system generated either a SCP or PCP. ImAxes [14] relied on virtual axes that could be manipulated in 3D space and combined to produce 2D and 3D visualizations. One limitation of ImAxes was the need for the user to move their body to interact with the plots in the 3D space. This led to lot of walking, crouching, and general movement to perform even simple analysis. The authors suggested that a zoom operation might permit the user to isolate axes, which would overcome the abovementioned limitation. VisTiles [33] also used orientation and arrangement to produce different visualizations but was designed for a collaborative VA workflow where multiple devices are spatially oriented and arranged to compose higher order views. The additional step of introducing multiple devices increases the friction between creating visualizations and generating insights. For ease of access, our workflow focuses on a single display.

3   Design Goals

Informed by our main research goals for VizInteract, which are to observe (a) users' VA behaviors with simple touch-based interactions on a tablet and (b) data exploration behaviors on a large touch display, we developed VizInteract with three main design goals in mind: (1) allow rapid multi-touch composition and editing of visualizations, (2) leverage easy-to-use and -learn interactions, and (3) provide a flexible yet powerful interface. In the following, we discuss these design goals in detail.

3.1   Rapid Multi-touch Composition and Editing of Visualizations

Studies have shown that touch interaction is beneficial for a diverse range of plots, such as bar charts and stacked graphs [6, 19]. However, all presented methods work only well for single data attribute visualization and do not allow for rapid switching between primitive and higher-order visualization idioms. Touch interaction has also been used for data transformation and filtering operations, e.g., in TouchPivot [31] and PanoramicData [57]. However, these tools do not support rapid visualization composition for easy multi-dimensional analysis workflows. Some tools like iVoLVER [40], Data Illustrator [37], and Charticulator [44] facilitate both visualization creation and editing. Instead of transforming data from multiple sources or providing a new visual language, VizInteract focuses on rapid data exploration via existing visualization paradigms. Also, many desktop VA tools do not generalize well to touchscreens, e.g., Data Illustrator and Charticulator. VizInteract's interface leverages the benefits of direct manipulation [18], which suggests avoiding menus, forms, and toolbars, whose profusion can increase the complexity of any application. VizInteract affords multi-touch interaction as a first-class construct to enable rapid and easy exploration of high-dimensional data. Motivated by the encouraging results of using a tablet for interacting with a single type of visualization [48], we explore multi-touch affordances for constructing and editing multiple types of visualizations on touch-enabled displays. Examples include interactions like adding filters or altering the configuration of individual dimensions.

VizInteract currently supports SCPs, PCPs, Radar charts, and SPLOMs. SCPs offer a simple visual representation of two-dimensional data as they show every data point individually. As a result, they easily highlight groupings, outliers, and trends [12]. PCPs have relatively low representational complexity [29] and are effective for multi-dimensional data visualization. Radar charts support many variables next to each other, with each variable having the same resolution [23]. SPLOMs are simple to evaluate perceptually, as they show scatter plots for all combinations of dimensions. Thus, analyzing bivariate correlations, classifications, clusters, or trends is relatively easy with SPLOMs and they are appropriate for both novice and expert user [36].

3.2 Easy-To-Learn Set of Interactions

Unlike many VA tools that use complex gestures for interacting with multiple visualizations (such as Tangere [47] and its touch-based hold-and-swipe gesture), VizInteract relies on the same simple interaction vocabulary that most touch-based systems support, which most users are intricately familiar with. We rely on the Direct Combination interaction paradigm [26], which focuses on pairs of interaction objects, in our case (initially simple) visualizations that are then combined to form more advanced ones. VizInteract also affords the frequently used brushing-and-linking method of multi-dimensional visualization systems [7] through a simple single-finger touch-and-drag operation. As the barrier to construct, edit, or remove visualizations is thus very low, users can quickly correct any mistakes in their choices. VizInteract also supports rapid modification of the visual mappings, which encourages users to explore different data configurations. This design decision was motivated by documented user behaviors, which show that they iteratively refine data mappings and tend to ignore finer control [24]. Novice users have also shown a tendency to think about data attributes and visual structures separately [24]. A blank canvas where data attributes can be independently placed and visualized thus enables the users to compose the elements as visual structures. As identified by Grammel et al. [24], participants want to link the data space with the visual space, as they are generally aware about the need to create links between the two. VizInteract builds on the metaphor of providing independent attributes which can be 'linked' easily, through simple composition with multi-touch interaction.

3.3 Flexible yet Powerful Interface

Our last design goal was to build an interface for a range of expertise levels, from novice users to experts with advanced VA requirements. To support workflows that require advanced data queries, we added brushing-and-linking, numerical and categorical filters, and functionality for the duplication of filters in VizInteract. Our design builds on previous work on filter bubbles [41] that are linked to visualizations, which can be easily constructed, manipulated, and duplicated to other charts through drag-and-drop. Multiple copies of the same dimension can be present on the canvas, each of which can be manipulated and combined with others. Together with the pinch-to-zoom interaction this design overcomes the limitations of working with only single chart at a time [49] and thus provides a simple canvas that still supports advanced workflows. VizInteract also supports visualizations like radar charts and SPLOMs for advanced VA queries. Unlike the axis representations for immersive analytics proposed by Fonnet et al. [22], which cater to advanced data querying use cases but require a 3D grid-based representations of coordinate systems, VizInteract uses a simple, infinite 2D canvas, where the orientation of each dimension can be chosen freely. This design affords more freedom while at the same time providing flexibility for detailed VA tasks. Our work is also inspired by interactive systems to generate visualizations [11, 14]. However, instead of mechanically drawing links or in 3D space [14], we manipulate the axes through touch on a 2D canvas. We also support a touch-based zoom operation to facilitate isolated analysis of single plots. As the 3D grid of Fonnet et al. [22] had a negative impact on speed for retrieving coordinate information, we believe that in contrast a 2D interactive canvas reduces the barriers for data exploration, by reducing friction between ideation and constructing visualizations for advanced queries.

4   VizInteract Interactions

A typical workflow for data analysis in VizInteract involves eight primary interactions: A user loads a.csv file and *adds dimensions from the sidebar* onto the canvas which show up as frequency histograms.

Fig. 2. a) VizInteract Interface: 1) dimension Sidebar, 2) interactive Canvas, and 3) trash area at bottom b) dragging a dimension onto the canvas constructs a frequency histogram.

Each histogram can be *rotated to change its orientation*. To visualize correlations between two dimensions, a user *combines two orthogonal histograms to create a scatter plot*. For visualizing data relationships as *parallel coordinate plots, they combine multiple parallel attributes*. Another option is to *combine multiple dimensions at varying orientations to form a radar plot*. To get an overview of the correlations of four or more attributes, they can form two scatter plots and bring them in proximity to *form a scatter plot matrix.* During their analysis, *they add numerical or categorical filters* by dropping dimensions as filter attributes onto a chart. Throughout, they *can freely zoom and pan the canvas* to fluidly explore the data.

4.1 Adding Dimensions

The two main components of the VizInteract interface are the dimension sidebar and the interactive canvas (See Fig. 2). After loading a dataset through the top-right popup menu, the (scrolling) sidebar is populated with the dimensions of the data set. Each dimension also has an associated color, used for axes or filter bubbles. Both categorical and numerical attributes are listed in the sidebar. Dragging a dimension's name onto the canvas creates the corresponding frequency histogram (See Fig. 2). Histograms can be dropped into a "trash" area at the bottom of the screen to remove them (See Fig. 2).

4.2 Changing the Orientation of a Histogram

The default orientation for a histogram is vertical, but its orientation can be changed through a two-finger touch rotation gesture to any multiple of 45° (See Fig. 3a).

4.3 Combining Views to Create Scatter Plots

Combining histograms creates multi-dimensional views, depending on the orientation of each histogram. If two different histograms with orthogonal orientations are overlapped (by more than 80%), VizInteract creates a single SCP with the interacting dimensions (see Fig. 3b). To decompose a SCP, the user swiftly drags across the SCP. That separates the SCP into the individual dimensions, which revert to histograms (and similarly for other plots below). This retains the fluid nature of composition and decomposition of visualizations in VizInteract.

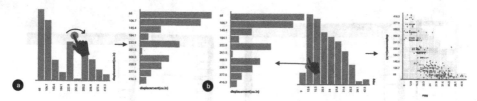

Fig. 3. a) Rotate dimension to change orientation, b) create scatter plot by combining histograms at orthogonal orientations.

4.4 Combining Views to Create Parallel Coordinate Plots

If the user brings two unique histograms with vertical orientation into proximity, a PCP is constructed between the interacting dimensions (see Fig. 4a). To improve the visibility of the PCP lines, each histogram is shown at 50% transparency. When creating larger PCPs, users can chain dimensions in the desired order (see Fig. 4b). A swift drag across a PCP dimension affords not only removal of that dimension, but also reordering.

Fig. 4. a) Combining vertically oriented dimensions results in a PCP, b) adding a 3rd dimension.

4.5 Combining Dimensions to Create Radar Charts

If two dimensions are brought into proximity without being orthogonal or parallel, VizInteract creates a radar chart (See Fig. 5a). Dimensions can be added by dropping them onto the chart or removed by dragging them away (See Fig. 5b). Radar charts also support a filter to specify how many data points are shown.

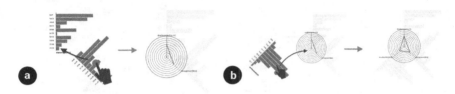

Fig. 5. a) Creating a radar chart, b) Adding attributes to a radar chart.

4.6 Filtering Operations

All charts in VizInteract support filters. If a dimension is dragged directly onto an existing visualization, VizInteract adds a filter corresponding to the dragged attribute to the visualization.

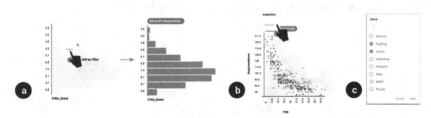

Fig. 6. a) Filter addition – drag dimension to visualization to add filter bubble, b) filter interaction through range slider for numerical, and c) searchable multi-select list for categorical dimensions.

As a visual aid, hovering over any chart displays a temporary popup "Add as filter" while dragging a dimension (see Fig. 6a). VizInteract supports both numerical (with a range slider, see Fig. 6b) and categorical filters (with a searchable multi-select list, see Fig. 6c). If an existing filter is dropped over a chart, VizInteract duplicates the filter. Filters can be removed by dragging them onto empty canvas space.

4.7   Combining Views to Create Scatter Plot Matrices

VizInteract also supports SPLOMs. If two SCPs are brought close to each other, the system generates a SPLOM corresponding to the combined attributes (See Fig. 7). Removing any participating SCP destroys the SPLOM.

4.8   Canvas Operations

VizInteract allows the user to use a one-finger drag on the canvas for brushing-and-linking, which creates a rectangular selection box that highlights all selected points in yellow that are then also highlighted in all other visualizations (See Fig. 8a). To clear the selection, the user can double-tap on the canvas.

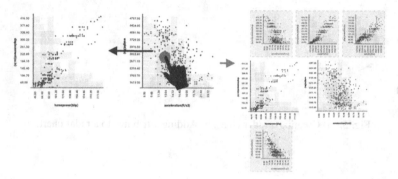

Fig. 7. Combining multiple SCPs by dragging them to overlap creates a SPLOM.

A pinch-to-zoom gesture on the canvas scales or a two-finger drag pans it. A 'touch-and-hold' on the canvas triggers a lens view to make it easier to read individual data point/line values, which brings up a magnifying lens view that can be dragged around. Values contained in it are displayed above the lens (See Fig. 8b).

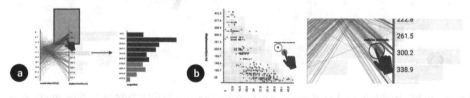

Fig. 8. a) Brushing-and-linking with rectangle selection, and b) single finger touch-and-hold to bring up a lens view to read values.

5   User Study I

We conducted an exploratory study to investigate how and how well VizInteract supports data analysis activities. The goal was to understand how users benefit from rapid interactive construction of multivariate data visualizations and how they use touch-based interaction to solve VA tasks. We also wanted to evaluate the usability of VizInteract. The study aimed to answer the following two main questions. **RQ1.1**: What usage patterns are observable while users complete visual data analysis tasks via VizInteract's interactions to construct charts and add or edit filters on the visualizations? **RQ1.2**: Do users find interacting with VizInteract to be easy and learnable?

5.1 Participants

We recruited 16 participants for the study, seven females, aged between 22 and 28. Ten were undergraduate students who participated for course credit, others were graduate students. We pre-screened participants to ensure familiarity with interpreting data from visualizations. All participants had some experience with basic multi-dimensional data analysis and multi-touch interactions. To minimize potential biases, we made sure that participants had not participated in any VA studies using touch-based visualization systems before. On average participants were familiar with at least one and at most two desktop visualization systems, e.g., Tableau, Microsoft Excel, or Power BI.

5.2 Apparatus and Datasets

All studies were performed before the COVID-19 pandemic. VizInteract ran on a 10", 1920×1200 pixel Galaxy Tab A tablet running Android O. We used the Auto dataset from the ISLR package [59] for the training session (397 cars with 8 dimensions) and a subset of the Video Game Sales 2019 dataset [62] (600 games with 13 dimensions) for the main session. With user consent, we recorded user interactions using a camera. The software also logged all user interaction, but we used an auxiliary computer to record survey answers and a digital audio device to record the post-task interviews.

5.3 Study Design

First, participants filled out an informed consent form and a demographic questionnaire. A short freeform interview with each participant was used to assess their familiarity with visualizations, VA, and multi-dimensional data. The experimenter then demonstrated the capabilities of VizInteract. The tutorial used the Cars dataset. Subsequently, participants were given the opportunity to freely explore this dataset for 10 min, guided by practice exploration tasks. Then, the main tasks were presented. For this part of the session, we used the Video Games sales 2019 dataset, with a total of five tasks.

- Q1: Your colleague wants to add video games to their community pop culture store. She wants suggestions for high-selling and highly rated adventure or puzzle games. Create a chart for this and record the names of 3 such games. *(Scenario Introduction)*
- Q2: Her community has a lot of European (EU) residents. She is curious about factors that impact EU game sales *(Explore how users create charts and use filters)*
- Q3: She wants to know how the North American (NA) game market compares to the global market for adventure games. *(Explore how users analyze relationships)*

- Q4: She has a lot of vintage game collectors as customers. Thus, she wants to know if the NA market has higher sales for an older platform like PS2 and NES, compared to Japan and EU. *(Explore how users analyze relationships)*
- Q5: Some customers requested top-ranking titles published by EA and Nintendo for PlayStation and Xbox platforms with high sales in NA. Does she have any options? *(Explore how users utilize views to find high performing variables)*

We chose these tasks to explore a range of multi-dimensional data queries. The questions also probe the usefulness of rapid SCP, PCP, radar chart, and SPLOM creation and the use of interactions for specific analysis. We asked participants to write down each insight they gathered and, once a task was completed, also to verbally explain their approach for arriving at that insight. The study ended with a semi-structured interview with each participant about their experience when using VizInteract. We focused on the usability of the interactions and the usefulness of the tool. The open-ended part of the interview encouraged participants to reflect on their experience with VizInteract and to provide additional feedback. We also captured usability feedback using a 7-point Likert type [15] questionnaire. Participants were also free to suggest areas of improvement for VizInteract. Answers were recorded and later encoded for analysis. As several studies had already established the benefits of touch-based visualization tools over desktop tools [39, 43, 55], we chose not compare VizInteract with a desktop-based system.

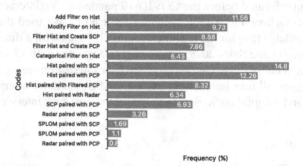

Fig. 9. Low level interaction codes and their frequency for Study 1.

Table 1. Coded findings for Study 1.

Initial Codes	Focused Theme	# Particpants
Add or modify Filter on Hist, Filter Hist and Compose SCP or PCP, Categorical Filter on Hist	Bottom-up approach for filter-based queries	12
Hist paired with SCP, PCP, Filtered PCP, or with Radar	Overview-and-detail arrangement	9
SPLOM with SCP or PCP, Radar with SCP, SCP with PCP	Validating higher-order visualizations	5

5.4 Results

To answer our research questions, we narrowed our analysis to focus only on the main interactions related to visualization construction, data querying, and filtering. We considered for this analysis: creation of charts, adding and manipulation of filters, and brushing-and-linking. We identified and analyzed all such interactions (See Fig. 9). The group of filter-based interactions represented the most frequently used actions, followed by the creations of different types of plots. Histogram and SCP/PCP arrangements were also frequent. Individual Histograms were also paired frequently with PCPs, and the histograms often had filters on them. Further analysis led us to the identification of a set of three over-arching patterns (see Table 1).

Bottom-up Approach for Constructing Filter-Based Queries. In this usage pattern and rather than adding filters on multi-dimensional visualizations, the participants first constructed and edited filters right on a *histogram* and then combined filtered representations to build combined views. For example, for Q4, participant P7 brought in the 'NA_Sales' dimension and directly applied the 'Platform' filter on it and then used that filtered dimension to construct a SCP with 'Global_Sales'. When asked for the rationale, the participant said, *"It is easy to construct the parameter at the beginning and then its associations with other attributes"*. Participant P3 also exhibited the same pattern for Q3 where they created the histogram, added the 'Genre' filter, and then constructed a PCP. P11 mentioned that *'Focusing on the primary attribute and selecting values for the filters makes it easy for building up the query. This matches my thinking.'* This pattern was the most frequent pattern, observed in 12 of the participants.

Overview-and-Detail Arrangement. We observed that for many analytical tasks participants arranged their charts in a repetitive manner. While some participants analyzed individual, isolated visualizations on the canvas, many created a side-by-side arrangement of histograms and multi-dimensional charts. Participant P2 used such an arrangement for Q3, where they placed the 'Genre' frequency histogram on one side of the display and on the other side constructed a SCP for 'NA_Sales vs Global_Sales'. When asked for their motivation they said, *"it was easier to analyze [the data] in this way"*. P5 showcased the same pattern for answering Q1, where they kept 'Critic_Score' on one side and a PCP of 'NA_Sales' and 'Global_Sales' on the other. They later added a 'Genre' filter on the PCP and brushed the two highest intervals on 'Critic_Score'. This highlighted the corresponding values on the SCP and allowed P5 to complete the task. In the interview, P5 indicated that *"I wanted to see the distribution for the critic ratings before I made my selection"*. This was the second-most repeated usage pattern, with nine participants creating a kind of overview and detail arrangement.

Validating Higher-Order Views. Some participants first constructed a Radar chart and then immediately coupled it with multiple SCPs. P6, P11, and P13 each constructed a Radar chart for Q4 comprising of attributes 'NA_Sales', 'PAL_Sales', and 'Global_Sales'. P6 immediately followed up with the construction of three SCPs, using all combination of the above attributes. P11 and P13 interacted with the radar data filter and then rearranged the dimensions to form individual SCPs. P13 mentioned that *"I didn't know if the radar web represented the properties of the whole table, I wanted* *to be sure before I answered*". Similarly, for Q2, participant P4 constructed two SCPs, 'PAL_Sales vs Critic Score' and 'Global_Sales vs Critic Score' and combined them to form a SPLOM. After adding a filter to see the impact of 'Genre' in the SPLOM, they immediately reset the canvas, constructed the two SCPs again and added the filter back to each SCP. P4 reported in the post task interview that "*I wanted to check if the filters were correctly applied to individual plots or not*". This usage pattern shows that participants were attempting to validate correlations visible in the higher-order multivariate visualizations. This pattern was observed for five participants.

Learnability and Usability. Participants stated that VizInteract's interactions were overall easy to learn. P8 mentioned that "*Not much explanation was needed for understanding the interactions*", P4 said that only a single explanation was enough, and P1 noted that "*only 5 min* *needed to learn the interface and its capabilities*". Participant P4 even commented that the radar chart and PCP interactions felt 'magical'. On the used 7-point Likert scales, SCP (14 strongly agreed and 2 agreed) and PCP (11 strongly agreed and 5 agreed) had the highest ratings in terms of ease-of-use and learnability. Radar chart interactions were also comparatively easy to learn ($\mu = 5.1$, sd $= 0.83$) and use ($\mu = 5.31$, sd $= 1.11$). The SPLOM had good ratings for learnability ($\mu = 5.24$, sd $= 0.74$) but ease-of-use was not as strong ($\mu = 3.17$, sd $= 1.04$). We attribute this at least partially to the computational delay associated with constructing SPLOMs and the subsequent automatic rescaling of the canvas. Participants also liked the filter interactions, which had a very high ease-of-use ($\mu = 6.1$, sd $= 1.21$) and learnability rating ($\mu = 5.9$, sd $= 0.63$). P8 remarked that "*I found the multiple option popup for selecting game genre really useful*". This confirms that VizInteract's interaction set is easy-to-use and easy-to-learn.

Dimensional Awareness and Data Comprehension. In the post-task interview, 10 participants mentioned that the ability to easily create multi-dimensional views made them (better) aware of the dimensional relationships. Participant P7 said that "*[the] interdependence of Video game sales in different regions and Genre makes sense now*". Participant P15 noted that "*it's visually very easy to see the relationships between the different attributes*". Another noteworthy observation was that users appreciated the comprehensiveness of the supported charts to address the specific analysis tasks. P6 remarked that "*the different types of views are helpful, findings from a radar chart can be coupled with other view types to support your hunch*".

5.5   Discussion

Our findings for VizInteract largely support our overall design goals to build a tool that provides: D1) rapid multi-touch composition and editing of visualizations, D2) leverages easy to use and learn interactions, and D3) a flexible yet powerful interface. For our research question RQ1.1 (*What usage patterns are observable while users complete visual data analysis tasks*), we found that participants successfully created multiple multi-dimensional charts and were easily able to "drill down" into the data for specific queries. Interestingly, we also identified that participants frequently used filters in a bottom-up approach for constructing queries. We believe this behavior matches the mental model of users who follow an atomic VA workflow, where visualization *composition* is a second-order step. This finding supports our design goal of providing a flexible yet powerful interface (D3). We also found people utilized an 'overview-and-detail' style arrangement of charts while rapidly and interactively constructing complex visualizations to address their data queries. VizInteract's interaction set did not seem to have hindered the user's processes for visualizing dimensional relationships and comprehending the data. This rapid and fluid composition and editing of visualizations using multi-touch interactions validates our first goal (D1). The participants also identified that the interactions were easy to learn and agreed in general with the ease-of-use for the interactions for constructing multi-dimensional visualizations. This confirms RQ1.2 *(Do users find interacting with VizInteract to be easy and learnable?)* and demonstrates that VizInteract's interaction set is easy-to-use and easy-to-learn (D2).

6   User Study II

Building on related work [4, 5], our main research question was: how does a larger display change user data exploration strategy while they are rapidly constructing and editing visualizations? And with the interactions afforded by VizInteract, do they exhibit different usage patterns on the large display?

6.1   Apparatus and Participants

We used an 85" Samsung 4K 60 Hz display with a PQ Labs G5 multi-touch panel, connected to a PC running a bootable USB image of Android X86. We patched the OS to add support for the PQ Labs panel (now part of the Android X86 distribution). Interaction logs were saved to the USB drive. With user consent, a video camera was used to record interactions. An auxiliary computer was used to record survey answers and an audio recorder for post-task interviews. For the training and free exploration phases, we used the same dataset as in Study I [59]. For the main session, we used a subset of the Video Game Sales 2019 Dataset [62]. We ran the study with 16 new participants. Twelve were undergraduate students who took part for course credits, while the rest were graduate students. We pre-screened participants to ensure that they had familiarity with data visualization. To mentally prepare them for study, participants were told that they would be required to stand for 40 min. The display was mounted on a movable stand, adjusted to a comfortable height for every person.

6.2   Study Design

The participants were asked to fill a consent form and answer basic demographic questions. We then conducted a short freeform interview to assess their familiarity with visualizations, VA tasks, multi-touch interaction, and multi-dimensional data analysis. This whole phase lasted 5 min. Then we introduced the experimental setting and demonstrated VizInteract's interactions. The tutorial used the sample Cars dataset and participants were then given a set of practice tasks to explore the system. For the main part of the study overall task objectives were similar to Study I (See Appendix Table 2) and participants had 30 min to perform five tasks on a subset of the Video Games sales dataset. Even though the attributes involved in the tasks differed slightly from Study I, we believe that this difference did not affect the outcomes in a notable way. After all, we did not focus on task completion nor performance metrics, but on user behaviors when interacting with VizInteract. Once participants completed a task, they were asked to explain their approach to arrive at each insight. After the tasks, we conducted a semi-structured interview with each participant, to understand their experience when using VizInteract. We focused on their opinions on the usability of the interactions and the usefulness of the tool. We quantified some of the feedback through the System Usability Scale [9]. If consent to record had been given, audio and video recordings were later encoded for thematic analysis.

6.3 Results

In this section, we report our qualitative findings for the usage patterns and list the interaction codes observed in Fig. 10.

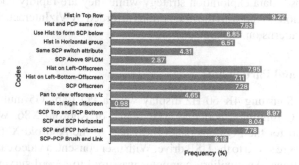

Fig. 10. Low-level interaction codes and their frequency for Study II.

The primary spatial arrangement observed was individual histograms placed above a SCP. Two or more histograms were often placed on the same "upper row" and were brought "down" individually to construct or edit a SCP below. We also saw that off-screen space was utilized to temporarily store visualizations. Additionally, we observed a specific arrangement for the pairing of SCPs and PCPs, where frequently a SCP was on top and a PCP at the bottom. Pairs of SCPs, however, were arranged side-by-side. Through further analysis, we identified three major emerging themes, see Table 2.

Staging Visualizations. We observed that participants constructed visualizations by bringing histograms for the attributes involved in the task into a single row, high up on the display, in a "staging" area. This allowed users to later take these histograms and combine them into desired multi-dimensional visualizations below that row. For example, for Q2, participant P3 brought in 'Critic rating', 'Global sales', and 'NA_Sales' attributes as histograms one beside the other. They then paired attributes into SCPs below the histogram staging row. When questioned, P3 said, "*Having attributes separated*

Table 2. Coded findings for Study 1.

Initial Codes	Focused Theme	# Particpants
Hist in Top Row, Hist and PCP same row, Use Hist to form SCP below, Hist in Horizontal group, Same SCP switch attribute, SCP above SPLOM	Staging visualizations	10
Hist on Left- Offscreen, Hist on Left-Bottom-Offscreen, SCP Offscreen, pan to view offscreen viz, Hist on Right Offscreen	Docking visualizations	8
SCP top and PCP bottom, SCP and SCP horizontal, SCP and PCP horizontal, SCP-PCP brush and link	Simultaneous PCP and SCP analysis	7

makes it easy to quickly replace the dimensions in the charts". For Q4, P6 put 'Console', 'Europe_Sales', 'NA_Sales', 'JP_Sales' histograms into a row. Then, they created 3 SCPs below the row before arriving at their conclusion. They said that *"It's like a mental map where [I] save these attributes that [I] want to analyze for later"*.

Docking Visualizations. Another observed behavior concerned the way participants 'docked' their visualizations beyond the viewport. They created a visualization, moved it offscreen, brought other attributes into the empty space, and then constructed new visualizations. Later, they would bring the offscreen visualization back to refer to it or to compare it with the current one before drawing conclusions for the task. For Q3, participant P7 constructed a 'Genre' vs 'Europe Sales' SCP, docked it to the left side, and then created 'Europe Sales' vs 'Global Sales' with a 'Genre' filter on it. When asked about it, they remarked *"I want to know if there are peculiarities with the way Europe reacts to different categories of the games. I spotted [that] co-op games have [a] higher frequency count. I was curious and wanted to compare it to global but have 3 attributes in the equation, that other visualization was for cross referencing"*.

Simultaneous PCP and SCP. Most pairings that combined PCPs and SCPs involved an arrangement with the PCP for correlational insights on top and the SCP on the bottom. P2, P10, and P14 used a PCP for Q3 where they made a PCP for 'Europe_Sales' and 'Genre' at the top and then constructed a SCP for 'Europe_Sales' vs 'Global_Sales' with a filter at the bottom. P10 followed this up with a two-finger canvas move operation to vertically align the plots at the center. This pattern supports the benefits of pairing a SCP with a PCP for data analysis [27]. P2 and P14 also rearranged the dimensions between the PCP and SCP, but the layout still remained a vertically separated PCP and SCP. P14 mentioned in their interview that *"The dots view gives me a better detailed picture but having the patterns in the connected lines be visible at the same time is useful"*. P2 reported in the post task interview that *"The scatter plot has some advantages but pairing it [with] another view validates your instinct about the pattern"*.

Temporal Patterns. When we analyzed the temporal distribution of actions during the tasks, some additional behavioral patterns emerged. Every dimension drop was almost always followed by brushing-and-linking. Analyzing such interactions in more detail via the trace log and video also identified that participants preferred brushing on isolated histogram ranges and linking on existing SCPs. It is also interesting that the press-and-hold interaction to bring up the lens view mostly happened when a visualization was constrained by filters. Also, the frequency of lens interactions kept increasing towards the end of a task, which might suggest that even somewhat less common touch interactions, such as the press-and-hold, quickly can become routine. We also saw that people spent more time on filter modification with PCPs than SCPs.

Learnability and Usability. With VizInteract running on the large display, participants found the interactions easy-to-learn and easy-to-use. P7 found the interface to be fluid and remarked that "*Seeing correlations so quickly from a dataset is good, user-experience wise*". P13 commented that not having a lot of "*calls to action*" (buttons) makes it a "*one-step process*" to think about the problem and create relevant visualizations. P4 claimed that it "*only took a single demonstration to get the hang of each interaction*" and they found the quick creation of charts exciting. In their words "*The number of steps from thinking about the problem and [then] actually creating the graph is [much] less*". Some people experienced issues with the lens view implementation. P8 thought the "*lens could be zoomed [more] in as it was a large screen*". Some participants were happy that the interactions on a large screen felt "phone-like" to them. P4 said that it felt like "*I was using a phone scaled up*". This indicates that the system is very learnable. VizInteract's System Usability Scale [9] score on the large display was 75.83, i.e., a highly usable system. Participants found the system very easy-to-use ($\mu = 4.1$, sd = 0.6) and agreed that it was easy-to-learn ($\mu = 4.2$, sd = 0.97). P8 remarked that "*It's so easy to compose something here that making a mistake doesn't really feel risky*".

6.4 Discussion

Our findings from this study characterize the exploration strategies used by people while using VizInteract on a large touch-enabled display. It shows participants were able to easily learn and use the multi-touch interactions for creating and editing multi-dimensional data visualizations (See Design Goal 3.2), even on a large display. Yet, the patterns observed on the large display in Study II reveal a distinct characteristic relative to Study I, as people used unique spatial arrangements for their visualizations. This answer our RQ for User Study II, i.e., that large displays elicit different usage patterns with VizInteract. We observed that people were 'staging' various visualizations in rows and picking and composing multi-dimensional visualizations using such staged attributes. This points to potential arrangement-related features, e.g., by enabling quick visualization of pairwise combinations of all attributes placed on screen. We also observed that users used offscreen space for storing visualizations for quick reference. As our use case focuses on a single user comparing visualizations, without involving a collaborative setting, this behavior is fundamentally different from the territoriality observed in large tabletop configurations [50]. One implication of this finding is that touch-enabled large display VA tools should enable quick comparisons with already created multivariate visualizations to speed the referencing process. We also note that this observation aligns with our goal of rapidly composing and editing visualizations (See Design goal 3.1). The additional vertical space on the large display also afforded a unique arrangement of PCPs and SCPs: a PCP on top and a SCP at the bottom. Without prompting from the experimenter's side, many participants repeatedly and seemingly naturally created such arrangements. This arrangement supports correlation analysis in the PCP in combination with detailed analysis through the SCP. The possible implication for this behavior is to support an ad-hoc creation of SCPs, like an embedded SCP visualization, similar to previous work [27]. This behavior also in line with our goal to provide a flexible yet powerful interface (See Design goals 3.2).

6.5 Challenges

Confirming that there is always room for improvements, VizInteract faced some challenges on the large display. First, interaction with the lens view could be improved, e.g., by increasing the zoom factor, potentially through an associated user setting. To support the quick staging and arrangement of previously constructed visualizations, a fast interaction method could be introduced to enable saving and restoring of visualizations. Currently, displaying tens of thousands of data points simultaneously in VizInteract can cause visual clutter and too many data dimensions (multiple dozens) can cause performance issues on a tablet. However, large dataset strategies like sampling, aggregation, tuning/tweaking, and/or segmentation could be utilized to address this issue. A built-in short tutorial would also reduce the need for a training phase for VizInteract.

7 Conclusion and Future Work

Overall, we found that VizInteract's multi-touch interface affords the rapid construction and editing of multi-dimensional visualization. Both studies confirmed that users easily understood how to create visualizations through combination. Users were quickly able to complete realistic VA tasks and to derive valid insights from the data. As the basic interaction of combining attributes worked very well, we are planning to increase the scope of visualization options by implementing support for adding additional dimensions to SCPs and SPLOMs, through color or size encodings. Several users also requested trendlines and sorting of axes in VizInteract to facilitate identification of insights. Moreover, we are planning to explore the automatic display of associated SCPs for a PCP. Based on our findings, and instead of relying on simple visualizations, the next version of VizInteract could guide users to use filters on higher-order multi-dimensional visualizations. This might also point to a need for mechanisms to quickly generate alternate visualization of selected dimensions. Finally, we plan to explore how device displacement or changing the display orientation affects usage patterns.

Appendix

A1. Tasks for Study II (Table 3).

Table 3. Tasks for Study II.

Question	Objective
Your video game archivist friend is in town, but she is only aware about indie game titles. She needs your suggestions about game trends and specific titles that are a little more mainstream. Show her some visualizations that can help her understand your choices for each of the below-mentioned tasks	Introducing the scenarios
Q1: Your friend wants suggestions on high-selling and highly rated shooting and RPG games. Create a corresponding chart and record the names of 3 such games	Explore how users create charts and use filter interactions
Q2: She wants to identify insights for mainstream popular North American titles. Specifically, what factors impact the North American game market?	Explore how users analyze dimensional relationships
Q3: She wants to know how European sales compare in the global market, especially for mainstream Co-op games?	Explore how users analyze dimensional relationships
Q4: A lot of popular publishers are still making games for slightly older consoles like Xbox 360 and PS3. Between Japan, Europe, and North America, she wants to know which gaming region has higher adoption for these games?	Explore how users utilize views to find high performing variables
Q5: Knowing about the recent rising popularity of Epic and Tencent Games, she is curious about the popular games from these companies in the North American market which are also highly rated by critics and are exclusively available on PC and PlayStation. Are there any options for her?	Check how users query for specific details and interact with numerical and categorical filters combined

References

1. Agarwal, M., et al.: VisWall: visual data exploration using direct combination on large touch displays (2019)
2. Ahlberg, C., Shneiderman, B.: Visual information seeking: tight coupling of dynamic query filters with starfield displays. In: The Craft of Information Visualization, pp. 7–13. Elsevier (2003). https://doi.org/10.1016/B978-155860915-0/50004-4
3. Amar, R., et al.: Low-level components of analytic activity in information visualization. In: IEEE Symposium on Information Visualization, 2005. INFOVIS 2005 (2005). https://doi.org/10.1109/INFVIS.2005.1532136
4. Andrews, C., et al.: Information visualization on large, high-resolution displays: issues, challenges, and opportunities. Inf. Vis. **10**(4), 341–355 (2011). https://doi.org/10.1177/147387 1611415997
5. Andrews, C., et al.: Space to think. In: Proceedings of the 28th international conference on Human factors in computing systems - CHI 2010, p. 55 ACM Press, New York, New York, USA (2010). https://doi.org/10.1145/1753326.1753336
6. Baur, D., et al.: TouchWave: kinetic multi-touch manipulation for hierarchical stacked graphs. In: Proceedings of the 2012 ACM International Conference on Interactive Tabletops Surfaces, pp. 255–264 (2012). https://doi.org/10.1145/2396636.2396675
7. Becker, R.A., Cleveland, W.S.: Brushing scatterplots. Technometrics **29**(2), 127–142 (1987)
8. Bikakis, N., Sellis, T.: Exploration and visualization in the web of big linked data: a survey of the state of the art. In: CEUR Workshop Proceedings, p. 1558 (2016)
9. Brooke, J.: SUS-A quick and dirty usability scale. Usability Eval. Ind. **189**, 4–7 (1996)
10. Browne, J., et al.: Data analysis on interactive whiteboards through sketch-based interaction. In: Proceedings of the ACM International Conference on Interactive Tabletops Surfaces - ITS 2011, December 2014, p. 154 (2011). https://doi.org/10.1145/2076354.2076383
11. Claessen, J.H.T., Van Wijk, J.J.: Flexible linked axes for multivariate data visualization. IEEE Trans. Vis. Comput. Graph. **17**(12), 2310–2316 (2011). https://doi.org/10.1109/TVCG.201 1.201
12. Cleveland, W.S., McGill, R.: The many faces of a scatterplot. J. Am. Stat. Assoc. **79**(388), 807–822 (1984). https://doi.org/10.1080/01621459.1984.10477098
13. Cook, K.A., Thomas, J.J.: Illuminating the path: The research and development agenda for visual analytics (2005)
14. Cordeil, M., et al.: ImAxes. In: Proceedings of the 30th Annual ACM Symposium on User Interface Software and Technology - UIST 2017, pp. 71–83 (2017). https://doi.org/10.1145/ 3126594.3126613
15. Creswell, J.W.: Chapter One, "A Framework for Design". Research Design: Qualitative, Quantitative, and Mixed Methods Approaches, pp. 3–26 (2003). https://doi.org/10.3109/089 41939.2012.723954
16. Crotty, A., et al.: Vizdom : interactive analytics through pen and touch. In: Proceedings of the 41st International Conference on Very Large Data Bases, vol. 8, no. 12, pp. 2024–2027 (2015). https://doi.org/10.14778/2824032.2824127
17. Crotty, A., et al.: Vizdom: interactive analytics through pen and touch. In: Proceedings of the VLDB Endow 8, no. 12, pp. 2024–2027 (2015). https://doi.org/10.14778/2824032.2824127
18. van Dam, A.: Post-WIMP user interfaces. Commun. ACM. **40**(2), 63–67 (1997). https://doi.org/10.1145/253671.253708
19. Drucker, S.M. et al.: TouchViz: a case study comparing two interfaces for data analytics on tablets. Proc. SIGCHI Conference on Human Factors in Computing Systems, pp. 2301–2310 (2013). https://doi.org/10.1145/2470654.2481318

20. Dunne, C., et al.: GraphTrail. In: Proceedings of the 2012 ACM annual conference on Human Factors in Computing Systems - CHI 2012, p. 1663. ACM Press, New York, New York, USA (2012). https://doi.org/10.1145/2207676.2208293

21. Elmqvist, N., et al.: DataMeadow: a visual canvas for analysis of large-scale multivariate data. In: VAST IEEE Symposium on Visual Analytics Science and Technology 2007, Proceedings January, pp. 187–194 (2007). https://doi.org/10.1109/VAST.2007.4389013

22. Fonnet, A., et al.: Axes and coordinate systems representations for immersive analytics of multi-dimensional data. In: Proceedings of the 4th International Symposium on Big Data Visual and Immersive Analytics, pp. 91–100 (2018). https://doi.org/10.1109/BDVA.2018.8533892

23. Friendly, M., Kwan, E.: Effect ordering for data displays. Comput. Stat. Data Anal. 43(4), 509–539 (2003). https://doi.org/10.1016/S0167-9473(02)00290-6

24. Grammel, L., et al.: How information visualization novices construct visualizations. IEEE Trans. Vis. Comput. Graph. 16(6), 943–952 (2010). https://doi.org/10.1109/TVCG.2010.164

25. Hinckley, K., et al.: Pen + touch = new tools. In: Proceedings of the 23nd Annual ACM Symposium on User Interface Software and Technology - UIST 2010, p. 27 (2010). https://doi.org/10.1145/1866029.1866036

26. Holland, S., Oppenheim, D.: Direct combination, pp. 262–269 (2003). https://doi.org/10.1145/302979.303057

27. Holten, D., Van Wijk, J.J.: Evaluation of cluster identification performance for different PCP variants. Comput. Graph. Forum. 29(3), 793–802 (2010). https://doi.org/10.1111/j.1467-8659.2009.01666.x

28. Huang, D., et al.: Personal visualization and personal visual analytics. IEEE Trans. Vis. Comput. Graph. 21(3), 420–433 (2015). https://doi.org/10.1109/TVCG.2014.2359887

29. Inselberg, A.: Multidimensional detective. In: Proceedings of the VIZ 1997 Visualization Conference, Information Visualization Symposium and Parallel Rendering Symposium, pp. 100–107 (1997). https://doi.org/10.1109/INFVIS.1997.636793

30. Isenberg, P., et al.: Data visualization on interactive surfaces: a research agenda. IEEE Comput. Graph. Appl. 33(2), 16–24 (2013). https://doi.org/10.1109/MCG.2013.24

31. Jo, J., et al.: TouchPivot: blending wimp & post-wimp interfaces for data exploration on tablet devices. In: Proceedings of the 2017 CHI Conference on Human Factors in Computing Systems - CHI 2017, pp. 2660–2671 (2017). https://doi.org/10.1145/3025453.3025752

32. Kosara, R., et al.: Parallel sets: interactive exploration and visual analysis of categorical data. IEEE Trans. Vis. Comput. Graph. 12(4), 558–568 (2006). https://doi.org/10.1109/TVCG.2006.76

33. Langner, R., et al.: VisTiles: coordinating and combining co-located mobile devices for visual data exploration. IEEE Trans. Vis. Comput. Graph. 24(1), 626–636 (2018). https://doi.org/10.1109/TVCG.2017.2744019

34. Lee, B., et al.: Beyond mouse and keyboard: expanding design considerations for information visualization interactions. IEEE Trans. Vis. Comput. Graph. 12, 2689–2697 (2012)

35. Lee, B., et al.: SketchInsight: natural data exploration on interactive whiteboards leveraging pen and touch interaction. In: IEEE Pacific Visualization Symposium 2015-July, Figure 1, pp. 199–206 (2015). https://doi.org/10.1109/PACIFICVIS.2015.7156378

36. Lehmann, D.J., et al.: Selecting coherent and relevant plots in large scatterplot matrices. Comput. Graph. Forum. 31(6), 1895–1908 (2012). https://doi.org/10.1111/j.1467-8659.2012.03069.x

37. Liu, Z., et al.: Data illustrator. In: Proceedings of the 2018 CHI Conference on Human Factors in Computing Systems - CHI 2018, pp. 1–13. ACM Press, New York, New York, USA (2018). https://doi.org/10.1145/3173574.3173697

38. Mackinlay, J.: Automating the design of graphical presentations of relational information. ACM Trans. Graph. 5(2), 110–141 (1986). https://doi.org/10.1145/22949.22950

39. Martin, A.R., Ward, M.O.: High dimensional brushing for interactive exploration of multivariate data. In: Proceedings of the Visualization 1995. June, p. 271 (2014). https://doi.org/10.1109/VISUAL.1995.485139
40. Méndez, G.G., et al.: iVoLVER: interactive visual language for visualization extraction and reconstruction. In: Proceedings of the SIGCHI Conference on Human Factors in Computing Systems, pp. 4073–4085 (2016). https://doi.org/10.1145/2858036.2858435
41. El Meseery, M., et al.: Multiple Workspaces in Visual Analytics. 2018 International Symposium on Big Data Visual and Immersive Analytics BDVA 2018, pp 1–12 (2018). https://doi.org/10.1109/BDVA.2018.8534019
42. North, C., Shneiderman, B.: Snap-together visualization. In: Proceedings of the Working Conference on Advanced Visual Interfaces - AVI 2000, pp. 128–135. ACM Press, New York, New York, USA (2000). https://doi.org/10.1145/345513.345282
43. Perry, D., et al.: VizDeck: streamlining exploratory visual analytics of scientific data. In: iConference 2013, pp. 338–350 (2013). https://doi.org/10.9776/13206
44. Ren, D., et al.: Charticulator: interactive construction of bespoke chart layouts. IEEE Trans. Vis. Comput. Graph. 25(1), 789–799 (2018). https://doi.org/10.1109/TVCG.2018.2865158
45. Rzeszotarski, J.M., Kittur, A.: Kinetica. In: Proceedings of the 32nd Annual ACM Conference on Human Factors in Computing Systems - CHI 2014, pp. 897–906 (2014). https://doi.org/10.1145/2556288.2557231
46. Sadana, R., et al.: OnSet: a visualization technique for large-scale binary set data. IEEE Trans. Vis. Comput. Graph. 20(12), 1993–2002 (2014). https://doi.org/10.1109/TVCG.2014.2346249
47. Sadana, R., et al.: Touching Data: A Discoverability-based Evaluation of a Visualization Interface for Tablet Computers (2018). arXiv:1806.06084v1
48. Sadana, R., Stasko, J.: Designing and implementing an interactive scatterplot visualization for a tablet computer. In: Proceedings of the 2014 International Working Conference on Advanced Visual Interfaces - AVI 2014, pp. 265–272 (2014). https://doi.org/10.1145/2598153.2598163
49. Sadana, R., Stasko, J.: Designing multiple coordinated visualizations for tablets. Comput. Graph. Forum. 35(3), 261–270 (2016). https://doi.org/10.1111/cgf.12902
50. Scott, S.D., et al.: Territoriality in collaborative tabletop workspaces. In: Proceedings of the ACM Conference on Computer Supported Cooperative Work CSCW, pp. 294–303 (2004). https://doi.org/10.1145/1031607.1031655
51. Tukey, J.W., Tukey, P.A.: The Collected Works of John W. Tukey: Graphics: 1965–1985. CRC Press, Boca Raton (1988)
52. Walny, J., et al.: Understanding pen and touch interaction for data exploration on interactive whiteboards. IEEE Trans. Vis. Comput. Graph. 18(12), 2779–2788 (2012). https://doi.org/10.1109/TVCG.2012.275
53. Wong, P.C., Bergeron, R.D.: 30 Years of multidimensional multivariate visualization. In: Scientific Visualization: Overviews, Methodologies, and Techniques Proceedings, pp. 3–33 (1997)
54. Wongsuphasawat, K., et al.: Voyager: exploratory analysis via faceted browsing of visualization recommendations. IEEE Trans. Vis. Comput. Graph. 22(1), 649–658 (2016). https://doi.org/10.1109/TVCG.2015.2467191
55. Wongsuphasawat, K., et al.: Voyager 2. In: Proceedings of the 2017 CHI Conference on Human Factors in Computing Systems - CHI 2017, pp. 2648–2659 (2017). https://doi.org/10.1145/3025453.3025768
56. Yee, K.-P., et al.: Faceted metadata for image search and browsing. In: Proceedings of the conference on Human factors in computing systems - CHI 2003, p. 401. ACM Press, New York, New York, USA (2003). https://doi.org/10.1145/642611.642681
57. Zgraggen, E., et al.: PanoramicData: data analysis through pen touch. IEEE Trans. Vis. Comput. Graph. 20(12), 2112–2121 (2014). https://doi.org/10.1109/TVCG.2014.2346293

58. D3.js. https://d3js.org/
59. Introduction to Statistical Learning. http://www-bcf.usc.edu/~gareth/ISL/data.html. Accessed 17 Jan 2019
60. Microsoft Excel spreadsheet software. https://products.office.com/en-ca/excel. Accessed 13 Jan 2019
61. Tableau - Business Intelligence and Analytics Software. https://www.tableau.com/. Accessed 13 Jan 2019
62. Video Games Sales 2019 | Kaggle. https://www.kaggle.com/ashaheedq/video-games-sales-2019. Accessed 19 Sep 2019
63. VTK - The Visualization Toolkit. https://vtk.org/. Accessed 13 Jan 2019

Interaction Design and Cultural Development

Blend in or Pop Out? Designing an Embedded Interface for a Historical Cemetery

Linda Hirsch⬥ and Andreas Butz(✉)

LMU Munich, Munich, Germany
{linda.hirsch,butz}@ifi.lmu.de

Abstract. Historical cemeteries are under-explored design spaces within Human-Computer Interaction (HCI), even though they are visited for many reasons nowadays. We present our strategy to embed interfaces into this sensitive environment and report on interim results and the potential of such interfaces to support these places' preservation. We followed an iterative design approach by (1) brainstorming various ideas and (2) creating four low-fidelity prototypes to (3) discuss them in two expert interviews. This led to a final prototype resembling a birdhouse, a reoccurring and tolerated object in the cemetery. We (4) tested our prototype in a field study, asking passers-by about their interaction and perception. Our results show that our design approach is suitable and unobtrusive for the culturally-sensitive target environment. Further, embedded interfaces seem to facilitate and are more inviting to visitors to inform themselves about the place's characteristics and historical meaning, supporting its preservation.

Keywords: Historic cemetery · Design opportunities · Embedded interfaces · Community space

1 Introduction

Historical cemeteries, such as Xoxocotlan in Mexico or Père-Lachaise in France[1] are popular tourism locations for their architecture, the graves of famous people, and their representation of culture and history. Nowadays, such cemeteries are often used as park-like areas for personal recreation, sports, or other activities [3, 4] besides paying your respect for the deceased. Despite the visitors' feedback that more details about the location and the deceased would be appreciated [1,8], municipalities are still reluctant to offer interactive content at those sites, mostly fearing to destroy the solemn atmosphere.

---

[1] www.pandotrip.com/top-10-impressive-cemeteries-around-the-world-18694/, accessed Dec. 29th 2020.

© IFIP International Federation for Information Processing 2021
Published by Springer Nature Switzerland AG 2021
C. Ardito et al. (Eds.): INTERACT 2021, LNCS 12934, pp. 635–645, 2021.
https://doi.org/10.1007/978-3-030-85613-7_40

Current, non-embedded solutions use virtual reality (VR), Augmented Reality (AR), or simple mobile applications. Yet, only a few HCI researchers looked at tangible, embedded interfaces due to these places' cultural-sensitivity. Häkkilä et al. [3], for example, turned a tombstone into an interactive display, inspired by commercially available displays[2] or QR codes[3] on gravestones. However, their study also revealed that participants perceived a digital display as rather obtrusive and unsuitable for the environment. In comparison, due to being culturally-sensitive places, cemeteries require interfaces to be physically and culturally unobtrusive [3]. We approach the research gap to identify design opportunities and requirements for embedded interfaces at historical cemeteries by looking at one historical cemetery in particular.

In our work, we focused on embedded, physical interfaces integrated into the environment for three main reasons: (1) Mobile applications offer easy and ubiquitous use, but do not allow an embodied, multi-sensory experience, nor is their handling fully culturally-accepted yet [9–11]. (2) Embedded interfaces facilitate an embodied experience of a place [12] and allow users to focus on their surroundings, instead of on the technology [13]. (3) There is little research about embedded interfaces at historical cemeteries, which we aim to enrich with our study results.

We approached the topic by first conducting a brainstorming to gather various ideas and requirements for an installation considering the target environment. Then, we created a set of four low-fidelity prototypes to discuss them in two expert interviews and built one interactive, birdhouse-inspired prototype to be tested in an in situ survey and guerrilla test. Our results show the need to preserve such places' meanings by making them relevant and accessible to their visitors and the potential of embedded interfaces to support this process.

2   Related Work

We build on existing work on technology in historical landmarks and cemeteries and consider general work about unobtrusive design briefly introducing it below.

2.1   Historical Landmarks and Technology

The preservation of historical landmarks serves as the living memory of a society supporting local identities [14,15]. Previous work often focused on the digitization of information [16–18] or enhanced cultural heritage sites via mobile applications [19–21]. The digitization process includes the creation of virtual 3D models of cultural heritage objects [16,17], digital storytelling [25], and web-based documentation [17]. Augmented Reality (AR) is a well-established technology for enhancing heritage sites [23,24]. However, mobile applications are still challenged by imprecise position tracking, varying daylight conditions [19] and require the

---

[2] www.funeralguide.co.uk/blog/digital-gravestones, accessed Jan. 1st 2021.

[3] www.bbc.com/news/uk-england-somerset-31525144/, accessed Jan. 1st 2021.

user to preinstall the application. They also make the user focus mainly on the device display instead of the environment [22]. Krösche et al. [20] emphasized the difficulty in raising awareness toward cultural heritage: The "lacking interest and perception" of the public is also caused by a lack of information directly provided at the monuments themselves. Hence, we see potential in exploring embedded interfaces that can capture and guide the user's attention.

2.2 Interactivity at Cemeteries

The primary purpose of a cemetery is to serve as a community place [27]. While research shows changes in the intention of visiting cemeteries, technology use and opportunities are still limited [4]. Ciolfi and Petrelli [26] researched design opportunities for the cultural heritage of a historical cemetery. The authors covered a range of ideas regarding information richness, (peripheral) interaction, and the level of obtrusiveness. However, they did not include any solutions embedded in the context. Other HCI projects concentrated on mobile applications [2,29,30] or used a tombstone as an interface [3,28]. The latter, however, was considered disrespectful and unacceptable by study participants as it would be too directly connected to the physical remains. The authors [3] emphasized the need for a physically and culturally unobtrusive design for embedded interfaces.

2.3 Unobtrusive Design

Unobtrusive interfaces are defined as non-disruptive and quickly moving from the periphery of attention to the focus and back as needed [5,31–34]. They also aim for a "natural interaction" that can be easily understood, executed, and ignored by others, and hence, are culturally unobtrusive. This includes the consideration of more implicit interaction modalities [36] as well as a context-dependent natural look of the interface [35], considering the requirements for physical unobtrusiveness. In this study, we want to contribute to this still limited research status by exploring the design space for embedded interfaces by considering the requirements for an unobtrusive interface.

3 Iterative Approach and Results

We applied an iterative, user-centered design approach using qualitative user research methods. As a first step, we brainstormed design opportunities and requirements among four Media Informatics and Human-Computer Interaction students, all female. Based on the results, we created four low-fidelity prototypes considering a natural design approach [35]. We evaluated these with two experts in independent semi-structured interviews who confirmed the birdhouse-inspired prototype's suitability for the target environment. Finally, we developed a first interactive prototype according to the gathered requirements and tested it at the target location. Each participant was informed about their data privacy rights according to the GDPR and gave their consent to being audio-recorded and photographed. Below, we report on our methods and key results which influenced our further design decisions.

3.1 Brainstorming and Low-Fidelity Prototypes

Method. We conducted a brainstorming using the Lotus Flower method by Michalko [37] which supports the creative thinking process through an iterative, structured approach. Moderators start with eight core categories for their overall design goal, and brainstorming participant gather another eight ideas for each of these categories. We prepared the following eight categories that we considered essential to define interaction and interface concepts for the historical cemetery: (1) available information about the deceased, (2) interesting stories from a user perspective, (3) information presentation, (4) embedding interfaces at the target location, (5) guiding the user attention to the interface, (6) contextual limitations and considerations, (7) preferred interaction modalities and (8) the potential influence of the user's cultural background. We presented pictures of our target environment so that participants could better relate to it.

Results. Overall, participants agreed on an unobtrusive design and to avoid big displays or signs as "[...] it has something touristy about it. I wouldn't want this.", participant 2. Instead, the interface should *blend in* by using natural materials or objects similar to those already existing in the target environment, such as wood or stone, and objects, such as grave lanterns or birdhouses. They further suggested avoiding sound as an interaction modality as it could be disruptive and perceived as disrespectful. Instead, the focus should be on touch interaction with mainly visual output. To make the unobtrusive interfaces obvious enough, participants suggested using *pop-out* effects as in web design, using color, shape, or size differences [6]. This also includes the interfaces' positioning. Information about a particular person should be close to the grave. Hence, the lantern or the birdhouse could be suitable interface objects[4]. The birdhouse interaction (Fig. 1, left picture) might be more comfortable as it would hang at eye-height and the lantern would require to kneel (Fig. 1, right picture). Participants also discussed "[...] us[ing] stones to trigger an information display" with low salience like an e-ink display (Fig. 1, second picture from the left). Depending on the size and the information, this could either be placed in the cemetery's central areas or embedded into a grave's decoration. In comparison, information about the cemetery should be placed in distance to individual graves. Here, participants suggested redesigning the information boards at the cemetery's entrance attached to the outer walls or introducing smaller walls as paths' divisions within the cemetery. The idea targeted attentive visitors who could discover hidden notes and information by moving stones as in a mosaic (Fig. 1, second picture from the right). Lastly, participants emphasized the relevance of sharing information about the persons' roles and works and how those influenced the city's development.

Combining the different suggestions, we implemented four low-fidelity prototypes as presented in Fig. 1, further considering the natural design approach according to Schlacht [35]. This approach finds mimicries of nature, such as

---

[4] The target environment included many trees and natural vegetation between the tombs and information boards at the entrances.

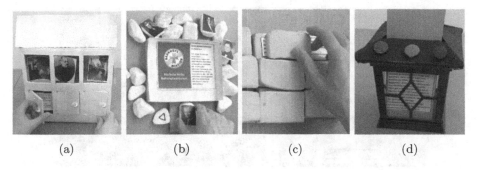

(a)   (b)   (c)   (d)

Fig. 1. Each prototype was inspired by reoccurring objects on European cemeteries: (a) birdhouse, (b) pebble stones, (c) brick wall, and (d) grave lantern.

organic shapes and biological structures, and local artifacts that are typical for the target environment to achieve a natural design.

3.2   Expert Interviews

Method. We discussed the prototypes in semi-structured interviews with a manager from the municipal cemetery administration (MCA) and a cemetery guide (CG) in independent sessions. The interviews focused on the meaning and usage of the historical cemetery and their opinions of the prototypes. The MCA manager had over 36 years of working experience in his job, the CG about 14 years. Both were male and consented to provide their data according to GDPR. We transcribed the interview recordings afterward and translated citations from the mother tongue into English.

Results. Both experts saw issues with the grave lantern idea (a) as there would not be any in current use at our target location. Hence, it would "change the cemetery's appearance massively" (MCA). Birdhouses (b), however, were already part of the current cemetery and hence, could be acceptable. However, neither saw a benefit in (c) the brick wall prototype, as "there is sufficient, textual information along the outer walls. Elderly people wouldn't understand that [how to interact]" (CG). Lastly, (d) the scanning sign idea of engraving pictures or symbols on stones reminded the MCA of a ritual for children's graves: Relatives and friends say good-bye to the departed child by coloring and writing messages on rocks, placing them on the grave. The ritual would support families in their grief. However, as there would be no burials at the historical cemetery, the screens would face the same issue as the grave lanterns. But that "depends on where exactly it would be positioned" (MCA). Both experts emphasized the need to guard historical cemeteries due to their cultural and historical value. They would need to be made more accessible and understandable for visitors to preserve their original purpose of mourning and visiting the deceased. But they would also have to be developed to adapt to current community needs, such as tourism and recreational and sportive activities.

Fig. 2. Left: The birdhouse-inspired mid-fidelity prototype can display text via an LED matrix connected to an Arduino UNO triggered by four touch buttons. A portrait of the person is carved into the wood from the backside. When somebody approaches the object, an ultrasonic distance sensor triggers its illumination from behind and makes the portrait appear on the translucent wood. Right: The prototype in context.

From our expert interviews, we derived the following main insights: (1) Historical cemeteries' relevance has to be made more accessible and understandable to visitors. (2) The place's original purpose should be retained and supported. (3) The birdhouse-inspired prototype seemed to be the most promising to iterate.

3.3   In Situ Survey and Guerrilla Test

Birdhouses are reoccurring, accepted objects in the cemetery and allow certain mobility: They can be placed at different heights, positions, and distances to a grave while all electronics can be hidden inside. We developed an interactive prototype using the materials as presented in Fig. 2. It included translucent wood displaying a picture of the person whose grave we chose as a testing environment and textual information. We decided on four information themes, the person's importance for the city, works, relationships, and place of residence.

Method. First, we conducted a survey and a semi-structured interview with 19 passers-by (11 female, eight male) who were spontaneously recruited. We asked them to rate the prototype's appropriateness for the context, how natural it looked, and how well it caught their attention using a 5-point Likert scale (1=totally disagree to 5=totally agree) and open interview questions. The prototype was attached to a tree trunk next to a grave. We analyzed the results of the survey questions using descriptive statistics. Nine participants (three female, six male) agreed to participate in a follow-up guerrilla test. Guerrilla testing is used as a practical, rapid method to test the usability of a system with few users only [40,43]. During this optional part of the interview, we asked all participants to use the Think-Aloud method [39] while interacting with the prototype. Afterward, we asked them for qualitative feedback about the prototype's usability.

Results. Overall, our prototype was perceived as *blending in* by being unobtrusive (75% agreed or strongly agreed) as well as seamlessly integrated (75% agreed or strongly agreed) and rather culturally fitting (50% agreed or strongly agreed, 30% were neutral) for the environment. The reasons mentioned were its small size, its close position relative to the grave, and the plain design. However, three participants also stated that they would not have noticed it as an interface they could interact with (e.g. "It looks like a donation box. I would have just ignored it." p.13). All participants considered it essential to maintain the natural image and atmosphere of the cemetery. Twelve out of 19 participants preferred our prototype to digital displays or phone applications because it provided information in the environment and appeared as a part of the cemetery. This also offered users to receive information without them originally intending to do so, which was positively acknowledged. However, four participants would have preferred no changes to the location at all. In comparison, the remaining 15 participants appreciated the opportunity to interact with their environment instead of just visiting it. However, the sunny conditions limited the translucent picture display's visibility, and the meaning of the icons remained partly unclear. Nonetheless, eight of nine guerrilla study participants agreed or strongly agreed to the prototype's usability. The remaining person ranked it neutral. They further appreciated the prepared information of the buried person that was displayed on the button push.

4 Discussion and Limitations

4.1 Limitations

There are several limitations showing our initial status. We tested the interface in context with individuals but not its effect on third persons, limiting our findings regarding the prototype's unobtrusiveness. Also, our prototype hangs in trees, which not every cemetery has. Yet, we could imagine it suitable for cemeteries with similar vegetation. Lastly, the prototype is still on a primary status requiring further iteration toward a high-fidelity version.

4.2 Suitability of the Birdhouse-Inspired Prototype

Our prototype's goal was to provide individuals with more information if desired by using an interface that can easily be ignored and preserves the place's natural and historical conditions. Participants found the birdhouse prototype to be rather attention-inviting, but not demanding [41], and adapted to the context [38]. We also placed it at the periphery of perception [5,42]. Furthermore, the material (wood) and object (birdhouse) choices supported the unobtrusive design [31] that we were aiming for by redesigning a naturally appearing object [35]. Participants rated the interface as non-interrupting and unobtrusive for the cemetery's atmosphere, making it compliant to the required physical and culturally-sensitive unobtrusiveness [3]. In comparison, it was partly perceived as being too unobtrusive, showing the need to let it *pop out* more. Nonetheless, the birdhouse-inspired interface proved to be unobtrusive, embedded, and natural for our target environment. It further shows the effectiveness of the natural design approach to achieve an unobtrusive design. This can be adapted according to the context, taking other reoccurring, natural objects as interface inspiration.

4.3   Untouched Preservation Versus Encouraged Engagement

In some historical cemeteries, it is prohibited to introduce any changes, as was the case in Ciolfi and Petrelli's work [26]. Yet, we see significant benefit in an embedded, physical interface as it makes information available at the spot. This further supports directing visitors' attention and awareness, which is one of the main difficulties for historic landmarks [20]. In our study, we also had visitors with initially no intention of informing themselves about the place but still appreciated the possibility of doing so. It raises a question about preservation approaches considering whether it is more important to leave a place physically untouched or extend it unobtrusively, offering immediate information. Considering our experts' feedback, there is a clear need to make the historical meaning of such places accessible and understandable to a broader audience. Our study also identified the need to preserve historical cemeteries in their role as community place [27]. We see further research potential in these topics to support the communication of historical cemeteries' meanings and their roles as community spaces to their visitors.

5   Summary, Conclusion and Next Steps

Our work used an iterative approach to explore the design space for embedded interfaces at a historical cemetery. Considering the limitations of preserved, historical landmarks, our prototype confirmed to blend in well while even requiring to pop out a bit more for future design iterations.

We used a natural design approach to adapt the interface's shape and appearance to a reoccurring object (a birdhouse) from the target environment [35], which caused our prototype to be considered unobtrusive, barely distracting, and well-adapted to its natural and historical surrounding. Our results further show that even participants who did not intend to inform themselves about the location appreciated prepared information available at the spot. We also identified the need and, hence, design opportunities for HCI to support historical cemeteries preservation in conjunction with its original role as community space.

In the following steps, we want to iterate on our prototype and deepen our understanding of the adequate level of embeddedness by exploring different strategies and designs. Additionally, we want to research more solutions to bridge their historical, social and cultural roles. With our current work status, we hope to spark a discussion about the role of embedded interfaces at historical cemeteries, including the design opportunities to emphasize such places' historical value and their communal character.

References

1. Häkkilä, J., Colley, A.: Graveyards as a Design Context for Unobtrusive Interaction (2016)
2. Häkkilä, J., Forsman, M.T., Colley, A.: Navigating the graveyard: designing technology for deathscapes. MUM 2018 (2018)
3. Häkkilä, J., Colley, A., Kalving, M.: Designing an interactive gravestone display. PerDis 2019 (2019)
4. Nordh, H., Evensen, K.H.: Qualities and functions ascribed to Urban cemeteries across the capital cities of scandinavia. In: Urban Forestry & Urban Greening, vol. 33 (2018)
5. Bakker, S., Hausen, D., Selker, T. (eds.).: Peripheral Interaction: Challenges and Opportunities for HCI in the Periphery of Attention. Springer, Berlin (2016)
6. Goldstein, E.B., Brockmole, J.: Sensation and perception. In: Cengage Learning (2016)
7. Butz, A., Krüger, A.: Mensch-Machine-Interaktion, 2nd edn., pp 21–23. De Gruyter Oldenburg, Berlin (2017)
8. Hirsch, L.: Designing interactive interfaces by keeping the natural beauty of public places. UbiComp/ISWC 2019 Adjunct (2019)
9. Farrelly, G.: Claiming Places: An Exploration of People's Use of Locative Media and the Relationship to Sense of Place (2017)
10. Brown, K.W., Ryan, R.M.: The benefits of being present: mindfulness and its role in psychological well-being. J. Pers. Soc. Psychol. **84**, 822–848 (2003)
11. Love, S., Perry, M.: Dealing with mobile conversations in public places: some implications for the design of socially intrusive technologies. In: CHI EA 2004 (2004)
12. Boari, D., Fraser, M.: Taking shortcuts: embedded physical interfaces for spatial navigation. TEI 2009 (2009)
13. Schmidt, A., Kranz, M., Holleis, P.: Interacting with the ubiquitous computer: towards embedding interaction. In: SOC-EUSAI 2005 (2005)
14. Bandarin, F., Van Oers, R.: The Historic Urban Landscape Managing Heritage in an Urban Century, 1st edn., p. XIII. Wiley-Blackwell, Hoboken (2012)
15. Kuipers, M., De Jonge, W.: Designing from Heritage - Strategies for Conservation and Conversion, p. 33. Basic Books, Delft, NY (2017)
16. Koeva, M., Luleva, M., Maldjanski, P.: Integrating spherical panoramas and maps for visualization of cultural heritage objects using virtual reality technology. Sensors (Basel, Switz.) **17**(4), 829 (2017)
17. Albourae, A.T., Armenakisa, C., Kyan, M.: Architectural heritage visualization using interactive technologies. In: ISPRS - International Archives of the Photogrammetry, Remote Sensing and Spatial Information Sciences, vol. XLII-2/W5, pp. 7–13 (2017)
18. Ahn, J., Wohn, K.Y.: Interactive scan planning for heritage recording. Multimed. Tools Appl. **75**(7), 3655–3675 (2015)
19. Duguleana, M., Voinea, G.D.: Enhancing the experience of visiting outdoor heritage sites using handheld AR. In: Stephanidis, C. (eds.) HCI International 2018 – Posters' Extended Abstracts. HCI 2018. Communications in Computer and Information Science, vol. 852, pp. 184–191. Springer, Cham (2018). https://doi.org/10. 1007/978-3-319-92285-0_26
20. Krosche, J., Baldzer, J., Boll, S.: MobiDENK - mobile multimedia in monument conservation. IEEE Multimed. **11**(2), 72–77 (2004)

21. Barazzetti, L., Banfi, F.: Historic BIM for mobile VR/AR applications. In: Ioannides, M., Magnenat-Thalmann, N., Papagiannakis, G. (eds.) Mixed Reality and Gamification for Cultural Heritage, pp. 271–290. Springer, Cham (2017). https://doi.org/10.1007/978-3-319-49607-8_10

22. Butz, A.: Taming the urge to click. In: 10. GI-Workshop "Adaptivität und Benutzermodellierung in interaktiven Softwaresystemen" (2002)

23. Hollerer, T., Feiner, S., Pavlik, J.: Situated documentaries: embedding multimedia presentations in the real world. In: IEEE, Digest of Papers. Third International Symposium on Wearable Computers, pp. 79–86 (1999)

24. Hollerer, T., Feiner, S., Terauchi, T., Rashid, G., Hallaway, D.: Exploring MARS: developing indoor and outdoor user interfaces to a mobile augmented reality system. Comput. Graphics 23(6), 779–785 (1999)

25. Rizvić, S.: How to breathe life into cultural heritage 3d reconstructions. Eur. Rev. 25(1), 39–50 (2017)

26. Ciolfi, L., Petrelli, D.: Studying a community of volunteers at a historic cemetery to inspire interaction concepts. C&T 2015 (2015)

27. Rugg, J.: Defining the place of burial: what makes a cemetery a cemetery? Mortality 5(3), 259–275 (2000)

28. Foong, P.S.: Designing Technology for Sensitive Contexts: Supporting End-of-Life Decision Making (2008)

29. Newton, O.N., Deshan, C., Pang, N., Nakatsu, R.: Mobile augmented reality for Bukit Brown cemetery navigation. VRCAI 2012 (2012)

30. Dow, S., Lee, J., Oezbek, C., MacIntyre, B., Bolter, J.D., Gandy, M.: Exploring spatial narratives and mixed reality experiences in Oakland Cemetery. ACE 2005 (2005)

31. Kim, H., Lee, W.: Designing unobtrusive interfaces with minimal presence. In: CHI EA 2009 (2009)

32. Gil, M., Giner, P., Pelechano, V.: Personalization for unobtrusive service interaction. Pers. Ubiquitous Comput. 16(5), 543–561 (2012)

33. Luria, M., Hoffman, G., Zuckerman, O.: Comparing social robot, screen and voice interfaces for smart-home control. In: CHI 2017 (2017)

34. Börner, D., Kalz, M., Specht, M.: Lead me gently: facilitating knowledge gain through attention-aware ambient learning displays. Comput. Educ. 78, 10–19 (2014)

35. Schlacht, I.L.: Space extreme design. Pers. Ubiquitous Comput. 15, 487–489 (2011)

36. Leifer, L.: The design of implicit interactions: making interactive systems less obnoxious. Des. Issues 24, 72–84 (2008)

37. Michalko, M.: Thinkpak: A Brainstorming Card Deck; [a Creative-thinking Toolbox]. Ten Speed Press (2006)

38. Riekki, J., Isomursu, P., Isomursu, M.: Evaluating the calmness of ubiquitous applications. In: Bomarius, F., Iida, H. (eds.) Product Focused Software Process Improvement. PROFES 2004. Lecture Notes in Computer Science, vol. 3009, pp. 105–119. Springer, Berlin, Heidelberg (2004). https://doi.org/10.1007/978-3-540-24659-6_8

39. Martin, B., Hanington, B., Hanington, B.M.: Universal Methods of Design: 100 Ways to Research Complex Problems, Develop Innovative Ideas, and Design Effective Solutions, p. 180. Rockport Publishers, Beverly (2012)

40. Kauhanen, O., et al.: Assisting immersive virtual reality development with user experience design approach. AcademicMindtrek (2017)

41. Dublon, G., Portocarrerro, E.: ListenTree: Audio-Haptic Display in the Natural Environment (2014)
42. Kučera, J., Scott, J., Chen, N.: Probing calmness in applications using a calm display prototype. In: UbiComp 2017 (2017)
43. Klein, L.: UX for Lean Startups: Faster, Smarter User Experience Research and Design, pp. 31–32. O'Reilly Media, Sebastopol (2012)

Cognitive Limitations of Older E-Commerce Customers in Product Comparison Tasks

Klara Rydzewska[2], Justyna Pawłowska[1,2(✉)], Radosław Nielek[1],
Adam Wierzbicki[1], and Grzegorz Sedek[2]

[1] Polish-Japanese Academy of Information Technology, Warsaw, Poland
{nielek,adamw}@pja.edu.pl
[2] SWPS University of Social Sciences and Humanities, Warsaw, Poland
{krydzewska1,jpawlowska2,gsedek}@swps.edu.pl

Abstract. The number of older consumers making e-commerce purchasing decisions is constantly rising. We examined the impact of age-related cognitive limitations on older adults' choices in a series of multi-attribute choice tasks designed to mimic the process of products comparison and selection on e-commerce platforms. 135 older, middle-aged and younger adults were asked to participate in an on-line experiment. We found significant age-related limitations in solving simple and moderately difficult tasks, especially in the older adults group. The mediational model indicated an interplay between the age-related limitation and the role of additional variables (Helplessness of Contracting an Infectious Disease and Numeracy) in explaining the relationship between aging and performance in the multi-attribute choice task.

Keywords: Aging · Multi-attribute choice · Helplessness · Numeracy · E-commerce

1 Introduction

Since the pandemic, older adults are confined at home, and the value of their e-commerce purchases (which was high even before the pandemic's onset) is expected to rise. This is also due to the aging of population in all developed countries in the world. Monetary considerations aside, older consumers become increasingly dependent on e-commerce platforms because of their enforced isolation. The Internet becomes one of the main platforms for social interaction for older adults - luckily, according to the Pew Research Institute study, in 2019 73% of US citizens aged over 65 were connected to the Internet [26]. However, this raises the question - how well are current e-commerce web sites adapted to requirements of older adults?

While the user interfaces of e-commerce web sites are usually adapted for older consumers [22], these are mainly superficial changes, affecting such aspects

© IFIP International Federation for Information Processing 2021
Published by Springer Nature Switzerland AG 2021
C. Ardito et al. (Eds.): INTERACT 2021, LNCS 12934, pp. 646–656, 2021.
https://doi.org/10.1007/978-3-030-85613-7_41

as navigation and readability. The underlying mechanics of product comparison, recommendation, and purchasing decision support is the same for older and younger consumers. This situation has been recognized as harmful by HCI researchers, who appealed against conflating aging with accessibility [16]. In this article we consider the question - do cognitive limitations due to aging affect consumer choices significantly? If the answer to this question turns out to be positive, then the underlying recommendation mechanisms of e-commerce will have to be modified to adapt to older consumers. We seek an answer to our research question by the means of an experiment that uses a decision task similar to the ubiquitous function of product comparison in e-commerce systems. The experiment setup and data uses methodology from psychology to investigate the effects of age and age-related cognitive limitations on the performance of participants in product comparison tasks.

2 Related Work

2.1 Older Adults, E-Commerce, Multi-attribute Choice

Research on the use of e-commerce systems by older adults is focused mostly on two interconnected areas: accessibility and acceptance [17,18,23]. Deeper adaptation of existing e-commerce systems to the needs and limitations of older adults has only recently been considered. El Shamy et al. [8] proposed an experiment to measure the impact of recommender systems and comparison matrices on older adults' e-commerce decisions' quality, but no final results have been published yet. Pawłowska et al.[24] used multi-agent simulation to verify the existence of harmful feedback loop in typical recommendation algorithms, if used by older adults with cognitive limitations. Von Helversen et al. [13] studied the influence of on-line reviews on purchasing decisions of older adults and revealed statistically significant differences in how older and younger people respond to negative reviews. It is important to note that such consideration of the needs, preferences, and abilities of older adults in the context of e-commerce systems is beneficial to all of its users, not only to the older population [7].

2.2 Age-Related Cognitive and Motivational Changes

A vast array of research findings indicate gradual decline in basic fluid cognitive abilities such as processing speed of information and working memory capacity throughout adult life span [9,28,31]. Therefore, maintaining high level of performance in cognitively demanding tasks may require much effort. In response, related compensatory mechanisms may arise, with older adults conserving their limited cognitive resources by simplifying interactions with the environment, both in terms of the quantity and complexity of the attended information [1,14].

In line with the idea that costs for searching and storing information increase due to age-related cognitive decline, which in turn leads to a decrease in intrinsic motivation [14], older adults put less value on informational gain and more on achieving a satisfactory decision outcome. While younger adults are often quite likely to be systematic and use maximizing decision strategies, older adults often search for information only for as long as it is sufficient [6]. Both age-related decline in cognitive resources and motivational changes may contribute to the reduction in information search among older adults.

Emotion Regulation, Helplessness and Anxiety of Contracting an Infectious Disease, and Numeracy. Besides cognitive and motivational factors, emotion regulation and numeracy are important parts of decision-making competence [3]. A number of both financial and health-related decisions require making choices between alternatives that are characterized by numerous attributes. Therefore, in the current multi-attribute choice study we have used Subjective [10] and Objective Numeracy [19] measures to assess numerical skills of the participants, because numerical abilities are important for calculating various attribute weights and values for several alternatives. Individuals highly confident about their mathematical competences may use the emotions that result from analyzing numerical information to make better decisions. On the other hand, less confident individuals are directed by emotions that are irrelevant for effective decision making [25]. In the context of the COVID-19 pandemic, we also included our own measures of helplessness and anxiety of contracting an infectious disease as additional scales that may indicate the dysfunctional role of a high level of maladaptive emotions when making rational choices. The Scale of Helplessness of Contracting an Infectious Disease was inspired by the Intellectual Helplessness Scale initially developed for the education setting, where one tries to solve a task without understanding it for a prolonged period of time and a lack of control ultimately leads to intellectual helplessness in the domain related to that task [27]. Similarly, emotions that accompany the uncontrollable situation of the pandemic may lead to the feelings of helplessness and anxiety, and overshadow rational choices. Our previous research indicate that intellectual helplessness toward math is a strong predictor of low achievement in math [2]. Additionally, anxiety toward math was highly correlated with intellectual helplessness toward math, but only intellectual helplessness (not anxiety) was a significant predictor of low math achievement [30].

2.3 Strategies in Multi-attribute Choice Tasks

Despite the fact that the value of older adults' e-commerce purchases is most likely going to rise, the age-related limitations in performance of decision making tasks and in particular multi-attribute choice tasks, seem to be quite stable and universal. Numerous research has indicated that older adults perform worse than younger adults in cognitively demanding experimental decision making tasks. It is especially evident for the multi-attribute choice tasks that demand the use of a more complex strategy requiring thorough information processing [20,21]. Weighted Additive (WADD) is an information-intensive strategy, which involves multiplication of cue values by cue validities and addition of them for each alternative. The alternative with the largest sum is being selected. This strategy

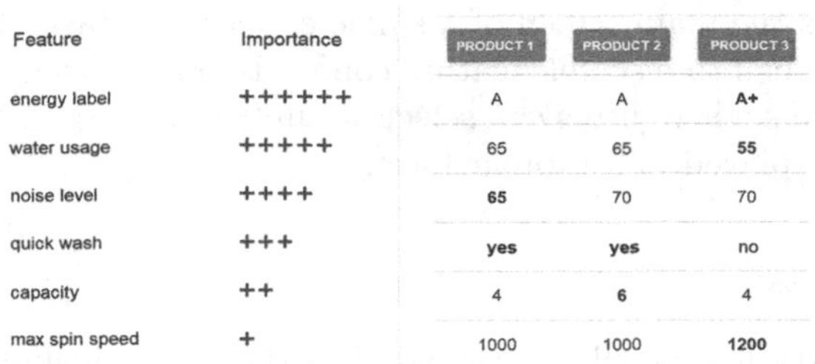

Feature	Importance	PRODUCT 1	PRODUCT 2	PRODUCT 3
energy label	++++++	A	A	A+
water usage	+++++	65	65	55
noise level	++++	65	70	70
quick wash	+++	yes	yes	no
capacity	++	4	6	4
max spin speed	+	1000	1000	1200

Fig. 1. Experiment screen showing the single multi-attribute choice task. On the left are the washing machine features and their importance expressed as a number of plus signs. On the right are the 3 products and their features.

allows for compensation, where two cues favoring one alternative can counterbalance other cue favoring another alternative. Another, yet simpler, compensatory strategy is TALLY [11], where cue weights are ignored and cue values are added for each alternative. Again, the alternative with the largest sum is the one that is being selected.

Take The Best (TTB) is the simplest of the strategies considered here, it is a strategy based on one, most important information. That means making decision by looking at the cue with the highest validity and its respective values. If the most predictive cue (one with the highest validity) is not discriminative, then TTB involves looking at the cue with the second-highest validity and so on.

Older adults have difficulty applying decision rules that are necessary for selection of an alternative from a set of choices [15]. In multi-attribute choice tasks older adults have considerable problems with learning value of cues [5] and options [29].

Following previous work, we formulate the hypothesis of a significant age-related decrease in the performance of multi-attribute choice task. Moreover, we test new hypotheses that numeracy and the Scales of Helplessness and Anxiety of Contracting an Infectious Disease may be significant predictors of decision making performance.

3 Experiment Design

The design of our experiment aimed at replicating the product comparison function which is ubiquitous in e-commerce platforms. In order to investigate our research question, we needed an objective ground truth - a best choice in each product comparison. This was achieved by instructing experiment participants to select the best washing machine out of 3 available products taking into account multiple features of varying importance. The importance of each feature was specified in the experiment using a simple metaphor - a number of plus signs associated with each feature, ranging from 1 (least important) to 6 (most important). Participants had to repeat the product comparison task 32 times.

Figure 1 shows the main screen of a single experiment task. The experiment interface was designed to resemble feature comparison table available on many e-commerce platforms where users can select a number of product for comparison, which then are displayed in a tabular form.

3.1   Participants

One hundred thirty five people participated in the study, including 49 younger adults (26 women; age range 20–30; mean age = 25.65, SD = 2.96; mean years of education = 14.76, SD = 2.45), 45 middle-age adults (24 women; age range 42–52; mean age = 46.38, SD = 3.02; mean years of education = 14.98, SD = 2.55) and 41 older adults (23 women; age range 65–76; mean age = 69.27, SD = 3.00; mean years of education = 15.41, SD = 2.94). Participation in the study took between 1 and 2 h, participants were remunerated for their participation. The study was approved by the Ethics Committee of the SWPS University of Social Sciences and Humanities in Warsaw.

3.2   Materials

Measures of Helplessness and Anxiety of Contracting an Infectious Disease, and Numeracy. Participants completed the Scales of Helplessness and Anxiety of Contracting an Infectious Disease (Rydzewska & Sedek, in preparation). Each of these scales was composed of ten items with answers on a 5-point Likert Scale ranging from 1 = "never" to 5 = "always". An exemplary item from the Scale of Helplessness was "I feel helpless in the face of the possibility of contracting an infectious disease" and a sample from the Scale of Anxiety was "I am concerned when someone around me sneezes without covering their mouth". The reliabilities of these scales were impressively high: Cronbach's alpha = .92 and Cronbach's alpha = .93, respectively for the Scale of Helplessness and the Scale of Anxiety of Contracting an Infectious Disease.

Finally, participants also completed Scales of Subjective Numeracy [10] and Objective Numeracy [19]. Scale of Subjective Numeracy consisted of seven questions measuring subjective view on cognitive abilities in relation to fractions and percentages, and preferences for displaying numeric information. The Objective Numeracy Scale was comprised of three open-ended questions measuring numerical skills and an additional warm-up question. The reliability of the Subjective Numeracy Scale was satisfactory (Cronbach's alpha = .83), the reliability of the Objective Numeracy Scale was also satisfactory considering it is a 3-item only scale (Cronbach's alpha = .65).

Product Comparison in Multi-attribute Choice Tasks. On the screens preceding the task, participants were given a brief description of the meaning of each feature and its relative importance for an average consumer expressed as a number of plus signs, ranging from 1 plus sign for the least important feature (max spin speed) to 6 for the most important one (energy label). The participants

Table 1. Correlation table of dependent and independent variables. Simple = simple decision tasks; Moderate = moderately difficult decision tasks; Difficult = difficult decision tasks; S_Numeracy = Subjective Numeracy Scale; O_Numeracy = Objective Numeracy Scale; Helplessness = Scale of Helplessness of Contracting an Infectious Disease; Anxiety = Scale of Anxiety of Contracting an Infectious Disease. Note: *p < .05, **p < .01.

Variable	1	2	3	4	5	6	7	8
1. Age	-							
2. Simple	$-.24^{**}$	-						
3. Moderate	-.11	.01	-					
4. Difficult	.04	.12	$.38^{**}$	-				
5. S_Numeracy	-.10	$.25^{**}$	.13	.06	-			
6. O_Numeracy	-.05	$.39^{**}$	$.19^{*}$	.16	$.53^{**}$	-		
7. Helplessness	$.23^{**}$	$-.23^{**}$	$-.17^{*}$	-.13	.01	$-.19^{**}$	-	
8. Anxiety	-.08	-.12	$-.22^{**}$	-.09	-.01	$-.20^{**}$	$.80^{**}$	-

were explicitly instructed to follow the preferences of an average consumer. On the left side of the screen depicted on the Fig. 1 the list of features is presented in a descending importance order. On the right side there are 3 washing machines and their feature values. If for a given feature one or two washing machines had a better feature value, for example a lower noise level preferred by most of the customers, the feature value was printed in bold.

We designed 32 task sets of 3 products each. The values of the features were chosen to realistically reflect washing machines currently available on e-commerce platforms, which is new for a multi-attribute choice task (as the values are usually presented as dichotomous yes/no). For 17 of the tasks, marked as 'simple', washing machine feature values were selected to model a non-compensatory choice. In these tasks, using either a simpler TTB or TALLY strategy, or using the WADD strategy allowed the user to select the same correct answer. The remaining 15 tasks were constructed to model a compensatory choice. 8 compensatory choice tasks were marked as 'moderately difficult'. A user could determine the correct answer using both the TALLY and WADD strategy. In the remaining 7 tasks, marked as a 'difficult', only the WADD strategy allowed to choose the correct answer.

3.3   Experiment Procedure

The experiment was conducted online. The participants were redirected from a research participant recruitment agency portal to the experiment website. At the beginning of the study, participants filled out a personal questionnaire. Subsequently, the instruction was displayed to the participants, followed by four training trials for the multi-attribute choice tasks. In each task, the participants were instructed to select the best products guided by the importance of the given feature (number of pluses). Afterwards the participants were informed that the training part has finished, and were directed to the core part of the experiment where they have to solve 32 multi-attribute product choice tasks. There was no feedback regarding the correctness of the chosen answers. Finally, participants filled in the questionnaires listed in the Materials section.

4   Results and Discussion

4.1   Age-Related Differences in Accuracy of Multi-attribute Choice Tasks

In the first part we will describe main results of the effects of age and parameters of tasks on the accuracy of performance. Next, we will overview the correlation matrix of the main variables. Finally, we will demonstrate the role of cognitive and emotional variables as potential mediators and covariates of the relationship between age and multi-attribute decision making task performance.

Proportion of Correct Decisions. The key measure of performance in the multi-attribute product choice task is the proportion of correct decisions. For the record, the participants did not receive feedback concerning the accuracy of their decision making, except for the training tasks. A 3×3 (Age [younger adults, middle-age adults, older adults] x Decision Difficulty [simple, moderately difficult, difficult; within-subject variable]) mixed ANOVA on the proportion of correct decisions yielded one main effect and an interaction effect. Importantly, the assumption of equality of error variances was not violated because Levene's test was not significant across age groups. There was a main and strong effect of decision difficulty, $F(2, 264) = 92.22$, MSE $= .055$, $p < .001$, $\eta_p^2 = .411$, with the significant differences ($p < .001$, Sidak post-hoc tests) between all decision tasks – the more difficult was the task, the worse the performance. This main effect was qualified by the significant Age x Decision Difficulty interaction, $F(2, 264) = 3.47$, MSE $= .055$, $p = .01$, $\eta_p^2 = .050$. As shown in Fig. 2, for the simple decision task the performance of younger adults was significantly higher than of both the middle-age group ($p = .005$) and the older adults group ($p = .006$). For the moderately difficult decision task the performance was higher in the middle-age group than in the older adults group ($p = .04$). There were no significant age differences for the most difficult decision tasks. For decision difficulty comparisons within the age groups, there were significant differences between three levels of difficulty for younger adults ($p < .01$) and middle age adults groups ($p < .05$). However, for the older adults group there was no significant difference in performance between the moderately difficult and the difficult decisions, but significantly better performance ($p < .001$) for the simple decision tasks in comparison to the moderately difficult decisions (see Fig. 2). The discovered age-related limitations in solving simple and moderately difficult multi-attribute product choice tasks, especially in the older adults group, confirm previous findings [20,21]. Interestingly, age differences are observed even between younger

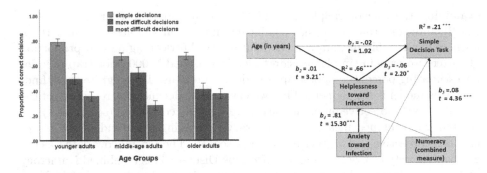

Fig. 2. Performance of decision task as the function of age and decision difficulty and model of the mediational effect of age via the Scale of Contracting an Infectious Disease on simple decision task. Error bars represent the standard errors of the mean. Entries are unstandardized regression coefficients with t-test values. *p < .05, **p < .01, ***p < .001

and middle-age groups in relatively simple tasks. This suggests that problems with learning values of cues and options that were previously demonstrated in older adults [5,29] could be also identified among the middle-age group.

Mediation Analysis for the Simple Decision Task. The correlation table between accuracy of the decisions, age, and questionnaire measures (see Table 1) indicates that age (in years) significantly and negatively correlates with the performance of simple decisions and age positively correlates with the Helplessness Scale. Additionally, numeracy scales, Scales of Helplessness and Anxiety significantly (although not systematically) correlate with accuracy for simple and moderately difficult decision tasks. The results indicating that numeracy is related to the accuracy of decisions in multi-attribute choice task are in line with the previous findings that numeracy is an important predictor of performance in many decision tasks. The significant correlations between objective numeracy and both anxiety and helplessness confirmed the predicted link between low level of numeracy and emotions that are irrelevant for effective decision making [25]. The results showing that feelings of helplessness and anxiety of contracting an infectious disease are significant predictors of accuracy of multi-attribute choice task performance are to our knowledge the novel and original demonstration (specific to the COVID-19 pandemic) of the dysfunctional role of such negative emotions when making rational multi-attribute choice in the domain of e-commerce.

Although the above correlational analyses indicated (in rather indirect way) the important role of numeracy scales and Scales of Helplessness and Anxiety of Contracting an Infectious Disease in explaining the age-related limitation on accurate solving of the simple decision task, only the Scale of Helplessness of Contracting an Infectious Disease appeared to be the classical mediation variable. Namely, the mediation analysis (applying the Process software) [12] examining the role of Helplessness of Contracting an Infectious Disease (see Fig. 2), indicates that aging has significant impact on Helplessness, and Helplessness is a reliable mediator of the relationship between aging and proportion of correct answers in simple decision tasks. We applied 10000 bootstrap samples for estimating percentile bootstrap confidence intervals. To integrate these findings, this model is supplemented by two covariates. Because the responses of the subjective and objective numeracy scales were highly correlated (see Table 1), we created the combined measure of Numeracy (averaging the standardized scores for both subjective and objective numeracy scales). The second covariate was the Scale of Anxiety of Contracting an Infectious Disease. This combined Numeracy scale was a strong, additional predictor of the simple decision accuracy. Even though the Scale of Anxiety was strongly related to the Scale of Helplessness, it did not significantly predict the accuracy of simple decision task.

In sum, the mediational model with covariates nicely integrates the correlational analysis and indicates the interplay between the age-related limitation and the role of additional variables (especially Helplessness and Numeracy) in explaining the relationship between aging and performance in simple multi-attribute decision making task. However, we are aware that this mediational model, although original, is still preliminary and elucidating psychological mechanisms behind the role of intellectual helplessness as a mediator demands further experimental work (e.g., experimental manipulation of the intensity of a mediator, see [4]).

5   Conclusions

In this article, we have considered the question of how cognitive limitations of older consumers affect their choices when using a popular user interface function in e-commerce systems: product comparison.

We have found significant aging effects, especially for moderately difficult decisions, when the proportion of correct decisions of older adults drops as low as 40%. This effect is mediated by feelings of helplessness that are enhanced by the pandemic. This effect can have a severe adverse impact on the training and functioning of recommendation systems. To mitigate this effect, we recommend that content-based recommendation systems should not be used for older adults as these are particularly sensitive to individual choices that may be - as shown in this article - 60% incorrect. Instead, it is better to use collaborative or hybrid recommendation systems, in particular specially designed algorithms that would take into account age diversity.

All these questions will be the subject of our future research. This article is also a call to arms to designers of e-commerce recommendation systems to adapt them for older consumers with cognitive limitations.

Acknowledgements. This research was supported by grant 2018/29/B/HS6/02604 from the National Science Centre of Poland.

References

1. Baltes, P.B., Baltes, M.M.: Psychological perspectives on successful aging: The model of selective optimization with compensation. In Baltes, P.B., Baltes, M.M. (eds.) Successful aging: Perspectives from the behavioral sciences, pp. 1–34. Cambridge University Press (1990). https://doi.org/10.1017/CBO9780511665684.003
2. Bedyńska, S., Krejtz, I., Sedek, G.: Chronic stereotype threat and mathematical achievement in age cohorts of secondary school girls: mediational role of working memory, and intellectual helplessness. Soc. Psychol. Educ. **22**(2), 321–335 (2019)
3. Bruine de Bruin, W., Parker, A.M., Fischhoff, B.: Decision-making competence: more than intelligence? Curr. Dir. Psychol. Sci. **29**(2), 186–192 (2020)
4. Bullock, J.G., Green, D.P., Ha, S.E.: Yes, but what's the mechanism?(don't expect an easy answer). J. Pers. Soc. Psychol. **98**(4), 550 (2010)
5. Chasseigne, G., et al.: Aging and probabilistic learning in single-and multiple-cue tasks. Exp. Aging Res. **30**(1), 23–45 (2004)
6. Chen, Y., Sun, Y.: Age differences in financial decision-making: using simple heuristics. Educ. Gerontol. **29**(7), 627–635 (2003)
7. Czaja, S.J., Boot, W.R., Charness, N., Rogers, W.A.: Designing for Older Adults: Principles and Creative Human Factors Approaches. CRC Press, Boca Raton (2019)
8. El Shamy, N., Hassanein, K.: The impact of age and cognitive style on e-commerce decisions: the role of cognitive bias susceptibility. In: Davis, F.D., Riedl, R., vom Brocke, J., Léger, P.-M., Randolph, A.B. (eds.) Information Systems and Neuroscience. LNISO, vol. 25, pp. 73–83. Springer, Cham (2018). https://doi.org/10.1007/978-3-319-67431-5_9
9. Engle, R.W., Sedek, G., Von Hecker, U., McIntosh, D.N.: Cognitive Limitations in Aging and Psychopathology. Cambridge University Press, Cambridge (2005)
10. Fagerlin, A., Zikmund-Fisher, B.J., Ubel, P.A., Jankovic, A., Derry, H.A., Smith, D.M.: Measuring numeracy without a math test: development of the subjective numeracy scale. Med. Decis. Making **27**(5), 672–680 (2007)
11. Gigerenzer, G., Goldstein, D.G.: Reasoning the fast and frugal way: models of bounded rationality. Psychol. Rev. **103**(4), 650 (1996)
12. Hayes, A.F.: Introduction to Mediation, Moderation, and Conditional Process Analysis: A Regression-Based Approach. Guilford publications, New York (2017)
13. von Helversen, B., Abramczuk, K., Kopeć, W., Nielek, R.: Influence of consumer reviews on online purchasing decisions in older and younger adults. Decis. Support Syst. **113**, 1–10 (2018)
14. Hess, T.M.: Selective engagement of cognitive resources: motivational influences on older adults' cognitive functioning. Perspect. Psychol. Sci. **9**(4), 388–407 (2014)
15. Hess, T.M., Queen, T.L., Patterson, T.R.: To deliberate or not to deliberate: interactions between age, task characteristics, and cognitive activity on decision making. J. Behav. Decis. Mak. **25**(1), 29–40 (2012)
16. Knowles, B., et al.: The harm in conflating aging with accessibility. Commun. ACM **64**, 66–71 (2020)
17. de Lara, S.M.A., de Mattos Fortes, R.P., Russo, C.M., Freire, A.P.: A study on the acceptance of website interaction aids by older adults. Univers. Access Inf. Soc. **15**(3), 445–460 (2016)
18. Lian, J.W., Yen, D.C.: Online shopping drivers and barriers for older adults: age and gender differences. Comput. Hum. Behav. **37**, 133–143 (2014)

19. Lipkus, I.M., Samsa, G., Rimer, B.K.: General performance on a numeracy scale among highly educated samples. Med. Decis. Making **21**(1), 37–44 (2001)
20. Mata, R., Schooler, L.J., Rieskamp, J.: The aging decision maker: cognitive aging and the adaptive selection of decision strategies. Psychol. Aging **22**(4), 796 (2007)
21. Mata, R.: Learning to choose: cognitive aging and strategy selection learning in decision making. Psychol. Aging **25**(2), 299 (2010)
22. Nielsen-Norman: UX Design for Seniors (Ages 65 and older). Nielsen Norman Group (2020). https://www.nngroup.com/reports/senior-citizens-on-the-web/
23. Osman, R., Hwang, F.: An instrument for assessing e-commerce web object designs against guidelines for older adults. In: Proceedings of the 32nd International BCS Human Computer Interaction Conference 32, pp. 1–6 (2018)
24. Pawlowska, J., Nielek, R., Wierzbicki, A.: Lost in online stores? Agent-based modeling of cognitive limitations of elderly online consumers. In: Thomson, R., Bisgin, H., Dancy, C., Hyder, A. (eds.) SBP-BRiMS 2019. LNCS, vol. 11549, pp. 204–213. Springer, Cham (2019). https://doi.org/10.1007/978-3-030-21741-9_21
25. Peters, E., Västfjäll, D., Slovic, P., Mertz, C., Mazzocco, K., Dickert, S.: Numeracy and decision making. Psychol. Sci. **17**(5), 407–413 (2006)
26. Pew-Research: Internet/Broadband Fact Sheet. Pew Research Center (2021). https://www.pewresearch.org/internet/fact-sheet/internet-broadband/
27. Rydzewska, K., Rusanowska, M., Krejtz, I., Sedek, G.: Uncontrollability in the classroom: The intellectual helplessness perspective. In: Bukowski, M., Fritsche, I., Guinote, A., Kofta, M. (eds.) Current Issues in Social Psychology: Coping with Lack of Control in a Social World, pp. 62–80. Taylor & Francis Groups (2016)
28. Salthouse, T.A.: Mental exercise and mental aging: evaluating the validity of the "use it or lose it" hypothesis. Perspect. Psychol. Sci. **1**(1), 68–87 (2006)
29. Samanez-Larkin, G.R., Gibbs, S.E., Khanna, K., Nielsen, L., Carstensen, L.L., Knutson, B.: Anticipation of monetary gain but not loss in healthy older adults. Nat. Neurosci. **10**(6), 787–791 (2007)
30. Sedek, G., McIntosh, D.N.: Intellectual helplessness. In: Kofta, M., Weary, G., Sedek, G. (eds.) Personal Control in Action. The Springer Series in Social Clinical Psychology, pp. 419–443. Springer, Boston, MA (1998). https://doi.org/10.1007/978-1-4757-2901-6_17
31. Sedek, G., Verhaeghen, P., Martin, M.: Social and Motivational Compensatory Mechanisms for Age-Related Cognitive Decline. Psychology Press, London (2012)

Multisensory Experiences for Art Appreciation

Sakshi Arora[✉] (iD)

Pearl Academy, New Delhi 110027, India

Abstract. This study aims at understanding multisensory interactions, from visual or bimodal to all senses, to design user experiences for art appreciation. Museum experiences are not just an encounter between an eager visiting public who soaks up the knowledge articulated by the curatorial team. It is a multilayered journey that is proprioceptive, sensory, intellectual, aesthetic, and social, leading to learning and reflection [1]. The target users for this study are people who are not well versed with the context of a visual artwork and are unable to interpret it. Based on secondary readings, it is essential to determine what sensory experiences we can design for and how we can meaningfully stimulate such experiences, when interacting with technology, while understanding the limitations that come into play when users need to monitor more than one sense at a time [2]. The research conducted for this study involved evaluation of simple everyday life activities for multisensorial interactions, through both qualitative and quantitative data collection. The observations from these activities and secondary readings of the subject, have further been tested in the context of visual art experiences, through auditory and visual art prototypes. The key finding of the study is that any multisensory experiences should be designed by isolating the secondary sense modalities. The experience through unconscious senses should be induced involuntarily, by associating a narrative with the entire experience. Based on these findings, a set of principles for designing multisensory experiences have been formed. These principles can further be tested in different contexts for designing intuitive immersive experiences.

Keywords: Multisensory interfaces · Sensory isolation · Immersive art experiences

1 Introduction

The senses that we use while interacting with technology are mostly restricted to vision and audition. In order to translate these experiences, be it conscious or unconscious, to HCI, we can design multisensory experiences by evaluating different experiences in real life and implementing those in our designs [2]. These design interfaces should take into account the relationships between the senses and understand what limitations come into

Electronic supplementary material The online version of this chapter (https://doi.org/10.1007/978-3-030-85613-7_42) contains supplementary material, which is available to authorized users.

play when users must monitor information from more than one sense simultaneously [3].

This study focuses on identifying different principles for designing multisensory interfaces from everyday experiences and applying those in a specific context to build meaningful experiences.

1.1 Research Design

The research has been done in the following two phases:

- Informal research, through quick prototyping for everyday activities, has been conducted with 5 individuals. Both qualitative and quantitative data is collected through observation and conversations during the course of the activities. The raw data obtained is supported with visual and auditory references of the process to draw observational insights.
- Testing of audio-visual prototypes of visual artworks, based on the learnings from the first phase. These prototypes were specifically created in the context of art appreciation for people who are not well versed with the context of visual artworks. The responses were collected from 8 users, through formal interviews.

1.2 Designing Multisensory Experiences by Secondary Sense Isolation

Multisensory experiences should be designed by isolating the secondary sense modalities. Human physical interaction is inherently multisensory [4]. As participants, one may not be aware of the senses that they are engaging with. For instance, when sipping a cup of coffee, it is not just the smell and taste of coffee that constitutes the experience. The involvement of temperature, color, texture or the material of the cup, sounds in the background, feeling and the overall environment, contributes to the experience as well. These may not be obvious to a user when participating in an activity but can alter the user behavior and experience. In this case, the senses of smell and taste are primary or the conscious senses of interaction. While the ones which are less obvious, are the secondary or the unconscious senses. Isolation of senses means enhancing the experience with secondary sense, while eliminating the interaction with primary sense. Playing the sound of crunching of chips, to provide an experience of the activity or the environment, where one usually eats chips, is a simple example of isolation.

In order to understand conscious and unconscious sensory interactions in everyday life, a research activity was conducted. This was based on the 5 senses graph by Jinsop Lee and the idea of experimenting and designing intuitive interactions with Hidden Senses exhibit curated in Milan Design Week, 2018. The idea of designing interactions to tap two different layers of experience: the immediate experience of actually interacting with the technology and the past, familiar experiences that populate people's memories was showcased in the Hidden senses exhibit [5]. Jinsop Lee, an industrial designer, proposed his five senses theory where one can grade in the intensity of every experience with respect to each sense [6]. With these graphs as a tool to collect responses, we have tested everyday prompts, like crunching chips, reading a book, making coffee etc. for the following activities:

Activity 1. For each prompt, a user rates the intensity of experience with each sense modality. The data is collected for both before and after the activity. During the activity, the users are asked to observe the senses intentionally (Fig. 1).

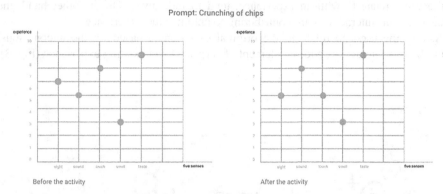

Before the activity   After the activity

Fig. 1. Intensity graphs for before and after an activity. The x-axis represents the five senses, while the intensity of interaction is mapped on a scale of 0–10 on y-axis, respectively.

Activity 2. The conscious or the obvious mode of interaction for each prompt is hidden and a user describes the interaction with other i.e. the unconscious senses. The emotional value for each interaction is plotted on a similar graph. For example (Fig. 2):

- Smell through visual
- Sound through visuals
- Visual through sound

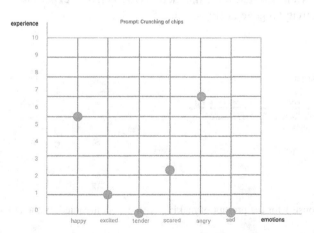

Fig. 2. This is an emotion graph, which was created when the activity of crunching of chips is identified by the secondary sense of sound. The x-axis represents different emotions, while the y-axis rates the intensity of the emotional experience on a scale of 0–10, respectively.

Based on the above research activity, conducted as a part of this study, we found the following:

- During an everyday activity, the impact of obvious sensory interactions, which the users relate to with an experience, tend to fade away. On the other hand, the unconscious interactions are contributing to enhance the experience.
- Asking the users to relate to the original experience, based on the unconscious/ unobvious interaction, adds an element of surprise to an existing experience (Fig. 3).

ACTIVITY 1

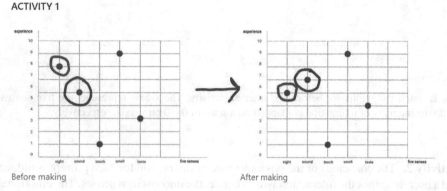

Before making   After making

Fig. 3. Intensity graphs for Activity 1 for the prompt of making coffee. In this case, the intensity of experience with sound (secondary sense) rises, with decline in the intensity of sight (primary sense).

This showed that the emotional response to a sensory interaction changes with change in primary sense modality but lies in a similar range for different users. During the experience, users tend to relate these interactions to a personal experience or the expected nature of the activity in general (Figs. 4 and 5).

RESPONSE 1

Sound of sipping a warm drink- maybe
Coffee, Tea
The coffee is very hot and someone is sipping
it slowly, maybe this is from a cold morning
Brown, black, white

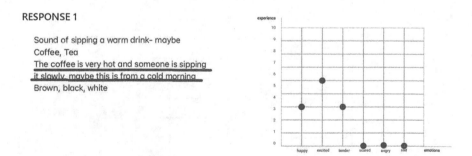

Fig. 4. Response 1 for the prompt of making coffee, accompanied by the emotion graphs.

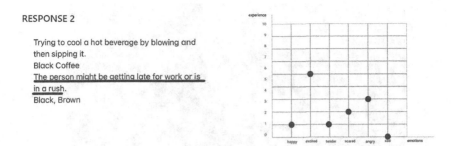

RESPONSE 2

Trying to cool a hot beverage by blowing and
then sipping it.
Black Coffee
The person might be getting late for work or is
in a rush.
Black, Brown

Fig. 5. Response 2 for the prompt of making coffee, accompanied by the emotion graphs.

Of course, there is a possibility that when repeated frequently, experience with the unconscious senses could turn out to be less engaging like the primary sensory interactions in real life. Therefore, when designing multi-sensorial experiences, using the idea of isolation, one time-sensory interactions should be preferred over repetitive interactions.

2 Narrative Based Multisensory Experiences for Art Appreciation

There is a growing international interest in more immersive media (multisensory) experiences [7]. For users, non-linear stories stay with them because they demand careful thinking about all the pieces presented. When one completes that puzzle, they feel a real sense of achievement [8].

The experience through unconscious senses should be induced involuntarily, by associating a narrative with the entire experience, because not only would the narrative help in enhancing the experience by engaging unconscious senses, but also give a direction or flow for the user journey. "Multisensory stimulation, along with interactive components and dynamic displays, has a strong influence on the visitor experience, especially in terms of the visitor's sense of flow and immersion" [9].

This is also evident from the testing of visual art prototypes with multiple soundscapes and audio commentaries to describe the artworks, done with the users. To understand the user behavior and experience with visual artworks, created by Amrita Sher Gil in different settings, visual and auditory prototypes have been created. These prototypes add an additional auditory experience to visual artworks by combining soundscapes associated with the elements of the artworks. There are multiple soundscapes associated with each artwork. These soundscapes could be ambient sounds with still or moving visuals and audio commentary. The purpose of these soundscapes could be satisfying the visual experience or creating a disturbing experience overall. Here, sound becomes the primary sensory mode of communication and can alter the visual interpretation or experience of the prototype (Figs. 6, 7 and 8).

Fig. 6. This is the first art prototype for Notre Dame (1932), an artwork by Amrita Sher Gil. The auditory input supports the visual cue of church tower blocking the view of the impressionist river and the city. The sound of church bells dominates over the city sounds and the river.

Fig. 7. This is the second art prototype for Notre Dame (1932), an artwork by Amrita Sher Gil. The soundscape associated with the background, depicts the idea of a quiet city by a river with natural and calming sounds which aligns with the visuals in the artwork. The interpretation of the artwork with both visual and sound, contradicts with the idea of the setting being at a busy location in Paris.

Fig. 8. This is the final art prototype for Notre Dame (1932), an artwork by Amrita Sher Gil. This version aims to create a disturbing experience by expressing different message through both sensory modalities. The soundscape signifies the setting of a busy tourist spot of the city of Paris, where this artwork was originally created by the artist.

Within this activity, most users could engage with secondary senses effectively, when accompanied with a conversation during the interviews. The main observations from these interviews are as follows:

- A user, who is not well versed with the context of an artwork, finds the visual experience to be minimal and less relatable.
- Ambient soundscapes turned out to be useful in connecting and directing the users in the initial phase of experiencing the artworks, while keeping the scope of interpretation open.
- Audio commentaries on the other hand, provided clearer ideas about the context but were a bit overwhelming or too informative in terms of experience (Figs. 9 and 10).

Fig. 9. This is a art prototype for Hungarian Peasant (1938), an artwork by Amrita Sher Gil. Ambient soundscape is associated with the visual here.

Fig. 10. This is a art prototype for Hungarian Peasant (1938), an artwork by Amrita Sher Gil. Here, an audio commentary is associated with the visual artwork [10].

Based on these, one could mention that audio commentaries are informative and are very common in museum exhibits and may not be treated as multisensory interaction. That may be true, and audio commentary could be added after the immersive multisensory experience with the artwork like those museums. But they should not be a part of the narrative that is created specifically for the purpose of art appreciation, because of their conclusive and informative nature. The multisensory artworks should rather be open to interpretation where every user can have a unique experience with the same artwork.

3 Conclusion

The above stated arguments form on the following design principles, which must be followed to design a multisensory art experience:

- Secondary sense should be isolated to design multisensory experience.
- Create a narrative to engage with the unconscious/ inactive senses of a user.
- Background interactions for every sensory modality, should be considered.
- One-time sensory experiences should be preferred over repetitive interactions.
- Experience with either sense, primary or secondary, should be ambient and not overwhelmingly informative.
- Any essential information, which may not be communicated through the ambient sensory experience, can be shared after the multisensorial experience.

Based on these design considerations, I am working on conceptualizing a virtual reality multisensory prototype, with three sets of visual artworks by Amrita Sher Gil. These sets are based on time periods and locations of the creation of these artworks. Soundscapes and smells based on the narrative of an artwork or the context would be an additional element to an existing visual experience. The idea of experiencing an artwork in a VR environment by participating would be more of a learning experience, where everyone has an inclusive and memorable experience, paving the path for art appreciation.

Considering these design principles as an elementary framework, we can design more immersive user experiences in future. These experiences would not only be meaningful for every user, but would also lead to valuable insights and opportunities, as to how multisensory simulations can influence human computer interaction.

References

1. Levant, N., Leone, A.P.: The Multisensory Museum: Cross-disciplinary Perspectives on Touch, Sound, Smell, Memory. Plymouth: Rowman & Littlefield. (Obrist, Gatti, Maggioni, Vi, & Velasco, 2017) (2014)
2. Obrist, M., et al.: Touch taste, & smell user interfaces: the future of multisensory HCI, pp. 3285–3292 (2016)
3. Obrist, M., Gatti, E., Maggioni, E., Vi, C.T., Velasco, C.: Multisensory experience in HCI. IEE Multimed. 9–12 (2017)
4. Pai, D.K.: Multisensory interaction: real and virtual. In: Dario, P., Chatila, R. (eds.) Robotics Research. The Eleventh International Symposium. STAR, vol. 15, pp. 489–498. Springer, Heidelberg (2005). https://doi.org/10.1007/11008941_52

5. Sony Design: Hidden Senses Concept/Stories/Sony Design (2019). https://www.sony.com/en/SonyInfo/design/stories/hidden_senses/. Accessed 15 Apr 2021
6. Kate Torgovnick. The 5 senses showdown: Designer Jinsop Lee grades 6 great experiences | TED Blog. [online] @tedtalks, May 2013. https://blog.ted.com/the-5-senses-showdown-how-to-grade-your-experiences/. Accessed 15 Apr 2021
7. Obrist, M.: Multi-sensory media experiences, pp. 221–221 (2015). https://doi.org/10.1145/2745197.2783433
8. Motionographer: No Particular Order: Thoughts on Non-Linear Storytelling (2015). https://motionographer.com/2015/10/19/no-particular-order-thoughts-on-non-linear-storytelling/. Accessed 15 Apr 2021
9. Harvey, M.L., et al.: The influence of museum exhibit design on immersion and psychological flow. Environ. Behav. **30**(5), 601–627 (1998)
10. Shakeel, T.: Amrita Sher Gil and her commentaries (2001). http://ir.amu.ac.in/3390/1/T%205867.pdf. Accessed 10 Mar 2021

Older Auctioneers: Performance of Older Users in On-Line Dutch Auctions

Radoslaw Nielek[1](✉), Klara Rydzewska[2], Grzegorz Sedek[2], and Adam Wierzbicki[1]

[1] Polish-Japanese Academy of Information Technology, Warsaw, Poland
{nielek,adamw}@pja.edu.pl
[2] SWPS University of Social Sciences and Humanities, Warsaw, Poland
{krydzewska1,gsedek}@swps.edu.pl

Abstract. The number of older adults using e-commerce platform has grown rapidly in recent years. This has created a whole lot of challenges and research problems in the field of adapting e-commerce systems and algorithms to the needs of older adults. In the current study We have conducted an experiment involving 60 older adults whose task was to participate in realistically modeled Dutch auctions. Results show that more advanced age has a clear, statistically significant adverse impact on the overall performance in Dutch auctions, and that need for cognitive closure is correlated with decreased performance in auctions.

Keywords: Older adults · Dutch auction · e-commerce · Decision · Risk

1 Introduction

In 2018 people aged 65+ comprise about one fifth of the entire European Union member states' population. The already significant and increasing number of older adults has a high potential as a target group on the digital market. The current value of the so-called "silver economy" is estimated at about 7 trillion dollars per year, which makes it the third largest economy in the world. Older adults living independently will have the largest commercial transaction value of the entire population in the developed countries. Growing part of it take place online.

In this article, we investigate how older adults deal with the risk of looking for bargains on the Internet in the context of time pressure and an awareness of the existence of competition. We decided to use simulated Dutch auctions that are sometimes applied by e-commerce platforms for selling tickets for events or trips[1]. Our results, to some extent, can also be interpolated to e-commerce

---

[1] https://www.berksmontnews.com/news/tickets-now-on-sale-for-dutch-auction-on-oct/article_af0f6a68-aad4-11e8-b3d7-8f583153923f.html.

© IFIP International Federation for Information Processing 2021
Published by Springer Nature Switzerland AG 2021
C. Ardito et al. (Eds.): INTERACT 2021, LNCS 12934, pp. 667–676, 2021.
https://doi.org/10.1007/978-3-030-85613-7_43

scenarios where users have to make decisions regarding an acceptable level of risk in the context of a possible reward under time pressure, and at the same time, learn to predict the behaviour of other users.

We have carried out an experiment involving 60 older adults who participated in simulated Dutch auctions with a realistic user interface. Our research was designed to study the actual behaviour of older adults in a controlled environment, enabling a rigorous statistical analysis. We have investigated several factors known from literature, such as cognitive and motivation factors or competition in the auction itself, which might influence older adults' performance in Dutch auctions. To the best of our knowledge, this is the first study of this kind reported in literature.

Our findings show that the performance of older adults in Dutch auctions clearly deteriorates with age. Moreover, this phenomenon is strengthened by the tendency of older adults to avoid uncertainty, which we measured using a psychological scale.

2   Related Work

2.1   Older Adults, E-Commerce, and Dutch Auctions

Research on the use of e-commerce systems by older adults is focused mostly on two interconnected areas: accessibility and acceptance. With help of the Unified Theory of Acceptance and Use of Technology, Lian et al. studied barriers among older adults in Taiwan, and found that performance expectation and social influence have between a strong and moderate positive influence on intentions to shop online [18]. On the other hand, usage barrier, tradition barrier, and risk barrier negatively affect older adults' intentions to shop online. An extensive overview of theoretical and practical studies regarding e-commerce acceptance by older adults can be found in work done by Zhang et al. [29].

Many researchers have studied practical aspects of designing e-commerce systems that would be more older adults friendly. De Lara et al. measured the influence of almost 20 different techniques to make e-commerce web sites more accessible, i.a. explanation of images, selection of colour of links in navigation menus and summarise content [17]. Other researchers proposed a formal framework for assessing e-commerce web object design against guidelines for older adults [21].

Work on deeper adaptation of existing e-commerce systems to the need and limitation of older adults has started only recently. El Shamy et al. [6] proposed an experiment to measure impact of recommender systems and comparison matrices on older adults' e-commerce decisions' quality, but no final results have been published yet. Pawlowska et al. used multi-agent simulation to verify the existence of harmful feedback loop in typical recommendation algorithms, if used by older adults with cognitive limitations [23]. Von Helversen et al. studied the influence of on-line reviews on purchasing decisions of older adults and revealed statistically significant differences in how older and younger people respond to negative reviews [11].

Dutch auctions have been thoroughly studied from a variety of perspectives, but to the best of our knowledge no research regarding behaviors of older adults in such an environment has yet been published. Cox et al. investigated the differences between predictions of theoretical models and bidders behaviour in Dutch auction [3]. Many factors affect bidders' behaviours, i.a. personality [5] and clock speed [12]. Adam et al. [1] have shown that participation in the Dutch auction can induce excitement, which in turn affects the acceptable level of risk and payoffs.

2.2   Search Demands as Moderator of the Effect of Aging on Decision Making

Gaining knowledge about possible choice options in complex decision making requires some effort. A number of research findings have indicated that older adults compared to younger ones have a tendency to search for less information in various decision making tasks. For instance, the review by Mara Mather concludes that older adults request less information than younger adults in research on consumer and medical decisions [20]. Additionally, older adults in comparison to younger adults tend to rely more on recognition heuristic and discard further information [22]. Such reduction in information search among older adults may be connected to age-related decrease in cognitive resources and changes in motivation.

Following on that, Mata et al. [19] and Pachur et al. [22] suggest that older adults switch to simpler decision strategies requiring less information, and, therefore, they search less. Furthermore, performance of older adults is better on less complex tasks including smaller set sizes [24]. Therefore, because waiting in Dutch auctions is similar to the search in standard decision tasks, we generally predict that the actual performance in Dutch auctions will be worse in relatively older adults because of their aversion to prolonged information search. However, we predict that such worsening should be observable only in trials when prolonged waiting behaviour was optimal for the actual task performance.

2.3   Need for Cognitive Closure as Moderator of the Effect of Aging on Decision Making

Need for Cognitive Closure (NFC) is a classical and well established in psychology measure of the epistemic motivation on the inter-individual level. It was defined by Arie Kruglanski as a desire for a definite answer to a question or for any firm answer rather than confusion, uncertainty, or ambiguity, even at the expense of that answer's quality [15,28]. High NFC individuals prefer order and structure, clarity and certain knowledge. Moreover, they tend to make simplistic decisions, and have problems with adding new knowledge to their views. On the contrary, low NFC individuals are more flexible and open to new information, analyse situations systematically, deal well with uncertainty and ambiguity, and make complex decisions [14,15,25].

Hotel Beang Resort SPA **

The hotel offers accommodation in Phuket, just a few steps from the beach. A restaurant and spa are available. Free WiFi is available.

All rooms have air conditioning and a flat-screen TV with satellite channels. Some have sea or city views. Each room has a private bathroom with bathrobes, slippers and free toiletries.

The reception is open 24 hours a day. The property also offers a gift shop, a shared lounge and childcare. You can also play billiards.

The largest cities are 18 km away. Distance from the airport is 23 km.

Fig. 1. Experiment screen showing the course of a single auction.

Several studies have indicated that there is a strong increase in NFC with age, and it is especially true for two NFC subscales, namely Preference for Order and Structure and Preference for Predictability [4,13,26]. Nevertheless, even among older adult groups, there can be found individuals with relatively low and relatively high need for cognitive closure. Previous research shows that relatively low NFC is beneficial for performance in the computerized sequential decision tasks, enabling older adults to be more flexible decision makers compared to their high NFC counterparts [26].

3   Experiment Design

Design of our experiment aimed at creating a realistic environment that would require the use of Dutch auctions. To this end, we created a simulated application where participants would bid for hotel rooms. The prices of hotel rooms were discounted over time, and, therefore, these rooms were sold in a Dutch auction. Figure 1 shows the main screen of the experiment. On the left side of the screen depicted on the Fig. 1 the start price and current price are presented. The current price drops by 10 PLN (ca. 2 euros) every half a second. On the right side of the screen the name of the hotel, brief description, and three photos are presented. Descriptions and photos were taken from the actual three and four-star hotels.

The Finometer (Finapress Medical Systems, Amsterdam, the Netherlands) was used to collect continuous measures of blood pressure.

Major goal of the experiment design was to create a controlled experiment, which would recreate the effect of competition in a Dutch auction. Letting the participants compete against each other would make it impossible for us to control the auction outcome. Instead, the auction was simulated, and for each auction there was a predetermined, but unknown for participants, closure price.

Table 1. Time in seconds for subsequent auctions in a decreasing risk scenario. For increasing risk scenario times are the same but in reverse order.

Auction	1	2	3	4	5	6	7	8	9	10	11	12	13	14	15
Time (s)	2.5	4	2	3	3.5	5.5	5	6.5	4.5	6	9	7.5	8.5	8	7
Auction	16	17	18	19	20	21	22	23	24	25	26	27	28	29	30
Time (s)	10.5	9.5	11	10	11.5	13	14	12	13.5	12.5	16.5	14.5	15	15.5	16

3.1 Participants

Sixty people participated in the study, including 28 older adults aged 65 to 68 (17 women; mean age = 66,82 years, SD = 1.16) and 32 older adults over 68 years old (23 women; mean age = 70,56 years, SD = 1.41). The level of education was similar for both age groups (mean years of education = 14.57, SD = 2.33 for younger older adults group and mean years of education = 14.75, SD = 2.31 for older adults group). Participants received 12 euros for their participation, which took approx. 1 h.

3.2 Used Questionnaires

MMSE and NFC. Participants were screened for signs of dementia and other impairments in cognitive functioning by using Mini-Mental State Examination (MMSE, [8]). Only those who scored 27 and more points (out of 30) participated in the study. MMSE examines time and space orientation, memory, attention, language, and ability to follow simple commands.

Participants completed the Need for Cognitive Closure–Short Scale (NFC [15]). In further analyses we used two subscales: Desire for Predictability, Preference for Order and Structure (in total six items). Participants rated how well each of the items described them on a 6-point scale ranging from 1 (totally disagree) to 6 (totally agree). The reliability of those subscales of NFC was satisfactory (Cronbach's alpha = .70).

3.3 Dutch Auction Task

Participants were asked to make bids in 30 online auctions of hotel rooms. The aim of the task was to make hotel room reservations at the lowest possible price, knowing that one may be forestalled in bidding. We created two subtasks: one with Decreased Risk of failures in auctions and the other one with Increased Risk of failures in auctions. Depending on the condition (between-participants), distribution of the risk of failures was either high at the beginning and decreased throughout the task (Decreased Risk of failures, modeling decreasing competition) or the risk was low at the beginning and increased as the task proceeded (Increased Risk of failures, modeling increasing competition). Participants were not informed about the different task types or aware that a change in the optimal

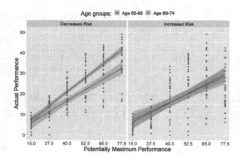

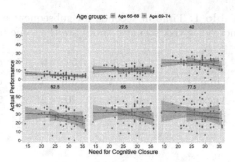

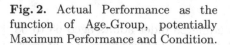

Fig. 2. Actual Performance as the function of Age_Group, potentially Maximum Performance and Condition.

Fig. 3. Actual Performance as the function of Need for Cognitive Closure (NFC) and Age_Group.

search length could occur. The payoff scheme is presented in Table 1. The possible savings are directly related to the auction time, because the price was falling by 2 euros every half second. For example, in action number 7, the participant could wait a maximum of 5 s and save 20 euros.

30 auctions were divided into six blocks with five auctions each. As the main behavioral measure in the Dutch auction task we used the sum of money saved in six phases of the auction task (actual performance).

3.4 Experiment Procedure

At the beginning of the study, participants filled in an informed consent form. Then MMSE was administered. Subsequently, participants were asked to read the instruction and completed three training trials for the computerised Dutch auction task. In each trial, a participant was to decide when to make a bid while prices within an auction were decreasing with every 0.5 s by 2 euros . Each auction could end either by a participant making a bid or because of someone else (i.e. computer) making a bid, as explained to research participants. If a given auction was over before participant made a bid, they had to make hotel room reservation at a standard price (highest price for a particular hotel room compared to the following auction prices), as each of the 30 hotel rooms had to have reservations made. After the Dutch auction task was completed, NFC scale was administered.

4   Results

In the analysis of the auction task data, we focused on actual performance, assessing whether or not participants managed to win Dutch auctions as measured by the sum of money earned in six phases (in total 30 trials) as a dependent variable. Given the structure of the task in which each individual completed 30 auctions grouped in six phases, we used linear-mixed models (LMMs) to investigate if participants differed in their auction behaviour depending on age, as well as individual differences, and how they adapted their behavior over time. Linear-mixed models can incorporate sources of correlation and variability between Dutch auction phases. Linear-mixed models were estimated using the lmer-function (lme4 package [2] and lmerTest package [16]) in R [27].

At the beginning we built a linear-mixed model for actual performance as dependent variable with Condition (Decreased Risk of failures in auctions vs. Increased Risk of failures in auctions) and Maximum Performance (six phases with regularly increased potential for auction wins) and Age_Group (Older Adults up to the age of 68 vs. Older Adults over the age 68) and their interaction as fixed effects, and Participants as random effect. We fit the linear-mixed models using the restricted maximum likelihood method (REML; [2]) and used the Satterthwaite approximations to estimate the degrees of freedom of the t-tests.

The LMM analysis for actual performance yielded a significant main effect of Maximum Performance, $b = .56, SE = 0.04, t(296) = 15.82, p < .001$ (the higher the potentially maximum performance, the higher the actual performance), a significant main effect of Condition $b = -6.60, SE = 1.91, t(56) = 3.46, p < .002$ (the actual performance in decreased risk condition is higher than in increased risk condition). Furthermore, results of this LMM analysis for actual performance that also yielded a significant main effect of Group_Age (worse performance of older adults over 68 years of age in comparison to younger older adults), $b = -5.12, SE = 1.83, t(56) = 2.80, p < .007$, and interesting and significant Group_Age x Condition x Maximum Performance interaction, $b = .15, SE = 0.07, t(296) = 2.03, p < .05$ (see Fig. 2).

The relationship between potentially maximum performance and actual performance was nearly identical for both age groups in the increased risk condition (see Fig. 2, right panel). However, the difference in actual performance between age groups (much better actual performance of older adults below the age of 69) is especially evident in the phases of potentially higher maximum performance (see Fig. 2, left panel).

To examine the predictions about the compensatory role of the NFC, we added this variable to the linear-mixed model for actual performance. Results of this extended LMM analysis for actual performance yielded significant Group_Age x NFC x Maximum Performance, $b = -.02, SE = 0.01, t(292) = 1.98, p = .05$ interaction (see Fig. 3). Inspection of Fig. 3 indicates that older adults aged over 68 have similar performance as relatively younger participants, but only when they have relatively low scores in the Need for Cognitive Closure. Increased level of NFC for older adults aged over 68 substantially decreased their actual performance.

Additionally, we assessed cognitive engagement by measuring cardiovascular response. Replicated research demonstrated that systolic blood pressure (sBP) is associated with task engagement (for recent review see [9]). Ennis et al. found that the sBP response (i.e., change from the baseline) was greater for participants reporting high levels of engagement in the tasks and this effect was much stronger in the older adults group than in the younger adults group [7].

Findings in our study show that the relation between continuously collected sBP response and performance in the auction task is moderated by experimental condition (significant interaction between sBP x condition, yielded by the Process software [10]; t = 2.03, p = .04). Namely, the higher sBP response among participants (i.e., the higher change from the baseline) the better performance but only in the increased risk condition (Pearson's correlation R = .36, p = .03, one-sided test). Such a relationship was not significant in the decreased risk condition. This interesting finding indicates that the role of subjective engagement is important in older adults only in the condition (increased risk) where in the beginning the optimal performance demanded relatively long waiting time with the stop response and then adaptive shortening waiting time in later phases. Further research (including younger adults) is needed to demonstrate age differences in engagement for performance of the Dutch auction task.

5   Conclusions

The goal of our work was to investigate how older adults perform in the Dutch auctions. Our findings can be summarized as follows: more advanced age has a clear, statistically significant adverse impact on the overall performance in Dutch auctions. Moreover, need for cognitive closure (measured by the subscales of Desire for Predictability, Preference for Order and Structure), a cognitive motivation variable that is known to increase with age, is also correlated with decreased performance in auctions. In short, older auctioneers often end up paying too much in Dutch auctions because of their cognitive limitations and high need for closure. Our results correspond well with previous findings, but they extend this theoretical knowledge to the domain of e-commerce research.

How can this finding be used to improve the design of Dutch auctions, a commonly used method of many e-commerce systems? Note that strategies in Dutch auctions are completely characterised by an amount of money that an auctioneer is willing to pay for the offered product or service. Theoretical work on auction strategies typically assumes that auctioneers will use a strategy to determine the maximum amount they are willing to pay, and then they will implement the strategy by just waiting for the price to drop to the selected amount. However, for older auctioneers, the waiting itself is the challenge.

Need for cognitive closure can be understood as a desire for quickly making a decision (any decision is better than none). This need of older auctioneers can be accommodated in the design of Dutch auctions in a simple manner. Consider a Dutch auction that allows its participants to look at the product, and then set the price that they are willing to pay for the product or service in advance, without requiring participants to actively wait for the price to drop. When the threshold price specified by an auctioneer is reached in such an auction, the auctioneer's software will automatically place a bid for the product at that price. Such interface would allow older auctioneers to make a decision quickly, and to avoid stressful waiting for the price to drop. Another idea would be to allow older auctioneers to observe auctions of choice without participating – making a decision of not participating, but learning about the bidding process instead.

In future work, we intend to test these ideas to see whether they will allow older auctioneers to improve their performance. We also wish to repeat our experiment with the participation of younger adults, in order to better understand the differences between their strategies and strategies of older auctioneers.

Acknowledgements. This research was supported by grant 2018/29/B/HS6/02604 from the National Science Centre of Poland.

References

1. Adam, M.T., Krämer, J., Weinhardt, C.: Excitement up! price down! measuring emotions in dutch auctions. Int. J. Electron. Commer. **17**(2), 7–40 (2012)
2. Bates, D., et al.: Package 'lme4'. Convergence **12**(1), 2 (2015)
3. Cox, J.C., Roberson, B., Smith, V.L.: Theory and behavior of single object auctions. Res. Exp. Econ. **2**(1), 1–43 (1982)
4. Czarnek, G., Kossowska, M., Sedek, G.: The influence of aging on outgroup stereotypes: the mediating role of cognitive and motivational facets of deficient flexibility. Exp. Aging Res. **41**(3), 303–324 (2015)
5. Deck, C., Lee, J., Reyes, J.: Personality and the consistency of risk taking behavior: Experimental evidence. Working papers, Chapman University, Economic Science Institute (2010)
6. El Shamy, N., Hassanein, K.: The impact of age and cognitive style on e-commerce decisions: the role of cognitive bias susceptibility. In: Davis, F.D., Riedl, R., vom Brocke, J., Léger, P.-M., Randolph, A.B. (eds.) Information Systems and Neuroscience. LNISO, vol. 25, pp. 73–83. Springer, Cham (2018). https://doi.org/10.1007/978-3-319-67431-5_9
7. Ennis, G.E., Hess, T.M., Smith, B.T.: The impact of age and motivation on cognitive effort: implications for cognitive engagement in older adulthood. Psychol. Aging **28**(2), 495 (2013)
8. Folstein, M.F., Folstein, S.E., McHugh, P.R.: "Mini-mental state": a practical method for grading the cognitive state of patients for the clinician. J. Psychiatr. Res. **12**(3), 189–198 (1975)
9. Gendolla, G.H., Wright, R.A., Richter, M.: Advancing Issues in Motivation Intensity Research. The Oxford handbook of human motivation, p. 373 (2019)
10. Hayes, A.F.: Introduction to Mediation, Moderation, and Conditional Process Analysis: A Regression-Based Approach. Guilford publications, New York (2017)
11. von Helversen, B., Abramczuk, K., Kopeć, W., Nielek, R.: Influence of consumer reviews on online purchasing decisions in older and younger adults. Decis. Support Syst. **113**, 1–10 (2018)
12. Katok, E., Kwasnica, A.M.: Time is money: the effect of clock speed on seller's revenue in dutch auctions. Exp. Econ. **11**(4), 344–357 (2008)
13. Koscielniak, M., Rydzewska, K., Sedek, G.: Effects of age and initial risk perception on balloon analog risk task: the mediating role of processing speed and need for cognitive closure. Front. Psychol. **7**, 659 (2016)
14. Kossowska, M., Orehek, E., Kruglanski, A.W.: Motivation towards closure and cognitive resources: an individual differences approach. In: Gruszka, A., Matthews, G., Szymura, B. (eds.) Handbook of Individual Differences in Cognition. The Springer Series on Human Exceptionality, pp. 369–382. Springer, New York, NY (2010). https://doi.org/10.1007/978-1-4419-1210-7_22

15. Kruglanski, A.W., Webster, D.M.: Motivated closing of the mind: "seizing" and "freezing". Psychol. Rev. **103**(2), 263 (1996)
16. Kuznetsova, A., Brockhoff, P.B., Christensen, R.H., et al.: lmertest package: tests in linear mixed effects models. J. Stat. Softw. **82**(13), 1–26 (2017)
17. de Lara, S.M.A., de Mattos Fortes, R.P., Russo, C.M., Freire, A.P.: A study on the acceptance of website interaction aids by older adults. Univers. Access Inf. Soc. **15**(3), 445–460 (2016)
18. Lian, J.W., Yen, D.C.: Online shopping drivers and barriers for older adults: age and gender differences. Comput. Hum. Behav. **37**, 133–143 (2014)
19. Mata, R., Schooler, L.J., Rieskamp, J.: The aging decision maker: cognitive aging and the adaptive selection of decision strategies. Psychol. Aging **22**(4), 796 (2007)
20. Mather, M.: A review of decision-making processes: weighing the risks and benefits of aging. In: Carstensen, L.L., Hartel., C.R. (eds.) When I'm 64, pp. 145–173. The National Academies Press (2006)
21. Osman, R., Hwang, F.: An instrument for assessing e-commerce web object designs against guidelines for older adults. In: Proceedings of the 32nd International BCS Human Computer Interaction Conference 32, pp. 1–6 (2018)
22. Pachur, T., Mata, R., Schooler, L.J.: Cognitive aging and the adaptive use of recognition in decision making. Psychol. Aging **24**(4), 901 (2009)
23. Pawlowska, J., Nielek, R., Wierzbicki, A.: Lost in online stores? Agent-based modeling of cognitive limitations of elderly online consumers. In: Thomson, R., Bisgin, H., Dancy, C., Hyder, A. (eds.) SBP-BRiMS 2019. LNCS, vol. 11549, pp. 204–213. Springer, Cham (2019). https://doi.org/10.1007/978-3-030-21741-9_21
24. Reed, A.E., Mikels, J.A., Simon, K.I.: Older adults prefer less choice than young adults. Psychol. Aging **23**(3), 671–675 (2008)
25. Roets, A., Kruglanski, A.W., Kossowska, M., Pierro, A., Hong, Y.Y.: The motivated gatekeeper of our minds: new directions in need for closure theory and research. In: Advances in experimental social psychology, vol. 52, pp. 221–283. Elsevier (2015)
26. Rydzewska, K., von Helversen, B., Kossowska, M., Magnuski, M., Sedek, G.: Age-related within-task adaptations in sequential decision making: considering cognitive and motivational factors. Psychol. Aging **33**(2), 297 (2018)
27. Team, R.C.: R foundation for statistical computing; vienna, austria: 2020. R: A language and environment for statistical computing, p. 2013 (2020)
28. Viola, V., et al.: Need for cognitive closure modulates how perceptual decisions are affected by task difficulty and outcome relevance. PloS one **10**(12), e0146002 (2015)
29. Zhang, F., Soto, C.G., et al.: Older adults on electronic commerce: a literature review. Int. J. Bus. Adm. **9**(3), 10–17 (2018)

Author Index

Printed in the United States
by Baker & Taylor Publisher Services